KU-734-032

Philips'
Modern School
Atlas

Seventy-sixth Edition

Edited by Harold Fullard M.Sc.

George Philip & Son Limited, London

© 1979

ISBN 0 540 05335 X

Printed in Great Britain by George Philip Printers Ltd., London

Preface

To justify its title and to continue to merit the reput-
ation it has gained over many years among teachers
of geography, each new edition of PHILIPS' MODERN
SCHOOL ATLAS receives most careful editing to en-
sure that every map is up to date and that its contents
meet the changing needs of the geography syllabus.

Philips' Modern School Atlas was first published in
1906 and now, more than seventy years later, the atlas bene-
fits from the improvements made over so many years
and for this edition the wider use of the
metric system has been reflected in conversion to,
or inclusion of metric equivalents where they had not
already been given in previous editions and particularly
on thematic maps and in climate graphs. All maps and
graphs have recently been reproduced afresh after
extensive revision and a new colour scheme has been
developed aimed at clear layer colouring on which the
legibility of names is yet further improved and hill
shading is added on the physical maps of the
continents, to give a graphic impression of principal
relief features.

The Modern School Atlas is designed to meet the
requirements of those intending to take the examina-
tion in Geography for the General Certificate; and
as the list of contents shows in detail the geology,
structure, relief, climate, vegetation and human conditions of the whole world are illustrated, whilst for
detailed regional study there are larger scale maps of
more important political and highly developed regions.

Modern spellings have been adopted in accordance
with the latest official lists, the rules of the Royal
Geographical Society Permanent Committee on Geographical Names, the decision lists of the United
States Board on Geographical Names and other
sources. A selective index of names appearing on the
maps have been included.

Where there are rival claims to territory the *de facto*
boundaries have been shown. This does not denote
international recognition of these boundaries but
shows the states which are administering the areas
on either side of the line.

HAROLD FULLARD

Contents

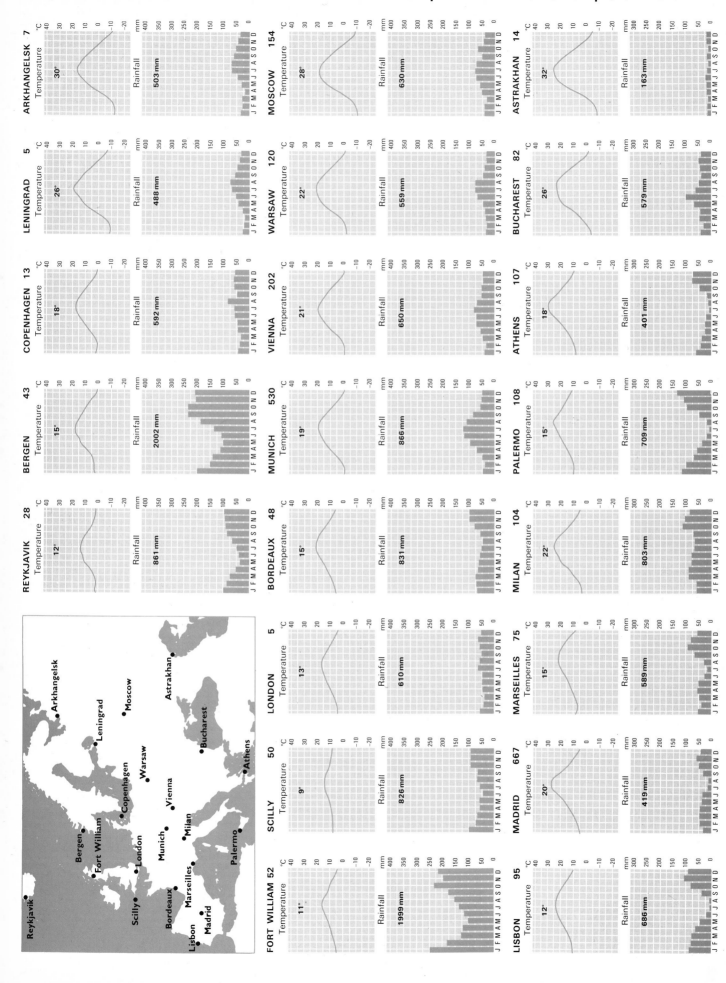

The climate graphs should be used in conjunction with the maps illustrating the climate of the World, and also the more detailed maps of the Continents. The stations have been selected to show the various types of climate to be found throughout the World. On each graph the name of the station is followed by its height in metres above sea-level, so that comparisons between stations can be made after allowing for elevation. The line on the temperature graphs shows the mean monthly temperatures. The mean annual range of temperature (in degrees Celsius) is given above the temperature graphs. The rainfall graphs show the average monthly rainfall and above them is given the average total annual rainfall (in millimetres).

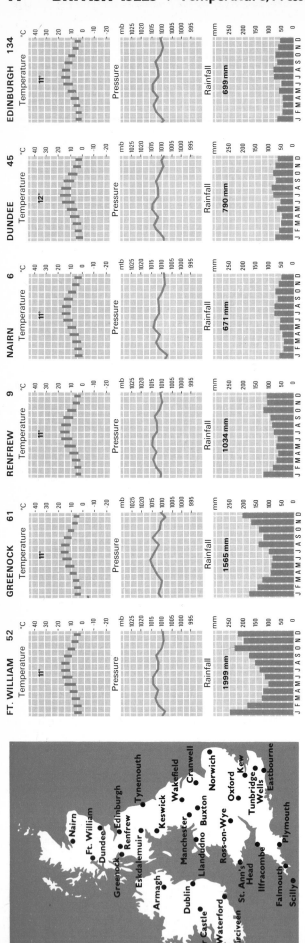

On these climate graphs of the British Isles, in addition to rainfall and temperature, mean monthly pressure is shown (in millibars and reduced to sea-level). Temperature is shown by a bar, the top of the bar representing the mean monthly maximum and the bottom of the bar the mean monthly minimum temperature. A mid point between these is the mean monthly temperature.

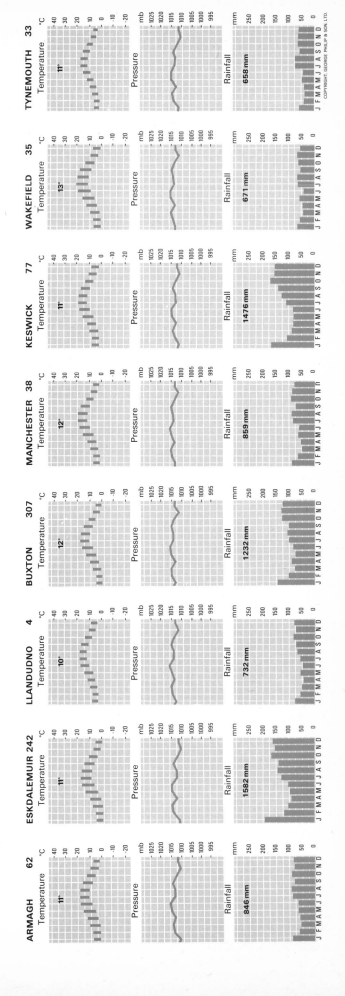

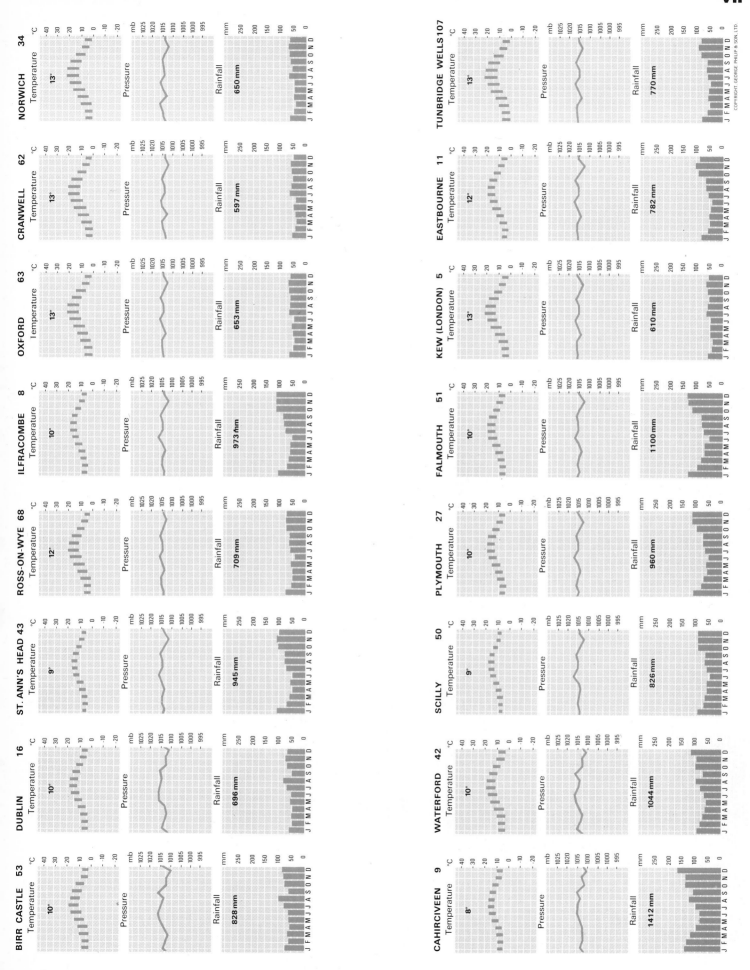

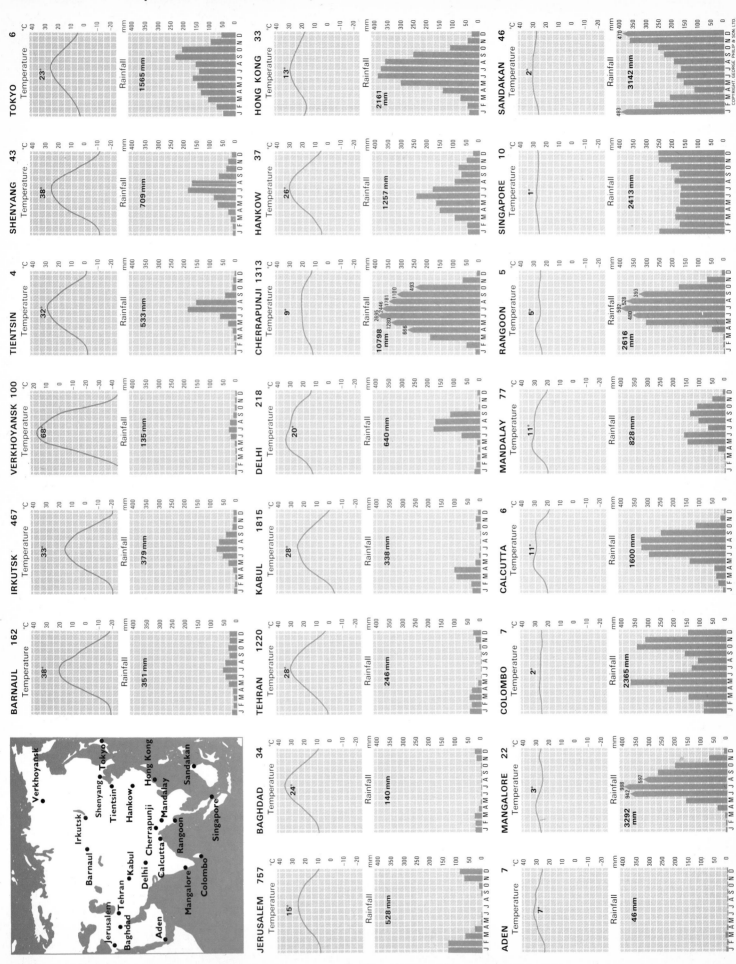

TOKYO 6 — Temperature 23° — Rainfall 1565 mm

HONG KONG 33 — Temperature 13° — Rainfall 2161 mm

SANDAKAN 46 — Temperature 2° — Rainfall 3142 mm (470, 400, 483)

SHENYANG 43 — Temperature 38° — Rainfall 709 mm

HANKOW 37 — Temperature 26° — Rainfall 1257 mm

SINGAPORE 10 — Temperature 1° — Rainfall 2413 mm

TIENTSIN 4 — Temperature 32° — Rainfall 533 mm

CHERRAPUNJI 1313 — Temperature 9° — Rainfall 10798 mm (2695, 2446, 1781, 1280, 493, 1100, 666)

RANGOON 5 — Temperature 5° — Rainfall 2616 mm (582, 528, 393, 480)

VERKHOYANSK 100 — Temperature 68° — Rainfall 135 mm

DELHI 218 — Temperature 20° — Rainfall 640 mm

MANDALAY 77 — Temperature 11° — Rainfall 828 mm

IRKUTSK 467 — Temperature 33° — Rainfall 379 mm

KABUL 1815 — Temperature 28° — Rainfall 338 mm

CALCUTTA 6 — Temperature 11° — Rainfall 1600 mm

BARNAUL 162 — Temperature 38° — Rainfall 351 mm

TEHRAN 1220 — Temperature 28° — Rainfall 246 mm

COLOMBO 7 — Temperature 2° — Rainfall 2365 mm

BAGHDAD 34 — Temperature 24° — Rainfall 140 mm

MANGALORE 22 — Temperature 3° — Rainfall 3292 mm (942, 988, 597)

JERUSALEM 757 — Temperature 15° — Rainfall 528 mm

ADEN 7 — Temperature 7° — Rainfall 46 mm

Verkhoyansk, Tokyo, Shenyang, Tientsin, Hong Kong, Hankow, Sandakan, Irkutsk, Barnaul, Kabul, Mandalay, Rangoon, Singapore, Delhi, Cherrapunji, Calcutta, Tehran, Baghdad, Jerusalem, Mangalore, Colombo, Aden

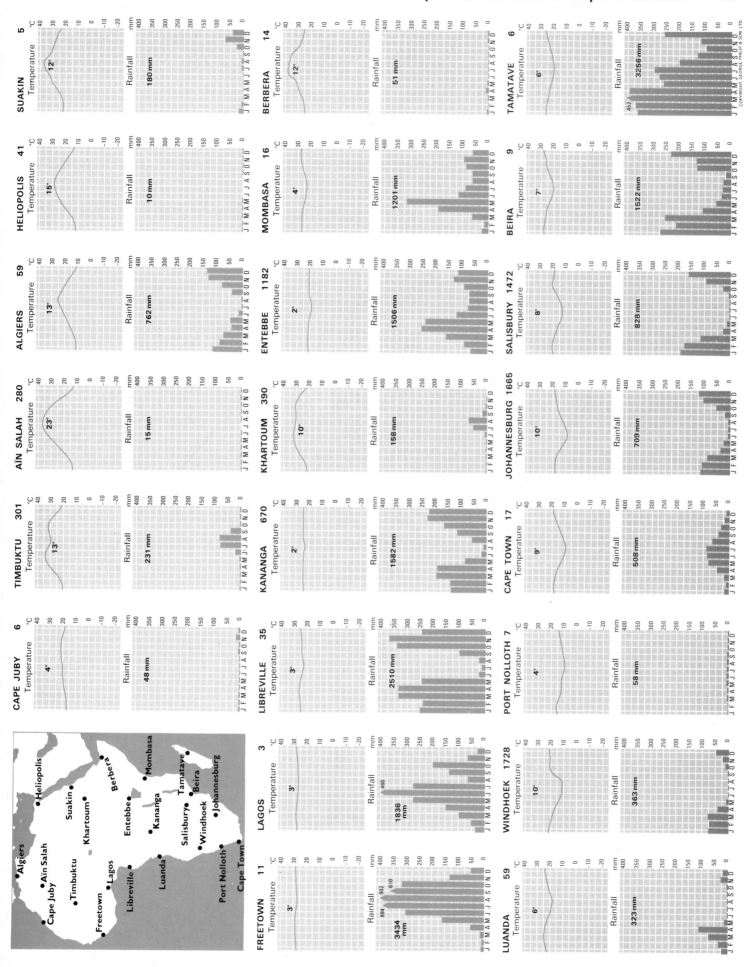

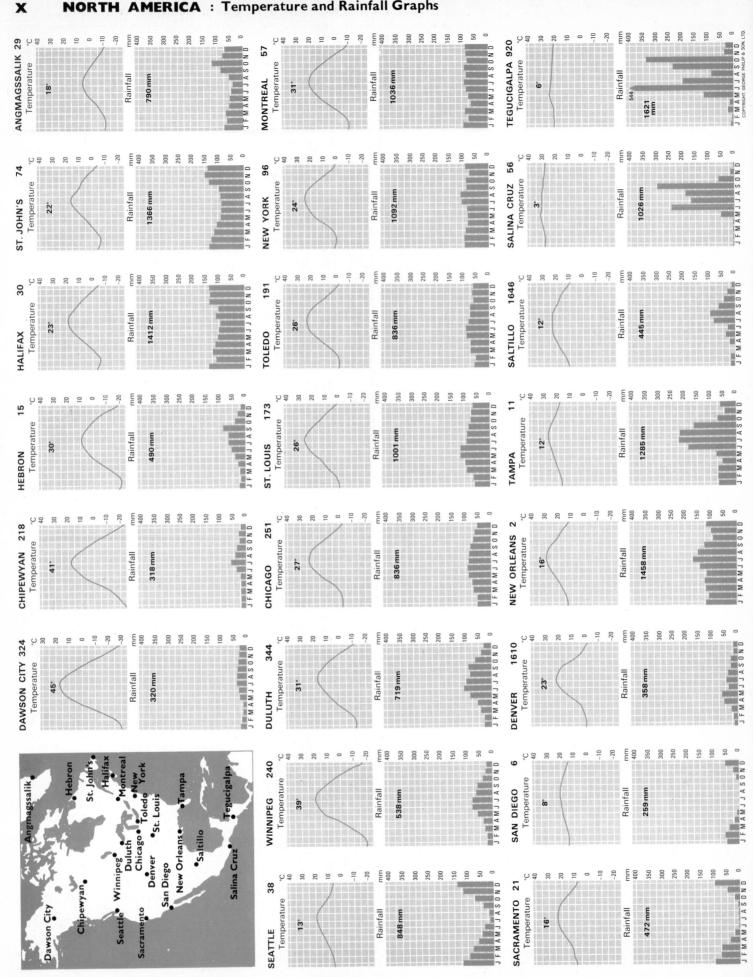

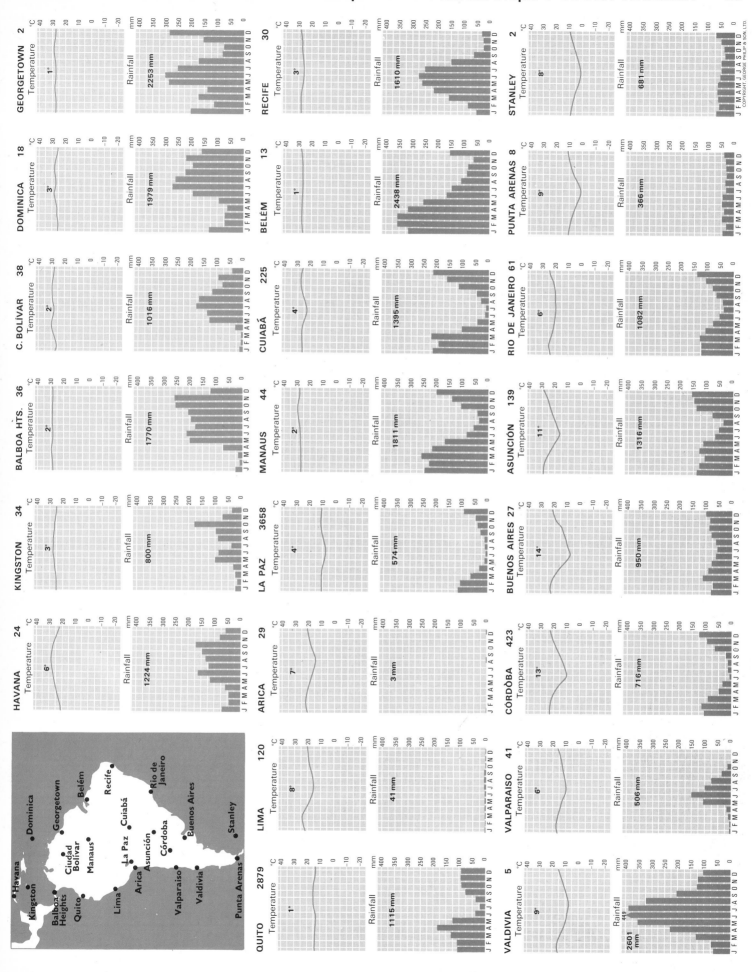

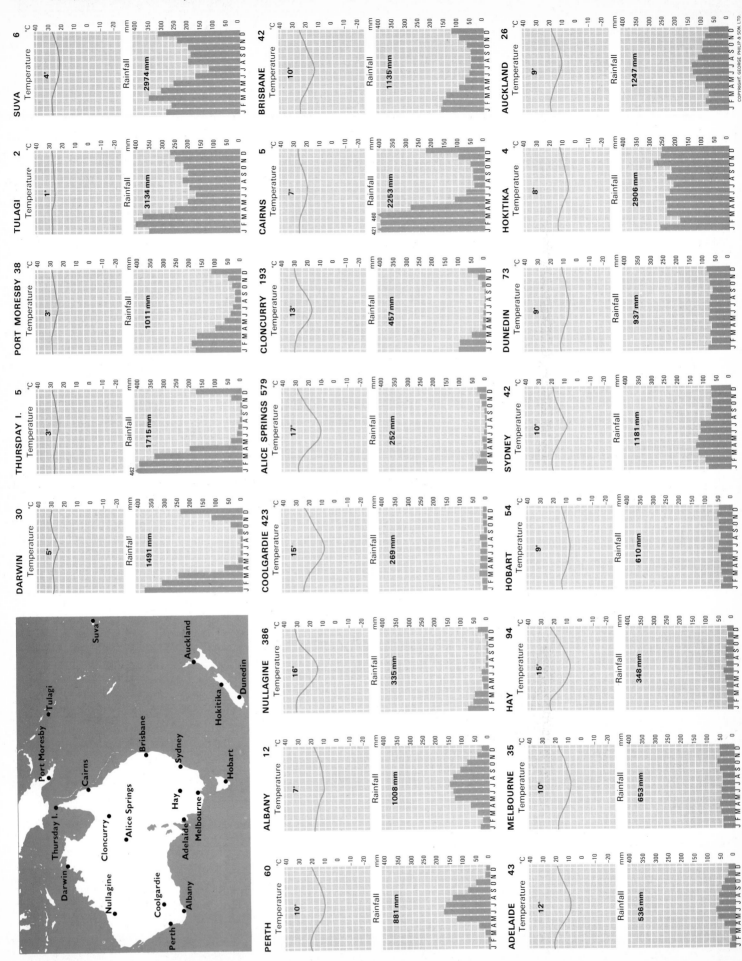

Chart of the Stars

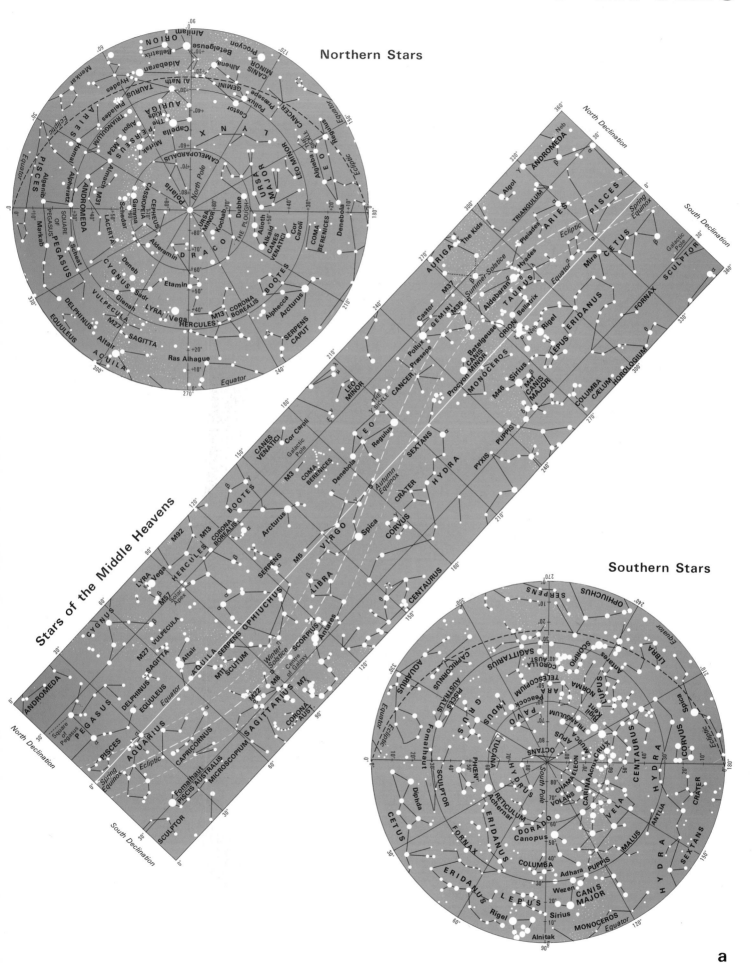

Northern Stars

Southern Stars

Stars of the Middle Heavens

The Evolution of the Continents

The origin of the earth is still open to much conjecture although the most widely accepted theory is that it was formed from a solar cloud consisting mainly of hydrogen. Under gravitation the cloud condensed and shrank to form our planets orbiting around the sun. Gravitation forced the lighter elements to the surface of the earth where they cooled to form a crust while the inner material remained hot and molten. Earth's first rocks formed over 3500 million years ago but since then the surface has been constantly altered.

Until comparatively recently the view that the primary units of the earth had remained essentially fixed throughout geological time was regarded as common sense, although the concept of moving continents has been traced back to references in the Bible of a break up of the land after Noah's floods. The continental drift theory was first developed by Antonio Snider in 1858 but probably the most important single advocate was Alfred Wegener who, in 1915, published evidence from geology, climatology and biology. His conclusions are very similar to those reached by current research although he was wrong about the speed of break-up.

The measurement of fossil magnetism found in rocks has probably proved the most influential evidence. While originally these drift theories were openly mocked, now they are considered standard doctrine.

The jigsaw
As knowledge of the shape and structure of the earth's surface grew, several of the early geographers noticed the great similarity in shape of the coasts bordering the Atlantic. It was this remarkable similarity which led to the first detailed geological and structural comparisons. Even more accurate fits can be made by placing the edges of the continental shelves in juxtaposition.

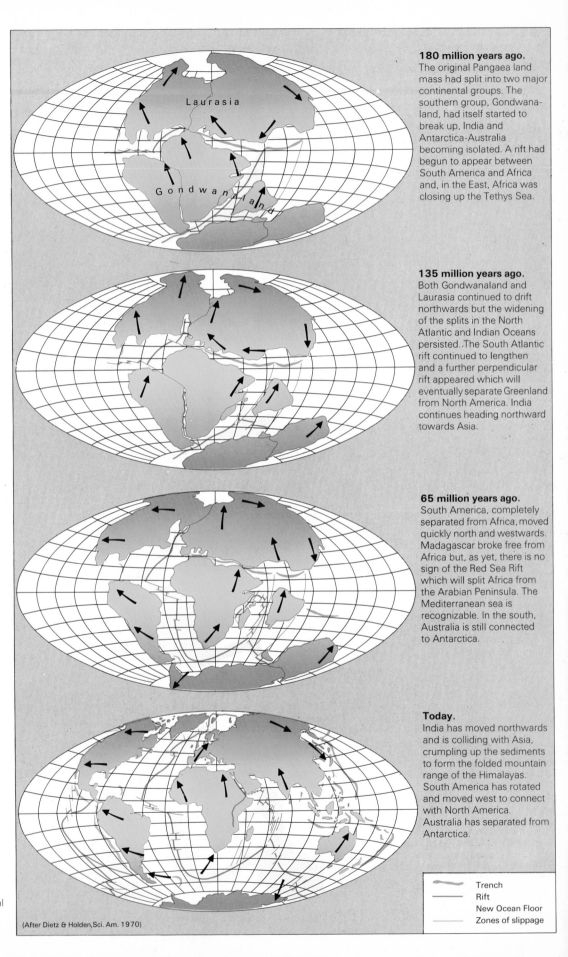

(After Dietz & Holden, Sci. Am. 1970)

180 million years ago.
The original Pangaea land mass had split into two major continental groups. The southern group, Gondwana-land, had itself started to break up, India and Antarctica-Australia becoming isolated. A rift had begun to appear between South America and Africa and, in the East, Africa was closing up the Tethys Sea.

135 million years ago.
Both Gondwanaland and Laurasia continued to drift northwards but the widening of the splits in the North Atlantic and Indian Oceans persisted. The South Atlantic rift continued to lengthen and a further perpendicular rift appeared which will eventually separate Greenland from North America. India continues heading northward towards Asia.

65 million years ago.
South America, completely separated from Africa, moved quickly north and westwards. Madagascar broke free from Africa but, as yet, there is no sign of the Red Sea Rift which will split Africa from the Arabian Peninsula. The Mediterranean sea is recognizable. In the south, Australia is still connected to Antarctica.

Today.
India has moved northwards and is colliding with Asia, crumpling up the sediments to form the folded mountain range of the Himalayas. South America has rotated and moved west to connect with North America. Australia has separated from Antarctica.

	Trench
	Rift
	New Ocean Floor
	Zones of slippage

b

Plate tectonics

The original debate about continental drift was only a prelude to a more radical idea; plate tectonics. The basic theory is that the earth's crust is made up of a series of rigid plates which float on a soft layer of the mantle and are moved about by convection currents in the earth's interior. These plates converge and diverge along margins marked by earthquakes, volcanoes and other seismic activity. Plates diverge from mid-ocean ridges where molten lava pushes upwards and forces the plates apart at a rate of up to 30 mm a year. Converging plates form either a trench, where the oceanic plate sinks below the lighter continental rock, or mountain ranges where two continents collide. This explains the paradox that while there have always been oceans none of the present oceans contain sediments more than 150 million years old.

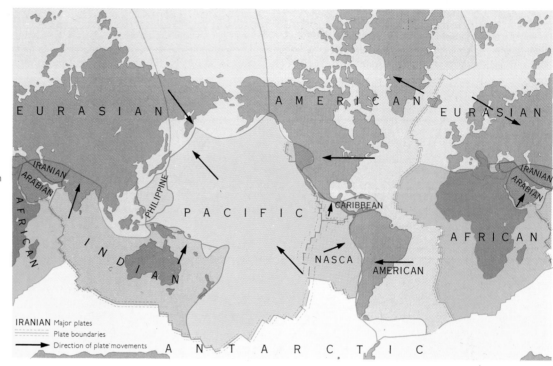

IRANIAN — Major plates
- - - - - Plate boundaries
→ Direction of plate movements

Trench boundary

The present explanation for the comparative youth of the ocean floors is that where an ocean and a continent meet the ocean plate dips under the less dense continental plate at an angle of approximately 45°. All previous crust is then ingested by downward convection currents. In the Japanese trench this occurs at a rate of about 120 mm a year.

Transform fault

The recent identification of the transform, or transverse, fault proved to be one of the crucial preliminaries to the investigation of plate tectonics. They occur when two plates slip alongside each other without parting or approaching to any great extent. They complete the outline of the plates delineated by the ridges and trenches and demonstrate large scale movements of parts of the earth's surface

Ridge boundary

Ocean rises or crests are basically made up from basaltic lavas for although no gap can exist between plates, one plate can ease itself away from another. In that case hot, molten rock instantly rises from below to fill in the incipient rift and forms a ridge. These ridges trace a line almost exactly through the centre of the major oceans.

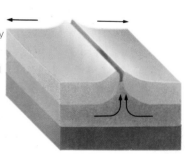

Destruction of ocean plates.

As the ocean plate sinks below the continental plate some of the sediment on its surface is scraped off and piled up on the landward side. This sediment is later incorporated in a folded mountain range which usually appears on the edge of the continent, such as the Andes. Similarly if two continents collide the sediments are squeezed up into new mountains.

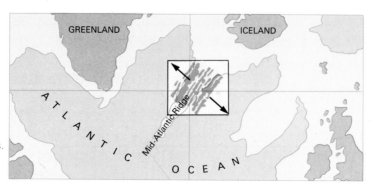

Sea floor spreading

Reversals in the earth's magnetic field have occured throughout history. As new rock emerges at the ocean ridges it cools and is magnetised in the direction of the prevailing magnetic field. By mapping the magnetic patterns either side of the ridge a symmetrical stripey pattern of alternating fields can be observed (see inset area in diagram). As the dates of the last few reversals are known the rate of spreading can be calculated.

The Unstable Earth

The earth's surface is slowly but continually being rearranged. Some changes such as erosion and deposition are extremely slow but they upset the balance which causes other more abrupt changes often originating deep within the earth's interior. The constant movements vary in intensity, often with stresses building up to a climax such as a particularly violent volcanic eruption or earthquake.

The crust (below and right)
The outer layer or crust of the earth consists of a comparatively low density, brittle material varying from 5 km to 50 km deep beneath the continents. Under this is a layer of rock consisting predominately of silica and aluminium; hence it is called 'sial'. Extending under the ocean floors and below the sial is a basaltic layer known as 'sima', consisting mainly of silica and magnesium.

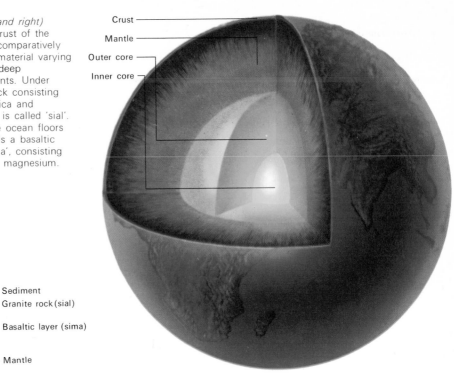

Crust
Mantle
Outer core
Inner core

Continental crust   Ocean crust

Sediment
Granite rock (sial)
Basaltic layer (sima)
Mantle

Volcanoes(right, below and far right)
Volcanoes occur when hot liquefied rock beneath the crust reaches the surface as lava. An accumulation of ash and cinders around a vent forms a cone. Successive layers of thin lava flows form an acid lava volcano while thick lava flows form a basic lava volcano. A caldera forms when a particularly violent eruption blows off the top of an already existing cone.

The mantle (above)
Immediately below the crust, at the mohorovicic discontinuity line, there is a distinct change in density and chemical properties. This is the mantle - made up of iron and magnesium silicates - with temperatures reaching 1 600 °C. The rigid upper mantle extends down to a depth of about 1 000 km below which is the more viscous lower mantle which is about 1 900 km thick.

The core (above)
The outer core, approximately 2 100 km thick, consists of molten iron and nickel at 2 000 °C to 5 000 °C possibly separated from the less dense mantle by an oxidised shell. About 5 000 km below the surface is the liquid transition zone, below which is the solid inner core, a sphere of 2 740 km diameter where rock is three times as dense as in the crust.

Shield volcano   **Cinder cone**   **Hornit cone**   **Caldera**

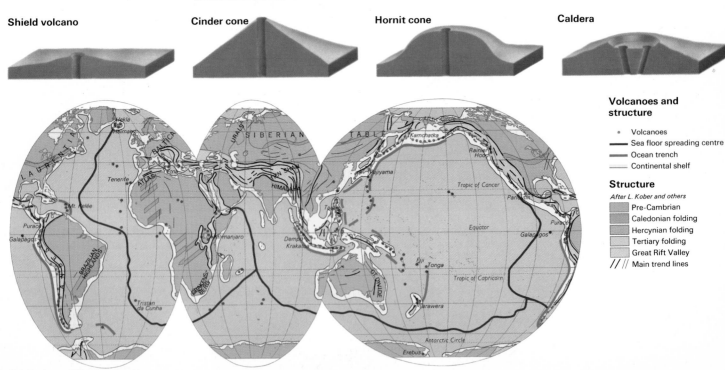

Volcanoes and structure

- Volcanoes
— Sea floor spreading centre
— Ocean trench
— Continental shelf

Structure
After L. Kober and others

Pre-Cambrian
Caledonian folding
Hercynian folding
Tertiary folding
Great Rift Valley
/// Main trend lines

Projection: *Interrupted Mollweide's Homolographic*

d

Major earthquakes in the last 100 years and numbers killed

Year	Location	Killed
1896	Japan (tsunami)	22 000
1906	San Francisco	destroyed
1906	Chile, Valparaiso	22 000
1908	Italy, Messina	77 000
1920	China, Kansu	180 000
1923	Japan, Tokyo	143 000
1930	Italy, Naples	2 100
1931	New Zealand, Napier	destroyed
1931	Nicaragua, Managua	destroyed
1932	China, Kansu	70 000
1935	India, Quetta	60 000
1939	Chile, Chillan	20 000
1939/40	Turkey, Erzincan	30 000
1948	Japan, Fukui	5 100
1956	N. Afghanistan	2 000
1957	W. Iran	10 000
1960	Morocco, Agadir	12 000
1962	N.W. Iran	10 000
1963	Yugoslavia, Skopje	1 000
1966	U.S.S.R., Tashkent	destroyed
1970	N. Peru	66 800
1972	Nicaragua, Managua	7 000
1974	N. Pakistan	10 000
1975	Turkey, Lice	2 300
1976	China, Tangshan	650 000
1976	Turkey, Van	3 800

World distribution of earthquakes

- Major earthquake zones
- Areas experiencing frequent earthquakes

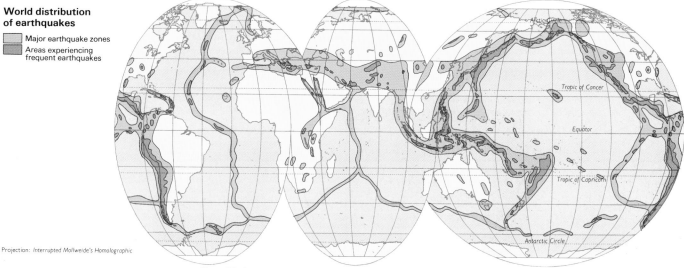

Projection: *Interrupted Mollweide's Homolographic*

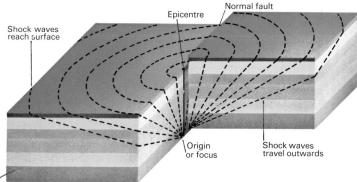

Earthquakes *(right and above)*

Earthquakes are a series of rapid vibrations originating from the slipping or faulting of parts of the earth's crust when stresses within build up to breaking point. They usually happen at depths varying from 8 km to 30 km. Severe earthquakes cause extensive damage when they take place in populated areas destroying structures and severing communications. Most loss of life occurs due to secondary causes i.e. falling masonry, fires or tsunami waves.

Alaskan earthquake, 1964

Tsunami waves *(left)*

A sudden slump in the ocean bed during an earthquake forms a trough in the water surface subsequently followed by a crest and smaller waves. A more marked change of level in the sea bed can form a crest, the start of a Tsunami which travels up to 60 km/h with waves up to 60 m high. Seismographic detectors continuously record earthquake shocks and warn of the Tsunami which may follow it.

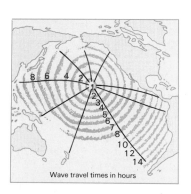

Wave travel times in hours

Seismic Waves *(right)*

The shock waves sent out from the focus of an earthquake are of three main kinds each with distinct properties. Primary (P) waves are compressional waves which can be transmitted through both solids and liquids and therefore pass through the earth's liquid core. Secondary (S) waves are shear waves and can only pass through solids. They cannot pass through the core and are reflected at the core-mantle boundary taking a concave course back to the surface. The core also refracts the P waves causing them to alter course, and the net effect of this reflection and refraction is the production of a shadow zone at a certain distance from the epicentre, free from P and S waves. Due to their different properties P waves travel about 1,7 times faster than S waves. The third main kind of wave is a long (L) wave, a slow wave which travels along the earth's surface, its motion being either horizontal or vertical.

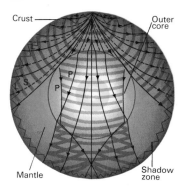

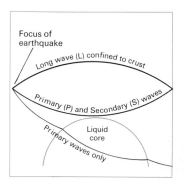

Principles of seismographs *(left)*

- M = Mass
- D = Drum
- P = Pivot
- S = Spring

Seismographs

are delicate instruments capable of detecting and recording vibrations due to earthquakes thousands of kilometres away. P waves cause the first tremors. S the second, and L the main shock.

The Atmosphere and Clouds

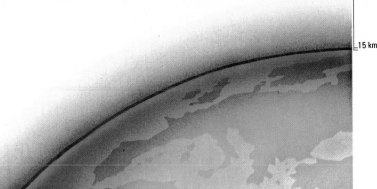

Earth's thin coating *(right)*
The atmosphere is a blanket of protective gases around the earth providing insulation against otherwise extreme alternations in temperature. The gravitational pull increases the density nearer the earth's surface so that 5/6ths of the atmospheric mass is in the first 15 kms. It is a very thin layer in comparison with the earth's diameter of 12 680 kms., like the cellulose coating on a globe.

Exosphere(1)
The exosphere merges with the interplanetary medium and although there is no definite boundary with the ionosphere it starts at a height of about 600 kms. The rarified air mainly consists of a small amount of atomic oxygen up to 600 kms. and equal proportions of hydrogen and helium with hydrogen predominating above 2 400 kms.

Ionosphere(2)
Air particles of the ionosphere are electrically charged by the sun's radiation and congregate in four main layers, D, E, F1 and F2, which can reflect radio waves. Aurorae, caused by charged particles deflected by the earth's magnetic field towards the poles, occur between 65 and 965 kms. above the earth. It is mainly in the lower ionosphere that meteors from outer space burn up as they meet increased air resistance.

Stratosphere(3)
A thin layer of ozone contained within the stratosphere absorbs ultra-violet light and in the process gives off heat. The temperature ranges from about -55°C at the tropopause to about -60°C in the upper part, known as the mesosphere, with a rise to about 2°C just above the ozone layer. This portion of the atmosphere is separated from the lower layer by the tropopause.

Troposphere(4)
The earth's weather conditions are limited to this layer which is relatively thin, extending upwards to about 8 kms. at the poles and 15 kms. at the equator. It contains about 85% of the total atmospheric mass and almost all the water vapour. Air temperature falls steadily with increased height at about 1°C for every 100 metres above sea level.

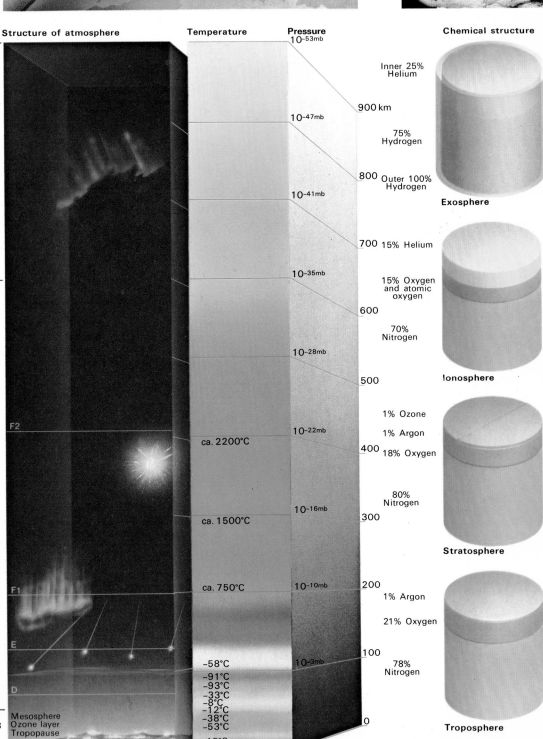

Structure of atmosphere

Temperature

Pressure

Chemical structure

600 km
15 km

10^{-53}mb
10^{-47}mb
10^{-41}mb
10^{-35}mb
10^{-28}mb
10^{-22}mb
10^{-16}mb
10^{-10}mb
10^{-3}mb
10^{3}mb

900 km
800
700
600
500
400
300
200
100
0

Inner 25% Helium
75% Hydrogen
Outer 100% Hydrogen
Exosphere

15% Helium
15% Oxygen and atomic oxygen
70% Nitrogen
Ionosphere

1% Ozone
1% Argon
18% Oxygen
80% Nitrogen
Stratosphere

1% Argon
21% Oxygen
78% Nitrogen
Troposphere

ca. 2200°C
ca. 1500°C
ca. 750°C
-58°C
-91°C
-93°C
-33°C
-8°C
-12°C
-38°C
-53°C
15°C

F2
F1
E
D

Mesosphere
Ozone layer
Tropopause

1
2
3
4

f

Pacific Ocean
Cloud patterns over the Pacific show the paths of prevailing winds.

Circulation of the air

30°N

Equator

30°S

Circulation of the air
Owing to high temperatures in equatorial regions the air near the ground is heated, expands and rises producing a low pressure belt. It cools, causing rain, spreads out then sinks again about latitudes 30° north and south forming high pressure belts.

High and low pressure belts are areas of comparative calm but between them, blowing from high to low pressure, are the prevailing winds. These are deflected to the right in the northern hemisphere and to the left in the southern hemisphere (Corolis effect). The circulations appear in three distinct belts with a seasonal movement north and south following the overhead sun.

Cloud types
Clouds form when damp air is cooled, usually by rising. This may happen in three ways: when a wind rises to cross hills or mountains; when a mass of air rises over, or is pushed up by another mass of denser air; when local heating of the ground causes convection currents.

Cirrus *(1)* are detached clouds composed of microscopic ice crystals which gleam white in the sun resembling hair or feathers. They are found at heights of 6 000 to 12 000 metres.

Cirrostratus *(2)* are a whitish veil of cloud made up of ice crystals through which the sun can be seen often producing a halo of bright light.

Cirrocumulus *(3)* is another high altitude cloud formed by turbulence between layers moving in different directions.

Altostratus *(4)* is a grey or bluish striated, fibrous or uniform sheet of cloud producing light drizzle.

Altocumulus *(5)* is a thicker and fluffier version of cirro cumulus, it is a white and grey patchy sheet of cloud.

Nimbostratus *(6)* is a dark grey layer of cloud obscuring the sun and causing almost continuous rain or snow.

Cumulus *(7)* are detached heaped up, dense low clouds. The sunlit parts are brilliant white while the base is relatively dark and flat.

Stratus *(8)* forms dull overcast skies associated with depressions and occurs at low altitudes up to 1500 metres.

Cumulonimbus *(9)* are heavy and dense clouds associated with storms and rain. They have flat bases and a fluffy outline extending up to great altitudes.

High clouds

Middle clouds

Low clouds

Thousands of metres

1 Cirrus

2 Cirrostratus

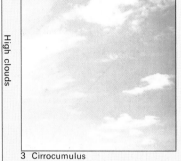

3 Cirrocumulus

4 Altostratus

5 Altocumulus

6 Nimbostratus

7 Cumulus

8 Stratus

9 Cumulonimbus

Time Zones

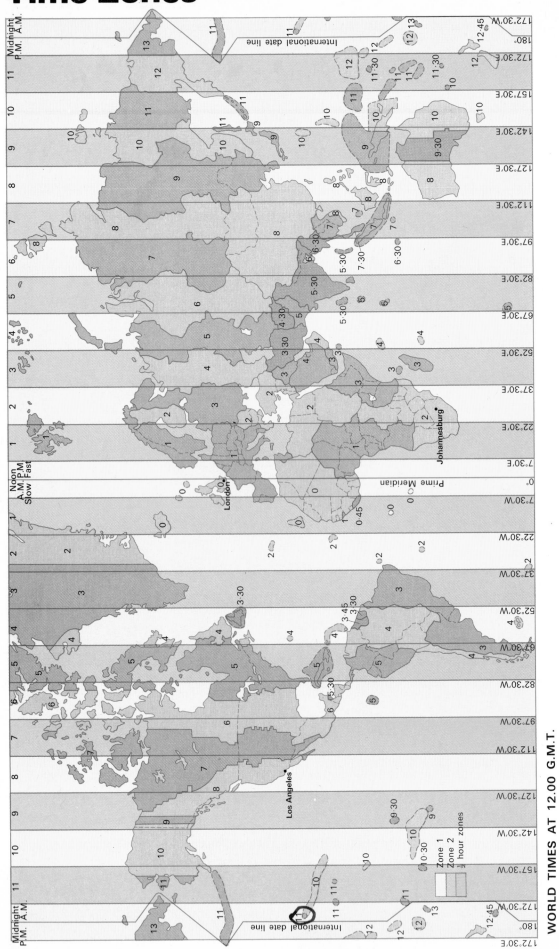

WORLD TIMES AT 12.00 G.M.T.

h

Time zones

The world is divided into 24 time zones, each centred on meridians at 15° intervals which is the longitudinal distance the sun appears to travel every hour. The meridian running through Greenwich passes through the middle of the first zone. Successive zones to the east of Greenwich zone are ahead of Greenwich time by one hour for every 15° of longitude, while zones to the west are behind by one hour.

The International Date Line

When it is 12 noon at the Greenwich meridian, 180° east it is midnight of the same day while 180° west the day is only just beginning. To overcome this the International Date Line was established, approximately following the 180° meridian. Thus, for example, if one travelled eastwards from Japan (140° East) to Samoa (170° West) one would pass from Sunday night into Sunday morning.

International date line

Watch must be put back 24 hrs.

Watch must be put forward 24 hrs.

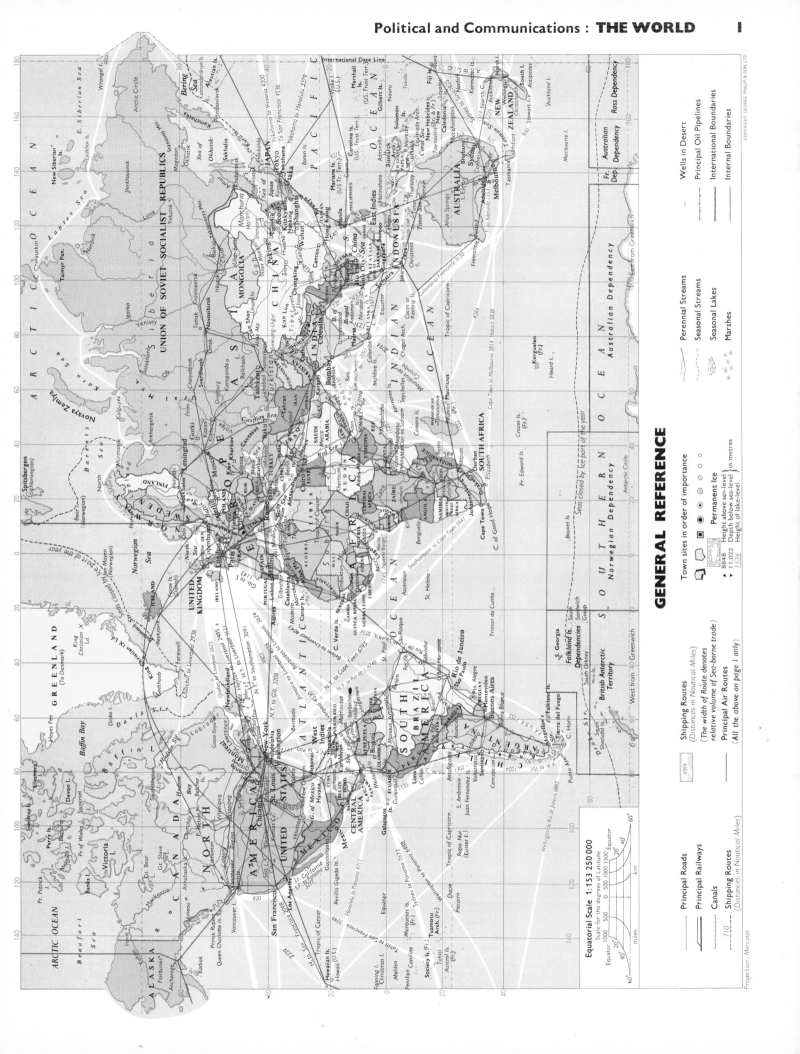

GENERAL REFERENCE

Principal Roads	
Principal Railways	
Canals	
Shipping Routes (Distances in Nautical Miles)	

Shipping Routes
(Distances in Nautical Miles)
(The width of Route denotes relative volume of Sea-borne trade)

Principal Air Routes
(All the above on page 1 only)

Town sites in order of importance

Height above sea-level
Depth below sea-level } in metres
Height of lake-level

8848 ▲
11,022 ▼
1,134

Seas closed by Ice part of the year

Permanent Ice

Perennial Streams
Seasonal Streams
Seasonal Lakes
Marshes
Wells in Desert
Principal Oil Pipelines
International Boundaries
Internal Boundaries

Equatorial Scale 1:153 250 000
Scale for the degrees of Latitude

Projection: Mercator

GEOLOGY
after
Beyschlag, Nalivkin and others

1:90 000 000

Ⓐ

Ⓒ GEOLOGICAL
CYCLES

Quaternary	Recent		
Tertiary (Cainozoic)	Pliocene	Alpine Folding	
	Miocene		
	Oligocene		
	Eocene		
Secondary (Mesozoic)	Cretaceous	Laramide Folding	
	Jurassic		
	Triassic		
Primary Upper (Palæozoic)	Permian	Hercynian Folding	
	Carboniferous		
Primary Lower (Palæozoic)	Devonian		
	Silurian	Caledonian Folding	
	Ordovician		
	Cambrian		
Archæan	Pre-Cambrian		

Ⓑ An Interpretation of
STRUCTURE
showing
the distribution of rigid masses and folded regions
after L. Kober and others

Pre-Cambrian tables composite in structure, rigid since the Cambrian period and forming stable elements separating the geo-synclines of later times.
Regions of Caledonian folding; Siluro-Devonian earth movements.
Regions of Hercynian folding; Carbo-Permian earth movements.
Regions of Tertiary folding; Cretaceo-Tertiary earth movements.
The Great Rift Valley
Main Trend lines

Projections: Interrupted Mollweide's Homolographic

LAURENTIA

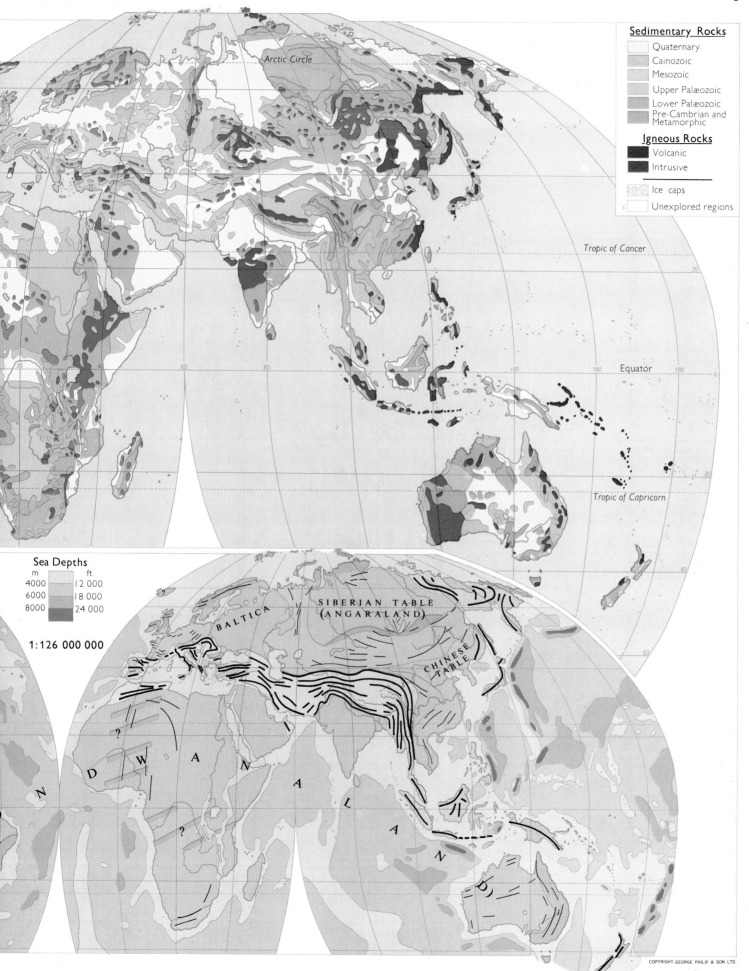

3

COPYRIGHT. GEORGE PHILIP & SON LTD.

Sedimentary Rocks

- Quaternary
- Cainozoic
- Mesozoic
- Upper Palæozoic
- Lower Palæozoic
- Pre-Cambrian and Metamorphic

Igneous Rocks

- Volcanic
- Intrusive

- Ice caps
- Unexplored regions

Arctic Circle

Tropic of Cancer

Equator

Tropic of Capricorn

60

20

80

60

140

160

180

0

20

40

60

Sea Depths

m	ft
4000	12 000
6000	18 000
8000	24 000

1:126 000 000

BALTICA

SIBERIAN TABLE (ANGARALAND)

CHINESE TABLE

G O N D W A N A L A N D

?

?

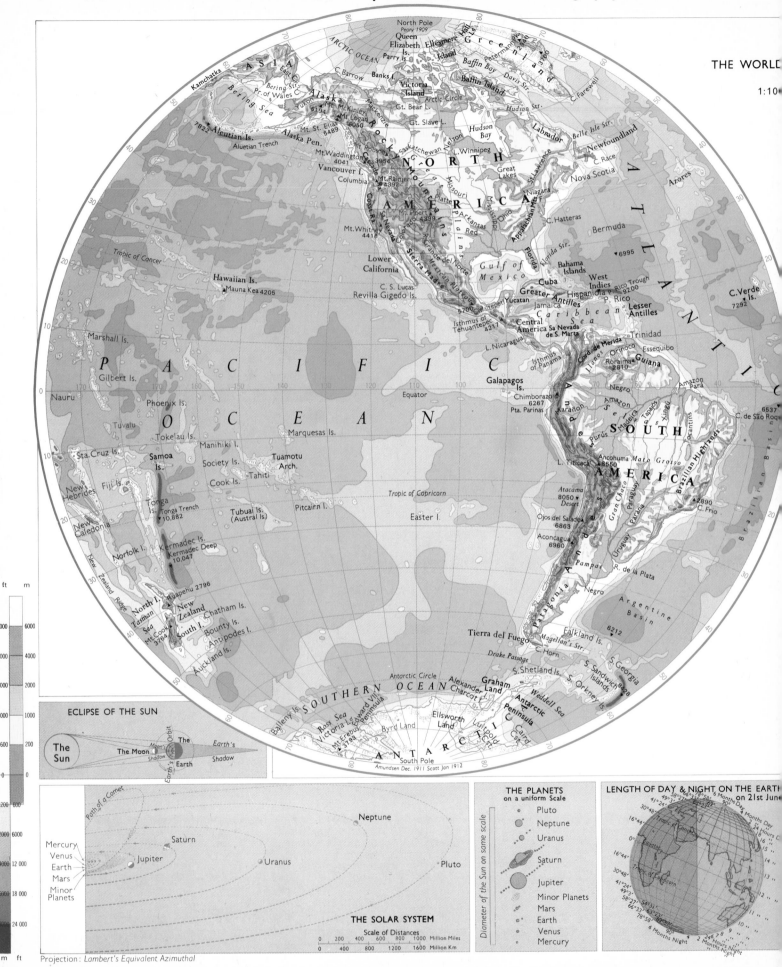

THE WORLD

1:10

ft   m

18 000   6000

12 000   4000

6000   2000

3000   1000

600   200

0   0

200   600

2000   6000

4000   12 000

6000   18 000

24 000

m   ft

ECLIPSE OF THE SUN

The Sun

The Moon

Moon's Orbit

The Earth

Earth's Shadow

Earth's Orbit

THE SOLAR SYSTEM

Path of a Comet

Neptune

Saturn

Jupiter

Uranus

Pluto

Mercury
Venus
Earth
Mars
Minor
Planets

Scale of Distances

0   200   400   600   800   1000 Million Miles
0   400   800   1200   1600 Million Km

THE PLANETS
on a uniform Scale

Pluto
Neptune
Uranus
Saturn
Jupiter
Minor Planets
Mars
Earth
Venus
Mercury

Diameter of the Sun on same scale

LENGTH OF DAY & NIGHT ON THE EARTH
on 21st June

Projection: *Lambert's Equivalent Azimuthal*

5

PHYSICAL

00 000

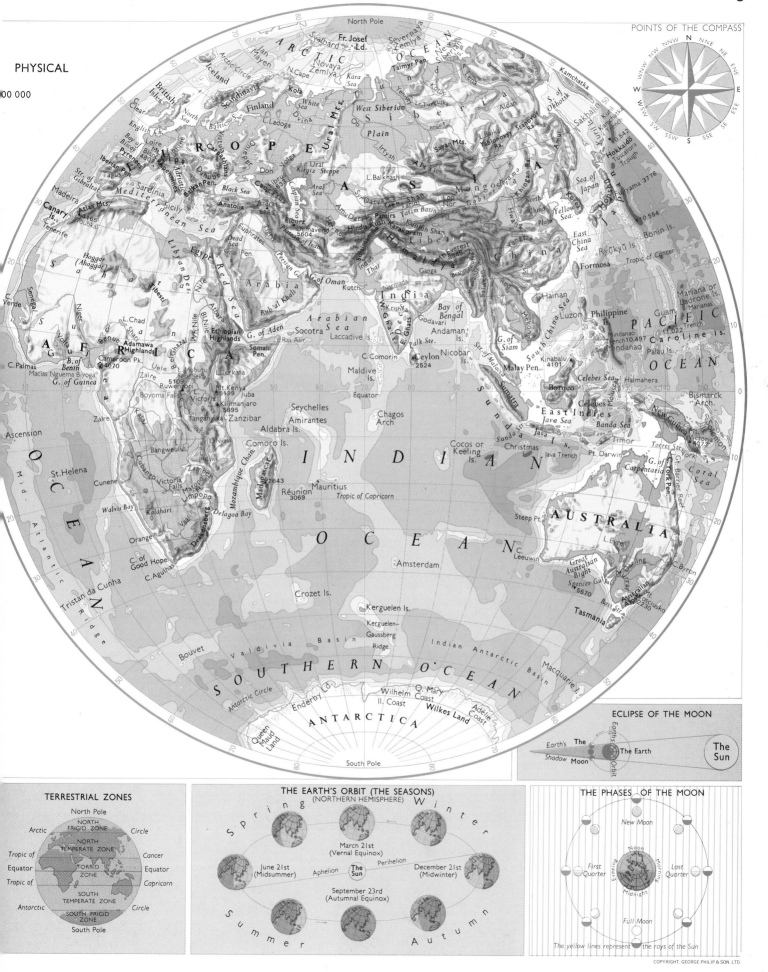

POINTS OF THE COMPASS

N NNE NE ENE
NNW
NW
WNW E
W
WSW ESE
SW SE
SSW SSE
S

North Pole

ARCTIC OCEAN
Fr. Josef Ld.
Severnaya Zemlya
Svalbard
Jan Mayen
N.Cape
Novaya Zemlya
New Siberian Is.
Iceland
Arctic Circle
Kara Sea
Taimyr Pen.
Kolyma
Kamchatka
British Isles
Scandinavia
Finland
White Sea
Dvina
West Siberian Plain
Lena
Aldan
Sea of Okhotsk
Sakhalin
Kuril Is.
C. Clear
North Sea
Baltic
L. Ladoga
Kola
Ural Mts.
Ob
Irtysh
S i b e r i a
Angara
Yenisey
Stanovoy Ra.
Amur
Sikhote Alin
Hokkaido
10,542
English Ch.
Loire
E U R O P E
Don
Volga
Kirgiz Steppe
L. Balkhash
Sayan Mts.
Yablonowy Ra.
L. Baikal
Gobi
Khingan Ra.
Sea of Japan
Fujiyama 3776
Bay of Biscay
Pyrenees
Alps
Carpathians
Danube
Caucasus
Caspian Sea
Aral Sea
Syr Darya
Tien Shan
Lop Nor
Tarim Basin
Mongolia
North China Plain
Hwang
Korea
J a p a n
10,554
Iberian Pen.
Tagus
Adriatic
Balkan Pen.
Black Sea
Elbruz 5633
Ararat 5165
Amu Darya
Pamirs
Kunlun Shan
T i b e t
Yangtze
Yellow Sea
East China Sea
Bonin Is.
Madeira
Atlas Mts.
Sardinia
Sicily
Mediterranean Sea
Anatolia
Syrian Des.
Tigris
Hindu Kush
Karakoram
H i m a l a y a
Everest 8848
Brahmaputra
C h i n a
Red
Si
Formosa
Tropic of Cancer
Canary Is.
Toubkal 4165
Tenerife
Libyan Des.
Egypt
Nile
Euphrates
Dead Sea
Sinai Pen.
Persian G.
Elburz 5604
Plateau of Iran
Indus
Thar
Ganga
Narmada
Iwo Jima
Hainan
Mariana or Ladrone Is.
Marianas
C. Verde
Senegal
S a h a r a
Hoggar (Ahaggar) 2918
Tibesti
Arabia
Rub' al Khali
G. of Oman
Kutch
I n d i a
Krishna
Godavari
Bay of Bengal
Andaman Is.
Nicobar Is.
11,022
Mindanao Trench 10,497
Philippine Trench 10,497
Guam
Mariana Trench
Caroline Is.
Niger
Benue
L. Chad
Shari
G. of Aden
Arabian Sea
Socotra
Ras Asir
Somali Pen.
Laccadive Is.
Deccan
E. Ghats
W. Ghats
Palk Str.
G. of Siam
Malay Pen.
Luzon
Philippine Is.
Palau Is.
PACIFIC OCEAN
C. Palmas
B. of Benin
Macias Nguema Biyoga
G. of Guinea
A F R I C A
Cameroon Pk. 4070
Adamawa Highlands
R.
Uele
Bahr el Ghazal
Wh. Nile
Bl. Nile
Atbara
Ethiopian Highlands
L. Turkana
C. Comorin
Ceylon 2524
Maldive Is.
Sunda Str.
Sumatra
Kinabalu 4101
Borneo
Celebes Sea
Halmahera
Bismarck Arch.
Ascension
Zaire
Boyoma Falls
L. Mobutu Seko
Ruwenzori 5109
Mt. Kenya 5199
Kilimanjaro 5895
Juba
Mt. Victoria 4073
Mt. Solomon
Zaire
L. Victoria
Seychelles
Amirantes
Chagos Arch.
E a s t I n d i e s
Celebes
Java Sea
Banda Sea
New Guinea
St. Helena
Kasai
L. Tanganyika
Zanzibar
Aldabra Is.
Comoro Is.
I N D I A N
Sunda Is.
Java
Timor
Java Trench
Torres Strait
C. York Pen.
Coral Sea
Bangweulu
L. Nyasa
Réunion 3069
Mauritius
Christmas
Pt. Darwin
G. of Carpentaria
Gt. Barrier Reef
M i d - A t l a n t i c R i d g e
Cubango
Victoria Falls
Zambezi
Mozambique Channel
Madagascar 2643
Tropic of Capricorn
O C E A N
A U S T R A L I A
Cunene
Matopo
Limpopo
Delagoa Bay
Walvis Bay
Kalahari
Vaal
Drakensberg
Amsterdam
Steep Pt.
C. Leeuwin
Great Australian Bight
Spencer Gulf 5670
L. Eyre
Murray
Darling
C. Byron
Orange
C. of Good Hope
C. Agulhas
Crozet Is.
Great Dividing Ra.
Australian Alps 2230
Bass Str.
Tristan da Cunha
Bouvet
Kerguelen Is.
Kerguelen-Gaussberg Ridge
Valdivia Basin
Indian Antarctic Basin
Tasmania
Macquarie I.
A T L A N T I C
S O U T H E R N O C E A N
Antarctic Circle
Enderby Ld.
Wilhelm II. Coast
Q. Mary Coast
Wilkes Land
Adélie Coast
Queen Maud Land
A N T A R C T I C A

South Pole

ECLIPSE OF THE MOON

Earth's Orbit
Earth's Shadow
The Moon
The Earth
The Sun

TERRESTRIAL ZONES

North Pole
Arctic Circle
NORTH FRIGID ZONE
Tropic of Cancer
NORTH TEMPERATE ZONE
Equator
TORRID ZONE
Tropic of Capricorn
SOUTH TEMPERATE ZONE
Antarctic Circle
SOUTH FRIGID ZONE
South Pole

THE EARTH'S ORBIT (THE SEASONS)
(NORTHERN HEMISPHERE)

Spring
Winter
March 21st (Vernal Equinox)
June 21st (Midsummer)
Aphelion
The Sun
Perihelion
December 21st (Midwinter)
September 23rd (Autumnal Equinox)
Summer
Autumn

THE PHASES OF THE MOON

New Moon
First Quarter
Noon
Evening
Morning
Last Quarter
Midnight
Full Moon

The yellow lines represent the rays of the Sun

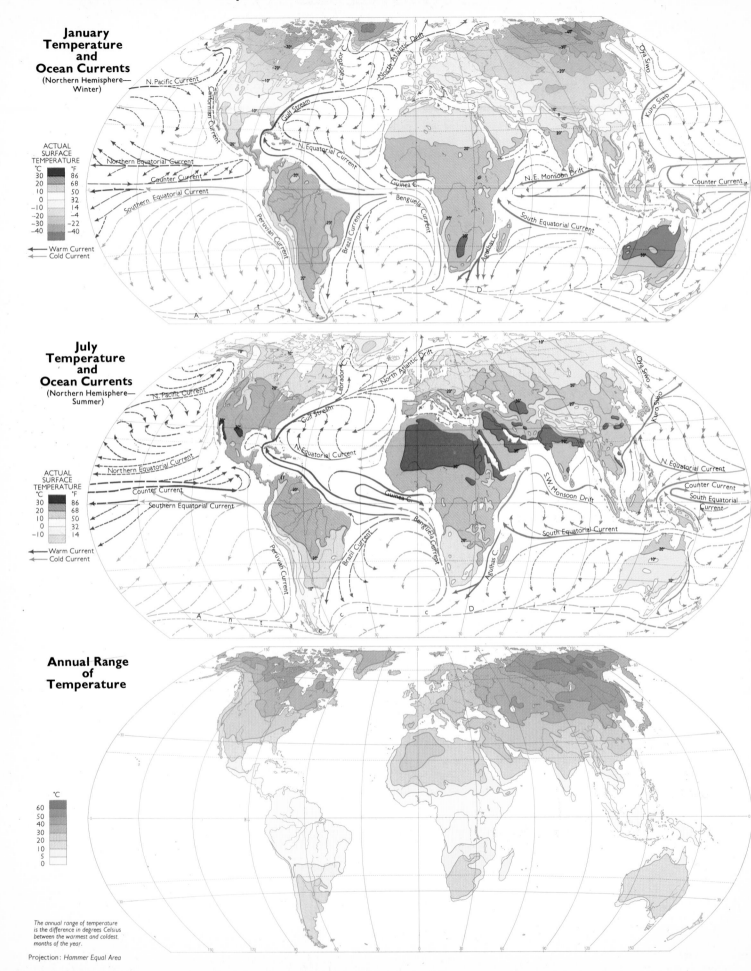

January Temperature and Ocean Currents
(Northern Hemisphere— Winter)

ACTUAL SURFACE TEMPERATURE

°C	°F
30	86
20	68
10	50
0	32
−10	14
−20	−4
−30	−22
−40	−40

← Warm Current
← Cold Current

July Temperature and Ocean Currents
(Northern Hemisphere— Summer)

ACTUAL SURFACE TEMPERATURE

°C	°F
30	86
20	68
10	50
0	32
−10	14

← Warm Current
← Cold Current

Annual Range of Temperature

°C
60
50
40
30
20
10
5
0

The annual range of temperature is the difference in degrees Celsius between the warmest and coldest months of the year.

Projection: *Hammer Equal Area*

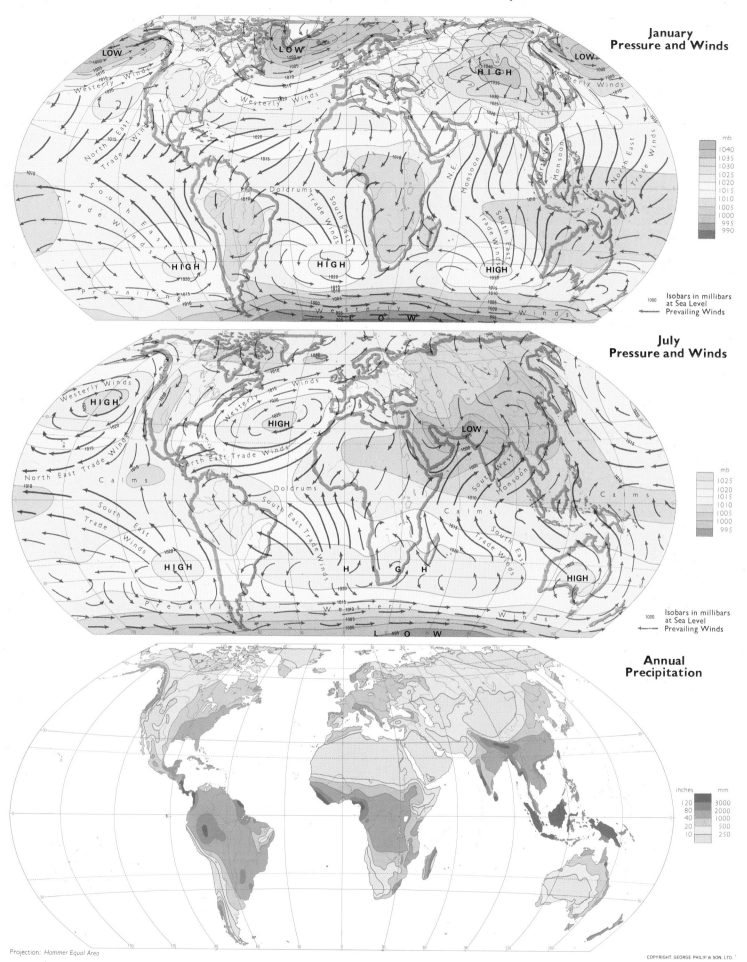

**January
Pressure and Winds**

**July
Pressure and Winds**

**Annual
Precipitation**

mb
1040
1035
1030
1025
1020
1015
1010
1005
1000
995
990

1000 Isobars in millibars
at Sea Level
Prevailing Winds

mb
1025
1020
1015
1010
1005
1000
995

1000 Isobars in millibars
at Sea Level
Prevailing Winds

inches   mm
120   3000
80   2000
40   1000
20   500
10   250

Projection: *Hammer Equal Area*

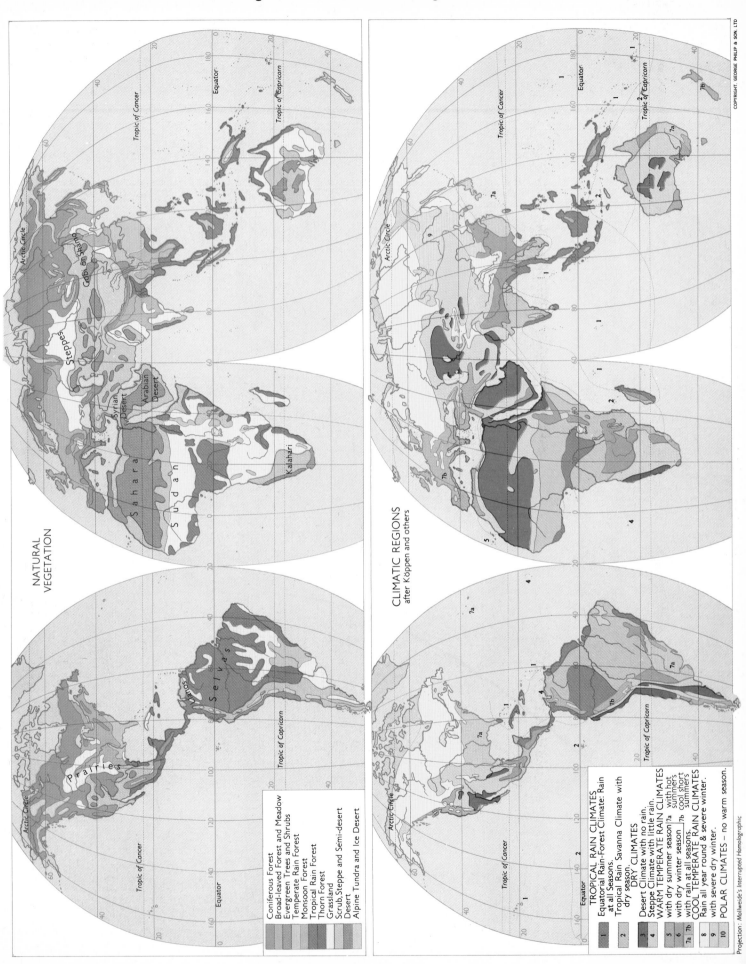

NATURAL VEGETATION

CLIMATIC REGIONS
after Köppen and others

Coniferous Forest
Broad-leaved Forest and Meadow
Evergreen Trees and Shrubs
Temperate Rain Forest
Monsoon Forest
Tropical Rain Forest
Thorn Forest
Grassland
Scrub, Steppe and Semi-desert
Desert
Alpine Tundra and Ice Desert

TROPICAL RAIN CLIMATES
Equatorial Rain-Forest Climate: Rain at all Seasons.
Tropical Rain Savanna Climate with dry season.
DRY CLIMATES
Desert Climate with no rain.
Steppe Climate with little rain.
WARM TEMPERATE RAIN CLIMATES
7a with dry summer season / with hot summers
7b with dry winter season / with cool short summers
with rain at all seasons.
COOL TEMPERATE RAIN CLIMATES
Rain all year round & severe winter.
with severe dry winter.
POLAR CLIMATES – no warm season.

COPYRIGHT. GEORGE PHILIP & SON, LTD

Projection: Mollweide's Interrupted Homolographic

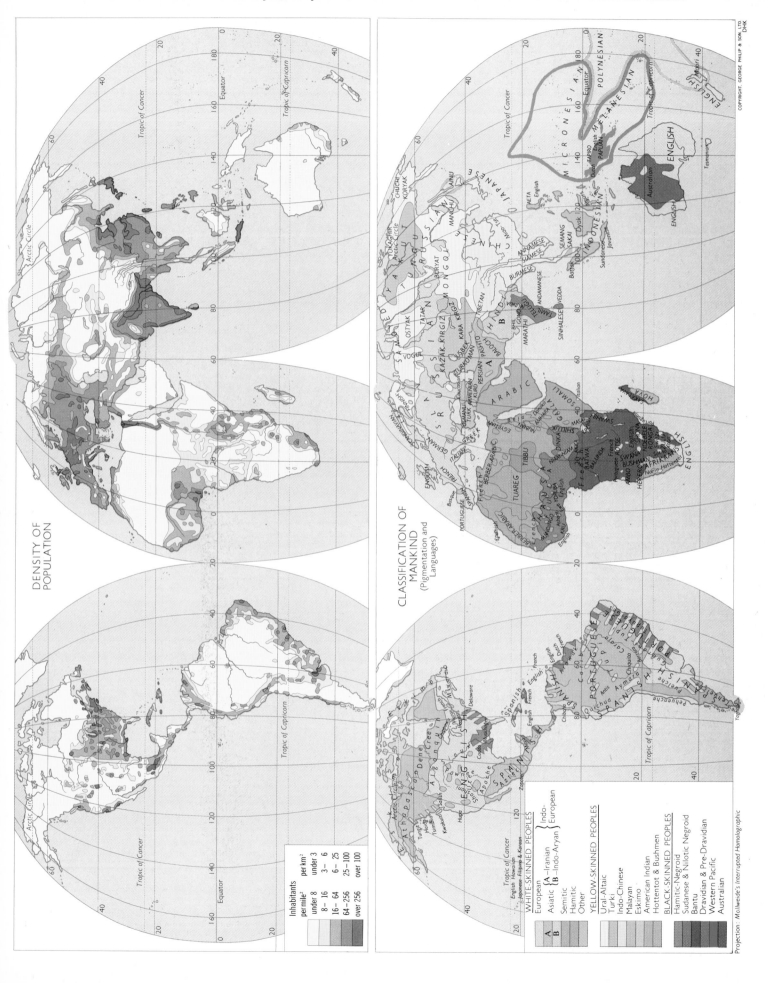

DENSITY OF POPULATION

CLASSIFICATION OF MANKIND
(Pigmentation and Languages)

Inhabitants

per mile²	per km²
under 8	under 3
8 – 16	3 – 6
16 – 64	6 – 25
64 – 256	25 – 100
over 256	over 100

WHITE-SKINNED PEOPLES

European
Asiatic { A – Iranian } Indo-
        { B – Indo-Aryan } European
Semitic
Hamitic
Other

YELLOW-SKINNED PEOPLES

Ural-Altaic
Turki
Indo-Chinese
Malayan
American Indian
Eskimo
Hottentot & Bushmen

BLACK-SKINNED PEOPLES

Hamitic-Negroid
Sudanese & Nilotic Negroid
Bantu
Dravidian & Pre-Dravidian
Western Pacific
Australian

Projection: Mollweide's Interrupted Homolographic

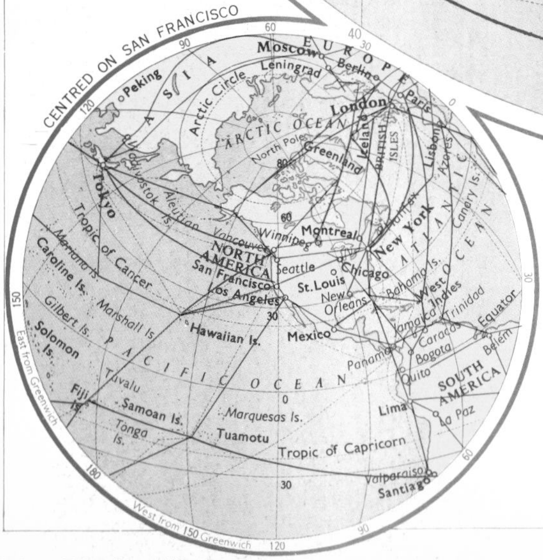

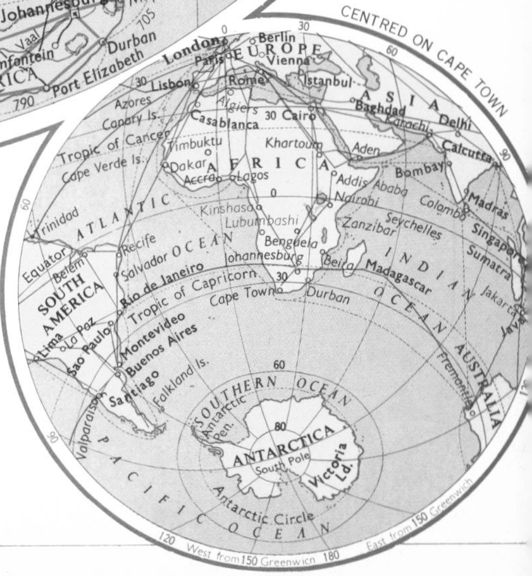

CENTRED ON LONDON

CENTRED ON SAN FRANCISCO

CENTRED ON CAPE TOWN

1 : 300 000 000

2000 1000 0 2000 4000 6000 miles

2000 0 2000 4000 6000 8000 km

3091 Principal Shipping Routes
(Distances in Nautical Miles)

Projection : Oblique Azimuthal Equidistant

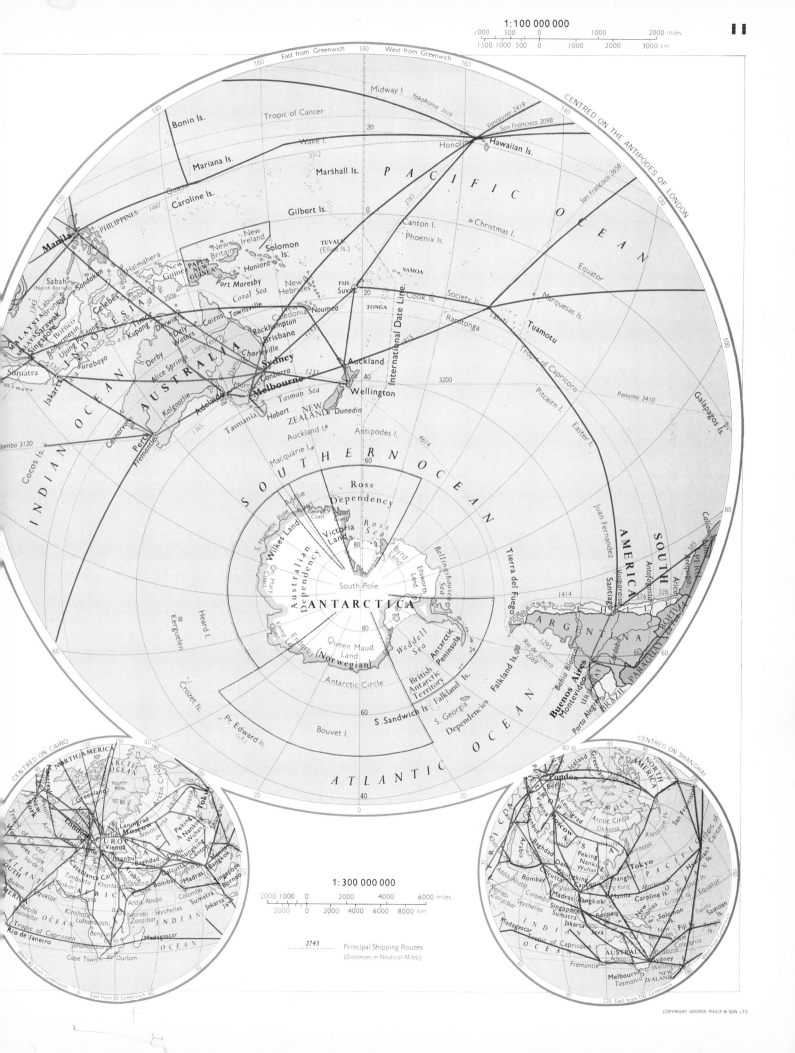

11

1:100 000 000

1000 500 0 1000 2000 miles
1500 1000 500 0 1000 2000 3000 km

CENTRED ON THE ANTIPODES OF LONDON

East from Greenwich 180 West from Greenwich

Midway I.
Bonin Is.
Tropic of Cancer
Yokohama 3419
Vancouver 2419
San Francisco 2098
Wake I.
Mariana Is.
3312
Honolulu Hawaiian Is.
Marshall Is.
PACIFIC OCEAN
Caroline Is.
1497
Manila
PHILIPPINES
Gilbert Is.
0
2783
Canton I.
Christmas I.
San Francisco 3658
Sabah
(North Borneo)
Sandakan
New
Ireland
New
Britain
Solomon
Is.
TUVALU
(Ellice Is.)
Phoenix Is.
Equator
MALAYSIA Sarawak
Brunei
Halmahera
PAPUA
NEW
GUINEA
Honiara
SAMOA
Marquesas Is.
INDONESIA
New Guinea
Port Moresby
FIJI
Suva
Society Is.
Singapore
Borneo
Celebes
Ambon
Coral Sea
New
Hebrides
Noumea
TONGA
Rarotonga
Tahiti
Tuamotu
Banjarmasin
Timor
Kupang
Darwin
Cairns Townsville
New
Caledonia
20
Tropic of Capricorn
Jakarta
Surabaya
Daly
Waters
3506
Rockhampton
Brisbane
Cook Is.
Pitcairn I.
Easter I.
Panama 3410
Galapagos Is.
Sumatra
Derby
Alice Springs
Longreach
Charleville
Sydney
Canberra
1232
Auckland
Wellington
3200
4614
80
INDIAN OCEAN
Kalgoorlie
Adelaide
Melbourne
Murray
Tasman Sea
NEW
ZEALAND
Dunedin
Callao
PERU
SOUTH AMERICA
Colombo 3120
Perth
Fremantle
1365
Tasmania
Hobart
Auckland I.
Antipodes I.
International Date Line
Antofagasta
Valparaiso
Santiago
Cocos Is.
Conaryong
Macquarie I.
SOUTHERN OCEAN
60
80
Arica
326
Kerguelen
S. Magnetic Pole
Wilkes Land
Ross
Dependency
Victoria
Land
Ross
Sea
Byrd
Land
Juan Fernandez
585
Heard I.
Adelie
George V
Coast
Oates
Coast
80
South Pole
Ellsworth
Land
Bellingshausen
Sea
Tierra del Fuego
SOUTH
AMERICA
80
Pr. Edward Is.
(S.A.)
On. Mary
Coast
Australian
Dependency
ANTARCTICA
Antarctic
Peninsula
1414
ARGENTINA
BOLIVIA
PARAGUAY
Crozet Is.
Kemp
Land
Enderby
Land
Queen Maud
Land
(Norwegian)
Weddell
Sea
British
Antarctic
Territory
60
60
Córdoba
Rio de Janeiro
2269
BRAZIL
Porto Alegre
Bahia Blanca
Buenos Aires
Montevideo
URUGUAY
1295
Bouvet I.
Antarctic Circle
60
Falkland Is.
S. Sandwich Is.
Falkland Is.
Dependencies
S. Georgia
ATLANTIC OCEAN
20
40
0
20
40

CENTRED ON CAIRO

NORTH AMERICA
ARCTIC OCEAN
North
Pole
Arctic Circle
Greenland
Vladivostok
Tokyo
New
York
Leningrad
Moscow
Novosibirsk
Peking
Nanking
Wuhan
Shanghai
London
Berlin
Vienna
EUROPE
Istanbul
Baghdad
Delhi
Chungking
Canton
West
Indies
Cape
Verde Is.
Azores
Lisbon
Rome
Casablanca
Cairo
Arabia
Mecca
Calcutta
Bombay
Madras
Bangkok
Timbuktu
Dakar
Khartoum
Aden
SOUTH
AMERICA
Recife
Salvador
Belém
AFRICA
Addis Ababa
Nairobi
Seychelles
Colombo
Sumatra
Singapore
Borneo
Jakarta
Java
ATLANTIC
OCEAN
Equator
Tropic of Cancer
Kinshasa
Lubumbashi
Zanzibar
INDIAN
OCEAN
Rio de Janeiro
Tropic of Capricorn
Benguela
Johannesburg
Cape Town
Durban

1:300 000 000

2000 1000 0 2000 4000 6000 miles
2000 0 2000 4000 6000 8000 km

2743 _ _ _ _ _ Principal Shipping Routes
(Distances in Nautical Miles)

CENTRED ON SHANGHAI

NORTH
AMERICA
Iceland
Greenland
Vancouver
London
Berlin
Vienna
Leningrad
Moscow
Arctic Circle
North
Pole
EUROPE
AFRICA
Arabia
Baghdad
Delhi
Peking
Nanking
Wuhan
Chungking
Irkutsk
Okhotsk
Vladivostok
Aleutian Is.
San Francisco
PACIFIC
OCEAN
Addis Ababa
Nairobi
Zanzibar
Bombay
Calcutta
Madras
Colombo
Seychelles
Singapore
Sumatra
Bangkok
Borneo
Tokyo
Shanghai
Hong Kong
Manila
Caroline Is.
Equator
Tropic of Cancer
Hawaiian Is.
Madagascar
Java
Jakarta
INDIAN
OCEAN
Tropic of Capricorn
New
Guinea
Solomon
Is.
New
Fiji
Samoa
Is.
Tuvalu
Gilbert Is.
AUSTRALIA
Fremantle
Adelaide
Sydney
Melbourne
Tasmania
Wellington
NEW ZEALAND

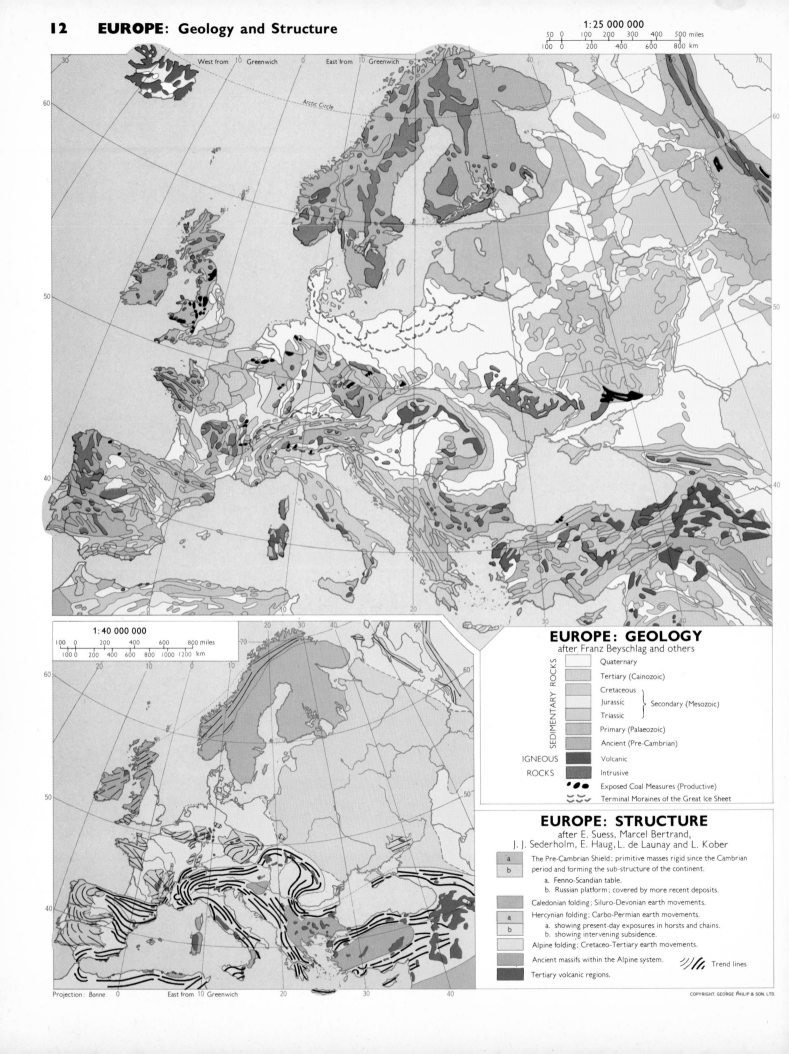

1:25 000 000

50 0 100 200 300 400 500 miles
100 0 200 400 600 800 km

EUROPE: GEOLOGY
after Franz Beyschlag and others

SEDIMENTARY ROCKS
- Quaternary
- Tertiary (Cainozoic)
- Cretaceous
- Jurassic — Secondary (Mesozoic)
- Triassic
- Primary (Palaeozoic)
- Ancient (Pre-Cambrian)

IGNEOUS ROCKS
- Volcanic
- Intrusive

- Exposed Coal Measures (Productive)
- Terminal Moraines of the Great Ice Sheet

EUROPE: STRUCTURE
after E. Suess, Marcel Bertrand,
J. J. Sederholm, E. Haug, L. de Launay and L. Kober

a
b — The Pre-Cambrian Shield; primitive masses rigid since the Cambrian period and forming the sub-structure of the continent.
    a. Fenno-Scandian table.
    b. Russian platform; covered by more recent deposits.

Caledonian folding; Siluro-Devonian earth movements.

Hercynian folding; Carbo-Permian earth movements.
a
b
    a. showing present-day exposures in horsts and chains.
    b. showing intervening subsidence.

Alpine folding; Cretaceo-Tertiary earth movements.

Ancient massifs within the Alpine system.

Tertiary volcanic regions.

Trend lines

1:40 000 000

100 0 200 400 600 800 miles
100 0 200 400 600 800 1000 1200 km

Projection: Bonne

1:20 000 000

100   0   100   200   300   400   500 miles
100   0   200   400   600   800 km

Ob

Ural Mountains

Obshchiyr

Volga Uplands

CASPIAN SEA
-28

Armenia
Kurdistan

Tundra

Ural

1894

Pechora
Kama
Ural
Volga
Volga
Don

Euphrates

Caucasus
5633
Rion
5165
L. Urmia
L. Van

Mezen
N. Dvina
Rybinsk Res.
Oka
Tsimlyansk Res.

Anatolia
Taurus
3770

Kanin Peninsula
White Sea
Kola Peninsula

Onega
L. Onega
Ladoga
L. Chudskoye
Neva

Central Russian Uplands

Sea of Azov
Kerch Str.
2211

BLACK SEA

Kizil Irmak
Bosporus

Cyprus 1951

North Cape
Nordkinn

Lapland
Finland

Plain
Don
Ukraine
Dnepr (Dnieper)
Bug

Danube
Prut
Dnestr (Dniester)

Wallachia
Danube

Rhodope
Balkan Peninsula

Aegean Sea

Crete

Gulf of Bothnia
Gulf of Finland
Gulf of Riga
Gotland

BALTIC SEA

Niemen

Pripyat Marshes
Pripyat (Pripet)

Carpathians
Transylvanian Alps
2665 Tatra
Plain of Hungary
Tisza
Drava
Sava
Morava

Balkans

Pindus
5121
C. Matapan

Scandinavia
2123

Glittertind 2469

Vesterålen
Lofoten

Ume
Indals
Mjøsen
Vänern
Vättern

North

Vistula
Wisła (Vistula)
Odra (Oder)

Sudetes
Erz Geb.
Morava
Bohemian For.
Harz 1142

Danube
Inn

Dinaric Alps
ALPS
Gran Sasso

ADRIATIC SEA
Str. of Otranto
Calabria
Ionian Sea

Morea

NORWEGIAN SEA
3734

Jutland
Skagerrak
Kattegat
Lindesnes
Weser
Elbe

Fisher

GERMAN BIGHT
Helgoland
Rhine
Weser
Black For.
Thur. For.
Vosges
Ardennes
Meuse

Apennines
2914
Mt. Blanc 4807
Vesuvius 1277

Ligurian Sea
Tyrrhenian Sea
Str. of Messina
Etna 3263
Sicily

Malta

NORTH SEA
Dogger Bank
VIKING
FORTIES
HUMBER
THAMES
Netherlands

Rhône
Saône
Jura

Corsica
Sardinia
C. Blanco

MEDITERRANEAN SEA

Maritime Atlas

Arctic Circle

Iceland
Öraefa Jökull
2119

SOUTH EAST ICELAND

Fisher Bank

FAEROES
Faroe Is.
Shetland Is.
Fair Isle
Orkney Is.

CROMARTY
FORTH
TYNE
DOGGER

Great Britain
Cheviot H.
Pennines 847
British Seas

Hebrides
HEBRIDES

Rockall
ROCKALL

BAILEY

British Isles
Ireland
Irish Sea
Snowdon 1085

HUMBER
THAMES
Seine

English Channel
FORTLAND
PLYMOUTH

Loire

Central Massif
1886
Cévennes

Maritime Alps

Hekla 1491

Fishguard

Land's End
FASTNET
LUNDY

Valentia
SHANNON
C. Clear

SOLE
PLYMOUTH
PORTLAND

Brittany

Bay of Biscay
4881

Garonne
Gironde

Pyrenees
3404

New Castile

Cantabrian Mts.
Old Castile
Iberian Peninsula
Sierra Morena
Guadalquivir
Andalusia
Sa. Nevada

Str. of Gibraltar
C. St. Vincent
C. Trafalgar
C. Spartel
Rif

Plateau of the Shotts

ATLANTIC OCEAN
FINISTERRE
FINISTERRE

ROCKALL
Rockall

Projection. Bonne   West from Greenwich 0 East from Greenwich
Sea areas named in
ROCKALL   weather forecasts

ft   m   4000   2000   1000   400   200   0   200-600
12 000   6000   3000   1200   600   0   2000   4000 12 000
ft   m

1 : 40 000 000

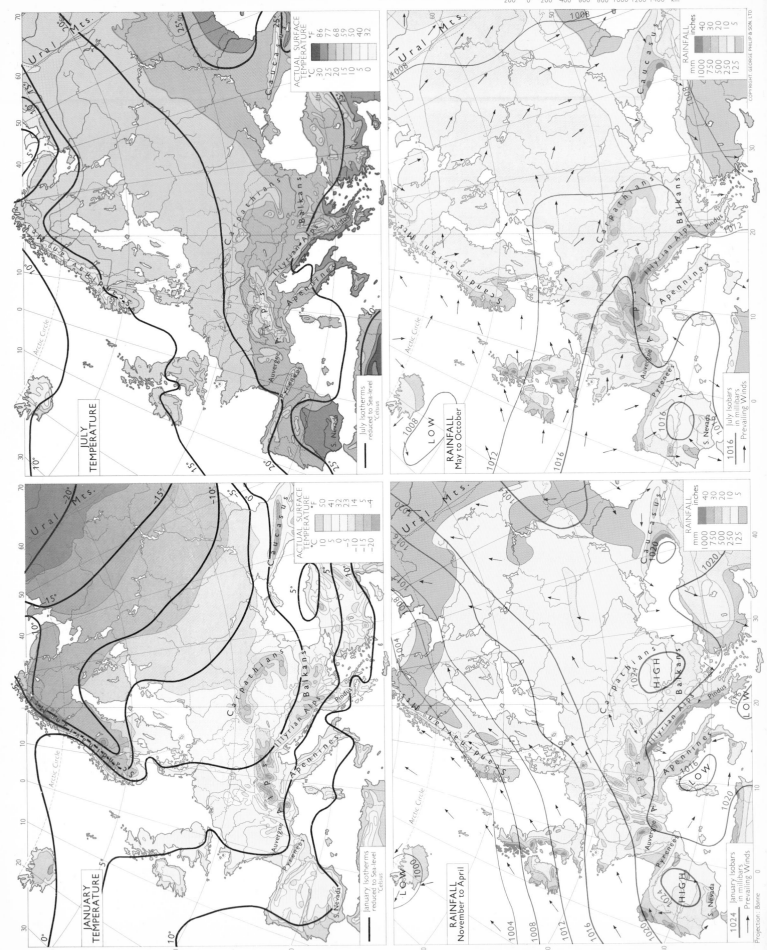

JULY TEMPERATURE

ACTUAL SURFACE TEMPERATURE

°C   °F
30   86
25   77
20   68
15   59
10   50
5   40
0   32

July Isotherms reduced to Sea-level °Celsius

RAINFALL
May to October

RAINFALL
inches
40
30
20
10
5

mm
1000
750
500
250
125

July Isobars in millibars
Prevailing Winds

LOW

1016

JANUARY TEMPERATURE

ACTUAL SURFACE TEMPERATURE

°C   °F
10   50
5   41
0   32
-5   23
-10   14
-15   5
-20   -4

January Isotherms reduced to Sea-level °Celsius

RAINFALL
November to April

RAINFALL
inches
40
30
20
10
5

mm
1000
750
500
250
125

January Isobars in millibars
Prevailing Winds

HIGH

LOW

1024

Projection: Bonne

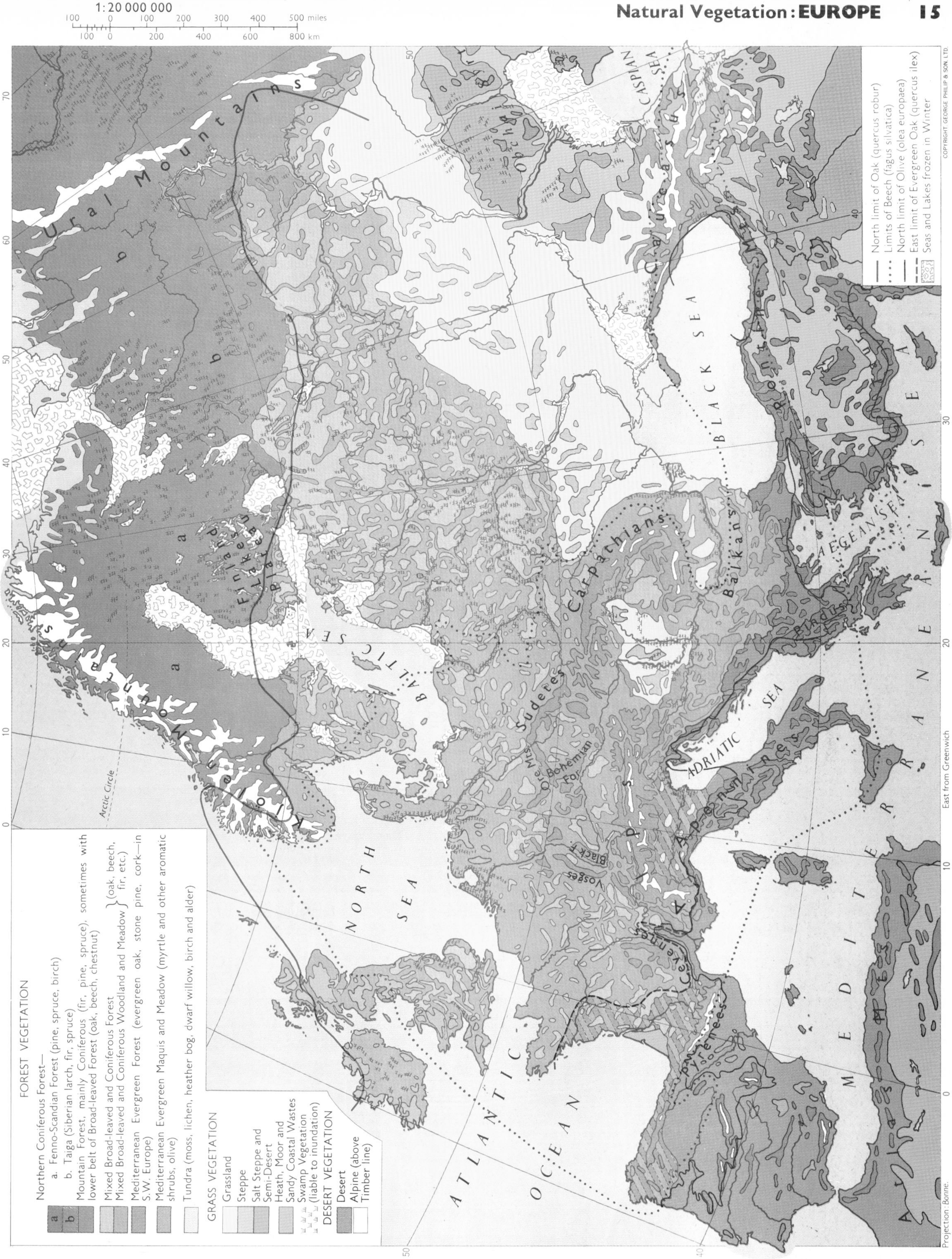

1:20 000 000

100   0   100   200   300   400   500 miles

100   0   200   400   600   800 km

FOREST VEGETATION

Northern Coniferous Forest—
  a. Fenno-Scandian Forest (pine, spruce, birch)
  b. Taïga (Siberian larch, fir, spruce)

Mountain Forest, mainly Coniferous (fir, pine, spruce), sometimes with lower belt of Broad-leaved Forest (oak, beech, chestnut)

Mixed Broad-leaved and Coniferous Forest } (oak, beech,
Mixed Broad-leaved and Coniferous Woodland and Meadow } fir, etc.)

Mediterranean Evergreen Forest (evergreen oak, stone pine, cork—in S.W. Europe)

Mediterranean Evergreen Maquis and Meadow (myrtle and other aromatic shrubs, olive)

Tundra (moss, lichen, heather bog, dwarf willow, birch and alder)

GRASS VEGETATION

Grassland

Steppe

Salt Steppe and Semi-Desert

Heath, Moor and Sandy Coastal Wastes

Swamp Vegetation (liable to inundation)

DESERT VEGETATION

Desert

Alpine (above Timber line)

North limit of Oak (quercus robur)

Limits of Beech (fagus silvatica)

North limit of Olive (olea europaea)

East limit of Evergreen Oak (quercus ilex)

Seas and Lakes frozen in Winter

Projection Bonne.

East from Greenwich

COPYRIGHT GEORGE PHILIP & SON LTD.

Ural Mountains

CASPIAN SEA

Volga

Caucasus

BLACK SEA

Carpathians

Balkans

Pindus

AEGEAN SEA

Scandinavian Mountains

Kjölen

Finnish Lakes

BALTIC SEA

Sudeten Mts.

O Bohemian For.

Vosges

Black F.

Jura

Alps

Apennines

ADRIATIC SEA

Cévennes

Pyrenees

M E D I T E R R A N E A N   S E A

NORTH SEA

ATLANTIC OCEAN

Arctic Circle

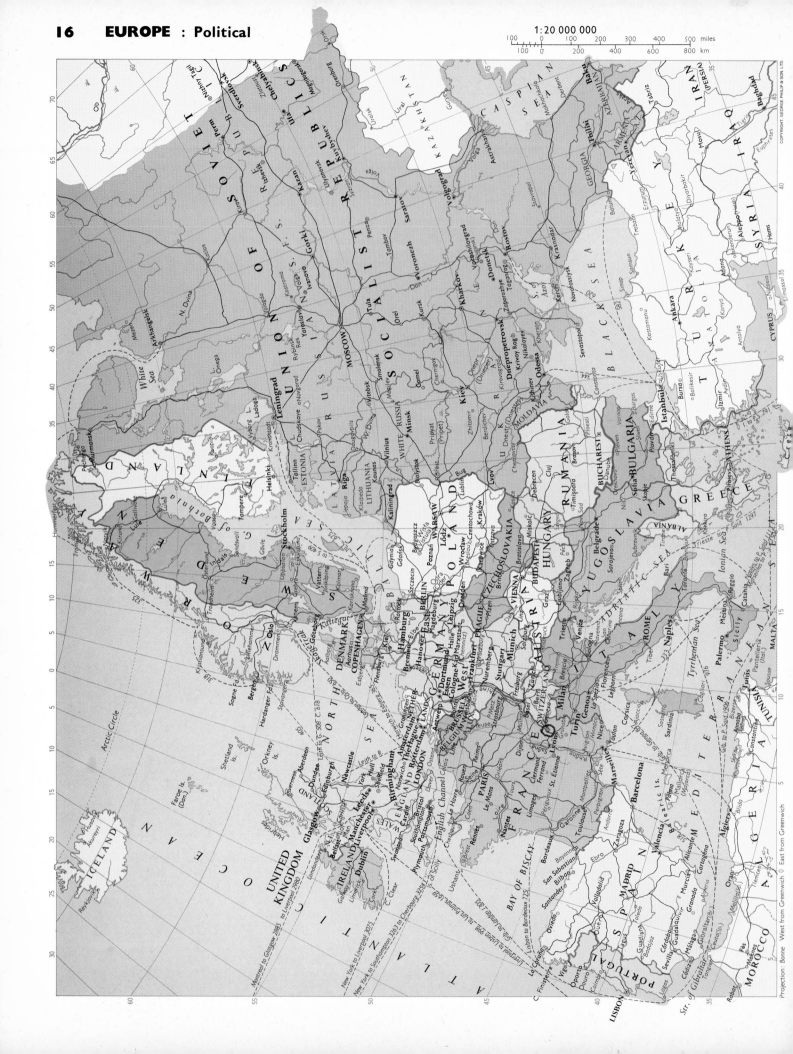

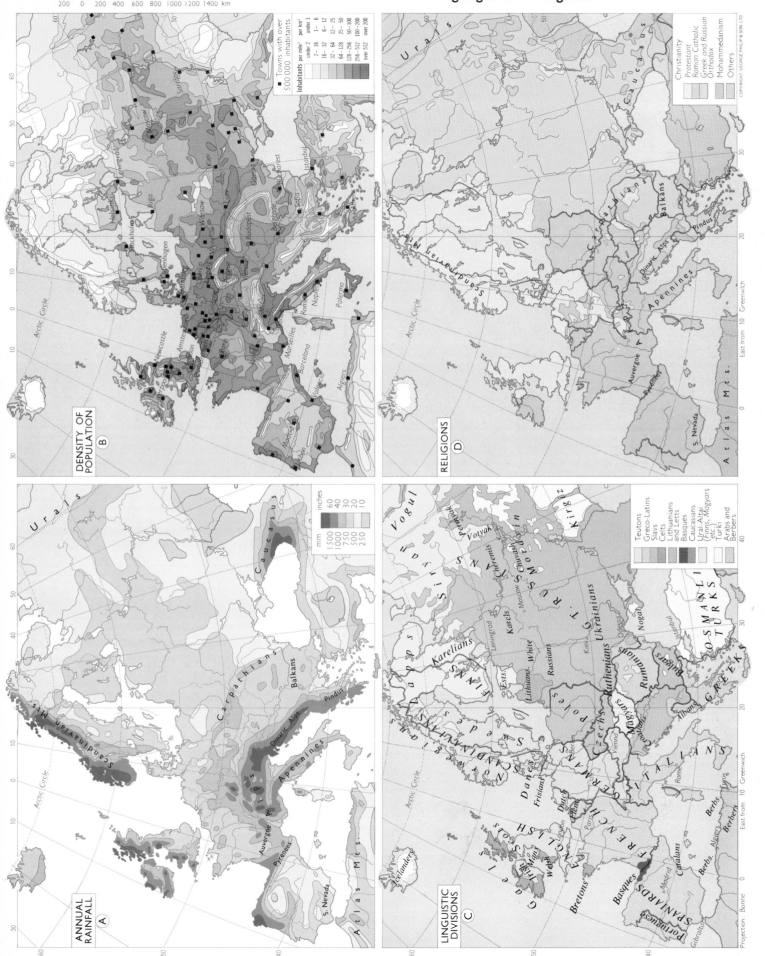

1:40 000 000

DENSITY OF POPULATION B

Towns with over 500 000 inhabitants

Inhabitants per mile² per km²
under 2 — under 1
2 – 16 — 1 – 6
16 – 32 — 6 – 12
32 – 64 — 12 – 25
64 – 128 — 25 – 50
128 – 256 — 50 – 100
256 – 512 — 100 – 200
over 512 — over 200

COPYRIGHT GEORGE PHILIP & SON LTD

RELIGIONS D

Christianity
Protestant
Roman Catholic
Greek and Russian Orthodox
Mohammedanism
Others

ANNUAL RAINFALL A

inches
60
40
30
20
10

mm
1500
1000
750
500
250

LINGUISTIC DIVISIONS C

Teutons
Greco-Latins
Slavs
Celts
Lithuanians and Letts
Basques
Caucasians
Ural-Altai (Finns, Magyars etc.)
Turki
Arabs and Berbers

Projection Bonne

1:5 000 000

20 0 20 40 60 80 100 miles
20 0 20 40 60 80 100 120 140 160 km

Shetland Is

Foula

Sumburgh Hd.

Fair I.

60

ATLANTIC OCEAN

Rona

Orkney Islands

Pentland Firth
C. Wrath   Dunnet Hd.   Duncansby Hd.

Flannan Is.

Butt of Lewis

Lewis
789 ▲

St. Kilda

Outer Hebrides

North Minch

Ben More Assynt ▲ 998   Shin

Ben Wyvis 1045 ▲   Moray Firth

58

Rockall Deep

Inner Hebrides

Skye   ▲ 1009   Carn Eige 1182   Glen Mor   L. Ness

Buchan Ness

Ben Macdhui ▲ 1311   Dee

238 ▲

North West Highlands

Ardnamurchan Pt.   Ben Nevis 1347 ▲

Grampians

Mull   Strathmore   Sidlaw Hills

F. of Tay

Firth of Lorn   974 ▲   Lomond   Ochil Hills   Fife Ness
Forth   Firth of Forth   Bass Rock

56

Islay   Arran   Clyde   Pentland Hills   Lammermuir Hills
Southern Uplands   Tweed

Giant's Causeway   Fair Hd.   Mull of Kintyre   Broad Law 840   The Cheviot ▲ 816

Tory I.   Malin Hd.

Firth of Clyde   Merrick 843 ▲   Cheviot Hills

Errigal 752 ▲   Derryveagh Mts.   Antrim Mts.   North Channel   Nith   Tyne

Donegal Bay   Bann   Neagh   Solway Firth   Cross Fell ▲ 893

Erris Hd.   Erne   Mull of Galloway   St. Bee's Hd.   Sca Fell   Cumbrian Mts. 978 ▲   Pennines

54

Achill I.   Mourne Mts. 852   I. of Man   Snaefell 620   737 ▲   N. York Moors 454
Flamborough Hd.

Mweelrea ▲ 819   L. Mask   Vale of York   Yorkshire Wolds   Holderness   Spurn Hd.

Connemara   L. Corrib   Central Plain   Morecambe Bay   Wharfe   Humber

Galway Bay   Boyne   IRISH SEA   Formby Pt.   Liverpool Bay   Aire   Don   Lincolnshire Wolds
Gt. Ormes Hd.   Mersey   The Peak 636   The Wash

Loop Hd.   Shannon   Slieve Bloom Mts.   Bog of Allen   Liffey   Anglesey   Cheshire Plain   Trent   Lincoln Heath   Breckland
Holy I.   Snowdon ▲ 1085   Wrekin ▲ 407   Yare   Lowestoftness

Golden Vale   Barrow   Wicklow Mts. 926   Menai Strait   Cambrian Mts.   Witham   The Fens

Galty Mts. 920   Suir   Cardigan Bay   892 ▲   Plynlimon 752   Welland   Nene   Gt. Ouse

52

Dunmore Hd.   Blackwater   Carnsore Pt.   Wye   Severn   Avon   Cotswolds   Chiltern Hills   Stour   The Naze
Macgillycuddy's Reeks 1041   Lee   St. George's Channel   St. David's Hd.   Brecon Beacons   Thames   Berks. Downs   Kennet   North Foreland

Cork Harbour   Milford Haven   Tywi   Marlboro Downs   North Downs   Thames
Bristol Channel   R. Severn   Mendip Hills   Avon   Hampshire Downs   The Weald   Strait of Dover

C. Clear   Lundy   Salisbury Plain   South Downs   Dungeness

Hartland Point   Exmoor 520   N. Dorset Downs   Needles   Beachy Hd.

Bodmin Moor   Dartmoor   Yes Tor ▲ 618   Exe   I. of Wight
Tamar   Portland Bill

Land's End   Lizard   Start Pt.   ENGLISH CHANNEL

Isles of Scilly

50

NORTH SEA

Dogger Bank

30

FRANCE

ft   m
3000   1000
1200   400
600   200   52
300   100
0   0
100   300
200   600
400   1200
600   1800
m   ft

Projection: Conical with two standard parallels

West from Greenwich 0 East from Greenwich   COPYRIGHT. GEORGE PHILIP & SON, LTD

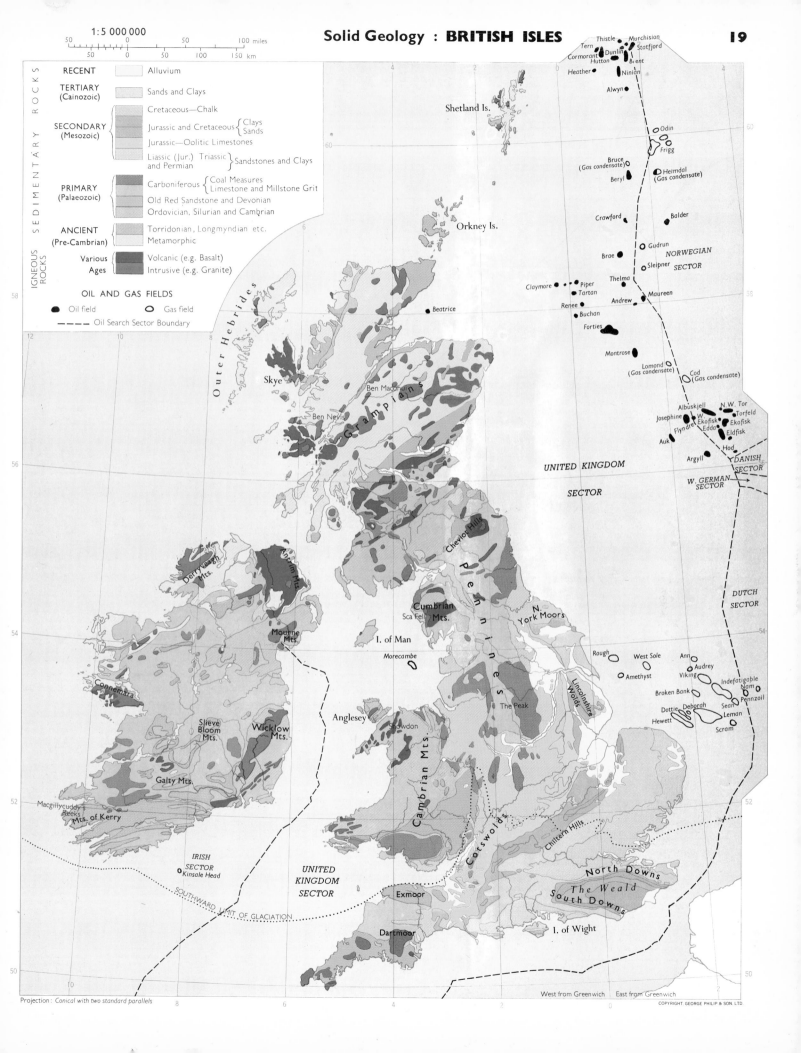

1:5 000 000

SEDIMENTARY ROCKS		
RECENT		Alluvium
TERTIARY (Cainozoic)		Sands and Clays
SECONDARY (Mesozoic)		Cretaceous—Chalk
	Jurassic and Cretaceous { Clays / Sands
	Jurassic—Oolitic Limestones
	Liassic (Jur.) Triassic and Permian } Sandstones and Clays
PRIMARY (Palaeozoic)		Carboniferous { Coal Measures / Limestone and Millstone Grit
	Old Red Sandstone and Devonian
	Ordovician, Silurian and Cambrian
ANCIENT (Pre-Cambrian)		Torridonian, Longmyndian etc.
	Metamorphic

IGNEOUS ROCKS

Various Ages { Volcanic (e.g. Basalt) / Intrusive (e.g. Granite)

OIL AND GAS FIELDS

● Oil field   ○ Gas field

- - - - Oil Search Sector Boundary

Thistle   Murchison
Cormorant   Dunlin   Statfjord
Hutton   Brent
Heather   Ninian

Alwyn

Odin
Frigg

Bruce
(Gas condensate)   Heimdal
Beryl   (Gas condensate)

Crawford   Balder

Brae   Gudrun   NORWEGIAN
                Sleipner   SECTOR

Claymore   Piper   Thelma
            Tartan
Renee   Andrew   Maureen
            Buchan
        Forties

    Montrose
            Lomond
            (Gas condensate)   Cod
                        (Gas condensate)

Shetland Is.

Orkney Is.

Beatrice

Outer Hebrides

Skye

Ben Macdhui's
Ben Nevis   Grampians

UNITED KINGDOM

SECTOR

Albuskjell   N.W. Tor
Josephine   W.   Torfeld
        Flyndra Ekofisk Ekofisk
        Eddo Eldfisk
Auk
                Hod
    Argyll   DANISH
                SECTOR
        W. GERMAN
        SECTOR

Antrim Mts.
Derryveagh
Mts.

Mourne
Mts.

Cheviot Hills

Pennines

Cumbrian
Mts.
Sca Fell   N.
            York Moors

I. of Man

Connemara

Morecambe

Lincolnshire
Wolds

DUTCH
SECTOR

Rough   West Sole   Ann
                    Audrey
        Amethyst   Viking   Indefatigable
                        Nom
Broken Bank   Pennzoil
        Dottie Deborah Sean
Hewett   Leman
                Scram

Slieve
Bloom   Wicklow
Mts.   Mts.

Anglesey   Snowdon

The Peak

Galty Mts.

Macgillycuddy's
Reeks
Mts. of Kerry

Cambrian Mts.

Cotswolds   Chiltern Hills

North Downs

IRISH
SECTOR
Kinsale Head

UNITED
KINGDOM
SECTOR

Exmoor

Dartmoor

The Weald
South Downs

I. of Wight

SOUTHWARD LIMIT OF GLACIATION

West from Greenwich   East from Greenwich

Projection: Conical with two standard parallels

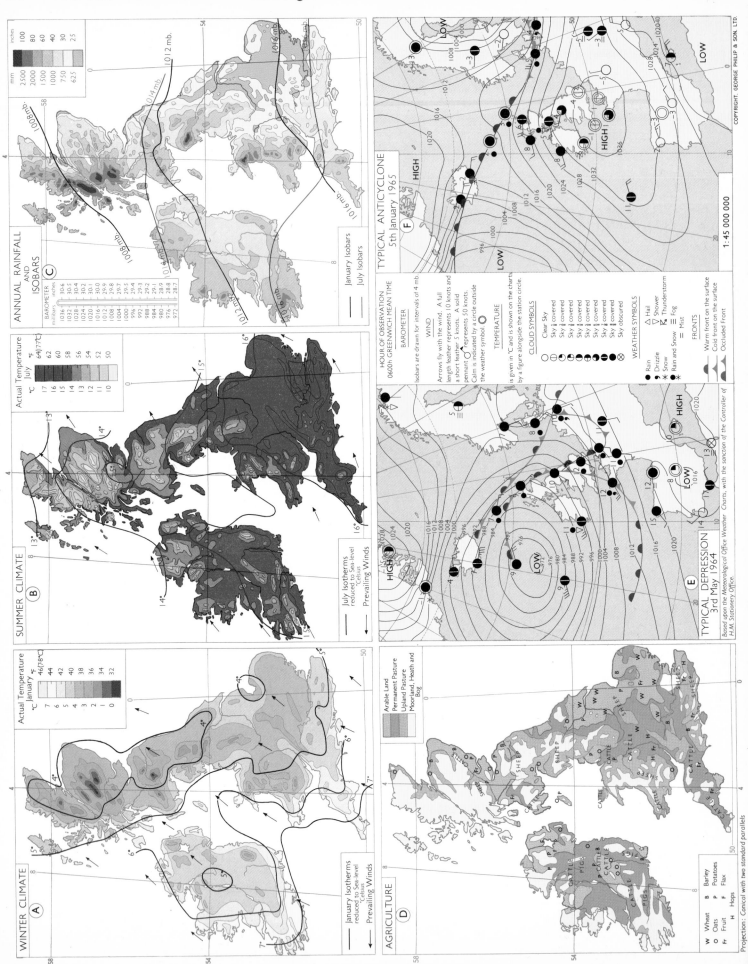

ANNUAL RAINFALL AND ISOBARS (C)

inches
100
80
60
40
30
25

mm
2500
2000
1500
1000
750
625

BAROMETER	
millibars	inches
1036	30.6
1032	30.5
1028	30.4
1024	30.2
1020	30.1
1016	30.0
1012	29.9
1008	29.8
1004	29.7
1000	29.5
996	29.4
992	29.3
988	29.1
984	29.0
980	28.9
976	28.8
972	28.7

—— January Isobars
—— July Isobars

SUMMER CLIMATE (B)

Actual Temperature July
°C   °F
17   64(?77°C)
16   62
15   60
14   58
13   56
12   54
11   52
      50

—— July Isotherms reduced to Sea-level °Celsius
→ Prevailing Winds

WINTER CLIMATE (A)

Actual Temperature January
°C   °F
7   46(7·8°C)
6   44
5   42
4   40
3   38
2   36
1   34
0   32

—— January Isotherms reduced to Sealevel °Celsius
→ Prevailing Winds

TYPICAL ANTICYCLONE 5th January 1965 (F)

1:45 000 000

HOUR OF OBSERVATION 0600h Greenwich Mean Time

BAROMETER
Isobars are drawn for intervals of 4 mb.

WIND
Arrows fly with the wind. A full length feather represents 10 knots and a short feather 5 knots. A solid pennant ⚑ represents 50 knots. Calm is indicated by a circle outside the weather symbol ◯

TEMPERATURE
is given in °C and is shown on the charts by a figure alongside the station circle.

CLOUD SYMBOLS
◯ Clear Sky
◔ Sky ¼ covered
◑ Sky ½ covered
etc. Sky covered
⊗ Sky obscured

WEATHER SYMBOLS
● Rain   △ Hail   ▽ Shower
, Drizzle   ⚡ Thunderstorm
✱ Snow   ≡ Fog   ∞ Mist
● Rain and Snow

FRONTS
▲▲ Warm front on the surface
▲▲ Cold front on the surface
▲▲ Occluded Front

TYPICAL DEPRESSION 3rd May 1964 (E)

Based upon the Meteorological Office Weather Charts, with the sanction of the Controller of H.M. Stationery Office.

AGRICULTURE (D)

Arable Land
Permanent Pasture
Upland Pasture
Moorland, Heath and Bog

W Wheat   B Barley
O Oats   P Potatoes
Fr Fruit   Fl Flax
H Hops

Projection: Conical with two standard parallels

COPYRIGHT. GEORGE PHILIP & SON. LTD.

1 : 5 000 000

| 20 | 0 | 20 | 40 | 60 | 80 miles |

| 20 | 0 | 40 | 80 | 120 km |

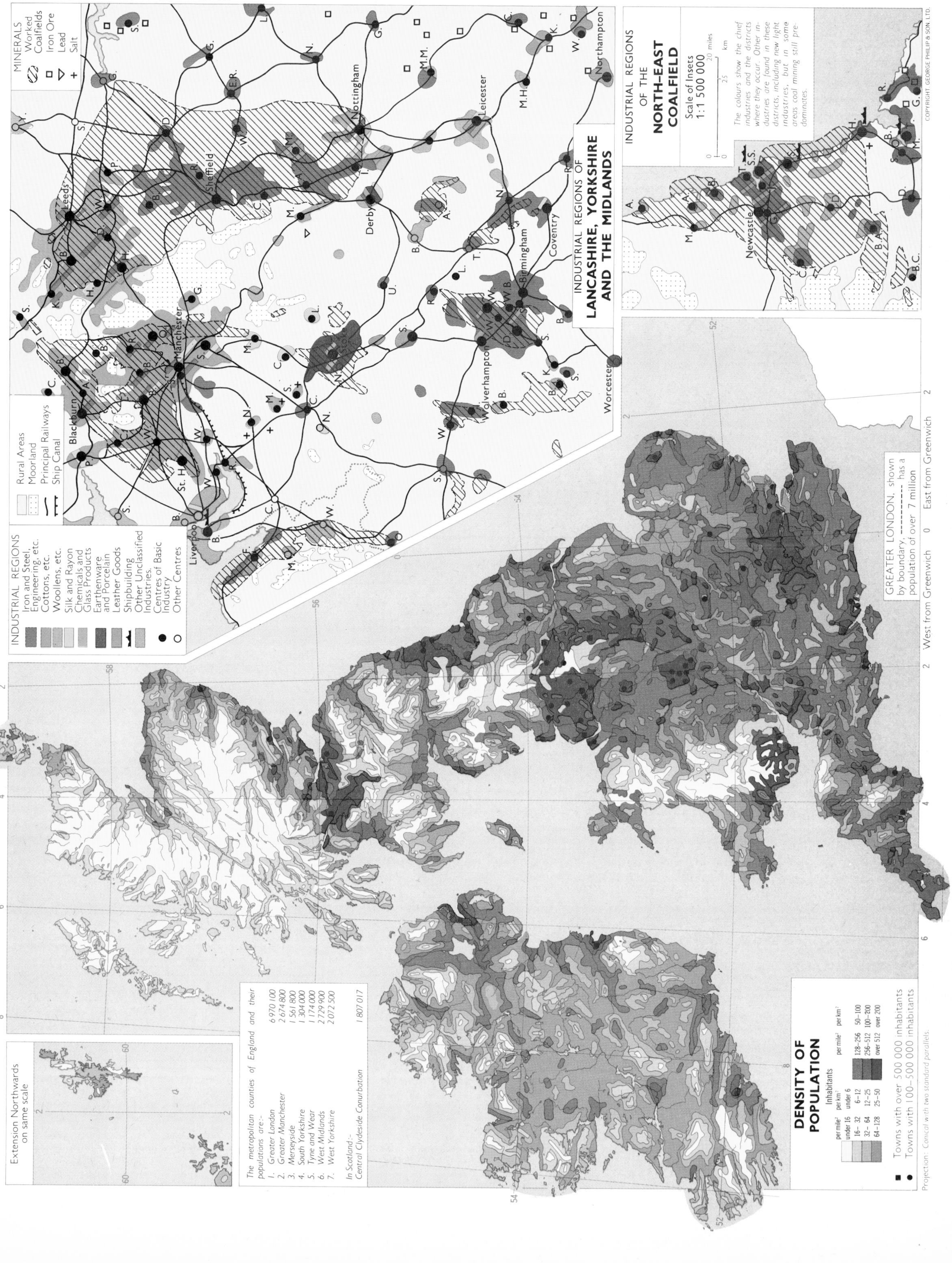

MINERALS

Worked
Coalfields
Iron Ore
Lead
Salt

**INDUSTRIAL REGIONS OF
LANCASHIRE, YORKSHIRE
AND THE MIDLANDS**

**INDUSTRIAL REGIONS
OF THE
NORTH-EAST
COALFIELD**

Scale of Insets
1:1 500 000

| 0 | 25 | km |
| 0 | 25 | 20 miles |

The colours show the chief industries and the districts where they occur. Other industries are found in these districts, including new light industries, but in some areas coal mining still predominates.

COPYRIGHT GEORGE PHILIP & SON LTD.

Newcastle

Leeds
Sheffield
Derby
Nottingham
Leicester
Manchester
Blackburn
Liverpool
Birmingham
Coventry
Wolverhampton
Worcester
Northampton

INDUSTRIAL REGIONS

Iron and Steel,
Engineering, etc.
Cottons, etc.
Woollens, etc.
Silk and Rayon
Chemicals and
Glass Products
Earthenware
and Porcelain
Leather Goods
Shipbuilding
Other Unclassified
Industries.
Centres of Basic
Industry
Other Centres

Rural Areas
Moorland
Principal Railways
Ship Canal

**Extension Northwards
on same scale**

The metropolitan counties of England and their
populations are:-

1.	Greater London	6 970 100
2.	Greater Manchester	2 674 800
3.	Merseyside	1 561 800
4.	South Yorkshire	1 304 000
5.	Tyne and Wear	1 174 000
6.	West Midlands	2 729 900
7.	West Yorkshire	2 072 500

In Scotland:-
Central Clydeside Conurbation   1 807 017

**DENSITY OF
POPULATION**

per mile²	per km²	Inhabitants
under 16	under 6	
16–32	6–12	
32–64	12–25	
64–128	25–50	
128–256	50–100	
256–512	100–200	
over 512	over 200	

● Towns with over 500 000 inhabitants
■ Towns with 100–500 000 inhabitants

GREATER LONDON, shown
by boundary, ——— has a
population of over 7 million

West from Greenwich   0   East from Greenwich

Projection: Conical with two standard parallels.

Projection : Conical with two
standard parallels

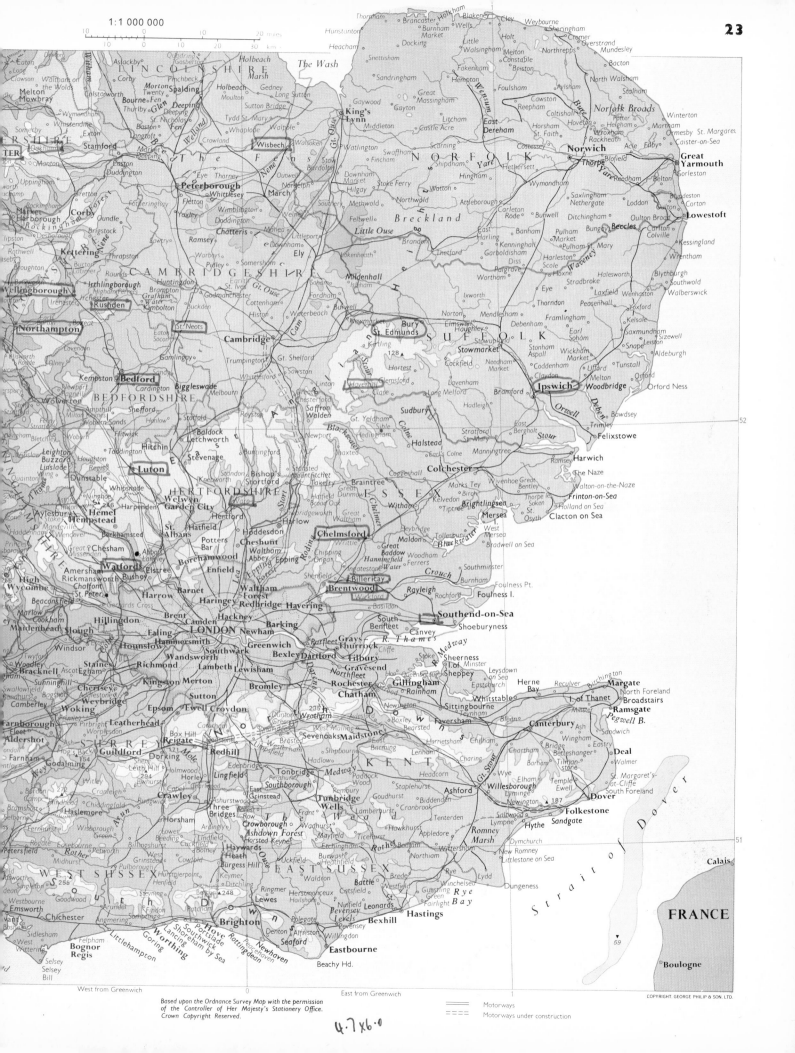

1:1 000 000

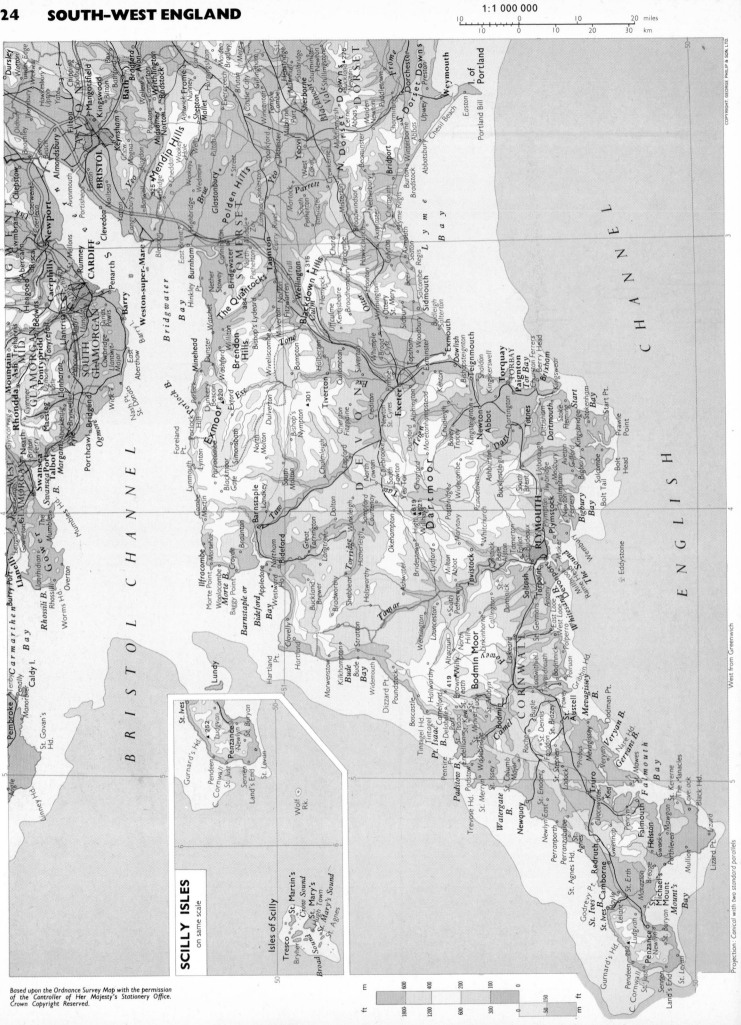

SCILLY ISLES on same scale

West from Greenwich

Projection: Conical with two standard parallels

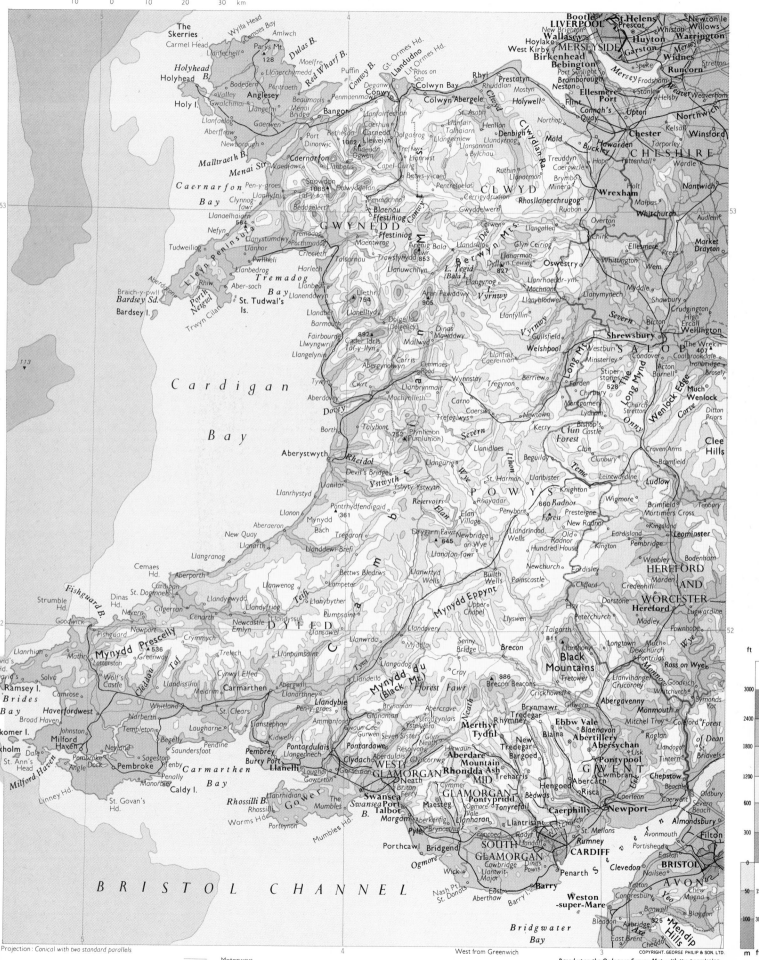

1:1 000 000

Projection: Conical with two standard parallels

West from Greenwich

COPYRIGHT. GEORGE PHILIP & SON. LTD.

Based upon the Ordnance Survey Map with the permission
of the Controller of Her Majesty's Stationery Office.
Crown Copyright Reserved.

DHK

Motorways
Motorways under construction

GALLOWAY

DUMFRIES AND GALLOWAY

Dumfries

IRISH

SEA

ISLE OF MAN

Snaefell 620

Douglas

Calf of Man

Luce Bay

The Machars

Wigtown Bay

Mull of Galloway

Solway Firth

Carlisle

CUMBRIA

Lake District

Workington

Whitehaven

Maryport

Cockermouth

Bassenthwaite

Skiddaw 931

Derwent Water

Keswick

Windermere

Kendal

Barrow

Morecambe

Lancaster

HADRIAN'S WALL

NORTHUM

DU

Bishop

Teesdale

Cross Fell 893

Appleby

Penrith

LANCASHIRE

Fleetwood

Blackpool

Preston

Blackburn

Burnley

Southport

Chorley

Bolton

Bury

Rochdale

GREATER MANCHESTER

MERSEYSIDE

Wigan

Salford

MANCHESTER

LIVERPOOL

Birkenhead

Warrington

Widnes

Runcorn

Stockport

Macclesfield

CHESHIRE

Chester

Crewe

Wrexham

CLWYD

GWYNEDD

Anglesey

Holyhead

Caernarfon

Snowdon 1085

Bangor

Conwy

Colwyn Bay

Rhyl

SALOP

STAFFORDSHIRE

STOKE ON TRENT

Newcastle under Lyme

ft	m	
3000	1000	
2400	800	
1800	600	
1200	400	
600	200	
	100	
0	0	
50	150	
m	ft	

Projection: Conical with two standard parallels

══ Motorways
════ Motorways under construction

1:1 000 000

10   0   10   20 miles
10   0   10   20   30 km

Continuation Northwards on same scale

NORTH SEA

TYNE AND WEAR

Whitley Bay · Tynemouth · Wallsend · South Shields · Jarrow · Gateshead · Sunderland · Houghton le Spring · Seaham · Murton · Easington Colliery · Horden · Peterlee · Chester le Street · Hetton le Hole · Durham

Hartlepool · Billingham · Stockton on Tees · Middlesbrough · Redcar · Marske by the Sea · Saltburn by the Sea · Eston · Skelton

CLEVELAND

Cleveland Hills 454 · Guisborough · Kettle Ness · Hinderwell · Staithes · Loftus · Lythe · Whitby · Hawsker · Robin Hood's Bay · Sleights · Fylingdales Moor

North York Moors

Rosedale Abbey · Eller Beck Bridge · Saltergate · Cloughton · Scalby Ness · **Scarborough**

YORKSHIRE

Hambleton Hills · Vale of Pickering · Rye · Northallerton · Thirsk · Helmsley · Rievaulx · Pickering · Thornton Dale · Ebberston · Snainton · Seamer · Filey · Filey Bay

Ripon · Boroughbridge · Aldborough · Easingwold · Malton · Norton · Sherburn · Rillington · Hunmanby · Flamborough · Flamborough Head

Harrogate · Knaresborough · York · Stamford Bridge · Driffield · Nafferton · Bridlington · Bridlington Bay

LEEDS · Wetherby · Harewood · Tadcaster · Pocklington · Market Weighton · Beverley · Hornsea

WEST YORKSHIRE · Castleford · Pontefract · Wakefield · Selby · Goole · Howden · Cottingham · South Cave · **HULL** · Hessle · Hedon · Withernsea

Barnsley · Doncaster · Thorne · Crowle · Scunthorpe · Barton upon Humber · Barrow upon Humber · New Holland · Keyingham · Patrington · Easington

SOUTH YORKSHIRE · Rotherham · **SHEFFIELD** · Maltby · Tickhill · Bawtry · Isle of Axholme · Epworth · Brigg · **Grimsby** · **Cleethorpes** · Spurn Hd. · Mouth of the Humber

Chesterfield · Bolsover · Worksop · East Retford · Gainsborough · Caistor · Market Rasen · Louth · Mablethorpe · Sutton-on-Sea

DERBYSHIRE · Matlock · Mansfield · Sutton in Ashfield · Kirkby-in-Ashfield · Newark-on-Trent · **Lincoln** · Horncastle · Alford · Willoughby · Skegness · Ingoldmells Pt.

NOTTINGHAM · Carlton · West Bridgford · Bingham · Grantham · Sleaford · **LINCOLNSHIRE** · Spilsby · Wainfleet All Saints · Gibraltar Pt.

Derby · Long Eaton · Beeston · Boston · The Wash

Holbeach · Snettisham · Heacham · Hunstanton · Brancaster · Wells · Blakeney · Cley · **NORFOLK** · Fakenham

West from Greenwich · East from Greenwich

Inset (Continuation Northwards):

BORDERS · Berwick on Tweed · Holy I. · Budle Bay · Farne Is. · Bamburgh · Seahouses · N. Sunderland · Beadnell · Embleton · Kelso · Coldstream · Wooler · The Cheviot 816 · Alnwick · Lesbury · Alnmouth · Warkworth · Amble · Coquet I.

NORTHUMBERLAND · Rothbury · Longframlington · Felton · Druridge B. · Widdrington · Ellington · Ashington · Newbiggin · Morpeth · Bedlington · **Blyth** · Rochester · Otterburn · Bellingham · Kielder · Cambo · Ponteland · Stannington · Seaton Delaval · **Whitley B.**

HADRIAN'S WALL · Haltwhistle · Haydon Bridge · Hexham · Prudhoe · **NEWCASTLE UPON TYNE** · **Tynemouth** · **South Shields** · **Wallsend** · **Jarrow** · **TYNE AND WEAR** · **Gateshead** · **Sunderland**

Allendale Town · Alston · Consett · Stanley · Chester le Street · Houghton le Spring · Hetton le Hole · Durham

1:2 500 000

10   5   0   10   20   30   40   50   60   miles
20 10   0   20   40   60   80   100 km

NORTH   SEA

IRISH   SEA

ENGLISH   CHANNEL

Bristol Channel

Cardigan Bay

SCOTLAND

Selected place and feature labels:

Berwick-on-Tweed, Holy I., Farne Is., Coldstream, Flodden, Peebles, Galashiels, Selkirk, Hawick, Jedburgh, The Cheviot 816, Broad Law 830, Alnwick, Coquet, Morpeth, NORTHUMBERLAND, Blyth, Tynemouth, Wallsend, Newcastle, Gateshead, South Shields, Sunderland, TYNE & WEAR, Houghton-le-Spring, Hexham, Blaydon, Durham, Bishop Auckland, Hartlepool, CLEVELAND, Billingham, Stockton, Middlesbrough, Redcar, Darlington, Whitby, Richmond, N. York Moors, Northallerton, Scarborough, Filey, Bridlington, Malton, Driffield, Hornsea, Withernsea, Spurn Hd., Cleethorpes, Grimsby, Mablethorpe, Skegness, Horncastle, Louth, Boston, The Wash, Hunstanton, Wells, Cromer, North Walsham, NORFOLK, Norwich, Great Yarmouth, Lowestoft, Beccles, Southwold, Aldeburgh, Orford Ness, SUFFOLK, Ipswich, Felixstowe, Harwich, Clacton, Colchester, ESSEX, Chelmsford, Southend, Shoeburyness, Basildon, Grays, Tilbury, Gravesend, Sheerness, Whitstable, Herne Bay, Margate, Ramsgate, Deal, Dover, Folkestone, Hythe, Dungeness, Rye, Hastings, Eastbourne, Beachy Hd., Newhaven, Brighton, Hove, Worthing, Littlehampton, Bognor Regis, Chichester, WEST SUSSEX, EAST SUSSEX

LONDON, Windsor, Maidenhead, Slough, Reading, BERKS, Newbury, Basingstoke, Aldershot, Farnborough, Guildford, SURREY, Reigate, Crawley, Tonbridge, Tunbridge Wells, Maidstone, Ashford, Canterbury, KENT, Rochester, Chatham, Gillingham

Cardiff, Newport, GWENT, Pontypool, Pontypridd, Rhondda, MID GLAMORGAN, W. GLAMORGAN, S. GLAMORGAN, Swansea, Port Talbot, Bridgend, Barry, Neath, Maesteg, Aberdare, Merthyr Tydfil, Ebbw Vale, Tredegar, Abergavenny, Monmouth, Ross, Forest of Dean, Gloucester, GLOUCESTER, Stroud, Cheltenham, Tewkesbury, Malvern, Evesham, Worcester, HEREFORD & WORCESTER, Hereford, Leominster, Ludlow, Kidderminster, Stourbridge, Dudley, Wolverhampton, Walsall, West Bromwich, Birmingham, WEST MIDLANDS, Coventry, Solihull, Redditch, WARWICK, Leamington, Stratford-on-Avon, Banbury, Rugby, Nuneaton, Hinckley, LEICESTER, Leicester, Loughborough, Coalville, Melton Mowbray, Oakham, Stamford, Corby, Kettering, Wellingborough, Rushden, NORTHAMPTON, Northampton, Daventry, Buckingham, BUCKS, Aylesbury, Bletchley, Milton, BEDFORD, Bedford, Luton, Dunstable, HERTFORD, Hitchin, Letchworth, Hemel Hempstead, St. Albans, Watford, Harlow, Hertford, Bishop's Stortford, Braintree, Saffron Walden, CAMBRIDGESHIRE, Cambridge, Newmarket, Bury St. Edmunds, Stowmarket, Huntingdon, St. Ives, St. Neots, Ely, Peterborough, Flitton, Spalding, Wisbech, Downham Market, King's Lynn, The Fens, Thetford

OXFORD, Oxford, Woodstock, Witney, Abingdon, Wantage, Swindon, WILTSHIRE, Chippenham, Devizes, Trowbridge, Marlborough, Salisbury, Salisbury Plain, Andover, Winchester, HAMPSHIRE, Eastleigh, Southampton, New Forest, Lymington, Portsmouth, Gosport, Fareham, I. OF WIGHT, Newport, Ryde, Ventnor, Cowes, Christchurch, Bournemouth, Poole, Swanage, I. of Purbeck, Weymouth, Portland I., Dorchester, DORSET, Blandford, Sherborne, Shaftesbury, Yeovil, Chard, Axminster, Bridport, Lyme Regis, Sidmouth, Exmouth, Teignmouth, Dawlish, Newton Abbot, Torquay, Paignton, TORBAY, Dartmouth, DEVON, Exeter, Honiton, Tiverton, Crediton, Okehampton, Dartmoor, Yes Tor 619, Tavistock, Launceston, Bodmin, Brown Willy 419, CORNWALL, St. Austell, Newquay, Padstow, Bude, Bideford, Barnstaple, Ilfracombe, Lynton, Minehead, Dunkery Hill 520, Exmoor, Taunton, Bridgwater, SOMERSET, Wells, Glastonbury, Frome, Radstock, Bath, AVON, Bristol, Avonmouth, Weston-super-Mare

Galloway, Stranraer, Larne, I. Magee, Belfast Lough, Bangor, Belfast, Newtownards, Newton Stewart, Castle Douglas, Dalbeattie, Kirkcudbright, Wigtown, Wigtown Bay, Whithorn, Mull of Galloway, Luce Bay, Dumfries, Annan, Gretna Green, Carlisle, Solway Firth, Maryport, Workington, Whitehaven, St. Bee's Hd., CUMBRIA, Skiddaw 931, Keswick, Penrith, Appleby, Ullswater, Ambleside, Sca Fell 978, Windermere, Kendal, Barnard Castle, Barrow, Ulverston, Furness, Morecambe Bay, Heysham, Morecambe, Lancaster, Fleetwood, Forest of Bowland, Blackpool, FYLDE, Preston, Southport, Formby Pt., LANCASHIRE, Skipton, Ingleborough 723, Pen-y-Ghent 693, Gt. Whernside 704, Ripon, Knaresborough, Harrogate, NORTH YORKSHIRE, York, Selby, Goole, HUMBERSIDE, Hull, Beverley, Holderness, Brigg, Scunthorpe, Immingham, Humber, Gainsborough, East Retford, Worksop, Mansfield, Sutton-in-Ashfield, NOTTS, Newark, LINCOLNSHIRE, Lincoln, Sleaford, Grantham, Witham, Nottingham, Beeston, Long Eaton, Ilkeston, Heanor, Alfreton, Matlock, DERBY, Derby, Burton-on-Trent, Uttoxeter, Ashby-de-la-Zouch, STAFFORD, Stafford, Stoke-on-Trent, Newcastle-under-Lyme, Crewe, CHESHIRE, Nantwich, Northwich, Macclesfield, Buxton, Chesterfield, Sheffield, Rotherham, SOUTH YORKSHIRE, Doncaster, Barnsley, WEST YORKSHIRE, Leeds, Bradford, Halifax, Huddersfield, Dewsbury, Wakefield, Pontefract, Keighley, Nelson, Colne, Burnley, Accrington, Blackburn, Rochdale, Oldham, Bury, Bolton, Wigan, St. Helens, MERSEYSIDE, Bootle, Wallasey, Liverpool, Birkenhead, Widnes, Runcorn, Warrington, Salford, MANCHESTER, Stockport, Glossop, Ashton-under-Lyne, Stalybridge, Sale, Altrincham, Chester, Flint, Mold, Ruthin, Denbigh, CLWYD, Wrexham, Llangollen, Oswestry, SALOP, Shrewsbury, Wellington, Telford, Wem, Market Drayton, Cannock, Tamworth, Lichfield

WALES, GWYNEDD, POWYS, DYFED, Anglesey, Holy I., Holyhead, Beaumaris, Amlwch, Llandudno, Colwyn Bay, Conwy, Rhyl, Caernarfon, Menai Strait, Bangor, Snowdon 1085, Festiniog, Bala L., Dolgellau, Cader Idris 892, Barmouth, Harlech, Pwllheli, Bardsey I., Aberdovey, Machynlleth, Newtown, Montgomery, Welshpool, Llanidloes, Plynlimon 752, Aberystwyth, Aberaeron, Cardigan, Fishguard, St. David's Hd., Haverfordwest, Milford Haven, Pembroke, Tenby, Carmarthen, Llanelli, Llandovery, Llandrindod Wells, Rhayader, New Radnor, Builth Wells, Brecon, Hay

ISLE OF MAN, Ramsey, Snaefell 620, Peel, Douglas, Castletown, Calf of Man

Kintyre, Arran, Goat Fell 873, Campbeltown, Mull of Kintyre, Ailsa Craig, Girvan, Ayr, Irvine, Kilmarnock, Saltcoats, Lanark, Carstairs, Firth of Clyde, North Channel, Sanquhar, Leadhills, Doon, Nith

Projection: Conical with two standard parallels

3   2   1   West from Greenwich 0 East from Greenwich

1:2 500 000

30 miles
km

Towns underlined in Northern Ireland give their
names to the Districts in which they stand
The remaining Districts are:-
1 Fermanagh   5 Castlereagh
2 Moyle   6 Ards
3 Newtownabbey   7 Down
4 North Down   8 Newry & Mourne

SHETLAND IS.
On same scale
SHETLAND

NORTHERN IRELAND

IRELAND

CONNACHT

LEINSTER

MUNSTER

ATLANTIC OCEAN

NORTH SEA

North Channel

ENGLAND

ORKNEY

SHETLAND IS.

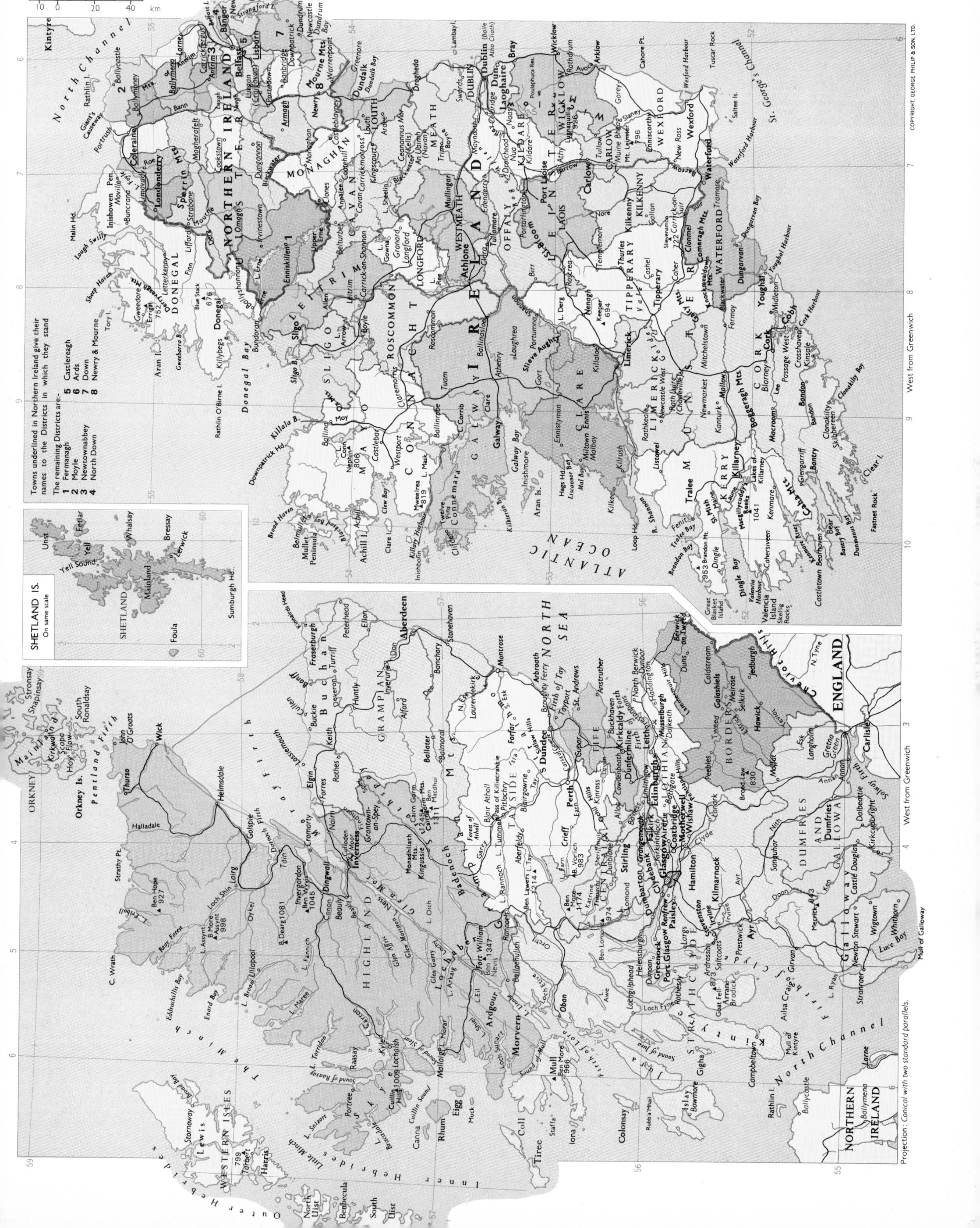

Projection : Conical with two standard parallels.

West from Greenwich

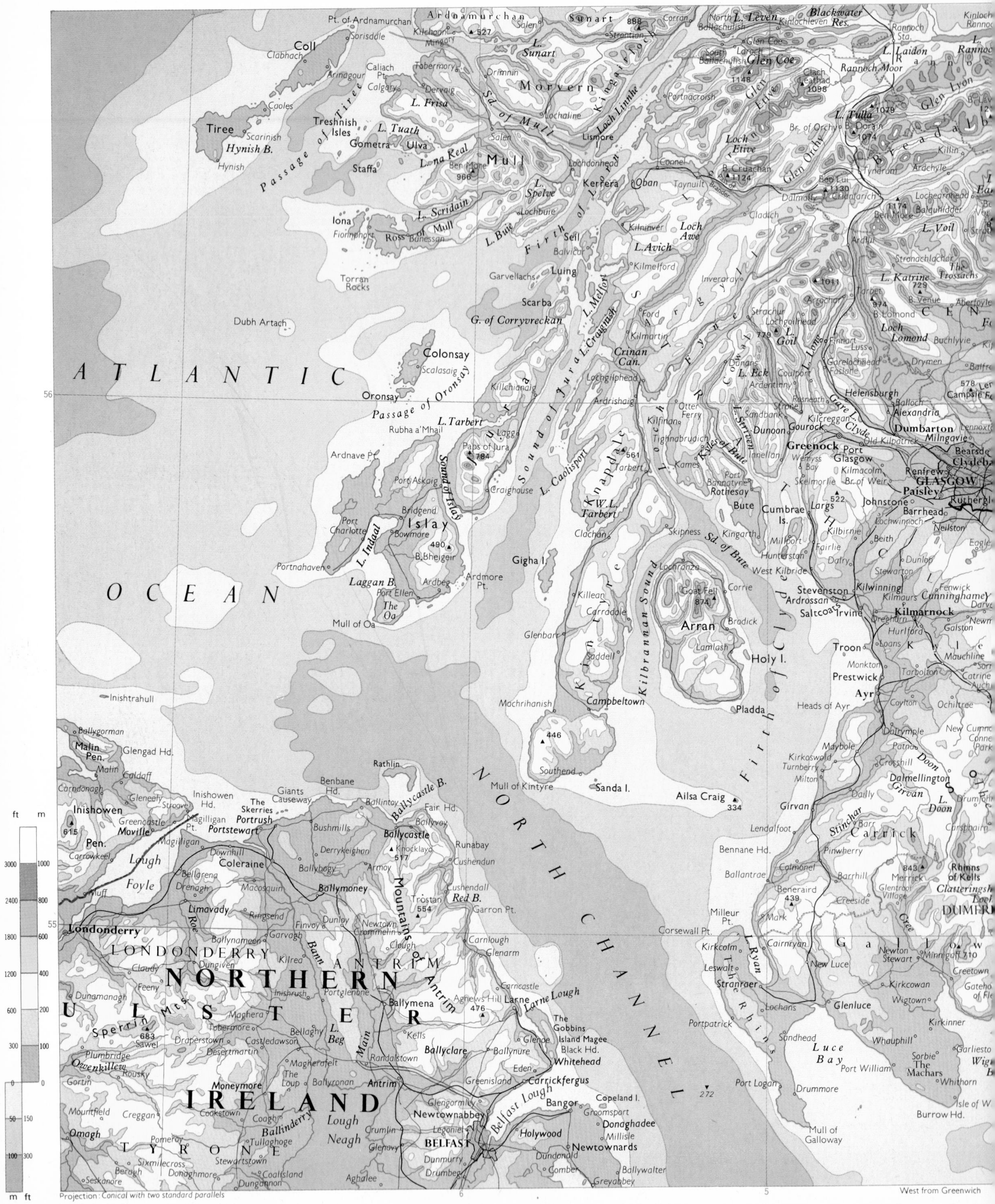

ATLANTIC

OCEAN

NORTH CHANNEL

NORTHERN IRELAND

ULSTER

LONDONDERRY

ANTRIM

TYRONE

BELFAST

Belfast Lough

Lough Neagh

Firth of Clyde

GLASGOW
Paisley
Renfrew
Dumbarton
Greenock
Port Glasgow
Gourock
Helensburgh
Alexandria
Milngavie
Bearsden
Rutherglen
Johnstone
Barrhead
Neilston
Kilbirnie
Beith
Dalry
Stewarton
Kilmaurs
Kilmarnock
Cunninghame
Galston
Hurlford
Mauchline
Catrine
Troon
Prestwick
Ayr
Coylton
Ochiltree
Tarbolton
Monkton
Maybole
Girvan
Ballantrae
Stranraer
Portpatrick
Newton Stewart
Glenluce
Wigtown
Whithorn
Port William

Mull
Iona
Tiree
Coll
Staffa
Ulva
Gometra
Treshnish Isles
Colonsay
Oronsay
Jura
Islay
Gigha I.
Arran
Bute
Cumbrae Is.
Holy I.
Pladda
Ailsa Craig
Sanda I.

Oban
Inveraray
Campbeltown
Machrihanish
Southend
Mull of Kintyre

Giants Causeway
Portrush
Portstewart
Coleraine
Ballymoney
Ballycastle
Cushendall
Cushendun
Ballymena
Ballyclare
Larne
Carrickfergus
Newtownabbey
Bangor
Newtownards
Holywood
Londonderry
Limavady
Omagh

Firth of Lorn
Sound of Mull
Loch Linnhe
Glen Coe
Loch Etive
Loch Awe
Loch Lomond
L. Katrine
L. Voil
Loch Fyne
Kilbrannan Sound
Sd. of Bute
Kyles of Bute
Luce Bay
Lough Foyle
Lough Neagh

Projection: Conical with two standard parallels

West from Greenwich

ft	m
3000	1000
2400	800
1800	600
1200	400
600	200
300	100
0	0
50	150
100	300
m	ft

1:1 000 000

10   0   10   20 miles
10 0   10 20 30 km

NORTH

SEA

56

55

Motorways
Motorways under construction

COPYRIGHT. GEORGE PHILIP & SON. LTD.

SHETLAND
ISLANDS
on same scale

Hecma Ness
Haroldswick
Baltasound
Bluemull Sd.
Unst
Balta
Cullivoe
Uyeasound
Mu Ness
Ramna
Stacks
Whale
Firth
Point of Fethaland
Fetlar
The Snap
The Faither
Mid Yell
North
Roe
Ronas Hill
450
Yell
Esha
Ness
Burravoe
Hillswick
Lunna Ness
S H E T L A N D
St. Magnus
Bay
Brae
Skaw Taing
Out
Skerries
Muckle Roe
Voe
Whalsay
Papa
Stour
The Haa
Sd. of Papa
Sandness
S Nesting
Bay
Walls
Score Hd.
Easter
Skeld
Lerwick
I. of Noss
Vaila
Gruting Voe
Scalloway
Bressay
Hamnavoe
Bressay Sd.
Bard Hd.
West
Burra
Helli
Ness
Mousa
Kettla Ness
Hoswick
St. Ninian's I.
Scousburgh
Boddam
Fitful Hd.
B. of Quendale
Sumburgh Hd.

C. Wrath
L. Inchard
L. Laxford
Handa I.
Scourie
Eddrachillis
Bay
Drumbeg
Pt. of Stoer
Quinag
Stoer
Assynt
Canisp
Butt of Lewis
Port of Ness
South Dell
Ness
Rhu Coigach
Enard
Bay
Lochinver
847
Borve
Cellar Hd.
Barvas
North Tolsta
Tolsta Hd.
Summer
Isles
L. Lurgainn
Shawbost
Carloway
291
Newmarket
Broad Bay
Tiumpan Hd.
Greenstone
Pt.
Gruinard B.
L. Broom
Gallan Hd.
Great
Bernera
Stornoway
Melbost
Portguiran
Eye
Peninsula
Mellon
Charles
Ullapool
Uig
Callanish
L E W I S
Bayble
Aultbea
Coigach
L. Roag
Lochs
Chicken Hd.
An Teallach
1062
Aird Brenish
575
Gisla
Balallan
Crossbost
Greenstone
L. Ewe
Poolewe
Fionn
Loch
Braemore
Loch
Langavat
Kintaravay
Cromore
Pt.
Melvaig
Scarp
Erisort
Park
Gravir
Kebock Hd.
Kerrysdale
Talladale
981
L.
Maree
Slioch
L.
Fannich
W
Husinish
N. Harris
571
L. Shell
Longa I.
Gairloch
Henderson
Kinlochewe
Achnasheen
Husinish
Pt.
Ardvourlie
Castle
799
Beinn Mhor
Sd. of Shiant
L. Gairloch
1053
Taransay
W. L. Tarbert
Ardhasig
L. Seaforth
Shiant Is.
Fasag
Torridon
Shieldaig
Toe Hd.
Sd. of Taransay
Torbert
W E S T E R N
Scalpay
Rubha Hunish
L. Torridon
Applecross
Forest
Coulags
Monar Forest
Carron
Scarastavore
S. Harris
E. L. Tarbert
Kilmaluag
Kilmaluag
Applecross
1052
L. Monar
Pabbay
Leverburgh
Rodel
Kilmaluag
Uig
Trotternish
Achnashellach
Sgurr na La
Sound of Harris
Berneray
Renish Pt.
Loch
Snizort
Waternish
Lochcarron
1150
Haskeir Is.
I S L E S
Vaternish Pt.
Stein
The Storr
719
Sound of Raasay
Kishorn
Mullardoc
Griminish Pt.
Dunvegan
Head
Rona
Inner Sound
Lochcarron
Carron
Sollas
Dunvegan
Waternish
Raasay
Toscaig
Plockton
Stromeferry
Carn Eige
1184
North Uist
L. Maddy
Milovaig
Lephin
488
Roskhill
Crowlin
Is.
Kyle of
Lochalsh
Glen
Paible
Clachan
Dunvegan
Bracadale
Coillore
L. Harport
Kyleakin
L. Alsh
Auchtertyre
Dornie
Chralaig
L.
Carinish
347 Eaval
L. Eport
Fernilea
Carbost
Scalpay
Glenelg
L.
Cluanie
Baleshare
Monach Is.
Sound of
Monach
Gramisdale
Ronay
L. Bracadale
Drynoch
Sligachan
Broadford
The Saddle
1010
Glen Shiel
Benbecula
Grimsay
Minginish
Bla Bheinn
928
Kylerhea
Invershiel
Glen
Ardivachar Pt.
Wiay
Cuillin
Hills
1009
Soay Sd.
Isle
Ornsay
L. Hourn
Quoich
L. Bee
Bagh nam
Faoileann
Rubh' an
Dunain
Soay
L. Scavaig
Elgol
Teangue
Tomdoun
Howmore
605 Hecla
Glenbrittle
Armadale
L. Glen Garry
South
Uist
820 B. Mhor
L. Eishort
Ardvasar
Knoydart
Rubha
Ardvule
L. Eynort
Cuillin Sound
Sound of Sleat
1040
Sgurr na
Ciche
Daliburgh
Lochboisdale
Canna
L. Nevis
Inver
L. Arkaig
L. Boisdale
Sanday Canna
Kintoch
Pt. of
Sleat
Mallaig
983
Culvain
Gairlochy
Sd. of Eriskay
Sd. of Barra
Eriskay
Sd. of Canna
Rhum
810
Morar
Arisaig
Glenfinnan
Caledonian
Canal
Greian
Hd.
Loch Morar
Lochailort
Corpach
Barra
384
Bruernish Pt.
Eigg
Kinlochmoidart
Castlebay
Sd. of Arisaig
882
Moidart
L. Eil
Vatersay
394
Shona
L. Shiel
Ben Ne
Sandray
Sd. of Eigg
L. Moidart
Muck
Pabbay
Ardnamurchan
527
Salen
Sunart
888
Corran
North
Mingulay
Kilchoan
Mingary
L. Sunart
Strontian
L. Leven
Berneray
Barra Head
Pt. of Ardnamurchan
Sorisdale
Morvern
1148
Coll
Clabhach
Arinagour
Tobermory
Drimnin
241
Calgary
Caliach
Pt.
Dervaig
Tiree
Scarinish
Treshnish
Isles
Coales
L. Frisa
Lochaline
Hynish B. Passage of Tree
L. Tuath
Sd. of Mull
Lismore I.
Hynish

Elevation scale
ft	m
3 000	1000
2 400	800
1 800	600
1 200	400
600	200
300	100
0	0
50	150
100	300

m ft

Projection: Conical with two standard parallels

1:1 000 000

10   0   10   20 miles
10   0   10   20   30 km

ORKNEY ISLANDS on same scale

Pentland Firth

Stroma
Dunnet Hd.
Holborn Hd. Dunnet B.
Scrabster Dunnet
Thurso Castletown
Strathy Pt.
Strathy Melvich Reay Dounreay
Portskerra Bettyhill
Craigtown Dalhalvaig
Halkirk Olgrinmore
Watten
Achavanich

John o'Groats
Duncansby Hd.
Mey Canisby Duncansby
Dunnet Freswick
Sortat Nybster
Hastigrow Keiss
Reiss Noss Head
Wick Staxigoe

Sinclair's B.

Thrumster
Ulbster

Lybster
Latheron
Dunbeath

Faraid Hd.
Whiten Hd.
Durness
Heilam
ness L. Eriboll
L. Hope
Tongue Borgie
Ben Hope 927
B. 763 Loyal
L. Loyal

Kyle of Tongue
Strath Halladale
Naver
Forsinain
Farsinard
Kinbrace

Strathmore
Loch Assynt
998 More
B. Hee Altnaharra
L. Naver B. Klibreck 961
L. nan Clar Kildonan

705 Morven
Braemore
Berriedale
Ousdale
Ord of Caithness

Kinloch
Lairg
Loch Shin

Brora
L. Brora
628 B. Dhorain
Helmsdale

Rosehall Auchness
Oykel Oykel Br.
Inveran Bonar bridge
Kincardine
Freewater Forest
Carron
Dearg

Torroboll
Culrain
Clashmore

Golspie
Fleet L. Fleet Embo
Brora
Dornoch
Tarbat Ness
Portmahomack

Easter Ross
Rosehall
Edderton
Tain
Fearn Balintore
B. Tharsuinn 692

Strathpeffer
L. Luichart
Contin
Strath
town
Dingwall
B. Wyvis 1045
Evanton
Alness
Nigg Balnapaling
Invergordon
Cromarty

Dornoch Firth

Moray Firth

Cromarty Firth
Balblair
Black Isle Rosemarkie
Fortrose Avoch
Canonbridge Nth. Kessock
Muir of Ord
Beauly Inverness
Culloden Moor

Branderburgh Spey B.
Lossiemouth Findochty Portknockie
Burghead Hopeman Portsoy
Burghead B. Spey Bay Buckie
Findhorn Garmouth Portgordon
Kinloss Lhanbryde Fochabers
Forres Elgin
Nairn Auldearn Kellas
Cawdor Littlemill Dallas Rothes
Ferness Craigellachie
Archiestown

Troup Hd. Rosehearty
Kinnairds Hd.
Fraserburgh
Inverallochy
St. Combs
Banff Macduff New Aberdour Rathen Rattray Hd.
Cullen Fordyce Witchyburn Strichen Crimond
Deveron Newbyth New Pitsligo St. Fergus
Aberchirder Turriff Buchan Peterhead
Keith Newmill Fortrie New Deer Maud Longside Boddam
Huntly Badenscoth Rothienorman Old Deer Buchan Ness
Colpy Fyvie Methlick Hatton Cruden Bay

Strathbogie
Rhynie Insch Tarves Ellon
Oldmeldrum Formartine Newburgh
Lumsden Alford Kennay Inverurie Newmachar
722 The Buck GRAMPIAN Monymusk Kintore Balmedie
803 Carn Mor Strathdon Kemnay Dyce Bankhead
Tomintoul Ladder Hills Don Bucksburn Bridge of Don
B. Avon 1171 Mar Tarland Lumphanan Echt **Aberdeen**
Morven 872 Torphins Peterculter Girdle Ness
Cairn Gorm 1245 Ordie Aboyne Banchory Cove Bay
Carn Ban Kincraig Crathie Dee Strachan Commachmore
941 Newtonmore Cairngorm Mts. 1295 Braeriach B. Macdhui 1311
Braemar Ballater Newtonhill
Balmoral Castle Mt. Keen 938 Muchalls
Lochnagar 1154 Stonehaven

Charlestown of Aberlour
Dufftown
840 Lettoch Spey
Laggan
Carn Glas-choire 659
Dulnain Bridge
Grantown-on-Spey
Spey Hills of Cromdale
Strath Avon
Cabrach
Glenlivet
Tomnavoulin

L. Duntelchaig
Torness
Farr
Tomatin
Carrbridge
Nethy Bridge
Boat of Garten
Aviemore Alvie
Kingussie Ruthven
Monadhliath Mts.
810
White Bridge
Carn na Saobhaidhe

GLEN MORE
Loch Ness
Foyers
Errogie
Invermoriston
Mealfuarvonie 696

Fort Augustus
Invergarry
Laggan

Creag Meagaidh 1128
Roybridge Glen
Spean Laggan
B. Alder 1148
L. Treig L. Ericht
L. Laggan
Lochlaggan Hotel
Dalwhinnie
Drumochter
B. Dearg 1008
Forest of Atholl
Beinn a' Ghlo 1121
Glen Garry Tilt
Blair Atholl
Pass of Killiecrankie
Kirkmichael

Blackwater Res.
Rannoch
L. Laidon
L. Rannoch Kinloch Rannoch
Rannoch Moor
Rannoch Sta.
Schiehallion 1083
Tummel L. Tummel Strath Tay
B. Lawers 1214
L. Lyon Fearnan Aberfeldy
Glen Lyon Kenmore
L. Tulla 1079 B. Dorain 1074
Breadalbane
Loch Tay
Killin

GRAMPIAN MOUNTAINS
Braes of Angus
Glas Maol 1067
Forest of Atholl
Glen Shee
Isla
Clova
Rottal

Glen Esk North Esk
South Esk
Howe of the Mearns
Fettercairn Laurencekirk
Edzell Marykirk
Brechin St. Cyrus
Dykehead
Kirriemuir
Forfar Glamis
Balthangie Pitlochry
Dunkeld
Blairgowrie
Coupar Angus
Rattray Sidlaw Hills 455
Bankfoot
Balholgie Muirdrum
Burrelton
Carmyllie
Dundee Broughty Ferry
Monifieth Buddon Ness

Auchenblae
Inverbervie
Gourdon
Johnshaven

Lunan B.
Inverkeilor
Marywell
Arbroath
Carnoustie

N O R T H   S E A

West from Greenwich

Based upon the Ordnance Survey Map with the permission
of the Controller of Her Majesty's Stationery Office.
Crown Copyright Reserved.

COPYRIGHT. GEORGE PHILIP & SON. LTD.

ORKNEY ISLANDS inset:

Mull Hd. Papa Westray
Noup Hd. Westray N. Ronaldsay
Pierowall N. Ronaldsay Firth
Berst Ness The North Sound Start Pt.
Westray Firth Eday Sanday
Rapness Sanday Sound
Sacquoy Hd. Papa Stronsay
Brough Hd. Rousay Egilsay Whitehall
Eynhallow Sd. Wasbister Stronsay
Twatt Wyre Gairsay Lamb Hd.
Redland Brinyan Stronsay Auskerry
Dounby Finstown Shapinsay
L. of Harray WIDE Y FIRTH
L. of Stenness Shapinsay Sd.
Stromness Mainland Kirkwall Mull Hd.
Graemsay Deer Sd. Deerness
Hoy Orphir St. Mary's Gritley
Old Man of Hoy Ward Hill 477 Pt. of Ayre
Rora Hd. Scapa Flow Copinsay
Rackwick Burray Rose Ness
Hoy Lyness Flotta St. Margaret's Hope
Hurliness South Ronaldsay
Tor Ness S. Walls Swona Cleat
Dunnet Hd. Stroma Pentland Skerries
Pentland Firth
Mey John o'Groats Duncansby Hd.
Canisby

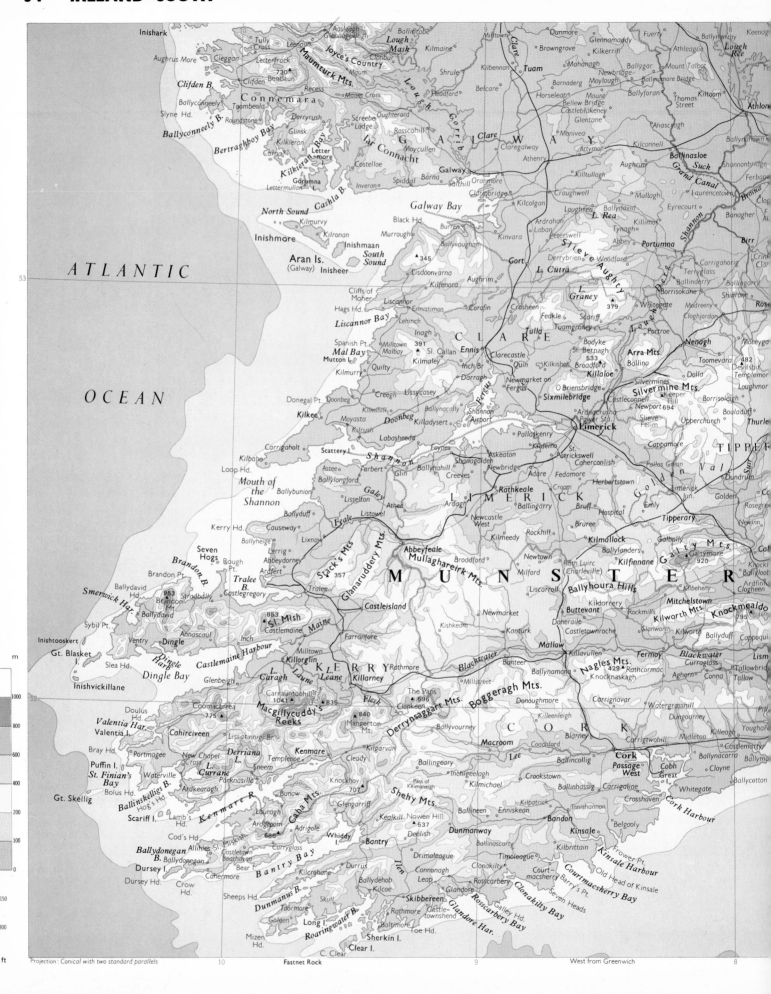

Inishark

Aasleagh
Glennadmagh
Joyce's Country

Milltown

Dunmore
Glennamaddy
Fuerty
Ballymurray
Keenagh

Tully Cross
Leenaun
Ballinrobe
Lough Mask
Kilmaine
Clonbur

Clare
Browngrove
Glenkerrin
Kilkerrin
Athleague
Lough Ree

Aughrus More
Cleggan
Maumturk Mts.
Maum
Shrule
Kilbennan
Tuam
Mahanagh
Barnaderg
Moylough
Newbridge
Ballymore Bridge
Mount Talbot

Clifden
Letterfrack
Recess
730 Benbaun
Maam Cross
Headford
Belcare
Horseleap
Bellew Bridge
Castleblakeney
Glentane
Street
Ballyforan
Kiltoom
Athlo

Ballyconneely
Connemara
Clifden B.
Derryrush
Screebe
Oughterard
GALWAY
Monivea
Attymon
Aughrim
Killconnell
Ballinasloe
Shannonbridge
Ferba

Slyne Hd.
Ballyconneely B.
Roundstone
Glinsk
Lodge
Rosscahill
Claregalway
Athenry
Killtullagh
Grand Canal
Suck
Clos

Bertraghboy Bay
Kilkieran Bay
Cashla
Costelloe
Galway
Oranmore
Killimor
Laurencetown
Brosna

Carna
Lettermore
Spiddal
Barna
Salthill
Clarinbridge
Loughrea
L. Rea
Eyrecourt
Banagher

Gorumna
Lettermullan
Inveran
Kilcolgan
Ardrahan
Laban
Petersweil
Tynagh
Portumna
Birr

North Sound
Galway Bay
Black Hd.
Burren
Kinvara
Stieve Aughty
Abbey
Shannon

Inishmore
Murrough
Ballyvaughan
Woodford
L. Graney
379
Borrisokane
Ballingarry

Aran Is.
Inishmaan
South Sound
345
Lisdoonvarna
Kilfenora
Crasheen
Scariff
Whitegate
Cloghjordan
Shinrone
Ros

(Galway) Inisheer
Cliffs of Moher
Liscannor
Ennistimon
Corofin
Fedkle
Tuamgraney
L. Derg
Borrisoleigh
Crin Clar

53

ATLANTIC
Hags Hd.
Lehinch
Inagh
Tulla
Bodyke
St. Bernagh
Nenagh
Moneyga

Liscannor Bay
Spanish Pt.
Milltown Malbay
391
Sl. Callan
Ennis
Clarecastle
Kilkishen
533
Arra Mts.
Toomevara
482 Devilsbit

Mal Bay
Mutton I.
Quilty
Kilmaley
Quin
Broadford
Killaloe
Silvermines
Templemor

OCEAN
Kilmurry
Darragh
Inch Br.
Newmarket on Fergus
O'Briensbridge
Silvermine Mts.
Loughmor

Donegal Pt.
Doonbeg
Creegh
Lissycasey
Fergus
Sixmilebridge
Castleconnell
Keeper
Upperchurch
Thurle

Kilkee
Kilmihil
Ballynacally
Shannon Airport
Ardnacrusha Power Sta.
Newport 694
Borrisoleigh

Moyasta
Killadysert
Slieve Felim

Kilrush
Labasheeda
Pallaskenry
Limerick
Cappamore
TIPPE

Carrigaholt
Scattery I.
Shannon
Foynes
Shanagolden
Kildemo
Patrickswell
Pallas Green
Dundru

Kilbaha
Astee
Tarbert
Ballyhahill
Newbridge
Askeaton
Caherconlish
Golden Vale

Loop Hd.
Mouth of the Shannon
Ballylongford
Glin
Creeves
Adare
Fedamore
Emly
Golden

Galey
Athea
LIMERICK
Croom
Herbertstown
Limerick Jun.
Rosegre

Ballybunion
Lisselton
Rathkeale
Ballingarry
Bruff
Hospital
Tipperary
Newinn

Ballyduff
Listowel
Newcastle West
Kilmeedy
Rockhill
Bruree
Kilmallock
Galbally
Cal

Kerry Hd.
Causeway
Feale
Abbeyfeale
Broadford
Newtown
Milford
Ballylanders
Galtymore
920

Seven Hogs
Ballyheige
Lerrig
Abbeydorney
Mullaghareirk Mts.
Rath Luirc (Charleville)
Kilfinnane
Galty Mts.

Brandon B.
Rough
Stack's Mts.
357
MUNSTER
Liscarroll
Ballyhoura Hills
Knocki

Brandon Pt.
Ardfert
Glanaruddery Mts.
Newmarket
Kikdorrery
Mitchelstown
Ardfinn

Tralee B.
Tralee
Castleisland
Kishkeam
Buttevant
Kilworth Mts.
Knockmealdo

Smerwick Har.
953 Brandon Mt.
Stradbally
Castlegregory
Farranfore
Kanturk
Doneraile
Castletownroche
Kilworth
795

Ballydavid Hd.
Ballydavid
Sl. Mish
Castlemaine
Mallow
Killavullen
Nagles Mts.
Fermoy
Blackwater

Sybil Pt.
Annascaul
Maine
Killorglin
Blackwater
429 Rathcormac
Aghern
Curraglass
Tallowbrid

Inishtooskert
Gt. Blasket I.
Ventry
Dingle
Inch
Castlemaine Harbour
Milltown
Rathmore
Banteer
Knocknaskagh
Conna
Tallow

Dingle Har.
Slea Hd.
L. Caragh
Laune
KERRY
Killarney
Millstreet
CORK
Watergrasshill
Pill

Dingle Bay
Glenbeigh
L. Leane
Flesk
The Paps
696
Boggeragh Mts.
Dungourney

Inishvickillane
Carrauntoohill
1041
835
Clonkeen
Donoughmore
Carrignavar
Youghal

52
Doulus Hd.
Coomacarrea
775
Macgillycuddy's Reeks
840
Derrynasaggart Mts.
Killeenleigh
Castlemartyr

Valentia Har.
Mangerton Mt.
Ballyvourney
Macroom
Blarney
Carrigtwohill
Killeagh

Valentia I.
Cahirciveen
Lissatinnig Br.
Kilgarvan
Coachford
Lee
Cork
Cobh
Cloyne

Bray Hd.
Kenmare
Cleady
Ballingeary
Ballincollig
Passage West
Great
Ballycotton

Puffin I.
New Chapel Cross
Derriana L.
Templenoe
Inchigeelagh
Crookstown
Midleton

St. Finian's Bay
Waterville
L. Currane
Sneem
Pass of Keimaneigh
Kilmichael
Carrigaline
Whitegate
Ballycotton

Bolus Hd.
Parknasilla
Knockboy 707
Shehy Mts.
Ballineen
Enniskean
Crosshaven
Cork Harbour

Gt. Skellig
Ballinskelligs B.
Ardkearagh
Bunow
Kealkill
Nowen Hill 537
Innishannon
Bandon

Scariff I.
Lamb's Hd.
Kenmare R.
Lauragh
Glengarriff
Deelish
Ballinhassig
Belgooly

Cod's Hd.
Ardgroom
686
Adrigole
Drimoleague
Dunmanway
Ballinascarty
Kinsale
Kilbrittain

Ballydonegan B.
Allihies
Sl. Miskish
Castletown Bearhaven
Caha Mts.
Whiddy I.
Bantry
Clonakilty
Frower Pt.
Kinsale Harbour

Dursey I.
Bear
Bantry Bay
Kilcrohane
Durrus
Ballydehob
Leap
Rosscarbery
Timoleague
Courtmacsherry
Old Head of Kinsale

Dursey Hd.
Crow Hd.
Sheeps Hd.
Dunmanus B.
Skull
Roaringwater B.
Tien
Kilcoe
Glandore
Barry's Pt.
Courtmacsherry Bay
Seven Heads

Mizen Hd.
Goleen
Toormore
Skibbereen
Castletownshend
Glandore Har.
Clonakilty Bay

Sherkin I.
Rathmore
Baltimore
Toe Hd.
Galley Hd.

C. Clear
Clear I.

ft m
3000 1000
2400 800
1800 600
1200 400
600 200
300 100
0 0
50 150
100 300
m ft

1:1 000 000

10   10   20 miles

10   0   10   20   30 km

WESTMEATH

L. Iron
Ballindlock
Ballynacargy
Rathconrath
more
Kildare
Castletown
Geoghegan
Horseleap
Clara
Kilbeggan
Durrow
Tullamore
Screggan

L. Owel
Mullingar
The Downs
L. Ennell
Dalystown
Ballynagore
Killavally
Kilbeggan
Daingean (Philipstown)
Ballinagar
Geashill

Delvin
Cloghan
Killucan
Rochfortbridge
Moyvalley
Carbury
Edenderry
Killane
Cushina

Athboy
Ballivor
Trim
Rathmolyon
Innfield
Johnstown Bridge
Clonard
Enfield
Timahoe

Dunshaughlin
Summerhill
Dunboyne
Kilcock
Clonee
Maynooth
Celbridge
Leixlip
Lucan

Ratoath
Ashbourne

Balbriggan
Skerries
Naul
Lusk
Rush
Donabate

Ardcath
Balscaddan
Ballyboghil
Swords
Malahide
Portmarnock
Baldoyle

Lambay I.

Cloghran
Ward
Finglas
Glasnevin

DUBLIN
Clontarf
Howth Hd.
Irelands Eye
Howth

DUBLIN (Baile Atha Cliath)
Blackrock
Dún Laoghaire (Dunleary)
Dalkey
Killiney

OFFALY
Kilcormac (Frankford)
Rosenallis
Cadamstown
Kinnitty
Slieve Bloom
Arderin ▲529

Portarlington
Barrow
Monasterevan
Kildare
Allenwood
Robertstown
Rathangan

KILDARE
Kilcullen
Ballymore Eustace
Hollywood

Clondalkin
Rathcoole
Dundrum

Bray
Bray Head
Greystones

Blessington
Brittas
Kippure ▲754
Enniskerry
Gt. Sugar Loaf ▲504

IRISH SEA

LEINSTER
Mountmellick
Port Laoise
New Inn
Vicarstown
Fontstown
Dunlavin

Slieve Bloom
Mountrath
Castletown
Stradbally
Athy
Timolin

Abbeyleix
Ballyroan
Ballylynan
Kilkea
Moone

Newtownmountkennedy
Newcastle
Donard
Lugnaquilla ▲926
Sally Gap
Roundwood
Poulaphouca Res.
Vartry Res.

Ballinaclea
Laragh
Glendalough
Rathnew
Wicklow
Wicklow Hd.

LAOIS
Borris in Ossory
Rathdowney
Ballycolla
Clogh
Castlecomer
Castledermot
Arless
Ballickmoyler
Rathvilly
Hacketstown
Knockananna
Aughrim
Glenealy
Kilbride

Graigue
Tullow
Clonmore
Tinahely
Avoca
Mizen Hd.
Wooden Br.
Glenart Castle
Arklow
Arklow Hd.

Johnstown
Freshford
CARLOW
Leighlinbridge
Fennagh
Ballon
Kiltegan
Aghavannagh
Rathdrum

Kilkenny
Muine Bheag (Bagenalstown)
Nurney
Whitehall
Old Leighlin

Shillelagh
Kildavin
Craanford
Coolgreany
Wicklow Gap
Kilmichael Pt.

Kilmanagh
Gowran
Bennettsbridge
Goresbridge
Borris
Mt. Leinster ▲796
Bunclody (Newtownbarry)
Carnew
Gorey
Courtown
Riverchapel

Callan
Kells
Thomastown
Graiguenamanagh
Ballymurphy ▲734
Kiltealy
Ballycarney
Camolin
Ballycanew
Ballygarrett
Cahore Pt.

Windygap
Inistioge
Glynn ▲519
Enniscorthy
Rathnure
Vinegar Hill

Slievenamon ▲722
Kilsheelan
Mullinavat
Ballywilliam
Cloonroche
Oilgate
Ford
Castlebridge
Blackwater

Clonmel
Carrickbeg
Carrick-on-Suir
Piltown
Fiddown
New Ross
Ballynabola
Killurin
WEXFORD
Taghmon
Wexford Harbour
Wexford
Rosslare

Comeragh Mts. ▲755
Portlaw
Mooncoin
Foulksmills
Wellington Bridge
Rosslare Harbour
Greenore Pt.
Killinick

Monavullagh Mts. ▲792
Kilbrien
Suir
Waterford
Kilmeadan
Mullinahone
Ninemilehouse

Kilmacthomas
WATERFORD
Tramore
Passage East
Fethard
Tintern Abbey
Duncormick
Bannow
Kilmore
Kilmore Quay
Bridgetown
Broadway
Churchtown
Carnsore Pt.
Tuskar Rock
Lady's I. Lake
Tacumshin L.

Ballylaneen
Stradbally
Annestown
Knockmahon
Dunmore East
Hook Hd.
Brownstown Hd.
Waterford Harbour
Bannow Bay
Baginbun Hd.
Saltee Is.
Crossfarnoge Pt.

Dungarvan Harbour
Helvick Hd.
Ringville
Tramore Bay
Mine Hd.

Ardmore
Ardmore Head
Bay

▼113

Continuation North-West on same scale

Benwee
Broad Haven
Portacloy
Downpatrick Hd.
Lenadoon Pt.
Erris Hd.
Belderg
Annagh Hd.
Belmullet
An Geata Mór (Binghamstown)
Glenamoy
▲380
Killala B.
Killala
Ross
Inniscrone

Mullet Pen.
Carrowmore L.
Owenmore
Belville
Crockets Town

Inishkea North
Inishkea South
Fallmore
Blacksod Bay
Blacksod Pt.
Bellacorick
Crossmolina
Ballina
Bunnyconnellan

Saddle Hd.
Ballycroy
Nephin Beg Range
Deel
L. Conn
Lahardaun
Nephin ▲806
Foxford
OX Mts.
Callow

Achill Hd.
Dooagh
Slievemore ▲672
Castlehill
▲714
Keel
Achill Mulrany
Achill I.
Dooega
Corraun Pen.
Glenisland
L. Feeagh
Beltra
L. Cullin
L. Beltra
Strade
Bellavary
Bohola

Achill Sd.
Achillbeg I.
Newport B.
Newport
Castlebar
Manulla
Kiltamagh

Clare I.
Clew Bay
Westport B.
Westport
MAYO
Mayo
Ballyglass

Caher I.
Louisburgh
Westport B.
Croaghpatrick ▲765
Kilfavally
Ballyglass

Inishturk
Creggánbaun
Sheefry Hills
Killadoon
L. Carra
Hollymount

Inishbofin
Killary Har.
Mweelrea ▲819
Aasleagh
Partry Mts.
Lough Mask
Ballinrobe
Kilmaine

Inishshark
Glennagevlagh
Joyce's Country
Lough Corrib
Shrule

Aughrus More
Cleggan
Tully Cross
Letterfrack
Feenaun
Maumturk Mts.
Maam
Clonbur

Clifden B.
▲730 Benbaun
Clifden
Maumturk Mts.

CONNACHT
Carra

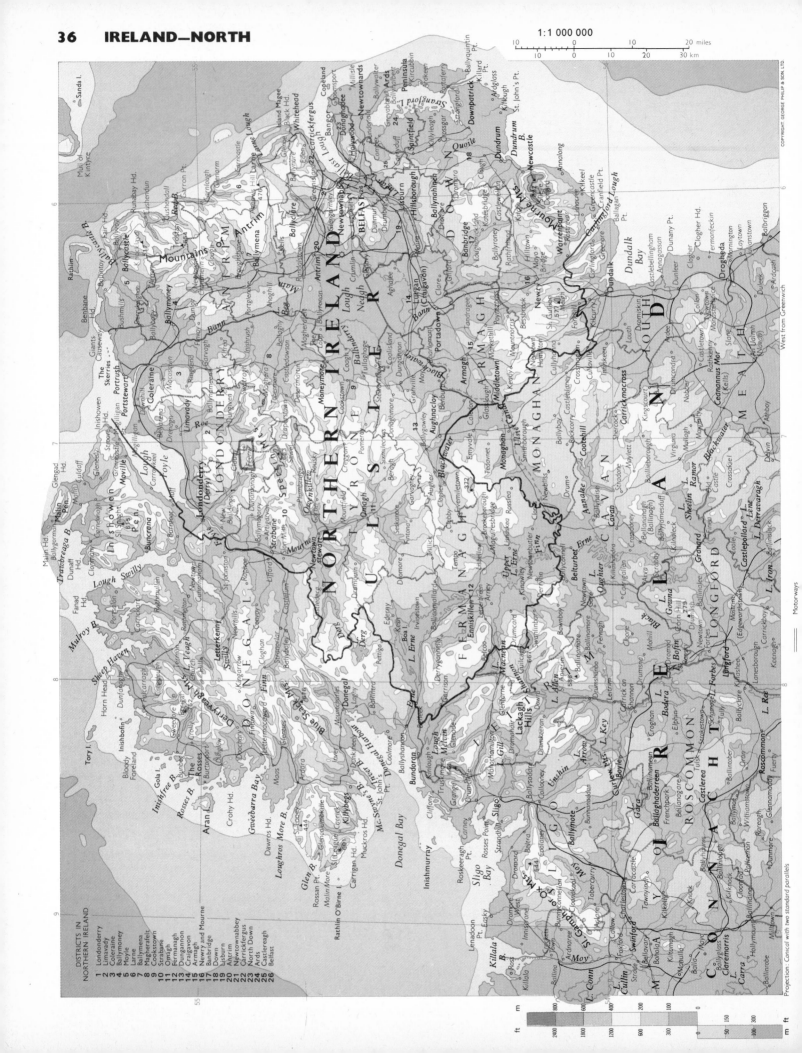

1:1 000 000

COPYRIGHT GEORGE PHILIP & SON, LTD.

DISTRICTS IN NORTHERN IRELAND
1 Londonderry
2 Limavady
3 Coleraine
4 Ballymoney
5 Moyle
6 Larne
7 Ballymena
8 Magherafelt
9 Cookstown
10 Strabane
11 Omagh
12 Fermanagh
13 Dungannon
14 Craigavon
15 Armagh
16 Newry and Mourne
17 Banbridge
18 Down
19 Lisburn
20 Antrim
21 Newtownabbey
22 Carrickfergus
23 North Down
24 Ards
25 Castlereagh
26 Belfast

Projection: Conical with two standard parallels

West from Greenwich

Motorways

Conical with two standard parallels

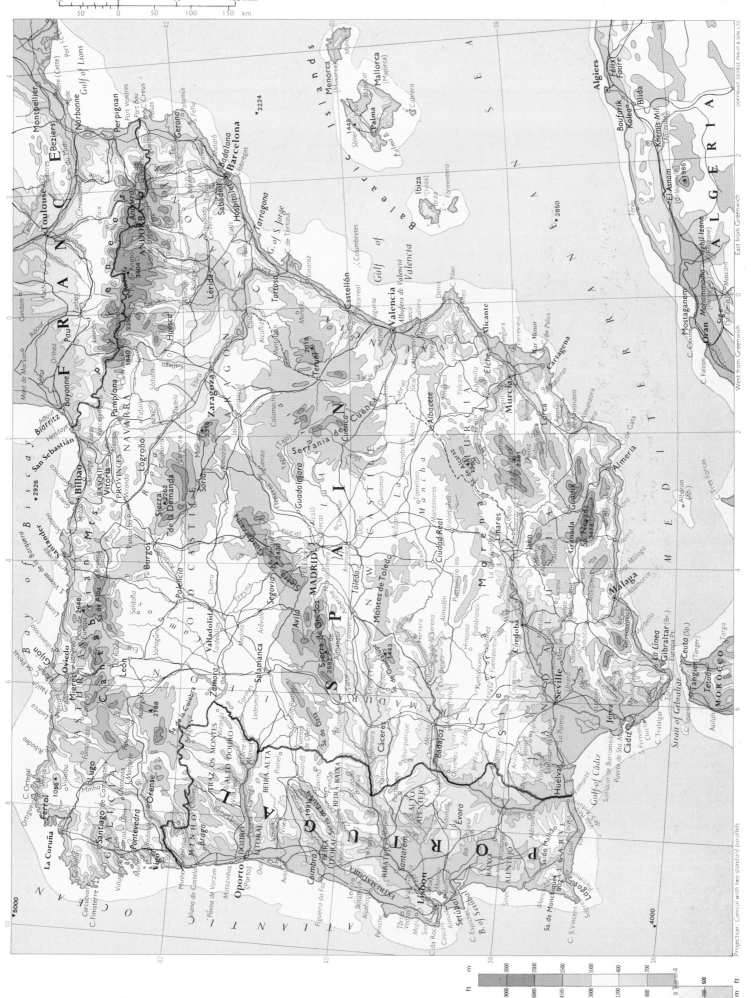

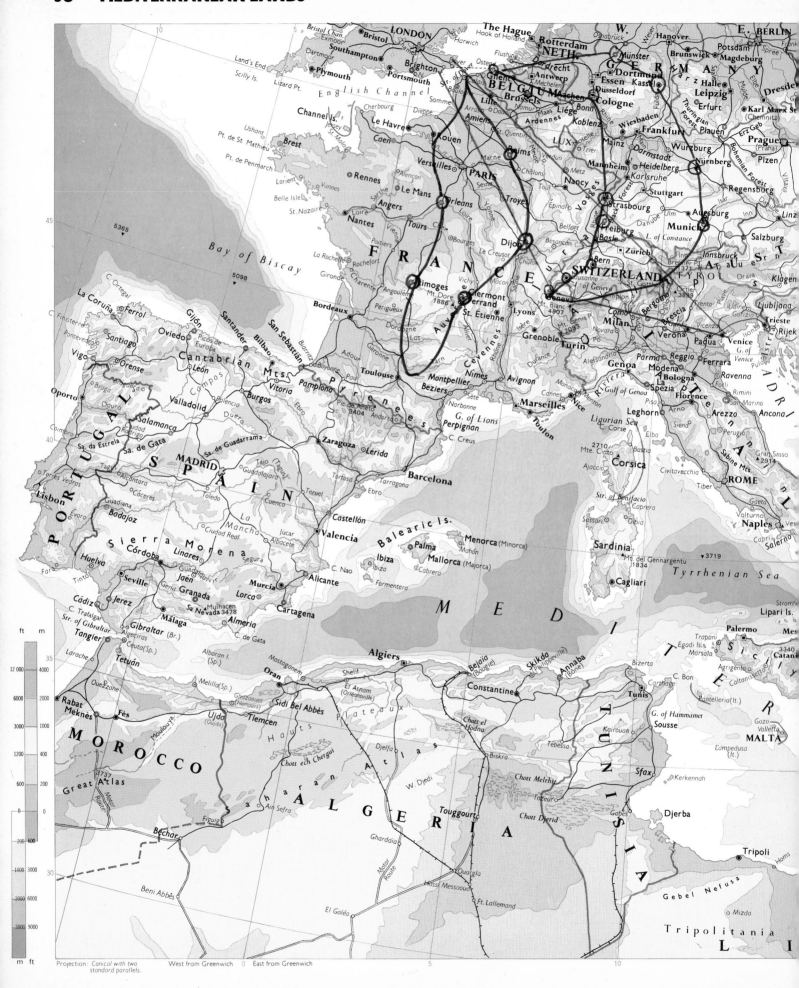

MALTA
1:1 000 000

S.E. EUROPE
POLITICAL
1:25 000 000

Projection: Conical with two standard parallels

CHANNEL ISLANDS

1:1 000 000

Over 300 ft. Over 100 m
0–300 ft. 0–100 m

FRANCE

CHANNEL ISLANDS

The Casquets
Burhou
Alderney
St. Anne
Cap de la Hague
St. Germain
Auderville
Urville
Jobourg
Anse de Vauville
Beaumont
Cherbourg
Virandeville 178
Breuville
Diélette
les Pieux
Bricquebec
GUERNSEY
Vale
Sampson
St. Martin
Herm
St. Peter Port
Herbourg Pt.
Sark
St. Jacques
Carteret
Forest
Torteval
Barneville
Portbail
Ecréhou Rocks
Baudreville
JERSEY
Bretteville
Grosnez Pt.
Trinity
St. Martin
St. Peter
Gorey
St. Germain
Corbière Pt.
la Rocque Pt.
Pirou
St. Brelade's
St. Helier
Gouville
Blainville
The Minquiers
Coutainville

West from Greenwich

FRANCE
DEPARTMENTS
1:8 000 000

1. VAL d'OISE
2. YVELINES
3. ESSONNE
4. HAUTS-DE-SEINE
5. SEINE-ST. DENIS
6. VAL-DE-MARNE
7. VILLE DE PARIS

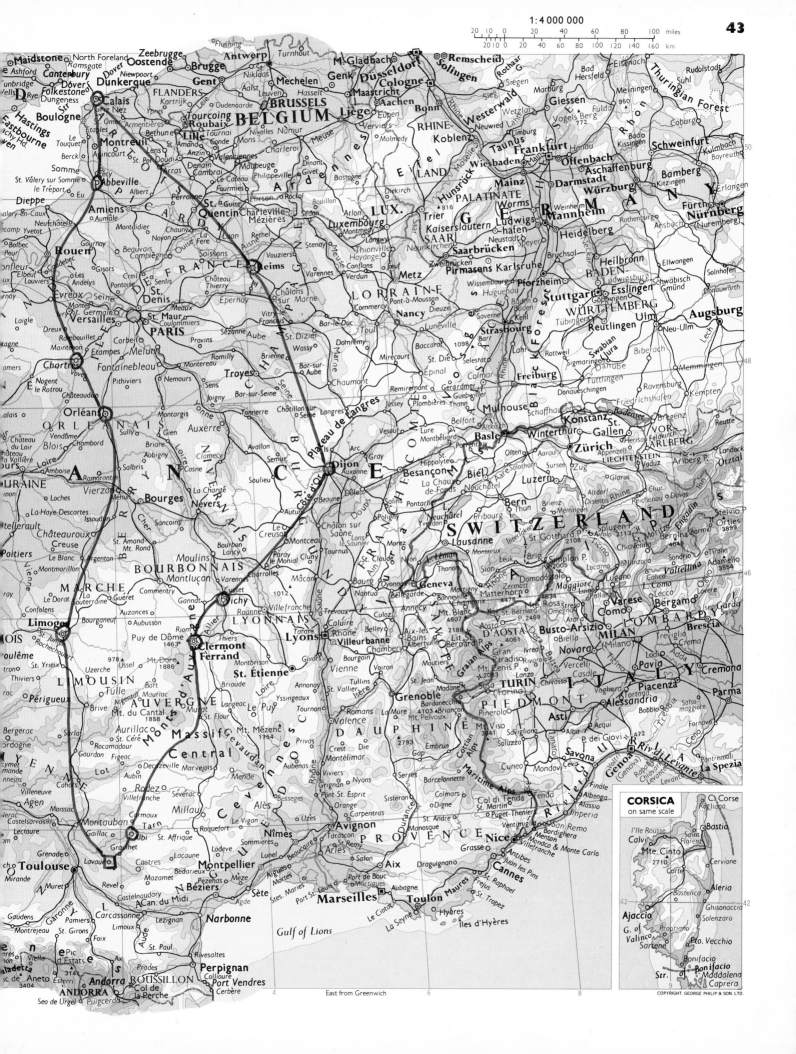

1 : 2 000 000

NORTH SEA

NETHERLANDS

BELGIUM

GERMANY

LUXEMBOURG

AMSTERDAM
THE HAGUE ('s Gravenhage)
ROTTERDAM
Utrecht
Haarlem
Leiden
Delft
Dordrecht
Breda
Tilburg
Eindhoven
Nijmegen
Arnhem
Zwolle
Groningen
Leeuwarden
Enschede
Hengelo
Apeldoorn
Amersfoort
Deventer
's Hertogenbosch

ANTWERP
Antwerp
Ghent
BRUSSELS (Brussel Bruxelles)
Brugge (Bruges)
Ostend (Oostende)
Mechelen
Leuven
Liège
Namur
Charleroi
Mons
Tournai
Kortrijk
Roeselare
Ypres
Aalst
Hasselt
Genk
Maastricht
Verviers
Aachen

COLOGNE (Köln)
Bonn
Düsseldorf
ESSEN
DORTMUND
Duisburg
Mülheim
Oberhausen
Bochum
Wuppertal
Solingen
Remscheid
Krefeld
Mönchen-Gladbach
Neuss
Leverkusen
Münster
Osnabrück
Emden
Oldenburg
Koblenz
Wiesbaden
Mainz
Trier
Saarbrücken

Lille
Roubaix
Tourcoing
Armentières
Arras
Cambrai
Valenciennes
Douai
Reims
Charleville-Mézières
St Quentin
Soissons
Compiègne
Luxembourg

Den Helder
Texel
Alkmaar
Zaandam
Hilversum
Gouda
Vlaardingen
Schiedam
Middelburg
Vlissingen (Flushing)
Terneuzen
Roosendaal
Bergen-op-Zoom
Oss
Venlo
Roermond
Weert
Helmond
Sittard
Heerlen

Emmen
Assen
Meppel
Veendam
Winschoten
Papenburg
Leer
Lingen
Nordhorn
Rheine
Gronau
Coesfeld
Borken
Bocholt
Emmerich
Kleve
Goch
Kevelaer
Geldern
Moers
Viersen
Erkelenz
Jülich
Düren
Stolberg
Eschweiler
Euskirchen
Siegburg
Brühl
Bergisch Gladbach
Opladen
Hagen
Iserlohn
Unna
Hamm
Soest
Werl
Lünen
Herne
Gelsenkirchen
Recklinghausen
Bottrop
Marl
Datteln
Lüdinghausen
Ahlen
Beckum
Warendorf

WESTFRIESCHE EILANDEN
Terschelling
Vlieland
Ameland
Schiermonnikoog
Texel
Wadden Zee
IJsselmeer
Noordoost Polder
FRIESLAND
DRENTHE
OVERIJSSEL
GELDERLAND
NOORD BRABANT
ZUID HOLLAND
NOORD HOLLAND
ZEELAND
FLANDRE
BRABANT
HAINAUT
ARDENNES
PICARDIE
PAS-DE-CALAIS
SOMME
OISE
AISNE
MEUSE
MEURTHE-ET-MOSELLE
MOSELLE
RHEINLAND PFALZ
NORDRHEIN WESTFALEN
NIEDERSACHSE
OSTFRIESLAND
SAUERLAND
WESTERWALD
HUNSRÜCK
EIFEL
Ruhr
Rhein
Maas
Mosel
Meuse
Sambre
Marne
Aisne
Oise

Projection: Conical with two standard parallels

East from Greenwich

COPYRIGHT. GEORGE PHILIP & SON. LTD.

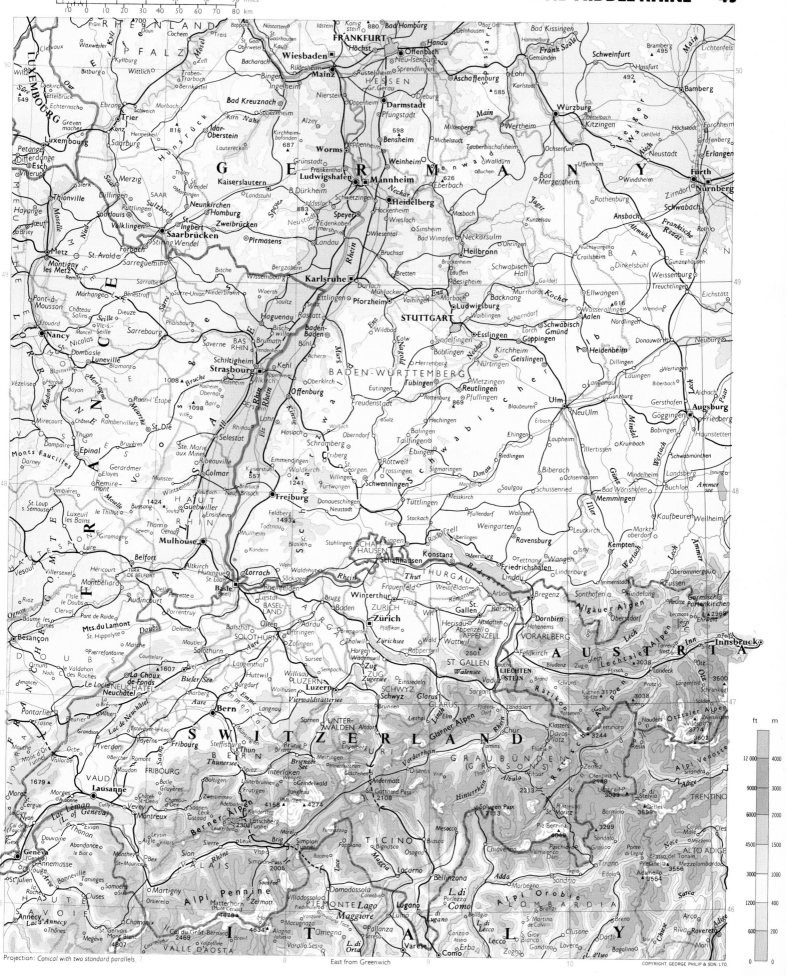

1:2 000 000

Projection: Conical with two standard parallels

East from Greenwich

COPYRIGHT. GEORGE PHILIP & SON. LTD.

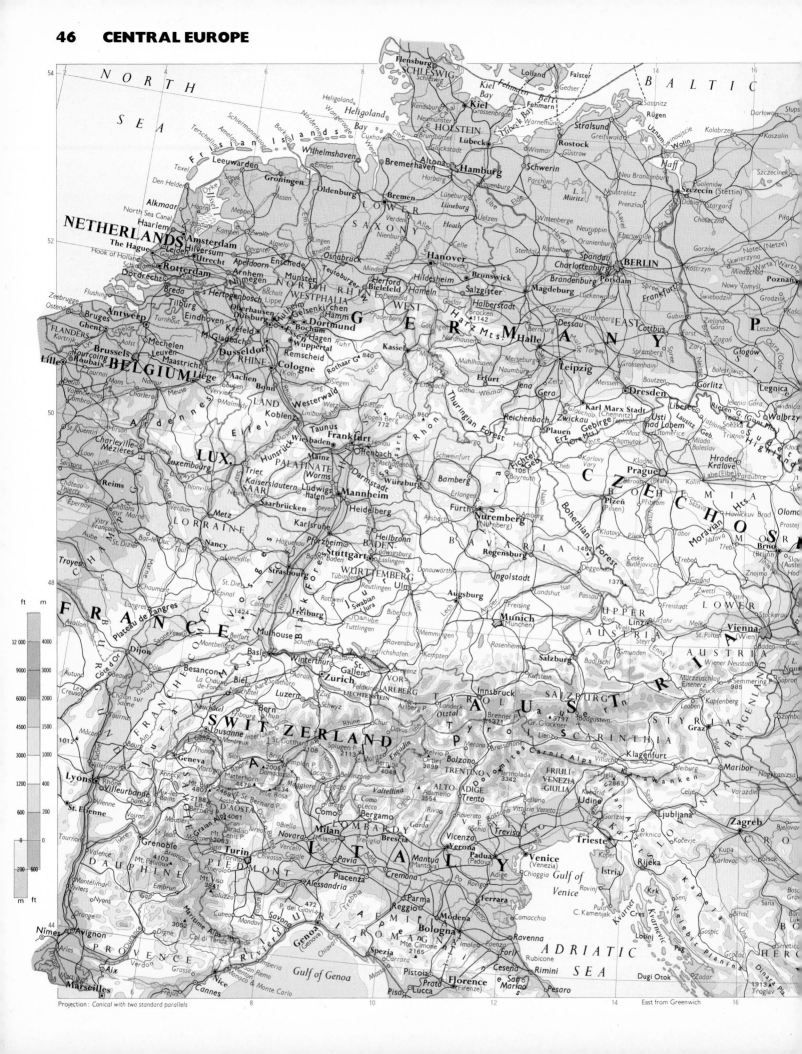

NORTH SEA

BALTIC

NETHERLANDS

BELGIUM

FLANDERS

LUX.

FRANCE

CHAMPAGNE

LORRAINE

GERMANY

WEST GERMANY

EAST GERMANY

LOWER SAXONY

NORTH RHINE WESTPHALIA

RHINE LAND

PALATINATE

SAAR

BADEN

WÜRTTEMBERG

BAVARIA

CZECHOSLOVAKIA

BOHEMIA

MORAVIA

LOWER

UPPER AUSTRIA

AUSTRIA

SWITZERLAND

LIECHTENSTEIN

TYROL

SALZBURG

STYRIA

CARINTHIA

BURGENLAND

ITALY

PIEDMONT

LOMBARDY

TRENTINO

ALTO-ADIGE

VENETO

FRIULI-VENEZIA-GIULIA

DAUPHINÉ

PROVENCE

ADRIATIC SEA

GULF OF VENICE

GULF OF GENOA

Berlin
Hamburg
Munich
Vienna
Prague
Amsterdam
Brussels
Zürich
Milan

Projection: Conical with two standard parallels

East from Greenwich

1:5 000 000

50 · 0 · 50 · 100 miles
50 · 0 · 50 · 100 · 150 km

CENTRAL EUROPE POLITICAL
1:25 000 000

Inset map (Central Europe Political): DENMARK · Copenhagen · Amsterdam · Hamburg · Berlin · EAST GERMANY · POLAND · Warsaw · U.S.S.R. · Kiev · Brussels · BELGIUM · WEST GERMANY · Bonn · Prague · CZECHOSLOVAKIA · Lvov · LUX. · FRANCE · Bern · SWITZ. · Liechtenstein · Vienna · AUSTRIA · Budapest · HUNGARY · RUMANIA · Bucharest · Trieste · ITALY · Belgrade · YUGOSLAVIA · Bucharest · BULGARIA · Sofia · Monaco · San Marino · Rome

Main map:

Gdansk Bay · Wejherowo · Sopot · Gdynia · Gdansk · Elblag · Zelenogradsk · Kaliningrad · Pregel · Chernyakhovsk · Gusev · LITHUANIA S.S.R. · Vilnius · Alitus · Varena · Suwalki · Augustów · Grodno · WHITE RUSSIA S.S.R. · Novogrudok · Lida · Volkovysk · Slonim · Shchara · Bereza

Starogard · Malbork · Kwidzyn · Olsztyn · Ketrzyn · Gizycko · 309 · Masurian Lakes Plateau · Mosty · Neman · Sokółka · 238 · Ostrów Mazowiecka · Bialystok · Hajnówka · Czeremcha · Zhabinka · Brest

Chelmza · Grudziadz · Chelmno · Wabrzezno · Rypin · Mlawa · Ciechanów · Pultusk · Bug · Ostrów · Bransk

Notec · Torun · Lipno · Plock · Wloclawek · Wisla (Vistula) · Lowicz · Warsaw (Warszawa) · Minsk Mazowiecki · Siedlce · Biala Podlaska · Brest

Gniezno · Kolo · Kutno · Leczyca · Pruszków · Zyrardów · Skierniewice · Gójec · Otwock · Łuków · Międzyrzec · Włodawa

Konin · Turek · Kalisz · Zdunska Wola · Lodz · Pilica · Radom · Kozienice · Pulawy · Chelm · Kovel · Pripyat · Sarny · 316 · Dubrovitsa · Pripyat Marshes · Uzh · Korosten · Desna

Ostrów · Wielun · Tomaszów Mazowiecki · Piotrków · Konskie · Kielce · Ostrowiec · Sandomierz · Lublin · Krasnik · Zamosc · Vladimir Volynski · Lutsk · Rovno · Styr · Sluch · Novograd Volynsk · Radomyshl

Opole · Tarnowskie Góry · Czestochowa · Radomsko · Jedrzejów · Pinczów · Tarnobrzeg · 390 · San · Przeworsk · Sokal · Brody · Dubno · Ostrog · Kremenets · Shepetovka · Zhitomir · Kiev · Borispol

Zabrze · Bytom · Gliwice · Sosnowiec · Chorzów · Katowice · Kraków · Wisla (Vistula) · Tarnów · Dabrowa Tarnowska · Rzeszów · Jaroslaw · Gorodok · Lvov · 471 · Zolochev · Ternopol · Khmelnitskiy · 384 · Vinnitsa · UKRAINE S.S.R. · Starokonstantinov · Berdichev · Kazatin · Belaya Tserkov

Raciborz · Ostrava · Cieszyn · Bielsko · Nowy Sacz · Jaslo · Krosno · Sanok · Przemysl · Sambor · Drogobych · Barislav · Stry · Dnestr · Buchach · Chortkov · Zaleshchiki · Kamenets Podolski · Mogilev-Podolski · Bug · Uman · Pervomaisk

Frýdek · Mistek · 550 · West Beskids · Jablunka P. · High Tatra 2655 · East Beskids · 1725 · Carpathian · Dukla P. 602 · Turka · Ivano-Frankovsk · Kolomyia · Snyatyn · Khotin · Yedintsy · Soroki · Kotovsk

Gottwaldov · Žilina · Ružomberok · Presov · SLOVAKIA · Low Tatra · Košice · 4380 · Uzhgorod · Ruthenia · Nadvornaya · 1881 · Pl. of the Tartars 931 · Chernovtsy · Stozhinets · MOLDAVIA S.S.R. · Beltsy · Dnestr · 429 · Kishinev · Bendery · Tiraspol

Kremnica · Banska Bystrica · Zvolen · Ore Mts. · Slovakian · Banska Stiavnica · Lucenec · Satoraljaujhely · Mukachevo · 2061 · Khust · Beregovo · Sighet · Baia Mare · Pietrosul 2305 · Radauti · Dorohoi · Botosani · Suceava · Vatra-Dornei

Nitra · N. Zámky · Hron · Komárno · Miskolc · Sajó · Hernad · Tokaj · Nyiregyhaza · Carei · Satu Mare · Bistrita · Pietrosul 2102 · Iasi · Odessa

Gyor · Tatabánya · Esztergom · Vác · Gyöngyös · Eger · Mezőkövesd · Hatvan · Jászberény · Hajdúböszörmény · Debrecen · Oradea · Cluj · Turda · Bistrita · Piatra Neamt · Roman · Vaslui · Bârlad · Belgorod Dnestrovsk

BUDAPEST · Ujpest · Bakony Forest · Székesfehérvár · Cegléd · Szolnok · Mezőtúr · Nagyvárad · Salonta · Black Crisu · Mures · Targu Mures · Praid · Odorhei · Ciuc · Bacau · Tecuci · Focsani

Dunaújváros · Kecskemét · Kiskunfélegyháza · Kiskőrös · Csongrád · Szentes · Békéscsaba · Gyula · Aiud · Mt. Bihor 1848 · Abrud · Transylvania · Sighisoara · Sf. Gheorghe · Bretcu

Dunaföldvár · HUNGARY · Kalocsa · Kiskunhalas · Hódmezővásárhely · Makó · Arad · White Crisu · Brad · Alba-Iulia · Deva · Medias · Mures · Siret · Ramnicu Sarat · Galati · Izmail

Szekszárd · Szeged · Subotica · RUMANIA · Timisoara · Lugoj · Hunedoara · Simeria · Sibiu · Fagaras · Mt. Negoiu 2535 · Omu 2507 · Transylvanian Alps · Braila · 467 · Tulcea · Sulina Mouth

Pécs · Mohács · Novi Sad · Banat · Becej · Zrenjanin · Caransebes · Resita · Transylvania · Peleaga 2509 · 2518 · Paringul Mare · Red Tower P. 350 · Petrosani · Cimpulung · Prahova · Campina · Buzau · Danube · St. George's Mouth · Portitei Mouth

Osijek · Vinkovci · Sombor · Sremska Mitrovica · Vršac · Bela Crkva · Porta Orientalis · Tirgu-Jiu · Rimnicu Valcea · Tirgoviste · Ploesti · Dobrogea · Cernavoda · Constanta

Brod · Odzak · Bosna · Brčko · Bijeljina · Tuzla · Zemun · Pancevo · Smederevo · Mehadia · Orsova · Iron Gate · Turnu-Severin · Jiu · Wallachia · Pitesti · Arges · Bucharest (Bucuresti) · Dambovita · Ialomita · Calarasi · Silistra · BLACK SEA

GOSLAVIA · Valjevo · 1346 · Sarajevo · Titovo Uzice · Cacak · Kragujevac · Zajecar · Morava · Timok · Vidin · Danube · Corabia · Turnu Magurele · Giurgiu · Ruse (Ruschuk) · Zimnicea · Oltenita · BULGARIA · Mangalia · Talbukhin

Han Pijesak · Craiova · Slatina · Olt · Caracal · Vedea · Negotin · Bor

18 · 20 · 22 · 24 · 26 · 28

COPYRIGHT. GEORGE PHILIP & SON. LTD.

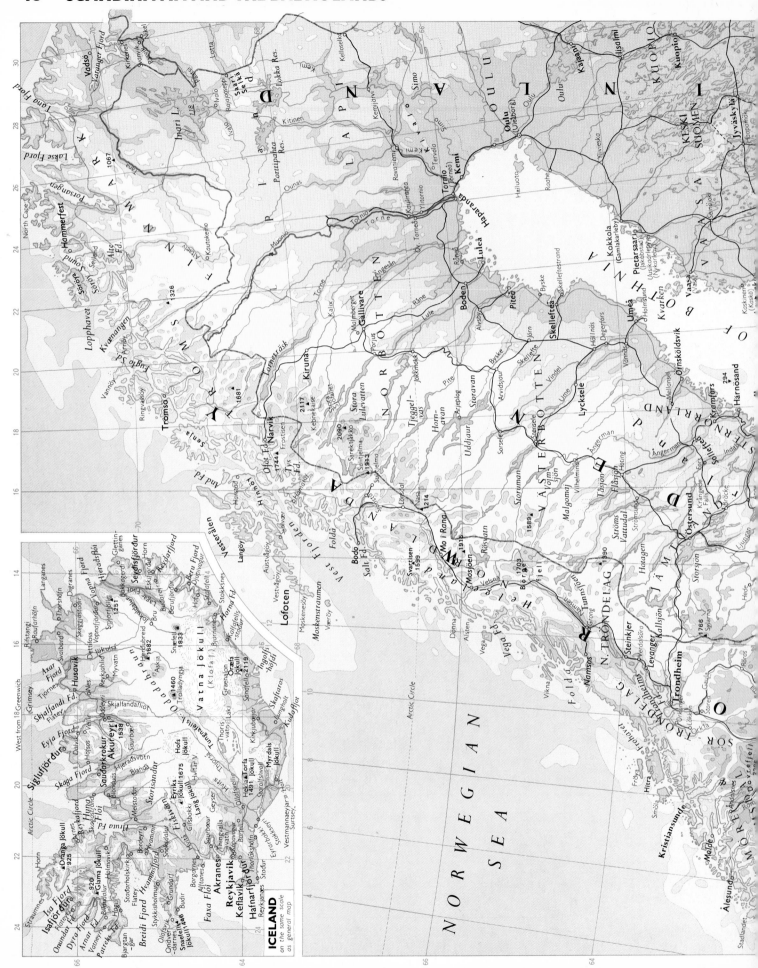

NORWEGIAN SEA

ICELAND
on the same scale
as general map

1:5 000 000

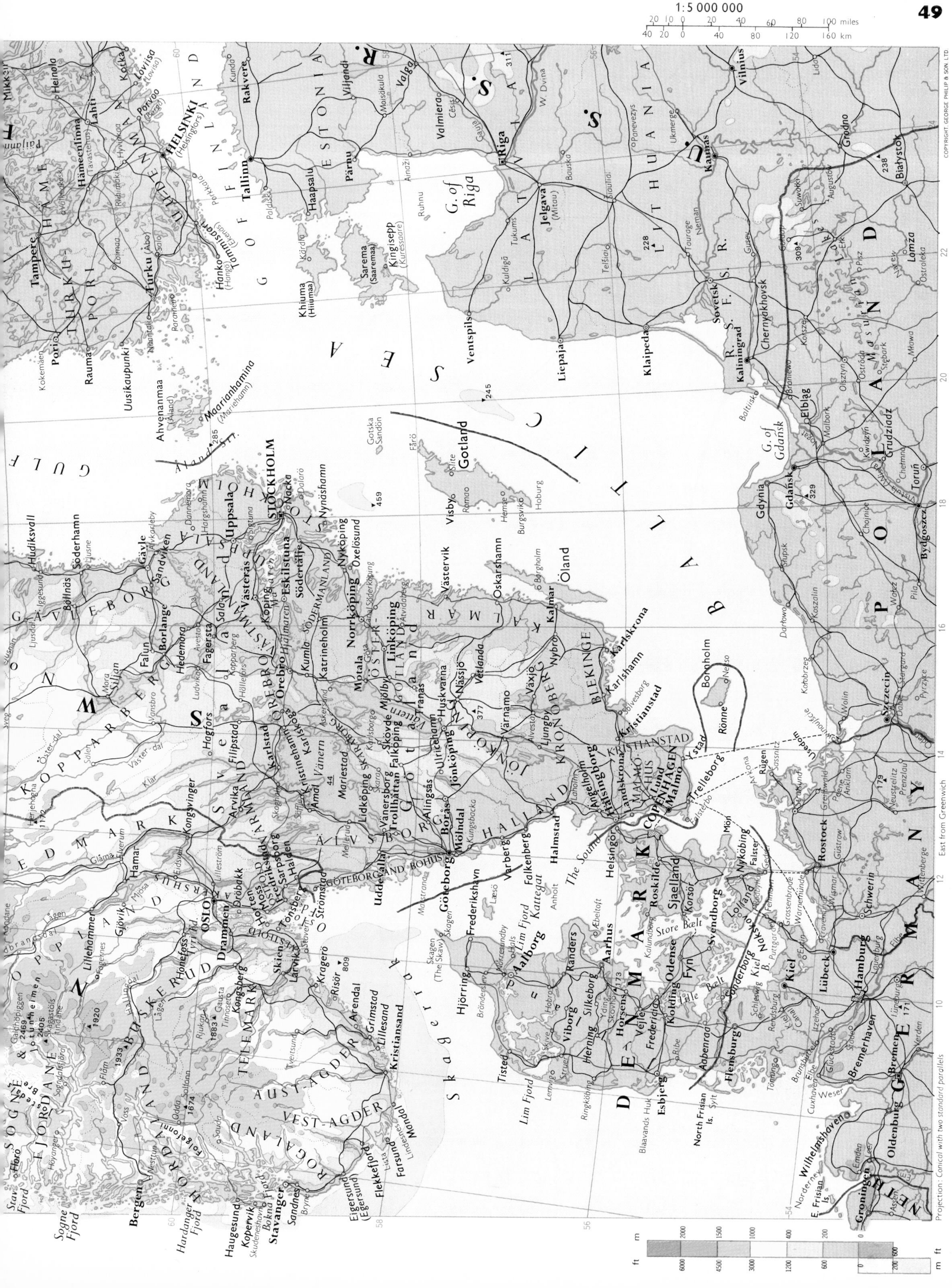

20 10 0 20 40 60 80 100 miles
40 20 0 40 80 120 160 km

COPYRIGHT. GEORGE PHILIP & SON, LTD.

East from Greenwich

Projection: Conical with two standard parallels

BALTIC SEA

GULF OF FINLAND

G. of Riga

Skagerrak

Kattegat

The Sound

The Skaw

FINLAND · ESTONIA · LATVIA · LITHUANIA · R.S.F.S.R. · POLAND · GERMANY · DENMARK · NORWAY · SWEDEN

Helsinki (Helsingfors) · Tampere · Pori · Turku (Åbo) · Rauma · Hanko (Hangö) · Hämeenlinna · Heinola · Kotka · Lovisa · Porvoo (Borgå)

Tallinn · Pärnu · Haapsalu · Valga · Valmiera · Riga · Jelgava (Mitau) · Ventspils · Liepaja

Vilnius · Kaunas · Klaipeda · Grodno · Białystok · Łomża · Ostrołęka

Kaliningrad · Chernyakhovsk · Sovetsk · Elbląg · Gdańsk · Gdynia · Toruń · Bydgoszcz · Grudziądz · Szczecin

Stockholm · Uppsala · Gävle · Västerås · Eskilstuna · Södertälje · Nacka · Norrköping · Nyköping · Oxelösund · Örebro · Linköping · Motala · Jönköping · Borås · Göteborg · Trollhättan · Vänersborg · Karlstad · Falun · Borlänge · Karlskrona · Karlshamn · Kalmar · Västervik · Oskarshamn · Visby · Gotland · Öland · Halmstad · Varberg · Helsingborg · Malmö · Lund · Landskrona · Kristianstad · Ystad · Trelleborg

Oslo · Drammen · Hamar · Lillehammer · Kongsvinger · Skien · Larvik · Kristiansand · Arendal · Stavanger · Bergen · Haugesund

Copenhagen · Aalborg · Aarhus · Odense · Esbjerg · Randers · Viborg · Horsens · Kolding · Vejle · Roskilde · Helsingør

Hamburg · Lübeck · Kiel · Rostock · Bremen · Bremerhaven · Flensburg · Schwerin · Wilhelmshaven · Oldenburg

Bornholm · Rügen · Rönne

Groningen

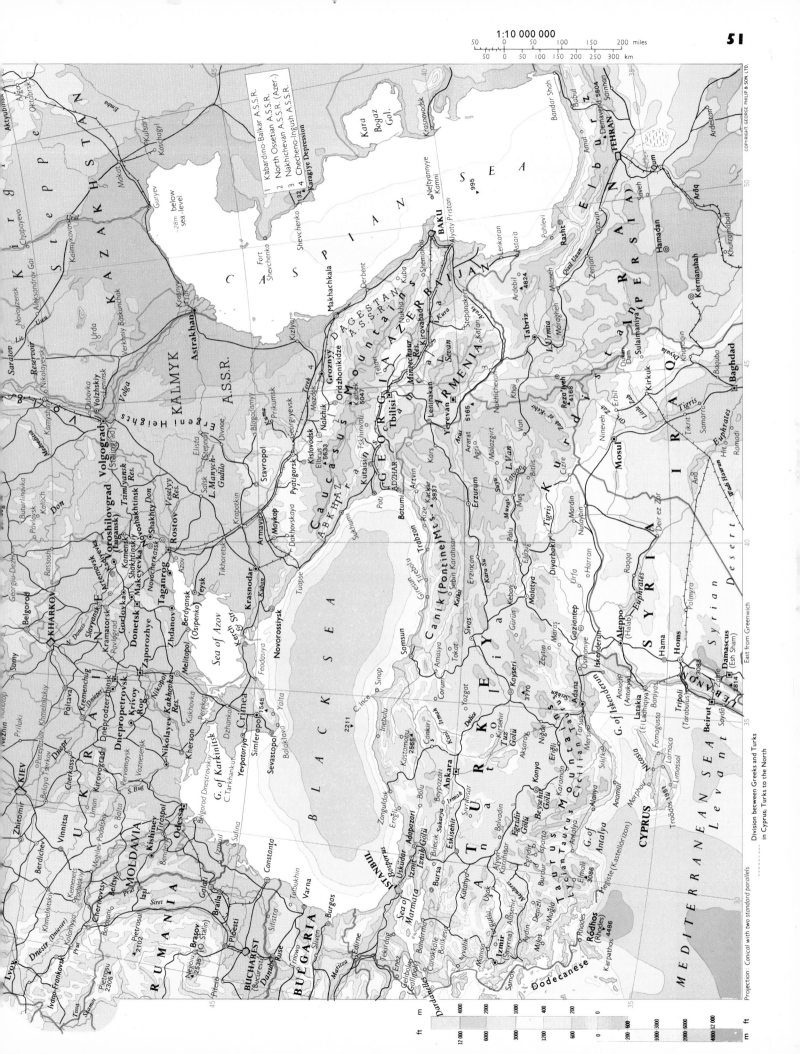

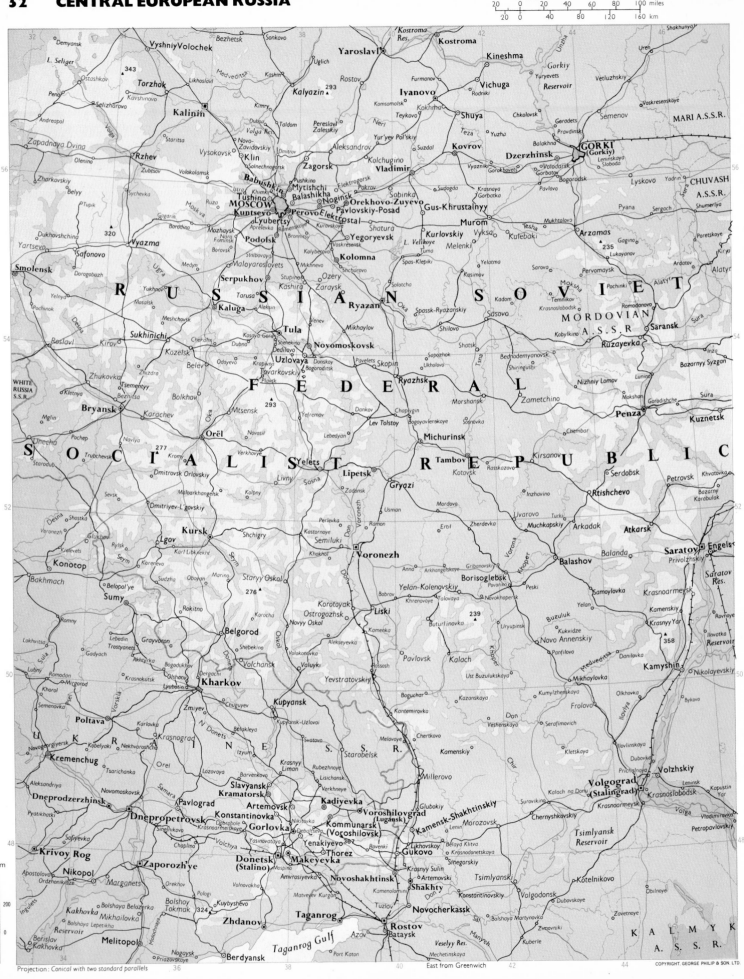

1:5 000 000

East from Greenwich

COPYRIGHT. GEORGE PHILIP & SON. LTD.

1:50 000 000

250   0   250   500   750   1000 miles
200   0   200 400 600 800 1000 1200 1400 1600 km

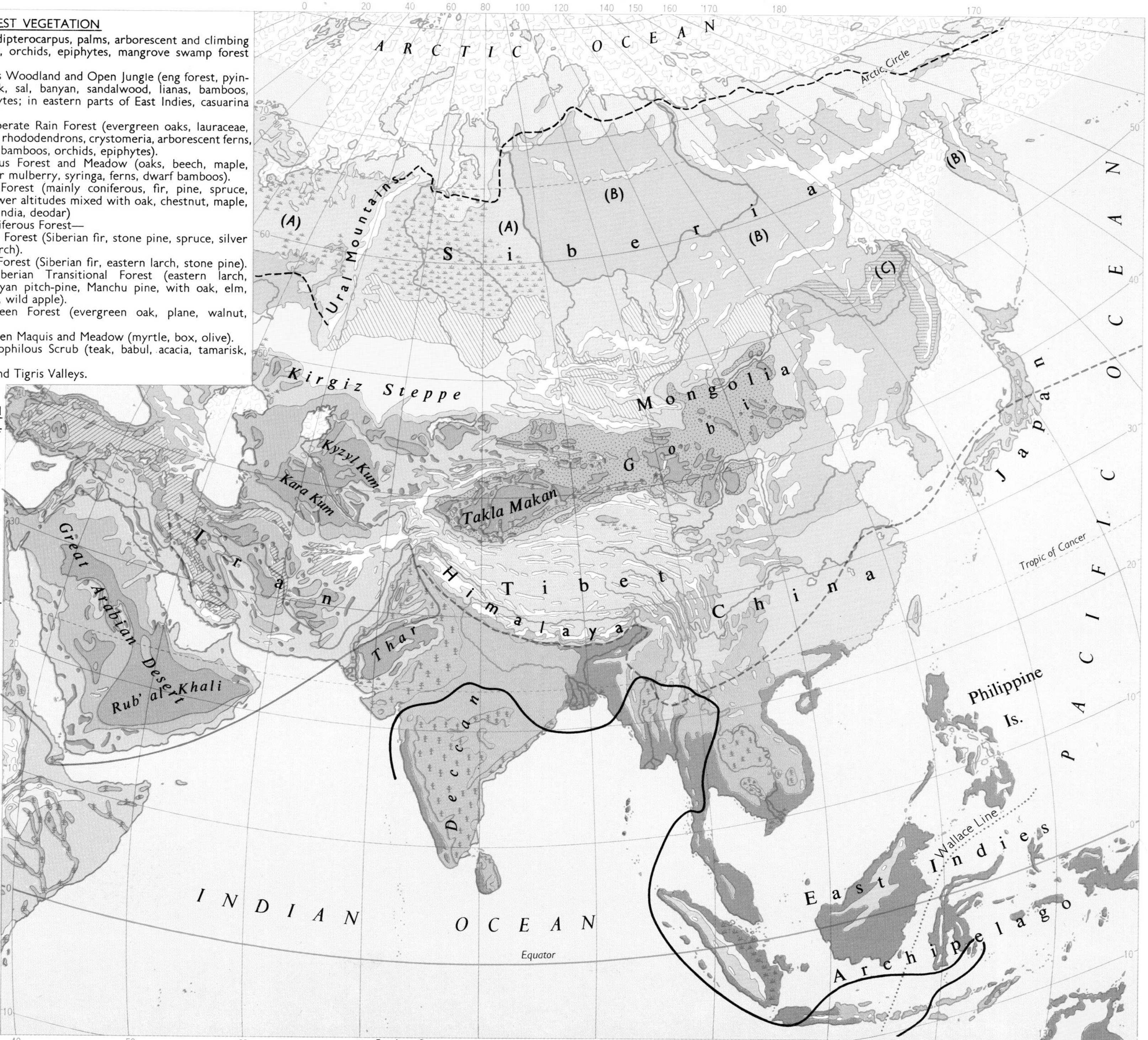

ARCTIC OCEAN

PACIFIC OCEAN

INDIAN OCEAN

Arctic Circle

Tropic of Cancer

Equator

East from Greenwich

Wallace Line

Japan

Siberia

Mongolia

Gobi

Tibet

Himalaya

China

Deccan

Iran

Philippine Is.

East Indies

Archipelago

Ural Mountains

Kirgiz Steppe

Takla Makan

Kyzyl Kum

Kara Kum

Thar

Great Arabian Desert

Rub' al Khali

N   C   E   A   N

Projection: Bonne

FOREST VEGETATION

Tropical Rain Forest (dipterocarpus, palms, arborescent and climbing ferns, lianas, bamboos, orchids, epiphytes, mangrove swamp forest on coast).

Monsoon Tropophilous Woodland and Open Jungle (eng forest, pyinkado (ironwood), teak, sal, banyan, sandalwood, lianas, bamboos, orchids, jungle, epiphytes; in eastern parts of East Indies, casuarina and eucalyptus).

Sub-tropical and Temperate Rain Forest (evergreen oaks, lauraceae, camellia, tea, magnolia, rhododendrons, crystomeria, arborescent ferns, palms, wistaria, lianas, bamboos, orchids, epiphytes).

Broad-leaved Deciduous Forest and Meadow (oaks, beech, maple, walnut, chestnut, paper mulberry, syringa, ferns, dwarf bamboos).

Temperate Mountain Forest (mainly coniferous, fir, pine, spruce, larch; sometimes at lower altitudes mixed with oak, chestnut, maple, birch; in North-West India, deodar).

Taiga or Northern Coniferous Forest—
(A) West Siberian Forest (Siberian fir, stone pine, spruce, silver fir, Siberian larch).
(B) East Siberian Forest (Siberian fir, eastern larch, stone pine).
(C) South-East Siberian Transitional Forest (eastern larch, Siberian fir, ayan pitch-pine, Manchu pine, with oak, elm, maple, walnut, wild apple).

Mediterranean Evergreen Forest (evergreen oak, plane, walnut, hornbeam).

Mediterranean Evergreen Maquis and Meadow (myrtle, box, olive).

Open Jungle and Xerophilous Scrub (teak, babul, acacia, tamarisk, tamarind, euphorbia).

Oases and Euphrates and Tigris Valleys.

GRASS VEGETATION

Transitional Zone of Wooded Steppe.

Temperate Grasslands and Steppe (stipa grass)

Savanna.

High Steppe (South-West Asia)

Steppe

Marsh Vegetation

DRY STEPPE & DESERT

Salt Steppe and Semi-desert (artemisia, saxaul, acacia, tamarisk).

Gobi and Central Asiatic Deserts (artemisia).

High Plateau Steppe and Desert (palaeoarctic vegetation).

Desert

Tundra (moss, lichen, heather bog, dwarf willow, birch and alder).

Alpine (ice desert).

Northern Limits of Siberian Larch (larix sibirica).

Limits of Date Palm (phœnix dactylifera).

Limits of Teak (tectona grandis).

Northern Limits of Palms.

Seas and Lakes frozen in Winter.

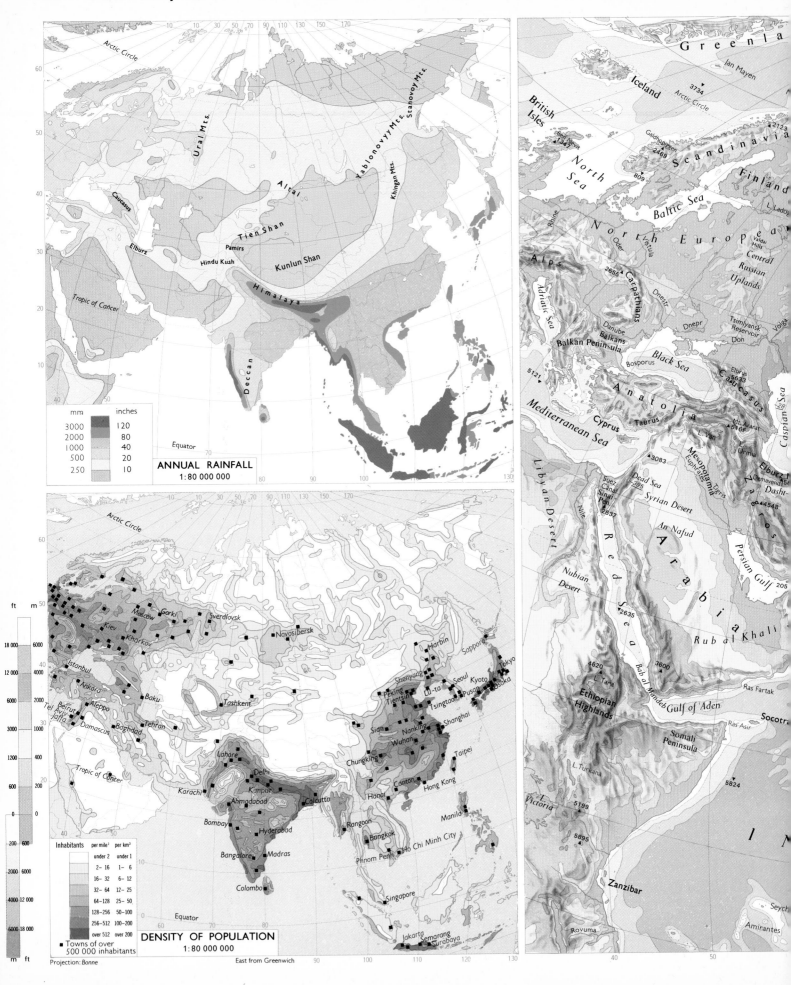

ANNUAL RAINFALL
1:80 000 000

mm	inches
3000	120
2000	80
1000	40
500	20
250	10

Arctic Circle

60

50

40

Ural Mts.

Caucasus

Elburz

Tien Shan

Pamirs

Hindu Kush

Altai

Yablonovyy Mts. Stanovoy Mts.

Khingan Mts.

Kunlun Shan

30

Himalaya

Tropic of Cancer

20

10

Deccan

Equator

70

80

90

100

110

120

130

DENSITY OF POPULATION
1:80 000 000

Inhabitants	per mile²	per km²
	under 2	under 1
	2– 16	1– 6
	16– 32	6– 12
	32– 64	12– 25
	64–128	25– 50
	128–256	50–100
	256–512	100–200
	over 512	over 200

■ Towns of over
500 000 inhabitants

Arctic Circle

Moscow Gorki Sverdlovsk

Kiev Kharkov

Novosibersk

Istanbul

Ankara Baku

Tashkent

Harbin

Sapporo

Tel Aviv Beirut Aleppo
Jaffa Damascus Baghdad Tehran

Shenyang Seoul Kyoto Tokyo
Peking Lü-ta Pusan Osaka
Tientsin Tsingtao

Sian Nanking Shanghai
Wuhan

Lahore

Delhi

Kanpur

Karachi

Ahmadabad Calcutta

Chungking Taipei

Canton Hong Kong

Bombay Hyderabad

Hanoi

Tropic of Cancer

Bangalore Madras

Rangoon

Bangkok

Manila

Phnom Penh Ho Chi Minh City

Colombo

Singapore

Equator

Jakarta Semarang
Surabaya

Projection: *Bonne*

East from Greenwich

Greenla

Iceland Jan Mayen

3734

Arctic Circle

British
Isles

Ben Nevis
1343 1342

Galdhøpiggen
2469

2123

Scandinavia

Finland

809

L. Ladoga

North
Sea

Baltic Sea

North Europe

Valdai
Hills

Central
Russian
Uplands

Alps

Rhine

Oder

Vistula

Carpathians
2655

Dnestr

Dnepr

Tsimlyansk
Reservoir

Volga

Adriatic
Sea

Danube

Balkans

Balkan Peninsula

Black Sea

Bosporus

Don

5121

Anatolia

Caucasus

Elbrus
5633

-28

Caspian Sea

Mediterranean Sea

Cyprus

Taurus

L. Van

Urmia

Mt. Ararat
516F

Elburz
Damavend
5604

Dasht-

4548

Zagros

3083

Mesopotamia

Euphrates

Tigris

Libyan Desert

Suez
Canal
Sinai
Pen.
2637

Dead Sea
-395

Syrian Desert

An Nafud

Persian Gulf

205

Nile

Arabia

Rub al Khali

Nubian
Desert

2635

Red
Sea

Ras Fartak

1620

L. Tana

3600

Ethiopian
Highlands

Bab el Mandeb Gulf of Aden

Ras Asir

Socotra

Somali
Peninsula

5824

L. Turkana

5199

L.
Victoria

5895

Zanzibar

Rovuma

I

Seych

Amirantes

40

50

1 : 40 000 000

200   0   200 400 600 800 1000 miles
200   0   200 400 600 800 1000 1200 1600 km

ARCTIC OCEAN

Svalbard
Bear I.
Fr. Josef Land
Severnaya Zemlya
New Siberian Is.
Wrangel I.
C. Dezhneva (East C.)
Bering Str.

Novaya Zemlya
Kara Sea
C. Chelyuskin
Taimyr Peninsula
Byrrang Mts.
Laptev Sea
Foddeyev
New Siberia
Lyakhov Is.
Bear I.
Kotelny
Indigirka
Kolyma Plain
Chukot Ra.
Koryk Ra. 2562
G. of Anadyr
Bering Sea

Kola Pen.
White Sea
Barents Sea
Kolguyev
Gydan Pen.
Yamal Pen.
G. of Ob
Putoran Mts.
Olenek
Verkhoyansk Ra.
Cherskiy Ra. 3147
Kolyma
Gydan Ra.
Shelokhor Bay
Sredinny Ra. 750
Kamchatka Peninsula
Kliuchevsk Vol.
Komandorskiye Is.

N. Dvina
Narodnaya 1894
West
Siberian
Central
Lower Tunguska
Lena
Stanovoy Ra. 2482
Dzhugdzhur Ra.
Shantar Is.
Sea of Okhotsk
C. Lopatka
7999
Kuril Islands

Ural Mountains
Yenisey
Siberian Plateau
Stony Tunguska
Stanovoy Ra. 2999
Aldan
Amur
Sakhalin
10,542

Kama
Ural
Irtysh
Angara
Plateau
Yablonovyy Ra.
Hsiao Khingan Shan
Tatary Str.
Sikhote Alin Ra.
La Pérouse Str.
2290
Hokkaido
Tsugaru Str.

Yaman Tau 1640
Kirgiz Steppe
Western Sayan
Eastern Sayan
L. Baikal 456
Ta Khingan Shan
Manchurian Plain
Khanka
Sungari Reservoir 2744
Sea of Japan
Honshu

Muyun Kum
L. Balkhash
Belukha 4506
Selenga
Plateau of Mongolia
Hsi-liao
Korea
Fuji Yama 3776

Aral Sea
Syr Darya
Kyzyl Kum
342
Chu
Altai 3957
Gobi
Ala Shan
Ordos Plateau 2894
G. of Chihli
Shantung Pen.
Yellow Sea
Koria Str.
Shikoku
10,554

Turanian Plain
Kara Kum
L. Issyk-Kul
Tien Shan 7439
Turfan Basin -154
Lop Nor
3015
Ordos Plateau
Hwang-Ho
Great Plain of China
Kyushu

Amu Darya
Communism Pk. 7495
Pamirs
Takla Makan
Tarim Basin
Altyn Tagh
Nan Shan 6346
Koko Nor
Chinling Shan 4107
Yangtze-kiang
Poyang
East China Sea
Ryukyu Islands 7507

Hindu Kush 7788
8611
Kunlun Shan 7723
Tsaidam
Bayan Kara Shan
China
7559

Karakoram Ra. 8126
Plateau of Tibet
Red Basin
Yangtze-kiang
Tung Ting L.
Nan Shan
Wu Shan
Formosa 3997
Tropic of Cancer

5143
Himal
Nam Tso
Tsangpo
7756
Minya Konka 7590
Ta Liang Shan
2710
Si-kiang
Bushi Chan.
Formosa Str.

Helmand
Sulaiman Ra.
Chenab
Sutlej
8221
Mt. Everest 8848
Kanchenjunga 8598
Brahmaputra
Naga Hills
3143
G. of Tonkin
Hainan
Babuyan Is.
8054

Thar
Aravalli Ra.
Indo-Gangetic Plain
Khasi Hills
Mt. Victoria 3053
Salween
Si-kiang
South China Sea
2828
Luzon
Philippine Islands

Saihan Ra.
Indus
Chambal
Yamuna
Ganga
India
Vindhya Mts.
Narmada
Arakan Yoma
Irrawaddy
Mekong
5245
Samar
Cape Johnson Deep 10,497

Ras al Hadd
Vindhya Mts.
Satpura Ra.
Godavari
Deccan
Ganges Delta
Bay of Bengal
3280
Mindoro
Panay
Leyte
Mindanao

Arabian Sea
Krishna
Western Ghats
Eastern Ghats
Salween
Blue Tseng R.
Phanom Dong Rak
Tonle Sap
Andaman Sea
Palawan
Negros 5576
Mt. Apo 2954
5842

Laccadive Is.
Malabar Coast
Coromandel Coast
G. of Martaban
Andaman Is.
G. of Siam
Ca Mau Pt.
Sulu Sea
Kinabalu 4101
Celebes Sea
Morotai
Halmahera

Anai Mudi 2698
Palk Str.
Ceylon
Pidurutalagala 2524
Isthmus of Kra
Malay Peninsula
Natuna Is.
Celebes
Buru 2655
Ceram 7440

5875
C. Comorin
G. of Mannar
Dondra Head
Nicobar Is.
Sumatra
Borneo
Makassar Str.
New Guinea

Maldive Is.
INDIAN OCEAN
Str. of Malacca
3466
Sunda Islands
East Indies
3455
Banda Sea

Chagos Arch.
Equator
Sumatra 3800
Java Sea
Timor
Sumba
Arafura Sea

Java 6073
Semeru 3676
Bali
Lombok 3726
Sumbawa 5123
Flores
Australia

East from 80 Greenwich
COPYRIGHT. GEORGE PHILIP & SON. LTD.

PACIFIC OCEAN

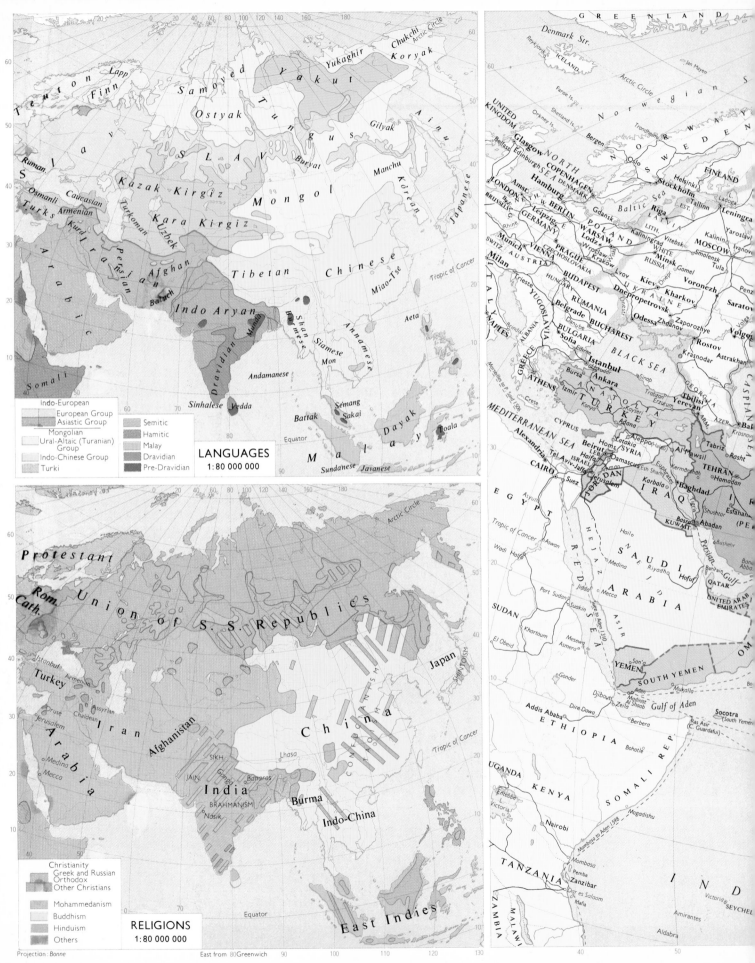

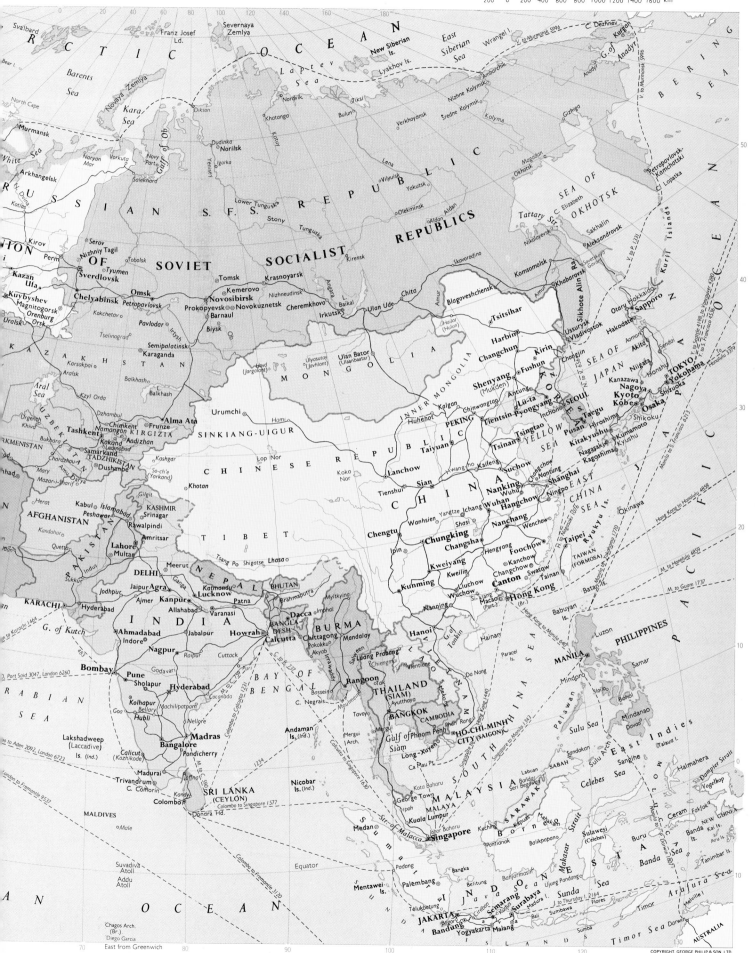

1:40 000 000

200   0   200   400   600   800   1000 miles
200   0   200   400   600   800 1000 1200 1400 1600 km

A R C T I C   O C E A N

Svalbard
Bear I.
North Cape
Murmansk
White Sea
Arkhangelsk
Barents Sea
Novaya Zemlya
Franz Josef Ld.
Severnaya Zemlya
Laptev Sea
New Siberian Is.
Lyakhov Is.
East Siberian Sea
Wrangel I.
C. Dezhnev
G. of Anadyr
Kara Sea
Dikson
North Dvina
Kirov
Perm
Serov
Nizhniy Tagil
Sverdlovsk
Tyumen
Tobolsk
Kazan
Ufa
Kuybyshev
Magnitogorsk
Orenburg
Chelyabinsk
Omsk
Petropavlovsk
Kemerovo
Novosibirsk
Prokopyevsk
Novokuznetsk
Barnaul
Biysk
Tomsk
Krasnoyarsk
Nizhneudinsk
Cheremkhovo
Irkutsk
Ulan Ude
Chita
Blagoveshchensk
Amur
Khabarovsk
Komsomolsk
Nikolayevsk
Sakhalin
Aleksandrovsk
Sovetskaya Gavan
Sikhote Alin
Ussuriysk
Vladivostok
SEA OF OKHOTSK
Tartary Str.
C. Elizabeth
Magadan
Okhotsk
Petropavlovsk-Kamchatski
Kurgan
Kamchatka
C. Lopatka
Kuril Islands
B E R I N G   S E A
Norilsk
Igarka
Dudinka
Salekhard
Gulf of Ob
Yenisey
Lower Tunguska
Stony Tunguska
Angara
Katanga
Vilyuy
Lena
Olekminsk
Yakutsk
Aldan
Nizhne Kolymsk
Sredne Kolymsk
Kolyma
Verkhoyansk
Tiksi
Bulun
Khatanga

R U S S I A N   S. F. S. R.

S O V I E T   S O C I A L I S T
R E P U B L I C S

Naryan Mar
Vorkuta
Kotlas
Uralsk
Orsk
Aktyubinsk
Aralsk
Aral Sea
Kzyl Orda
Tselinograd
Pavlodar
Semipalatinsk
Karaganda
Balkhash
L. Balkhash
Karsakpai
Kokchetav
Irtysh
K A Z A K H S T A N
Dzhambul
Frunze
Alma Ata
Chimkent
Tashkent
Namangan
Andizhan
Kokand
KIRGIZIA
Urumchi
Hami
Ulan Bator (Ulaanbaatar)
Ulyasutay (Javhlant)
Uliassutai (Jargalant)
Hovd (Jargalant)
M O N G O L I A
Kalgan
Huhehot
Chinwangtao
Antung
Mukden
Changchun
Kirin
Harbin
Tsitsihar
Hailar (Hulun)
Chongjin
K N.
KOREA
SEA OF JAPAN
Otaru
Hakodate
Hokkaido
Sapporo
Akita
Aomori
Niigata
Kanazawa
Sendai
Honshu
TOKYO
Yokohama
Nagoya
Kyoto
Kobe
Osaka
Shizuoka
SEOUL
Inchon
Pyongyang
Antung
INNER MONGOLIA
PEKING
Tientsin
Tsinan
Taiyuan
Shenyang (Mukden)
Fushun
Lü-ta
Tsingtao
YELLOW SEA
Pusan
Taegu
Hiroshima
Kitakyushu
Nagasaki
Kagoshima
Kyushu
Shikoku
JAPAN
P A C I F I C
O C E A N
Aral Sea
TURKMENISTAN
Urgench
Khiva
Chardzhou
Bukhara
Samarkand
UZBEKISTAN
TADZHIKISTAN
Dushanbe
Amu Darya
Mary
Mazar-i-Sharif
Herat
Kandahar
Kabul
Quetta
AFGHANISTAN
Peshawar
Islamabad
Rawalpindi
KASHMIR
Srinagar
Gilgit
Kashgar
So-ch'e (Yarkand)
Khotan
C H I N E S E   R E P U B L I C
SINKIANG-UIGUR
Lop Nor
Koko Nor
Tienshui
Lanchow
Sian
Chengtu
Wanhsien
Shasi
Ichang
Yangtze
Chungking
Ipin
Kunming
Kweiyang
Kweilin
Liuchow
Wuchow
Nanning
Si Kiang
Canton
Swatow
Macao (Port.)
Hong Kong (Br.)
Hainan
G. of Tonkin
Hanoi
Da Nang
VIETNAM
LAOS
Vientiane
Luang Prabang
Chiengmai
THAILAND (SIAM)
Ayutthaya
BANGKOK
CAMBODIA
Phnom Penh
Gulf of Siam
Long Xuyen
HO-CHI-MINH CITY (SAIGON)
Ca Mau Pt.
Swatow
TAIWAN (FORMOSA)
Taipei
Ryukyu Is.
Okinawa
EAST CHINA SEA
Ningpo
Wenchow
Foochow
Kanchow
Changchow
Nanchang
Hengyang
Changsha
Wuhan
Hangchow
Shanghai
Nantung
Nanking
Wuhu
Suchow
Chengchow
Kaifeng
Kwang-ho
CHINA
Hyderabad
KASHMIR
Amritsar
Lahore
Multan
Jodhpur
Ajmer
Jaipur
Agra
DELHI
Meerut
PAKISTAN
Indus
Sukkur
KARACHI
G. of Kutch
Hyderabad
Ahmadabad
Indore
Nagpur
Raipur
Jabalpur
Kanpur
Lucknow
Allahabad
Varanasi
Patna
Ganga
NEPAL
Katmandu
BHUTAN
Brahmaputra
Shigatse
Lhasa
Tsang Po
T I B E T
I N D I A
BANGLA-DESH
Dacca
Calcutta
Howrah
Chittagong
Imphal
Myitkyina
Mandalay
Akyab
Pakokku
BURMA
Irrawaddy
Salween
Rangoon
Bassein
C. Negrais
Tavoy
Moulmein
Mergui Arch.
Bombay
Pune
Sholapur
Hyderabad
Kolhapur
Bellary
Hubli
Goa
Godavari
Machilipatnam
Nellore
Madras
Bangalore
Pondicherry
Calicut (Kozhikode)
Madurai
C. Comorin
Trivandrum
Jaffna
Kandy
Colombo
SRI LANKA (CEYLON)
Dondra Hd.
Lakshadweep (Laccadive) Is. (Ind.)
MALDIVES
Male
Suvadiva Atoll
Addu Atoll
Chagos Arch. (Br.)
Diego Garcia
B A Y   O F   B E N G A L
Andaman Is. (Ind.)
Nicobar Is. (Ind.)
A R A B I A N   S E A
BHARAT
I N D I A N   O C E A N
Mentawei Is.
Sumatra
Padang
Palembang
Bangka
Belitung
Medan
Str. of Malacca
Singapore
Johor Baharu
Kuala Lumpur
MALAYA
George Town
Ipoh
Kota Baharu
Penang
M A L A Y S I A
SARAWAK
SABAH
Kuching
Pontianak
Banjarmasin
Balikpapan
Bandjarmasin
Borneo
Kapuas
Labuan
Bandar Seri Begawan
Sandakan
Sulu Sea
Sulu Arch.
Zamboanga
Davao
Mindanao
PHILIPPINES
Manila
Luzon
Mindoro
Samar
Iloilo
Panay
Cebu
Bohol
Palawan
Babuyan
Batan Is.
SOUTH CHINA SEA
Paracel Is.
Celebes Sea
Sulawesi (Celebes)
Makasar
Makasar Strait
Ujung Pandang
I N D O N E S I A
E A S T   I N D I E S
JAKARTA
Bandung
Bogor
Cirebon
Semarang
Surabaya
Yogyakarta
Malang
Java
Bali
Madura I.
Lombok
Sumbawa
Flores
Sumba
Timor
Timor Sea
Ceram Sea
Ceram
Buru
Banda Sea
Banda Is.
Kai Is.
Aru Is.
Tanimbar Is.
NEW GUINEA
Vogelkop
Halmahera
Talaud
Sangihe
Morotai
Fakfak
Dampier Strait
Melville I.
Darwin
A U S T R A L I A
Arafura Sea
Equator

COPYRIGHT. GEORGE PHILIP & SON. LTD.
DHK

East from Greenwich

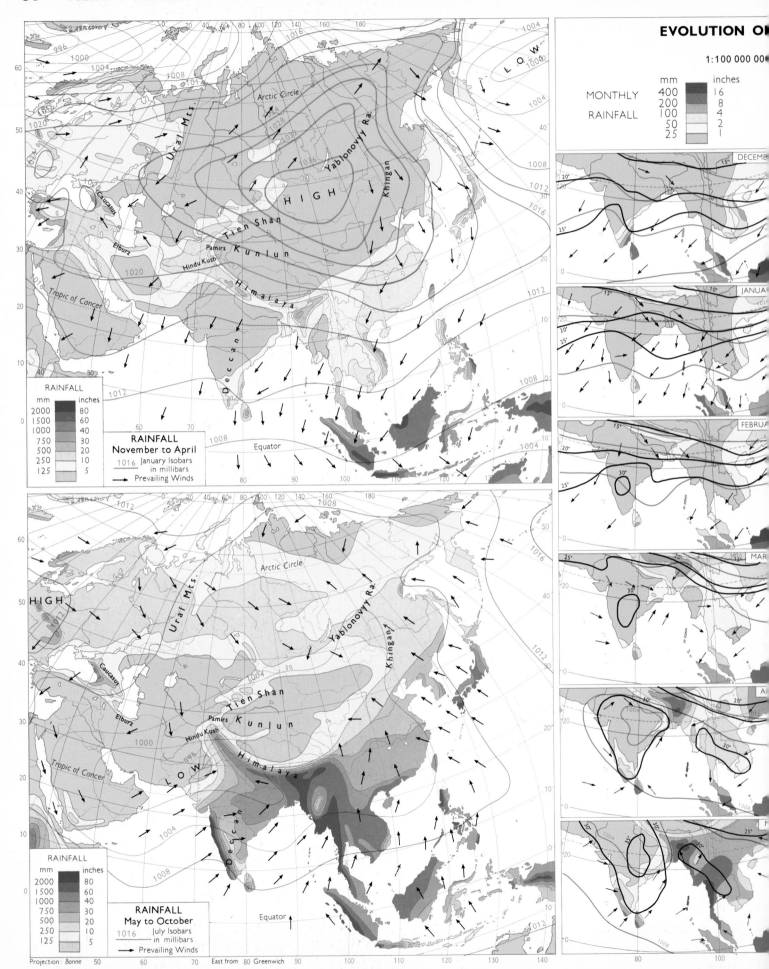

RAINFALL
mm   inches
2000   80
1500   60
1000   40
750   30
500   20
250   10
125   5

RAINFALL
November to April
1016 January Isobars
      in millibars
→   Prevailing Winds

RAINFALL
mm   inches
2000   80
1500   60
1000   40
750   30
500   20
250   10
125   5

RAINFALL
May to October
1016 July Isobars
      in millibars
→   Prevailing Winds

Projection: Bonne

EVOLUTION O

1:100 000 000

MONTHLY
RAINFALL
mm   inches
400   16
200   8
100   4
50   2
25   1

DECEMB

JANUA

FEBRUA

MAR

A

M

`1:80 000 000

400   0   400   800   1200   1600 miles
400   0   400 800 1600 2000 2400 km

THE MONSOON

0   500   1000   1500   2000 miles
500 0 500 1000 1500 2000 2500 3000 km

———— Isotherms
reduced to Sea-level °Celsius

1016 ———— Isobars in millibars

———→ Winds.

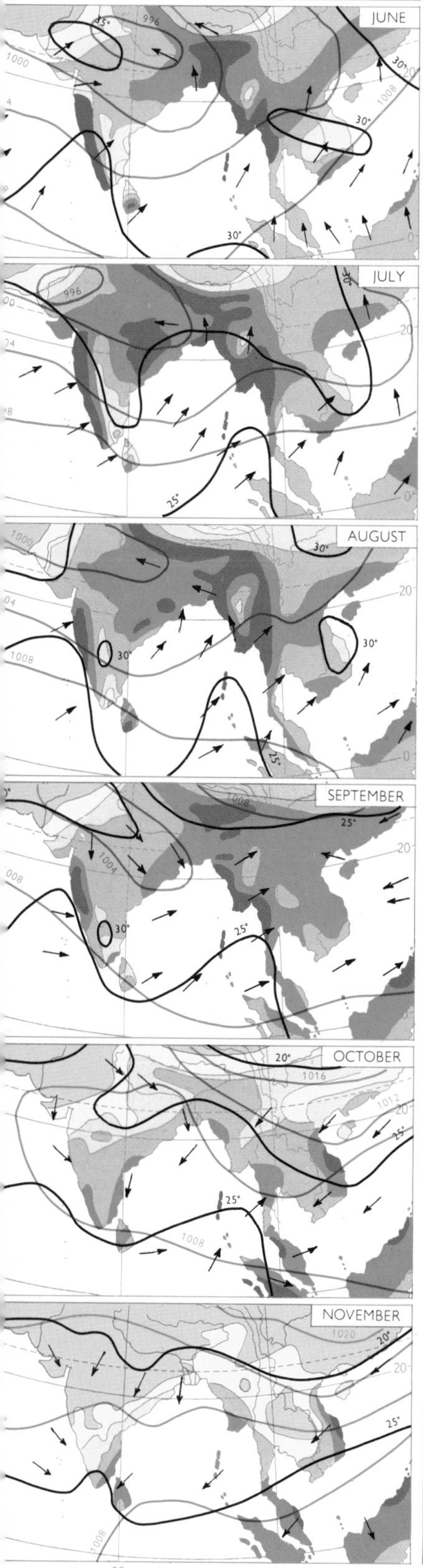

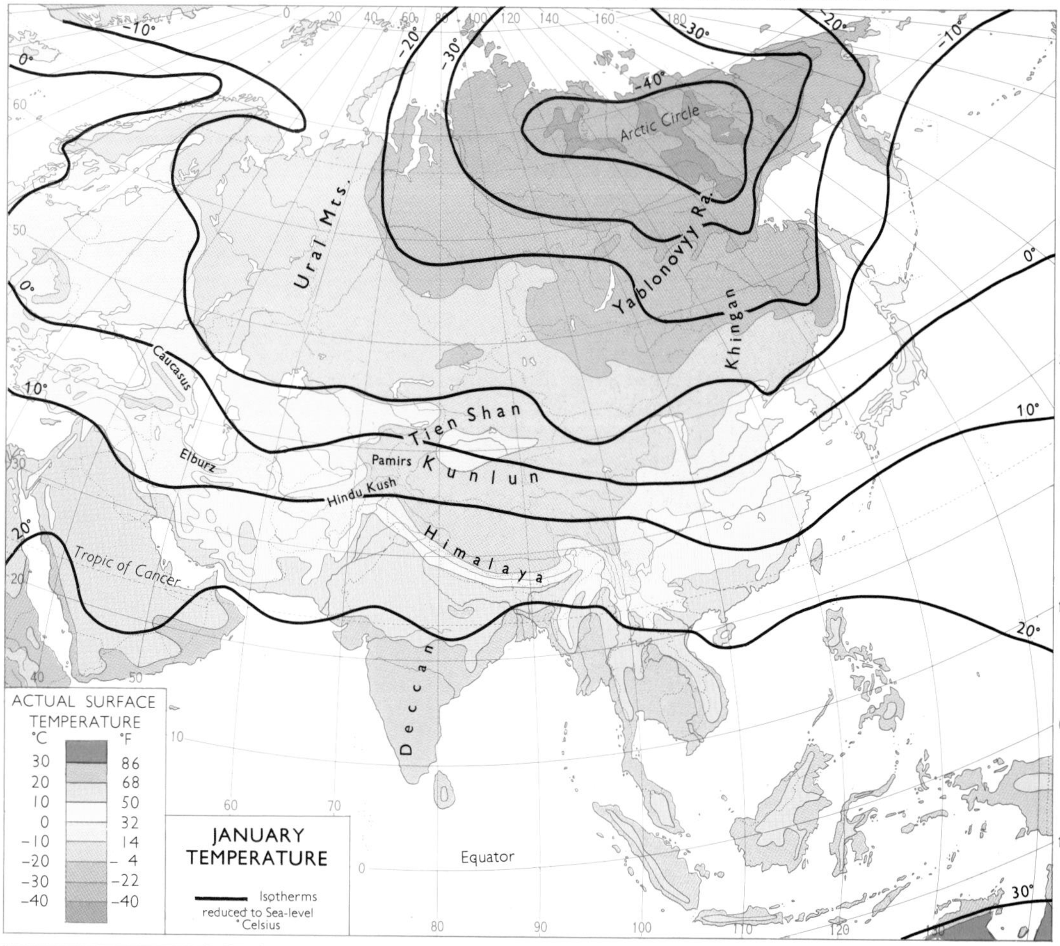

JUNE

JULY

AUGUST

SEPTEMBER

OCTOBER

NOVEMBER

Ural Mts.
Caucasus
Elburz
Tien Shan
Pamirs   Kunlun
Hindu Kush
Himalaya
Yablonovyy Ra.
Khingan
Deccan
Arctic Circle
Tropic of Cancer
Equator

ACTUAL SURFACE
TEMPERATURE
°C   °F
30   86
20   68
10   50
0   32
-10   14
-20   - 4
-30   -22
-40   -40

JANUARY
TEMPERATURE

———— Isotherms
reduced to Sea-level
°Celsius

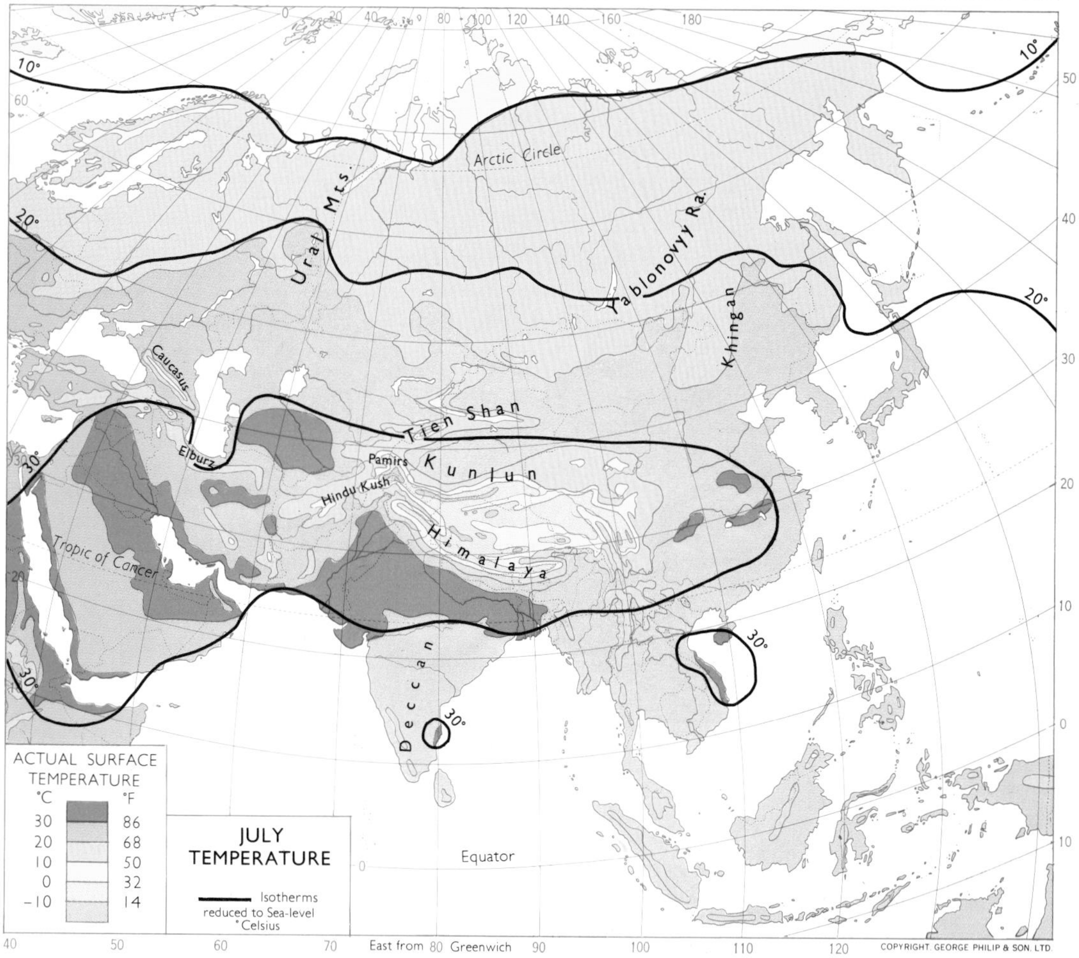

Ural Mts.
Caucasus
Elburz
Tien Shan
Pamirs   Kunlun
Hindu Kush
Himalaya
Yablonovyy Ra.
Khingan
Deccan
Arctic Circle
Tropic of Cancer
Equator

ACTUAL SURFACE
TEMPERATURE
°C   °F
30   86
20   68
10   50
0   32
-10   14

JULY
TEMPERATURE

———— Isotherms
reduced to Sea-level
°Celsius

East from Greenwich

COPYRIGHT GEORGE PHILIP & SON LTD.

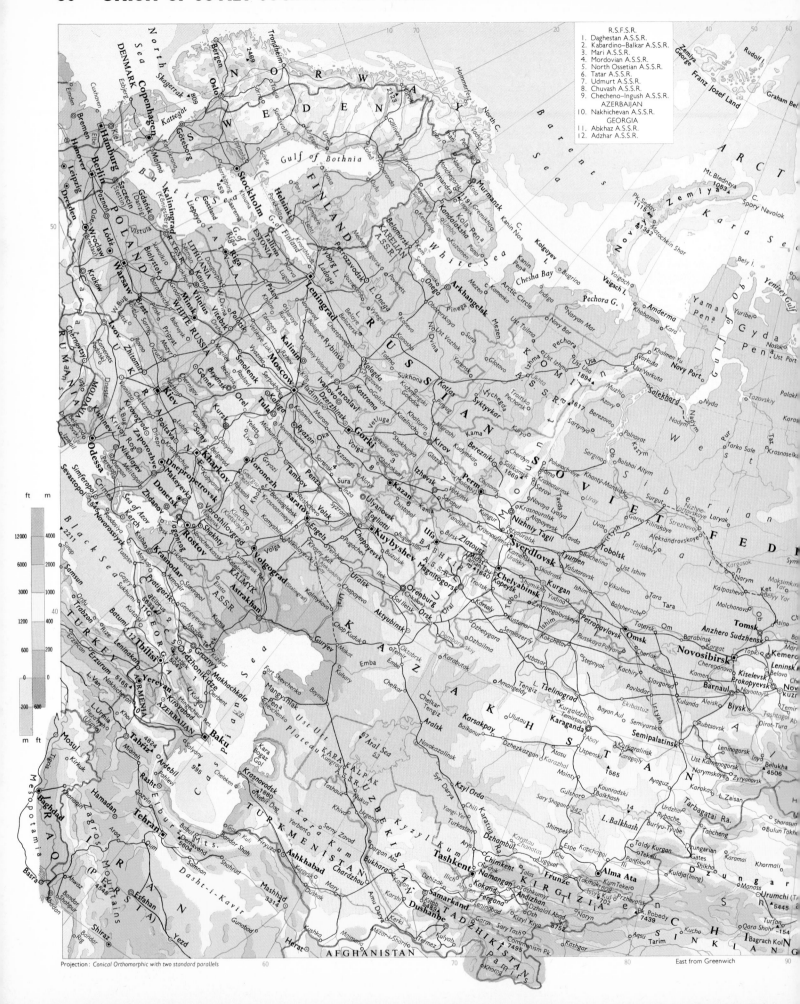

R.S.F.S.R.
1. Daghestan A.S.S.R.
2. Kabardino–Balkar A.S.S.R.
3. Mari A.S.S.R.
4. Mordovian A.S.S.R.
5. North Ossetian A.S.S.R.
6. Tatar A.S.S.R.
7. Udmurt A.S.S.R.
8. Chuvash A.S.S.R.
9. Checheno–Ingush A.S.S.R.
   AZERBAIJAN
10. Nakhichevan A.S.S.R.
    GEORGIA
11. Abkhaz A.S.S.R.
12. Adzhar A.S.S.R.

Projection: Conical Orthomorphic with two standard parallels

East from Greenwich

1:15 000 000

100   0   100   200   300 miles
100   0   100   200   300   400   500 km

UZBEKISTAN S. S. R. Dzhizak · Samarkand
Khiva · Amu Darya · Bukhara · Pendzhikent · **TADZHIKISTAN**
CHINA
Ashkhabad · Kara Kum · Kerki · Dushanbe · Pamir · Kashmir
MENISTAN · Mary · Karshi · Faizabad · Gilgit
Mashhad · Kushka · Balkh · Tashkurghan · Indus · Srinagar
Sabzawar · Mazar-i-Sharif · **Kabul** · Jalalabad · **Rawalpindi** · Jammu
Herat · Koh-i-Sangan · Ghazni · Khyber Pass · **Peshawar** · Sialkot
AFGHANISTAN · Koh-i-Mazar · Kohat · Lahore
Kandahar · Dera Ismail Khan · Multan
Quetta · Bolan Pass · Sukkur · Khanpur
PAKISTAN · **INDIA**
Kerman · Zahedan · Kalat · Jacobabad · Larkana · Nawabshah
Kuh-i-Taftan · Dalbandin · Sibi · Khairpur · Shikarpur
Bampur · Mashkel · **Hyderabad** · Kotri
Bandar Abbas · **Karachi**
Qishm I. · Makran
Gulf of Oman
Sharjah · As Sohar · Al Khabura · **Muscat** · Sonmiani · Ormara · Pasni · Gwadar
Buraimi · Tropic of Cancer
Dhank · **Arabian Sea**
Sur · Ras al Hadd
Al Masira · **Gulf of Masira**
Al Ain · Ras al Madraka
Al Juwara · Sauqra Bay
Dhofar · Kuria Muria Is.
Salala · Marbat
Socotra (South Yemen) · The Brothers

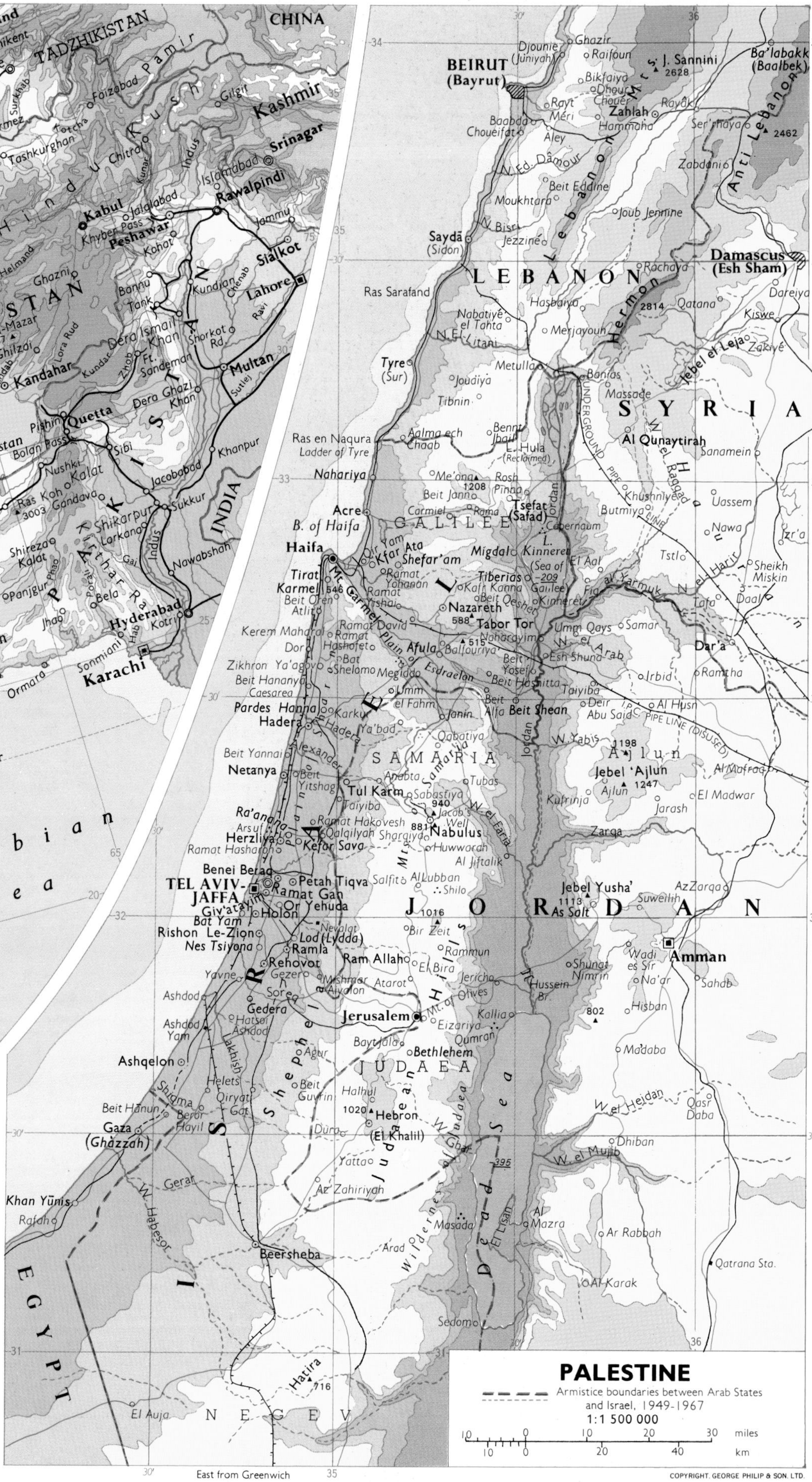

East from Greenwich

BEIRUT (Bayrut) · Djounie (Juniyah) · Ghazir · Raifoun · J. Sannini 2628 · **Ba'labakk (Baalbek)**
Bikfaiya · Dhour · Zahlah · Ser'aiya 2462
LEBANON · Aley · Hammana · Rayak
Saydā (Sidon) · Jezzine · Hermon 2814 · **Damascus (Esh Sham)**
Ras Sarafand · Nabatiyé · Hasbaiya · Qatana · Kiswe
Tyre (Sur) · Metulla · Massade · Al Quneytirah · **SYRIA**
Nahariya · Rosh Pinna · L. Hula · Khushniyeh
Acre · B. of Haifa · **GALILEE** · Tsefat (Safad) · Capernaum · Nawa
Haifa · Kfar Ata · Shefar'am · Migdal · Kinneret (Sea of Galilee) · Dar'a
Tirat Karmel · Nazareth · Tiberias · Irbid
Atlit · Ramat David · Afula · Tabor Tor · Umm Qays · Ramtha
Zikhron Ya'aqov · Megiddo · Plain of Esdraelon · Beit Shean · Al Husn
Pardes Hanna · Hadera · **SAMARIA** · Ajlun · Jebel 'Ajlun 1247
Netanya · Tul Karm · Nablus · Jarash
Herzliya · Kefar Sava · Qalqilya · Zarqa
Ra'anana · **JORDAN** · As Salt · **Amman**
TEL AVIV-JAFFA · Petah Tiqva · Ramat Gan · Shiloh
Bat Yam · Holon · Ramallah · Jericho · Mt. of Olives
Rishon Le-Zion · Lod (Lydda) · Ramla · El Bira
Rehovot · Ram Allah · Kallia
Ashdod · **Jerusalem** · Eizariya · Qumran
Ashqelon · Bethlehem · **JUDAEA** · Madaba
Gaza (Ghazzah) · Beit Guvrin · Hebron (El Khalil) · Dead Sea
Khan Yunis · Gerar · Masada · Al Mazra
Rafah · Beersheba · Arad · Ar Rabbah
EGYPT · **NEGEV** · Sedom · Al-Karak
El Auja · Hatira 716 · Qatrana Sta.

PALESTINE
- - - Armistice boundaries between Arab States and Israel, 1949-1967
1:1 500 000
10   0   10   20   30 miles
10   0   10   20   30   40 km

COPYRIGHT. GEORGE PHILIP & SON. LTD.

U.S.S.R.

Afghanistan

BADGHIS · FARYAB · BALKH · SAMANGAN · TAKHAR · BADAKHSHAN · HINDU KUSH · Karakoram Range

Paropamisus Range · Herat · HERAT · GHOR · BAMIAN · PARWAN · KAPISA · LAGHMAN · KUNAR · SWAT · PESHAWAR · JAMMU · LADAKH Range

Kabul · Kabul · WARDAK · LOGAR · NANGARHAR · Khyber Pass · Peshawar · Rawalpindi · Islamabad · Srinagar · KASHMIR

URUZGAN · GHAZNI · Ghazni · PAKTYA · DERA ISMAIL KHAN · Kohat · RAWALPINDI · ZASKAR Range

ZABUL · Kalat · KATTAWAZ-URGUN · Dera Ismail Khan · Mianwali · Jhelum · Gujrat · Sialkot · Pathankot · HIMACHAL PRADESH

Kandahar · KANDAHAR · Toba Kakar Hills · Fort Sandeman · SARGODHA · LAHORE · Lahore · Amritsar · Jullundur · Simla

Khash Desert · Dasht-i-Margo · REGISTAN · Quetta · Multan · PUNJAB · Ludhiana · Chandigarh · Ambala · Dehra Dun

CHAKHANSUR · Chagai Hills · QUETTA · BALUCHISTAN · BAHAWALPUR · Ferozepore · Patiala · Saharanpur · Hardwar

Sandy Desert · KALAT · Siahan Range · Central Makran Range · Kirthar Range · Sukkur · KHAIRPUR · Bikaner · Great Indian Desert (Thar Desert) · DELHI · Meerut · Moradabad

Makran Coast Range · KARACHI · Hyderabad · HYDERABAD · RAJASTHAN · Jodhpur · Jaipur · Agra · Gwalior

ARABIAN SEA · Mouths of the Indus · Rann of Kutch · Udaipur · Kota · Jhansi

GUJARAT · Little Rann · Ahmadabad · Indore · MADHYA PRADESH · Bhopal

Jamnagar · Rajkot · Vadodara

Junagadh · Bhavnagar · Bharuch · Surat · Satpura Range

Diu · Gulf of Cambay · Daman · Nagpur · Amraoti · Wardha

BOMBAY · Nasik · Aurangabad · MAHARASHTRA

Pune (Poona) · Ahmadnagar

Kolhapur · Sholapur · Gulbarga · Hyderabad · ANDHRA PRADESH

Inset (Continuation Southwards on same scale)

GOA · Dharwar · Gadag · Kurnool · Ongole

Hubli · Bellary · Nellore

KARNATAKA · Bangalore · Kolar · Madras · Pulicat Lake

Mangalore · Mysore · Vellore · Coromandel Coast

Calicut (Kozhikode) · Coimbatore · Salem · TAMIL NADU · Pondicherry · Cuddalore

Trichur · Tiruchirappalli · Thanjavur · Nagappattinam

Ernakulam · Madurai · Karaikkudi · Palk Strait

Alleppey · Rajapalaiyam · Jaffna · Palk Bay

Quilon · Gulf of Mannar · Trincomalee

Trivandrum · Nagercoil · Cape Comorin · Anuradhapura

SRI LANKA · Colombo · Kandy · Moratuwa · Galle · Dondra Head

Tropic of Cancer

ft m 18 000 6000 12 000 4000 9000 3000 6000 2000 4500 1500 3000 1000 1200 400 600 200 0 200 600 m ft

Continuation Southwards on same scale

Projection: Conical with two standard parallels

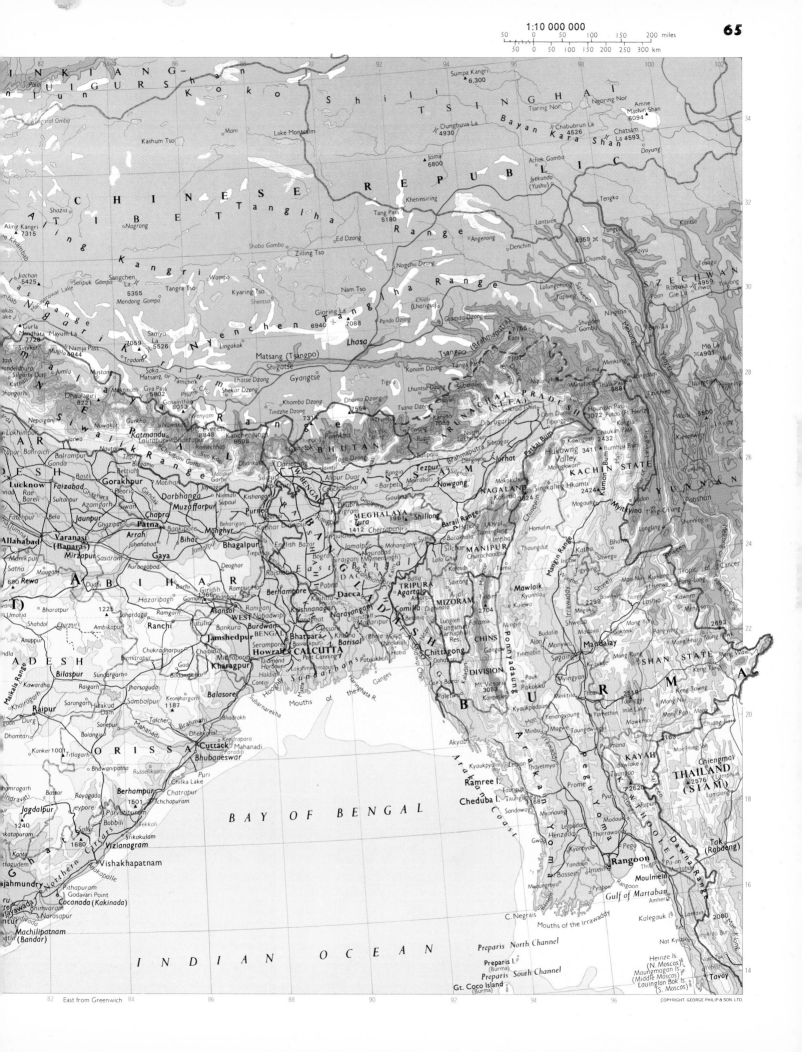

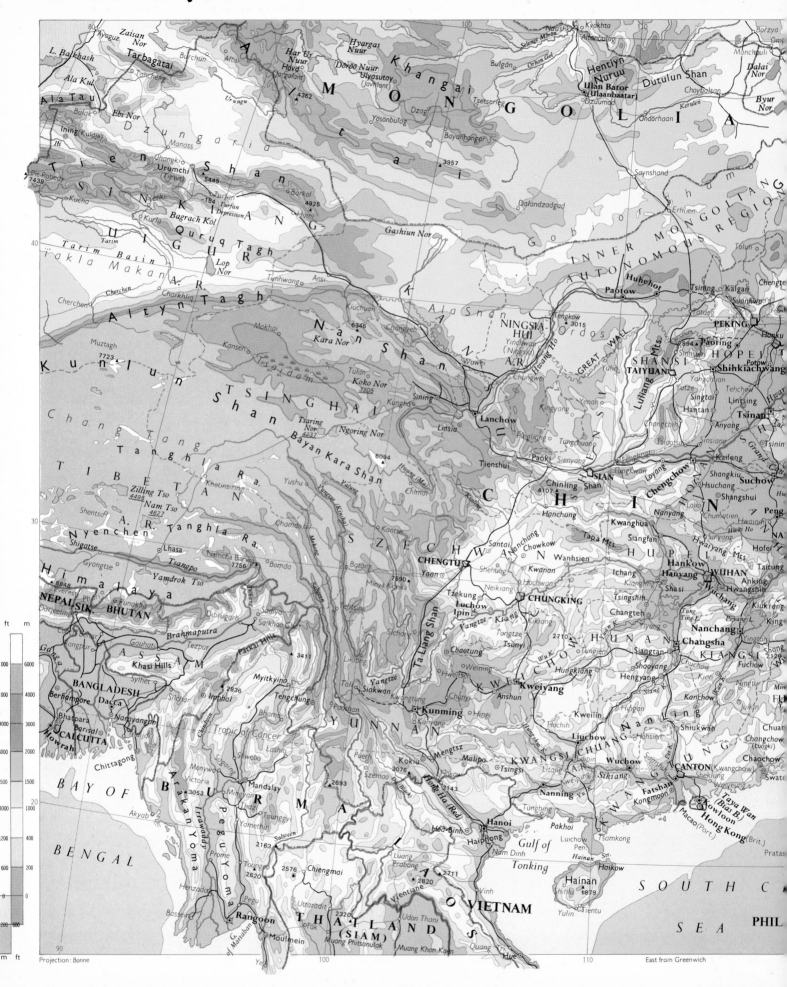

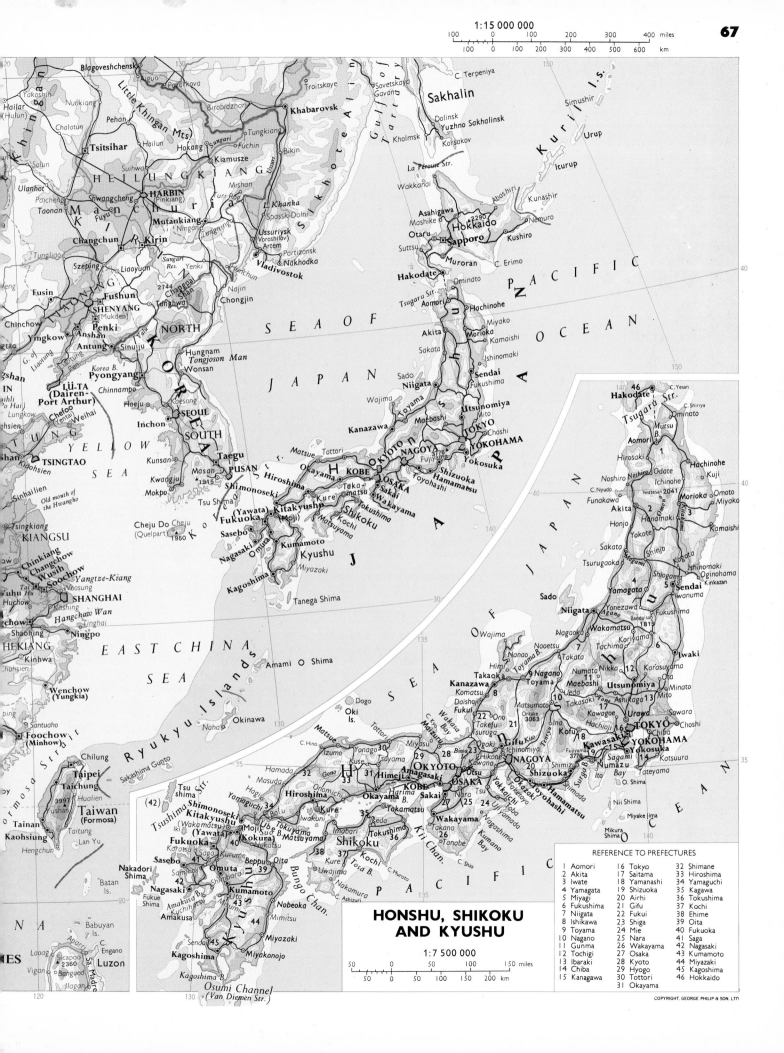

1:15 000 000

100   0   100   200   300   400 miles
100   0   100   200   300   400   500   600 km

HONSHU, SHIKOKU AND KYUSHU

1:7 500 000

50   0   50   100   150 miles
50   0   50   100   150   200 km

REFERENCE TO PREFECTURES

1 Aomori	16 Tokyo	32 Shimane
2 Akita	17 Saitama	33 Hiroshima
3 Iwate	18 Yamanashi	34 Yamaguchi
4 Yamagata	19 Shizuoka	35 Kagawa
5 Miyagi	20 Airhi	36 Tokushima
6 Fukushima	21 Gifu	37 Kochi
7 Niigata	22 Fukui	38 Ehime
8 Ishikawa	23 Shiga	39 Oita
9 Toyama	24 Mie	40 Fukuoka
10 Nagano	25 Nara	41 Saga
11 Gunma	26 Wakayama	42 Nagasaki
12 Tochigi	27 Osaka	43 Kumamoto
13 Ibaraki	28 Kyoto	44 Miyazaki
14 Chiba	29 Tottori	45 Kagoshima
15 Kanagawa	30 Tottori	46 Hokkaido
	31 Okayama	

COPYRIGHT. GEORGE PHILIP & SON. LTD

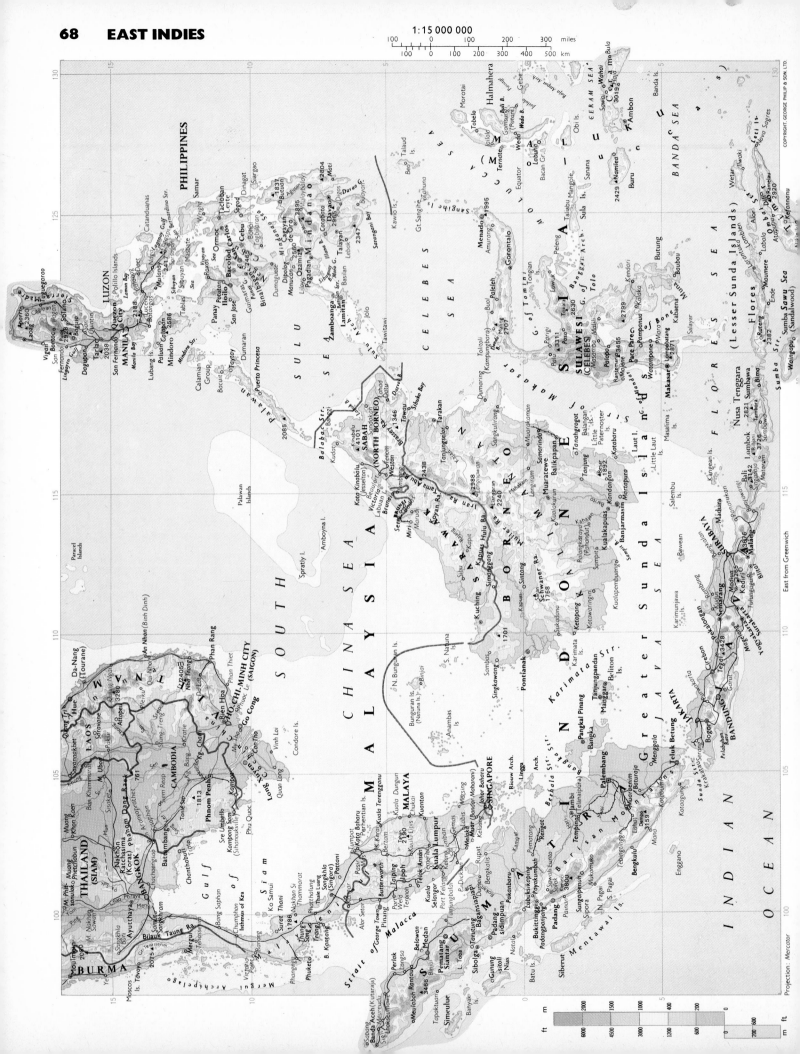

1:15 000 000

Projection: Mercator

COPYRIGHT. GEORGE PHILIP & SON LTD.

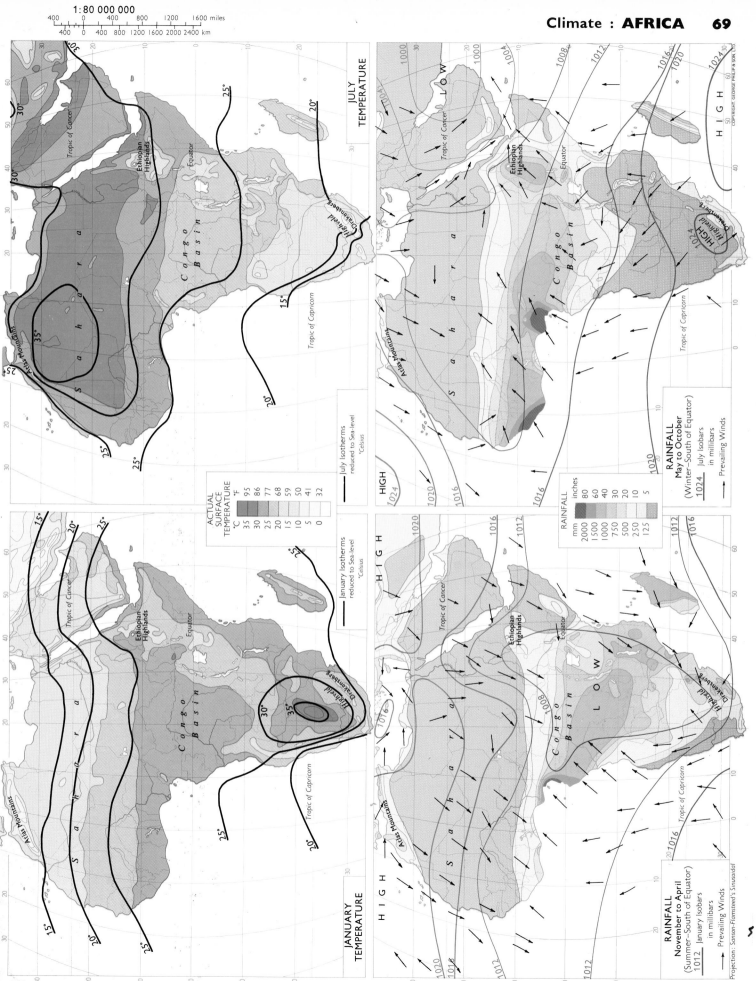

1 : 80 000 000

400   0   400   800   1200   1600 miles
400   0 400 800 1200 1600 2000 2400 km

JULY TEMPERATURE

ACTUAL SURFACE TEMPERATURE
°C   °F
35   95
30   86
25   77
20   68
15   59
10   50
5   41
0   32

July Isotherms reduced to Sea-level °Celsius

January Isotherms reduced to Sea-level °Celsius

JANUARY TEMPERATURE

RAINFALL
May to October
(Winter–South of Equator)
1024 July Isobars in millibars
Prevailing Winds

RAINFALL
mm   inches
2000   80
1500   60
1000   40
750   30
500   20
250   10
125   5

RAINFALL
November to April
(Summer–South of Equator)
1012 January Isobars in millibars
Prevailing Winds

COPYRIGHT: GEORGE PHILIP & SON LTD.

Projection: Sanson-Flamsteed's Sinusoidal

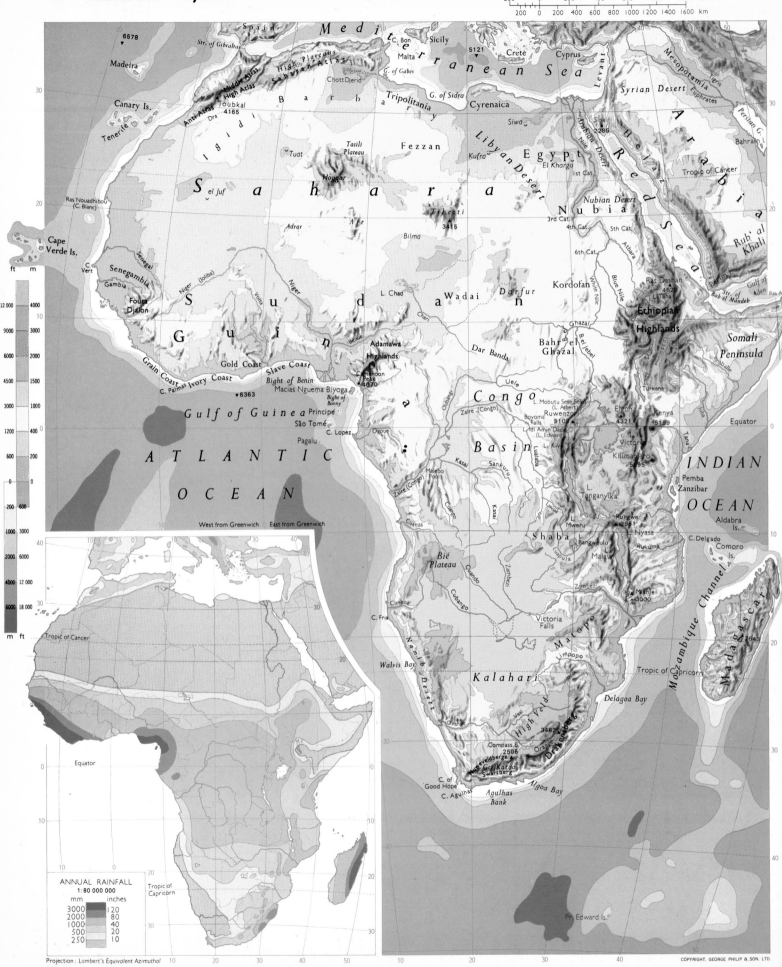

1 : 40 000 000

200   0   200   400   600   800   1000 miles
200   0   200 400 600 800 1000 1200 1400 1600 km

ANNUAL RAINFALL
1 : 80 000 000

mm	inches
3000	120
2000	80
1000	40
500	20
250	10

Projection : Lambert's Equivalent Azimuthal

COPYRIGHT. GEORGE PHILIP & SON. LTD.

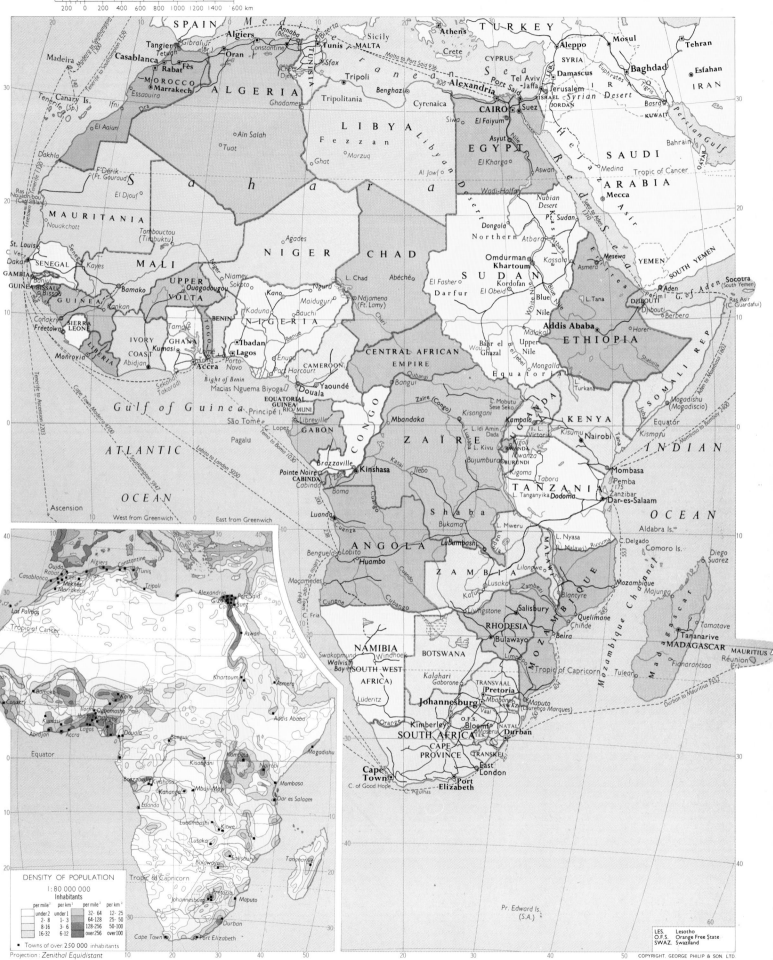

1:40 000 000

200   0   200   400   600   800   1000 miles
200   0   200 400   600 800 1000 1200 1400   600 km

SPAIN   Mediterranean   SICILY   TURKEY
Madeira   Algiers   Annaba Athens   Aleppo   Mosul   Tehran
Tangier Gibraltar(Br) Constantine Crete   CYPRUS   SYRIA   Baghdad   Esfahan
Casablanca Rabat Fès Oran Tunis MALTA   Tel Aviv Damascus   IRAN
MOROCCO Marrakech   Tripoli Benghazi Alexandria ISRAEL JORDAN
Essaouira   ALGERIA   Tripolitania   Cyrenaica CAIRO Suez   SAUDI
Ifni   Ghadames   El Faiyum EGYPT   Medina   Tropic of Cancer   ARABIA
Canary Is.   Aswan   Mecca
Tenerife (Sp.)   S   a   h   a   r   a   El Kharga   Asir
Dakhla   El Djouf   Wadi Halfa   Nubian Desert
MAURITANIA   Ain Salah   Fezzan   Marzuq   Al Jawf   Dongola Northern
Nouakchott   Tuat   Ghat   Pt Sudan   YEMEN
St. Louis   Omdurman Atbara   SOUTH YEMEN Socotra
Dakar SENEGAL Tombouctou Agades   Khartoum Kassala Asmera   Aden G. of Aden
GAMBIA Kayes MALI (Timbuktu) NIGER CHAD SUDAN Kordofan Blue Nile L.Tana DJIBOUTI
GUINEA-BISSAU Bamako UPPER Niamey Sokoto L.Chad Abéché El Fasher Darfur El Obeid White Nile ETHIOPIA
GUINEA Kankan VOLTA Ouagadougou Kaduna Maiduguri Ndjamena Bahr el Addis Ababa
SIERRA LEONE Freetown BENIN Kano Bauchi (Ft. Lamy) Ghazal Malakal Harer
Conakry IVORY GHANA NIGERIA Benue CENTRAL AFRICAN Upper SOMALI REP
LIBERIA COAST Kumasi Lagos Enugu CAMEROON EMPIRE Nile Mongalla
Monrovia Abidjan Accra Porto-Novo Port Harcourt Yaoundé Bangui Equatoria L.Turkana
Bight of Benin Macias Nguema Biyoga Douala Zaïre (Congo) L.Mobutu Mogadishu
Gulf of Guinea EQUATORIAL GUINEA Principé I. Libreville CONGO Kisangani KENYA
São Tomé RIO MUNI GABON Mbandaka L.Idi Amin Nairobi INDIAN
Pagalu ZAÏRE Kampala Equator
ATLANTIC Brazzaville Kinshasa RWANDA L.Victoria Mombasa
OCEAN Pointe Noire CABINDA Kasai BURUNDI TANZANIA Zanzibar
Ascension Boma Shaba Tabora Dodoma Dar-es-Salaam
Luanda Cuanza Bukama L.Tanganyika Pemba
ANGOLA Lubumbashi L.Mweru OCEAN
Benguela Lobito Huambo ZAMBIA L.Nyasa Comoro Is.
Moçamedes Lusaka Lilongwe MALAWI Diego Suarez
Cunene Kafue Blantyre Mozambique Majunga
NAMIBIA Livingstone Salisbury Quelimane MADAGASCAR MAURITIUS
Swakopmund Windhoek RHODESIA Beira Tananarive Réunion
Walvis Bay (SOUTH-WEST AFRICA) BOTSWANA Bulawayo Tropic of Capricorn Tulear Fianarantsoa
Lüderitz Kalahari Gaborone TRANSVAAL Maputo
Johannesburg Pretoria SWAZILAND
Orange Kimberley O.F.S. Bloemfontein NATAL Durban
Cape Town SOUTH AFRICA CAPE PROVINCE TRANSKEI East London
C. of Good Hope C. Agulhas Port Elizabeth

Pr. Edward Is. (S.A.)

LES. Lesotho
O.F.S. Orange Free State
SWAZ. Swaziland

DENSITY OF POPULATION
1:80 000 000
Inhabitants
per mile² per km²   per mile² per km²
under 2 under 1   32-64   12-25
2-8   1-3   64-128   25-50
8-16   3-6   128-256 50-100
16-32 6-12   over256 over100
● Towns of over 250 000 inhabitants

Projection: Zenithal Equidistant

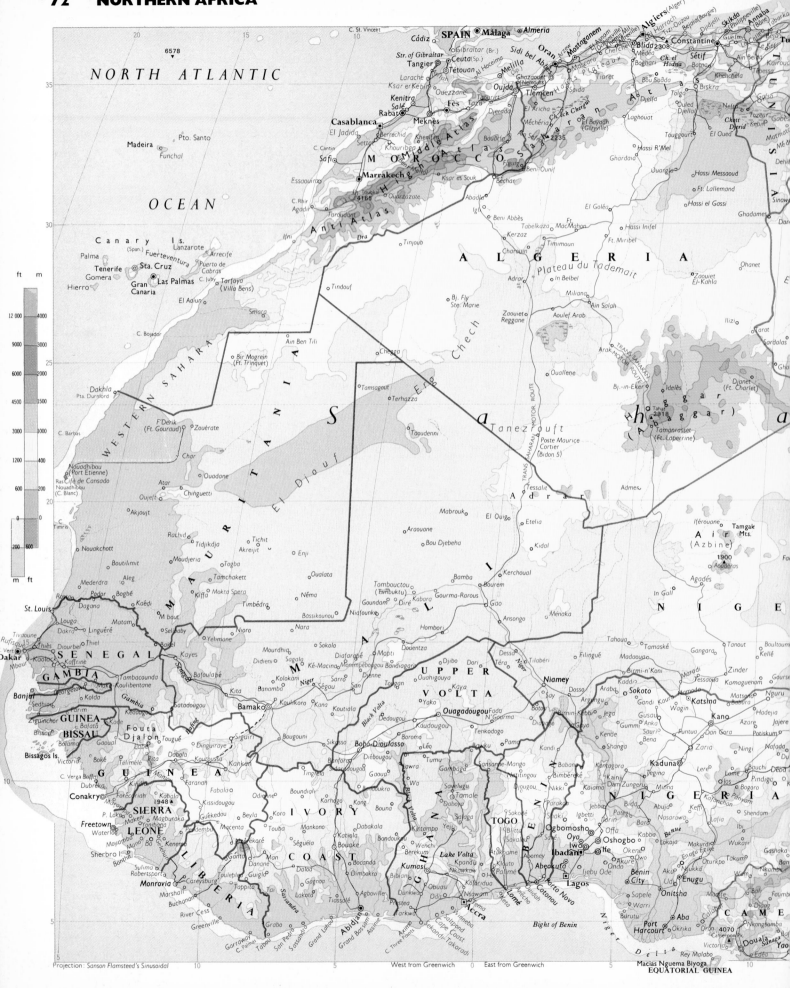

100   100   200   300   400 miles
100   0   100   200   300   400   500   600 km

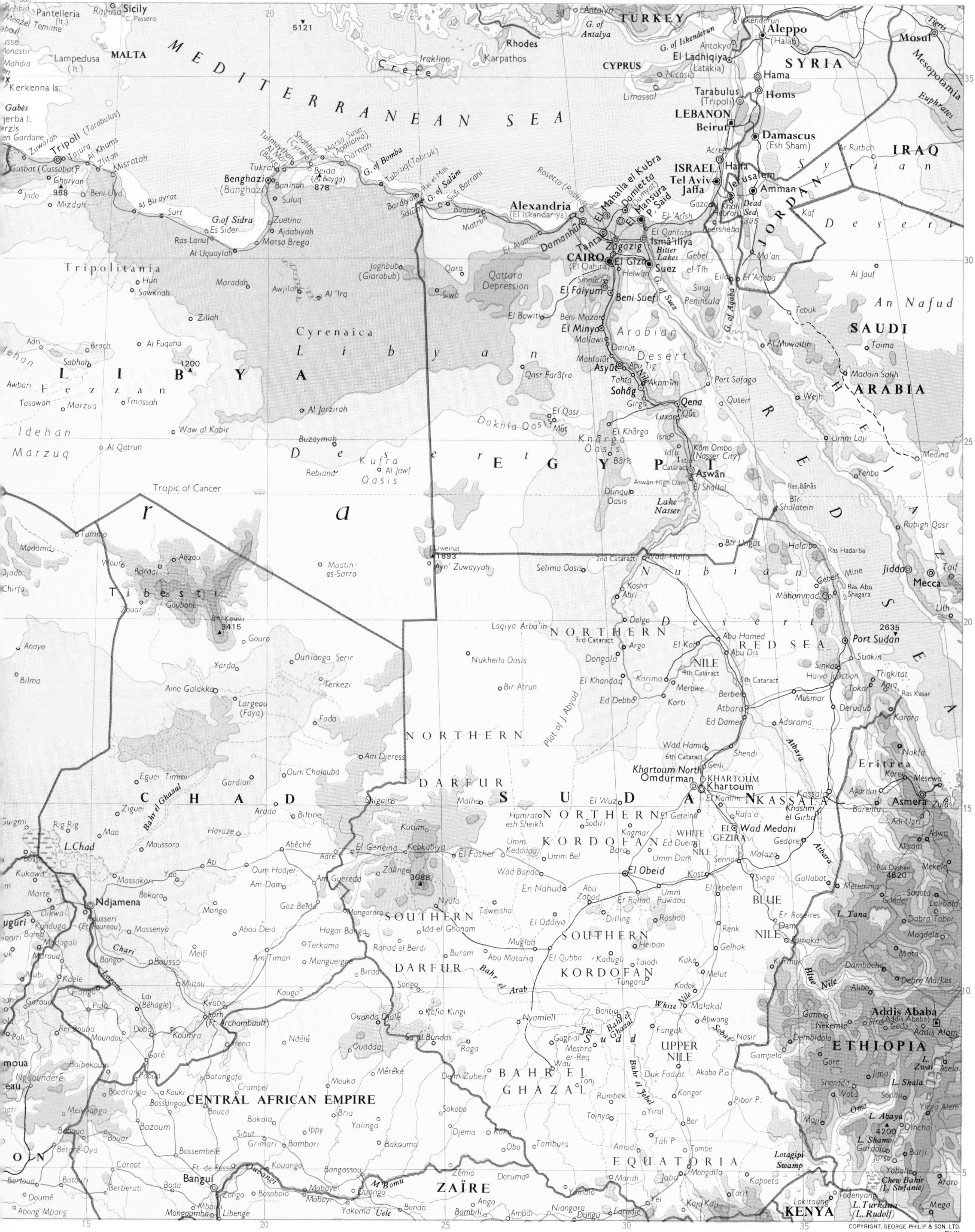

MEDITERRANEAN SEA

TURKEY
G. of Antalya
Rhodes
Karpathos
Crete
Iraklion
CYPRUS
Nicosia
Limassol
Latakia (Ladhiqiya)
El Ladhiqiya
Antakya
G. of Iskenderun
Kenderun
Aleppo (Halab)
Mosul
Tigris
SYRIA
Hama
Homs
Mesopotamia
Euphrates
Tarabulus (Tripoli)
LEBANON
Beirut
Damascus (Esh Sham)
Acre
Haifa
Ar Rutbah
IRAQ
Syrian
Tel Aviv
Jaffa
Jerusalem
Amman
ISRAEL
Gaza
Hebron
JORDAN
Beersheba
Dead Sea -395
Ma'an
Kaf
Al Jauf
Desert

MALTA
Sicily
Ragusa
C. Passero
Pantelleria (It.)
Lampedusa
Kerkenna Is.
Gabès
Jerba I.

Tripoli (Tarabulus)
Tajura
Al Khums
Zlitan
Misratah
Benghazi (Banghazi)
Baninah
Darnah
Tubruq (Tobruk)
G. of Bomba
Marsa Susa (Apollonia)
Shahhat (Cyrene)
Beida (Al Bayda)
878
Tukrah
Suluq
Ajdabiyah
Marsa Brega
Al Uquaylah
Es Sider
Ras Lanuf
G. of Sidra
Zuetina
Surt
Bardiya
Sidi Barrani
Ras el Milh
Sallum
G. of Salum
Buqbuq
Matruh
Mersa Matruh
El Alamein
Rosetta (Rashid)
Damietta (Dumyat)
P. Said
El Arish
El Qantara
Alexandria (El Iskandariya)
Damanhur
Tanta
Zagazig
Ismailiya
Bitter Lakes
El Qahira
CAIRO
El Giza
Suez
Helwan
Gebel el Tih
Eilat
El Aqaba
Tebuk

LIBYA
Tripolitania
Hun
Sawknah
Zillah
Maradah
Awjilah
Jaghbub (Giarabub)
Qara
Qattara Depression
Siwa
El Faiyum
Beni Suef
Sinai Peninsula
G. of Aqaba
SAUDI
An Nafud
Al Muwailh
Taima
Madain Salih
ARABIA
Hejaz

Cyrenaica
Libyan
El Bawiti
El Minya
Mallawi
Beni Mazar
Arabian
Desert
Port Safaga
Quseir
Wejh
Jado
968
Beni Ulid
Mizdah
Al Bu'ayrat
Adri
Brach
Al Fuqaha
1200
Al Jarzirah
Qasr Farafra
Asyut
Abu Tig
Manfalut
Dairut
Tahta
Sohag
Akhmim
Girga
Qena
Qus
Luxor
Isna
Idfu
Kom Ombo (Nasser City)
1st Cataract
Aswan
Aswan High Dam
El Shallal
Ras Banas
Bir Shalatein
Rabigh
Yenbo
Medina

FEZZAN
Sabhah
Tmassah
Marzuq
Waw al Kabir
Buzaymah
Dakhla Oasis
Mut
El Qasr
El Kharga
Kharga Oasis
Baris
Dunqul Oasis
Lake Nasser
Bir Ungat
Halaib
Ras Hadarba
Jidda
Mecca
Taif
Idehan
Marzuq
Al Qatrun
Rebiana
Kufra Oasis
Al Jawf
DESERT
E G Y P T
Uweinat
1893
Ayn Zuwayyah
Selima Oasis
Wadi Halfa
2nd Cataract
Nubian
Gebel Elba
Muhammad Qol
Ras Abu Shagara
Mine
Lith

Tropic of Cancer
Tumma
Modama
Aozou
Bardai
Maatin-es-Sarra
Djado
Chirfa
Anaye
Tibesti
Zouar
Goubone
Emi Koussi 3415
Gouro
Ounianga Serir
Yarda
Aine Galakka
Bilma
Largeau (Faya)
Fada
Terkezi
Kosha
Abri
Delgo
Argo
Dongola
El Kab
Abu Hamed
Abu Dis
3rd Cataract
NORTHERN
DESERT
NILE
Karima
Merowe
4th Cataract
Berber
Atbara
Musmar
Derudeb
Port Sudan
2635
Suakin
Trinkitat
Agig
Ras Kasar
Haiya Junction
Sinkat
Tokar
RED SEA

NORTHERN
Nukheila Oasis
Bir Atrun
El Khandaq
Ed Debba
Korti
5th Cataract
Karora
Ed Damer
Adorama
Eritrea
Nakfa
DARFUR
Am Djeress
Plat. of J. Abyad
Wad Hamid
6th Cataract
Shendi
Geili
Kassala
Keren
Mesewa
Agordat
Asmera
Zula
Adwa
Aksum
CHAD
Eguei Timmi
Oum Chalouba
Gardian
Khartoum North
Omdurman
KHARTOUM
Kamlin
Atbara
Barentu
Adi Ugri
Ziguei
Biltine
Shigaib
Malha
Kutum
Hamrat esh Sheikh
Sodiri
Khashm el Girba
Ras Dashen 4620
Mekele
Ras Dashan
L. Chad
Mao
Moussoro
Ati
Abéché
Adre
El Geneina
Kebkabiya
El Fasher
NORTHERN
Kaja Umm Kedddada
WHITE NILE
GEZIRA
El Wuzu
Sennar
Gedaref
Gallabat
Metemma
Gonder
L. Tana
Debra Tabor
Dikwa
Yao
Bokoro
Oum Hadjer
Am-Dam
Am Guereda
Nyala
Zalingei
3088
Wad Banda
Umm Bel
En Nahud
El Obeid
Singa
Mafaza
BLUE NILE
Er Roseires Dam
Lalibela
Magdala
Kuka
Marte
Massakori
Mongororo
Goz Beida
SOUTHERN
Idd el Ghanam
Buram
Abu Matariq
El Qubba
KORDOFAN
En Nahud
Abu Zabad
Er Rahad
Ruwaba
Dilling
Rashad
Renk
Kurmuk
Damazin
Gimbi
Nekemte
Addis Ababa
Ethiopia
ETHIOPIA
Addis Alam
L. Zwai
Ndjamena
Mousso
Chari
Massenya
Melfi
Am Timan
Mangueigne
Birao
DARFUR
Songo
Bahr el Arab
Kadugli
Talodi
Kaka
Melut
Heiban
Tungaru
Malakal
White Nile
Kuruk
Gore
Jima
L. Abaya
Dambech
Debr Markos
Alibo
Mota
CENTRAL AFRICAN EMPIRE
Bahr el Ghazal
Ouanda Djale
Kafia Kingi
Raga
Nyamlell
Wau
Meshra er-Req
Gogrial
Aweil
Bentiu
BAHR EL GHAZAL
Tonj
Rumbek
Yirol
Bor
Fangak
Abwong
Nasir
UPPER NILE
Akobo
Gambela
Dembidolo
L. Shala
4200
L. Shamo
Gardolo
Bangui
Zemio
Tambura
Amadi
Maridi
Juba
Torit
EQUATORIA
Lotagipi Swamp
Mega
Dincha
L. Abaya
Chew Bahir L. Stefanie
ZAIRE
M. Bomu
Uele
Yambio
Dungu
Kapoeta
Lokichokio
L. Turkana (L. Rudolf)
Todenyang
KENYA

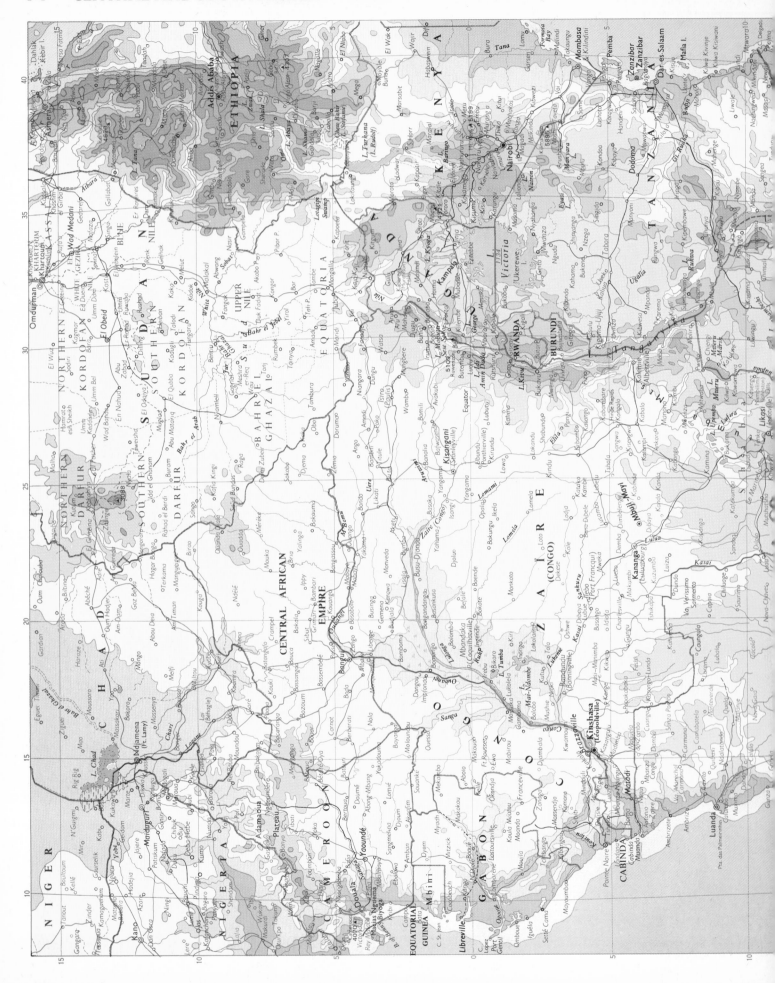

1:15 000 000

100   0   100   200   300   400 miles
100 0 100 200 300 400 500 600 km

MADAGASCAR
On same scale as General Map

INDIAN OCEAN

Tropic of Capricorn

Diego Suarez

Nossi Bé
Hell-Ville

Majunga

Tananarive
Antananarivo

Tamatave

Fianarantsoa

Tuléar

Fort-Dauphin

RHODESIA

Salisbury

Bulawayo

Lusaka

ZAMBIA

BOTSWANA

Kalahari

Gaborone

NAMIBIA
(SOUTH WEST AFRICA)

Windhoek

Namaland

Damaraland

Owambo

Etosha Pan

Swakopmund
Walvis Bay

SOUTH AFRICA

CAPE PROVINCE

Great Karoo

Cape Town
C. of Good Hope

Port Elizabeth

East London

TRANSKEI

NATAL

Durban
Pietermaritzburg

LESOTHO

ORANGE FREE STATE

Bloemfontein

Kimberley

TRANSVAAL

Pretoria
Johannesburg
Krugersdorp
Vereeniging

SWAZILAND

Maputo

Limpopo

Beira

Blantyre
Lilongwe

MALAWI

MOZAMBIQUE

INDIAN OCEAN

ATLANTIC OCEAN

Tropic of Capricorn

East from Greenwich

Benguela
Lobito

Caprivi Strip

ft m
18 000 6000
12 000 4000
9000 3000
6000 2000
4500 1500
3000 1000
1200 400
600 200
0

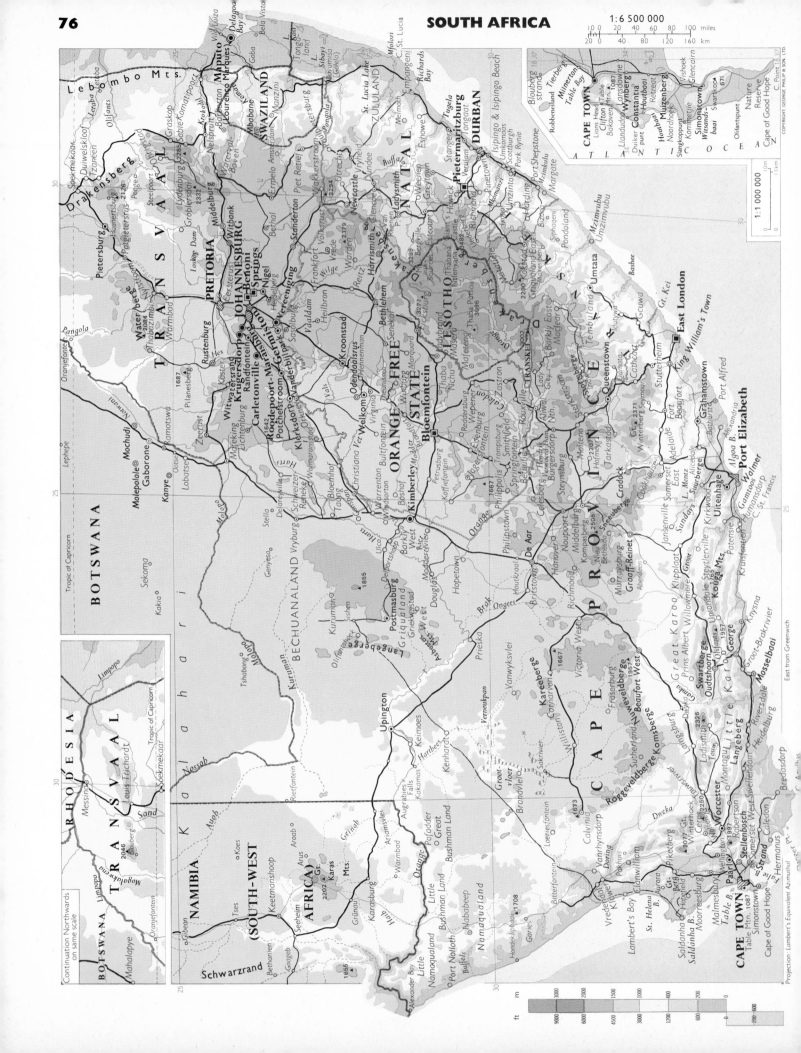

1:6 500 000

100   0   20   40   60   80   100 miles

20   0   40   80   120   160 km

Projection: Lambert's Equivalent Azimuthal

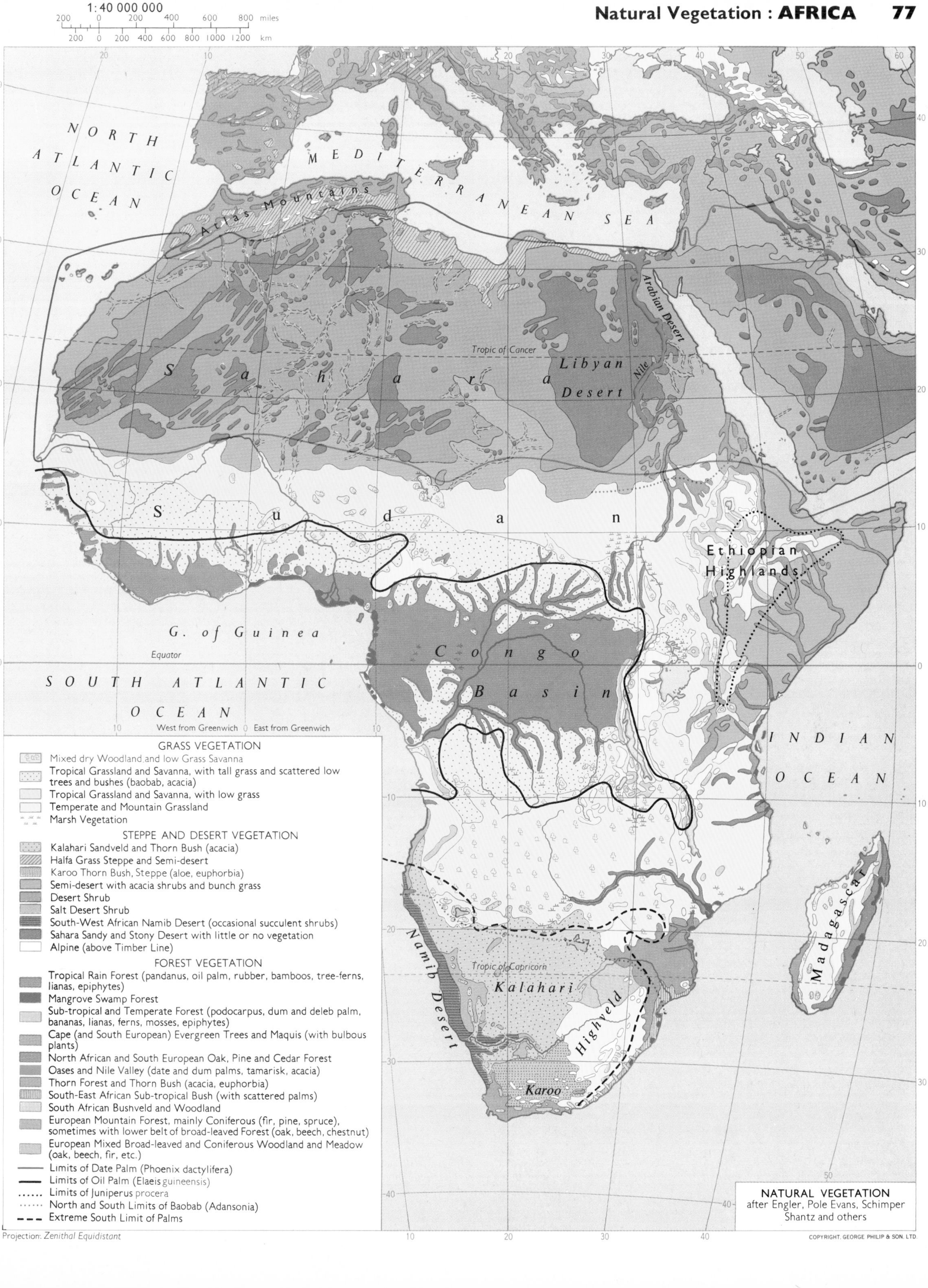

1:40 000 000

200   0   200   400   600   800 miles
200   0   200 400 600 800 1000 1200 km

Projection: *Zenithal Equidistant*

NORTH
ATLANTIC
OCEAN

MEDITERRANEAN SEA

Atlas Mountains

Arabian Desert

Tropic of Cancer

*Libyan
Desert*

S a h a r a

Nile

S u d a n

G. of Guinea

Equator

Ethiopian
Highlands

C o n g o

B a s i n

SOUTH ATLANTIC

OCEAN

West from Greenwich   East from Greenwich

INDIAN

OCEAN

Namib Desert

Tropic of Capricorn

Kalahari

Highveld

Karoo

Madagascar

GRASS VEGETATION
- Mixed dry Woodland and low Grass Savanna
- Tropical Grassland and Savanna, with tall grass and scattered low trees and bushes (baobab, acacia)
- Tropical Grassland and Savanna, with low grass
- Temperate and Mountain Grassland
- Marsh Vegetation

STEPPE AND DESERT VEGETATION
- Kalahari Sandveld and Thorn Bush (acacia)
- Halfa Grass Steppe and Semi-desert
- Karoo Thorn Bush, Steppe (aloe, euphorbia)
- Semi-desert with acacia shrubs and bunch grass
- Desert Shrub
- Salt Desert Shrub
- South-West African Namib Desert (occasional succulent shrubs)
- Sahara Sandy and Stony Desert with little or no vegetation
- Alpine (above Timber Line)

FOREST VEGETATION
- Tropical Rain Forest (pandanus, oil palm, rubber, bamboos, tree-ferns, lianas, epiphytes)
- Mangrove Swamp Forest
- Sub-tropical and Temperate Forest (podocarpus, dum and deleb palm, bananas, lianas, ferns, mosses, epiphytes)
- Cape (and South European) Evergreen Trees and Maquis (with bulbous plants)
- North African and South European Oak, Pine and Cedar Forest
- Oases and Nile Valley (date and dum palms, tamarisk, acacia)
- Thorn Forest and Thorn Bush (acacia, euphorbia)
- South-East African Sub-tropical Bush (with scattered palms)
- South African Bushveld and Woodland
- European Mountain Forest, mainly Coniferous (fir, pine, spruce), sometimes with lower belt of broad-leaved Forest (oak, beech, chestnut)
- European Mixed Broad-leaved and Coniferous Woodland and Meadow (oak, beech, fir, etc.)

— Limits of Date Palm (Phoenix dactylifera)
— Limits of Oil Palm (Elaeis guineensis)
..... Limits of Juniperus procera
······ North and South Limits of Baobab (Adansonia)
- - - Extreme South Limit of Palms

NATURAL VEGETATION
after Engler, Pole Evans, Schimper
Shantz and others

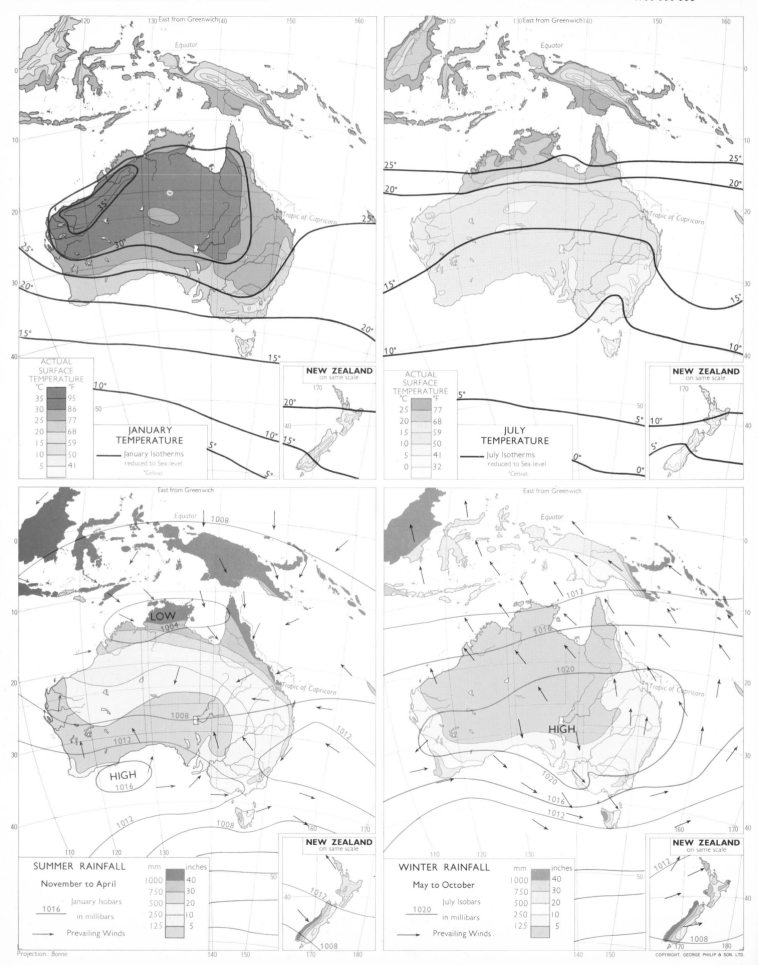

ACTUAL
SURFACE
TEMPERATURE
°C	°F
35	95
30	86
25	77
20	68
15	59
10	50
5	41

**JANUARY
TEMPERATURE**

January Isotherms
reduced to Sea-level
°Celsius

NEW ZEALAND
on same scale

ACTUAL
SURFACE
TEMPERATURE
°C	°F
25	77
20	68
15	59
10	50
5	41
0	32

**JULY
TEMPERATURE**

July Isotherms
reduced to Sea-level
°Celsius

NEW ZEALAND
on same scale

SUMMER RAINFALL

November to April

	mm	inches
	1000	40
	750	30
	500	20
	250	10
	125	5

_1016_ January Isobars
in millibars

→ Prevailing Winds

NEW ZEALAND
on same scale

WINTER RAINFALL

May to October

	mm	inches
	1000	40
	750	30
	500	20
	250	10
	125	5

_1020_ July Isobars
in millibars

→ Prevailing Winds.

NEW ZEALAND
on same scale

Projection: Bonne

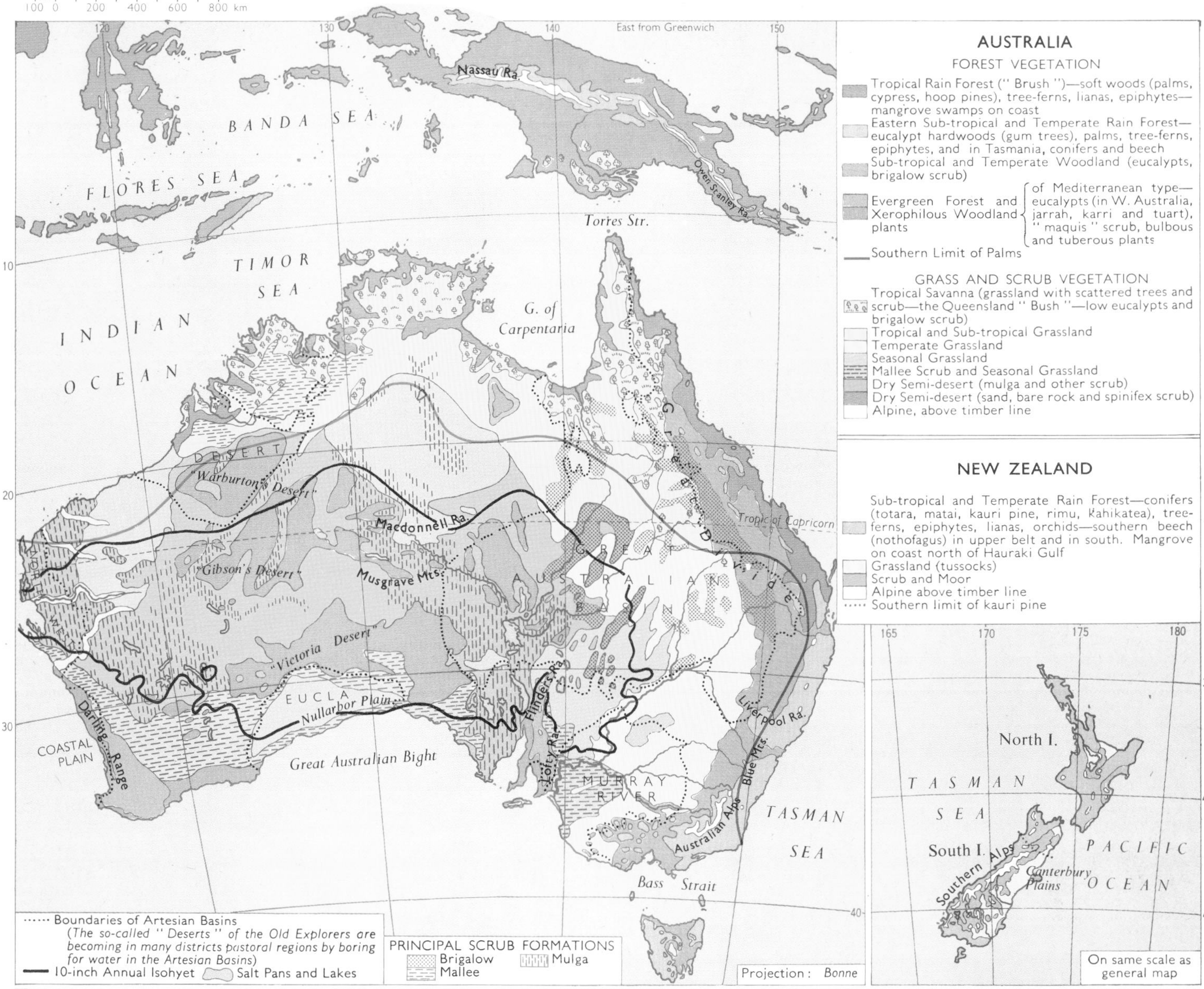

1:30 000 000

100   0   100   200   300   400   500 miles
100   0   200   400   600   800 km

East from Greenwich

AUSTRALIA

FOREST VEGETATION

Tropical Rain Forest (" Brush ")—soft woods (palms, cypress, hoop pines), tree-ferns, lianas, epiphytes—mangrove swamps on coast

Eastern Sub-tropical and Temperate Rain Forest—eucalypt hardwoods (gum trees), palms, tree-ferns, epiphytes, and in Tasmania, conifers and beech

Sub-tropical and Temperate Woodland (eucalypts, brigalow scrub)

Evergreen Forest and Xerophilous Woodland plants { of Mediterranean type—eucalypts (in W. Australia, jarrah, karri and tuart), " maquis " scrub, bulbous and tuberous plants

—— Southern Limit of Palms

GRASS AND SCRUB VEGETATION

Tropical Savanna (grassland with scattered trees and scrub—the Queensland " Bush "—low eucalypts and brigalow scrub)

Tropical and Sub-tropical Grassland
Temperate Grassland
Seasonal Grassland
Mallee Scrub and Seasonal Grassland
Dry Semi-desert (mulga and other scrub)
Dry Semi-desert (sand, bare rock and spinifex scrub)
Alpine, above timber line

NEW ZEALAND

Sub-tropical and Temperate Rain Forest—conifers (totara, matai, kauri pine, rimu, kahikatea), tree-ferns, epiphytes, lianas, orchids—southern beech (nothofagus) in upper belt and in south. Mangrove on coast north of Hauraki Gulf

Grassland (tussocks)
Scrub and Moor
Alpine above timber line
.... Southern limit of kauri pine

North I.

TASMAN SEA

South I.

PACIFIC OCEAN

Southern Alps

Canterbury Plains

On same scale as general map

BANDA SEA

FLORES SEA

Nassau Ra.

TIMOR SEA

Tortes Str.

INDIAN OCEAN

G. of Carpentaria

Owen Stanley Ra.

DESERT

Warburton Desert

Gibson's Desert

Macdonnell Ra.

Musgrave Mts.

Victoria Desert

EUCLA
Nullarbor Plain

Darling Range

COASTAL PLAIN

Great Australian Bight

Tropic of Capricorn

GREAT AUSTRALIAN

GREAT DIVIDING RANGE

Flinders Ra.

Liverpool Ra.

Blue Mts.

MURRAY RIVER

Australian Alps

TASMAN SEA

Bass Strait

..... Boundaries of Artesian Basins
(The so-called " Deserts " of the Old Explorers are becoming in many districts pastoral regions by boring for water in the Artesian Basins)

—— 10-inch Annual Isohyet   Salt Pans and Lakes

PRINCIPAL SCRUB FORMATIONS
Brigalow   Mulga
Mallee

Projection : Bonne

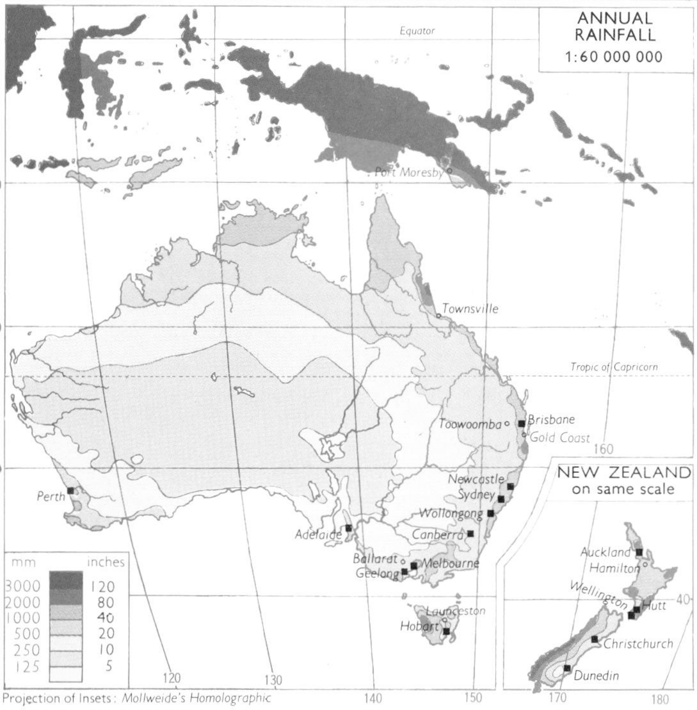

ANNUAL RAINFALL
1:60 000 000

Equator

Port Moresby

Townsville

Tropic of Capricorn

Perth

Toowoomba   Brisbane
Gold Coast

Newcastle
Sydney
Wollongong
Canberra

Adelaide

Ballarat   Melbourne
Geelong

Hobart

NEW ZEALAND
on same scale

Auckland
Hamilton
Wellington   Hutt

Christchurch

Dunedin

mm	inches
3000	120
2000	80
1000	40
500	20
250	10
125	5

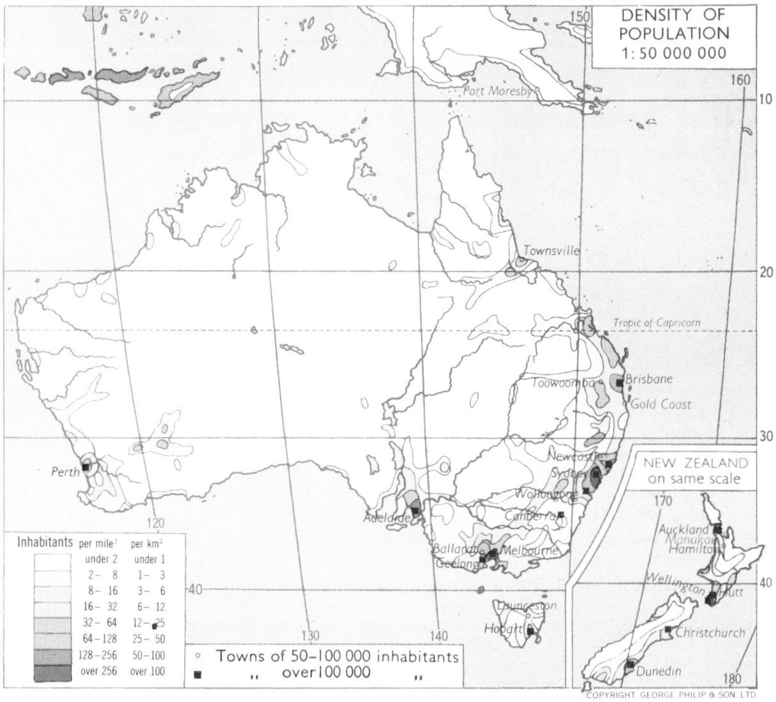

DENSITY OF POPULATION
1:50 000 000

Port Moresby

Townsville

Tropic of Capricorn

Perth

Toowoomba   Brisbane
Gold Coast

Newcastle
Sydney
Wollongong
Canberra

Adelaide

Ballarat   Melbourne
Geelong

Launceston

Hobart

NEW ZEALAND
on same scale

Auckland
Manukau
Hamilton
Wellington   Hutt

Christchurch

Dunedin

Inhabitants	per mile²	per km²
	under 2	under 1
	2- 8	1- 3
	8- 16	3- 6
	16- 32	6- 12
	32- 64	12- 25
	64-128	25- 50
	128-256	50-100
	over 256	over 100

○ Towns of 50-100 000 inhabitants
■   "   over 100 000   "

Projection of Insets: Mollweide's Homolographic

Boundaries of Artesian basins -- -- -- --

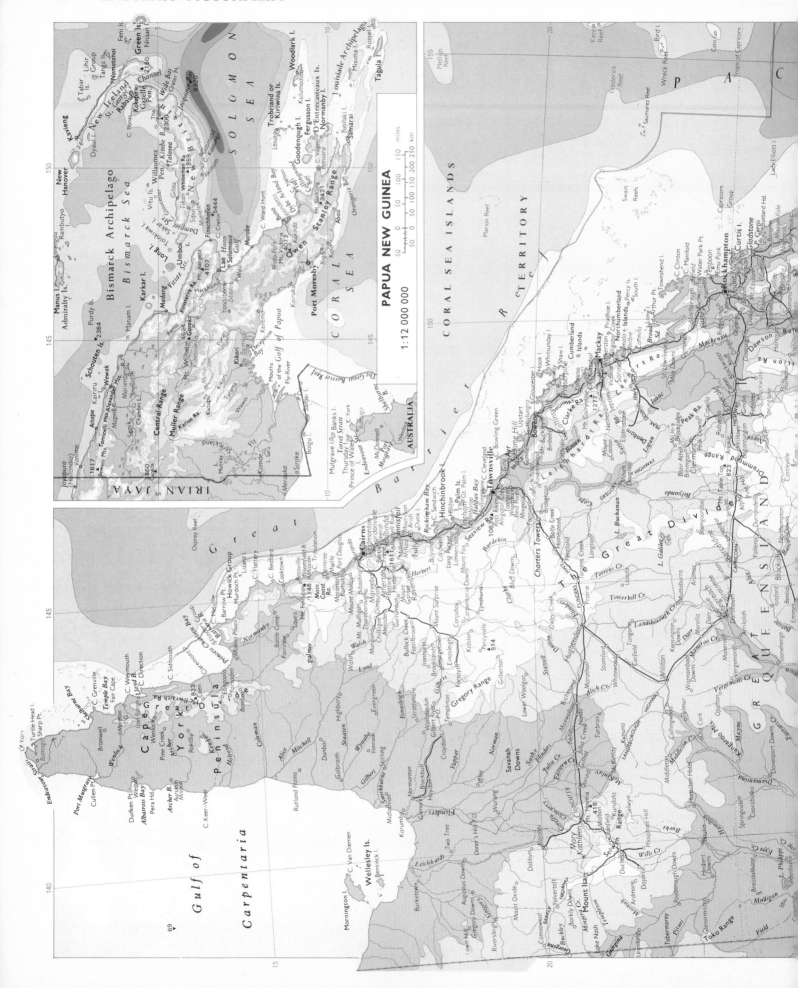

PAPUA NEW GUINEA

1:12 000 000

miles
0 50 100 150

km
0 50 100 150 200 250

1:7 500 000

50   0   50   100   150   200 miles

50   0   50   100   150   200   250   300 km

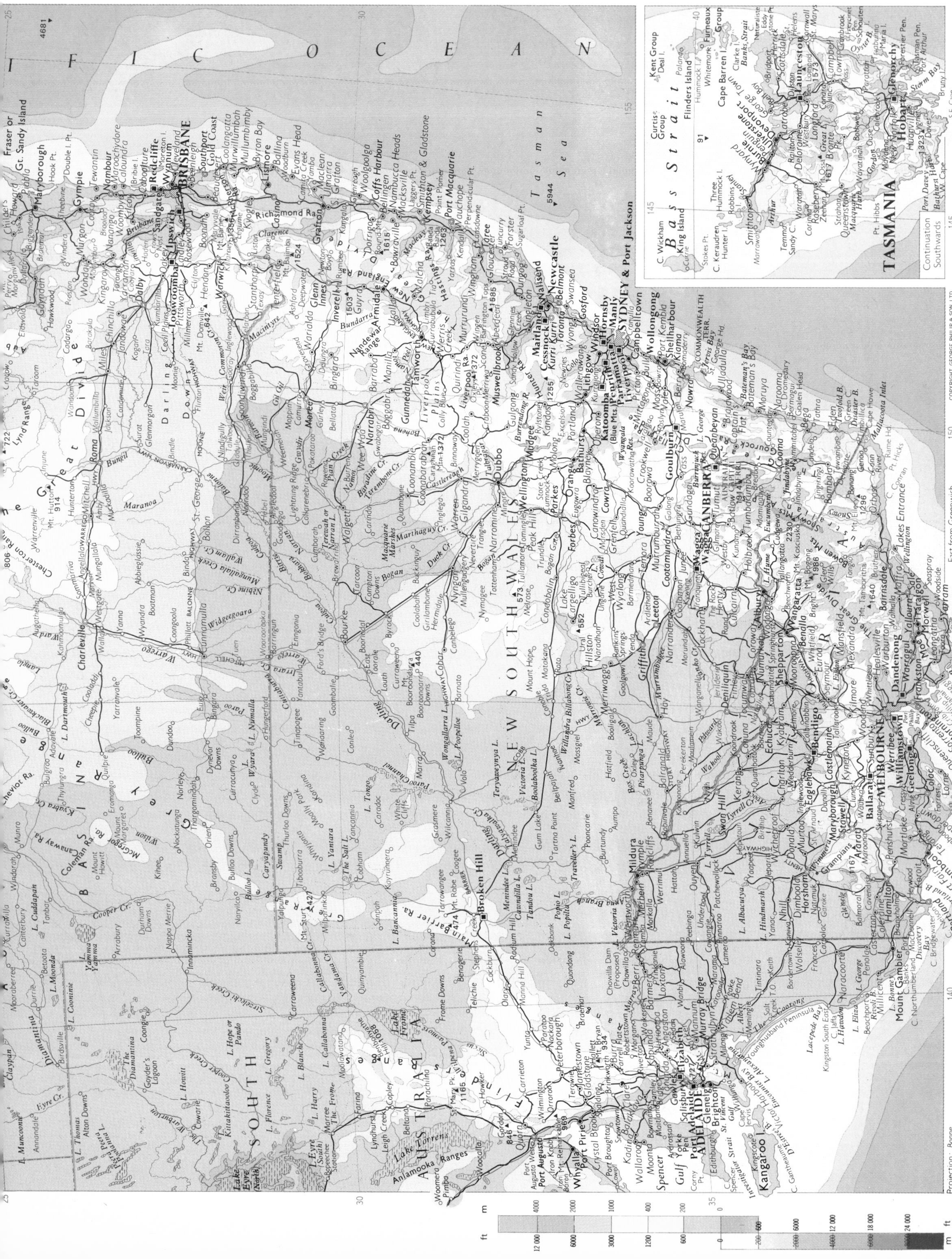

PACIFIC OCEAN

Tasman Sea

BASS STRAIT

KENT GROUP
FURNEAUX GROUP
Flinders Island
Cape Barren Island
King Island

TASMANIA

Launceston
Devonport
Burnie
Hobart

QUEENSLAND

Brisbane
Maryborough
Gympie
Ipswich
Toowoomba
Gold Coast
Southport
Redcliffe

Fraser or Gt. Sandy Island

NEW SOUTH WALES

SYDNEY & Port Jackson
Newcastle
Maitland
Cessnock
Wollongong
Coffs Harbour
Grafton
Armidale
Tamworth
Dubbo
Bathurst
Orange
Wagga Wagga
Albury
Broken Hill
Bourke

CANBERRA
AUSTRALIAN CAPITAL TERR.

The Great Dividing Range
Darling Downs
Great Artesian Basin
Murray R.
Darling R.
Lake Eyre
Lake Torrens
Lake Frome

VICTORIA

MELBOURNE
Ballarat
Bendigo
Geelong
Mildura

SOUTH AUSTRALIA

ADELAIDE
Port Augusta
Port Pirie
Whyalla
Kangaroo I.
Spencer Gulf
Gulf St. Vincent
Flinders Ranges

East from Greenwich

Projection: Bonne

COPYRIGHT GEORGE PHILIP & SON LTD.

1:6 000 000

20 0 20 40 60 80 100 miles
20 0 40 80 120 160 km

NEW ZEALAND & DEPENDENCIES
1:60 000 000

200 0 200 400 600 800 miles
200 0 400 800 1200 km

New Zealand Territory
Self-governing Territory

Projection: Conical with two standard parallels

SAMOA ISLANDS
1:12 000 000

SAMOA
Savaii Apia Upolu
American Samoa
Pago Pago Manua Is.
Tutuila Rose I.

FIJI AND TONGA ISLANDS
1:12 000 000

50 0 50 100 150 miles
50 0 50 100 150 200 250 km

COPYRIGHT. GEORGE PHILIP & SON. LTD

Inset — New Zealand & Dependencies
Tokelau or Union Group
WESTERN SAMOA Tutuila (U.S.)
Savaii Upolu
Rakahanga
Tongareva (Penrhyn) I.
Pukapuka (Danger) Nassau Suwarrow Manihiki
Rotuma (Fiji)
Vanua Levu
FIJI
Viti Levu Fiji Is.
Lau or Eastern Group
TONGA (Friendly) Is.
Northern Group
Cook Is.
Niue
Iles de la Société
Palmerston Atoll Aitutaki
Lower Group Mitiaro
Rarotonga Atiu Mauke
Mangaia
PACIFIC OCEAN
Tropic of Capricorn
Kermadec Is.
Macauley Raoul (Sunday) I.
Curtis
Three Kings Is.
Auckland
NORTH I.
NEW ZEALAND
SOUTH I.
Wellington
Christchurch
Chatham I. Chatham Is. Pitt I.
Tasman Sea
Dunedin Bounty Is.
Stewart I. Antipodes Is.
Snares
Auckland Is.
Campbell I.
Macquarie I. (Austr.)
SOUTHERN OCEAN

North Island
Three Kings Is.
C. Reinga North C.
C. Maria van Diemen
Houhora Rangaunu Bay
Doubtless Bay
Ahipara B. Mangonui Whangaroa Harb.
Kaitaia B. of Islands
Reef Pt. Rawene C. Brett
Hokianga Harb. Opua
Donnelly's Crossing Kaikohe Hikurangi
NORTHLAND Whangarei
Dargaville Waipu Whangarei Harb.
Bream Hd. Bream Bay
Kaipara Harb. Lit. Barrier I.
Gt. Barrier I.
Warkworth C. Rodney
Helensville C. Colville Cuvier I.
Takapuna Hauraki Gulf Coromandel
CENTRAL AUCKLAND Devonport Whitianga
AUCKLAND Thames
Onehunga Manukau Papakura Mayor I.
Waiuku Mercer Waihi Tauranga Harb.
Waikato Paeroa White I. Runaway
Huntly Te Aroha Mt. Maunganui Bay of Plenty
Raglan Morrinsville Tauranga Te Puke Whakatane Opotiki
Hamilton Cambridge SOUTH AUCKLAND Raukumara
Kawhia Harb. Te Awamutu BAY OF PLENTY Murupara
Otorohanga Rotorua Tarawera EAST COAST
Te Kuiti Kinleith KAINGAROA Tolaga
Mokau Mokai FOREST Opotiki Tokomaru Tolaga
Kaimanawa Mts. Gisborne
North Taranaki Taumarunui Taupo Ongarue Waikaremoana Poverty Bay
Bight Ohakune Waikokopu
New Plymouth Waitara Whangamomona Ruapehu Wairoa Mahia Peninsula
Inglewood Mt. Egmont 2518 Raetihi Ohakune Bay Hawke Bay
Stratford View
Opunake Eltham Napier
Kaponga C. Kidnappers
Hawera Taihape Hastings
South Taranaki Mangaweka HAWKE'S BAY Waipawa
Bight Pated Waipukurau
Wanganui Marton Hunterville C. Turnagain
Bulls Halcombe Feilding Danneyirke
Palmerston N. Woodville
Foxton Shannon Pahiatua
Levin Eketahuna
Otaki TARARUA RA.
Te Horo Castle Pt.
Featherston WELLINGTON
Up. Hutt Masterton
Petone Greytown Carterton
Lr. Hutt Martinborough
Eastbourne Wairarapa
WELLINGTON
Cook Strait

South Island
C. Farewell
Collingwood Golden Bay D'Urville I.
Takaka Tasman Bay French Pass
Tasman Mts. Motueka Pelorus Kapiti I.
Nelson Havelock Picton Sd.
Karamea Tadmor Richmond Blenheim
Bight Wakefield Seddon
Seddonville Murchison MARLBOROUGH
Granity Lyell Ra. Ward
Westport Lyell Inangahua Junction 2885 Tapuaenuku
Reefton Kaikoura
Blackball Spenser Mts.
Runanga Hanmer Clarence
Greymouth Brunner Amuri Kaikoura
Kumara L. Brunner
Hokitika Jackson Waiau
Ross Reefton Culverden
WESTLAND Waikari Waipara PACIFIC OCEAN
Abut Hd. Amberley
Okarito Oxford Pegasus Bay
Rangiora Kaiapoi
Franz Josef New Brighton
Whitecliffs Christchurch
Mt. Cook 3764 Springburn Riccarton Lyttelton
SOUTHERN ALPS Methven Lincoln Banks Peninsula
Jackson B. Haast Little River
Fairlie Akaroa
Geraldine L. Ellesmere
Canterbury Plains Southbridge
Mt. Aspiring L. Tekapo Rakaia Leeston
Wanaka Ashburton Bight
Hawea Temuka Canterbury Bight
Milford Sd. Timaru
Bligh Sd. St. Andrews
George Sd. Mt. Earnslaw Queenstown Kurow Waimate
Arrowtown Kakanui
Secretary I. Cromwell Naseby Oamaru
Doubtful Sd. Wakatipu Clyde Maheno
Breaksea Sd. Alexandra Hampden
Resolution I. Roxburgh Duback Palmerston
Dusky Sd. OTAGO Waikouaiti Port Chalmers
SOUTHLAND Lawrence Mosgiel Dunedin Otago Harbour
Chalky Clinton Green Island St. Kilda C. Saunders
Inlet Gore Milton
Preservation Mataura Balclutha Kaitangata
Inlet Winton Clydevale Owaka
Te Waewae B. Wyndham Nugget Pt.
Orepuki Waikawa Waikawa Harb.
Riverton Owaka
Invercargill Bluff
Foveaux Str. Ruapuke I.
Stewart I.
S.W. Cape Port Pegasus

Scale bar (elevation)
ft m
12 000 4000
9000 3000
6000 2000
3000 1000
1200 400
600 200
0 0
200 600
m ft

Fiji (inset)
Futuna (Fr.)
Thikombia
Niuafo'ou (Tonga)
Lambasa
FIJI Vanua Levu Taveuni
Yasawa Group Koro
Lautoka Levuka Ovalau Vanua Mbalavu
Nandi Viti Levu Koro Sea Lau or Eastern Group
Suva Ngau Lakemba
Moala
Kandavu Moala Vatoa
Vava'u
TONGA
Tonga (Friendly) Is.
Tofua I.
Tongatapu Nuku'alofa

Other labels
PACIFIC OCEAN
TASMAN SEA
SOUTHERN ALPS
NORTH ISLAND
SOUTH ISLAND

1:32 000 000

Projection: *Polyconic*

NATURAL VEGETATION
after Harschberger, Shantz,
Zon, Fernow and others
FOREST VEGETATION

Northern Coniferous Forest
Sub-Arctic and Northern
Forest (pine, spruce, fir,
tamarack, balsam, poplar,
larch; willow and birch
undergrowth)
North-East Coniferous
Forest (white, jack and red
pines, spruce, balsam, pop-
lar, tamarack, birch)
Central and Eastern
Hardwoods
Central (oak, hickory)
Alleghanian (oak, chestnut,
yellow poplar)
Piedmont (oak, pine)
North-Eastern (beech, birch,
maple, hemlock)
Appalachian Mountain
Forest
Broad-leaved Forest (beech,
chestnut, maple, oak)
Coniferous Forest (hemlock,
pine, fir, spruce)
Atlantic Pine Barrens
South-Eastern Pine Forest
(longleaf and loblolly pines)
South-Eastern Swamp Forest
(cypress, magnolia, white
cedar)
Pacific Coniferous Forest
Northern Zone (spruce,
hemlock)
Central Zone (Douglas fir,
hemlock)
Southern Zone (sequoia
(redwood), cypress, Douglas
fir, oak)
Cordilleran and Rocky
Mountain Coniferous Forest
Yellow Pine and Douglas Fir
Lodgepole, Yellow and Sugar
Pine Forest
Pinon-Juniper Coniferous
Woodland
Californian Chaparral
(broad-leaved Woodland)
Mexican and Central Ameri-
can Pine and Oak Forest
Sub-tropical and Tropical
Forest (palms, bamboo, tree-
ferns, lianas, orchids, etc.)
Sub-tropical and Tropical
Chaparral
Northern Limit of Douglas
Fir
Limit of White Pine
Limit of Sugar Maple
Limit of Yucca
Northern Limit of Coastal
Mangrove Swamps

GRASS VEGETATION
Temperate Grasslands
Sub-tropical and Tropical Grass-
lands and Savanna
Semi-desert Mesquite Grass-
lands
Semi-desert Mesquite Savanna
Swamp and Marsh Vegetation

STEPPE, SCRUB AND
DESERT VEGETATION
Sage Brush
Creosote Shrub (yucca)
Mexican Plateau Shrub (yucca,
agave, cactus)
Salt Desert Shrub (greasewood)

Ice Desert, Tundra (moss, lichen, heather
bogs, dwarf willow, birch and alder, etc.).
Alpine (above timber line)
Seas and Lakes frozen in Winter

West from Greenwich

1 : 40 000 000

200 0 200 400 600 800 1000 miles
200 0 200 400 600 800 1000 1200 1400 1600 km

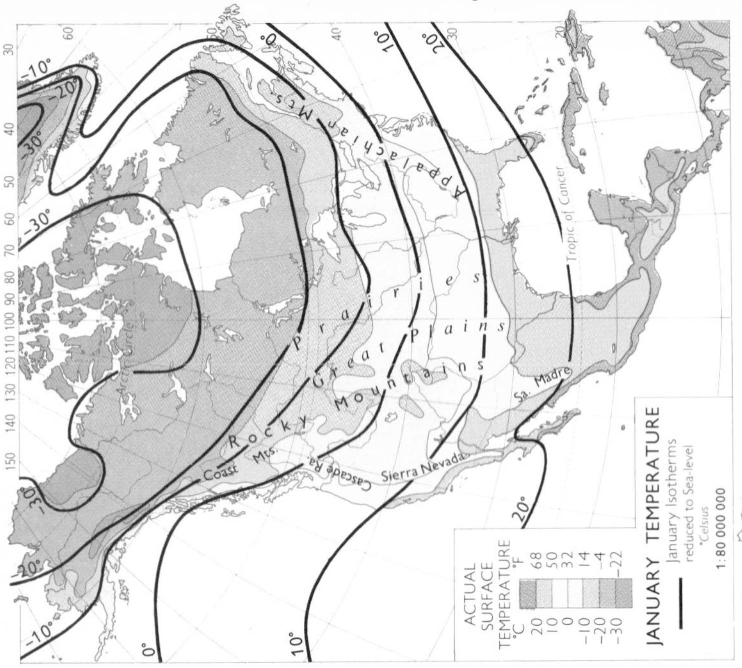

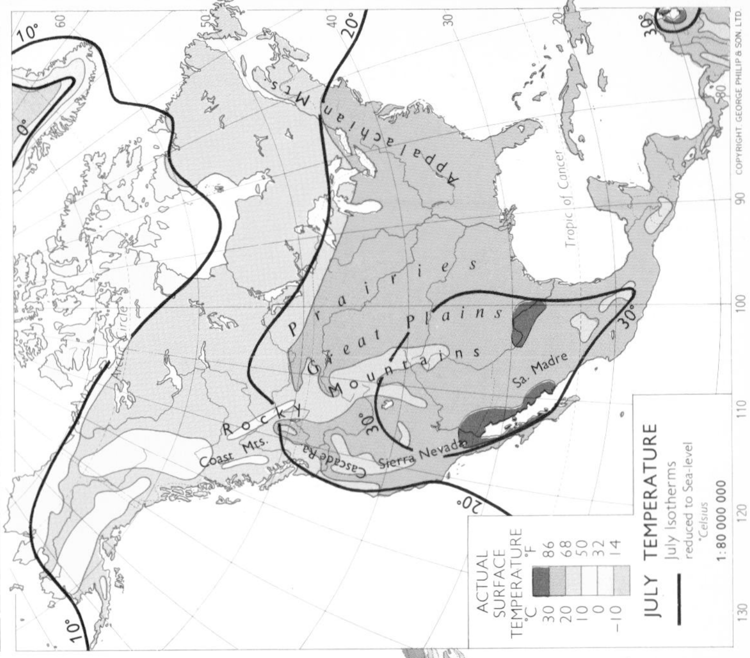

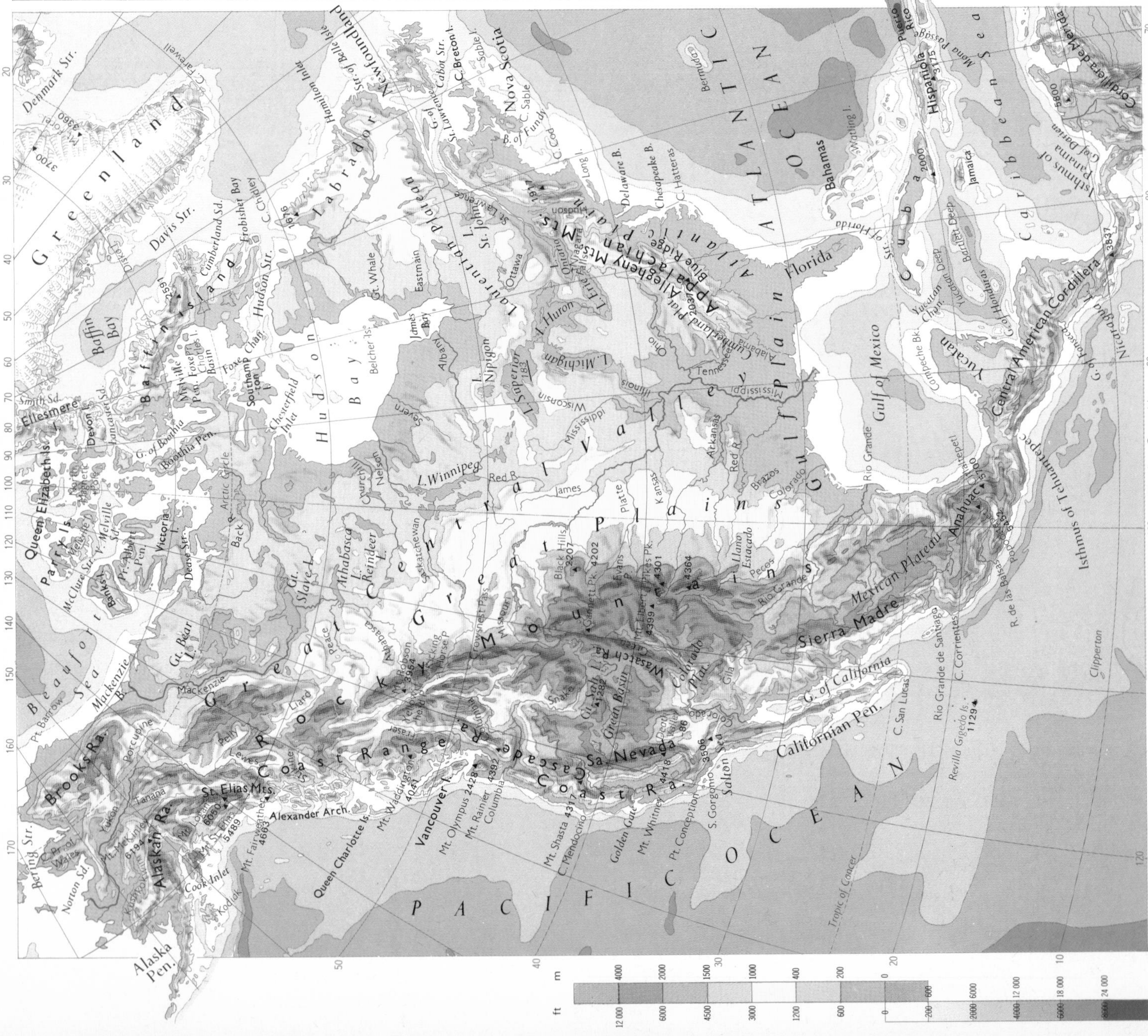

COPYRIGHT GEORGE PHILIP & SON LTD.

JANUARY TEMPERATURE
January Isotherms reduced to Sea-level
°Celsius
1 : 80 000 000

ACTUAL SURFACE TEMPERATURE
°C °F
20 68
10 50
-10 32
-20 14
-30 -4
-22

JULY TEMPERATURE
July Isotherms reduced to Sea-level
°Celsius
1 : 80 000 000

ACTUAL SURFACE TEMPERATURE
°C °F
30 86
20 68
10 50
0 32
-10 14

Tropic of Cancer

Appalachian Mts.
Prairies
Great Plains
Rocky Mountains
Coast Mts.
Cascade Ra.
Sierra Nevada
Sa. Madre

PACIFIC OCEAN

ATLANTIC OCEAN

Greenland
Denmark Str.
Baffin Bay
Davis Str.
Labrador
Newfoundland
Hudson Bay
Laurentian Plateau
Great Central Plain
Great Plains
Rocky Mountains
Brooks Ra.
Alaskan Ra.
Coast Range
Cascade Ra.
Sa. Nevada
Coast Ra.
Great Basin
Mexican Plateau
Sierra Madre
Gulf of Mexico
Gulf Coastal Plain
Atlantic Coastal Plain
Appalachian Mts.
Allegheny Mts.
Blue Ridge
Cumberland Plat.
Florida
Bahamas
Cuba
Hispaniola
Jamaica
Puerto Rico
Caribbean Sea
Yucatan
Isthmus of Panama
Central American Cordillera
Californian Pen.
G. of California

Mississippi
Missouri
Mackenzie
Rio Grande
Colorado
St. Lawrence
L. Superior
L. Michigan
L. Huron
L. Winnipeg
L. Erie
L. Ontario

Projection: Lambert's Equivalent Azimuthal
West from Greenwich

m 4000 2000 1500 1000 400 200 0 200 600 1000 6000 12 000 18 000 24 000 m
ft 12 000 6000 4500 3000 1200 600 0 600 2000 4000 12 000 18 000 24 000 ft

1:40 000 000

200   0   200   400   600   800   1000 miles
200   0   200 400 600 800 1000 1200 1400 1600 km

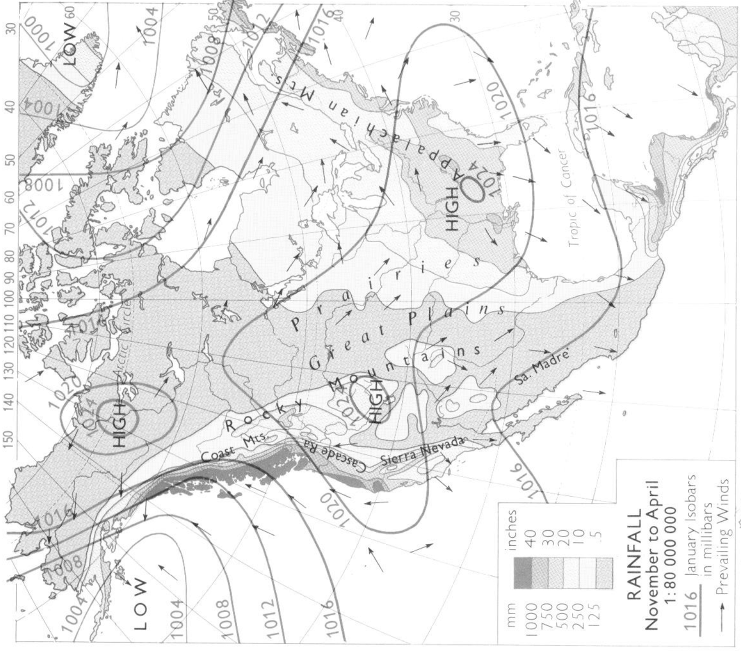

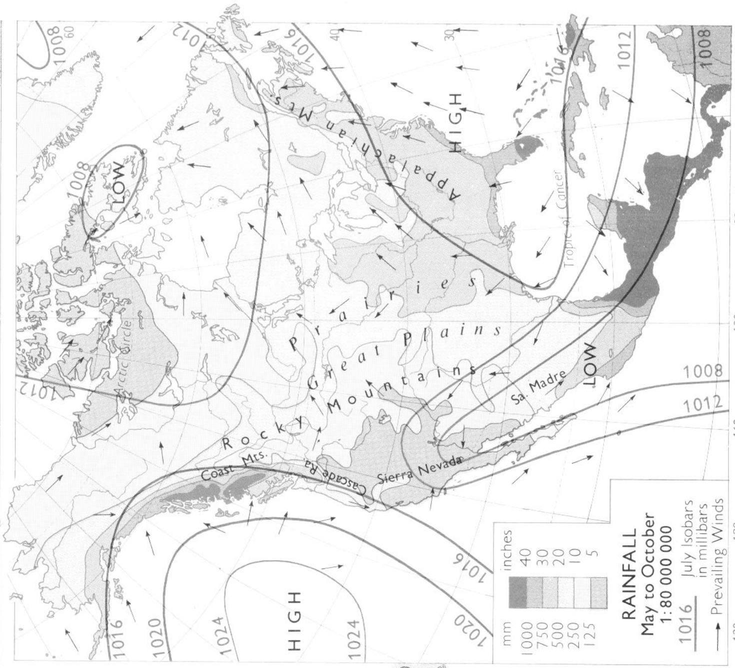

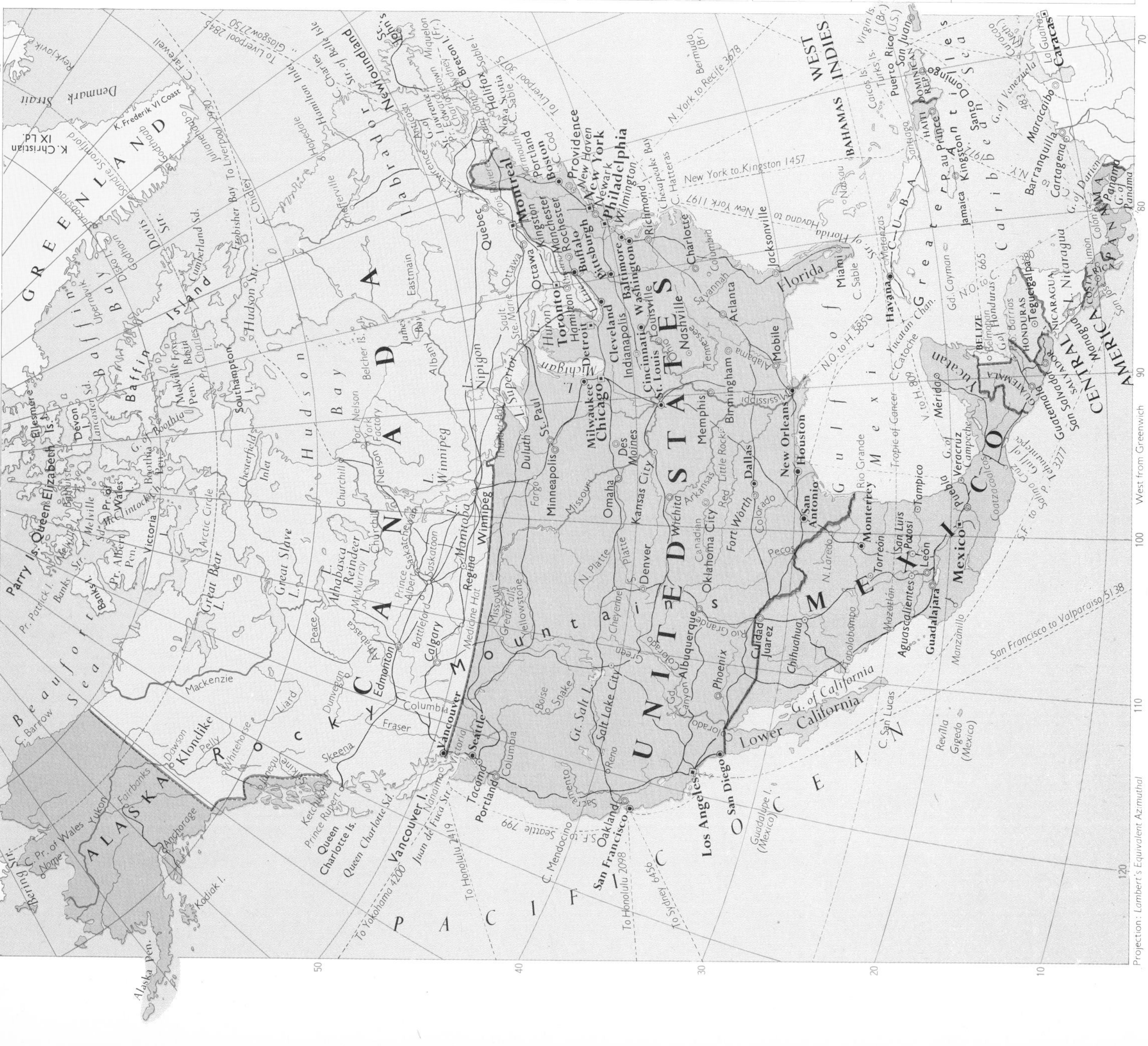

RAINFALL
November to April
1:80 000 000
1016 January Isobars in millibars
→ Prevailing Winds

inches
40
30
20
10
5

mm
1000
750
500
250
125

RAINFALL
May to October
1:80 000 000
1016 July Isobars in millibars
→ Prevailing Winds

inches
40
30
20
10
5

mm
1000
750
500
250
125

Appalachian Mts.
Prairies
Great Plains
Rocky Mountains
Coast Mts.
Cascade Ra.
Sierra Nevada
Sa. Madre
Tropic of Cancer
HIGH
LOW

(Upper-left weather map isobar values: 1000, 1004, 1008, 1012, 1016, 1020, 1024)

(Upper-right weather map isobar values: 1008, 1012, 1016, 1020, 1024)
HIGH
LOW

GREENLAND
Denmark Strait
Reykjavik
K. Frederik VI Coast
K. Christian IX Ld.

CANADA
Baffin Bay
Baffin Island
Hudson Bay
Davis Str.
Devon
Ellesmere
Queen Elizabeth Is.
Parry Is.
Victoria I.
Banks I.
Beaufort Sea
Arctic Circle
Great Bear L.
Great Slave L.
Athabasca L.
Reindeer L.
Mackenzie
Edmonton
Calgary
Regina
Winnipeg
Saskatoon
Prince Albert
Battleford
Medicine Hat
L. Winnipeg
L. Manitoba
Churchill
Port Nelson
Nelson
Southampton
Chesterfield Inlet
Boothia
Cumberland Sd.
James Bay
Belcher Is.
Eastmain
Albany
Nipigon
L. Nipigon
L. Superior
Port Arthur
Duluth
St. Paul
Minneapolis
Ottawa
Montreal
Quebec
Sault Ste. Marie
Toronto
Hamilton
Labrador
Newfoundland
Anticosti I.
Gulf of St. Lawrence
C. Breton I.
Prince Edward I.
Halifax
C. Sable
Nova Scotia
Miquelon (Fr.)

UNITED STATES
Seattle
Portland
Tacoma
Vancouver I.
Queen Charlotte Is.
Prince Rupert
Skeena
Fraser
Columbia
Snake
Boise
Gt. Salt Lake
Salt Lake City
Reno
Sacramento
Oakland
San Francisco
Los Angeles
San Diego
Phoenix
Denver
Cheyenne
N. Platte
Platte
Colorado
Albuquerque
Santa Fe
Missouri
Yellowstone
Great Falls
Billings
Fargo
Des Moines
Omaha
Kansas City
St. Louis
Chicago
Milwaukee
Detroit
Cleveland
Cincinnati
Indianapolis
Louisville
Nashville
Memphis
Little Rock
Oklahoma City
Wichita
Dallas
Fort Worth
Arkansas
Red
Canadian
Pecos
Rio Grande
San Antonio
Houston
New Orleans
Mississippi
Birmingham
Atlanta
Savannah
Columbia
Charlotte
Richmond
Washington
Baltimore
Philadelphia
Wilmington
New York
Newark
New Haven
Providence
Boston
Portland
Buffalo
Rochester
Pittsburgh
Kingston
Chesapeake Bay
C. Hatteras
Jacksonville
Mobile
Florida
Miami
C. Sable
Gulf of Mexico
L. Michigan
L. Huron
L. Erie
L. Ontario
Tropic of Cancer

MEXICO
Monterrey
Torreón
Chihuahua
Ciudad Juárez
N. Laredo
Tampico
San Luis Potosí
Guadalajara
León
Aguascalientes
Mexico
Veracruz
Campeche
Mérida
Yucatán
Mazatlán
Manzanillo
Gulf of California
Lower California
C. San Lucas
Guadalupe I. (Mexico)
Revilla Gigedo (Mexico)
Rio Grande

CENTRAL AMERICA
GUATEMALA
BELIZE
HONDURAS
Br. Honduras
EL SALVADOR
NICARAGUA
COSTA RICA
PANAMA
Gulf of Honduras
Tegucigalpa
San Salvador
Managua
San José
Panama
Gulf of Panama

WEST INDIES
BAHAMAS
CUBA
Havana
HAITI
JAMAICA
Kingston
DOMINICAN REP.
Santo Domingo
PUERTO RICO (U.S.)
Greater Antilles
Lesser Antilles
Caribbean Sea
Gulf of Venezuela
Maracaibo
Barranquilla
Cartagena
Caracas
COLOMBIA
VENEZUELA
Bermuda (Br.)
Virgin Is.
Turks Is.
Caicos Is.
Cayman Is.
Yucatan Chan.
Windward Passage

ALASKA
Fairbanks
Anchorage
Nome
Klondike
Dawson
Whitehorse
Yukon
Kodiak I.
Alaska Pen.
C. Barrow
Pr. of Wales
Pelly
Liard

ROCKY MOUNTAINS

PACIFIC OCEAN

To Liverpool 2845
To Liverpool 3750
Glasgow 2750
To Liverpool
New York to Bermuda
New York to Recife 3678
New York to Kingston 1457
Havana to...
New York 1197
N.O. to H.880
N.O. to 665
San Francisco to Valparaiso 5138
To Yokohama 4200
To Honolulu 2408
To Honolulu 2456
To Sydney 6456
Seattle 799

West from Greenwich

Projection: Lambert's Equivalent Azimuthal

ALASKA
1 : 30 000 000

100   0   100   200   300 miles
100   0   200   400 km

Projection: Bonne

1:15 000 000

100 50 0   100   200   300   400 miles

100   0   100   200   300   400   500   600 km

GREENLAND

King Frederick VI Coast

Angmagssalik

ATLANTIC

Devon Island
Lancaster Sound

Baffin Bay

2136

Bylot I.
Pond Inlet

Brodeur
Peninsula

Milne
Inlet

Scott I.

Svartenhuk
Peninsula

Disko I.

Disko
B.

Sondre Stromfjord

2850

Sukkertoppen

Holsteinsborg

C. Hewett

Home B.

Fury & Hecla Str.

Melville
Peninsula

Prince
Charles
I.

Foxe

C. Dyer

Cumberland
Peninsula

2591

Godthaab

Fiskenaesset

Foxe
Basin

Nettilling L.

Cumberland Sd.

Hoare B.

C. Mercy

Frederikshaab

Ivigtut

Commandeer B.

Rae Isthmus

C. Dorchester

Amadjuak
L.

Amadjuak

Frobisher

Julianehaab

Nanortalik

Sydproven

Southampton
I.

Foxe
Channel

Foxe
Penin.

Frobisher Bay

Resolution I.

C. Farewell

Wager
B.

Bell
Pen.

Coats
I.

Digges Is.

Hudson   Strait

C. Chidley

terfield Inlet

Southampton
I.

Mansel
I.

Ivugivik
(Notre-Dame
d'Ivugivic)

Saglouc
(Sugluk)

Koartac
(Notre Dame
de Koartac)

Akpatok
I.

1676

Port Nouveau-Quebec
(George R.)

Hebron

Maricourt
(Wakeham
Bay)

Bellin
(Payne Bay)

Nutak

Hudson

Ottawa
Is.

Ungava

Payne   L.

Ungava Bay

Nain

N

Bay

257

Portland
Promontory

Peninsula

Inoucdjouac
(Port Harrison)

Leaf

Larch

Koksoak

Ft. Chimo

George

E

C. Harrison

Hopedale

Indian Harbour

W

Sleeper Is.

King George Is.

Baker's
Dozen

Clearwater
L.

L. Minto

Lower Seal L.

Whale

Rigolet

Melville
L.

1128

Cartwright

F

Belle Isle

Ft. Severn

Belcher
Is.

Gr. Whale
Poste de
la Baleine
(Great Whale River)
Fort George

Lac Bienville

Scheffeville
Petitsikapau
L.

Michikamau
L.

North West R.

Goose
Bay

O

Battle Hbr.

U

Big
Trout L.

C. Henrietta
Maria

C. Jones

Ft. George

Fort George

Kaniapiskau

Lobstick
L.

Churchill
Falls

Churchill

LABRADOR

N

Notre Dame B.

Twillingate

Bonavista

Winisk

James Bay

Akimiski
I.

Nouveau Comptoir
(Paint Hills)

Eastmain

1128

Ashuanipi
L.

St. Augustin

D

Natashquan

L

Twillingate

Lewisporte

Gander

Trinity B.

Carbonear

St. John's

Severn

A

Attawapiskat

Ft. Albany

Charlton
I.

East Main

Fort Rupert
(Rupert
House)

Rupert

L. Albanel

Mistassini
L.

Wabush City

Gagnon

Romaine

Natashquan

Millertown Jc.

Grand
Falls

Buchans

Placentia

Grand
Bay
Placentia

NEWFOUNDLAND

St. Pierre

Str. of Belle Isle

Nataskshuan

Moisie

Mingan

Anticosti

aux Basques

Harbour Grace

Bell I.

Trepassey

C. Race

Albany

Moosonee

Missinaibi

Chibougamau

Peribonca

L. Minto

Baie Comeau

Sept Iles

Moisie

Port Cartier

Corner Brook

814

Gulf of
St. Lawrence

Ray

C. North

TARIO

St. Joseph

Nakina

Kenogami

Matagami

Dolbeau

St. John

Saguenay

R. St. Lawrence

Matane

C. Gaspé

Gaspé Pen.

Magdalen Is.

Cabot Str.

Cape Breton I.

strong

Longlac

Hearst

Cochrane

L. Abitibi

Tascheereau

Senneterre
Doucet

Roberval

Tadoussac

Riviere
du Loup

Rimouski

Campbellton

Dalhousie

Sunnyside

St. North

Glace Bay

L.
gon

Heron Bay

Oba

Timmins

Noranda
Rouyn

Val d'Or

Weymont

La Tuque

Jonquière
Chicoutimi

Edmundston

St. Leonard

Newcastle

Bathurst

Chatham

Tignish

Summerside

Charlottetown

Sydney

Nipigon

Thunder Bay

Michipicoten

Hr.

Franz

Haileybury

Cobalt

Temiskaming

Cabonga
Reservoir

Gouin
Reservoir

1190

Quebec

Levis

Trois Rivières

Thetford Mines

Woodstock

Fredericton

PR. EDWARD I.

Northumberland St.

Amherst

New Glasgow

Pictou

Port Hawkesbury

Mulgrave

C. Canso

Lake   Superior

Laurium
Keweenaw
Calumet
Bay

Marquette

Sault Ste. Marie

Coppercliff

Sudbury

North
Bay

Shawinigan

Sorel

St. Hyacinthe

NEW
BRUNSWICK

Moncton

Springhill

Truro

Windsor

NOVA

Dartmouth

Ironwood

Sault Ste. Marie

North Chan.

Parry
Sound

Pembroke

Arnprior

MONTREAL

Lachine

Sherbrooke

Saint
John

SCOTIA

Halifax

ES

Manistique

Cheboygan

Georgian
Bay

Orillia

Ottawa

Hull

Cornwall

L. Champlain

Granby

Raymond

1917

Fredericton

MAINE

B. of Fundy

Digby

Kentville

Bridgewater

lander

Iron Mt.

Antigo

Menominee

Lake
Huron

Owen Sound

Peterboro

Belleville

Kingston

Burlington

VERMONT

Bangor

Yarmouth

Liverpool

Shelburne

C. Sable

Sable I.
(Nova Scotia)

6309

NSIN

Wausau

Green
Bay

Appleton

Traverse

Cadillac

TORONTO

Oshawa

Cobourg

Watertown

NEW
HAMPSHIRE

Concord

Manchester

Portland

C. Cod

Shawano

Sheboygan

Saginaw

Guelph

Kitchener
Stratford

L. Ontario

Rochester

Syracuse

Utica

Albany

Glens
Falls

Worcester

Lowell

MASS.

Boston

Milwaukee

Racine

Grand
Rapids

London

Brantford

Hamilton

St. Catharines

Niagara
Falls

Buffalo

NEW   YORK

Elmira

Binghamton

Scranton

Springfield

Hartford

Waterbury

CONN.

Providence

R.I.

Kenosha

Kalamazoo

Sarnia

Chatham

Windsor

DETROIT

Erie

Jamestown

Williamsport

Bridgeport

New Haven

Evanston

South Bend

Toledo

Cleveland

Youngstown

PENNSYLVANIA

Allentown

Newark

New York

Jersey City

NEW JERSEY

CHICAGO

Gary

INDIANA

ILLINOIS

OHIO

Akron

Reading

Trenton

HAWAII
1:10 000 000

Projection: Albers' Equal Area with two standard parallels.
West from Greenwich

1:12 000 000

50   0   50   100   150   200   250   300 miles
50   0   50   100 150 200 250 300 350 400 450 km

ATLANTIC OCEAN

GULF OF MEXICO

BAHAMAS

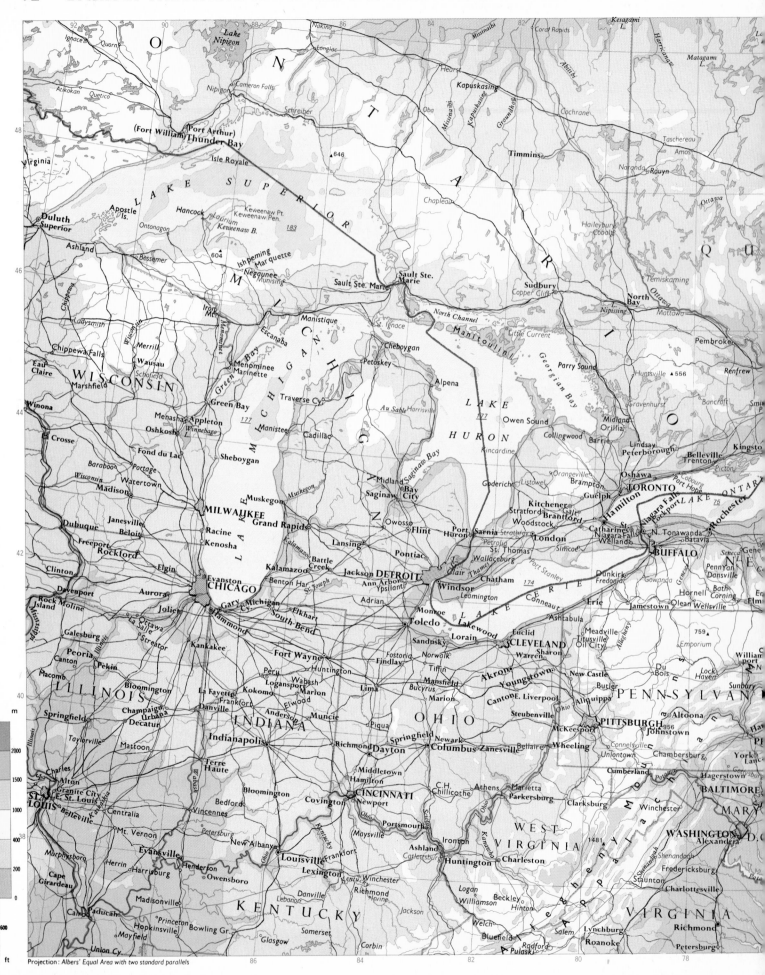

Projection: Albers' Equal Area with two standard parallels

1:6 000 000

50   0   50   100   150 miles

50   0   50   100   150   200   km

Port Cartier   West Pt.   *A n t i c o s t i I.*   Jupiter   Heath Pt.

Chibougamau   Chibougamau L.   556 ▲   Pipmuacan L.   South Pt.

Dolbeau   Peribonca   Cap Chat   Matane   Shickshock Mts.   1310   Gaspé   C. Gaspé   **GULF OF**   ▼ 572

Gouin Res.   St. Félicien   Roberval   Lac St. Jean   Mont Joli   Gaspé Peninsula   Miscou I.   **ST. LAWRENCE**   Brion I.

Chambord   Jonquiere   Chicoutimi   Saguenay   Rimouski   Shippigan   Magdalen Is. (Quebec)   Grindstone I.   St. Paul I.   C. North

Parent   Lac Bouchette   Bagotville   Tadoussac   Trois Pistoles   Campbellton   Baie de Chaleur   Tracadie   Tignish   **PRINCE EDWARD**   Ingonish

La Tuque   Lac Edouard   St. Siméon   Rivière du Loup   Edmundston   **NEW**   819   Newcastle   North Pt.   Miramichi B.   **ISLAND**   532 ▲   **Cape Breton**

QUEBEC   La Malbaie   Baie St. Paul   St. Leonard   Fort Kent   Grand Falls   **BRUNSWICK**   Chatham   Summerside   Charlottetown   **Glace Bay**   **Island**

Grand'Mère   Quebec   Levis   Montmagny   Caribou   Presque Isle   Richibucto   Georgetown   Souris   East Pt.   Inverness   **Sydney**

Shawinigan   960 ▲   Plessisville   Houlton   Woodstock   Grand L.   Chipman   Buctouche   Northumberland Str.   Port Hood   Bras d'Or

Trois Rivieres   Victoriaville   Thetford Mines   Mt. Katahdin   Fredericton   **Moncton**   Shediac   Murray Hbr.   Chedabucto B.   Madame I.

Joliette   Drummondville   1606   Moosehead L.   Springhill   Pictou   **New Glasgow**   Canso

Hawkesbury   St. Jérome   St. Hyacinthe   Mégantic   Sussex   **NOVA**   Stellarton   Sherbrooke

Ottawa   Lachute   Sorel   Sherbrooke   **MAINE**   Parrsboro   **Truro**   Sheet Hr.

MONTREAL   Magog   Chignecto B.   Minas Basin

Ottawa   St. Jean   Coaticook   Bangor   **Saint John**   Windsor   **Dartmouth**

Cornwall   Valleyfield   Newport   Rongeley   Farmington   Calais   St. Stephen   Bay of Fundy   **Halifax**

Ogdensburg   Plattsburg   Machias   Eastport   Annapolis Royal   Mahone Bay

Watertown   Burlington   Waterville   Ellsworth   Grand Manan I.   Digby   Lunenburg

L. Champlain   Montpelier   Augusta   Belfast   Mt. Desert   St. Mary Bay   Bridgewater

Adirondack Mts.   1629   Barre   Penobscot B.   L. Rossignol   Shelburne

L. George   1917   Auburn   Lewiston   Rockland   Yarmouth   C. Sable

Rome   Utica   Rutland   Laconia   Portland   Biddeford

Glens Falls   Concord   Rochester   Dover   Portsmouth

Gloversville   Saratoga Sps.   Keene   Manchester   Haverhill

Schenectady   Amsterdam   Fitchburg   Nashua   Lawrence   Lowell

YORK   Waterlvliet   Troy   Bennington   Gardner   Salem

Albany   Pittsfield   **MASS.**   Clinton   Newton   Lynn   **Massachusetts**

Hudson   **Worcester**   **BOSTON**   Bay

Binghamton   Catskill Mts.   1281   Holyoke   **Cambridge**   Quincy   C. Cod

Kingston   **Springfield**   **Brockton**

Torrington   **Hartford**   Pawtucket   **Providence**   Cape Cod B.

Poughkeepsie   New Britain   Woonsocket   **Fall River**

Newburgh   Waterbury   Meriden   **New Bedford**

Middletown   **CONN.**   Bristol   Newport   Nantucket Sd.

Wilkes Barre   Peekskill   **New Haven**   New London   Nantucket I.

Hazleton   Bridgeport   Block I.   Martha's Vineyard

Easton   Stamford   Greenwich   **Long Island**   Montauk Pt.

Bethlehem   Yonkers   Paterson

Allentown   **Newark**   **NEW YORK**

Reading   Jersey City   Elizabeth

PHILADELPHIA   Trenton   **NEW JERSEY**

Camden   Chester   Wilmington

Bridgeton   **Atlantic City**

Dover   Cape May   **ATLANTIC OCEAN**

Cape Charles   West from Greenwich   COPYRIGHT. GEORGE PHILIP & SON. LTD.

Density of Population inset:

Vancouver, Seattle, Portland, Edmonton, Winnipeg, Ottawa, Montreal, Boston, St. Paul, M., Buffalo, Pitts., New York, San Francisco, Omaha, Chicago, Ind., Philadelphia, Denver, Kansas City, St. Louis, Cin., Washington, Los Angeles, Oklahoma City, Memphis, Atlanta, San Diego, Dallas, Fort Worth, Jacksonville, Houston, New Orleans, Miami, Monterrey, Tropic of Cancer, Havana, Guadalajara, Mexico, Puebla, Port au Prince, Guatemala

Inhabitants

per mile²	per km²
under 2	under 1
2–8	1–3
8–16	3–6
16–32	6–12
32–64	12–25
64–128	25–50
128–256	50–100
256–512	100–200
over 512	over 200

■ Towns of over 500 000 Inhabitants

DENSITY OF POPULATION

1:50 000 000

PANAMA CANAL
1:1 000 000

Canal Zone

JAMAICA
1:5 000 000

TRINIDAD AND TOBAGO
1:5 000 000

LEEWARD ISLANDS
1:5 000 000

WINDWARD ISLANDS
1:5 000 000

Projection: Bonne

1:40 000 000

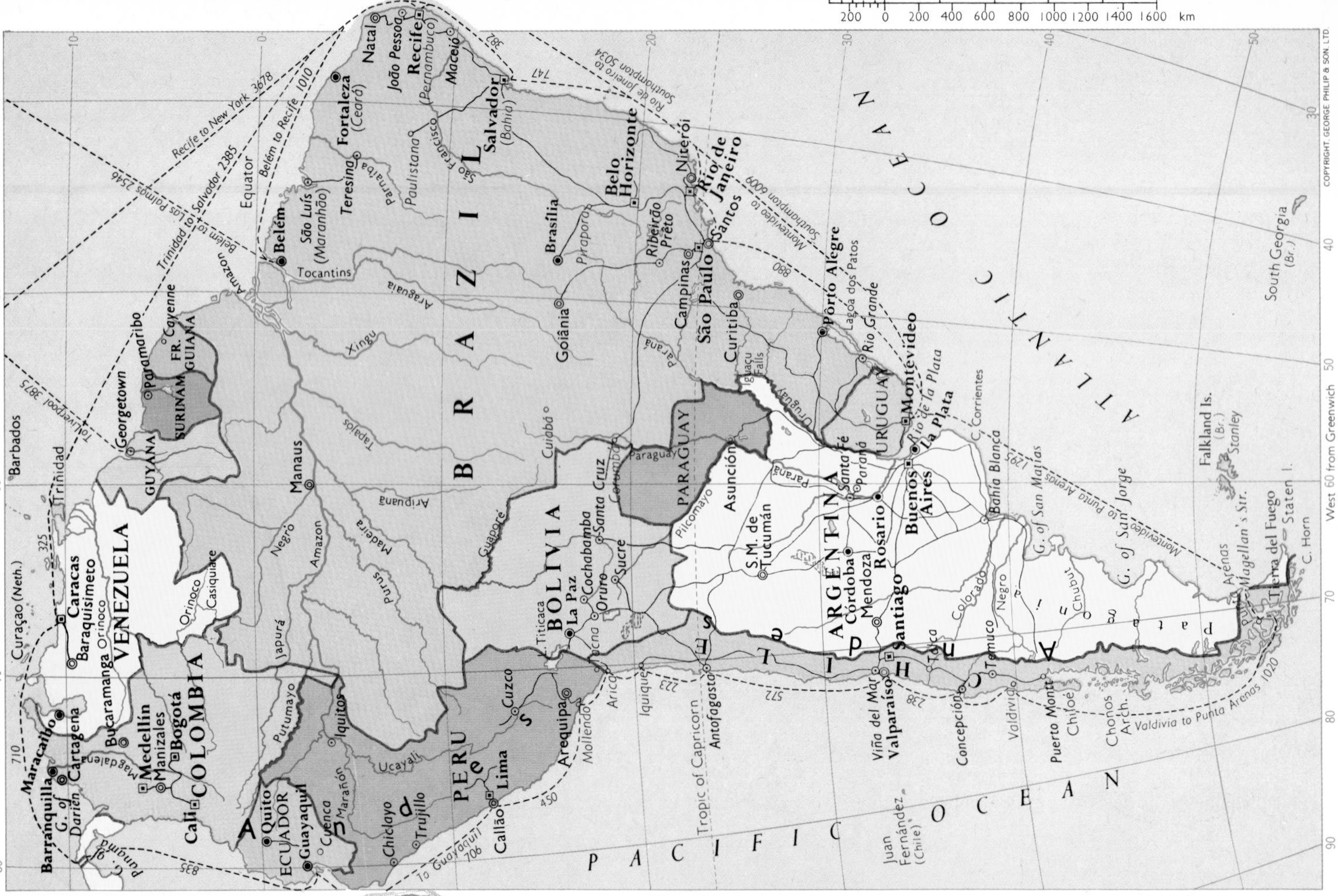

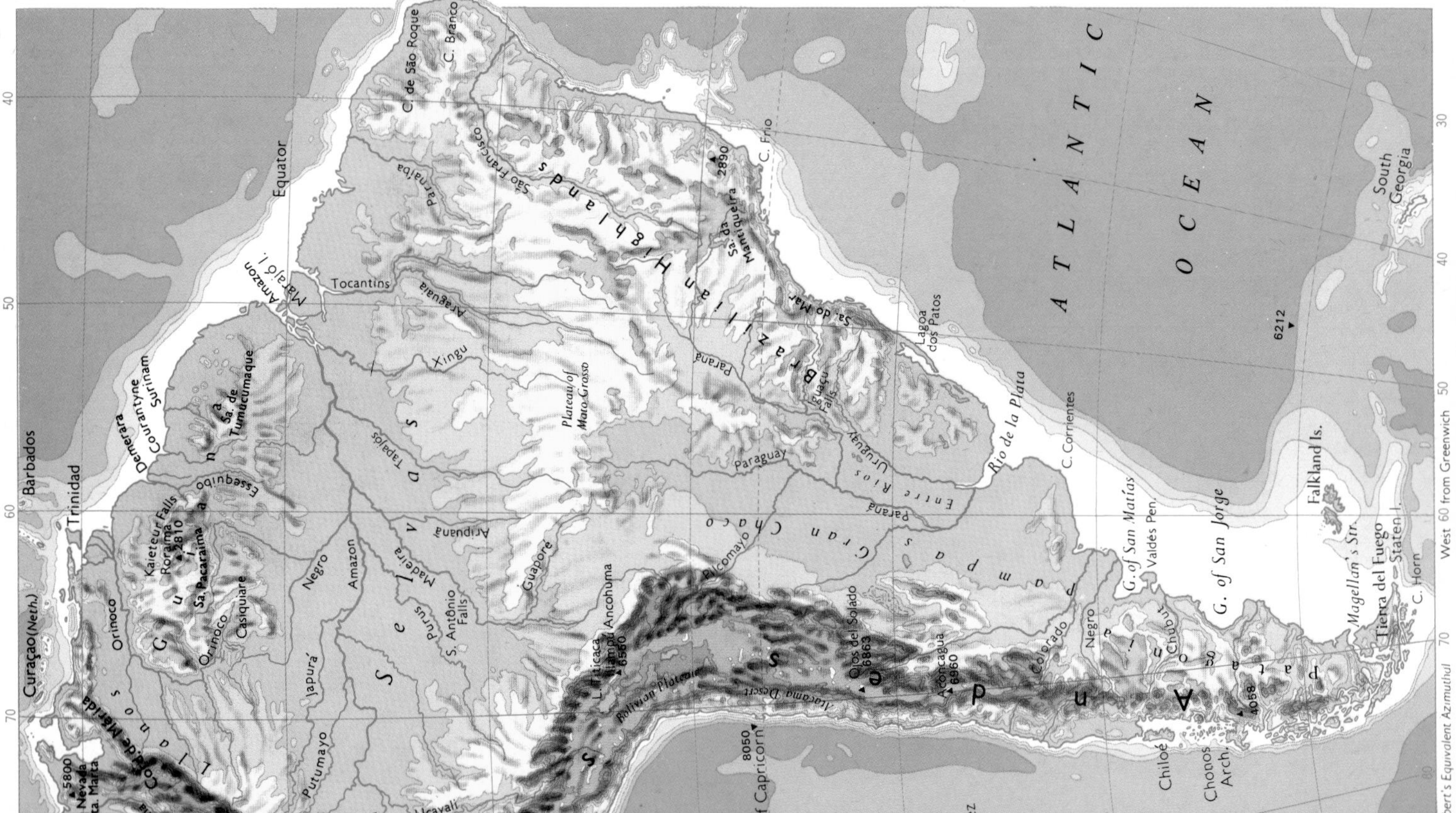

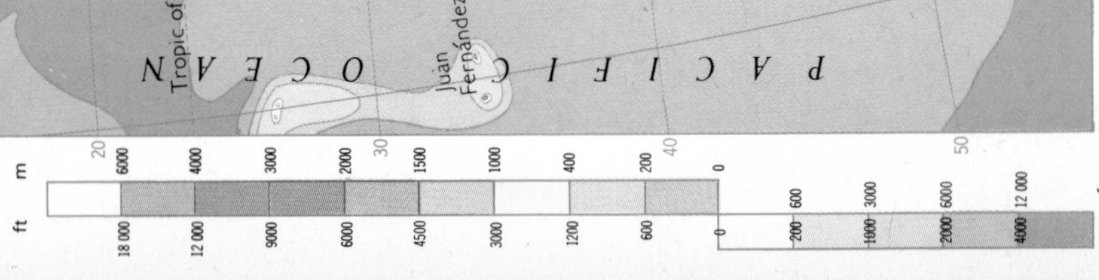

200   0   200   400   600   800   1000 miles
200 0 200 400 600 800 1000 1200 1400 1600 km

COPYRIGHT GEORGE PHILIP & SON LTD

Political map (top)

BRAZIL

VENEZUELA
COLOMBIA
ECUADOR
PERU
BOLIVIA
PARAGUAY
URUGUAY
ARGENTINA
CHILE
GUYANA
SURINAM
FR. GUIANA

Natal, João Pessoa, Recife (Pernambuco), Maceió, Salvador (Bahia), Fortaleza (Ceará), Teresina, São Luís (Maranhão), Belém, Brasília, Belo Horizonte, Niterói, Rio de Janeiro, Campinas, Ribeirão Prêto, São Paulo, Santos, Curitiba, Pôrto Alegre, Goiânia

Georgetown, Paramaribo, Cayenne

Caracas, Barquisimeto, Maracaibo, Barcelona, Cartagena, Medellín, Manizales, Bogotá, Cali, Quito, Guayaquil, Cuenca, Chiclayo, Trujillo, Lima, Callao, Arequipa, Cuzco, La Paz, Oruro, Cochabamba, Sucre, Santa Cruz

Asunción, Montevideo, La Plata, Buenos Aires, Rosario, Córdoba, S.M. de Tucumán, Mendoza, Santiago, Valparaíso, Viña del Mar, Concepción, Valdivia, Puerto Montt

Barbados, Trinidad, Curaçao (Neth.), Falkland Is., Stanley, South Georgia (Br.)

Equator, Tropic of Capricorn

PACIFIC OCEAN, ATLANTIC OCEAN

Amazon, Orinoco, Negro, Madeira, Tapajós, Xingu, Paraná, Paraguay, Pilcomayo, Uruguay, Colorado, Río de la Plata

West 60 from Greenwich

Recife to New York 3678, Belém to Recife 1010, Trinidad to Cayenne 2385, Las Palmas 2546, Rio de Janeiro to Southampton 5034, to Southampton 6009, Montevideo to Punta Arenas 1375, Valdivia to Punta Arenas

Physical map (bottom)

A N D E S
BRAZILIAN HIGHLANDS
GUIANA HIGHLANDS
Mato Grosso
Gran Chaco
Pampas
Patagonia
Bolivian Plateau
Atacama Desert
Selvas

ATLANTIC OCEAN, PACIFIC OCEAN
Equator, Tropic of Capricorn

Aconcagua 6960, Cotopaxi 5897, Chimborazo 6267, Illampu, Illimani 6882, Lago Titicaca

Amazon, Orinoco, Negro, Madeira, Paraná, Paraguay, Xingu, Tapajós, Tocantins, São Francisco, Paraíba

Kaieteur Falls, Roraima 2810, Sa. Pacaraima

C. São Roque, C. Branco, C. Frio, Pta. Piedras
G. of San Matías, G. of San Jorge, Valdés Pen.
Tierra del Fuego, C. Horn, Magellan's Str., Chonos Arch., Chiloé, Staten I.
Falkland Is., South Georgia
Barbados, Trinidad, Curaçao (Neth.)

6212

West 60 from Greenwich
Projection Lambert's Equivalent Azimuthal

m: 6000 4500 3000 2000 1500 1000 600 400 200 0
ft: 18000 12000 9000 6000 4500 3000 2000 1200 600 0

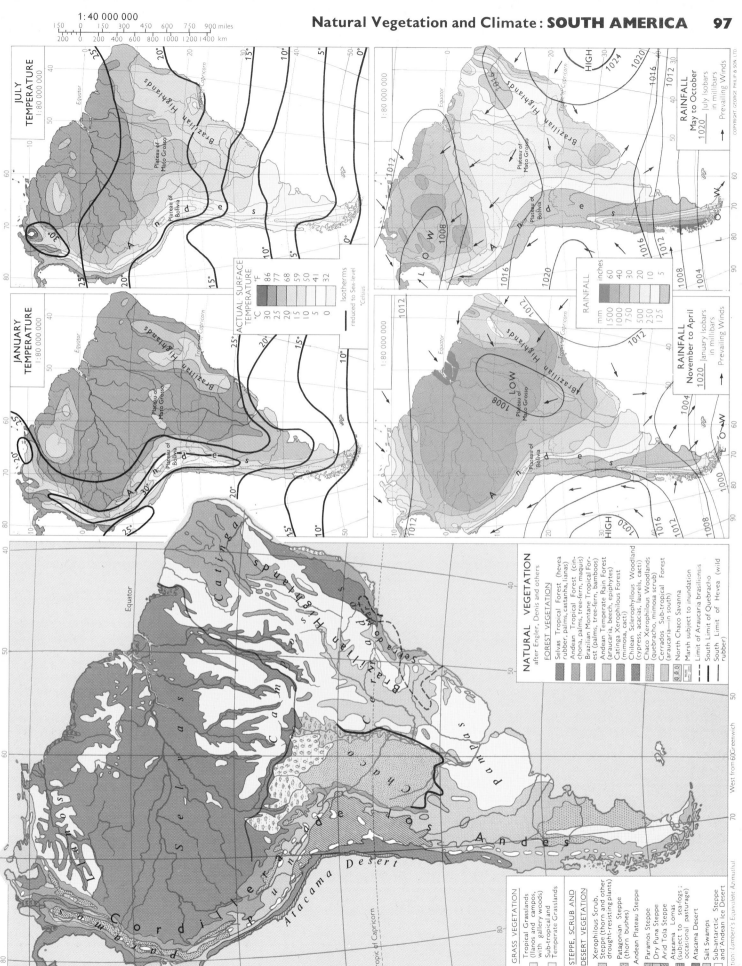

1:40 000 000

150   0   150 300   450   600   750   900 miles
200   0   200   400   600   800 1000 1200 1400 km

JULY TEMPERATURE 1:80 000 000

JANUARY TEMPERATURE 1:80 000 000

ACTUAL SURFACE TEMPERATURE
°C   °F
30   86
25   77
20   68
15   59
10   50
5   41
0   32

Isotherms reduced to Sea-level

RAINFALL May to October
1020 July Isobars in millibars
→ Prevailing Winds

RAINFALL November to April
1020 January Isobars in millibars
→ Prevailing Winds

RAINFALL
mm   inches
1500   60
1000   40
750   30
500   20
250   10
125   5

COPYRIGHT GEORGE PHILIP & SON LTD.

NATURAL VEGETATION after Engler, Denis and others

FOREST VEGETATION

Selvas Tropical Forest (hevea rubber, palms, castanha, lianas)
Andean Tropical Forest (cinchona, palms, tree-fern, maquis)
Brazilian Montane Tropical Forest (palms, tree-fern, bamboos)
Andean Temperate Rain Forest (araucaria, beech, epiphytes)
Catinga Xerophilous Forest (mimosa, cacti)
Chilean Sclerophyllous Woodland (cypress, acacias, laurels, cacti)
Chaco Xerophilous Woodlands (quebracho, mimosa scrub)
Cerrados Sub-tropical Forest (araucaria—in south)
North Chaco Savanna
Marsh subject to inundation
Limit of Araucaria brasiliensis
South Limit of Quebracho
South Limit of Hevea (wild rubber)

GRASS VEGETATION

Tropical Grasslands (llanos and campos, with gallery woods)
Sub-tropical and Temperate Grasslands

STEPPE, SCRUB AND DESERT VEGETATION

Xerophilous Scrub, Steppe (thorn and other drought-resisting plants)
Patagonian Steppe (thorn bushes)
Andean Plateau Steppe
Paramos Steppe
Dry Puna Steppe
Arid Tola Steppe
Atacama Lomas (subject to seafogs; occasional pasturage)
Atacama Desert
Sub-antarctic Steppe and Andean Ice Desert
Salt Swamps

Projection: Lambert's Equivalent Azimuthal.

West from 60°Greenwich

Tropic of Capricorn

Equator

Tropic of Capricorn

Brazilian Highlands

Plateau of Mato Grosso

Plateau of Bolivia

A n d e s

Selvas

Catinga

Campos

Pampas

Gran Chaco

Cordillera de los Andes

Atacama Desert

Patagonia

ATLANTIC OCEAN

CARIBBEAN SEA

LESSER ANTILLES

Windward Is.

Martinique (Fr.)
St. Lucia
St. Vincent
The Grenadines
Grenada
Barbados
Tobago
Trinidad
Curaçao (Neth.)
Aruba (Neth.)
Bonaire (Neth.)
La Blanquilla
Margarita
Los Roques
Orchila
La Tortuga

VENEZUELA
Caracas
Maracaibo
Cabimas
Valencia
Barquisimeto
Maracay
Barcelona
Cumaná
Ciudad Bolívar
Ciudad Guayana
El Tigre
Maturín
San Fernando de Apure
San Cristóbal
Puerto Ayacucho

COLOMBIA
Bogotá
Medellín
Cali
Barranquilla
Cartagena
Sta. Marta
Cúcuta
Bucaramanga
Barrancabermeja
Manizales
Pereira
Ibagué
Neiva
Florencia
Popayán
Pasto
Tunja
Villavicencio
Buenaventura
Quibdó

ECUADOR
Quito
Guayaquil
Cuenca
Machala
Ambato
Riobamba
Cotopaxi 5897

PANAMA
CANAL ZONE (U.S.A.)

GUYANA
Georgetown
New Amsterdam

SURINAM
Paramaribo
Nieuw Nickerie

FR. GUIANA
Cayenne

Guiana Highlands

Roraima 2810

BRAZIL
Belém (Pará)
Fortaleza (Ceará)
Recife (Pernambuco)
Salvador (Bahia)
Natal
João Pessoa
Maceió
Aracaju
Teresina
São Luís
Manaus
Brasília
FED. DIST.
Goiânia
Belo Horizonte
Vitória
São Roque

MARANHÃO
PIAUÍ
CEARÁ
RIO GRANDE DO NORTE
PARAÍBA
PERNAMBUCO
ALAGOAS
SERGIPE
BAHIA
MINAS GERAIS
ESPÍRITO SANTO
PARÁ
AMAPÁ
RORAIMA
AMAZONAS
MATO GROSSO
RONDÔNIA
ACRE

Mouths of the Amazon
I. de Marajó
I. de Maracá

MATO GROSSO
Plateau of Mato Grosso

Serra dos Parecis
Sa. do Norte
Sa. do Roncador
Sa. do Tombador
Sa. dos Gradaús
Sa. do Cachimbo
Sa. Estrondo

Capoeiras Falls
Salto Augusto

PERU
Lima
Callao
Iquitos
Trujillo
Chiclayo
Arequipa
Cuzco
Chimbote
Piura
Huancayo
Tacna
Cerro de Pasco
Nazca

Montaña

BOLIVIA
La Paz
Sucre
Cochabamba
Oruro
Potosí
Santa Cruz

Lake Titicaca

Amazonas (river)
Solimões
Negro
Branco
Madeira
Tapajós
Xingu
Tocantins
Purus
Juruá
Japurá
Içá
Putumayo
Napo
Marañón
Ucayali
Huallaga
Orinoco
Casiquiare
Magdalena

Equator

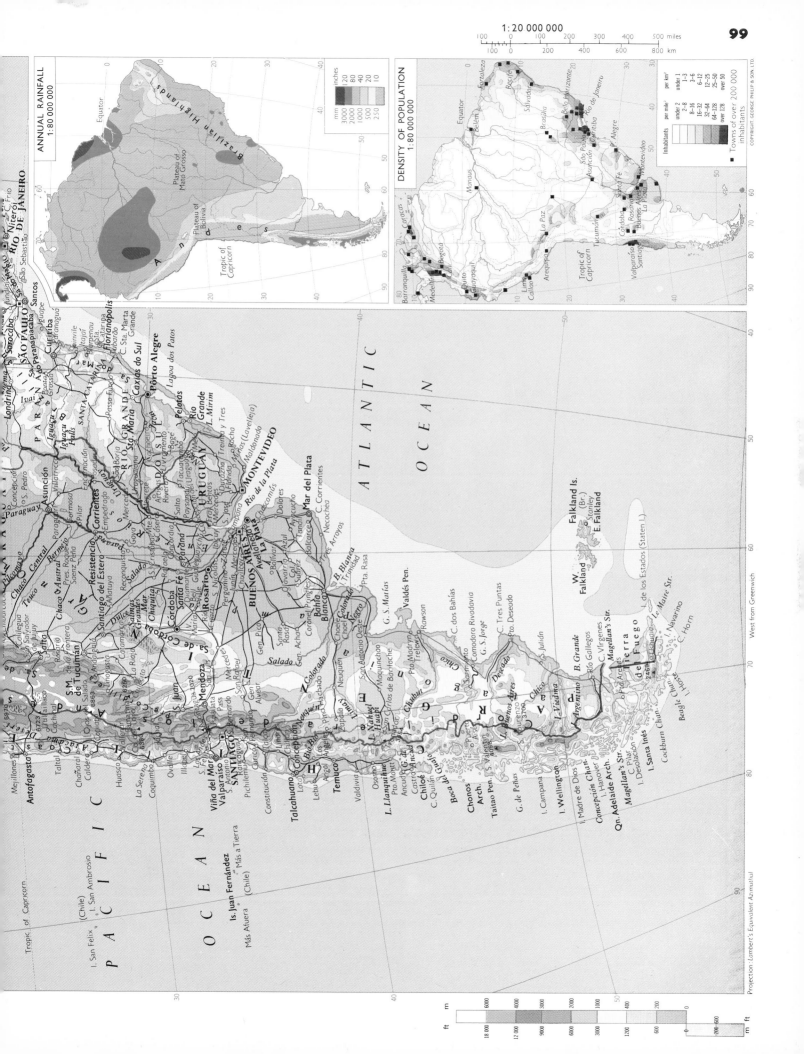

1:20 000 000

100   0   100   200   300   400   500 miles
100   0   200   400   600   800 km

ANNUAL RAINFALL
1:80 000 000

mm	inches
3000	120
2000	80
1000	40
500	20
250	10

DENSITY OF POPULATION
1:80 000 000

per km²			per mile²	
under 1			under 2	
1-3			2-8	
3-6			8-16	
6-12			16-32	
12-25			32-64	
25-50			64-128	
over 50			over 128	

inhabitants   inhabitants

■ Towns of over 200 000 inhabitants

COPYRIGHT GEORGE PHILIP & SON, LTD

Brazilian Highlands

Equator

Plateau of Mato Grosso

Plateau of Bolivia

Tropic of Capricorn

A n d e s

Equator

Fortaleza
Recife
Belém
Salvador
Manaus
Brasília
Belo Horizonte
São Paulo
Rio de Janeiro
Curitiba
Pôrto Alegre
Asunción
Santa Fé
Montevideo
Córdoba
Rosario
Buenos Aires
La Plata
Caracas
Bogotá
La Paz
Tucumán
Araguaína
Barranquilla
Medellín
Cali
Quito
Guayaquil
Lima
Callao
Arequipa
Valparaíso
Santiago

Tropic of Capricorn

ATLANTIC

OCEAN

RIO DE JANEIRO
Niterói
C. Frio
São Sebastião
Santos
SÃO PAULO
Sorocaba
Paranapiacaba
Curitiba

PARANÁ
Londrina
Ivaí
SANTA CATARINA
Joinville
Blumenau
Itajaí
Florianópolis
C. Sta. Marta Grande
Caxias do Sul
Pôrto Alegre
Lagoa dos Patos
Pelotas
Rio Grande
L. Mirim

RIO GRANDE DO SUL
Sta. Maria

PARAGUAY
Concepción
Asunción
Villarrica
Pilar

URUGUAY
Treinta y Tres
Rocha
Minas (Lavalleja)
Durazno
Florida
MONTEVIDEO
Maldonado

Corrientes
Resistencia
Paraná
Santa Fé
Rosario
Córdoba
BUENOS AIRES
Avellaneda
La Plata
Mar del Plata

Chaco Central
Chaco Austral
GRAN CHACO
Santiago del Estero

S.M. de Tucumán
Salta
S. Salvador de Jujuy

Antofagasta
Mejillones
Taltal
Chañaral

Mendoza
San Luis

Bahía Blanca
Río Colorado
Río Negro

Valdés Pen.
G. S. Matías

SANTIAGO
Valparaíso
Viña del Mar
Concepción
Talcahuano
Temuco
Valdivia
Osorno
Pto. Montt
Chiloé
Chonos Arch.
Taitao Pen.

PACIFIC

OCEAN

Tropic of Capricorn

I. San Félix (Chile)
I. San Ambrosio (Chile)
Is. Juan Fernández
Más a Tierra
Más Afuera

P A T A G O N I A

C. Tres Puntas
Comodoro Rivadavia
G. S. Jorge
Pto. Deseado
Deseado
Chico
L. Buenos Aires
Pto. Santa Cruz
S. Julián
Río Gallegos
B. Grande
C. Vírgenes
Magellan's Str.
Tierra del Fuego
Ushuaia
I. Navarino
C. Horn

Falkland Is. (Br.)
Stanley
E. Falkland
W. Falkland

I. de los Estados (Staten I.)
Le Maire Str.

ATLANTIC   OCEAN

West from Greenwich

Projection Lambert's Equivalent Azimuthal

m	ft
6000	18 000
4000	12 000
3000	9000
2000	6000
1000	3000
400	1200
200	600
0	0

1:50 000 000

200   0   200   400   600   800 miles
200   0   400   800   1200 km

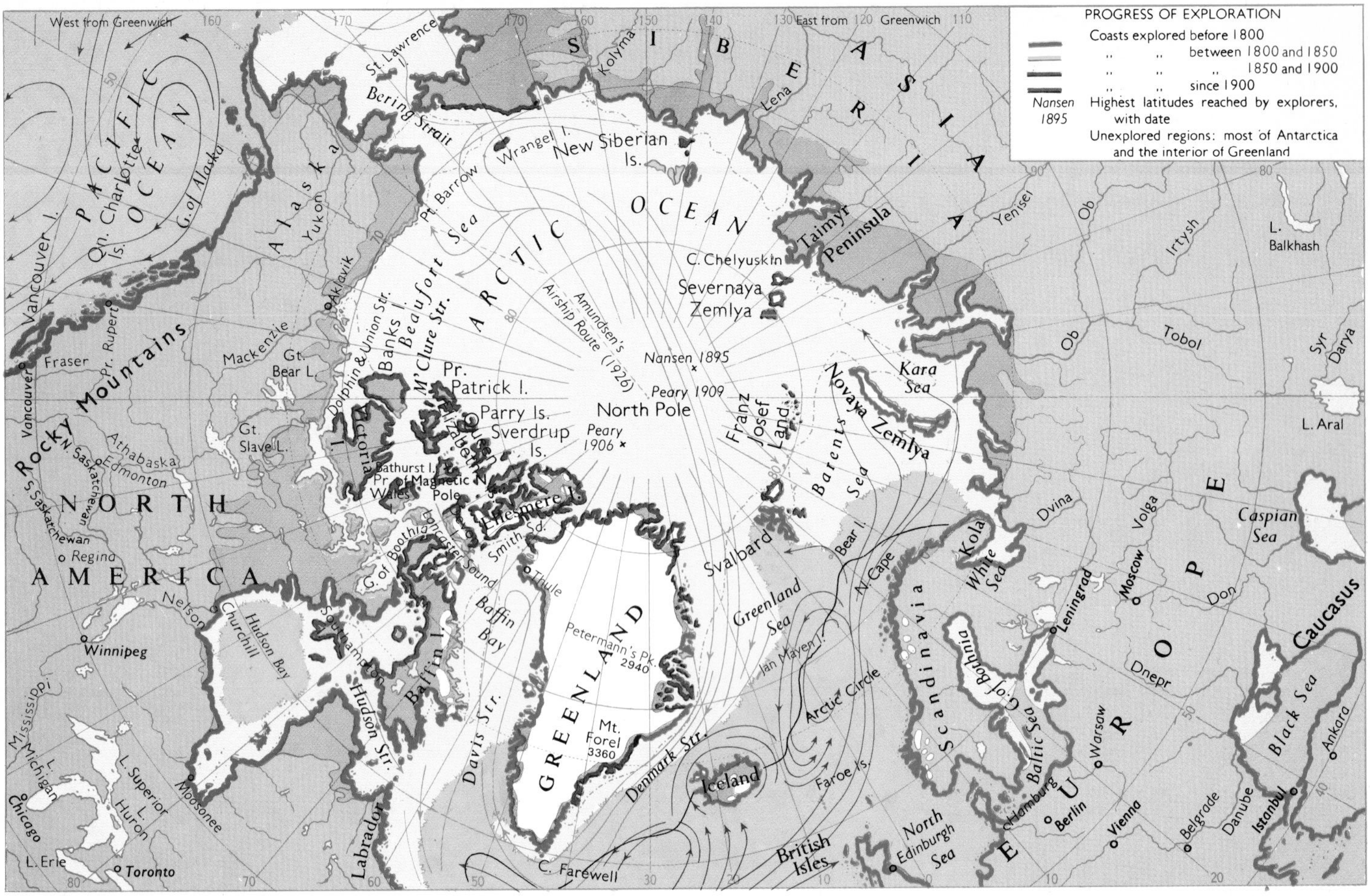

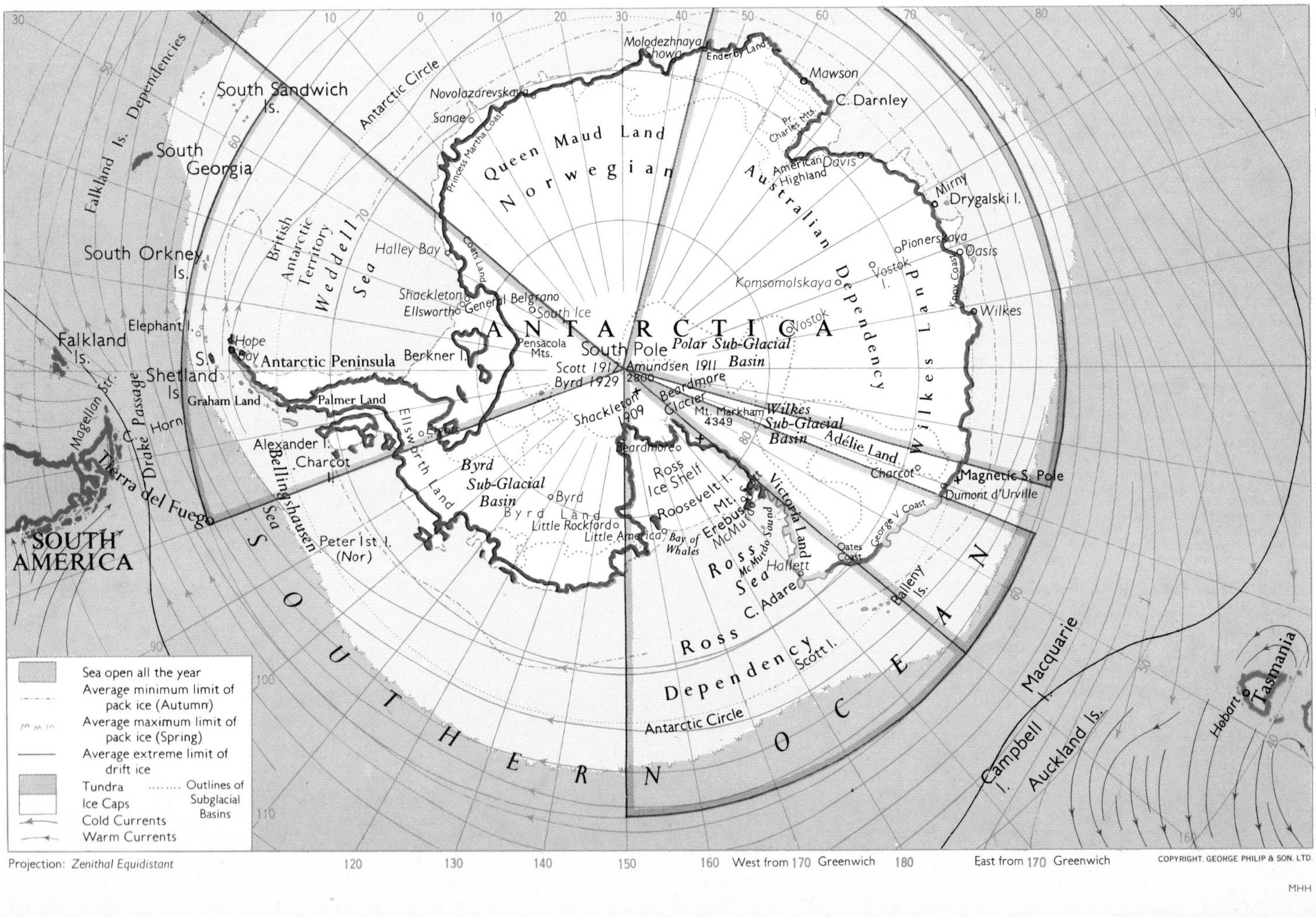

PROGRESS OF EXPLORATION

Coasts explored before 1800
    "   "   between 1800 and 1850
    "   "   "   1850 and 1900
    "   "   since 1900
Nansen 1895 Highest latitudes reached by explorers, with date
Unexplored regions: most of Antarctica and the interior of Greenland

Northern map

150   West from Greenwich   170   East from   Greenwich   110
150   80

S I B E R I A
A S I A

PACIFIC OCEAN
Vancouver I.
Qn. Charlotte Is.
G. of Alaska
St. Lawrence
Bering Strait
Wrangel I.
Kolyma
New Siberian Is.
Lena
ARCTIC OCEAN
Pt. Barrow
Beaufort Sea
C. Chelyuskin
Taimyr Peninsula
Severnaya Zemlya
Yenisei
Ob
Irtysh
L. Balkhash
Alaska
Yukon
Aklavik
Banks I.
M'Clure Str.
Amundsen's Airship Route (1926)
Nansen 1895
Peary 1909
Franz Josef Land
Novaya Zemlya
Kara Sea
Tobol
Mackenzie
Gt. Bear L.
Pr. Patrick I.
Dolphin & Union Str.
Victoria I.
North Pole
Peary 1906
Parry Is.
Sverdrup Is.
Barents Sea
Svalbard
Bear I.
N. Cape
Kola
Dvina
Volga
L. Aral
Caspian Sea
Athabaska
Edmonton
Gt. Slave L.
Bathurst I.
Pr. of Magnetic Pole
Pr. of Wales I.
Ellesmere I.
Lancaster Sound
Smith Sd.
Greenland Sea
Jan Mayen
White Sea
Moscow
Leningrad
Don
Dnepr
Caucasus
ROCKY MOUNTAINS
N. Saskatchewan
S. Saskatchewan
Regina
G. of Boothia
Thule
G. of Bothnia
Baltic Sea
Warsaw
Kiev
Vienna
Belgrade
Danube
Istanbul
Ankara
Black Sea
NORTH AMERICA
Nelson
Winnipeg
Hudson Bay
Churchill
Baffin I.
Baffin Bay
GREENLAND
Petermann's Pk. 2940
Mt. Forel 3360
Greenland Sea
Arctic Circle
Faroe Is.
Scandinavia
Gothenburg
Berlin
EUROPE
Mississippi
L. Michigan
L. Superior
L. Huron
Chicago
L. Erie
Toronto
Moosonee
Labrador
Hudson Str.
Davis Str.
Denmark Str.
Iceland
C. Farewell
British Isles
Edinburgh
North Sea

Southern map

30   10   0   10   20   30   40   50   60   70   80   90

Falkland Is. Dependencies
South Sandwich Is.
Antarctic Circle
Molodezhnaya
Showa
Enderby Land
Mawson
C. Darnley
South Georgia
Novolazarevskaya
Sanae
Queen Maud Land
Norwegian
Australian Dependency
American Highland
Davis
Mirny
Drygalski I.
South Orkney Is.
British Antarctic Territory
Weddell Sea
Halley Bay
Coats Land
Pr. Charles Mts.
Pionerskaya
Oasis
Vostok
Komsomolskaya
Knox Coast
Wilkes
Falkland Is.
Elephant I.
Shackleton
Ellsworth
General Belgrano
South Ice
Pensacola Mts.
ANTARCTICA
South Pole
Polar Sub-Glacial Basin
Vostok
S. Shetland Is.
Hope Bay
Antarctic Peninsula
Berkner I.
Scott 1912 Amundsen 1911
Byrd 1929   2800
Wilkes Sub-Glacial Basin
Mt. Markham 4349
Adélie Land
Wilkes Land
Graham Land
Palmer Land
Shackleton 1909
Beardmore Glacier
Charcot
Dumont d'Urville
Magnetic S. Pole
Alexander I.
Charcot
Ellsworth Land
Byrd Sub-Glacial Basin
Byrd
Byrd Land
Beardmore
Ross Ice Shelf
Roosevelt I.
Mt. Erebus
McMurdo
Victoria Land
George V Coast
Oates Coast
Bellingshausen Sea
Peter 1st I. (Nor)
Little Rockford
Little America
Bay of Whales
Ross Sea
Hallett
Balleny Is.
SOUTH AMERICA
Tierra del Fuego
C. Horn
Drake Passage
Magellan Str.
Ross Dependency
C. Adare
Scott I.
SOUTHERN OCEAN
Antarctic Circle
Macquarie
Campbell I.
Auckland Is.
Hobart
Tasmania

Legend

Sea open all the year
Average minimum limit of pack ice (Autumn)
Average maximum limit of pack ice (Spring)
Average extreme limit of drift ice
Tundra
Ice Caps
Cold Currents
Warm Currents
Outlines of Subglacial Basins

Projection: Zenithal Equidistant

West from 170 Greenwich   180   East from 170 Greenwich

COPYRIGHT. GEORGE PHILIP & SON. LTD.

MHH

A.R. – *Autonomous Region*
A.S.S.R. – *Autonomous Soviet Socialist Republic*
Afghan. – *Afghanistan*
Afr. – *Africa*
Ala. – *Alabama*
Alg. – *Algeria*
Amer. – *America*
Ang. – *Angola*
Antarc. – *Antarctic*
Arch. – *Archipelago*
Arg. – *Argentina*
Ark. – *Arkansas*
Atlant. – *Atlantic*
Austral. – *Australia*
B. – *Bay, Bight, (Baie, Baia, Bahia)*
Bangla. – *Bangladesh*
Belg. – *Belgium*
Br. – *British*
Braz. – *Brazil*
Bur. – *Burma*
C. – *Cape (Cabo)*
Cal. – *California*
Cam. – *Cameroon*
Can. – *Canada, Canal*
Cap. – *Capital*
Cent. – *Central*
Chan. – *Channel*
Ches. – *Cheshire*
Cn. – *Canton*
Co. – *County*
Col. – *Colony, Colombia*
Corn. – *Cornwall*
Cr. – *Creek*
Cumbs. – *Cumberland*
Cy. – *City*
Cz-slov. – *Czechoslovakia*
D.C. – *District of Columbia*
Dan. – *Danish*
Del. – *Delaware*
Den. – *Denmark*
Des. – *Desert*
Dept. – *Department*
Dist. – *District*
Div. – *Division*
Dom. Rep. – *Dominican Republic*
E. – *East*
Eng. – *England*
Eur. – *Europe*
F. – *Firth*
Fd. – *Fjord, Fiord*
Fed. – *Federal*
Fin. – *Finland*
Fla. – *Florida*
For. – *Forest*
Fr. – *French, France*
Fs. – *Falls*
G. – *Gulf, Gebel*
Ga. – *Georgia*
Ger. – *Germany*
Gr. – *Greater, Greece*
Gt. – *Great*
Guin.-B. – *Guinea-Bissau*
Guat. – *Guatemala*
Hants. – *Hampshire*
Hd. – *Head*
Herts. – *Hertfordshire*
Hr. – *Harbour, Harbor*
Hs. – *Hills*
Hts. – *Heights*
Hung. – *Hungary*
Hunts. – *Huntingdonshire*
I(s). – *Island(s), Isle, Ile(s)*
I.O.M. – *Isle of Man*
I.O.W. – *Isle of Wight*
Ice. – *Iceland*
Ill. – *Illinois*
Ind. – *Indian, Indiana*
Indon. – *Indonesia*
Ire. – *Ireland*
Isth. – *Isthmus*
It. – *Italy*
Jap. – *Japan*
Junc. – *Junction*
Kan. – *Kansas*
Ky. – *Kentucky*
L. – *Lake, Loch, Lough, Lago*
La. – *Louisiana*
Lag. – *Lagoon, Lagoa, Laguna*
Lancs. – *Lancashire*
Ld. – *Land*
Leb. – *Lebanon*
Leics. – *Leicestershire*
Lincs. – *Lincolnshire*
Lit. – *Little*
Lr. – *Lower*
Lux. – *Luxembourg*
Madag. – *Madagascar*
Mad. P. – *Madhya Pradesh*
Md. – *Maryland*
Me. – *Maine*
Medit. – *Mediterranean*
Mex. – *Mexico*
Mich. – *Michigan*
Minn. – *Minnesota*
Miss. – *Mississippi*
Mo. – *Missouri*
Mong. – *Mongolia*
Mozam. – *Mozambique*
Mt(s). – *Mountain(s), Mount(s)*
Mte. – *Monte*
N. – *North, Northern*
N.B. – *New Brunswick*
N.C. – *North Carolina*
N.H. – *New Hampshire*
N.J. – *New Jersey*
N.S.W. – *New South Wales*
N.Y. – *New York*
N.Z. – *New Zealand*
Neb. – *Nebraska*
Neth. – *Netherlands*
Newf. – *Newfoundland*
Nicar. – *Nicaragua*
Nor. – *Norway*
Northants. – *Northamptonshire*
O. – *Oasis*
O.F.S. – *Orange Free State*
Oc. – *Ocean*
Ont. – *Ontario*
Ore. – *Oregon*
Okla. – *Oklahoma*
P. – *Pass, Paso, Passo*
Pa. – *Pennsylvania*
Pac. Oc. – *Pacific Ocean*
Pak. – *Pakistan*
Pan. – *Panama*
Papua N.G. – *Papua New Guinea*
Para. – *Paraguay*
Pen. – *Peninsula*
Phil. – *Philippines*
Pk. – *Peak*
Pl. – *Plain, Planina*
Plat. – *Plateau*
Pol. – *Poland*
Port. – *Portuguese, Portugal*
Pref. – *Prefecture*
Prov. – *Province*
Pt. Pte. – *Point, Pointe*
R. – *River, Rio*
R.I. – *Rhode Island*
Ra. – *Range*
Reg. – *Region*
Res. – *Reservoir*
Rhod. – *Rhodesia*
Rum. – *Rumania*
S. – *South, Sea*
S.C. – *South Carolina*
S.D. – *South Dakota*
S.S.R. – *Soviet Socialist Republic*
S., St., Ste., Sta., Sto. – *Sao, Saint, Sainte, Santa, Santo*
Sa. – *Sierra, Serra*
Salop. – *Shropshire*
Scot. – *Scotland*
Sd. – *Sound*
Si Arabia – *Saudi Arabia*
Som. – *Somerset*
St. – *State*
Staffs. – *Staffordshire*
Str. – *Strait*
Switz. – *Switzerland*
Span. – *Spanish*
Tenn. – *Tennessee*
Terr. – *Territory*
Tex. – *Texas*
Thail. – *Thailand*
Tipp. – *Tipperary*
Trans. – *Transvaal*
Tur. – *Turkey*
U.S.A. – *United States of America*
U.S.S.R. – *Union of Soviet Socialist Republics*
Va. – *Virginia*
Val. – *Valley*
Ven. – *Venezuela*
Vic. – *Victoria*
Vol. – *Volcano*
Vt. – *Vermont*
W. – *West, Western, Wadi, Wady*
W.I. – *West Indies*
Wilts. – *Wiltshire*
Wis. – *Wisconsin*
Y.-slav. – *Yugoslavia*
Yorks. – *Yorkshire*

The latitudes and longitudes are intended primarily as a guide to finding the places on the map and in some cases are only approximate.

A

49 Aabenraa, Denmark 55 7N 9 20E
44 Aachen, Germany 50 49N 6 6E
49 Aalborg, Denmark 57 1N 9 45E
45 Aalen, Germany 48 50N 10 6E
63 Aalma ech Chaab, Leb. 33 6N 35 10E
44 Aalsmeer, Neth. 52 16N 4 45E
44 Aalst, Belgium 50 57N 4 3E
44 Aalten, Neth. 51 56N 6 35E
45 Aarau, Switzerland 47 24N 8 3E
45 Aarberg Switzerland 47 3N 7 17E
45 Aare, R., Switzerland 47 16N 7 45E
45 Aargau, Canton, Switz. 47 25N 8 10E
49 Aarhus, Denmark 56 9N 10 13E
44 Aarschot, Belgium 50 59N 4 50E
72 Aba, Nigeria 5 10N 7 19E
62 Abadan, Iran 30 22N 48 19E
72 Abadla, Algeria 31 0N 2 25W
61 Abakan, U.S.S.R. 53 59N 91 20E
98 Abancay, Peru 13 45S 72 45W
67 Abashiri, Japan 43 55N 144 15E
82 Abau, Papua N.G. 10 0S 148 50E
74 Abaya, L., Ethiopia 6 30N 37 50E
43 Abbeville, France 50 7N 1 50E
34 Abbeyfeale, Ireland 52 23N 9 19W
35 Abbeyside, Ireland 52 5N 7 36W
54 Abbottabad, Pakistan 34 10N 73 15E
73 Abéché, Chad 14 0N 20 40E
73 Abeokuta, Nigeria 7 0N 3 23E
25 Aberaeron, Wales 52 14N 4 16W
25 Abercarn, Wales 51 39N 3 9W
33 Aberchirder, Scotland 57 34N 2 40W
74 Abercorn, *see* Mbala
25 Abercrave, Wales 51 48N 3 42W
25 Aberdare, Wales 51 43N 3 28W
83 Aberdeen, Australia 32 5S 150 50E
33 Aberdeen, Scotland 57 9N 2 4W
90 Aberdeen, S. Dakota, U.S.A. 45 32N 98 30W
90 Aberdeen, Wash., U.S.A. 47 0N 123 47W
31 Aberdour, Scotland 56 2N 3 18W
25 Aberdovey, Wales 52 32N 4 2W
25 Aberdulais, Wales 51 41N 3 45W
31 Aberfeldy, Scotland 56 37N 3 50W
30 Aberfoyle, Scotland 56 11N 4 22W
25 Abergavenny, Wales 51 49N 3 0W
25 Abergele, Wales 53 18N 3 35W
25 Aberkenfig, Wales 51 33N 3 36W
25 Abersychan, Wales 51 43N 3 4W
25 Abertillery, Wales 51 43N 3 8W
25 Aberystwyth, Wales 52 24N 4 4W
62 Abha, Saudi Arabia 18 0N 42 34E
72 Abidjan, Ivory Coast 5 25N 3 58W
90 Abilene, U.S.A. 32 28N 99 45W
22 Abingdon, England 51 40N 1 16W
31 Abington, Scotland 55 30N 3 42W
9 Abitibi, L., Canada 49 40N 79 40W
51 Abkhaz, A.S.S.R., U.S.S.R. 43 0N 41 0E
49 Abo, *see* Turku.
74 Abolo, Congo (Fr.) 0 10N 13 10E
72 Abomey, Benin 7 5N 2 5E
73 Abong Mbang, Cameroon 4 0N 13 8E
73 Abou Deia, Chad 11 20N 19 20E
33 Aboyne, Scotland 57 5N 2 50W
62 Abqaiq, Saudi Arabia 26 0N 49 45E
37 Abrantes, Portugal 39 28N 8 10W
73 Abri, Sudan 20 45N 30 27E
98 Abrolhos Arch., Brazil 17 50S 38 35W
47 Abrud, Rumania 46 20N 23 0E
40 Abruzzi, Region, Italy 42 10N 14 0E
90 Absaroka Ra., U.S.A. 44 40N 110 0W
63 Abu Dhabi, U.A.E. 24 27N 54 18E
73 Abu Dist., Sudan 19 15N 33 38E
73 Abu Hamed, Sudan 19 35N 33 37E
73 Abu Matariq, Sudan 11 0N 26 10E
73 Abu Tig, Egypt 27 4N 31 15E
73 Abu Zabad, Sudan 12 28N 28 45E
72 Abuja, Nigeria 9 16N 7 2E
73 Abwong, Sudan 9 2N 32 14E
94 Acaponeta, Mexico 22 30N 105 20W
94 Acapulco, Mexico 17 0N 99 57W
72 Accra, Ghana 5 32N 0 12W
26 Accrington, England 53 46N 2 23W
65 Achak Gomba, China 33 35N 96 20E
35 Achill, Ireland 53 56N 9 55W
35 Achill Hd. & I., Ireland 53 58N 10 17W
61 Achinsk, U.S.S.R. 56 20N 90 20E
95 Acklin's I., Bahamas 22 15N 74 15W
99 Aconcagua, Mt., Arg. 32 37S 70 2W
43 Acqui, Italy 44 42N 8 29E
63 Acre, Israel 32 56N 35 4E
98 Acre, R., Brazil 10 45S 69 30W
98 Acre, st., Brazil 9 0S 71 0W
62 Ad Dam, Saudi Arabia 20 25N 44 30E
83 Adaminaby, Australia 36 0S 148 50E
64 Adam's Bridge, Sri Lanka 9 15N 79 30E
64 Adam's Pk., Sri Lanka 6 40N 80 40E
51 Adana, Turkey 37 10N 35 18E
51 Adapazari, Turkey 40 48N 30 25E
73 Adarama, Sudan 17 8N 34 58E
83 Adavale, Australia 25 46S 144 30E
43 Adda, R., Italy 45 15N 9 50E
74 Addis Ababa, Ethiopia 9 2N 38 43E
45 Adelboden, Switzerland 46 28N 7 36E
83 Adelaide, Australia 34 55S 138 43E
76 Adelaide, S. Africa 32 40S 26 20E
88 Adelaide, Pen., Canada 67 60N 98 0W
100 Adélie Ld., Antarctica 69 0S 140 0E
62 Aden, S. Yemen 12 45N 45 3E
62 Aden, G. of, Arabia 12 0N 48 0E
62 Adh Dharma, Si. Arabia 24 35N 46 12E
80 Adieu, C., Australia 32 0S 132 0E
64 Adilabad, India 19 50N 78 30E
93 Adirondack Mts., U.S.A. 43 50N 74 30W
72 Admer, Algeria 20 23N 5 20E
80 Admiralty G., Australia 14 20S 126 0E
82 Admiralty Is., Papua N.G. 2 0S 146 40E
64 Adoni, India 15 45N 77 20E
42 Adour, R., France 43 47N 0 50W
37 Adra, Spain 36 45N 3 1W
62 Adraj, Saudi Arabia 20 1N 51 0E
40 Adrano, Sicily, Italy 37 40N 14 49E
72 Adrar, Algeria 27 40N 0 12W
72 Adrar des Iforas, Plat., Mali 19 40N 1 40E
73 Adré, Chad 13 40N 22 20E
40 Adriatic Sea, Europe 43 0N 15 0E
73 Adwa, Ethiopia 14 13N 39 0E
27 Adwick le Street, Eng. 53 35N 1 12W
51 Adzhar, A.S.S.R., U.S.S.R. 42 0N 42 0E
49 Æbeltoft, Denmark 56 12N 10 41E
41 Ægean Sea, Medit. S. 38 0N 25 0E
62 Afars & Issas, Fr. Terr. of, Africa, see Djibouti
72 Affreville, *see* Khemis Miliana.
32 Affric, Glen & R., Scot. 57 16N 5 0W
64 Afghanistan, Asia 33 25N 66 0E
62 Afif, Saudi Arabia 23 53N 42 59E
70 Africa, Continent
63 Afula, Israel 32 36N 37 17E
51 Afyonkarahisar, Turkey 38 46N 30 33E
72 Agadés, Niger 16 58N 7 59E
72 Agadir, Morocco 30 32N 9 45W
65 Agartala, India 23 47N 91 15E
61 Agata, U.S.S.R. 66 50N 98 10E
72 Agboville, Ivory Coast 5 55N 4 15W
43 Agde, France 43 20N 3 28E
43 Agen, France 44 13N 0 37E
43 Agincourt, France 50 29N 2 7E
64 Agra, India 27 17N 78 0E
51 Agri, *see* Karaköse
40 Agrigento, Sicily 37 19N 13 33E
41 Agrinion, Greece 38 37N 21 27E
94 Agua Prieta, Mexico 31 25N 109 30W
94 Aguas Calientes, Mexico 22 0N 102 12W
95 Aguadilla, Puerto Rico 18 28N 67 5W
37 Aguilas, Spain 37 27N 1 39W
76 Agulhas C., S. Africa 34 50S 20 5E
43 Agur, Israel 31 41N 34 55E
84 Ahaura, N.Z. 42 20S 171 36E
44 Ahaus, Germany 52 6N 7 0E
84 Ahipara B., N.Z. 35 10S 173 0E
64 Ahiri, India 19 30N 80 0E
64 Ahmadabad, India 23 2N 72 30E
64 Ahmadnagar, India 19 0N 74 40E
64 Ahmadpur E., Pak. 29 0N 71 40E
36 Ahoghill, N. Ireland 54 52N 6 23W
62 Ahvaz, Iran 31 25N 48 40E
49 Ahvenanmaa, Is., Fin. 60 15N 20 0E
62 Ahwar, South Yemen 13 33N 46 37E
67 Aichi, Pref., Japan 35 0N 137 15E
45 Aigle, Switzerland 46 19N 6 58E
67 Aihun, China 49 59N 127 30E
65 Aijal, India 23 30N 92 55E
30 Ailsa Craig, I., Scotland 55 15N 5 6W
61 Aim, U.S.S.R. 59 0N 133 55E
42 Ain, Dépt., France 46 5N 5 30E
72 Ain Beida, Algeria 35 50N 7 29E
72 Ain Salah, Algeria 27 5N 2 30E
72 Ain Sefra, Algeria 32 46N 0 35W
73 Aine Galakka, Chad 18 5N 18 30E
72 Air, Mts., Niger 18 0N 8 20E
33 Aird, The, Scotland 57 26N 4 30W
31 Airdrie, Scotland 55 52N 3 59W
42 Aire, France 43 40N 0 20W
26 Aire, R., England 53 54N 2 0W
42 Aisne, Dépt., France 49 42N 3 40E
43 Aisne, R., France 49 25N 4 0E
82 Aitape, Papua N.G. 3 0S 142 5E
33 Aith, Scotland 59 8N 2 38W
41 Aitos, Bulgaria 42 40N 27 18E
43 Aix, France 43 34N 5 26E
43 Aix-les-Bains, France 45 40N 5 55E
41 Aiyina, tn. & G., Greece 37 40N 23 30E
41 Aíyion, Greece 38 15N 22 5E
43 Ajaccio, Corsica, Fr. 41 55N 8 40E
64 Ajanta Ra., India 20 20N 75 30E
43 Ajaccio, Corsica, Fr. 41 55N 8 40E
64 Ajanta Ra., India 20 20N 75 30E
62 Ajibba, Saudi Arabia 27 28N 44 28E
63 'Ajlun, Jordan 32 20N 35 44E
64 Ajmer, India 26 30N 74 39E
49 Akershus, Co., Norway 60 0N 11 0E
74 Aketi, Zaïre 2 38N 23 47E
41 Akhisar, Turkey 38 56N 27 48E
73 Akhmîm, Egypt 26 31N 31 47E
67 Akita, & Pref., Japan 39 45N 140 6E
72 Akjoujt, Mauritania 19 45N 14 10W
88 Aklavik, Canada 67 50N 135 0W
74 Akoafim, Cameroon 2 20N 12 50E
73 Akobo, Sudan 7 50N 33 1E
64 Akola, India 20 55N 76 59E
48 Akranes, Iceland 64 18N 21 53W
92 Akron, Ohio, U.S.A. 41 14N 81 31W
51 Aksaray, Turkey 38 19N 34 12E
61 Aksenovo Zilovskoye, U.S.S.R. 53 20N 117 40E
73 Aksum, Ethiopia 14 5N 38 40E
51 Aktyubinsk, U.S.S.R. 50 20N 57 10E
72 Aku, Nigeria 6 40N 7 18E
72 Akure, Nigeria 7 15N 5 5E
48 Akureyri, Iceland 65 37N 18 3E
65 Akyab, Burma 20 12N 92 58E
73 Al Bu'ayrat, Libya 31 20N 16 0E
62 Al Ghaidha, South Yemen 16 16N 52 7E
62 Al Hafr, Saudi Arabia 28 30N 46 0E
62 Al Hair, Saudi Arabia 24 18N 46 44E
62 Al Hamar, Saudi Arabia 22 23N 46 6E
62 Al Haraiba, Si. Arabia 28 7N 35 15E
62 Al Hataba, Saudi Arabia 19 30N 44 11E
72 Al Hoceima, Morocco, 35 8N 3 58W
63 Al Husn, Jordan 32 30N 35 55E
73 Al Jarzirah, Libya 25 55N 21 0E
73 Al Jawf, Libya 24 15N 23 30E
62 Al Jawf, Saudi Arabia 29 55N 39 37E
63 Al Jazir, Oman 18 30N 56 31E
63 Al Jiftalik, Jordan 32 10N 35 30E
63 Al Karak, Jordan 31 10N 35 42E
63 Al Khabura, Oman 23 57N 57 5E
63 Al Khalaf, Oman 20 30N 57 56E
62 Al Khobar, Saudi Arabia 25 30N 50 15E
73 Al Khums, Libya 32 32N 14 20E
62 Al Kuwayt, Kuwait 29 20N 48 0E
63 Al Lubban, Jordan 32 5N 35 14E
73 Al Marj (Barce), Libya 32 30N 20 50E
63 Al Masira, I. Oman 20 30N 58 0E
63 Al Mazra, Jordan 31 18N 35 32E
73 Al Muwaylih, Si. Arabia 27 35N 35 40E
73 Al Qatrun, Libya 24 45N 15 2E
62 Al Qunfidha, Si. Arabia 19 20N 41 10E
63 Al Qunaytirah, Syria 33 7N 35 50E
62 Al'Ula, Saudi Arabia 26 35N 38 0E
73 Al Uquaylah, Libya 30 10N 18 50E
63 Al Yarmuk, R., Syria 32 45N 35 40E
66 Ala Kul, L., U.S.S.R. 46 15N 81 50E
66 Ala Shan, Mts., China 39 45N 103 20E
66 Ala Tau, Mts., Asia 45 30N 80 40E
91 Alabama, st., & R., U.S.A. 32 40N 87 0W
98 Alagoas, st., Brazil 9 45S 35 47W
95 Alajuela, Costa Rica 10 0N 84 20W
90 Alamogordo, U.S.A. 32 55N 105 55W
90 Alamosa, U.S.A. 37 35N 105 55W
49 Aland Is., *see* Ahvenanmaa
49 Åland Str., Finland 60 10N 19 30E
51 Alanya, Turkey 36 36N 32 0E
60 Alapayevsk, U.S.S.R. 57 55N 62 0E
51 Alasehir, Turkey 38 20N 28 37E
88 Alaska, st., U.S.A. 65 0N 150 0W
88 Alaska Ra., Alaska 63 0N 150 0W
43 Alassio, Italy 44 0N 8 10E
50 Alatyr, U.S.S.R. 54 48N 46 32E
83 Alawoona, Australia 34 45S 140 30E
43 Alba, Italy 44 45N 8 0E
37 Alba, Sa. de, mts., Spain 43 5N 4 40W
47 Alba-Iulia, Rumania 46 2N 23 54E
37 Albacete, Spain 38 59N 1 53W
41 Albania, Europe 41 10N 20 0E
80 Albany, Australia 35 0S 117 52E
91 Albany, Georgia, U.S.A. 31 35N 84 16W
93 Albany, N.Y., U.S.A. 42 37N 73 50W
90 Albany, Oregon, U.S.A. 44 38N 123 0W
89 Albany, R., Canada 51 20N 86 30W
91 Albemarle Sd., U.S.A. 36 2N 76 0W
43 Albenga, Italy 44 4N 8 15E
43 Albert, France 50 0N 2 40E
83 Albert L., Australia 35 40S 139 20E
74 Albert L. *see* Mobutu Sese Seko, L.
88 Alberta, Prov., Canada 54 30N 115 0W
74 Albertville, *see* Kalemie
43 Albertville, France 45 40N 6 20E
43 Albi, France 43 57N 2 9E
37 Alboran I., Spain 35 58N 3 0W
90 Albuquerque, U.S.A. 35 3N 106 36W
37 Alburquerque, Spain 39 13N 6 55W
83 Albury, Australia 36 6S 146 59E
37 Alcalá de Henares, Spain 40 30N 3 19W
40 Alcamo, Sicily 38 0N 12 58E
37 Alcañiz, Spain 41 0N 0 10W
37 Alcántara, Spain 39 42N 6 54W
37 Alcaraz, Sa. de, mts., Spain 38 30N 2 30W
37 Alcaudete, Spain 37 38N 4 7W
37 Alcázar de S. Juan, Spain 39 33N 3 15W
37 Alcira, Spain 39 10N 0 30W
37 Alcobaça, Portugal 39 30N 9 0W
37 Alcoy, Spain 38 42N 0 29W
71 Aldabra Is., Indian Ocean 9 30S 46 15E
61 Aldan, U.S.S.R. 58 40N 125 30E
61 Aldan, R., U.S.S.R. 62 30N 135 30E
61 Aldanski Perezov, U.S.S.R. 62 5N 135 15E
23 Aldeburgh, England 52 9N 1 37E
22 Alderbury, England 51 4N 1 45W
42 Alderney I., Channel Is. 49 45N 2 15W
23 Aldershot, England 51 16N 0 45W
72 Aleg, Mauritania 17 15N 14 10W
99 Alegrete, Brazil 29 40S 56 0W
60 Aleisk, U.S.S.R. 52 40N 83 0E
51 Alexsandrov Gai, U.S.S.R. 50 30N 48 10E
61 Aleksandrovsk, U.S.S.R. 50 50N 142 10E
61 Aleksandrovski Zavod, U.S.S.R. 50 40N 117 50E
60 Aleksandrovskoye, U.S.S.R. 60 35N 77 50E
42 Alençon, France 48 25N 0 1E
37 Alentejo Alto, Prov., Portugal 39 0N 7 55W
37 Alentejo Baixo, Prov., Portugal 38 0N 8 20W
51 Aleppo (Halab), Syria 36 30N 37 22E
43 Alès, France 44 9N 4 5E
43 Alessandria, Italy 44 47N 8 40E
48 Ålesund, Norway 62 28N 6 5E
88 Aleutian Is., Pacific Oc. 52 0N 175 0W
75 Alexander B., S. Africa 28 20S 16 40E
100 Alexander I., Antarctica 68 0S 70 0W
63 Alexander, R., Israel 32 20N 34 55E
83 Alexandra, Australia 37 8S 145 40E
88 Alexandria, B.C., Can. 52 55N 122 20W
76 Alexandria, S. Africa 33 38S 26 25E
73 Alexandria, Egypt 31 5N 29 45E
30 Alexandria, Scotland 55 59N 4 34W
91 Alexandria La, U.S.A. 31 17N 92 29W
92 Alexandria, Va., U.S.A. 38 50N 77 5W

83 Alexandrina, L., Austral. 35 32S 139 12E
41 Alexandroúpolis, Greece 40 50N 25 55E
63 Aley, Lebanon 33 50N 35 36E
27 Alford, England 53 16N 0 10E
27 Alfreton, England 53 7N 1 24W
48 Alftanes, Iceland 64 29N 22 10W
37 Algarve, Prov., Portugal 37 20N 8 35W
37 Algeciras, Spain 36 11N 5 28W
37 Algemesi, Spain 39 15N 0 29W
72 Algeria, N. Africa 33 40N 3 0E
72 Algiers (Alger), Algeria 36 45N 3 5E
76 Algoa B., S. Africa 33 50S 26 0E
37 Alhama de Murcia, Spain 37 50N 1 30W
64 Alikhel, Afghanistan 33 50N 69 30E
74 Alibo, Ethiopia 9 52N 37 5E
37 Alicante, Spain 38 22N 1 28W
82 Alice, R., Australia 23 50S 145 0E
80 Alice Springs, Australia 23 42S 133 58E
75 Alicedale, S. Africa 33 16S 26 2E
64 Aligarh, India 27 42N 78 25E
65 Aling Kangri, Ra., Tibet, China 32 45N 81 5E
49 Alingsas Sweden 57 57N 12 36E
64 Alipur, Pakistan 29 25N 70 50E
65 Alipur Duar, India 26 35N 89 30E
47 Alitus, U.S.S.R. 54 20N 24 0E
37 Aljustrel, Portugal 37 55N 8 10W
44 Alkmaar, Netherlands 52 38N 4 44E
65 Allahabad, India 25 25N 81 50E
61 Allakh Yun, U.S.S.R. 60 50N 137 5E
31 Allan, Bridge of, Scotland 56 9N 3 56W
92 Allegheny Mts., U.S.A. 39 0N 79 0W
92 Allegheny, R., U.S.A. 42 0N 79 0W
35 Allen, Bog of, Ireland 53 13N 7 20W
36 Allen, L., Ireland 54 8N 8 2W
63 Allenby Bridge, *see* Hussein Bridge
27 Allendale, England 54 55N 2 16W
93 Allentown, U.S.A. 40 40N 75 25W
64 Alleppey, India 9 35N 76 25E
90 Alliance, Neb., U.S.A. 42 8N 102 55W
42 Allier, Dépt., France 46 25N 3 0E
43 Allier, R., France 44 50N 3 42E
31 Alloa, Scotland 56 7N 3 47W
60 Alma Ata, U.S.S.R. 43 20N 76 50E
37 Almada, Portugal 38 45N 9 10W
82 Almaden, Australia 17 22S 144 40E
37 Almadén, Spain 38 48N 4 48W
37 Almansa, Spain 38 50N 1 0W
37 Almazan, Spain 41 30N 2 30W
44 Almelo, Netherlands 52 21N 6 42E
37 Almendralejo, Spain 38 43N 6 28W
37 Almeria, Spain 36 53N 2 33W
24 Almondsbury, England 51 33N 2 34W
27 Aln, R., England 55 24N 1 57W
33 Alness, & R., Scotland 57 45N 4 20W
27 Alnwick, England 55 25N 1 42W
65 Alon, Burma 22 15N 95 10E
68 Alor, & I., Indonesia 8 10S 124 50E
68 Alor Star, Malaya 6 3N 100 25E
92 Alpena, U.S.A. 45 0N 83 35W
42 Alpes Maritimes, Dépt., Fr. 44 5N 7 0E
24 Alphington, England 50 41N 3 32W
45 Alpi Pennine, Mts., Switz. 46 4N 7 35E
90 Alpine, Texas, U.S.A. 30 25N 103 42W
46 Alps, The, Europe 46 to 47 0 N 6 to 10 0E
43 Alsace, Dist., France 48 30N 7 30E
26 Alsager, England 53 7N 2 20W
44 Alsdorf, Germany 50 48N 6 10E
32 Alsh, L., Scotland 57 17N 5 40W
26 Alston, England 54 49N 2 28W
66 Altai Mts., Central Asia 48 0N 90 0E
91 Altamaha, R., U.S.A. 31 45N 81 45W
66 Altanbulag, Mongolia 50 15N 106 25E
46 Altdorf, Switzerland 46 53N 8 38E
48 Alte Fjord, Norway 70 0N 23 25E
37 Altea, Spain 38 38N 0 1W
43 Altkirch, France 47 40N 7 15E
75 Alto Molocue, Mozam. 15 50S 37 35E
23 Alton, England 51 8N 0 59W
92 Alton, U.S.A. 38 54N 90 3W
46 Altona, Germany 53 34N 9 51E
92 Altoona, U.S.A. 40 32N 79 27W
26 Altrincham, England 53 24N 2 23W
46 Altstätten, Switzerland 47 23N 9 33E
90 Altus, U.S.A. 34 30N 99 25W
66 Altyn Tagh, Mts., Tibet 39 0N 89 0E
31 Alva, Scotland 56 9N 3 48W
94 Alvarado, Mexico 18 45N 95 50W
22 Alvechurch, England 52 22N 1 58W
49 Alvesta, Sweden 56 57N 14 30E
83 Alvie, Australia 38 15S 143 30E
49 Älvkarleby, Sweden 60 32N 17 40E
49 Alvsborg, Co., Sweden 58 0N 12 30E
48 Älvsby, Sweden 65 42N 21 0E
64 Alwar, India 27 43N 76 40E
51 Alyaty Pristan, U.S.S.R. 39 59N 49 28E
31 Alyth, Scotland 56 38 N 3 14W
47 Alytus, U.S.S.R. 54 25N 24 0E
73 Am-Dam, Chad 12 40N 20 35E
73 Am Djeress, Chad 16 15N 22 50E
73 Am Guereda, Chad 12 53N 21 14E
73 Am Timan, Chad 11 0N 20 10E
80 Amadeus, L., Australia 24 45S 130 45E
73 Amadi, Sudan 5 29N 30 25E
89 Amadjuak & L., Canada 64 0N 72 40W
67 Amagasaki, Japan 34 45N 135 25E
67 Amakusa B. & I., Japan 32 45N 130 5E
49 Amal, Sweden 59 5N 12 35E
64 Amalner, India 21 0N 74 58E
67 Amami O Shima, Is., Japan 27 0N 129 0E
60 Amangeldy, U.S.S.R. 50 10N 65 10E
98 Amapa, st., Brazil 2 0N 52 0W
62 Amara, Iraq 31 58N 47 5E
64 Amaravati, *see* Amraoti
90 Amarillo U.S.A. 35 6N 101 57W
40 Amaro, Mte., Italy 42 4N 14 5E
51 Amasya, Turkey 40 45N 36 10E
98 Amazon, R., Brazil 1 0S 59 0W
98 Amazonas, st., Brazil 4 30S 64 0W
64 Ambala, India 30 28N 76 50E
74 Amban, Cameroon 2 20N 11 15E
75 Ambanja, Madagascar 13 40S 48 27E
61 Ambarchik, U.S.S.R. 69 40N 162 20E
98 Ambato, Ecuador 1 40S 78 30W
75 Ambatolampy, Madag. 19 0S 47 35E
75 Ambatondrazaka, Madag. 17 55S 48 28E
46 Amberg, Germany 49 27N 11 52E
65 Ambikapur, India 23 10N 83 5E
75 Ambilobé, Madagascar 13 10S 49 3E
27 Amble, England 55 20N 1 36W
26 Ambleside, England 54 26N 2 56W
68 Ambon, Indonesia 3 50S 128 15E
43 Amboise, France 47 24N 1 2E
75 Ambositra, Madagascar 20 30S 47 25E
68 Amboyna, I., S. China Sea 7 0N 113 10E
75 Ambré, C'd', Madagascar 12 0S 49 20E
74 Ambriz, Angola 8 0S 13 0E
74 Ambrizète, Angola 7 18S 12 52E
60 Amderma, U.S.S.R. 69 45N 62 0E
94 Ameca, Mexico 20 26N 104 5W
44 Ameland, I., Netherlands 53 27N 5 45E
61 Amen, U.S.S.R. 68 50N 179 59E
1 America, N. and S., Continents
44 Amersfoort, Netherlands 52 10N 5 24E
23 Amersham, England 51 40N 0 38W
88 Amery, Canada 56 35N 94 5W
91 Ames, U.S.A. 42 3N 93 42W
22 Amesbury, England 51 10N 1 46W
61 Amga, R., U.S.S.R. 61 0N 132 0E
61 Amgu, U.S.S.R. 45 45N 137 15E
61 Amgun, R., U.S.S.R. 52 50N 138 0E
65 Amherst, Burma 16 0N 97 40E
89 Amherst, Canada 45 50N 64 30W
40 Amiata, Mt., Italy 42 49N 11 30E
43 Amiens, France 49 52N 2 15E
5 Amirante Is., Ind. Ocean 6 30S 53 0E
62 Amman, Jordan 31 57N 35 56E
25 Ammanford, Wales 51 48N 4 0W
67 Amoy, China 24 25N 118 15E
75 Ampanihy, Madagascar 24 40S 44 45E
62 Amran, Yemen 15 43N 43 57E
64 Amraoti, India 20 53N 77 15E
64 Amreli, India 21 40N 71 5E
64 Amritsar, India 31 40N 75 20E
64 Amroha, India 29 0N 78 25E
44 Amsterdam, Netherlands 52 23N 4 53E
76 Amsterdam, S. Africa 26 35S 30 40E
93 Amsterdam, U.S.A. 42 58N 74 6W
63 Amu Darya, R., U.S.S.R. 40 30N 62 0E
62 Amul, Iran 36 25N 52 10E
88 Amundsen Gulf, Canada 70 30N 123 0W
61 Amur, R., U.S.S.R. 52 0N 126 30E
68 Amurang, Indonesia 1 15N 124 30E
62 An Nafud, Des., Arabia 28 40N 42 0E
62 An Najaf, Iraq 32 0N 44 20E
62 An Nasiriyah, Iraq 31 0N 46 15E
68 An Nhon, Vietnam 13 40N 109 20E
36 An Uaimh, Ireland 53 40N 6 42W
63 Anabta, Jordan 32 19N 35 7E
90 Anaconda, U.S.A. 46 8N 112 58W
61 Anadyr & G., U.S.S.R. 64 40N 178 0E
61 Anadyr R., U.S.S.R. 65 0N 170 0E
90 Anaheim, U.S.A. 33 50N 118 0W
62 Anaiza, Saudi Arabia 26 4N 44 8E
65 Anakapalle, India 17 25N 82 50E
75 Analalava, Madagascar 14 35S 48 0E
68 Anambas Is., Indonesia 3 0N 106 0E
51 Anamur, Turkey 36 8N 32 58E
64 Anantnag, Kashmir 33 40N 75 3E
62 Anatolia, S.W. Asia 39 0N 32 30E
99 Anatuya, Argentina 28 20S 62 45W
73 Anaye, Niger. 19 28N 13 20E
42 Ancenis, France 47 23N 1 10W
88 Anchorage, Alaska 61 10N 150 0E
98 Anchohuma, Mt., Bolivia 16 0S 68 50W
94 Ancón, Panama Canal Zone (inset)
40 Ancona, Italy 43 38N 13 34E
99 Ancud & G., Chile 42 5S 73 48W
99 Andalgala, Argentina 27 25S 66 30W
48 Åndalsnes, Norway 62 35N 7 43E
37 Andalusia, Prov., Spain 37 20N 5 0W
91 Andalusia, U.S.A. 31 16N 86 30W
63 Andam, Wadi, Oman 21 30N 58 20E
65 Andaman Is., Indian Oc. 12 0N 92 40E
75 Andara, S.W. Africa 18 2S 21 9E
45 Andermatt, Switzerland 46 38N 8 37E
92 Anderson, Ind., U.S.A. 40 1N 85 40W
91 Anderson, S.C., U.S.A. 34 27N 82 36W
96 Andes, Mts., S. America 7 0N to 53 0S 65 0 to 80 0W
64 Andhra Pradesh, st., India 17 0N 81 0E
41 Andikithira I., Greece 35 40N 23 16E
60 Andizhan, U.S.S.R. 41 0N 72 37E
37 Andorra, Europe 42 28N 1 30E
22 Andover, England 51 12N 1 29W
88 Andreanof Is., Alaska 50 30N 178 0W
40 Andria, Italy 41 11N 16 17E
95 Andros I., Bahamas 24 40N 78 15W
41 Andros I., Greece 37 50N 24 53E
37 Andujar, Spain 38 0N 4 5W
72 Anécho, Togo 6 8N 1 32E
61 Angara, R., Siberia 55 0N 103 0E
61 Angarsk, U.S.S.R. 52 30N 104 0E
83 Angaston, Australia 34 28S 139 5E
48 Ånge, Sweden 62 31N 15 35E
49 Angelholm, Sweden 56 15N 12 58E
83 Angellala, Australia 26 20S 146 50E
65 Angenong, China 31 55N 94 10E
42 Angers, France 47 32N 0 38W
25 Anglesey I., Wales 53 20N 4 20W
89 Angmagssalik, Greenland 65 40N 37 20W
74 Ango, Zaïre 4 10N 26 5E
99 Angol, Chile 38 0S 72 45W
75 Angola, Port. Terr., Afr. 12 0S 19 0E
43 Angoulême, France 45 40N 0 10E
43 Angoumois, Dist., Fr. 45 43N 0 15E
60 Angren, U.S.S.R. 41 0N 69 10E
95 Anguilla I., W. Indies 18 0N 63 0W
33 Angus, Braes of, Scotland 56 45N 2 55W
49 Anholt, I., Denmark 56 43N 11 25E
66 Anhwei, Prov., China 32 0N 117 0E
64 Anjidiv I., India 14 45N 74 10E
42 Anjou, Prov., France 47 20N 0 50W
75 Anjozorobe, Madagascar 18 22S 47 52E
72 Anka, Nigeria 12 13N 5 58E
51 Ankara, Turkey 39 58N 32 28E
75 Ankazoabo, Madagascar 22 15S 44 45E
75 Ankazobe, Madagascar 18 17S 47 2E
66 Anking, China 30 40N 117 2E
49 Anklam, Germany 53 50N 13 40E
74 Ankoro, Zaïre 6 43S 26 45E
92 Ann Arbor, U.S.A. 42 12N 83 48W
72 Annaba (Bône), Algeria 36 55N 7 45E
68 Annam, reg., Vietnam 16 0N 107 0E
31 Annan, Scotland 55 0N 3 17W
31 Annandale, Dist. & R., Scotland 55 15N 3 25W
92 Annapolis, Md., U.S.A. 39 0N 76 15W
93 Annapolis Royal, Canada 44 45N 65 42W
43 Annecy, France 45 46N 6 5E
26 Annfield Plain, England 54 52N 1 45W
91 Anniston, U.S.A. 33 45N 85 50W
71 Annobon, I. *see* Pagalu
43 Annonay, France 45 15N 4 40E
94 Annotto Bay, Jamaica 18 17N 76 43W
83 Annuello, Australia 34 55S 142 55E
91 Anoka, U.S.A. 45 14N 93 29W
45 Ansbach, Germany 49 21N 10 37E
67 Anshan, China 41 2N 122 10E
66 Ansi, China 40 37N 95 50E
72 Ansongo, Mali 15 50N 0 25E
22 Anstey, England 52 41N 1 14W
31 Anstruther, Scotland 56 13N 2 41W
51 Antakya, Turkey 36 10N 36 15E
75 Antalaha, Madagascar 14 57S 50 20E
51 Antalya & G., Turkey 37 0N 30 43E
37 Antequera, Spain 37 4N 4 31W
72 Anti Atlas, Mts., Morocco 30 30N 7 0W
43 Antibes, France 43 40N 7 10E
93 Anticosti, I., Canada 49 30N 63 0W
91 Antigo, U.S.A. 45 10N 89 11W
95 Antigua, I., W. Indies 17 12N 61 45W
95 Antilla, Cuba 20 50N 75 50W
62 Antioch, *see* Antakya
98 Antioquia, Columbia 6 40N 76 0W
4 Antipodes I., S. Pac. Oc. 50 0S 178 0E
99 Antofagasta, Chile 23 45S 70 18W
75 Antonio Enes, Mozam. 16 8S 40 0E
36 Antrim, & Co., N. Ireland 54 42N 6 12W
36 Antrim, Mts. of N. Ire. 54 55N 6 4W
75 Antsalova, Madagascar 18 40S 44 37E
75 Antsirabe, Madagascar 19 55S 47 2E
75 Antsohihy, Madagascar 14 50S 47 50E
67 Antung, China 40 9N 124 22E
44 Antwerp, & Prov., Belg. 51 13N 4 25E
64 Anupgarh, India 29 10N 73 5E
64 Anuradhapura, Sri Lanka 8 25N 80 23E
80 Anxious, B., Australia 33 20S 134 40E
66 Anyang, China 36 15N 114 35E
60 Anzhero-Sudzhensk, U.S.S.R. 56 10N 85 40E
43 Anzin, France 50 20N 3 30E
40 Anzio, Italy 41 28N 12 37E
67 Aomori, & Pref., Japan 40 40N 140 40E
43 Aosta, Italy 45 46N 7 20E
72 Aoulef Arab, Algeria 27 0N 1 0E
91 Apalachee B., U.S.A. 30 0N 84 10W
91 Apalachicola, U.S.A. 29 47N 85 5W
68 Aparri, Philippines 18 15N 121 50E
44 Apeldoorn, Netherlands 52 13N 5 58E
40 Apennines, Mts., Italy 43 0N 13 0E
84 Apia, Upolu I., Samoa (Inset)
73 Apollonia (Marsa Susa), Libya 32 52N 21 59E
92 Apostle Is., U.S.A. 47 0N 90 45W
92 Appalachians, Mts., U.S.A. 37 0N 80 20W
44 Appenzell, & Cn., Switz. 47 20N 9 24E
44 Appingedam, Netherlands 53 17N 6 45E
26 Appleby, England 54 35N 2 30W
24 Appledore, Devon, England 51 3N 4 12W
23 Appledore, Kent, England 51 2N 0 47E
92 Appleton, U.S.A. 44 17N 88 27W
40 Apulia, Reg., Italy 40 40N 17 20E
95 Apure, R., Venezuela 7 30N 69 15W
98 Apurimac, R., Peru 13 0S 73 0W
73 Aqaba, & Gulf, Jordan 29 0N 35 0E
62 Aqiq, Sudan 18 10N 38 20E
62 Ar Rutbah, Iraq 33 0N 40 10E
62-63 Arab Emirates, Union of 23 50N 52 30E
72 Araba, Nigeria 13 7N 5 0E
62 Arabia, Asia 15 0 to 30 0N; 35 0 to 59 0E
73 Arabian Des., Egypt 28 0N 32 20E
57 Arabian Sea, Indian Oc. 17 0N 65 0E
98 Aracaju, Brazil 11 0S 37 0W
98 Aracati, Brazil 4 20S 37 45W
37 Aracena, Spain 37 53N 6 36W
98 Araçuai, Brazil 17 30S 42 0W
63 Arad, Israel 31 16N 35 13E
47 Arad, Rumania 46 10N 21 13E
37 Aragon, Prov., Spain 41 40N 0 40W
65 Arakan Coast Dist., Bur. 20 43N 93 20E
65 Arakan Yoma, Mts., Burma 20 0N 94 0E
51 Araks, R., Asia 39 0N 47 30E
60 Aral Sea, Cent. Asia 45 0N 59 0E
60 Aralsk, U.S.S.R. 46 50N 61 20E
82 Aramac, Australia 22 58S 145 14E
36 Aran I., Ireland 55 0N 8 32W
34 Aran Is, Ireland 53 5N 9 35W
37 Aranjuez, Spain 40 1N 3 38W
75 Aranos, S.W. Afr. 24 9S 19 7E
91 Aransas Pass, U.S.A. 27 55N 97 0W
72 Araouane, Mali 19 0N 3 30W
51 Araq, Iran 34 0N 49 50E
83 Ararat, Australia 37 30S 142 37E
51 Ararat, Mt., Turkey 39 40N 44 25E
98 Araripe, Sa. do, plat., Brazil 7 0S 40 0W
31 Arbroath, Scotland 56 33N 2 36W
42 Arcachon, France 44 39N 1 13W
37 Arcos, Spain 36 44N 5 47W
64 Arcot, India 12 50N 79 26E
100 Arctic Ocean
88 Arctic Red R., Canada 67 15N 134 0W
32 Ardcharnich, Scotland 57 52N 5 5W
51 Ardebil, Iran 38 24N 48 10E
42 Ardèche, Dépt., France 45 0N 4 40E
36 Ardee, Ireland 53 51N 6 32W
42 Ardennes, Dépt., France 49 33N 4 50E
44 Ardennes, Mts., Belg.-Fr. 50 0N 5 30E
51 Ardestan, Iran 33 22N 52 24E
34 Ardfinnan, Ireland 52 20N 7 53W
36 Ardglass, N. Ireland 54 15N 5 56W
32 Ardhasig, Scotland 57 55N 6 51W
36 Ardkeen, N. Ireland 54 27N 5 53W
35 Ardmore & Hd., Ire. 51 58N 7 44W
91 Ardmore, U.S.A. 34 11N 97 9W
34 Ardnacrusha, Ireland 52 42N 8 38W
32 Ardnamurchan Pt., Scot. 56 46N 6 14W
30 Ardrossan, Scotland 55 39N 4 49W
95 Areciba, Puerto Rico 18 28N 66 30W
49 Arendal, Norway 58 28N 8 43E
25 Arenig Fach, Mt., Wales 52 57N 3 46W
98 Arequipa, Peru 16 30S 71 25W
42 Arès, France 44 46N 1 10W
37 Arévalo, Spain 41 0N 4 45W
40 Arezzo, Italy 43 29N 11 54E
42 Argentan, France 48 43N 0 2W
43 Argentat, France 45 8N 2 0E
96 Argentina, S. Amer. 30 30S 65 0W
99 Argentino, L., Argentina 50 30S 72 54W
43 Argenton, France 46 35N 1 30E
47 Arges, R., Rumania 44 25N 25 40E
72 Argo, L., Sudan 19 30N 30 28E
41 Argolis, G. of, Greece 37 44N 22 54E
41 Argos, Greece 37 39N 22 42E
72 Argungu, Nigeria 12 55N 4 30E
30 Argyll, Dist., Scot. 56 20N 5 25W
98 Arica, Chile 18 37S 70 18W
80 Arid, C., Australia 34 0S 123 20E
42 Ariège, Dépt., France 43 20N 1 30E
94 Arima, Trinidad 10 40N 61 15W
98 Arinos, R., Brazil 12 0S 57 0W
98 Aripuana, R., Brazil 7 30S 60 0W
32 Arisaig, & Sd. of, Scot. 56 54N 5 48W
90 Arizona, st., U.S.A. 34 30N 111 30W
48 Arjeplog, Sweden 66 0N 18 0E
32 Arkaig, L., Scotland 56 58N 5 10W
90 Arkansas, R., U.S.A. 38 5N 103 0W
91 Arkansas, st., U.S.A. 35 0N 92 0W
91 Arkansas City, U.S.A. 37 9N 97 3W
50 Arkhangelsk, U.S.S.R. 64 35N 40 50E
35 Arklow, & Hd., Ireland 52 47N 6 9W
43 Arles, France 43 10N 4 42E
44 Arlon, Belgium 49 41N 5 49E
31 Armadale, Scotland 55 54N 3 42W
36 Armagh & Co., N. Ire. 54 20N 6 38W
51 Armavir, U.S.S.R. 45 0N 41 7E
51 Armenia, S.S.R., U.S.S.R. 40 0N 45 0E
43 Armentières, France 50 40N 2 55E
83 Armidale, Australia 30 30S 151 40E
48 Arnar Fjord, Iceland 65 45N 23 50W
48 Arnes, Iceland 66 2N 22 32W
44 Arnhem, Netherlands 51 59N 5 55E
80 Arnhem B., Austral. 12 15S 136 4E
80 Arnhem Ld., Australia 13 15S 133 30E
40 Arno, R., Italy 43 41N 10 40W
27 Arnold, England 53 0N 1 8W
48 Arnöy I., Norway 70 5N 20 30E
92 Arnprior, Canada 45 28N 76 26W
76 Aroab, S.W. Afr. 26 41S 19 39E
37 Aroche, Spain 37 58N 7 0W
43 Arona, Italy 45 48N 8 32E
62 Arqa, S. Yemen 13 35N 47 22E
34 Arra Mts., Ireland 52 50N 8 22W
65 Arrah, India 25 40N 84 38E
94 Arraijan, Panama 8 57N 79 38W
30 Arran I., Scotland 55 35N 5 15W
43 Arras, France 50 17N 2 40E
72 Arrecife, Canary Is. 28 58N 13 35W
42 Arrée, Mts. d', France 48 25N 3 35W
36 Arrow L., Ireland 54 3N 8 19W
67 Arshan, China 47 20N 119 55E
41 Arta, Greece 39 10N 20 59E
61 Artem, U.S.S.R. 43 50N 131 55E
52 Artemovsk, U.S.S.R. 48 25N 38 5E
61 Artemovski, U.S.S.R. 54 45N 93 35E
43 Artois, Prov., France 50 30N 2 20E
51 Artvin, Turkey 41 10N 41 3E
74 Arua, Uganda 3 1N 30 58E
95 Aruba I., Neth. W. Indies 12 30N 70 0W
23 Arun, R., England 51 0N 0 27W
65 Arunachal Pradesh, st., India 28 0N 95 0E
23 Arundel, England 50 52N 0 33W
74 Arusha, Tanzania 3 10S 36 50E
74 Aruwimi, R., Zaïre 1 30N 25 0E
45 Arve, R., France 45 56N 6 40E
49 Arvika, Sweden 59 43N 12 34E
60 Arys, U.S.S.R. 42 20N 68 30E
52 Arzamas, U.S.S.R. 55 30N 43 45E
72 Arzew, Algeria 35 50N 0 40W
63 As Rabbah, Jordan 31 10N 35 45E
62 As Sabya, Saudi Arabia 17 10N 42 37E
63 As Salt, Jordan 32 1N 35 44E
63 As Sohar, Oman 24 20N 56 40E
63 As Zahiriyah, Jordan 31 24N 34 56E
67 Asahigawa, Japan 43 50N 142 20E
5 Ascension I., Atlantic Oc. 7 55S 14 0W
45 Aschaffenburg, Germany 49 58N 9 10E
40 Ascoli Piceno, Italy 42 54N 13 37E
23 Ascot, England 51 24N 0 41W
62 Aseb, Ethiopia 13 5N 42 38E
74 Asela, Ethiopia 8 0N 39 0E
44 Asfeld, France 49 27N 4 5E
23 Ash, England 51 16N 0 18W
62 Ash Shihr, S. Yemen 14 50N 49 35E
62 Ashaira, Saudi Arabia 21 40N 40 40E
27 Ashbourne, England 53 1N 1 44W
24 Ashburton, England 50 31N 3 46W
84 Ashburton, N.Z. 53 59S 171 52E
80 Ashburton R., Australia 22 20S 115 12E
22 Ashby-de-la-Zouch, Eng. 52 45N 1 30W
63 Ashdod, Israel 31 49N 34 38E
63 Ashdod Yam, Israel 31 47N 34 39E
23 Ashdown Forest, Eng. 51 4N 0 10E
91 Asheville, U.S.A. 35 40N 82 33W
23 Ashford, England 51 8N 0 52E
67 Ashikaga, Japan 36 25N 139 20E
27 Ashington, England 55 12N 1 35W
63 Ashkhabad, U.S.S.R. 38 5N 58 22E
92 Ashland, Ky., U.S.A. 38 30N 82 42W
92 Ashland, Wis., U.S.A. 46 30N 91 0W
63 Ashquelon, Israel 31 40N 34 35E
92 Ashtabula, U.S.A. 41 55N 80 47W
26 Ashton-in-Makerfield, England 53 29N 2 39W
26 Ashton-under-Lyne, Eng. 53 30N 2 8W
5 Asia, Continent
51 Asia Minor, *see* Anatolia
72 Asilah, Morocco 35 30N 6 0W
60 Asino, U.S.S.R. 57 0N 86 0E
62 Asir, Dist., Saudi Arabia 18 25N 43 0E
49 Askersund, Sweden 58 58N 14 8E
25 Aslackby, England 52 53N 0 23W
74 Asmera, Ethiopia 15 20N 38 49E
26 Aspatria, England 54 45N 3 20W
84 Aspiring, Mt., N.Z. 44 31S 168 41E
65 Assam, st., India 25 20N 93 30E
44 Asse, Belgium 50 55N 4 12E
46 Assen, Netherlands 53 0N 6 35E
88 Assiniboia, Canada 49 36N 106 4W
88 Assiniboine R., Canada 49 45N 99 0W
72 Assinie, Ivory Coast 5 9N 3 15W
40 Assisi, Italy 43 5N 12 38E
32 Assynt, L. & Dist., Scot. 58 10N 5 1W
40 Asti, Italy 44 54N 8 15E
37 Astorga, Spain 42 28N 6 9E
90 Astoria, U.S.A. 46 10N 123 45E
51 Astrakhan, U.S.S.R. 46 25N 48 8W
37 Asturias, Prov., Spain 43 20N 5 50E
99 Asunción, Paraguay 25 25S 57 35E
73 Aswan, Egypt 24 12N 32 59W
73 Asyut, Egypt 27 15N 31 0S
99 Atacama Des., Chile 25 0S 70 0W
72 Atakpame, Togo 7 35N 1 0E
72 Atar, Mauritania 20 30N 13 0W
61 Atara, U.S.S.R. 63 10N 129 10E
60 Atasu, U.S.S.R. 48 30N 71 0E
73 Atbara, Sudan 17 20N 35 0E
73 Atbara, R., Sudan 13 50N 36 0E
60 Atbasar, U.S.S.R. 51 50N 68 25E
91 Atchison, U.S.A. 39 31N 95 10W
44 Ath, Belgium 50 39N 3 48E
88 Athabasca, Canada 54 48N 113 15W
88 Athabasca L. & R., Can. 59 20N 109 30W
35 Athboy, Ireland 53 38N 6 57W
34 Athenry, Ireland 53 19N 8 45W
41 Athens, Greece 37 59N 23 42E
91 Athens, Georgia, U.S.A. 33 57N 83 29W
92 Athens, Ohio, U.S.A. 39 28N 82 12W
91 Athens, Tenn., U.S.A. 35 29N 84 42W
22 Atherstone, England 52 35N 1 32W
82 Atherton, Australia 16 54S 145 3E
26 Atherton, England 53 32N 2 30W
34 Athleague, Ireland 53 34N 8 17W
34 Athlone, Ireland 53 27N 7 55W
33 Athol, Forest of, Scot. 56 51N 4 0W
41 Athos, Mt., Greece 40 9N 24 23E
35 Athy, Ireland 53 0N 7 0W
73 Ati, Chad 13 25N 17 0E
92 Atikokan, Canada 48 45N 91 43W
52 Atkarsk, U.S.S.R. 52 0N 45 3E
91 Atlanta, U.S.A. 33 45N 84 25W
93 Atlantic City, U.S.A. 39 24N 74 28W
10 Atlantic Ocean, N. 35 0N 40 0W
10 Atlantic Ocean, S. 20 0S 10 0W
72 Atlas Mts., Morocco 33 0N 1 0W
44 Attigny, France 49 29N 4 35E
23 Attleborough, England 52 32N 1 1E
64 Attock, Pakistan 33 58N 72 32E
68 Attopeu, Laos 14 50N 107 0E
64 Attur, India 11 35N 78 30E
43 Aubagne, France 43 20N 5 30E
42 Aube, Dépt., France 48 30N 4 0E
43 Aube, R., France 48 35N 4 30E
43 Aubenas, France 44 38N 4 20E
44 Aubenton, France 49 50N 4 11E
43 Aubigny, France 47 30N 2 25E
45 Aubonne, Switzerland 46 31N 6 42E
93 Auburn, Me., U.S.A. 44 0N 70 10W
92 Auburn, N.Y., U.S.A. 42 55N 76 38W
43 Auch, France 43 39N 0 32E

Auchinleck, Scotland 55 28N 4 18W
Auchterarder, Scotland 56 18N 3 43W
Auchterderran, Scotland 56 9N 3 16W
Auchtermuchty, Scotland 56 18N 3 15W
Auchtertyre, Scotland 57 17N 5 35W
Auckland, N.Z. 36 50S 174 42E
Auckland Is., S. Ocean 51 0S 168 0E
Aude, Dépt., France 43 2N 2 25E
Aude, R., France 42 47N 2 9E
Audierne, France 48 2N 4 38W
Aughnacloy, N. Ireland 54 26N 6 59W
Aughrus More, Ireland 53 34N 10 10W
Augsburg, Germany 48 26N 10 53E
Augusta, Australia 34 18S 115 12E
Augusta, Italy 37 14N 15 12E
Augusta, Me., U.S.A. 44 20N 69 45W
Augusta, Ga., U.S.A. 33 30N 82 0W
Augustow, Poland 53 51N 22 58E
Augustus, Mt., Australia 24 8S 117 0E
Aulnoye, France 50 10N 3 50E
Aumale, France 49 50N 1 45E
Aunis, Dist., France 46 9N 0 57W
Aurangabad, India 19 55N 75 30E
Auray, France 47 40N 3 0W
Aurillac, France 44 58N 2 27E
Aurora, Ill., U.S.A. 41 48N 88 15W
Aus, S.W. Africa 26 43S 16 12E
Aust-Agder, Co., Norway 59 0N 8 30E
Austin, Minn., U.S.A. 43 39N 92 59W
Austin, Tex., U.S.A. 30 20N 97 46W
Austral Downs, Australia 20 45S 137 40E
Austral Is., Pacific Ocean 23 0S 150 0W
Australia, Commonwealth of, 25 0S 135 0E
Australian Alps, Australia 37 0S 148 0E
Australian Cap. Terr., Australia 35 15N 149 8E
Austria, Europe 47 30N 13 20E
Austvågöy, I., Norway 68 25N 14 45E
Autun, France 47 1N 4 20E
Auvergne, Prov., France 45 30N 3 0E
Auvergne Monts d', France 45 30N 3 0E
Auxerre, France 47 48N 3 33W
Avakubi, Zaïre 1 16N 27 30E
Avallon, France 47 34N 3 49E
Aveh, Iran 35 40N 49 15E
Aveiro, Portugal 40 39N 8 39W
Avellino, Italy 41 0N 14 42E
Aversa, Italy 41 0N 14 10E
Avesnes, France 50 9N 3 55E
Avesta, Sweden 60 13N 16 4E
Aveyron, Dépt., France 44 10N 2 45E
Aviá Terai, Argentina 26 30S 60 45W
Avignon, France 43 58N 4 54E
Avila, Spain 40 39N 4 41W
Aviles, Spain 43 33N 6 0W
Avoca, Ireland 52 51N 6 12W
Avon, Co., England 51 25N 2 35W
Avon, R., Hants, Eng. 51 8N 1 48W
Avon, R., Warwick, Eng. 52 22N 1 25W
Avon, R., Scotland 57 15N 3 23W
Avon Downs, Australia 19 58S 137 25E
Avonmouth, England 51 30N 2 43W
Avranches, France 48 42N 1 18W
Awash, Ethiopia 9 8N 40 7E
Awe, L. & R., Scotland 56 17N 5 15W
Awjilah, Libya 29 8N 21 7E
Axar, Fd., Iceland 66 20N 16 45W
Axbridge, England 51 17N 2 50W
Axe, R., England 51 17N 2 50W
Axe Edge, England 53 13N 1 58W
Axholme, I. of, England 53 33N 0 50W
Axim, Ghana 4 58N 2 6W
Axminster, England 50 46N 3 0W
Ayacucho, Peru 12 58S 74 5W
Ayaguz, U.S.S.R. 48 10N 80 0E
Ayamonte, Spain 37 15N 7 26W
Ayan, U.S.S.R. 56 0N 137 0E
Aydin, Turkey 37 55N 27 55E
Ayios Evstratios, I., Gr. 39 30N 24 59E
Aylesbury, England 51 49N 0 48W
Aylesford, England 51 18N 0 29E
Aylsham, England 52 48N 1 16E
Ayr, Australia 19 36S 147 25E
Ayr, Scotland 55 27N 4 37W
Ayre, Pt. of, Isle of Man 54 25N 4 22W
Ayton, England 54 15N 0 29W
Ayutla, Mexico 17 0N 99 5W
Ayutthaya, Thailand 14 30N 100 40E
Ayvalik, Turkey 39 20N 26 50E
Azamgarh, India 26 15N 83 16E
Azare, Nigeria 11 55N 10 10E
Azerbaijan, S.S.R., U.S.S.R. 40 20N 48 0E
Azores Is., Atlantic Oc. 39 0N 29 0W
Azov, U.S.S.R. 47 3N 39 20E
Azov, S. of, U.S.S.R. 45 53N 35 35E
Azpeitia, Spain 43 13N 2 14W
Azua, Dominican Rep. 18 15N 70 40W
Azuaga, Spain 38 16N 5 42W
Azul, Argentina 36 25S 59 40W

B

Ba'âbda, Lebanon 33 50N 35 32E
Ba'labakk (Baalbek), Leb. 34 0N 36 12E
Baarle-Nassau, Neth. 51 27N 4 57E
Baarn, Neth. 52 13N 5 17E
Bab el Mandeb Str. 12 37N 43 22E
Babar Is., Indonesia 8 2S 128 58E
Babinda, Australia 17 27S 146 0E
Babine L., Canada 54 40N 126 10W
Baboua, Central Africa 5 49N 14 58E
Babul, Iran 36 40N 52 40E
Babushkin, U.S.S.R. 55 50N 38 0E
Babuyan Is., Philippines 19 20N 121 45E
68 Bacan Gr., Is., Indonesia 0 30S 127 0E
47 Bacau, Rumania 46 30N 26 59E
43 Baccarat, France 48 30N 6 45E
60 Bachelina, U.S.S.R. 57 45N 67 20E
45 Backnang, Germany 48 57N 9 26E
68 Bacolod, Philippines 10 40N 123 2E
68 Bacuit, Philippines 11 0N 119 25E
26 Bacup, England 53 44N 2 13W
43 Bad Hersfeld, Germany 50 50N 9 40E
45 Bad Homburg, Germany 50 15N 8 36E
46 Bad Ischl, Austria 47 40N 13 39E
45 Bad Kissingen, Germany 50 10N 10 10E
45 Bad Kreuznach, Germany 49 51N 7 50E
90 Bad Lands, U.S.A. 43 30N 102 10W
45 Bad Mergentheim, Ger. 49 29N 9 46E
64 Badagara, India 11 35N 75 35E
72 Badagri, Nigeria 6 25N 2 55E
37 Badajoz, Spain 38 51N 7 0W
64 Badakhshan, Dist., Afghanistan 36 40N 70 0E
37 Badalona, Spain 41 28N 2 30E
65 Badampahar, India 22 10N 86 10E
64 Baddo R., Pak. 28 20N 65 10E
46 Baden, Austria 48 0N 16 46E
45 Baden, Switzerland 47 29N 8 18E
45 Baden-Baden, Germany 48 44N 8 18E
33 Badenoch, Dist., Scot. 57 5N 4 0W
45 Baden-Württemberg, Länd, Germany 48 45N 9 0E
46 Badgastein, Austria 47 7N 13 9E
64 Badrinath, India 30 45N 79 25E
64 Badulla, Sri Lanka 6 48N 81 7E
89 Baffin B. & I., Canada 73 0N 70 0W
74 Bafia, Cameroon 4 40N 11 10E
72 Bafoulabe, Mali 13 45N 11 0W
63 Bafq, Iran 31 40N 55 28E
74 Bafwasende, Zaïre 1 20N 27 20E
68 Bagansiapiapi, Indonesia 2 5N 101 0E
99 Bagé, Brazil 31 10S 54 10W
35 Bagenalstown, *see* Muine Bheag
51 Baghdad, Iran 33 23N 44 30E
32 Bagh nam Faoileann, B., Scotland 57 22N 7 10W
42 Bagnères de Bigorre, Fr. 43 0N 0 5E
43 Bagnères de Luchon, Fr. 42 45N 0 35E
93 Bagotville, Canada 48 28N 70 58W
66 Bagrach Kol, China 42 0N 87 0E
23 Bagshot, England 51 21N 0 39W
68 Baguio, Philippines 16 17N 120 47E
91 Bahama Is., W. Indies 26 0N 77 30W
64 Bahawalpur, Pak. 29 0N 72 0E
98 Bahia Prov., Brazil 12 0S 42 0W
99 Bahia Blanca, Argentina 38 45S 62 25W
99 Bahias, C. dos, Argentina 45 0S 65 30W
62 Bahr el Abyad (White Nile), Sudan 13 30N 33 0E
62 Bahr el Azraq (Blue Nile), Sudan 14 30N 33 30E
73 Bahr el Ghazal, R., Sudan 9 0N 30 0E
73 Bahr el Jebel, R., Sudan 7 30N 30 35E
62 Bahra, Saudi Arabia 21 15N 39 30E
65 Bahraich, India 27 48N 81 30E
62 Bahrain I., Persian G. 26 0N 50 23E
64 Bahu Kalat, Iran 25 40N 61 15E
47 Baia Mare, Rumania 47 40N 23 32E
89 Baie Comeau, Canada 49 25N 68 20W
61 Baikit, U.S.S.R. 61 40N 96 5E
60 Baikonur, U.S.S.R. 47 48N 66 4E
27 Baildon, England 53 52N 1 46W
36 Baillieborough, Ireland 53 56N 6 59W
42 Bain, France 47 52N 1 40W
91 Bainbridge, U.S.A. 31 0N 84 30W
88 Baird Mts. Alaska 60 45 N 160 0W
83 Bairnsdale, Australia 38 0S 147 32E
65 Baitadi, Nepal, India 29 35N 80 25E
47 Baja, Hungary 46 10N 19 0E
74 Bakala, Central Africa 6 15N 20 20E
90 Baker, Ore., U.S.A. 44 45N 117 50W
88 Baker Lake, Canada 64 20N 96 0W
90 Baker, Mt., U.S.A. 48 45N 121 45W
89 Baker's Dozen, Is., Can. 56 45N 79 20W
90 Bakersfield, Calif., U.S.A. 35 22N 119 0W
27 Bakewell, England 53 12N 1 40W
48 Bakkagerdi, Iceland 65 33N 13 58W
47 Bakony Forest, Hungary 47 30N 18 0E
51 Baku, U.S.S.R. 40 27N 49 48E
61 Bala, U.S.S.R. 66 40N 133 5E
25 Bala, tn. & L., Wales 52 55N 3 37W
63 Ba'labakk, Lebanon 34 0N 36 12E
64 Balaghat Ra., India 18 58N 76 0E
37 Balaguer, Spain 41 52N 0 50E
83 Balaklava, Australia 34 2S 138 20E
51 Balaklava, U.S.S.R. 44 27N 33 44E
65 Balangir, India 20 50N 83 25E
52 Balashikha, U.S.S.R. 55 47N 37 59E
50 Balashov, U.S.S.R. 51 35N 43 5E
65 Balasore, India 21 31N 87 10E
47 Balaton, L., Hungary 46 47N 17 40E
31 Balbeggie, Scotland 56 26N 3 19W
94 Balboa, Panama Canal Zone (Inset)
35 Balbriggan, Ireland 53 36N 6 12W
99 Balcarce, Argentina 38 30S 58 0W
41 Balchik, Bulgaria 43 23N 28 11E
84 Balclutha, N.Z. 46 15S 169 50E
23 Baldock, England 51 59N 0 11W
90 Baldy Pk., U.S.A. 33 50N 109 30W
61 Baldzhikan, U.S.S.R. 49 20N 110 30E
37 Balearic Is., Spain 39 40N 3 0E
32 Baleshare I., Scotland 57 30N 7 21W
63 Balfouriya, Israel 32 38N 35 17E
30 Balfron, Scotland 56 4N 4 20W
62 Balhaf, South Yemen 14 0N 48 10E
74 Bali, Cameroon 5 54N 10 0E
68 Bali, I., Indonesia 8 30S 115 20E
41 Balikesir, Turkey 30 40N 28 2E
68 Balikpapan, Indonesia 1 10S 116 55E
33 Balintore, Scotland 57 45N 3 55W
65 Balipara, India 26 54N 92 51E
41 Balkan Mts., Bulgaria 42 50N 24 50E
60 Balkhash, L., U.S.S.R. 46 30N 76 0E
63 Balkh, Afghanistan 36 44N 66 47E
65 Balla, Bangladesh 24 10N 91 35E
30 Ballachulish, Scot., *see* N. Ballachulish
36 Ballaghaderreen, Ireland 53 55N 8 34W
30 Ballantrae, Scotland 55 6N 5 0W
83 Ballarat, Australia 37 37S 143 50E
33 Ballater, Scotland 57 3N 3 3W
26 Ballaugh, Isle of Man 54 20N 4 32W
100 Balleny Is., S. Ocean 64 0S 160 0E
83 Ballina, Australia 28 48S 153 40E
36 Ballina, Mayo, Ireland 54 8N 9 10W
34 Ballina, Tipperary, Ire. 52 50N 8 27W
36 Ballinalee, Ireland 53 46N 7 40W
36 Ballinamore, Ireland 54 3N 7 48W
36 Ballinasloe, Ireland 53 20N 8 12W
34 Ballincollig, Ireland 51 52N 8 35W
35 Ballindaggin, Ireland 52 34N 6 41W
36 Ballindine, Ireland 53 40N 8 57W
34 Ballineen, Ireland 51 44N 8 57W
34 Ballingarry, Limerick, Ire. 52 29N 8 50W
35 Ballingarry, Tipp., Ire. 53 1N 8 3W
36 Ballinlough, Ireland 53 45N 8 39W
31 Ballinluig, Scotland 56 38N 3 39W
34 Ballinrobe, Ireland 53 37N 9 12W
36 Ballintoy, Ireland 55 13N 6 20W
36 Ballintra, Ireland 54 35N 8 9W
35 Ballivor, Ireland 53 32N 6 58W
30 Balloch, Scotland 56 0N 4 35W
35 Ballon, Ireland 52 44N 6 47W
36 Ballybay, Ireland 54 8N 6 52W
36 Ballybofey, Ireland 54 48N 7 47W
34 Ballybunion, Ireland 52 31N 9 40W
35 Ballycanew, Ireland 52 37N 6 18W
36 Ballyconnell, Ireland 54 7N 7 35W
34 Ballycotton, Ireland 51 50N 8 0W
34 Ballycroy, Ireland 54 2N 9 49W
34 Ballydavid, Ireland 52 13N 10 21W
34 Ballydehob, Ireland 51 34N 9 29W
34 Ballyduff, Kerry, Ire. 52 27N 9 40W
34 Ballyduff, Waterford, Ire. 52 9N 8 2W
34 Ballyforan, Ireland 53 29N 8 16W
34 Ballygar, Ireland 53 33N 8 20W
35 Ballygarrett, Ireland 52 34N 6 15W
36 Ballygawley, N. Ireland 54 27N 7 2W
36 Ballyhaise, Ireland 54 3N 7 20W
36 Ballyhalbert, N. Ireland 54 30N 5 33W
36 Ballyhaunis, Ireland 53 47N 8 47W
34 Ballyheige, Ireland 52 24N 9 50W
36 Ballyjamesduff, Ireland 53 52N 7 11W
34 Ballylanders, Ireland 52 22N 8 21W
34 Ballylongford, Ireland 52 34N 9 30W
35 Ballylynan, Ireland 52 56N 7 3W
35 Ballymahon, Ireland 53 33N 7 47W
36 Ballymoe, Ireland 53 41N 8 28W
35 Ballymore, Ireland 53 29N 7 40W
35 Ballymore Eustace, Ire. 53 8N 6 38W
36 Ballymote, Ireland 54 5N 8 30W
35 Ballynacargy, Ireland 53 35N 7 32W
36 Ballynahinch, N. Ireland 54 25N 5 54W
36 Ballynure, N. Ireland 54 47 N 5 59W
36 Ballyragget, Ireland 52 47N 7 20W
35 Ballyroan, Ireland 52 57N 7 20W
36 Ballysadare, Ireland 54 12N 8 30W
36 Ballyshannon, Ireland 54 30N 8 10W
36 Ballyvaughan, Ireland 53 7N 9 9W
36 Ballywalter, N. Ireland 54 33N 5 30W
33 Balmoral Castle, Scotland 57 2N 3 14W
30 Balquhidder, Scotland 56 22N 4 22W
65 Balrampur, India 27 25N 82 20E
83 Balranald, Australia 34 40S 143 25E
94 Balsas, R., Mexico 18 30N 102 0W
45 Balsthal, Switzerland 47 20N 7 42E
49 Baltic Sea, Europe 57 0N 19 30E
49 Baltiisk, U.S.S.R. 54 40N 19 10E
36 Baltimore, Ireland 51 29N 9 20W
92 Baltimore, U.S.A. 39 25N 76 40W
64 Baluchistan, Reg., Pak. 27 30N 65 0E
63 Bam, Iran 29 5N 58 23E
72 Bamako, Mali 12 30N 7 45W
72 Bamba, Mali 17 0N 1 0W
74 Bambari, Central Africa 5 40N 20 35E
82 Bambaroo, Australia 18 57S 146 15E
45 Bamberg, Germany 49 53N 11 14E
27 Bamburgh, England 55 37N 1 42W
64 Bamian, Afghanistan 35 0N 67 53E
22 Bampton, England 51 44N 1 33W
63 Bampur, Iran 27 8N 60 8E
68 Ban Aranyaprathet, Thailand 13 40N 102 35E
68 Ban Khemmarat, Thail. 16 0N 105 20E
34 Banagher, Ireland 53 12N 7 59W
74 Banalia, Zaïre 1 40N 25 20E
65 Banaras, India *see* Varanasi
47 Banat, Dist., Rumania 45 27N 21 35E
36 Banbridge, N. Ireland 54 20N 6 16W
22 Banbury, England 52 4N 1 20W
33 Banchory, Scotland 57 3N 2 30W
75 Bancroft, Zambia, *see* Chililabombwe
68 Banda Aceh, Indonesia 5 35N 95 25E
68 Banda Sea, East Indies 6 0S 127 30E
67 Bandaisan, Mt., Japan 37 40N 140 30E
72 Bandama, R., Ivory Coast 7 0N 5 0W
63 Bandar Abbas, Iran 27 15N 56 23E
63 Bandar Rig, Iran 29 27N 50 47E
62 Bandar Shah, Iran 37 4N 54 0E
62 Bandar Shapur, Iran 30 10N 48 40E
72 Bandiagara, Mali 14 12N 3 29W
49 Bandirma, Turkey 40 21N 27 58E
34 Bandon, Ireland 51 45N 8 43W
74 Bandundu, Zaire 3 12S 17 12E
68 Bangung, Indonesia 6 48S 107 45E
88 Banff, Canada 51 14N 115 38W
33 Banff, Scotland 57 41N 2 32W
72 Banfora, Volta 10 40N 4 40W
64 Bangalore, India 12 58N 77 50E
74 Bangassou, Central Africa 4 50N 22 48E
68 Banggai, Arch., Indonesia 1 15S 123 0E
68 Bangka, I., Indonesia 2 20S 106 0E
68 Bangkalan, Indonesia 7 10S 112 50E
68 Bangkok, Thailand 13 55N 100 30E
65 Bangladesh, South Asia 24 0N 90 0E
36 Bangor, N. Ireland 54 39N 5 39W
91 Bangor, Me., U.S.A. 44 45N 68 40W
25 Bangor, Wales 53 14N 4 7W
74 Bangui, Central Africa 4 23N 19 20E
74 Bangweulu, L., Zambia 11 30S 30 5E
63 Banias, Syria 35 7N 36 2E
40 Banja Luka, Yugoslavia 44 45N 17 0E
68 Banjarmasin, Indonesia 3 20S 114 25E
72 Banjul, Gambia 13 20N 16 38W
31 Bankfoot, Scotland 56 30N 3 31W
73 Baninah, Libya 32 10N 20 15E
65 Bankipore, India 25 35N 85 10E
82 Banks I., Australia 10 5S 142 12E
88 Banks I., Canada 73 30N 122 0W
84 Banks Pen., N.Z. 43 47S 173 0E
83 Banks Str., Australia 40 40S 148 10E
65 Bankura, India 23 15N 85 5E
74 Banningville, *see* Bandundu
31 Bannockburn, Scotland 56 5N 3 55W
64 Bannu, Pakistan 33 0N 70 18E
47 Banská Bystrica, Cz.-slov. 48 46N 19 54E
47 Banská Stiavnica, Cz.-slov. 48 26N 18 54E
34 Banteer, Ireland 52 8N 8 53W
34 Bantry, & B., Ireland 51 1N 9 27W
74 Banyo, Cameroon 6 58N 11 50E
74 Banzyville (Mobayi), Zaïre 4 15N 21 8E
64 Bapatla, India 15 50N 80 30E
44 Bapaume, France 50 7N 2 49E
51 Baquba, Iraq 33 45N 44 50E
41 Bar, Yugoslavia 42 4N 19 7E
91 Bar Harbor, U.S.A. 44 20N 68 17W
43 Bar-le-Duc, France 48 45N 5 8E
43 Bar-s.-Aube, France 48 18N 4 45E
43 Bar-s.-Seine, France 48 6N 4 28E
60 Barabinsk, U.S.S.R. 55 30N 78 35E
92 Baraboo, U.S.A. 43 30N 89 48W
95 Baracoa, Cuba 20 20N 74 20W
95 Barahona, Dom. Rep. 18 0N 71 2W
65 Barail Ra., India 25 15N 93 0E
65 Barakhola, India 25 0N 92 40E
83 Barakula, Australia 26 30S 150 33E
64 Baramula, Kashmir 34 15N 74 25E
64 Baran, India 25 3N 76 30E
88 Baranof I., Alaska 57 0N 135 0W
50 Baranovichi, U.S.S.R. 53 10N 26 0E
98 Barbacena, Brazil 21 0S 44 0W
95 Barbados I., W. Indies 13 15N 59 30W
76 Barberton, Transvaal 25 42S 31 1E
42 Barbezieux, France 45 30N 0 12W
95 Barbuda I., W. Indies 17 43N 61 42W
82 Barcaldine, Australia 23 30S 145 17E
73 Barce (Al Marj), Libya 32 30N 20 50E
37 Barcelona, Spain 41 24N 2 9E
95 Barcelona, Venezuela 10 12N 64 45W
43 Barcelonnette, France 44 20N 6 35E
73 Bardai, Chad 21 15N 17 40E
73 Bardiyah, Libya 31 45 25 0E
27 Bardney, England 53 13N 0 19W
43 Bardonecchia, Italy 45 5N 6 40E
64 Bareilly, India 28 25N 79 32E
100 Barents Sea, Arctic Oc. 73 0N 42 0E
74 Barentu, Ethiopia 15 2N 37 35E
42 Barfleur, France 49 40N 1 20W
65 Barhi, India 24 20N 85 20E
40 Bari, Italy 41 7N 16 53E
64 Bari Doab, Pakistan 30 30N 73 0E
64 Bari Sadri, India 24 20N 74 27E
88 Baring C., Canada 70 0N 116 30W
74 Baringo, L., Kenya 0 35N 36 0E
65 Barisal, Bangladesh 22 50N 90 32E
68 Barisan Mts., Indonesia 4 0S 103 0E
23 Barking, Greater London, England 51 32N 0 5E
80 Barkly Tableland, Australia 19 40S 138 30E
66 Barkol, China 44 18N 90 48E
27 Barlby, England 53 48N 1 3W
80 Barlee L., Australia 29 10S 119 28E
40 Barletta, Italy 41 20N 16 17E
27 Barmby Moor, England 53 55N 0 47W
83 Barmedman, Australia 34 0S 147 16E
64 Barmer, India 25 49N 71 32E
31 Barmoor Castle, England 55 38N 2 0W
25 Barmouth, Wales 52 43N 4 3W
34 Barna, Ireland 53 14N 9 10W
26 Barnard Castle, England 54 33N 1 56W
83 Barnato, Australia 31 35S 145 0E
60 Barnaul, U.S.S.R. 53 10N 83 30E
83 Barnes, Australia 36 2S 144 40E
23 Barnet, Greater London, England 51 40N 0 11W
44 Barneveld, Neth. 52 7N 5 36E
42 Barneville, France 49 23N 1 45W
26 Barnoldswick, England 53 55N 2 11W
27 Barnsley, England 53 34N 1 29W
24 Barnstaple, England 51 5N 4 2W
24 Barnstaple or Bideford Bay, England 51 5N 4 20W
72 Baro, Nigeria 8 50N 6 25E
64 Baroda, *see* Vadodara
75 Barotse, Prov., Zambia 15 30S 23 30E
65 Barpeta, India 26 20N 91 0E
95 Barquisimeto, Venezuela 9 55N 69 15W
43 Barr, France 48 20N 7 20E
98 Barra, Brazil 10 30S 42 28W
32 Barra I., & Sd., Scotland 57 0N 7 30W
83 Barraba, Australia 30 12S 150 40E
65 Barrackpore, India 22 45N 88 30E
37 Barrancos, Portugal 38 10N 7 0W
95 Barranquilla, Colombia 10 49N 74 45W
93 Barre, U.S.A. 44 28N 72 25W
37 Barreiro, Portugal 38 42N 8 56W
75 Barren Is., Madagascar 18 30S 44 0E
30 Barrhead, Scotland 55 47N 4 24W
92 Barrie, Canada 44 30N 79 45W
26 Barrow, England 54 8N 3 12W
80 Barrow I., Australia 20 47S 115 25E
80 Barrow Ra., Mts., Austral. 26 0S 128 0E
27 Barrow upon Humber, England 53 41N 0 22W
26 Barrowford, England 53 51N 2 14W
25 Barry, Wales 51 24N 3 17W
65 Barsoi, India 25 48N 87 57E
91 Bartlesville, U.S.A. 36 48N 96 15W
86 Bartlett Deep, W. Indies 20 0N 85 0W
27 Barton-upon-Humber, England 53 41N 0 27W
64 Baruch, India 21 50N 73 10E
42 Bas-Rhin, Dépt., France 48 45N 7 35E
50 Bashkir, A.S.S.R., U.S.S.R. 54 0N 56 0E
68 Basilan, I., Philippines 6 40N 122 0E
23 Basildon, England 51 34N 0 29E
40 Basilicata, Prov., Italy 40 30N 16 0E
22 Basingstoke, England 51 16N 1 5W
80 Baskerville, C., Australia 17 0S 122 5E
45 Basle, & Cn., Switzerland 47 33N 7 34E
74 Basoka, Zaïre 1 20N 23 38E
37 Basque Provinces, Spain 43 20N 2 20W
62 Basra, Iraq 30 30N 47 50E
83 Bass Str., Australia 39 30S 146 0E
88 Bassano, Canada 50 45N 112 30W
40 Bassano, Italy 45 50N 11 40E
75 Bassas da India, Is., Ind. Oc. 21 45S 37 38E
94 Basse Terre, Guadeloupe 16 0N 61 45W
65 Bassein, Burma 17 0N 94 58E
42 Basses Alpes, Dépt., Fr. 44 40N 6 20E
42 Basses-Pyrénées, Dépt., France 43 17N 0 57W
43 Bassigny, Dist., France 48 3N 5 23E
65 Bastar, India 19 30N 81 30E
65 Basti, India 26 45N 82 58E
43 Bastia, Corsica 42 40N 9 20E
44 Bastogne, Belgium 50 0N 5 40E
23 Baston, England 52 43N 0 19W
75 Basutoland, *see* Lesotho
63 Bat Shelomo, Israel 32 36N 35 0E
63 Bat Yam, Israel 32 0N 34 44E
74 Bata, Rio Muni 1 57N 9 50E
95 Batabano, G., Cuba 22 20N 82 40W
37 Batalha, Portugal 39 40N 8 52W
67 Batan, Is., Philippines 20 25N 122 5E
66 Batang, China 30 20N 98 25E
68 Batangas, Philippines 13 50N 121 5E
92 Batavia, U.S.A. 43 0N 78 2W
52 Bataysk, U.S.S.R. 47 5N 39 45E
83 Bateman's Bay, Australia 35 40S 150 12E
22 Bath, England 51 24N 2 22W
91 Bath, Me., U.S.A. 43 57N 69 58W
63 Batha, Wadi, Oman 22 30N 59 0E
31 Bathgate, Scotland 55 55N 3 38W
83 Bathurst, Australia 33 28S 149 30E
93 Bathurst, Canada 47 37N 65 49W
72 Bathurst, Gambia *see* Banjul
88 Bathurst Inlet, Canada 67 30N 109 0W
27 Batley, England 53 44N 1 38W
83 Batlow, Australia 35 33S 148 10E
72 Batna, Algeria 35 32N 6 20E
91 Baton Rouge, U.S.A. 30 22N 90 50W
74 Batongafo, Central Africa 7 30N 18 20E
74 Batouri, Cameroon 4 30N 14 25E
68 Battambang, Cambodia 13 5N 103 8E
64 Batticaloa, Sri Lanka 7 50N 81 31E
23 Battle, England 50 55N 0 29E
92 Battle Creek, U.S.A. 42 17N 85 10W
89 Battle Harbour, Canada 52 13N 55 42W
88 Battleford, Canada 52 40N 108 12W
68 Batu Is., Indonesia 0 20S 98 5E
74 Batu, Mt., Ethiopia 6 50N 39 30E
51 Batumi, U.S.S.R. 41 40N 41 30E
68 Baturaja, Indonesia 4 10S 104 10E
98 Baturite, Brazil 4 0S 38 40W
74 Baudouinville (Moba), Zaïre 7 0S 29 48E
42 Bauge, France 47 35N 0 10W
45 Baume les Dames, France 47 21N 6 21E
98 Baurú, Brazil 22 12S 49 8W
49 Bauska, U.S.S.R. 56 24N 24 15E
46 Bautzen, Germany 51 14N 14 23E
46 Bavaria, land, Germany 49 0N 12 0E
72 Bawku, Ghana 11 3N 0 19W
65 Bawlake, Burma 19 0N 97 30E
92 Bay Cy., Mich., U.S.A. 43 38N 83 48W
95 Bayamo, Cuba 20 25N 76 40W
66 Bayan Khara Shan Mts., China 34 0N 98 0E
66 Bayanhongor, Mts., Mongolia 46 35N 99 45E
74 Bayanga, Central Africa 2 55N 16 15E
32 Bayble, Scotland 58 12N 6 13W
42 Bayeux, France 49 20N 0 44W
60 Bayhan Aul, U.S.S.R. 50 50N 75 50E
61 Baykal, L., U.S.S.R. 53 0N 108 0E
42 Bayonne, France 43 30N 1 30W
46 Bayreuth, Germany 49 57N 11 32E
37 Baza, Spain 37 31N 2 46W
52 Bazarnyy Syzgan, U.S.S.R. 53 45N 46 45E

83 Beachport, Australia 37 30S 140 0E
23 Beachy Hd., England 50 44N 0 17E
23 Beaconsfield, England 51 36N 0 39W
99 Beagle Chan, Chile 55 0S 68 30W
22 Beaminster, England 50 48N 2 46W
90 Bear, L. & R., U.S.A. 42 0N 111 20W
100 Beardmore, Antarc. 83 30S 175 0E
100 Beardmore Glacier, Antarctica 84 30S 170 0E
42 Béarn, Prov., France 43 20N 0 40W
30 Bearsden, Scotland 55 55N 4 19W
91 Beatrice, U.S.A. 40 20N 96 46W
31 Beattock, Scotland 55 19N 3 27W
43 Beaucaire, France 43 50N 4 35E
83 Beaudesert, Australia 28 0S 152 50E
68 Beaufort, Malaysia 5 25N 115 50E
100 Beaufort Sea, Arctic Oc. 75 0N 160 0W
43 Beaujolais, Dist., France 46 10N 4 30E
33 Beauly, & Firth, Scot. 57 28N 4 28W
25 Beaumaris, Wales 53 17N 4 6W
91 Beaumont, U.S.A. 30 4N 94 10W
43 Beaune, France 47 2N 4 50E
43 Beauvais, France 49 26N 2 2E
88 Beauval, Canada 55 10N 107 55W
91 Beaverdam, U.S.A. 43 30N 88 50W
26 Bebington, England 53 25N 3 1W
23 Beccles, England 52 28N 1 36E
41 Becejo, Yugoslavia 45 33N 20 2E
72 Bechar, Algeria 31 40N 2 17W
31 Beckfoot, England 54 50N 3 25W
27 Beckingham, England 53 24N 0 49W
92 Beckley, U.S.A. 37 44N 81 42W
27 Bedale, England 54 18N 1 35W
43 Bédarieux, France 43 40N 3 10E
23 Bedford, & Co., England 52 8N 0 28W
92 Bedford, Ind., U.S.A. 39 6N 86 37W
23 Bedford Level, England 52 50N 0 15W
27 Bedlington, England 55 9N 1 35W
25 Bedwas, England 51 36N 3 10W
22 Bedworth, England 52 28N 1 29W
83 Beenleigh, Australia 27 52S 153 0E
27 Beeston, England 52 55N 1 11W
74 Befale, Zaïre 0 5N 21 0E
36 Beg, L., N. Ireland 54 48N 6 25W
83 Bega, Australia 36 48S 149 55E
25 Begelly, Wales 51 45N 4 44W
61 Begichev I., U.S.S.R. 74 20N 112 30E
65 Behariganj, India 25 40N 87 0E
73 Beida (Al Bayda), Libya 32 35N 21 25E
62 Beihan al Daula, South Yemen 14 45N 45 15E
75 Beira, Mozambique 19 45S 35 0E
37 Beira-Alta, Prov., Port. 40 35N 7 35W
37 Beira-Baixa, Prov., Port. 40 0N 7 30W
37 Beira-Litoral Prov., Port. 40 5N 8 30W
63 Beirut (Bayrut), Lebanon 33 55N 35 30E
63 Beit Alfa, Israel 32 31N 35 25E
63 Beit Eddine, Lebanon 33 42N 35 35E
63 Beit Hanun, Israel 31 32N 34 31E
63 Beit Shean, Israel 32 30N 35 30E
63 Beit Yosef, Israel 32 34N 35 33E
75 Beitbridge, Rhodesia 22 12S 30 0E
30 Beith, Scotland 55 45N 4 38W
37 Beja, Portugal 38 2N 7 51W
72 Beja, Tunisia 36 55N 9 5E
72 Bejaia (Bougie), Algeria 36 49N 5 7E
47 Békéscaba, Hungary 46 40N 21 0E
41 Bela Crkva, Y.-slav. 44 54N 21 22E
68 Belawan, Indonesia 3 45N 98 45E
51 Belaya Tserkov, U.S.S.R. 49 40N 30 10E
89 Belcher Is., Canada 56 0N 80 30W
51 Belebei, Russia 54 10N 54 5E
98 Belem (Pará), Brazil 1 25S 48 20W
37 Belem, Portugal 38 40N 9 10W
52 Belev, U.S.S.R. 53 50N 36 5E
36 Belfast, & L., N. Ireland 54 35N 5 57W
93 Belfast, Me., U.S.A. 44 15N 69 0W
42 Belfort, France 47 41N 6 54E
42 Belfort, Dépt., France 47 38N 6 52E
64 Belgaum, India 15 42N 74 40E
44 Belgium, Europe 51 0N 4 10E
52 Belgorod, U.S.S.R. 50 30N 36 40E
51 Belgorod Dnestrovski, U.S.S.R. 46 11N 30 23E
41 Belgrade (Beograd), Yugoslavia 44 48N 20 33E
68 Beliton, I., Indonesia 3 0S 108 0E
94 Belize, St., Cent. America 17 0N 88 40W
94 Belize, Belize 17 28N 88 20W
83 Bell Bay, Australia 41 2S 146 48E
31 Bell Rock, Scot., 56 26N 2 24W
98 Bell Ville, Argentina 32 30S 62 50W
88 Bella Coola, Canada 52 25N 126 40W
36 Bellaghy, N. Ireland 54 50N 6 31W
45 Bellágio, Italy 45 55N 9 20E
92 Bellaire, Ohio, U.S.A. 40 1N 80 48W
36 Bellanagare, Ireland 53 49N 8 21W
36 Bellananagh, Ireland 53 53N 7 28W
64 Bellary, India 15 12N 77 5E
83 Bellata, Australia 29 58S 149 55E
36 Bellavary, Ireland 53 54N 9 10W
90 Belle Fourche R., U.S.A. 44 40N 104 0W
89 Belle I., Canada 52 10N 55 18W
42 Belle Ile, France 47 20N 3 12W
36 Belleek, N. Ireland 54 30N 8 6W
43 Bellegarde, France 46 4N 5 46E
89 Belleville, Canada 44 15N 77 37W
92 Belleville, Ill., U.S.A. 38 30N 90 7W
43 Belley, France 45 45N 5 45E
83 Bellingen, Australia 30 25S 152 50E
31 Bellingham, Eng., 55 9N 2 16W
90 Bellingham, U.S.A. 48 45N 122 48W
100 Bellingshausen Sea, Antarctica 65 0S 80 0W
45 Bellinzona, Switzerland 46 12N 9 1E
40 Belluno, Italy 46 8N 12 12E
37 Belmez, Spain 38 15N 5 15W
83 Belmont, Australia 33 0S 151 35E
94 Belmopan, Br. Honduras 17 12N 88 0W
35 Belmullet, Ireland 54 13N 9 58W
98 Belo Horizonte, Brazil 19 55S 44 0W
75 Belo sur Tsiribihina, Madagascar 19 40S 44 30W
50 Belomorsk, U.S.S.R. 64 35N 34 30E
65 Belonia, India 23 15N 91 25E
50 Beloretsk, U.S.S.R. 54 0N 58 0E
60 Belovo, U.S.S.R. 54 35N 86 27E
50 Beloye L., U.S.S.R. 60 10N 37 35E
27 Belper, England 53 2N 1 28W
27 Belton (Lincs.), England 53 33N 0 49W
23 Belton (Suff.), England 52 35N 1 39E
91 Belton, Texas, U.S.A. 31 30N 97 30W
36 Beltra, Sligo, Ireland 54 12N 8 36W
47 Beltsy, U.S.S.R. 47 48N 28 0E
36 Belturbet, Ireland 54 6N 7 25W
22 Bembridge, England 50 41N 1 4W
91 Bemidji, U.S.A. 47 30N 94 58W
33 Ben Alder, Scotland 56 49N 4 30W
33 Ben Avon, Scotland 57 7N 3 18W
31 Ben Chonzie, Scotland 56 27N 4 0W
30 Ben Cruachan, Scotland 56 27N 5 5W
33 Ben Dearg, Perth, Scot. 56 54N 3 50W
33 Ben Dhorain, Scotland 58 7N 3 50W
30 Ben Dorain, Scotland 56 30N 4 42W
33 Ben Hope, Scotland 58 26N 4 33W
30 Ben Lawers, Scotland 56 31N 4 17W
30 Ben Lomond, Scotland 56 10N 4 30W
33 Ben Loyal, Scotland 58 25N 4 25W
30 Ben Lui, Scotland 56 23N 4 45W
33 Ben Macdhui, Scotland 57 3N 3 30W
32 Ben Mhor, Lewis, Scot. 57 58N 6 30W
32 Ben Mhor, S. Uist., Scot. 57 16N 7 18W
30 Ben More, Perth, Scot. 56 20N 4 30W
33 Ben More Assynt, Suth., Dist., Scotland 58 9N 4 53W
32 Ben Nevis, Scotland 56 46N 5 0W
33 Ben Sgeirach, Scotland 58 4N 4 39W
32 Ben Sgritheall, Scotland 57 9N 5 34W
32 Ben Stack, Scotland 58 20N 4 58W
30 Ben Venue, Scotland 56 13N 4 28W
30 Ben Vorlich, Scotland 56 22N 4 15W
33 Ben Wyvis, Scotland 57 41N 4 40W
72 Bena, Nigeria 11 20N 5 50E
83 Benalla, Australia 36 34S 146 0E
83 Benanee, Australia 34 26S 142 56E
65 Benares, *see* Varanasi
34 Benbaun, Mt., Ireland 53 30N 9 50W
32 Benbecula I., Scotland 57 26N 7 20W
80 Bencubbin, Australia 30 56S 118 5E
90 Bend, U.S.A. 44 3N 121 15W
47 Bendery, U.S.S.R. 46 50N 29 28E
83 Bendigo, Australia 36 48S 144 13E
63 Benei Berag, Israel 32 5N 34 50E
40 Benevento, Italy 41 8N 14 50E
73 Benghazi, Libya 32 10N 20 5E
68 Bengkalis, Indonesia 1 38N 102 9E
75 Benguela, Angola 12 20S 13 10E
72 Beni Abbès, Algeria 30 10N 2 0W
73 Beni Mazâr, Egypt 28 32N 30 44E
72 Beni Mellal, Morocco 32 21N 6 14W
73 Beni Suef, Egypt 29 2N 30 58E
73 Beni Ulid, Libya 31 50N 14 20E
72 Benin, W. Africa 9 0N 2 0E
72 Benin City, Nigeria 6 20N 5 31E
68 Bengkulu, Indonesia 3 40S 102 40E
88 Bennett, Canada 59 50N 135 0W
61 Bennett I., U.S.S.R., 76 30N 150 0E
35 Bennettsbridge, Ireland 52 36N 7 12W
93 Bennington, U.S.A. 42 55N 73 16W
63 Bennt Jbail, Lebanon 33 7N 35 26E
76 Benoni, Trans. S. Africa 26 11S 28 18E
45 Bensheim, Germany 49 41N 8 36E
82 Bentinck I., Australia 17 15S 139 30E
73 Bentiu, Sudan 9 10N 29 55E
27 Bentley, Yorks., England 53 33N 1 9W
92 Benton Harbor, U.S.A. 42 8N 86 28W
72 Benue R., Nigeria 8 0N 7 30E
41 Beograd, *see* Belgrade
67 Beppu, Japan 33 15N 131 35E
94 Bequia, W. Indies 13 0N 61 15W
72 Ber Rechid, Morocco 33 0N 7 35E
36 Beragh, N. Ireland 54 34N 7 10W
41 Berat, Albania 40 40N 20 0E
73 Berber, Sudan 18 2N 34 2E
71 Berbera, Somali Rep. 10 30N 45 25E
45 Bercher, Switzerland 46 43N 6 43E
52 Berdichev, U.S.S.R. 49 50N 28 45E
52 Berdyansk, U.S.S.R. 46 42N 36 47E
47 Beregovo, U.S.S.R. 48 15N 22 45E
72 Berekum, Ghana 7 29N 2 34W
47 Bereza, U.S.S.R. 52 45N 25 0E
50 Berezniki, U.S.S.R. 59 25N 56 5E
50 Berezovo, U.S.S.R. 64 5N 65 0E
41 Bergama, Turkey 39 6N 27 20E
40 Bergamo, Italy 45 42N 9 40E
49 Bergen, Norway 60 21N 5 22E
44 Bergen Binnen, Neth. 52 40N 4 40E
44 Bergen-op-Zoom, Neth. 51 30N 4 17E
43 Bergerac, France 44 53N 0 26E
44 Bergum, Netherlands 53 12N 5 59E
76 Bergville, S. Africa 28 40S 29 20E
65 Berhampore, India 24 10N 88 20E
65 Berhampur, India 19 24N 84 50E
61 Bering Sea, Pacific Ocean 57 0N 173 0E
37 Berja, Spain 36 45N 3 0W
22 Berkeley, England 51 42N 2 27W
90 Berkeley, U.S.A. 38 6N 122 0W
23 Berkhamsted, England 51 45N 0 33W
22 Berks. Downs, England 51 30N 1 20W
22 Berkshire, Co., England 51 25N 1 15W
46 Berlin, Germany 52 31N 13 20E
93 Berlin, N.H., U.S.A. 44 28N 71 11W
100 Bermejo, R., Arg. 25 40S 59 40W
42 Bermeo, Spain 43 26N 2 46W
95 Bermuda Is., Atlantic Oc. 32 20N 65 0W
45 Bern and Cn., Switz. 46 57N 7 27E
43 Bernay, France 49 5N 0 32E
46 Bernburg, Germany 51 40N 11 42E
45 Berner Alpen, Mts., Switzerland 46 25N 7 30E
32 Berneray, I., Scotland 56 47N 7 40W
80 Bernier I., Australia 24 58S 113 0E
45 Bernina, Mt., Switzerland 46 22N 9 50E
63 Beror Hayil, Israel 31 34N 34 39E
75 Beroroha, Madagascar 21 40S 45 10E
46 Beroun, Cz.-slov. 50 0N 14 5E
83 Berri, Australia 34 12S 140 38E
33 Berriedale, Scotland 58 10N 3 31W
83 Berry, Australia 34 48S 150 48E
43 Berry, Prov., France 46 48N 2 5E
74 Bertoua, Cameroon 4 30N 13 45E
48 Beru Fjord, Iceland 64 40N 14 15W
48 Berufjordur, Iceland 64 47N 14 28W
31 Berwick-upon-Tweed, England 55 47N 2 2W
25 Berwyn Mts., Wales 52 54N 3 25W
75 Besalampy, Madagascar 16 43S 44 29E
43 Besançon, France 47 18N 6 0E
47 Beskids, E., Mts., Eur. 49 8N 22 10E
47 Beskids, W., Mts., Eur. 49 8N 19 0E
47 Bessarabia, reg., U.S.S.R. 47 20N 28 20E
36 Bessbrook, N. Ireland 54 11N 6 23W
43 Bességes, France 44 20N 4 2E
92 Bessemer, U.S.A. 46 30N 90 0W
73 Betaré-Oya, Cameroon 5 40N 14 15E
76 Bethanien, S.W. Africa 26 32S 17 11E
63 Bethlehem, Jordan 31 42N 35 12E
76 Bethlehem, S. Africa 28 5S 28 30E
93 Bethlehem, Pa., U.S.A. 40 25N 75 30W
76 Bethulie, S. Africa 30 30S 26 0E
43 Béthune, France 50 30N 2 40E
75 Betioky, Madag. 23 48S 44 20E
89 Betsiamites, Canada 48 53N 68 46W
23 Betteshanger, England 51 13N 1 20E
65 Bettiah, India 26 59N 84 38E
64 Betul, India 21 50N 77 50E
25 Betws-y-Coed, Wales 53 5N 3 50W
44 Beveren, Belgium 51 14N 4 16E
80 Beverley, Australia 32 25S 116 58E
27 Beverley, England 53 51N 0 27W
44 Beverwijk, Netherlands 52 28N 4 38E
45 Bex, Switzerland 46 16N 7 2E
23 Bexhill, England 50 50N 0 27E
23 Bexley, Gt. London, Eng. 51 26N 0 10E
41 Beykoz, Turkey 41 6N 29 8E
72 Beyla, Guinea 8 35N 8 30W
41 Beypazari, Turkey 40 11N 31 50E
51 Beysehir Gölü L., Tur. 37 50N 31 30E
52 Bezhitsa, U.S.S.R. 53 25N 34 18E
43 Beziers, France 43 27N 3 15E
64 Bhachau, India 23 20N 70 16E
65 Bhadrakh, India 21 0N 86 30E
65 Bhagalpur, India 25 12N 86 52E
65 Bhamo, Burma 24 16N 96 50E
65 Bhamragarh, India 19 30N 80 30E
64 Bhandara, India 21 8N 79 40E
64 Bharatpur, India 27 19N 77 50E
65 Bhatpara, India 23 0N 88 30E
64 Bhavnagar, India 21 59N 72 19E
64 Bhima, R., India 17 25N 76 0E
65 Bhimvaram, India 16 30N 81 30E
64 Bhiwandi, India 19 15N 72 55E
65 Bhola, Bangladesh 22 45N 90 35E
64 Bhopal, India 23 15N 77 30E
65 Bhubaneswar, India 20 10N 85 50E
64 Bhuj, India 23 10N 69 45E
64 Bhusawal, India 21 10N 75 56E
65 Bhutan, Asia 27 30N 90 20E
74 Biafra, B. of, *see* Bonny, B. of
47 Biala Podlaska, Poland 52 2N 23 0E
47 Bialystok, Poland 53 4N 23 12E
42 Biarritz, France 43 30N 1 32W
45 Biasca, Switzerland 46 22N 8 39E
45 Biberach, Germany 48 5N 9 45E
72 Bibiani, Ghana 6 30N 2 8W
82 Biboohra, Australia 16 35S 145 27E
22 Bibury, England 51 46N 1 50W
22 Bicester, England 51 55N 1 9W
25 Bicton, England 52 43N 2 47W
72 Bida, Nigeria 9 2N 6 12E
64 Bidar, India 17 58N 77 35E
23 Biddenden, England 51 7N 0 40E
26 Biddulph, England 53 8N 2 11W
24 Bideford, England 51 1N 4 13W
22 Bidford on Avon, Eng. 52 9N 1 53W
72 Bidon 5, *see* Poste Maurice Cortier
75 Bié, Angola 12 16S 16 5E
75 Bié Plateau, Angola 13 0S 16 40E
45 Biel, Switzerland 47 9N 7 15E
46 Bielefeld, Germany 52 2N 8 17E
45 Bieler See, Switzerland 47 7N 7 18E
47 Bielsko, Poland 49 50N 19 10E
68 Bien Hoa, Vietnam 11 0N 107 0E
91 Big Belt, Mts., U.S.A. 46 40N 111 30W
88 Big Salmon, Canada 61 50N 136 0W
90 Big Spring, U.S.A. 32 14N 101 32W
91 Big Stone L., U.S.A. 45 30N 96 30W
89 Big Trout L., Canada 54 30N 90 0W
24 Bigbury, tn. & B., England 50 17N 3 52W
88 Biggar, Canada 52 6N 108 0W
31 Biggar, Scotland 55 38N 3 31W
83 Biggenden, Australia 25 30S 152 0E
23 Biggleswade, England 52 5N 0 17W
90 Bighorn, Mts., U.S.A. 44 30N 107 30W
45 Bignasco, Switzerland 46 20N 8 36E
40 Bihac, Yugoslavia 44 46N 15 57E
65 Bihar, st., India 23 0N 85 30E
65 Bijapur, Mad. P., India 18 50N 80 50E
64 Bijapur, Mysore, India 16 55N 75 57E
62 Bijar, Iran 32 52N 47 35E
41 Bijeljina, Yugoslavia 44 42N 19 15E
64 Bikaner, India 28 1N 73 40E
63 Bikfaïya, Lebanon 33 55N 35 40E
61 Bikin, U.S.S.R. 46 50N 134 15E
74 Bikoro, Zaïre 0 48S 18 15E
64 Bilara, India 26 20N 73 58E
65 Bilaspur, Mad. P., India 22 2N 82 14E
68 Bilauk Taung Ra., Thail. 13 30N 99 15W
37 Bilbao, Spain 43 16N 2 53W
48 Bildudalur, Iceland 65 20N 23 40W
51 Bilecik, Turkey 40 16N 29 52E
61 Bilir, U.S.S.R. 65 40N 131 20E
23 Billericay, England 51 38N 0 25E
23 Billesdon, England 52 38N 0 56W
27 Billingham, England 54 36N 1 18W
90 Billings, U.S.A. 45 58N 108 30W
73 Bilma, Niger 18 5N 13 20E
82 Biloela, Australia 24 25S 150 35E
91 Biloxi, U.S.A. 30 32N 89 0W
22 Bilston, England 52 34N 2 7W
73 Biltine, Chad 14 40N 20 50E
82 Bilyana, Australia 18 5S 145 50E
72 Bimbéreké, Benin 10 11N 2 43E
64 Bina-Etawah, India 24 11N 78 12E
44 Binche, Belgium 50 25N 14 12E
83 Binda, Australia 27 50S 147 20E
75 Bindura, Rhodesia 17 15S 31 20E
83 Bingara, Australia 29 40S 150 40E
27 Bingham, England 52 57N 0 55W
93 Binghampton, U.S.A. 42 5N 75 48W
26 Bingley, England 53 51N 1 50W
68 Binh-dinh, *see* An Nhon
68 Binjai, Indonesia 3 30N 98 30E
99 Bio Bio, R., Chile 37 40S 71 30W
64 Bir, India 19 4N 75 58E
63 Bir, Iran 25 26N 59 47E
73 Bir Atrun, Sudan 28 15N 26 40E
62 Bir Terfawi, Egypt 22 7N 28 10E
73 Bir Ungat, Egypt 22 8N 33 48E
63 Bir Zeit, Jordan 31 59N 35 11E
73 Birao, Central Africa 10 20N 22 40E
23 Birch, England 51 50N 0 54E
83 Birdsville, Australia 25 58S 139 20E
80 Birdum, Australia 15 30S 133 0E
63 Birjand, Iran 32 52N 59 7E
26 Birkdale, England 53 38N 3 2W
26 Birkenhead, England 53 23N 3 3W
47 Birlad, Rumania 46 15N 27 38E
22 Birmingham, England 52 29N 1 54W
91 Birmingham, U.S.A. 33 37N 86 45W
65 Birmitrapur, India 22 30N 84 10E
72 Birnin-Kebbi, Nigeria 12 32N 4 12E
61 Birobidzhan, U.S.S.R. 48 50N 132 50E
50 Birsk, U.S.S.R. 55 23N 55 35E
31 Birtley, England 54 55N 1 33W
27 Birtley, England 55 5N 2 12W
64 Birur, India 13 30N 75 55E
40 Birzebbuga, Malta 35 52N 14 31E
13 Biscay, B. of, Atlantic Oc. 46 20N 4 0W
27 Bishop Auckland, Eng. 54 40N 1 41W
22 Bishop's Cleeve, England 51 56N 2 3W
24 Bishop's Nympton, Eng. 50 58N 3 44W
23 Bishop's Stortford, Eng. 51 53N 0 10E
24 Bishopsteignton, Eng. 50 32N 3 32W
72 Biskra, Algeria 34 50N 5 45E
90 Bismarck, U.S.A. 46 52N 100 45W
82 Bismarck Arch., Papua N.G. 2 0S 148 0E
82 Bismarck Sea, Papua N.G. 4 30S 149 0E
72 Bissagos Is., Guinea-B., 11 0N 16 0W
72 Bissau, Guinea-Bissau 11 50N 15 37W
47 Bistrita, Rumania 47 7N 24 32E
44 Bitburg, Germany 49 59N 6 32E
51 Bitlis, Turkey 38 30N 42 17E
41 Bitola (Monastir) Y.-slav. 41 1N 21 14E
73 Bitter Lakes, Egypt 30 10N 32 0E
76 Bitterfontein, S. Africa 31 0S 18 28E
90 Bitterroot Ra., U.S.A. 46 30N 115 0W
67 Biwa, L., Japan 35 15N 135 45E
60 Biysk, U.S.S.R., 52 40N 85 0E
76 Bizana, S. Africa 30 55S 29 50E
72 Bizerte, Tunisia 37 20N 9 45E
48 Bjargtangar, Iceland 65 30N 24 30W
48 Bjarnanes, Iceland 64 18N 15 10W
40 Bjelovar, Yugoslavia 46 0N 16 45E
49 Blaavands Huk, Denmark 55 33N 8 2E
22 Blaby, England 52 34N 1 10W
47 Black Crisul, R., Rumania 46 40N 22 0E
26 Black Fell, Mt., England 54 47N 2 34W
45 Black Forest, *see* Schwarzwald, Ger.
27 Black Hills, England 53 33N 1 45W
90 Black Hills, U.S.A. 44 0N 104 0W
33 Black Isle, Scotland 57 35N 4 15W
25 Black Mt., *see* Mynydd du
25 Black Mts., Wales 51 52N 3 5W
66 Black (Da) R., Viet Nam 21 30N 104 0E
90 Black Range, Mts., U.S.A. 33 0N 107 45W
51 Black Sea, Europe 43 0N 34 0E
72 Black Volta R., W. Africa 10 0N 3 0W
82 Blackall, Australia 24 20S 145 30E
84 Blackball, New Zealand 42 20S 171 35E
82 Blackbull, Australia 18 0S 141 7E
26 Blackburn, England 53 46N 2 30W
24 Blackdown Hills, Eng. 50 57N 3 15W
90 Blackfoot, U.S.A. 43 14N 112 22W
31 Blackford, Scotland 56 15N 3 48W
24 Blackmoor Vale, England 50 54N 2 18W
26 Blackpool, England 53 50N 3 3W
82 Blackwater, Australia 23 35S 149 0E
35 Blackwater, Ireland 52 27N 6 20W
34 Blackwater, R., Cork, Ire. 52 6N 8 30E
23 Blackwater, R., England 51 47N 0 38E
36 Blackwater, R., N. Ireland 54 26N 7 5W
31 Blackwood, Scotland 55 40N 3 56W
25 Blaenavon, Wales 51 46N 3 5W
51 Blagodarnoye, U.S.S.R. 45 0N 43 45E
61 Blagoveshchensk, U.S.S.R. 50 30N 127 55E
42 Blain, France 47 30N 1 42W
25 Blaina, Wales 51 46N 3 10W
42 Blainville, France 49 5N 1 32W
82 Blair Athol, Australia 22 50S 147 0E
33 Blair Atholl, Scotland 56 46N 3 50W
31 Blairgowrie, Scotland 56 36N 3 20W
88 Blairmore, Canada 49 40N 114 25W
23 Blakeney, Norfolk, England 52 57N 1 1E
72 Blanc, C., Mauritania 20 40N 17 0W
83 Blanche, L., Australia 29 15S 139 40E
94 Blanchisseuse, Trinidad 10 45N 61 18W
44 Blankenberge, Belgium 51 18N 3 8E
95 Blanquilla I., Venezuela 12 0N 64 30W
75 Blantyre, Malawi 15 50 35 1E
34 Blarney, Ireland 51 58N 8 35W
27 Blaydon, England 54 56N 1 47W
42 Blaye, France 45 8N 0 40W
83 Blayney, Australia 33 35S 149 10E
60 Blednaya, Mt., U.S.S.R. 75 50N 65 30E
46 Bleiburg, Austria 46 40N 14 55E
49 Blekinge, Co., Sweden 56 27N 15 10E
84 Blenheim, New Zealand 41 38S 174 5E
23 Bletchley, England 52 0N 0 45W
72 Blida, Algeria 36 30N 2 50E
68 Blitar, Indonesia 8 12S 112 25E
93 Block, I., U.S.A. 41 12N 71 32W
76 Bloemfontein, S. Africa 29 12S 26 15E
76 Bloemhof, S. Africa 27 30S 25 36E
23 Blofield, England 52 38N 1 25E
43 Blois, France 47 37N 1 19E
48 Blonduös, Iceland 65 40N 20 12W
36 Bloody Foreland, Ireland 55 9N 8 18W
92 Bloomington, Ill., U.S.A. 40 28N 88 59W
92 Bloomington, Ind., U.S.A. 39 10N 86 32W
83 Blue Mts., *see* Katoomba
90 Blue Mts., U.S.A. 45 0N 119 5W
80 Blue Mud B., Australia 13 30S 136 10E
73 Blue Nile, Dist., Sudan 12 40N 33 30E
73 Blue Nile, R., N.E. Africa 10 35N 35 0E
91 Blue Ridge Mts., U.S.A. 35 0N 82 0W
92 Bluefield, U.S.A. 37 28N 81 4W
95 Bluefields, Nicaragua 12 0N 83 45W
36 Blue Stack, Mt., Ireland 54 45N 8 9W
84 Bluff, New Zealand 46 32S 168 20E
99 Blumenau, Brazil 27 0S 49 0W
23 Blundeston, England 52 33N 1 42E
27 Blyth, England 55 7N 1 31W
31 Blyth Bridge, Scotland 55 41N 3 22W
27 Blyth R., England 55 6N 1 56W
23 Blythburgh, England 52 19N 1 36E
92 Blytheville, U.S.A. 35 56N 89 58W
72 Bo, Sierra Leone 7 55N 11 50W
98 Boa Vista, Brazil 2 55N 60 15W
65 Bobbili, India 18 35N 83 30E
45 Bobbio, Italy 44 50N 9 25E
72 Bobo-Dioulasso, Volta 11 20N 4 0W
46 Bobr, R., Poland 51 30N 15 28E
50 Bobruysk, U.S.S.R. 53 0N 30 0E
72 Bocanda, Ivory Coast 7 5N 4 31W
74 Bocaranga, Central Africa 7 0N 15 35W
44 Bocholt, Germany 51 51N 6 37E
44 Bochum, Germany 51 30N 7 15E
74 Boda, Central Africa 4 19N 17 26E
61 Bodaibo, U.S.S.R. 57 50N 114 0E
33 Boddam, Scotland 57 28N 1 46W
32 Boddam, Shetland Is., Scotland 59 55N 1 16W
48 Boden, Sweden 65 48N 21 45E
45 Bodensee, L., Germany 47 33N 9 30E
64 Bodhan, India 18 45N 77 50E
24 Bodmin Moor, England 50 33N 4 36W
48 Bodö, II, Norway 67 21N 14 20E
47 Bodrog, R., Hungary 48 20N 21 45E
74 Boende, Zaïre 0 15S 21 12E
35 Bog of Allen, Ireland 53 13N 7 20W
91 Bogalusa, U.S.A. 30 51N 89 56W
82 Bogan, R., Australia 31 0S 147 2E
83 Bogan Gate, Australia 33 0S 147 52E
75 Bogenfels, S.W. Africa 27 31S 15 33E
83 Boggabilla, Australia 28 40S 150 20E
83 Boggabri, Australia 30 45S 150 0E
34 Boggeragh, Mts., Ireland 52 2N 8 55W
72 Boghé, Mauritania 16 45N 14 10W
23 Bognor Regis, England 50 48N 0 42W
68 Bogor, Indonesia 6 30S 106 58E
72 Bogoro, Nigeria 9 37N 9 29E
98 Bogota, Colombia 4 38N 74 15W
60 Bogotol, U.S.S.R. 56 15N 89 50E
65 Bogra, Bangladesh 24 48N 89 24E
44 Bohain, France 49 59N 3 28E
46 Bohemia dist., Cz. 49 50N 51 0E
46 Bohemian For., Cz. 49 15N 13 20E
68 Bohol, I., Philippines 9 45N 124 20E
90 Boise, U.S.A. 43 54N 116 12W
72 Bojador, C., Span. Sahara 26 20N 14 55W
72 Boké, Guinea 10 56N 14 17W
49 Bokna Fd., Norway 59 12N 5 30E
74 Bokote, Zaïre 0 12S 21 8E
74 Bokungu, Zaïre 0 49S 23 12E
72 Bolama, Guinea-B. 11 30N 15 35W
43 Bolbec, France 49 35N 0 30E
46 Bolesawiec, Poland 51 17N 15 37E
47 Bolgrad, U.S.S.R. 45 40N 28 40E
99 Bolivar, Argentina 36 0S 61 0W
98 Bolivia, South America 16 0S 64 30W

49 Böllnäs, Sweden 61 24N 16 27E
83 Bollon, Australia 28 0S 147 36E
74 Bolobo, Zaïre 2 65S 16 20E
40 Bologna, Italy 44 29N 11 23E
50 Bologoye, U.S.S.R. 57 55N 34 5E
74 Bolomba, Zaïre 0 35N 19 0E
40 Bolsena, L., Italy 42 40N 12 0E
60 Bolshereche, U.S.S.R. 56 5N 74 40E
61 Bolshevik I., U.S.S.R. 78 30N 102 0E
60 Bolshoi I., U.S.S.R. 73 30N 142 0E
61 Bolshoi Altym, U.S.S.R. 62 25N 66 50E
61 Bolshoi Mamyr, U.S.S.R. 56 20N 102 55E
44 Bolsward, Netherlands 53 4N 5 31E
24 Bolt Hd., England 50 13N 3 48W
45 Boltigen, Switzerland 46 37N 7 24E
26 Bolton, England 53 25N 2 25W
26 Bolton Abbey, England 53 59N 1 53W
26 Bolton-by-Bowland, Eng. 53 56N 2 21W
51 Bolu, Turkey 40 46N 31 38E
34 Bolus Hd., Ireland 51 47N 10 21W
51 Bolvadin, Turkey 38 45N 31 57E
40 Bolzano, Italy 46 30N 11 23E
74 Boma, Zaïre 5 57S 12 40E
83 Bomaderry, Australia 34 55S 150 35E
83 Bombala, Australia 37 0S 149 3E
64 Bombay, India 18 55N 73 0E
66 Bomda, China 30 10N 95 10E
74 Bomongo, Zaïre 1 27N 18 21E
73 Bon, C., Tunisia 37 0N 11 0E
88 Bona Mt., Canada 61 20N 140 0W
98 Bonaire I., Neth. W.I. 12 12N 68 15W
83 Bonang, Australia 37 15S 150 35E
80 Bonaparte Arch., Austral. 13 0S 124 0E
33 Bonarbridge, Scotland 57 53N 4 20W
89 Bonavista, Canada 48 42N 53 5W
72 Bône, Algeria, see Annaba
68 Bone, G. of, Indonesia 4 38S 120 10E
31 Bo'ness, Scotland 56 1N 3 5W
74 Bongandanga, Zaïre 1 30N 21 0E
73 Bongor, Chad 10 35N 15 20E
43 Bonifacio, & Str., of, Medit. 41 18N 9 10E
5 Bonin Is., Pacific Oc. 27 0N 142 0E
44 Bonn, W. Germany 50 43N 7 7E
43 Bonneville, France 46 0N 6 30E
80 Bonnie Rock, Australia 30 10S 118 5E
74 Bonny, B. of, W. Africa 3 40N 9 30E
31 Bonnyrigg, Scotland 55 52N 3 8W
72 Bonthé, Sierra Leone 7 30N 12 33W
68 Bontoc, Philippines 17 10N 121 0E
44 Boom, Belgium 51 5N 4 22E
83 Boonah, Australia 28 0S 152 27E
83 Boorindal, Australia 30 25S 146 10E
83 Boorowa, Australia 34 26S 148 47E
26 Boot, England 54 24N 3 18W
88 Boothia, G. & Pen., Can. 70 0N 90 0W
26 Bootle, Cumberland, Eng. 54 17N 3 24W
26 Bootle, Lancs., England 53 28N 3 0W
74 Booué, Gabon 0 5S 11 55E
41 Bor, Yugoslavia 44 16N 22 3E
49 Boras, Sweden 57 46N 12 55E
62 Borazjan, Iran 29 22N 51 10E
42 Bordeaux, France 44 45N 0 38W
31 Borders, Reg., Scotland 55 30N 2 50W
83 Bordertown, Australia 36 21S 140 50E
48 Bordeyri, Iceland 65 12N 21 8E
43 Bordighera, Italy 43 50N 7 40E
72 Bordj-in-Eker, Algeria 24 5N 5 10E
23 Borehamwood, England 51 40N 0 15W
48 Borgarnes, Iceland 64 33N 21 55W
48 Börgefjell Mts., Norway 65 20N 13 30E
44 Borger, Netherlands 52 55N 6 46E
90 Borger, U.S.A. 35 43N 101 25W
49 Borgholm, Sweden 56 55N 16 40E
61 Boris Vilkitski Strait, U.S.S.R. 77 40N 105 0E
47 Borislav, U.S.S.R. 49 5N 23 26E
52 Borisoglebsk, U.S.S.R. 51 21N 42 5E
50 Borisov, U.S.S.R. 54 14N 28 20E
44 Borken, Germany 51 50N 6 50E
46 Borkum I., Germany 53 38N 6 41E
49 Borlänge, Sweden 60 28N 14 33E
45 Bormio, Italy 46 30N 10 20E
68 Borneo, I. Asia 1 0N 114 30E
49 Bornholm I., Denmark 55 9N 14 55E
72 Boromo, Volta 11 56N 2 59W
72 Bororen, Australia 24 13S 151 33E
50 Borovichi, U.S.S.R. 58 25N 33 58E
35 Borris, Ireland 52 36N 6 57W
35 Borris-in-Ossory, Ire. 52 57N 7 40W
34 Borrisokane, Ireland 53 0N 8 8W
34 Borrisoleigh, Ireland 52 48N 7 58W
81 Borroloola, Australia 16 7S 136 28E
26 Borrowdale, England 54 30N 3 9W
43 Bort, France 45 20N 2 30E
25 Borth, Wales 52 29N 4 3W
32 Borve, Scotland 58 25N 6 28W
56 Borzya, U.S.S.R. 50 25N 116 0E
40 Bosa, Sardinia, Italy 40 20N 8 25E
40 Bosanska Gradiska, Yugoslavia 45 20N 17 20E
41 Bosna, R., Yugoslavia 45 0N 18 10E
40 Bosnia, & Hercegovina, Fed. Unit, Yugoslavia 44 20N 17 40E
74 Bosobolo, Zaïre 4 14N 19 50E
41 Bosporus, Turkey 41 10N 29 6E
74 Bossangoa, Central Africa 6 35N 17 30E
74 Bossembelé, Cen. Africa 5 25N 17 40E
27 Boston, England 53 0N 0 3W
93 Boston, U.S.A. 42 18N 71 0W
93 Boston Mts., U.S.A. 36 0N 94 0W
49 Bothnia, G. of, Europe 62 0N 19 30E
83 Bothwell, Australia 42 28S 147 2E
47 Botosani, Rumania 47 42N 26 42E
75 Botswana, Africa 22 30S 24 0E
27 Bottesford, England 52 47N 0 48W
72 Botou, Upper Volta 12 45N 2 5E
44 Bottrop, Germany 51 34N 6 59E
72 Bou Arfa, Morocco 33 0N 2 0W
72 Bouaké, Ivory Coast 7 45N 5 0W
42 Bouches du Rhône, Dépt., France 43 28N 5 22E
72 Bougie, Algeria, see Bejaia
72 Bougouni, Mali 11 22N 7 12W
44 Bouillon, Belgium 49 50N 5 2E
80 Boulder, Australia 30 55S 121 28E
90 Boulder, U.S.A. 40 0N 105 0W
82 Boulia, Australia 23 0S 139 50E
43 Boulogne, France 50 42N 1 33E
90 Bountiful, U.S.A. 41 0N 111 58W
4 Bounty I., S. Ocean 48 0S 179 0E
61 Bour Khaya, C., U.S.S.R. 71 50N 133 10E
43 Bourbon Lancy, France 46 39N 3 45E
43 Bourbonnais, Prov., Fr. 46 20N 2 55E
72 Bourem, Mali 17 1N 0 30W
43 Bourg, France 46 14N 5 17E
43 Bourganeuf, France 45 55N 1 46E
43 Bourges, France 47 9N 2 25E
42 Bourgneuf, France 47 5N 1 58W
43 Bourgoin, France 45 38N 5 15E
83 Bourke, Australia 30 8S 145 59E
23 Bourne, England 52 47N 0 21W
23 Bournemouth, England 50 43N 1 54W
22 Bourton-on-the-Water, England 51 53N 1 45W
44 Boussu, Belgium 50 25N 3 42E
72 Boutilimit, Mauritania 17 30N 14 40W
1 Bouvet, Is., S. Atlantic 55 0S 3 30E
24 Bovey Tracey, England 50 36N 3 40W
44 Bovigny, Belgium 50 12N 5 55E
82 Bowen, Australia 19 59S 148 18E
83 Bowen, Mts., Australia 37 5S 148 0E
31 Bowes, England 54 31N 1 59W
27 Bowland Forest, England 54 0N 2 30W
92 Bowling Green, U.S.A. 36 59N 86 25W
83 Bowmans, Australia 34 15S 138 10E
30 Bowmore, Scotland 55 45N 6 17W
83 Bowral, Australia 34 27S 150 30E
83 Bowraville, Australia 30 40S 152 40E
23 Box Hill, England 51 16N 0 16W
44 Boxtel, Netherlands 51 37N 5 17E
36 Boyle, Ireland 53 59N 8 20W
41 Bozca 'Ada I., Turkey 39 50N 26 10E
90 Bozeman, U.S.A. 45 45N 111 5W
74 Bozoum, Central Africa 6 25N 16 35E
44 Brabant, N., Netherlands 51 37N 5 0E
44 Brabant, Prov., Belgium 50 47N 4 30E
40 Brac., I., Yugoslavia 43 20N 16 40E
32 Bracadale, L., Scotland 57 19N 6 30W
40 Bracciano, L., Italy 42 5N 12 15E
73 Brach, Libya 27 50N 14 50E
48 Bräcke, Sweden 62 50N 15 12E
22 Brackley, England 52 3N 1 10W
23 Bracknell, England 51 24N 0 45W
31 Braco, Scotland 56 16N 3 55W
47 Brad, Rumania 46 10N 22 45E
91 Bradenton, U.S.A. 27 30N 82 33W
26 Bradford, Yorks., Eng. 53 48N 1 46W
22 Bradford-on-Avon, Eng. 51 21N 2 15W
23 Bradwell-on-Sea, Eng. 51 44N 0 55E
32 Brae, Scotland 60 23N 1 20W
83 Braemar, Queens., Australia 25 35S 152 15E
83 Braemar, S. Australia 33 15S 139 35E
33 Braemar, Scotland 57 0N 3 24W
33 Braeriach, Mt., Scotland 57 6N 3 45W
31 Braes of Angus, Scotland 56 52N 3 0W
37 Braga, Portugal 41 34N 8 28W
99 Bragança, Brazil 0 56S 47 0W
37 Bragança, Portugal 41 48N 6 51W
65 Brahmani, R., India 20 52N 85 40E
65 Brahmanbaria, Bangla. 23 55N 91 15E
65 Brahmaputra, R., India 26 45N 93 0E
64 Brahmaur, India 32 28N 76 32E
83 Braidwood, Australia 35 28S 149 57E
47 Braila, Rumania 45 18N 27 57E
27 Brailsford, England 52 58N 1 35W
91 Brainerd, U.S.A. 46 16N 94 10W
23 Braintree, England 51 53N 0 33E
76 Brak, R., S. Africa 29 55S 23 12E
64 Bramhapuri, India 20 40N 79 30E
92 Brampton, Canada 43 40N 79 58W
26 Brampton, England 54 57N 2 46W
96 Branco, C., Brazil 7 20S 36 0W
46 Brandenburg, Germany 52 24N 12 31E
33 Branderburgh, Scotland 57 43N 3 17W
76 Brandfort, S. Africa 28 36S 26 28E
88 Brandon, Canada 49 50N 99 57W
47 Braniewo, Poland 54 25N 19 50E
47 Bransk, Poland 52 45N 22 50E
89 Brantford, Canada 43 17N 80 20W
83 Branxholme, Australia 38 0S 141 52E
98 Brasilia (Fed. Dist.), Braz. 16 0S 48 10W
47 Brasov, Rumania 45 35N 25 35E
45 Brasschaat, Belgium 51 17N 4 30E
46 Bratislava, Cz-slov. 48 7N 17 2E
61 Bratsk, U.S.S.R. 56 10N 101 30E
24 Braunton, England 51 6N 4 9W
90 Brawley, U.S.A. 32 58N 115 35W
34 Bray, Ireland 53 11N 6 6W
96 Brazil, S. America 0 0 to 30 0S; 35 0 to 75 0W
90 Brazos, R., U.S.A. 32 30N 97 30W
74 Brazzaville, Congo (Fr.) 4 7S 15 15E
41 Brcko, Yugoslavia 44 55N 18 40E
30 Breadalbane, Dist., Scot. 56 35N 4 15W
84 Bream, B., & Hd., N.Z. 35 56S 174 35E
31 Brechin, Scotland 56 46N 2 30W
23 Breckland, England 52 30N 1 20W
25 Brecon, Wales 51 57N 3 24W
25 Brecon Beacons, Wales 51 55N 3 30W
44 Breda, Netherlands 51 36N 4 46E
83 Bredbo, Australia 36 0S 148 40E
46 Bregenz, Austria 47 28N 9 45E
48 Breidi Fd., Iceland 65 15N 24 0W
49 Bremen, Germany 53 6N 8 51E
49 Bremerhaven, Germany 53 36N 8 40E
45 Bremgarten, Switzerland 47 21N 8 20E
40 Brenner Pass, Austra-Italy 47 1N 11 30E
45 Breno, Italy 45 57N 10 19E
23 Brent, Gt. London, Eng. 51 33N 0 15W
23 Brentwood, England 51 37N 0 19W
40 Brescia, Italy 45 35N 10 17E
42 Bressanone, Italy 46 43N 11 39E
32 Bressay, I. & Sd., Scot. 60 8N 1 5W
43 Bresse, Dist., France 46 25N 5 10E
42 Bressuire, France 46 50N 0 30W
42 Brest, France 48 26N 4 32W
47 Brest, U.S.S.R. 52 10N 23 40E
47 Bretcu, Rumania 46 2N 26 10E
91 Breton Sd., U.S.A. 29 30N 89 15E
84 Brett, C., N.Z. 35 12S 174 20W
42 Bretteville, France 49 18N 1 35W
42 Breuville, France 49 32N 1 40W
83 Brewarrina, Australia 30 0S 146 53E
22 Brewood, England 52 41N 2 10W
43 Briançon, France 44 53N 6 35E
43 Briare, France 47 40N 2 45E
83 Bribie I., Australia 26 55S 153 17E
75 Brickaville, Madagascar 18 49S 49 4E
31 Bridge of Allan, Scotland 56 9N 3 56W
31 Bridge of Earn, Scotland 56 22N 3 21W
30 Bridge of Orchy, Scot. 56 32N 4 46W
25 Bridgend, Wales 51 31N 3 35W
93 Bridgeport, U.S.A. 41 15N 73 13W
93 Bridgeton, U.S.A. 39 30N 75 15W
80 Bridgetown, Australia 33 59S 116 8E
94 Bridgetown, Barbados 13 5N 59 35W
93 Bridgewater, Canada 44 27N 64 30W
24 Bridgwater, England 51 8N 3 1W
22 Bridgnorth, England 52 32N 2 25W
27 Bridlington, England 54 7N 0 12W
83 Bridport, Australia 41 0S 147 32E
22 Bridport, England 50 44N 2 46W
43 Brienne, France 48 23N 4 30E
45 Brienz, Switzerland 46 47N 8 2E
22 Brierley Hill, England 52 29N 2 7W
44 Briey, France 49 15N 5 56E
45 Brig, Switzerland 46 20N 8 0E
27 Brigg, England 53 34N 0 30W
90 Brigham City, U.S.A. 41 35N 111 58W
27 Brighouse, England 53 42N 1 46W
83 Bright, Australia 36 48S 147 0E
23 Brightlingsea, England 51 48N 1 2E
83 Brighton, Australia 35 0S 138 30E
23 Brighton, England 50 49N 0 9W
25 Brimfield, England 52 18N 2 42W
41 Brindisi, Italy 40 40N 17 55E
83 Brinkworth, Australia 33 40S 138 20E
33 Brinyan, Scotland 59 8N 3 0W
93 Brion, I., Canada 47 50N 61 30W
43 Brioude, France 45 18N 3 25E
44 Briquebec, France 49 28N 1 39W
83 Brisbane, Australia 27 30S 153 1E
83 Brisbane R., Australia 27 0S 152 30E
22 Bristol, England 51 28N 2 36W
93 Bristol, R.I., U.S.A. 41 40N 71 15W
24 Bristol Chan., England 51 20N 4 0W
100 British Antarctic Terr. 65 0S 50 0W
88 British Columbia, Prov. Canada 54 0N 125 0W
95 British Guiana, see Guyana
94 British Honduras, see Belize
13 British Isles, Europe 55 0N 5 0W
25 Briton Ferry, Wales 51 37N 3 50W
76 Britstown, South Africa 30 33S 23 32E
42 Brittany, Prov., France 48 0N 2 10W
35 Brittas, Ireland 53 14N 6 29W
43 Brive, France 45 10N 1 30E
24 Brixham, England 50 23N 3 32W
82 Brixton, Australia 23 32S 144 52E
23 Brixworth, England 52 20N 0 54W
46 Brno (Brünn), Cz. 49 19N 16 38E
64 Broach, see Baruch
35 Broad Haven, Ireland 54 18N 9 54W
25 Broad Haven, Wales 51 46N 5 6W
31 Broad Law, Mt., Scot. 55 27N 3 20W
82 Broad Sd., Australia 22 10S 149 40E
34 Broadford, Ireland 52 48N 8 38W
23 Broadstairs, England 51 21N 1 27E
22 Broadway, England 52 2N 1 51W
88 Brochet, Manitoba, Can. 57 55N 101 40W
46 Brocken, Mt., Germany 51 48N 10 50E
22 Brockenhurst, England 50 49N 1 34W
93 Brockton, Mass., U.S.A. 42 4N 71 0W
41 Brod, Yugoslavia 45 9N 18 0E
89 Brodeur Pen., Canada 72 0N 88 0W
30 Brodick, Scotland 55 33N 5 8W
47 Brody, U.S.S.R. 50 7N 25 8E
83 Broken Hill, Australia 31 59S 141 25E
75 Broken Hill, see Kabwe
26 Bromborough, England 53 20N 3 0W
23 Bromley, England 51 24N 0 2W
27 Brompton, England 54 22N 1 25W
22 Bromsgrove, England 52 20N 2 1W
22 Bromyard, England 52 12N 2 30W
49 Bronderslev, Denmark 57 17N 9 55E
83 Bronte Park, Australia 42 8S 146 30E
36 Brookeborough, N. Ire. 54 19N 7 23W
91 Brookhaven, U.S.A. 31 48N 90 27W
91 Brookings, S. Dak., U.S.A. 44 25N 96 40W
80 Brookton, Australia 32 15S 117 0E
83 Brooloo, Australia 26 28S 152 30E
80 Broome, Australia 18 8S 122 15E
33 Brora, & R., Scotland 58 0N 3 51W
22 Broseley, England 52 35N 2 28W
34 Brosna, R., Ireland 53 20N 7 50W
36 Broughshane, N. Ireland 54 54N 6 12W
27 Broughton, Lincs., Eng. 55 33N 0 33W
23 Broughton, Northants., England 52 22N 0 45W
27 Broughton, Yorks., Eng. 54 26N 1 8W
31 Broughton, Scotland 55 37N 3 25W
31 Broughty Ferry, Scotland 56 27N 2 51W
44 Brouwershaven, Neth. 51 45N 3 53E
24 Brown Willy, Mt., Eng. 50 35N 4 35W
22 Brownhills, England 52 38N 1 57W
91 Brownsville, Tex., U.S.A. 26 0N 97 20W
90 Brownwood, U.S.A. 31 42N 99 2W
31 Broxburn, Scotland 55 56N 3 23W
48 Brú, Iceland 65 5N 15 25W
80 Bruce, Mt., Australia 22 40S 117 30E
45 Bruchsal, Germany 49 10N 8 45E
46 Bruck, Austria 47 27N 15 15E
24 Brue R., England 51 11N 2 50W
34 Bruff, Ireland 52 29N 8 35W
44 Bruges, Belgium, see Brugge
45 Brugg, Switzerland 47 28N 8 12E
44 Brugge, Belgium 51 12N 3 10E
44 Bruhl, Germany 50 49N 6 51E
68 Brunei, Borneo 4 55N 114 52E
45 Brunig Pass, Switzerland 46 48N 8 10E
46 Brünn, see Brno
45 Brunnen, Switzerland 47 0N 8 18E
84 Brunner, & L., N.Z. 42 30S 171 23E
46 Brünsbüttel, Germany 53 55N 9 14E
46 Brunswick, Germany 52 17N 10 36E
91 Brunswick, Ga., U.S.A. 31 10N 81 31W
80 Brunswick B., Australia 15 15S 125 0E
83 Bruny I., Australia 43 20S 147 15E
34 Bruree, Ireland 52 35N 8 40W
44 Brussels, Belgium 50 51N 4 22E
83 Bruthen, Australia 37 55S 147 49E
44 Bruxelles, see Brussels
91 Bryan, Texas, U.S.A. 30 17N 96 5W
52 Bryansk, U.S.S.R. 53 25N 34 22E
25 Bryncethin, Wales 51 32N 3 34W
49 Bryne, Norway 58 46N 5 38E
25 Brynmawr, Wales 51 50N 3 8W
47 Brzeg, Poland 50 52N 17 30E
68 Buayan, Philippines 6 5N 125 20E
95 Bucaramanga, Colombia 6 55N 72 58W
47 Buchach, U.S.S.R. 49 5N 25 25E
72 Buchanan, Liberia 5 57N 10 2W
89 Buchans, Canada 48 50N 57 30W
47 Bucharest (Bucuresti), Rumania 44 25N 26 2E
45 Buchs, Switzerland 47 10N 9 30E
33 Buck, The, Mt., Scot. 57 9N 3 0W
31 Buckhaven, Scotland 56 10N 3 2W
33 Buckie, Scotland 57 40N 2 58W
93 Buckingham, Canada 45 40N 75 36W
23 Buckingham & Co., Engl 52 0N 0 59W
25 Buckley, Wales 53 10N 3 5W
30 Bucklyvie, Scotland 56 7N 4 20W
33 Bucksburn, Scotland 57 10N 2 10W
93 Buctouche, Canada 46 30N 64 47W
92 Bucyrus, U.S.A. 40 52N 83 0W
65 Budalin, Burma 22 25N 95 5E
46 Budapest, Hungary 47 33N 19 3E
48 Budareyri, Iceland 65 3N 14 10W
64 Budaun, India 28 15N 79 6E
31 Buddon Ness, Scotland 56 28N 2 43W
24 Bude, England 50 50N 4 32W
48 Budir, Iceland 64 48N 23 21W
74 Budjala, Zaïre 2 50N 19 40E
24 Budleigh Salterton, Eng. 50 37N 3 19W
95 Buenaventura, Colombia 3 55N 77 5W
99 Buenos Aires, Argentina 34 50S 58 37W
92 Buffalo, N.Y., U.S.A. 42 57N 78 50W
90 Buffalo, Wyoming, U.S.A. 44 20N 106 42W
47 Bug, R., Poland 52 39N 21 35E
51 Bug., R., U.S.S.R. 48 17N 30 0E
50 Bugulma, U.S.S.R. 54 35N 52 45E
30 Buie, L., Scotland 56 20N 5 55W
25 Builth Wells, Wales 52 8N 3 24W
44 Buitenpost, Netherlands 53 15N 6 6E
74 Bujumbura, Burundi 3 30S 29 30E
61 Bukachacha, U.S.S.R. 52 55N 116 50E
74 Bukama, Zaïre 9 10S 25 50E
74 Bukavu, Zaïre 2 20S 28 52E
74 Bukene, Tanzania 4 13S 33 0E
60 Bukhara, U.S.S.R. 39 50N 64 10E
68 Bukittingi, Malaysia 0 25S 100 25E
74 Bukoba, Tanzania 1 15S 31 50E
66 Bulak, Sinkiang, China 45 0N 82 0E
64 Bulandshahr, India 28 30N 77 58E
75 Bulawayo, Rhodesia 20 7S 28 38E
66 Bulgan, Mongolia 48 45N 103 0E
83 Bulgroo, Australia 25 40S 143 57E
41 Bulgaria, Europe 42 35N 25 0E
61 Bulinski, U.S.S.R. 68 10N 123 5E
61 Bulkur, U.S.S.R. 71 50N 126 30E
45 Bulle, Switzerland 46 35N 7 6E
80 Bullfinch, Australia 31 10S 119 0E
83 Bulli, Australia 34 12S 150 59E
82 Bullock Creek, Australia 17 40S 144 30E
84 Bulls, N.Z. 40 10S 175 21E
64 Bulsar, India 21 28N 72 35E
61 Bulun, U.S.S.R. 70 37N 126 0E
27 Bulwell, England 53 1N 1 12W
65 Bumhpa Bum Mt., Burma 26 45N 97 10E
74 Buna, Kenya 2 58N 39 30E
82 Buna, Papua N.G. 8 35S 148 30E
80 Bunbury, Australia 33 18S 115 40E
35 Bunclody (Newtownbarry), Ireland 52 40N 6 38E
36 Buncrana, Ireland 55 8N 7 25W
83 Bundaberg, Australia 24 54S 152 22E
36 Bundoran, Ireland 54 29N 8 16W
23 Bungay, England 52 27N 1 27E
67 Bungo Chan., Japan 33 0N 132 15E
68 Bunguran Is., Indonesia 3 45N 108 15E
74 Bunia, Zaïre 2 0N 30 20E
36 Bunnanaddan, Ireland 54 3N 8 35W
23 Buntingford, England 51 57N 0 1W
23 Bunwell, England 52 30N 1 9E
74 Bura, Kenya 1 0S 40 0E
62 Buraida ,Saudi Arabia 26 3N 44 0E
22 Buraimi, U.A.E. 24 15N 55 43E
22 Burbage, Wilts., England 51 21N 1 40W
90 Burbank, U.S.A. 34 14N 118 28W
83 Burcher, Australia 33 30S 147 10E
66 Burchun, Sinkiang, China 47 50N 86 30E
51 Burdur, Turkey 37 40N 30 17E
65 Burdwan, India 23 18N 87 50E
61 Bureya, R., U.S.S.R. 50 35N 132 0E
62 Burgan, Kuwait 29 0N 47 59E
41 Burgas, Bulgaria 42 36N 27 26E
45 Burgdorf, Switzerland 47 4N 7 38E
46 Burgenland, Prov., Austria 47 20N 16 20E
76 Burgersdorp, South Africa 31 0S 26 20E
23 Burgess Hill, England 50 57N 0 7W
22 Burghclere, England 51 19N 1 20W
37 Burgos, Spain 42 21N 3 40W
49 Burgsvik, Sweden 57 2N 18 14E
43 Burgundy Prov., France 47 0N 4 50E
50 Burguruslan, U.S.S.R. 53 22N 52 22E
42 Burhou Rocks, Channel Is. 49 45N 2 12W
74 Burji, Ethiopia 5 29N 37 51E
82 Burketown, Australia 17 45S 139 33E
27 Burley, England 53 55N 1 46W
90 Burley, U.S.A. 42 30N 113 55W
91 Burlington, Iowa, U.S.A. 41 0N 91 10W
93 Burlington, Vt., U.S.A. 44 30N 73 12W
60 Burlyu-Tyube, U.S.S.R. 46 30N 79 10E
65 Burma, Asia 21 30N 97 0E
23 Burnham, Essex, England 51 37N 0 50E
83 Burnie, Australia 41 0S 146 0E
26 Burnley, England 53 49N 2 16W
31 Burnmouth, Scotland 55 50N 2 4W
88 Burnside, R., Canada 66 20N 110 0W
31 Burntisland, Scotland 56 3N 3 12W
32 Burravoe, Scotland 60 31N 1 5W
33 Burray I., Scotland 58 50N 2 54W
83 Burren, Australia 30 10S 148 55E
83 Burrinjuck Res., Australia 35 0S 149 0E
25 Burry Port, Wales 51 41N 4 17W
41 Bursa, Turkey 40 8N 29 1E
24 Burton Bradstock, Eng. 50 41N 2 43W
23 Burton Latimer, Eng. 52 23N 0 41W
22 Burton-upon-Trent, Eng. 52 48N 1 38W
83 Burtundy, Australia 33 40S 142 20E
68 Buru, I., Indonesia 3 30S 126 30E
62 Burujird, Iran 33 55N 48 50E
74 Burundi, Africa 3 30S 30 0E
72 Burutu, Nigeria 5 20N 5 29E
26 Bury, England 53 36N 2 18W
23 Bury St. Edmunds, Eng. 52 14N 0 43E
61 Buryat, A.S.S.R., U.S.S.R. 51 0N 104 0E
62 Busaiya, Iraq 30 1N 46 10E
62 Bushire, Iran 29 0N 50 50E
36 Bushmills, N. Ireland 55 14N 6 32W
74 Businga, Zaïre 3 30N 20 50E
49 Buskerud, Co., Norway 60 20N 9 0E
62 Busra, Syria 32 30N 38 27E
80 Busselton, Australia 33 40S 115 20E
44 Bussum, Netherlands 52 18N 5 10E
43 Busto Arsizio, Italy 45 40N 8 50E
74 Buta, Zaïre 2 50N 24 53E
30 Bute, I., & Kyles of, Scotland 55 50N 5 5W
30 Bute, Sd. of, Scotland 55 45N 5 10W
74 Butembo, Zaïre 0 9N 29 18E
63 Butmiya, Syria 32 57N 35 53E
32 Butt of Lewis, Scotland 58 30N 6 16W
90 Butte, Montana, U.S.A. 46 0N 112 32W
31 Buttermere, England 54 32N 3 16W
68 Butterworth, Malaya 5 20N 100 35E
34 Buttevant, Ireland 52 14N 8 40W
68 Butuan, Philippines 9 0N 125 35E
68 Butung, I., Indonesia 5 0S 123 0E
52 Buturlinovka, U.S.S.R. 50 50N 40 35E
26 Buxton, England 53 16N 1 56W
61 Buyaga, U.S.S.R. 59 50N 127 0E
66 Buyr Nor, L., Mongolia 47 40N 17 40E
47 Buzau, & R., Rumania 45 10N 26 48E
73 Buzaymah, Libya 24 35N 22 0E
50 Buzuluk, U.S.S.R. 52 48N 52 5E
47 Bydgoszcz, Poland 53 7N 17 59E
89 Bylot I., Canada 73 0N 78 0W
100 Byrd, Antarctica 80 5S 120 0W
100 Byrd Basin, Antarctica 80 0S 110 0W
100 Byrd Land, Antarctica 79 30S 125 0W
83 Byrock, Australia 30 40S 146 28E
83 Byron Bay, Australia 28 30S 153 30E
61 Byrrang Mts., U.S.S.R. 75 0N 100 0E
48 Byske, & R., Sweden 64 57N 21 15E
61 Bysyttakh, U.S.S.R. 69 30N 124 10E
47 Bytom, Poland 50 23N 18 58E

C

98 Cabedelo, Brazil 6 45S 35 0W
74 Cabinda, Angola 5 10S 12 10E
89 Cabonge, Res., Canada 47 10N 77 0W
83 Caboolture, Australia 27 5S 152 47E
89 Cabot Str., Canada 47 20N 60 0W
33 Cabrach, Scotland 57 20N 3 0W
37 Cabrera I., Spain 39 8N 2 58E

41 Cacak, Yugoslavia 43 51N 20 22E
37 Caceres, Spain 39 29N 6 22W
99 Cachoeira, Brazil 30 3S 52 53W
99 Cachoeiro, Brazil 20 45S 41 0W
75 Caconda, Angola 13 40S 15 9E
35 Cadamstown, Ireland 53 7N 7 39W
25 Cader Idris, Mt., Wales 52 40N 3 50W
91 Cadillac, U.S.A. 44 15N 85 28W
37 Cadiz, Spain 36 33N 6 20W
42 Caen, France 49 15N 0 27W
27 Caenby Corner, England 53 23N 0 32W
25 Caerleon, Wales 51 37N 2 57W
25 Caernarfon, Wales 53 9N 4 15W
25 Caernarfon B., Wales 53 4N 4 28W
25 Caerphilly, Wales 51 34N 3 13W
25 Caerwent, Wales 51 37N 2 47W
63 Caesarea, Israel 32 30N 34 54E
68 Cagayan, R., Philippines 17 30N 121 40E
68 Cagayan de Oro, Phil. 8 32N 124 35E
40 Cagliari, & G., Italy 39 19N 9 8E
95 Caguas, Puerto Rico 18 15N 66 0W
35 Caha Mts., Ireland 51 47N 9 40W
34 Caherconlish, Ireland 52 36N 8 30W
35 Cahir, Ireland 52 21N 7 56W
35 Cahirciveen, Ireland 51 57N 10 14W
43 Cahors, France 44 28N 1 21E
98 Caiapó, Sa. do, Mts., Brazil 17 0S 52 0W
95 Caicos Is., W. Indies 21 45N 72 0W
33 Cairn Gorm Mt., Scot. 57 9N 3 40W
31 Cairn Table, Mt., Scot. 55 30N 4 0W
33 Cairn Toul, Mt., Scotland 57 1N 3 49W
33 Cairngorm Mts., Scotland 57 6N 3 38W
30 Cairnryan, Scotland 54 59N 5 0W
82 Cairns, Australia 17 0S 145 42E
73 Cairo (El Qâhira), Egypt 30 1N 31 14E
91 Cairo, Ill., U.S.A. 37 0N 89 20W
23 Caister-on-Sea, England 52 38N 1 43E
27 Caistor, England 53 31N 0 18W
98 Cajamarca, Peru 7 0S 78 18W
72 Calabar, Nigeria 4 59N 8 23E
40 Calabria, Reg., Italy 39 10N 16 20E
41 Calafat, Rumania 43 59N 22 54E
37 Calahorra, Spain 42 20N 2 0W
43 Calais, France 50 59N 1 55E
93 Calais, U.S.A. 45 6N 67 14W
99 Calama, Chile 22 20S 69 0W
95 Calamar, Colombia 10 0N 75 0W
68 Calamian Group, Phil. 11 30N 120 0E
37 Calamocha, Spain 40 57N 1 8W
68 Calapan, Philippines 13 15N 121 15E
47 Calarasi, Rumania 44 35N 27 25E
37 Calatayud, Spain 41 20N 1 40W
68 Calauag, Philippines 14 0N 122 20E
65 Calcutta, India 22 38N 88 21E
26 Calder Hall, England 54 25N 3 30W
99 Caldera, Chile 27 12S 70 48W
90 Caldwell, Idaho, U.S.A. 43 42N 116 45W
36 Caledon, N. Ireland 54 23N 6 52W
81 Caledon B., Australia 12 57S 136 50E
32 Caledonian Can., Scot. 57 28N 4 22W
26 Calf of Man, Isle of Man 54 4N 4 49W
88 Calgary, Canada 51 2N 114 5W
32 Calgary, Scotland 56 34N 6 17W
95 Cali, Colombia 3 30N 76 45W
65 Calicut, India 11 15N 75 43E
94 California, G. of, Mexico 28 0N 112 0W
90 California, st., U.S.A. 37 0N 120 0W
94 California, Lower, Mex. 28 0N 114 0W
82 Callabonna L., Australia 29 45S 140 0E
35 Callan, Ireland 52 33N 7 23W
31 Callander, Scotland 56 14N 4 12W
98 Callao, Peru 11 48S 77 15W
82 Callide, Australia 24 23S 150 33E
82 Calliope, Australia 24 0S 151 16E
22 Calne, England 51 27N 1 55W
83 Caloundra, Australia 26 45S 153 10E
40 Caltagirone, Italy 37 14N 14 33E
40 Caltanisetta, Italy 37 29N 14 7E
74 Calumbo, Angola 9 0S 13 0E
91 Calumet, U.S.A. 47 18N 88 28W
42 Calvados, Dépt., France 49 5N 0 20W
76 Calvinia, S. Africa 31 29S 19 59E
74 Camabatela, Angola 8 20S 15 26E
95 Camaguey, Cuba 21 17N 78 10W
64 Cambay, & G., India 22 27N 72 42E
23 Camberley, England 51 20N 0 44W
68 Cambodia, S.E. Asia 11 45N 105 0E
24 Camborne, England 50 12N 5 17W
44 Cambrai, France 50 11N 3 13E
25 Cambrian Mts., Wales 52 20N 3 30W
23 Cambridge, Eng. 52 11N 0 8E
23 Cambridge, England 52 15W 0 5E
94 Cambridge, Jamaica 18 16N 77 53W
84 Cambridge, N.Z. 37 52S 175 28E
93 Cambridge, Mass., U.S.A. 42 40N 71 3W
88 Cambridge Bay, Canada 69 10N 105 0W
80 Cambridge G., Australia 14 30S 128 30E
23 Camden Gr. London, Eng. 51 32N 0 8W
91 Camden, Ark., U.S.A. 33 36N 92 52W
91 Camden, N.J., U.S.A. 39 58N 75 0W
92 Cameron Falls, Canada 49 5N 88 16W
74 Cameroon, Mt., Camer. 4 30N 8 55E
74 Cameroon, Africa 6 0N 12 0E
24 Camerton, England 51 18N 2 27W
37 Caminha, Portugal 41 50N 8 50W
83 Camira Creek, Austral. 29 15S 152 58E
98 Camocim, Brazil 2 55S 40 50W
35 Camolin, Ireland 52 37N 6 26W
82 Camooweal, Australia 19 59S 138 8E
99 Campana, Argentina 34 10S 58 40W
99 Campaña I., Chile 48 30S 75 30W
40 Campania, Prov., Italy 40 50N 14 45E
100 Campbell I., Southern Oc. 52 0S 169 0E
83 Campbell Town, Austral. 42 0S 147 50E
93 Campbellton, Canada 48 0N 66 57W
83 Campbelltown, Australia 34 5S 150 48E
30 Campbeltown, Scotland 55 26N 5 37W
94 Campêche, & G., Mexico 19 50N 90 30W
83 Camperdown, Australia 38 11S 143 12E
98 Campina Grande, Brazil 7 15S 36 0W
99 Campinas, Brazil 22 50S 47 0W
74 Campo, Cameroon 2 25N 9 55E
98 Campo Grande, Brazil 20 27S 54 40W
40 Campobasso, Italy 41 37N 14 44E
99 Campos, Brazil 21 45S 41 35W
30 Campsie Fells, Scotland 56 2N 4 25W
88 Camrose, Canada 53 0N 112 57W
83 Camurra, Australia 29 25S 149 58E
68 Can Tho, Vietnam 10 0N 105 40E
88-89 Canada, N. America 42 0 to 70 0N; 60 0 to 140 0W
90 Canadian, R., U.S.A. 35 15N 102 0W
41 Canakkale, Turkey 40 5N 26 30E
94 Cananea, Mexico 31 0N 110 25W
72 Canary Is., Atlantic Oc. 28 0N 16 0W
98 Canastra, Sa. da, Mts., Brazil 9 30S 46 30W
95 Canaveral, C., U.S.A., see Kennedy, C.
83 Canaway Ra., Australia 25 50S 142 40E
83 Canbelego, Australia 31 28S 146 27E
83 Canberra, Australia 35 15S 149 10E
42 Cancale, France 48 40N 2 0W
41 Candia, see Iraklion, Greece
98 Cañete, Peru 13 10S 76 25W
37 Cangas, Spain 43 13N 6 31W
75 Canicado, Mozam., 24 45S 33 15E
63 Cankiri, Turkey 40 43N 33 35E
83 Cann River, Australia 37 40S 149 10E
32 Canna I., Scotland 57 5N 6 35W
64 Cannanore, India 11 59N 75 32E
43 Cannes, France 43 35N 0 0E
80 Canning Basin, Austral. 19 50S 124 0E
24 Cannington, England 51 8N 3 4W
22 Cannock, England 52 42N 2 2W
22 Cannock Chase, Hs., Eng. 52 40N 2 0W
88 Canora, Canada 51 48N 102 36W
83 Canowindra, Australia 33 31S 148 50E
93 Canso, & C., Canada 45 30N 61 0W
37 Cantabrian Mts., Spain 43 12N 5 20W
42 Cantal, Dépt., France 45 5N 3 0E
23 Canterbury, England 51 15N 1 6E
84 Canterbury, Dist., N.Z. 44 0S 171 0E
84 Canterbury Bight, N.Z. 44 20S 172 0E
84 Canterbury Plains, N.Z. 43 30S 172 0E
66 Canton, China 23 15N 113 30E
91 Canton, Miss., U.S.A. 32 37N 90 7W
92 Canton, Ohio, U.S.A. 40 48N 81 20W
23 Canvey, Eng., 51 32N 0 35E
93 Cap Chat, Canada 49 3N 66 40W
95 Cap Haitien, Haiti 20 50N 72 20W
83 Cape Barren I. Austral. 40 25S 148 15E
89 Cape Breton I., Canada 46 25N 61 0W
72 Cape Coast, Ghana 5 5N 1 0W
91 Cape Fear, R., U.S.A. 34 30N 78 30W
92 Cape Girardeau, U.S.A. 37 19N 89 38W
55 Cape Johnson Deep, Pacific Ocean 10 0N 128 0E
76 Cape Province, S. Afr. 32 0S 24 0E
76 Cape Town, S. Africa 33 59S 18 30E
70 Cape Verde Is., Atlantic Oc. 16 0N 24 0W
82 Cape York Pen., Austral. 13 0S 142 30E
25 Capel-Curig, Wales 53 6N 3 55W
82 Capella, Australia 23 2S 148 1E
63 Capernaum, Israel 32 53N 35 34E
98 Capoeiras Falls, Fs., Brazil 7 0S 57 45W
40 Caporetto, Yugoslavia, see Kobarid
34 Cappamore, Ireland 52 38N 8 20W
34 Cappoquin, Ireland 52 9N 7 49W
40 Capri, I., Italy 40 35N 14 18E
75 Caprivi Strip, S.W. Africa 17 50S 23 0E
83 Captain's Flat, Australia 35 35S 149 30E
47 Caracal, Rumania 44 10N 24 20E
95 Caracas, Venezuela 10 25N 66 50W
83 Caradoc, Australia 30 35S 142 58E
47 Caransebes, Rumania 45 30N 22 15E
98 Caravelas, Brazil 17 45S 39 0W
40 Carbonara, C., Italy 39 10N 9 33E
89 Carbonear, Canada 47 42N 53 13W
43 Carcassonne, France 43 13N 2 22E
88 Carcross, Canada 60 20N 134 40W
64 Cardamon Hills, India 9 30N 77 0E
95 Cardenas, Cuba 23 0N 81 30W
25 Cardiff, Wales 51 29N 3 10W
25 Cardigan, Wales 52 6N 4 38W
25 Cardigan B., Wales 52 30N 4 40W
37 Cardona, Spain 41 56N 1 40E
88 Cardston, Canada 49 15N 113 28W
82 Cardwell, Australia 18 14S 146 2E
47 Carei, Rumania 47 45N 22 33E
42 Carentan, France 49 20N 1 20W
80 Carey, L., Australia 29 0S 122 20E
72 Careysburg, Liberia 6 34N 10 30W
42 Carhaix, France 48 20N 2 40W
95 Caribbean Sea, W. Indies 15 30N 73 0W
91 Caribou, U.S.A. 46 52N 68 2W
44 Carignan, France 49 37N 5 10E
83 Carinda, Australia 30 27S 147 52E
46 Carinthia, Prov., Austria 46 50N 14 0E
22 Carisbrooke, England 50 42N 1 19W
93 Carleton Place, Canada 45 4N 76 7W
76 Carletonville, S. Africa 26 25S 27 15E
36 Carlingford, & L., Ireland 54 2N 6 8W
26 Carlisle, England 54 54N 2 57W
31 Carlops, Scotland 55 47N 3 20W
35 Carlow, & Co., Ireland 52 50N 6 56W
90 Carlsbad, U.S.A. 32 25N 104 13W
27 Carlton, England 52 58N 1 6W
31 Carluke, Scotland 55 44N 3 50W
88 Carmacks, Canada 62 0N 136 0W
88 Carman, Canada 49 30N 98 0W
25 Carmarthen, & Co., Wales 51 52N 4 18W
24 Carmarthen B., Wales 51 37N 4 30W
43 Carmaux, France 44 1N 2 5E
63 Carmel, Mt., Israel 32 45N 35 0E
82 Carmila, Australia 21 53S 149 5E
37 Carmona, Spain 37 28N 5 43W
31 Carmyllie, Scotland 56 36N 2 41W
32 Carn Eige, Mt., Scotland 57 17N 5 9W
33 Carn Glas-choire, Mt., Scotland 57 18N 3 50W
33 Carn na Caim, Mt., Scotland 56 54N 4 10W
42 Carnac, France 47 39N 3 3W
80 Carnarvon, Austral. 24 49S 113 40E
76 Carnarvon, S. Africa 31 0S 22 10E
64 Carnatic, Dist., India 12 30N 79 30E
80 Carnegie, L., Australia 26 0S 122 30E
35 Carnew, Ireland 52 43N 6 30W
26 Carnforth, England 54 8N 2 46W
40 Carnic Alps, Italy 46 34N 12 50E
36 Carnlough, N. Ireland 54 59N 6 0W
73 Carnot, Central Africa 5 0N 15 57E
31 Carnoustie, Scotland 56 30N 2 43W
31 Carnwath, Scotland 56 42N 3 38W
5 Caroline Is., Pacific Ocean 6 0N 146 0E
98 Caroni, R., Venezuela 7 0N 63 0W
47 Carpathian Mts., E. Eur. 48 0N 24 0E
82 Carpentaria, G. of, Australia 15 0S 138 0E
43 Carpentras, France 44 0N 5 0E
83 Carpolac, Australia 36 45S 141 20E
35 Carra, L., Ireland 53 43N 9 15W
40 Carrara, Italy 44 3N 10 9E
83 Carraweena, Australia 29 10S 139 55E
33 Carrbridge, Scotland 57 16N 3 48W
94 Carriacou I., W. Indies 12 30N 61 28W
30 Carrick, Dist., Scotland 55 10N 4 40W
36 Carrick-on-Shannon, Ire. 53 58N 8 5W
35 Carrick-on-Suir, Ireland 52 21N 7 24W
36 Carrickboy, Ireland 53 36N 7 40W
36 Carrickfergus, N. Ireland 54 43N 5 48W
36 Carrickmacross, Ireland 53 59N 6 45W
83 Carrieton, Australia 32 27S 138 30E
34 Carrigaholt, Ireland 52 37N 9 42W
34 Carrigaline, Ireland 51 49N 8 22W
36 Carrigallen, Ireland 53 59N 7 40W
32 Carron, L. & R., Scotland 57 22N 5 35W
31 Carronbridge, Scotland 55 16N 3 46W
36 Carryduff, N. Ireland 54 32N 5 52W
25 Carreg Cennen, Wales 51 50N 3 55W
90 Carson City, U.S.A. 39 6N 119 37W
90 Carson Sink, L., U.S.A. 39 45N 118 40W
30 Carsphairn, Scotland 55 13N 4 15W
31 Carstairs, Scotland 55 42N 3 40W
78 Carstenz, Mt., New Guinea, see Sukarno Pk.
95 Cartagena, Colombia 10 21N 75 35W
37 Cartagena, Spain 37 38N 0 55W
95 Cartago, Colombia 4 30N 76 10W
95 Cartago, Costa Rica 9 50N 83 50W
42 Carteret, France 49 23N 1 48W
91 Carthage, Mo., U.S.A. 37 4N 94 18W
89 Cartwright, Canada 53 40N 56 40W
95 Carúpano, Venezuela 10 40N 63 25W
44 Carvin, France 50 30N 2 56E
72 Casablanca, Morocco 33 30N 7 35W
43 Casale, Italy 45 6N 8 32E
90 Cascade Ra., U.S.A. 45 0N 122 0W
37 Cascais, Portugal 38 45N 9 35W
40 Caserta, Italy 41 8N 14 23E
34 Cashel, Ireland 52 30N 7 52W
83 Casino, Australia 29 0S 152 49E
95 Casiquiare, R., Venezuela 2 40N 66 15W
37 Caspe, Spain 41 15N 0 0
90 Casper, U.S.A. 42 57N 106 30W
51 Caspian Sea, U.S.S.R. 42 30N 51 0E
42 Casquets, The, Channel Is. 49 45N 2 20W
88 Cassiar, Mts., Canada 58 30N 129 0W
75 Cassinga, Angola 15 5S 16 20E
42 Casteljaloux, France 44 20N 0 0
40 Castellammare, Italy 38 1N 12 52E
43 Castelnaudary, France 43 20N 2 0E
37 Castelo Branco, Portugal 39 50N 7 32W
43 Castelsarrasin, France 44 0N 1 5E
40 Castelvetrano, Italy 37 42N 12 47E
83 Casterton, Australia 37 32S 141 25E
37 Castile, New, Prov., Spain 40 0N 3 20W
37 Castile, Old, Prov., Spain 41 30N 3 40W
31 Castle Douglas, Scotland 54 56N 3 57W
36 Castlebellingham, Ireland 53 53N 6 22W
36 Castleblayney, Ireland 54 6N 6 50W
35 Castlebridge, Ireland 52 23N 6 28W
35 Castlecomer, Ireland 52 45N 7 12W
34 Castleconnell, Ireland 52 44N 8 30W
36 Castledawson, N. Ireland 54 47N 6 30W
36 Castlederg, N. Ireland 54 43N 7 36W
35 Castledermot, Ireland 52 55N 6 50W
34 Castlegregory, Ireland 52 15N 10 1W
34 Castleisland, Ireland 52 14N 9 28W
83 Castlemaine, Australia 37 0S 144 15E
34 Castlemaine, Ireland 52 10N 9 44W
34 Castlemaine Hr., Ireland 52 8N 9 52W
34 Castlemartyr, Ireland 51 54N 8 3W
36 Castlepollard, Ireland 53 40N 7 20W
36 Castlereagh, Ireland 53 47N 8 29W
83 Castlereagh R., Australia 31 20S 148 0E
26 Castleton, England 53 22N 1 40W
26 Castletown, I.o.M. 54 4N 4 41W
36 Castletown, Meath, Ire. 53 47N 6 41W
35 Castletown, Laois, Ire. 52 58N 7 30W
35 Castletown, Westmeath, Ireland 53 26N 7 25W
33 Castletown, Scotland 58 35N 3 22W
34 Castletownroche, Ire. 52 10N 8 28W
34 Castletownshend, Ireland 51 31N 9 11W
36 Castlewellan, N. Ireland 54 16N 5 57W
43 Castres, France 43 40N 2 13E
94 Castries, Windward Is. 14 0N 61 0W
99 Castro, Chile 42 30S 73 40W
37 Castro, Spain 37 46N 4 30W
91 Cat I., Bahamas 24 25N 75 30W
99 Catalão, Brazil 18 8S 47 50W
37 Catalonia, Prov., Spain 41 40N 1 30E
99 Catamarca, Argentina 28 28S 65 47W
68 Catanduanas, Phil. 13 45N 124 20E
40 Catania, Italy 37 33N 15 7E
40 Catanzaro, Italy 38 59N 16 34E
23 Caterham, England 51 16N 0 4W
92 Catlettsburg, U.S.A. 38 28N 82 33W
94 Catoche, C., Mexico 21 45N 87 0W
94 Catorce, Mexico 23 50N 100 55W
93 Catskill, Mts., U.S.A. 42 18N 74 30W
27 Catterick, England 54 23N 1 38W
51 Caucasus, Mts., U.S.S.R. 43 0N 44 0E
43 Caudebec, France 49 20N 1 0E
44 Caudry, France 50 7N 3 22E
74 Caungula, Angola 8 15S 18 50E
42 Cauterets, France 43 0N 0 12W
65 Cauvery, R., India 11 0N 78 0E
36 Cavan, & Co., Ireland 54 0N 7 21W
83 Cavendish, Australia 37 35S 142 5E
98 Caviana I., Brazil 0 15N 50 30W
33 Cawdor, Scotland 57 32N 3 53W
64 Cawnpore, see Kanpur
98 Caxias, Brazil 4 50S 43 2W
99 Caxias do Sul, Brazil 29 25S 51 10W
98 Cayenne, French Guiana 4 45N 52 15W
92 Cayuga, L., U.S.A. 42 42N 76 35W
36 Ceanannus Mor, Ireland 53 40N 6 55W
98 Ceará, see Fortaleza
98 Ceará, st., Brazil 4 30S 39 30W
68 Cebu & I., Philippines 10 20N 123 50E
83 Cecil Plains, Australia 27 32S 151 4E
90 Cedar City, U.S.A. 37 40N 113 7W
91 Cedar Falls, U.S.A. 42 33N 92 30W
91 Cedar Rapids, U.S.A. 42 0N 91 39W
80 Ceduna, Australia 32 0S 133 54E
40 Cefalu, Italy 38 0N 14 0E
37 Cehegin, Spain 38 6N 1 48W
94 Celaya, Mexico 21 0N 101 0W
35 Celbridge, Ireland 53 20N 6 31W
68 Celebes, I., Indonesia, see Sulawesi
68 Celebes Sea, Indonesia 4 0N 122 0E
40 Celje, Yugoslavia 46 20N 15 20E
46 Celle, Germany 52 39N 10 3E
25 Cemaes Road, Wales 52 39N 3 41W
43 Cenis, Mt., France 45 17N 7 0E
43 Ceno, R., Italy 44 42N 9 48E
31 Central, Reg., Scotland 54 10N 4 5W
74 Central African Empire, Africa 7 0N 20 0E
84 Central Auckland, Dist., N.Z. 37 0S 174 50E
13 Central Massif, mts., Fr. 45 0N 2 30E
64 Central Makran Ra., Pakistan 26 30N 64 0E
13 Central Russian Uplands, U.S.S.R. 53 0N 35 0E
61 Central Siberian Plat, U.S.S.R. 65 0N 105 0E
92 Centralia, Ill., U.S.A. 38 30N 89 10W
90 Centralia, Wash., U.S.A. 46 40N 122 55W
41 Cephalonia, I., see Kefallinia
68 Ceram, I., Indonesia 3 10S 129 30E
68 Ceram Sea, Indonesia 2 20S 129 0E
43 Cerbère, France 42 25N 3 10E
76 Ceres, Cape Prov., S. Afr. 33 21S 19 18E
40 Cerignola, Italy 41 18N 15 58E
41 Cerigo, I., Greece, see Kithira
40 Cerknica, Yugoslavia 45 47N 14 40E
47 Cernavoda, Rumania 44 20N 28 5E
98 Cerro de Pasco, Peru 10 45S 77 0W
37 Cervera, Spain 41 40N 1 5E
43 Cervione, France 42 17N 9 30E
40 Cesena, Italy 44 10N 12 15E
49 Cesis, U.S.S.R. 57 20N 25 15E
47 Cesky Tesin, Cz-slov. 49 45N 18 39E
41 Cesme, Turkey 38 20N 26 20E
83 Cessnock, Australia 33 0S 151 0E
41 Cetinje, Yugoslavia 42 23N 18 54E
72 Ceuta, Morocco 35 50N 5 20W
43 Ceva, Italy 44 25N 8 0E
43 Cevennes, mts., France 44 30N 4 0E
64 Ceylon, see Sri Lanka
98 Chachapoyas, Peru 6 15S 77 35W
68 Chachoengsao, Thailand 13 45N 101 12E
64 Chachran, Pakistan 28 55N 70 30E
99 Chaco Central, Argentina 24 0S 61 0W
73 Chad (Tchad), Afr. 13 0N 14 0E
73 Chad, L., Chad 13 50N 14 30E
90 Chadron, U.S.A. 42 52N 103 4W
64 Chagai Hills, Afghan. 29 40N 64 0E
61 Chagda, U.S.S.R. 58 30N 130 45E
55 Chagos Is., Indian Ocean 6 0S 72 0W
64 Chahar Burjak, Afghan. 30 20N 62 0E
63 Chahbar, Iran 25 22N 60 33E
65 Chaibasa, India 22 42N 85 49E
64 Chakhansur, Prov., Afghan. 30 0N 62 0E
65 Chakradharpur, India 22 50N 85 40E
66 Chalainor, China 49 25N 117 30E
67 Chalatun, China 48 0N 122 40E
93 Chaleur, B. de, Canada 47 50N 65 10W
23 Chalfont St. Peter, Eng. 51 36N 0 33W
64 Chalisgaon, India 20 30N 75 0E
42 Challans, France 46 50N 1 58W
43 Châlon-s-Saône, France 46 51N 4 52E
42 Chalonnes, France 47 20N 0 44W
43 Châlons-s-Marne, France 49 0N 4 20E
64 Chaman, Pakistan 30 55N 66 50E
64 Chamba, India 32 35N 76 15E
75 Chamba, Tanzania 11 40S 37 0E
64 Chambal, R., India 26 0N 76 55E
43 Chambéry, France 45 35N 5 54E
93 Chambord, Canada 48 27N 72 3W
42 Chamborn, France 47 38N 1 30E
66 Ch'amdo, China 31 30N 97 35E
66 Chamdo, Prov., China 31 0N 95 0E
43 Chamonix, France 45 55N 6 50E
42 Champagne, Dist., France 49 0N 4 30E
92 Champaign, U.S.A. 40 12N 88 17W
80 Champion Bay, Australia 28 30S 114 30E
93 Champlain, L., U.S.A. 44 30N 73 20W
99 Chanaral, Chile 26 16S 70 45W
64 Chanda, India 19 59N 79 15E
64 Chandigarh, India 30 32N 76 55E
65 Chandpur, Bangladesh 23 6N 90 35E
66 Changchih, China 36 15 113 0E
66 Changchow, Fukien, China 24 36N 117 40E
67 Changchow, Kiangsu, China 31 55N 119 50E
67 Changchun, China 43 20N 126 30E
66 Changki, Sinkiang, China 44 10N 87 0E
67 Changpai Shan, Mts., China 42 0N 126 30E
66 Changsha, China 28 10N 112 59E
66 Chang Tang, Tibet 34 0N 88 0E
66 Changteh, China 29 2N 111 45E
66 Changyeh, China 39 15N 100 15E
66 Chankiang, see Tsamkong, China
64 Channapatna, India 12 40N 77 5E
42 Channel Is., U.K. 49 20N 2 20W
37 Chantada, Spain 42 40N 7 48W
68 Chanthaburi, Thailand 12 35N 102 5E
66 Chanyi, China 25 50N 103 20E
66 Chaochow, China 23 42N 116 25E
66 Chaotung, China 27 22N 103 34E
60 Chap Kuduk, U.S.S.R. 48 40N 55 5E
98 Chapada dos Veadeiros, plat., Brazil 15 0S 48 0W
94 Chapala, L. de, Mexico 20 20N 103 10W
50 Chapayevsk, U.S.S.R. 53 0N 49 50E
26 Chapel-en-le-Frith, Eng. 53 19N 1 54W
65 Chapra, India 25 58N 84 39E
63 Charak, Iran 26 40N 54 50E
98 Charaña, Bolivia 17 45S 69 10W
100 Charcot, I., Antarctica 70 0S 78 0W
24 Chard, England 50 52N 2 57W
60 Chardzhou, U.S.S.R. 39 0N 63 15E
42 Charente, Dépt., France 46 0N 0 30E
42 Charente-Maritime, Dépt., France 46 5N 0 48W
64 Charikar, Afghan, 35 5N 69 0E
66 Charkhlik, China 39 30N 88 10E
44 Charleroi, Belgium 50 25N 4 27E
93 Charles, C., U.S.A. 37 12N 75 43W
91 Charles City, U.S.A. 43 2N 92 43W
91 Charleston, S.C., U.S.A. 32 48N 80 0W
92 Charleston, W. Va., U.S.A. 38 24N 81 36W
91 Charleston Hr., U.S.A. 32 45N 79 55W
36 Charlestown, Ireland 53 58N 8 48W
95 Charlestown, Nevis, W.I. 17 10N 62 35W
74 Charlesville, Zaïre 5 27S 20 59E
83 Charleville, Australia 26 27S 146 14E
43 Charleville-Mézières, France 49 46N 4 42E
91 Charlotte, N.C., U.S.A. 35 16N 80 50W
95 Charlotte Amalie, Virgin Is. 18 0N 65 0W
80 Charlotte Waters, Australia 25 55S 134 59E
46 Charlottenburg, Ger. 52 31N 13 15E
92 Charlottesville, U.S.A. 38 0N 78 31W
89 Charlottetown, Canada 46 20N 63 22W
83 Charlton, Australia 36 20S 143 30E
89 Charlton I., Canada 52 0N 79 20W
22 Charlton Kings, Eng. 51 52N 2 3W
22 Charnwood Forest, Eng. 52 45N 1 18W
72 Charouin, Algeria 29 10N 0 15W
43 Charrolles, France 46 27N 4 16E
82 Charters Towers, Austral. 20 0S 146 13E
43 Chartres, France 48 30N 1 33E
61 Chasovnya Uchurskaya, U.S.S.R. 57 5N 133 20E
45 Château-d'Oex, Switz. 46 28N 7 10E
43 Château du Loir, France 47 40N 0 30E
42 Château Gontier, France 47 40N 0 42W
43 Château la Vallière, Fr. 47 30N 0 15E
44 Château Porcien, France 49 32N 4 14E
44 Château Thierry, France 49 0N 3 28E
42 Châteaubriant, France 47 45N 1 23W
43 Châteaudun, France 48 0N 1 20E
43 Châteauroux, France 46 51N 1 39E
43 Châtellerault, France 46 46N 0 30E
45 Chatel-St.-Denis, Switz. 46 32N 6 55E
89 Chatham, N.B., Canada 47 0N 65 31W
92 Chatham, Ont., Canada 42 20N 82 18W
23 Chatham, England 51 21N 0 32E
4 Chatham Is., Pacific Oc. 44 0S 176 40W
43 Châtillon-s.-Seine, France 47 50N 4 35E
65 Chatrapur, India 19 25N 84 55E
91 Chattahoochee R., U.S.A. 32 10N 85 7W
91 Chattanooga, U.S.A. 35 2N 85 10W
23 Chatteris, England 52 27N 0 3E
31 Chatton, England 55 34N 1 55W
44 Chaulnes, France 49 48N 2 47E
43 Chaumont, France 48 7N 5 10E
43 Chauny, France 49 40N 3 15E
37 Chaves, Portugal 41 45N 7 35W
75 Chavuma, Zambia 13 10N 22 55E
64 Chayul, Tibet 28 20N 92 50E
26 Cheadle, Ches. Eng. 53 23N 2 14W

26 Cheadle, Staffs., Eng. 43 0N 1 58W
26 Cheadle Hulme, Eng. 53 22N 2 12W
46 Cheb, Czechoslovakia 50 9N 12 20E
50 Cheboksary, U.S.S.R. 56 8N 47 30E
91 Cheboygan, U.S.A. 45 29N 84 15W
72 Chech, Erg, des., Algeria 25 0N 7 0W
51 Checheno-Ingush, A.S.S.R., U.S.S.R. 43 30N 46 0E
22 Cheddar, England 51 16N 2 47W
26 Cheddleton, England 53 5N 2 2W
65 Cheduba, I., Burma 18 48N 93 43E
83 Cheepie, Australia 26 39S 145 0E
67 Chefoo (Yehtai), China 37 30N 121 25E
72 Chegga, Mauritania 25 15N 5 40W
90 Chehalis, U.S.A. 46 35N 122 55W
67 Cheju, Korea 33 30N 126 20E
67 Cheju Do. I. (Quelpart), Korea 33 20N 126 30E
67 Chekiang, Prov., China 29 10N 120 0E
62 Cheleken, I., U.S.S.R. 39 25N 53 15E
60 Chelkar, U.S.S.R. 47 50N 59 32E
47 Chelm, Poland 51 12N 23 39E
47 Chelmno, Poland 53 20N 18 30E
23 Chelmsford, England 51 43N 0 27E
47 Chelmza, Poland 53 10N 18 45E
22 Cheltenham, England 51 54N 2 4W
60 Chelyabinsk, U.S.S.R. 55 20N 61 15E
50 Chemikovsk, U.S.S.R. 54 55N 56 0E
66 Chengchow, China 34 55N 113 40E
66 Cheng-teh, China 41 3N 118 0E
66 Chengtu, China 30 50N 104 5E
22 Chepstow, Wales 51 39N 2 41W
43 Cher, R. & Dépt., France 47 0N 2 15E
42 Cherbourg, France 49 39N 1 40W
66 Cherchen, China 38 13N 85 27E
66 Cherchen, R., China 39 20N 86 0E
50 Cherdyn, U.S.S.R. 60 20N 56 20E
61 Cheremkhovo, U.S.S.R. 53 5N 103 0E
50 Cherepovets, U.S.S.R. 59 10N 37 50E
51 Cherkassy, U.S.S.R. 49 20N 32 10E
50 Chernigov, U.S.S.R. 51 35N 31 15E
51 Chernovtsy, U.S.S.R. 48 21N 25 58E
61 Chernoye, U.S.S.R. 70 30N 89 10E
49 Chernyakhovsk, U.S.S.R. 54 29N 21 48E
91 Cherokee, U.S.A. 42 46N 95 39W
65 Cherrapunji, India 25 18N 91 57E
61 Cherskiy Ra., U.S.S.R. 64 0N 145 0E
22 Cherwell, R., England 51 55N 1 18W
91 Chesapeake B., U.S.A. 37 0N 76 0W
23 Chesham, England 51 42N 0 36W
26 Cheshire, Co. & Plain, Eng. 53 15N 2 30W
23 Cheshunt, England 51 42N 0 1W
22 Chesil Beach, England 50 38N 2 35W
26 Chester, England 53 12N 2 53W
27 Chesterfield, England 53 15N 1 26W
88 Chesterfield Inlet, Can. 63 45N 92 0W
81 Chesterfield Is., Pac. Oc. 19 52S 158 0E
27 Chester-le-Street, Eng. 54 52N 1 34W
83 Chesterton Ra., Australia 25 50S 146 55E
31 Cheviot Hills, England 55 20N 2 30W
74 Chew Bahir, L., Ethiopia 4 45N 36 50E
90 Cheyenne, U.S.A. 41 20N 104 57W
90 Cheyenne, R., U.S.A. 44 30N 101 45W
64 Chhatarpur, India 25 0N 78 35E
64 Chhindwara, India 22 6N 78 59E
65 Chiali, China 30 25N 93 0E
65 Chiang Mai, Thailand 19 0N 99 55E
65 Chiang Rai, Thailand 19 30N 99 50E
94 Chiapa, R., Mexico 16 45N 92 58W
40 Chiavari, Italy 44 20N 9 20E
40 Chiavenna, Italy 46 20N 9 26E
67 Chiba, & Pref., Japan 35 40N 140 6E
75 Chibia, Angola 15 10S 13 50E
73 Chibuk, Nigeria 10 52N 12 50E
92 Chicago, U.S.A. 41 50N 87 50W
88 Chichagof I., Alaska 57 50N 136 0W
23 Chichester, England 50 50N 0 47W
90 Chickasha, U.S.A. 35 2N 98 0W
37 Chiclana, Spain 36 23N 6 10W
98 Chiclayo, Peru 7 0S 79 30W
99 Chico, R., Argentina 49 0S 70 0W
75 Chicoa, Mozambique 15 35S 32 20E
89 Chicoutimi, Canada 48 24N 71 2W
64 Chidambaram, India 11 20N 79 40E
74 Chiengi, Zambia 8 38S 29 10E
44 Chiers, R., France 49 30N 5 20E
40 Chieti, Italy 42 21N 14 12E
66 Chihli, G., China 40 0N 116 30E
94 Chihuahua, Mexico 28 47N 106 20W
64 Chik Ballapur, India 13 20N 77 40E
65 Chikmagalur, India 13 20N 75 52E
64 Chilaw, Sri Lanka 7 30N 79 50E
83 Childers, Australia 25 15S 152 17E
90 Childress, U.S.A. 34 25N 100 15W
99 Chile, S. America 17 30S to 55 0S 71 15W
99 Chilecito, Argentina 29 0S 67 40W
50 Chili, U.S.S.R. 44 20N 66 59E
75 Chililabombwe, Zambia 12 10S 28 0E
65 Chilka, L., India 19 40N 85 28E
82 Chillagoe, Australia 17 0S 144 10E
99 Chillán, Chile 36 48S 72 12W
91 Chillicothe, Mo., U.S.A. 39 46N 93 34W
92 Chillicothe, Ohio, U.S.A. 39 28N 83 1W
99 Chiloe, I., Chile 43 0S 73 30W
23 Chiltern Hills, England 51 45N 0 45W
66 Chimai, China 33 30N 100 45E
44 Chimay, Belgium 50 2N 4 20E
98 Chimborazo, Mt. Ecuador 1 10S 79 5W
98 Chimbote, Peru 8 55S 78 33W
50 Chimkent, U.S.S.R. 42 40N 69 25E
66 China, Asia 55 0N to 18 30N; 70 0E to 133 0E
94 Chinandega, Nicaragua 12 34N 87 5W
98 Chincha Alta, Peru 13 20S 76 0W
83 Chinchilla, Australia 26 40S 150 8E
37 Chinchon, Spain 40 10N 3 29W
67 Chinchow, China 41 10N 121 2E
75 Chinde, Mozambique 18 45S 36 25E
65 Chindwin, R., Burma 25 0N 95 0E
67 Chingkiang, China 32 7N 119 32E
75 Chingola, Zambia 12 31S 27 53E
72 Chinguetti, Mauritania 20 35S 12 25W
64 Chiniot, Pakistan 31 45N 72 55E
67 Chinnampo, Korea 39 10N 126 0E
43 Chinon, France 47 12N 0 15E
65 Chins Division, Burma 22 30N 93 30E
74 Chinsali, Zambia 10 35S 32 3E
67 Chinwangtao, China 39 58N 119 30E
40 Chioggia, Italy 45 13N 12 17E
75 Chipata, Zambia 13 29S 32 36E
93 Chipman, Canada 46 10N 65 55W
22 Chippenham, England 51 28N 2 7W
91 Chippewa Falls, U.S.A. 44 55N 92 30W
22 Chipping Campden, Eng. 52 4N 1 48W
22 Chipping Norton, Eng. 51 57N 1 33W
64 Chirala, India 15 45N 80 20E
60 Chirchik, U.S.S.R. 41 40N 69 10E
25 Chirk, Wales 52 57N 3 4W
65 Chirmiri, India 23 15N 82 20E
75 Chiromo, Malawi 16 25S 35 12E
75 Chisamba, Zambia 14 55N 28 20E
65 Chisapani Garhi, Nepal 27 30N 84 2E
50 Chistopol, U.S.S.R. 55 22N 50 37E
61 Chita, U.S.S.R. 52 15N 113 50E
75 Chitembo, Angola 13 30S 16 50E
64 Chitorgarh, India 24 58N 74 36E
64 Chitral, India 35 57N 71 46E
95 Chitré, Panama 7 50N 80 25W
65 Chittagong, E. Pak. 22 25N 91 43E
64 Chittoor, India 13 8N 79 5E
40 Chiusi, Italy 43 2N 11 56E
43 Chivasso, Italy 45 15N 7 55E
99 Chivilcoy, Argentina 35 0S 60 4W
75 Chobe Swamp, Botswana 18 25S 24 25E
99 Choele Choel, Argentina 39 15S 65 30W
49 Chojnice, Poland 53 44N 17 40E
22 Cholsey, England 51 34N 1 10W
75 Choma, Zambia 16 57S 26 58E
46 Chomutov, Cz-slov. 50 28N 13 23E
67 Chongjin, Korea 41 40N 129 40E
99 Chonos Arch., Chile 45 0S 74 0W
26 Chorley, England 53 39N 2 38W
47 Chortkov, U.S.S.R. 49 2N 25 46E
47 Chorzow, Poland 50 20N 19 0E
67 Choshi, Japan 35 50N 140 48E
46 Choszczno, Poland 53 7N 15 25E
64 Chotila, India 22 30N 71 3E
72 Chott Djerid, Tunisia 34 10N 8 0E
72 Chott el Hodna, Algeria 35 30N 4 30E
62 Choueifat, Lebanon 33 48N 35 30E
83 Chowilla, Australia 33 58S 140 45E
66 Chowkow (Shangshui), China 31 10N 105 45E
66 Choybalsan, Mongolia 48 9N 114 30E
66 Chowkow, China 33 40N 115 0E
22 Christchurch, England 50 44N 1 47W
84 Christchurch, N.Z. 43 30S 172 43E
76 Christiana, S. Africa 27 57S 25 8E
95 Christiansted, St. Croix, W. Indies 17 45N 64 45W
5 Christmas I., Indian Oc. 10 0S 105 0E
11 Christmas I., Pac. Oc. 1 58N 157 27W
67 Chüanchow, China 25 0N 118 33E
66 Chuchow, China 27 45N 113 10E
61 Chuckchi or Chukot Sea, U.S.S.R. 69 0N 177 0E
24 Chudleigh, England 50 35N 3 36W
50 Chudskoye L., U.S.S.R. 58 0N 27 30E
67 Chühsien, China 28 55N 119 0E
68 Chukai, Malaysia 4 10N 103 30E
61 Chulman, U.S.S.R. 57 5N 124 50E
66 Chumatien, China 33 0N 114 10E
61 Chumikan, U.S.S.R. 54 45N 135 20E
68 Chumphon, Thailand 10 35N 99 20E
66 Chunking, China 29 32N 106 45E
65 Chungtien, China 27 50N 99 50E
66 Chungwei, China 38 0N 105 0E
74 Chunya, Tanzania 8 20S 34 0E
99 Chuquicamata, Chile 22 30S 69 0W
45 Chur, Switzerland 46 51N 9 33E
22 Church Stretton, Eng. 52 32N 2 49W
22 Churchdown, England 51 53N 2 9W
88 Churchill, & C., Canada 58 45N 94 0W
88 Churchill L., Canada 56 0N 108 30W
89 Churchill Falls, Canada 53 35N 65 20W
88 Churchill R., Canada 55 30N 104 0W
64 Churu, India 28 25N 75 0E
50 Chusovoy, U.S.S.R. 58 15N 57 30E
64 Chusul, Kashmir 33 40N 78 40E
50 Chuvash, A.S.S.R., U.S.S.R. 55 40N 47 0E
47 Ciechanów, Poland 52 55N 20 35E
98 Cienaga, Colombia 11 0N 74 15W
95 Cienfuegos, Cuba 22 13N 80 30W
47 Cieszyn, Poland 49 45N 18 40E
37 Cieza, Spain 38 15N 1 25W
62 Cilician Gates, Turkey 37 20N 34 52E
91 Cimarron, R., U.S.A. 37 10N 102 0W
47 Cîmpina, Rumania 45 10N 25 45E
47 Cîmpulung, Rumania 45 18N 25 0E
37 Cinca, R., Spain 42 20N 0 10E
92 Cincinnati, U.S.A. 39 17N 84 25W
22 Cinderford, England 51 49N 2 30W
44 Ciney, Belgium 50 19N 5 5E
68 Cirebon, Indonesia 6 5S 108 30E
22 Cirencester, England 51 44N 1 58W
94 Citlaltepetl, Mt., Mexico 19 3N 97 16W
95 Ciudad Bolivar, Venezuela 8 0N 63 30W
94 Ciudad Camargo, Mexico 27 40N 105 10W
94 Ciudad del Carmen, Mex. 18 45N 91 45W
95 Ciudad Guayana, Ven. 8 25N 62 30W
94 Ciudad Juaréz, Mexico 31 40N 106 28W
94 Ciudad Madero, Mexico 22 40N 98 10W
94 Ciudad Mante, Mexico 22 40N 99 2W
94 Ciudad Obregon, Mex. 27 40N 109 50W
37 Ciudad Real, Spain 39 0N 3 55W
37 Ciudad Rodrigo, Spain 40 38N 6 33W
94 Ciudad Victoria, Mex. 23 50N 99 0W
40 Civitanova, Italy 43 20N 13 40E
40 Civitavecchia, Italy 42 6N 11 51E
43 Civray, France 46 10N 0 15E
51 Cizre, Turkey 37 27N 42 3E
30 Clachan, Arg., Scot. 55 45N 5 35W
32 Clachan, Invern., Scot. 57 33N 7 20W
31 Clackmannan, Scot. 56 6N 3 45W
23 Clacton-on-Sea, England 51 48N 1 9E
30 Cladich, Scotland 56 21N 5 5W
43 Clamecy, France 47 27N 3 30E
88 Claire L., Canada 58 30N 112 0W
35 Clane, Ireland 53 18N 6 40W
76 Clanwilliam, S. Africa 32 13S 18 59E
35 Clara, Ireland 53 20N 7 38W
83 Clare, Australia 33 47S 138 30E
23 Clare, England 52 5N 0 36E
34 Clare, Co., Ireland 52 52N 8 55W
35 Clare, I., Ireland 53 48N 10 0W
34 Clare, R., Ireland 53 30N 8 53W
36 Claremorris, Ireland 53 42N 8 58W
84 Clarence, R., N.Z. 42 15S 173 30E
34 Clarinbride, Ireland 53 13N 8 55W
83 Clarke I., Australia 40 32S 148 10E
90 Clark Fork, R., U.S.A. 46 45N 114 0W
92 Clarksburg, U.S.A. 39 30N 80 15W
91 Clarksdale, U.S.A. 34 14N 90 31W
91 Clarksville, U.S.A. 36 35N 87 15W
33 Clashmore, Scotland 57 53N 4 8W
36 Claudy, N. Ireland 54 55N 7 10W
27 Clay Cross, England 53 11N 1 26W
23 Claydon, England 52 6N 1 7E
34 Clear, C. & I., Ireland 51 26N 9 30W
91 Clearwater, U.S.A. 28 0N 82 47W
89 Clearwater, L., Canada 56 20N 75 0W
90 Clearwater, R., U.S.A. 46 15N 115 30W
33 Cleat, Scotland 58 45N 2 56W
26 Cleator Moor, England 54 31N 3 32W
91 Cleburne, U.S.A. 32 21N 97 27W
25 Cleddau, R., Wales 51 55N 4 44W
22 Clee Hills, England 52 26N 2 37W
27 Cleethorpes, England 53 33N 0 2W
22 Cleeve Cloud, mt., Eng. 51 57N 2 0W
82 Clermont, Australia 22 45S 147 30E
43 Clermont Ferrand, Fr. 45 46N 3 10E
44 Clervaux, Luxembourg 50 3N 6 2E
83 Cleveland, Australia 27 35S 153 0E
27 Cleveland, Co., Eng. 54 32N 1 10W
91 Cleveland, Miss., U.S.A. 33 45N 90 50W
92 Cleveland, Ohio, U.S.A. 41 25N 81 40W
91 Cleveland, Tenn., U.S.A. 35 10N 84 35W
27 Cleveland Hills, England 54 25N 1 11W
35 Clew B., Ireland 53 50N 9 45W
34 Clifden, & B., Ireland 53 30N 10 1W
84 Clifden, New Zealand 46 5S 167 30E
36 Cliffony, Ireland 54 27N 8 31W
22 Clifford, England 52 6N 3 6W
34 Cliffs of Moher, Ireland 52 59N 9 25W
83 Clifton, Australia 27 58S 151 40E
76 Clifton Bakoven, S. Africa 33 57S 18 20E
91 Clinch, Mts., U.S.A. 36 30N 83 0W
88 Clinton, Canada 51 0N 121 40W
84 Clinton, New Zealand 46 24S 169 23E
92 Clinton, Iowa, U.S.A. 41 50N 90 15W
90 Clinton, Okla., U.S.A. 35 30N 98 58W
88 Clinton Colden L., Can. 64 0N 107 0W
26 Clitheroe, England 53 52N 2 24W
80 Cloates, Pt., Australia 22 30S 113 40E
36 Cloghan, Donegal, Ireland 54 48N 7 57W
34 Clogheen, Ireland 52 17N 8 0W
36 Clogher, N. Ireland 54 23N 7 11W
36 Clogher Hd., Ireland 53 47N 6 13W
34 Cloghjordan, Ireland 52 57N 8 2W
34 Clonakilty, & B., Ireland 51 38N 8 52W
82 Cloncurry, Australia 20 38S 140 30E
35 Clondalkin, Ireland 53 20N 6 25W
35 Clonee, Ireland 53 25N 6 28W
36 Clones, Ireland 54 10N 7 13W
34 Clonkeen, Ireland 51 59N 9 20W
36 Clonmany, Ireland 55 16N 7 24W
35 Clonmel, Ireland 52 22N 7 40W
35 Clonroche, Ireland 52 27N 6 42W
35 Cloonfad, Ireland 53 41N 8 45W
31 Closeburn, Scotland 55 13N 3 45W
36 Clough, N. Ireland 54 18N 5 50W
90 Clovis, U.S.A. 34 25N 103 16W
27 Clowne, England 53 16N 1 16W
34 Cloyne, Ireland 51 52N 8 8W
32 Cluanie, L., Scotland 57 8N 5 6W
47 Cluj, Rumania 46 42N 23 36E
22 Clun, England 52 26N 3 1W
83 Clunes, Australia 37 20S 143 45E
43 Cluny, France 46 32N 4 43E
45 Cluses, France 46 4N 6 35E
45 Clusone, Italy 45 54N 9 58E
85 Clutha R., N.Z. 45 39S 168 55E
25 Clwyd, Co., Wales 53 10N 3 20W
25 Clwyd, R., Wales 53 15N 3 25W
84 Clyde, New Zealand 45 12N 169 20E
31 Clyde, R., Scot. 55 38N 3 47W
30 Clyde, Firth of, Scotland 55 35N 5 0W
30 Clydebank, Scotland 55 54N 4 25W
31 Clydesdale, Dist., Scot. 55 30N 3 35W
34 Coachford, Ireland 51 57N 8 56W
36 Coagh, N. Ireland 54 40N 6 37W
22 Coalbrookdale, Eng. 52 40N 2 25W
36 Coalisland, N. Ireland 54 33N 6 42W
22 Coalville, England 52 43N 1 21W
88 Coast Mts., Canada 56 0N 130 0W
99 Coast Ra., Chile 24 0S 70 0W
90 Coast Ra., N. America 42 0N 123 0W
80 Coastal Plains Basin, Australia 30 30S 115 30E
31 Coatbridge, Scotland 55 51N 4 2W
93 Coaticook, Canada 45 7N 71 50W
88 Coats I., Canada 62 30N 83 0W
100 Coats Ld., Antarctica 78 0S 25 0W
94 Coatzacoalcos, Mexico 18 7N 94 35W
89 Cobalt, Canada 47 30N 79 42W
83 Cobar, Australia 31 29S 145 45E
34 Cobh, Ireland 51 52N 8 17W
83 Cobham, Australia 30 10S 142 5E
83 Cobram, Australia 35 58S 145 35E
75 Cóbuè, Mozambique 12 0S 34 58E
46 Coburg, Germany 50 16N 10 57E
65 Cocanada, India 17 0N 82 10E
98 Cochabamba, Bolivia 17 30S 66 27W
68 Cochin China, Vietnam 10 0N 106 0E
89 Cochrane, Canada 49 12N 81 37W
83 Cockburn, Australia 31 58S 141 8E
99 Cockburn Chan., Chile 54 30S 72 30W
31 Cockburnspath, Scotland 55 56N 2 23W
31 Cockenzie, Scotland 55 58N 2 59W
26 Cockerham, England 53 58N 2 49W
26 Cockermouth, England 54 41N 3 19W
23 Cockfield, England 52 8N 0 47E
95 Coco, R., Cent. Amer., *see* Wanks R.
5 Cocos Is., Indian Ocean 12 10S 96 50E
93 Cod, C., U.S.A. 42 8N 70 10W
23 Coddenham, England 52 8N 1 8E
94 Codrington. Barbuda, 17 40N 61 11W
82 Coen, Australia 13 55S 143 15E
44 Coesfeld, Germany 51 57N 7 11E
90 Coeur d'Alene, U.S.A. 47 58N 116 57W
44 Coevorden, Netherlands 52 29N 6 45E
83 Coff's Harbour, Austral. 30 17S 152 51E
40 Coghinas, R., Sardinia, It. 40 30N 8 50E
42 Cognac, France 45 42N 0 20W
83 Cohuna, Australia 35 57S 144 8E
95 Coiba, I., Panama 7 30N 81 50W
32 Coigach, Scotland 58 0N 5 10W
64 Coimbatore, India 11 0N 77 0E
37 Coimbra, Portugal 40 17N 8 26W
37 Coin, Spain 36 42N 4 46W
45 Col de Faucille, France 46 21N 6 0E
43 Col de la Perche, Spain 42 30N 2 0E
43 Col di Tenda, France 44 10N 7 30E
83 Colac, Australia 38 18S 143 40E
83 Colbinabbin, Australia 36 40S 144 45E
23 Colchester, England 51 53N 0 55E
26 Cold Fell, Mt., England 54 56N 2 38W
31 Coldingham, Scotland 55 53N 2 29W
31 Coldstream, Scotland 55 40N 2 14W
24 Colebrooke, England 50 45N 3 44W
22 Coleford, England 51 46N 2 38W
88 Coleman, Canada 49 36N 114 30W
83 Coleraine, Australia 37 47S 141 42E
36 Coleraine, N. Ireland 55 7N 6 39W
22 Coleshill, England 52 30N 1 42W
43 Colico, Italy 46 9N 9 24E
94 Colima, & Vol., Mex. 19 30N 103 50W
30 Coll I., Scotland 56 40N 6 35W
83 Collarenebri, Austral. 29 33S 148 36E
80 Collie, Australia 33 18S 116 5E
80 Collier B., Australia 16 0S 124 0E
26 Collier Law, mt., Eng. 54 47N 1 59W
84 Collingwood, N.Z. 40 40S 172 40E
82 Collinsville, Australia 20 35S 147 50E
43 Collioure, France 42 30N 3 0E
36 Collon, Ireland 53 46N 6 29W
83 Colly Blue, Australia 31 30S 150 2E
43 Colmar, France 48 0N 6 43E
43 Colmars, France 44 10N 6 40E
26 Colne, England 53 52N 2 12W
23 Colne, R., England 51 55N 0 45E
44 Cologne (Köln), Germany 50 56N 6 58E
98 Colombia, Rep., S. Amer. 7 40N 75 0W
64 Colombo, Sri Lanka 6 56N 79 58E
95 Colon, Cuba 22 55N 80 55W
95 Colón, Panama 9 22N 80 12W
30 Colonsay I., Scotland 56 4N 6 13W
94 Colorado I., Panama Canal Zone (Inset)
99 Colorado, R., Argentina 39 30S 63 0W
90 Colorado, R., U.S.A. 38 0N 109 30W
90 Colorado, st., U.S.A. 39 15N 105 30W
90 Colorado Springs, U.S.A. 38 57N 104 59W
33 Colpy, Scotland 57 23N 2 35W
92 Columbia, Dist. of, 38 50N 77 0W
91 Columbia, S.C., U.S.A. 33 59N 81 0W
91 Columbia, Tenn., U.S.A. 35 38N 86 59W
90 Columbia Plat., U.S.A. 47 0N 118 0W
90 Columbia R., U.S.A. 46 15N 124 0W
37 Columbretes Is., Spain 39 53 0 45E
91 Columbus, Ga., U.S.A. 32 30N 84 58W
91 Columbus, Miss., U.S.A. 33 31N 88 17W
91 Columbus, Neb., U.S.A. 41 27N 97 20W
92 Columbus, Ohio, U.S.A. 39 57N 83 2W
25 Colwyn, Wales 53 17N 3 43W
25 Colwyn Bay, Wales 53 19N 3 44W
40 Comacchio, Italy 44 42N 12 17E
94 Comayagua, Honduras 14 10N 87 40W
44 Comblain, Belgium 50 27N 5 34E
35 Comeragh Mts., Ireland 52 16N 7 34W
65 Comilla, Bangladesh 23 27N 91 15E
40 Comino I., Malta 36 0N 14 21E
43 Commentry, France 46 20N 2 45E
43 Commercy, France 48 46N 5 30E
83 Commonwealth Territory, Austral. 35 10S 151 0E
45 Como, & L., Italy 45 49N 9 8E
99 Comodoro Rivadavia, Argentina 45 45S 67 30W
64 Comorin, C., India 8 5N 77 40E
71 Comoro Is., Mozam. Chan. 11 30S 43 17E
88 Comox, Canada 49 50N 125 5W
43 Compiègne, France 49 25N 2 49E
22 Compton, England 51 2N 1 19W
83 Compton Downs, Australia 30 30S 146 35E
31 Comrie, Scotland 56 22N 4 0W
83 Conara Junction, Australia 41 50S 147 20E
72 Conakry, Guinea 9 25N 13 56W
42 Concarneau, France 47 55N 3 55W
99 Concepción, Chile 36 48S 73 5W
75 Conception B., S.W. Afr. 23 55S 14 22E
90 Conceptión Pt., U.S.A. 34 21N 120 40W
99 Conception del Uruguay, Argentina 33 0S 58 40W
93 Concord, U.S.A. 43 7N 71 30W
99 Concordia, Argentina 31 0S 57 48W
83 Condamine, Australia 26 55S 150 5E
42 Condé, Calvados, Fr. 48 55N 0 35W
44 Condé, Nord, France 50 25N 3 35E
83 Condobolin, Australia 33 1S 147 13E
68 Condore Is., Vietnam 8 35N 106 30E
22 Condover, England 52 39N 2 46W
43 Conflans, France 49 10N 5 45E
43 Confolens, France 46 0N 0 45E
26 Congleton, England 53 10N 2 13W
74 Congo, Dem. Rep. of, *see* Zaïre
74 Congo, Africa 0 0 16 0E
74 Congo, R., Africa 2 0N 22 0E
70 Congo Basin, Africa 1 0S 22 0E
27 Conisbrough, England 53 29N 1 12W
26 Coniston Water, Eng. 54 20N 3 7W
82 Conjuboy, Australia 18 35S 144 45E
36 Conn, L., Ireland 54 0N 9 15W
35 Connacht, Prov., Ireland 53 42N 8 55W
25 Connah's Quay, Wales 53 13N 3 6W
92 Conneaut, U.S.A. 41 57N 80 32W
93 Connecticut, st., U.S.A. 41 35N 72 40W
92 Connelsville, U.S.A. 40 0N 79 33W
34 Connemara, Dist., Ire. 53 27N 9 48W
82 Connors Ra., Australia 21 40S 149 10E
83 Conoble, Australia 33 0S 144 45E
26 Consett, England 54 52N 1 50W
45 Constance, L., Switz.-Ger., *see* Bodensee
72 Constantine, Algeria 36 23N 6 29E
47 Constanta, Rumania 44 12N 28 39E
37 Constantina, Spain 37 55N 5 43W
99 Constitución, Chile 35 18S 72 30W
98 Contas, R., Brazil 13 40S 40 30W
36 Convoy, Ireland 54 52N 7 40W
91 Conway, U.S.A. 35 5N 92 30W
25 Conwy, & B., Wales 53 18N 3 52W
25 Conwy, R., Wales 53 0N 3 50W
65 Cooch Behar, India 26 30N 89 20E
11 Cook Is., Pacific Ocean 18 0S 164 0W
84 Cook, Mt., N.Z. 43 30S 170 12E
84 Cook Str., N.Z. 41 15S 174 30E
23 Cookham, England 51 33N 0 42W
76 Cookhouse, S. Africa 32 43S 25 45E
36 Cookstown, N. Ireland 54 39N 6 44W
82 Cooktown, Australia 15 35S 145 10E
83 Coolabah, Australia 30 52S 146 54E
83 Cooladdi, Australia 26 35S 145 28E
83 Coolah, Australia 31 36S 149 50E
83 Coolamon, Australia 34 46S 147 8E
83 Coolangatta, Australia 28 0S 153 5E
36 Coolaney, Ireland 54 11N 8 35W
80 Coolgardie, Australia 30 55S 121 7E
35 Coolgreany, Ireland 52 46N 6 14W
83 Cooma, Australia 36 13S 149 10E
83 Coonabarabran, Austral. 31 5S 149 50E
83 Coonamble, Australia 31 0S 148 21E
64 Coondapoor, India 13 30N 74 40E
83 Coongie, Australia 27 10S 140 5E
83 Coongoola, Australia 27 48S 146 0E
83 Cooper Cr., Australia 27 30S 139 17E
83 Cooroy, Australia 26 18S 152 50E
83 Cootamundra, Australia 34 40S 148 2E
36 Cootehill, Ireland 54 6N 7 3W
83 Cooyar, Australia 27 0S 151 48E
49 Copenhagen, Denmark 55 40N 12 35E
99 Copiapó, Chile 27 15S 70 20W
83 Copley, Australia 30 35S 138 20E
92 Coppercliff, Canada 46 25N 81 6W
88 Coppermine, Canada 68 0N 116 0W
27 Coquet, R. & I., England 55 18N 1 45W
74 Coquilhatville, *see* Mbandaka
99 Coquimbo, Chile 29 50S 71 27W
47 Corabia, Rumania 43 45N 24 30E
98 Coracora, Peru 15 0S 73 40W
91 Coral Gables, U.S.A. 25 46N 80 16W
82 Coral Sea, Australasia 18 0S 152 30E
40 Corato, Italy 41 10N 16 27E
43 Corbeil, France 48 38N 2 30E
26 Corbridge, England 54 58N 2 6W
23 Corby, Lincs., England 52 49N 0 31W
23 Corby, Northants., Eng. 52 30N 0 41W
37 Corcubion, Spain 42 55N 9 14W
91 Cordele, U.S.A. 31 51N 83 49W
99 Cordoba, Argentina 31 22S 64 12W
37 Cordoba, Spain 37 54N 4 48W
99 Cordoba, Sierra de, Arg. 31 30S 65 0W
88 Cordova, Alaska 60 36N 145 45W
22 Corfe Castle, England 50 38N 2 3W
22 Corfe Mullen, England 50 45N 2 0W
82 Corfield, Australia 21 40S 143 21E
41 Corfu, *see* Kérkira
40 Corigliano, Italy 39 37N 16 32E

41 Corinth, Greece 37 40N 22 58E
91 Corinth, U.S.A. 34 54N 88 35W
34 Cork, & Co., Ireland 51 54N 8 28W
34 Cork Harbour, Ireland 51 48N 8 16W
89 Corner Brook, Canada 49 0N 58 0W
83 Cornwall, Australia 41 35S 148 0E
93 Cornwall, Canada 45 2N 75 10W
24 Cornwall Co., England 50 20N 4 50W
95 Coro, Venezuela 11 23N 69 45W
98 Corocoro, Bolivia 17 25S 68 25W
34 Corofin, Ireland 52 52N 9 11W
84 Coromandel, N.Z. 36 33S 175 28E
64 Coromandel Coast, India 13 0N 80 20E
88 Coronation G., Canada 68 0N 110 0W
99 Coronel Pringles, Arg. 38 0S 61 30W
83 Corowa, Australia 36 7S 146 30E
94 Corozal, Belize 17 20N 88 30W
91 Corpus Christi, U.S.A. 27 50N 97 28W
99 Corral, Chile 40 0S 73 40W
42 Corrèze Dépt., France 45 28N 2 5E
35 Corrib, Lough, Ireland 53 30N 9 20W
99 Corrientes, Argentina 27 15S 58 45W
98 Corrientes, C., Columbia 5 30N 77 30W
94 Corrientes, C., Mexico 20 20N 105 40W
27 Corringham, England 53 25N 0 41W
30 Corryvreckan, G. of, Scot. 56 10N 5 44W
43 Corse, C., Corsica 43 0N 9 20E
42 Corse-du-Sud, Dépt. Fr. 42 0N 9 0E
22 Corsham, England 51 25N 2 11W
42 Corsica I., Mediterranean 42 0N 9 0E
91 Corsicana, U.S.A. 32 5N 96 31W
31 Corsock, Scotland 55 4N 3 56W
43 Corte, France 42 17N 9 8E
90 Cortez, U.S.A. 37 25N 108 45W
93 Cortland, U.S.A. 42 35N 76 12W
40 Cortona, Italy 43 19N 12 1E
51 Corum, Turkey 40 35N 35 5E
98 Corumba, Brazil 19 0S 57 20W
37 Corunna, see La Coruña, Spain
22 Corve, R., Eng. 52 27N 2 43W
25 Corwen, Wales 52 58N 3 22W
22 Coseley, England 52 33N 2 6W
40 Cosenza, Italy 39 20N 16 13E
22 Cosham, England 50 51N 1 3W
43 Cosne, France 47 22N 3 0E
95 Costa Rica, Cen. Amer. 10 0N 84 0W
34 Costelloe, Ireland 53 17N 9 33W
23 Costessey, England 52 40N 1 11E
68 Cotabato, Philippines 7 0N 124 10E
43 Côte d'Or, Dépt. & Dist., France
47 40N 4 45E
91 Coteau des Prairies, U.S.A.
45 0N 95 30W
43 Cotentin, Dist., France 49 20N 1 30W
42 Côtes du Nord, Dépt., Fr. 48 25N 2 45W
72 Cotonou, Benin 6 25N 2 20E
98 Cotopaxi Vol., Ecuador 0 40S 78 30W
22 Cotswold Hills, England 51 45N 2 10W
46 Cottbus, Germany 51 45N 14 24E
23 Cottenham, England 52 18N 0 8E
43 Cottian Alps, France 44 40N 6 50E
27 Cottingham, England 53 47N 0 25W
43 Coulommiers, France 48 46N 3 5E
91 Council Bluffs, U.S.A. 41 22N 95 50W
31 Coupar Angus, Scotland 56 33N 3 15W
95 Courentyne, R., S. Amer. 6 0N 57 3W
44 Courmayeur, Italy 45 47N 7 0E
45 Courtelary, Switzerland 47 10N 7 5E
34 Courtmacsherry, & B., Ire. 51 38N 8 41W
35 Courtown, Ire. 52 37N 6 14W
43 Coutainville, France 49 2N 1 32W
33 Cove Bay, Scotland 57 5N 2 5W
22 Coventry, England 52 25N 1 31W
37 Covilha, Portugal 40 20N 7 27W
92 Covington, U.S.A. 39 0N 84 38W
30 Cowal, Dist., Scotland 56 5N 5 8W
80 Cowan, L., Australia 31 50S 121 50E
83 Cowangie, Australia 35 20S 141 25E
25 Cowbridge, Wales 51 27N 3 28W
31 Cowdenbeath, Scotland 56 7N 3 20W
83 Cowell, Australia 33 35S 136 50E
22 Cowes, England 50 46N 1 18W
22 Cowley, England 51 43N 1 12W
83 Cowra, Australia 33 50S 148 37E
65 Cox's Bazaar, Bangladesh 21 30N 92 5E
94 Cozumel I. de, Mexico 20 30N 87 0W
83 Craboon, Australia 32 2S 149 30E
76 Cradock, S. Africa 32 5S 25 38E
36 Craigavon, N. Ireland 54 28N 6 20W
31 Crail, Scotland 56 16N 2 38W
47 Craiova, Rumania 44 20N 23 49E
27 Cramlington, England 55 5N 1 37W
83 Cranbrook, Australia 42 0S 147 10E
88 Cranbrook, Canada 49 28N 115 58W
23 Cranbrook, England 51 6N 0 33E
23 Cranleigh, England 51 8N 0 29W
31 Cranshaws, Scotland 55 51N 2 30W
27 Cranwell, England 53 2N 0 28W
44 Craonne, France 49 27N 3 42E
98 Crateus, Brazil 5 5S 40 43W
33 Crathie, Scotland 57 2N 3 13W
98 Crato, Brazil 7 0S 39 12W
34 Craughwell, Ireland 53 14N 8 44W
22 Craven Arms, England 52 26N 2 45W
31 Crawford, Scotland 55 28N 3 39W
23 Crawley, England 51 7N 0 12W
33 Creag Meagaidh, Scot. 56 57N 4 37W
43 Crécy, France 50 17N 1 53E
44 Crécy s. Serre, France 49 45N 3 35E
22 Credenhill, England 52 6N 2 48W
24 Crediton, England 50 48N 3 39W
43 Creil, France 49 18N 2 30E
43 Crema, Italy 45 22N 9 40E
43 Cremona, Italy 45 10N 10 1E
44 Crépy, France 49 37N 3 32E
40 Cres, I., Yugoslavia 44 50N 14 25E
83 Cressy, Australia 38 10S 143 48E
43 Crest, France 44 40N 5 0E
91 Creston, U.S.A. 41 2N 94 21W
41 Crete, I., Greece 35 15N 25 0E
37 Creus, C., Spain 42 18N 3 21E
42 Creuse, Dépt., France 45 57N 1 53E
43 Creuse, France 46 40N 1 20E
26 Crewe, England 53 8N 2 23W
24 Crewkerne, England 50 54N 2 48W
30 Crianlarich, Scotland 56 23N 4 36W
25 Crickhowell, Wales 51 52N 3 8W
22 Cricklade, England 51 39N 1 51W
31 Crieff, Scotland 56 23N 3 51W
31 Criffel, Mt., Scotland 54 57N 3 45W
51 Crimea, Pen., U.S.S.R. 45 30N 34 0E
33 Crimond, Scotland 57 35N 1 53W
30 Crinan Canal, Scotland 56 4N 5 30W
94 Cristobal, Panama Canal Zone (Inset)
47 Crisul, Black, R., Rum. 46 40N 22 0E
47 Crisul, White, R., Rum. 46 20N 22 0E
41 Crna, R., Yugoslavia 41 20N 21 59E
41 Crna Gora Mts., Y.-Slav. 42 20N 21 30E
35 Croaghpatrick, Mt., Ire. 53 45N 9 42W
40 Croatia, Fed. unit, Y.-slav. 45 30N 16 0E
32 Comalt Hill, Scotland 58 0N 5 0W
33 Cromarty, Scotland 57 41N 4 2W
33 Cromarty Firth, Scot. 57 40N 4 10W
23 Cromer, England 52 57N 1 19E
84 Cromwell, New Zealand 45 0S 169 12E
23 Crondall, England 51 14N 0 52W
83 Cronulla, Australia 33 58S 151 4E
27 Crook, England 54 44N 1 45W
83 Crookwell, Australia 34 30S 149 28E
34 Croom, Ireland 52 31N 8 44W
31 Crosby, Cumb., Eng. 54 45N 3 25W
26 Crosby, Lancs., Eng. 53 28N 3 2W
27 Cross Fell, mt., England 54 44N 2 32W
88 Cross Sd., Alaska 58 20N 136 30W
35 Crossakiel, Ireland 53 43N 7 1W
36 Crossgar, N. Ireland 54 24N 5 46W
34 Crosshaven, Ireland 51 48N 8 17W
35 Crossmolina, Ireland 54 6N 9 19W
40 Crotone, Italy 39 5N 17 6E
23 Crouch, R., England 51 39N 0 40E
23 Crowborough, England 51 4N 0 9W
83 Crowes, Australia 38 55S 143 22E
27 Crowle, England 53 36N 0 50W
88 Crows Nest P., Canada 49 35N 115 0W
82 Croydon, Australia 18 30S 142 15E
23 Croydon, England 51 21N 0 6W
5 Crozet Is., Indian Ocean 46 0S 51 0E
42 Crozon, France 48 18N 4 30W
33 Cruden Bay, Scotland 57 24N 1 51W
26 Crummock Water L. Eng. 54 34N 3 19W
34 Crusheen, Ireland 52 57N 8 54W
98 Cruzeiro do Sul, Brazil 7 30S 72 30W
83 Crystal Brook, Australia 33 20S 138 7E
47 Csongrad, Hungary 46 43N 20 12E
75 Cuangar, Angola 17 28S 18 30E
74 Cuango, Congo 6 20S 16 50E
95 Cuba, West Indies 21 30N 79 30W
75 Cubango, R., Angola 17 30S 18 0E
75 Cuchi, Angola 14 40S 17 5E
23 Cuckfield, England 51 1N 0 9W
27 Cudworth, England 53 34N 1 26W
95 Cúcuta, Colombia 7 40N 72 40W
64 Cuddalore, India 11 42N 79 50E
64 Cuddapah, India 14 30N 78 50E
83 Cudgewa, Australia 36 10S 147 48E
80 Cue, Australia 27 25S 118 0E
98 Cuenca, Ecuador 2 46S 79 10W
37 Cuenca, Spain 40 8N 2 5W
37 Cuenca, Sa. de, mts., Spain 40 20N 1 50W
91 Cuero, U.S.A. 29 20N 97 30W
98 Cuiaba, Brazil 15 30S 56 6W
36 Cuilcagh, Mt., Ireland 54 16N 8 0W
32 Cuillin Hills & Sd., Scot. 57 13N 6 6W
75 Cuima, Angola 13 0S 15 50E
83 Culcairn, Australia 35 40S 147 0E
36 Culdaff, Ireland 55 16N 7 8W
37 Culebra, Sa. de la, mts., Spain
42 0N 6 30W
94 Culiacan, Mexico 24 49N 107 20W
33 Cullen, Scotland 57 42N 2 48W
37 Cullera, Spain 39 10N 0 15W
35 Cullin, L., Ireland 53 57N 9 11W
32 Cullivoe, Scotland 60 42N 1 1W
33 Culloden Moor, Scotland 57 29N 4 8W
24 Cullompton, England 50 52N 3 23W
45 Cully, Switzerland 46 30N 6 44E
43 Culoz, France 45 50N 5 50E
31 Culross, Scotland 56 3N 3 38W
33 Cults, Scotland 57 7N 2 10W
32 Culvain Mt., Scotland 56 55N 5 19W
95 Cumanà, Venezuela 10 30N 64 10W
88 Cumberland, Canada 49 34N 125 0W
26 Cumberland, Co., see Cumbria
92 Cumberland, U.S.A. 39 45N 78 57W
82 Cumberland Is., Austral. 20 25S 149 0E
89 Cumberland Pen., Can. 67 0N 65 0W
91 Cumberland Plat., U.S.A. 36 0N 84 40W
91 Cumberland, R., U.S.A. 36 15N 85 0W
89 Cumberland Sd., Canada 65 0N 65 0W
31 Cumbernauld, Scotland 55 57N 3 59W
30 Cumbrae, Is., Scot. 55 46N 4 55W
26 Cumbria, Co., England 54 30N 3 0W
83 Cumnock, Australia 32 55S 148 40E
30 Cumnock, Scotland 55 27N 4 16W
22 Cumnor, England 51 44N 1 21W
31 Cumwhinton, England 54 51N 2 49W
75 Cunene, R., Angola 17 0S 15 0E
43 Cuneo, Italy 44 23N 7 32E
83 Cunnamulla, Australia 28 0S 145 42E
30 Cunninghame, Dist., Scot. 55 40N 4 25W
31 Cupar, Scotland 56 19N 3 2W
95 Curaçao, I., Neth. W. I. 12 12N 69 0W
99 Curicó, Chile 35 0S 71 15W
99 Curitiba, Brazil 52 25S 49 45W
34 Currane, L., Ireland 51 50N 10 8W
83 Curraweena, Australia 30 45S 145 55E
31 Currie, Scotland 55 53N 3 17W
82 Curtis I., Australia 23 45S 151 17E
94 Curundu, Panama Can. Zone (Inset)
36 Cushendall, N. Ireland 55 5N 6 4W
91 Cushing, U.S.A. 35 56N 96 50W
43 Cusset, France 46 10N 3 30E
65 Cuttack, India 20 30N 85 57E
49 Cuxhaven, Germany 53 54N 8 42E
98 Cuzco, Peru 13 30S 72 8W
22 Cwmbran, Wales 51 39N 3 0W
25 Cwrt, Wales 52 35N 3 55W
41 Cyclades, Is., see Kikladhes
83 Cygnet, Tasmania 43 5S 147 3E
62 Cyprus I., Medit. Sea 35 0N 33 0E
73 Cyrenaica, Prov., Libya 28 0N 22 0E
73 Cyrene (Shahhat), Libya 32 39N 21 18E
46-47 Czechoslovakia, Eur. 49 0N 17 0E
47 Czegléd, Hungary 47 15N 19 45E
47 Czeremcha, Poland 52 32N 23 20E
47 Czestochowa, Poland 50 49N 19 4E

D

68 Da Lat, Vietnam 12 0N 108 30E
68 Da-Nang (Tourane), Vietnam
16 20N 108 0E
63 Daal, Syria 32 45N 36 8E
62 Dabat, Ethiopia 13 0N 37 50E
46 Dabie, Poland 53 27N 14 45E
72 Dabola, Guinea 10 50N 11 5W
74 Dabra Tabor, Ethiopia 11 50N 38 0E
47 Dabrowa, Poland 50 10N 21 0E
65 Dacca, Bangladesh 23 49N 90 25E
64 Dadu, Pakistan 26 45N 67 35E
68 Daet, Philippines 14 3N 122 59E
62 Dafina, Saudi Arabia 23 11N 42 0E
72 Dagana, Sénégal 16 30N 15 20W
51 Dagestan, A.S.S.R., U.S.S.R.
43 0N 47 0E
68 Dagupan, Philippines 16 0N 120 20E
62 Dahlak Arch., Red Sea 16 0N 40 10E
72 Dahomey, see Benin
35 Daingean (Philipstown), Ireland
53 19N 7 18W
67 Dairen-Port Arthur, China, see Lü-ta
73 Dairut, Egypt 27 34N 30 43E
67 Daishoji, Japan 36 15N 136 16E
82 Dajarra, Australia 21 47S 139 20E
72 Dakar, Sénégal 14 45N 17 8W
72 Dakhla, W. Sahara 23 55N 15 50W
73 Dakhla Oasis, Egypt 25 55N 27 30E
51 Dakhovskaya, U.S.S.R. 44 15N 40 15E
90 Dakota N. & S., see N. & S. Dakota
41 Dakovica, Yugoslavia 42 25N 20 26E
72 Dakra, Sénégal 15 30N 15 20W
49 Dal, R., Sweden 60 12N 16 40E
66 Dalai Nor, L., China 48 0N 116 30E
66 Dalandzadagad, Mong. 43 55N 104 10E
49 Dalarö, Sweden 59 10N 18 23E
64 Dalbandin, Pakistan 29 0N 64 23E
31 Dalbeattie, Scotland 54 56N 3 50W
83 Dalby, Australia 27 6S 151 18E
33 Dalhalvaig, Scotland 58 27N 3 52W
93 Dalhousie, Canada 48 0N 66 21W
31 Dalkeith, Scotland 55 53N 3 4W
83 Dallarnil, Australia 25 25S 152 0E
90 Dallas, Oregon, U.S.A. 44 50N 123 20W
91 Dallas, Texas, U.S.A. 32 44N 96 55W
30 Dalmally, Scotland 56 24N 4 58W
40 Dalmatia, Prov., Y.-slav. 43 10N 17 10E
30 Dalmellington, Scotland 55 19N 4 24W
61 Dalnegorsk, U.S.S.R. 44 30N 135 57E
61 Dalnerechensk, U.S.S.R. 45 50N 133 50E
30 Dalry, Scotland 55 43N 4 43W
26 Dalton, Lancs., England 54 12N 3 12W
27 Dalton, Yorks., England 54 28N 1 32W
48 Dalvik, Iceland 66 2N 18 20W
80 Daly, R., Australia 14 0S 130 50E
80 Daly Waters, Australia 16 5S 133 30E
64 Daman, India 20 20N 72 59E
75 Damara Ld., S.W. Africa 22 25S 17 0E
63 Damascus (Esh Sham), Syria
33 30N 36 18E
74 Damba, Angola 6 44S 15 29E
73 Dambacha, Ethiopia 10 40N 37 10E
62 Damghan, Persia 36 5N 54 20E
73 Damietta, Egypt 31 30N 31 32E
62 Damman, Saudi Arabia 26 27N 50 3E
64 Damoh, India 23 58N 79 30E
80 Dampier, Austral. 20 30S 116 40E
80 Dampier Downs, Austral. 18 5S 124 10E
82 Dampier Str., Indonesia 0 30S 131 15E
72 Dan Gora, Nigeria 11 30N 8 7E
64 Dandeli, India 15 5N 74 30E
65 Dandeldhura, Nepal 29 25N 80 30E
83 Dandenong, Australia 38 10S 145 14E
64 Dankhar Gompa, India 32 10N 78 10E
49 Dannemora, Sweden 60 13N 17 50E
84 Dannevirke, N.Z. 40 8S 176 10E
92 Dansville, U.S.A. 42 35N 77 40W
47 Danube, R., Europe 45 0N 28 0E
92 Danville, Ill., U.S.A. 40 10N 87 35W
92 Danville, Ken., U.S.A. 37 40N 84 50W
74 Dar es Salaam, Tanzania 6 48S 39 12E
72 Daraj, Libya 30 5N 10 30E
65 Darbhanga, India 26 15N 85 55E
41 Dardanelles (Hellespont), Str., Turkey
40 10N 26 0E
63 Dareiya, Syria 33 28N 36 14E
64 Dargai, India 34 20N 71 50E
60 Dargan Ata, U.S.S.R. 40 40N 62 20E
84 Dargaville, N.Z. 36 0S 173 59E
94 Darien, Panama Canal Zone (Inset)
95 Darien, G. of, Colombia 9 0N 77 0W
65 Darjeeling, India 27N 88 18E
22 Darlaston, England 52 35N 2 1W
83 Darling Downs, Australia 27 45S 150 0E
83 Darling, R., Australia 32 0S 143 0E
80 Darling Ra., Australia 32 0S 116 0E
27 Darlington, England 54 33N 1 34W
46 Darlowo, Poland 54 13N 16 19E
45 Darmstadt, Germany 49 52N 8 40E
73 Darnah, Libya 32 40N 22 25E
100 Darnley, C., Antarctica 68 0S 70 0E
82 Darr, Australia 24 34S 144 52E
24 Dart, R., England 50 28N 3 45W
23 Dartford, England 51 26N 0 15E
24 Dartmoor, England 50 39N 3 55W
93 Dartmouth, Canada 44 50N 63 30W
24 Dartmouth, England 50 21N 3 37W
27 Darton, England 53 36N 1 32W
30 Darvel, Scotland 55 37N 4 20W
26 Darwen, England 53 42N 2 28W
80 Darwin, Australia 12 28S 131 0E
62 Darya yi Namak, L., Iran 34 40N 51 30E
63 Dasht-i-Kavir, Des., Iran 35 0N 55 0E
63 Dasht-i-Lut, Des., Iran 31 0N 58 30E
64 Dasht-i-Margo, Des., Afghan.
30 40N 62 30E
50 Daugavpils, U.S.S.R. 56 0N 26 30E
60 Daukara, U.S.S.R. 45 55N 59 30E
64 Daulat Yar, Afghan. 34 35N 65 40E
63 Daulatabad, Afghanistan 32 46N 62 34E
63 Daulatabad, Iran 28 22N 56 38E
88 Dauphin, Canada 51 13N 100 3W
43 Dauphiné, Prov., France 45 5N 5 30E
64 Davangere, India 14 30N 75 50E
68 Davao, & G., Philippines 7 15N 125 35E
92 Davenport, U.S.A. 41 33N 90 34W
22 Daventry, England 52 15N 1 10W
100 Davis, Antarctica 69 10S 79 0E
89 Davis Str., N. America 67 0N 58 0W
45 Davos-Platz, Switzerland 46 50N 9 50E
62 Dawasir, Si. Arabia 20 25N 45 30E
24 Dawlish, England 50 35N 3 29W
65 Dawna Ra., Burma 16 30N 98 30E
88 Dawson, Canada 64 10N 139 30W
88 Dawson Cr., Canada 55 45N 120 15W
82 Dawson Ra., Australia 24 45S 149 55E
42 Dax, France 43 41N 1 0W
92 Dayton, Ohio, U.S.A. 39 47N 84 12W
91 Daytona Beach, U.S.A. 29 7N 81 2W
76 De Aar, S. Africa 30 46S 23 54E
80 De Grey R., Australia 20 32S 120 0E
61 De Long Is., U.S.S.R. 77 0N 155 0E
63 Dead Sea, Jordan-Israel 31 30N 35 25E
80 Deakin, Australia 30 34S 129 0E
23 Deal, England 51 13N 1 24E
22 Dean, Forest of, England 51 47N 2 35W
88 Dease Arm, Canada 66 45N 120 6W
88 Dease, R. & L., Canada 59 10N 129 50W
90 Death Valley, U.S.A. 36 0N 117 0W
43 Deauville, France 49 20N 0 0
72 Deba Habe, Nigeria 10 14N 11 20E
41 Debar, Yugoslavia 41 30N 20 30E
23 Deben, R., England 52 12N 1 13E
74 Debre Markos, Ethiopia 10 20N 37 45E
47 Debrecen, Hungary 47 37N 21 54E
91 Decatur, Alabama, U.S.A.
34 29N 86 43W
91 Decatur, Georgia, U.S.A. 33 42N 84 21W
92 Decatur, Ill., U.S.A. 39 53N 88 56W
43 Decazeville, France 44 37N 2 15E
65 Deccan, Reg., India 17 0N 78 30E
72 Dedougou, Volta 12 35N 3 40W
33 Dee, R., Scotland 57 7N 2 10W
25 Dee, R., Wales 52 50N 3 30W
83 Deepwater, Australia 29 25S 151 50E
64 Deesa, India 24 25N 72 20E
25 Deganwy, Wales 53 18N 3 49W
48 Degerfors, Sweden 64 10N 19 48E
46 Deggendorf, Germany 48 49N 12 59E
64 Deh Titan, Afghan. 33 45N 63 50E
72 Dehibat, Tunisia 32 0N 10 10E
64 Dehra Dun, India 30 24N 78 5E
73 Deim Zubeir, Sudan 7 47N 26 20E
44 Deinze, Belgium 50 59N 3 30E
63 Deir Abu Sa'id, Jordan 32 30N 35 42E
51 Deir ez Zor, Syria 35 19N 40 15E
74 Dekese, Zaïre 3 20S 21 21E
90 Del Rio, U.S.A. 29 22N 100 55W
62 Delami, Sudan 11 50N 30 25E
93 Delaware, R., U.S.A. 42 0N 75 15W
91 Delaware, st. & B., U.S.A. 38 45N 75 20W
83 Delegate, Australia 37 14N 148 58E
45 Delemont, Switzerland 47 20N 7 20E
44 Delft, Netherlands 52 1N 4 21E
44 Delfzijl, Netherlands 53 20N 6 55E
74 Delgado, C., Mozambique 10 40S 40 43E
62 Delgo, Sudan 20 1N 30 20E
64 Delhi, India 28 42N 77 20E
51 Delice, R., Turkey 39 45N 34 15E
94 Delicias, Mexico 27 25N 105 0W
83 Deloraine, Australia 41 30S 146 45E
76 Delportshoop, S. Africa 28 25S 24 20E
35 Delvin, Ireland 53 37N 7 4W
37 Demanda, Sa. de la, mts., Spain
42 8N 3 0W
51 Demavend, Mt., Iran 35 50N 52 12E
74 Dembra, Zaïre 5 25S 22 20E
74 Dembidolo, Ethiopia 8 34N 34 50E
44 Demer, R., Belgium 51 0N 5 10E
90 Deming, U.S.A. 32 17N 107 48W
44 Den Burg, Netherlands 53 5N 4 47E
44 Den Helder, Netherlands 52 58N 4 46E
44 Denain, France 50 20N 3 22E
25 Denbigh, Wales 53 11N 3 26W
65 Denchin, China 31 35N 95 10E
37 Denia, Spain 38 50N 0 5E
83 Deniliquin, Australia 35 31S 144 59E
51 Denizli, Turkey 37 57N 28 41E
48 Denmark, Europe 55 45N 10 20E
100 Denmark Str., N. Atlantic Ocean
66 0N 30 0W
31 Denny, Scotland 56 1N 3 55W
26 Denton, Lancs., England 53 26N 2 10W
23 Denton, Leics., England 52 55N 0 42W
23 Denton, Sussex, England 50 48N 0 5E
91 Denton, U.S.A. 33 10N 97 14W
82 D'Entrecasteaux Is., Papua N.G.
9 30S 151 0E
90 Denver, U.S.A. 39 50N 104 57W
65 Deoghar, India 24 40N 86 40E
64 Deolali, India 19 55N 73 45E
65 Deoria, India 26 35N 83 50E
64 Dera Ghazi Khan, Pak. 30 5N 70 53E
64 Dera Ismail Khan, Pak. 31 46N 70 54E
62 Deraheib, Sudan 21 58N 35 7E
51 Derbent, U.S.S.R. 42 0N 48 23E
80 Derby, Australia 17 18S 123 40E
27 Derby, & Co., England 52 56N 1 28W
35 Derg, L., Ireland 53 0N 8 18W
36 Derg, L. & R., Ireland 54 40N 7 40W
65 Dergaon, India 26 40N 94 0E
36 Derry, N. Ireland, see Londonderry
36 Derrygonnelly, N. Ire. 54 25N 7 50W
34 Derryrush, Ireland 53 23N 9 40W
36 Derryveagh Mts., Ireland 55 0N 8 3W
73 Derudub, Sudan 17 30N 36 30E
27 Derwent, R., Derby, Eng. 53 15N 1 38W
27 Derwent, R., Yorks., Eng. 53 50N 1 0W
26 Derwent Water, L., Eng. 54 35N 3 9W
91 Des Moines, & R., U.S.A.
41 42N 93 34W
74 Dese, Ethiopia 10 58N 39 45E
99 Deseado, R., Argentina 47 0S 68 0W
94 Désirade, I., Leeward Is. 16 15N 61 0W
50 Desna, R., U.S.S.R. 51 30N 32 30E
99 Desolación I., Chile 53 0S 74 30W
72 Dessa, Niger 14 44N 1 6E
46 Dessau, Germany 51 41N 12 14E
46 Detmold, Germany 51 55N 8 50E
92 Detroit, U.S.A. 42 22N 83 7W
48 Dettifoss, Iceland 65 50N 16 0W
44 Deurne, Belgium 51 13N 4 27E
44 Deurne, Netherlands 51 27N 5 47E
42 Deux Sèvres, Dépt., Fr. 46 30N 0 30W
47 Deva, Rumania 45 55N 22 50E
64 Devakottai, India 9 55N 78 40E
44 Deventer, Netherlands 52 16N 6 10E
33 Deveron, R., Scotland 57 22N 3 0W
22 Devizes, England 51 21N 1 59W
24 Devon, Co., England 50 47N 3 40W
89 Devon Island, Canada 4 30N 85 0W
83 Devonport, Australia 41 8S 146 30E
24 Devonport, England 50 22N 4 10W
84 Devonport, N.Z. 36 49S 174 49E
64 Dewas, India 23 0N 76 0E
27 Dewsbury, England 53 42N 1 38W
61 Dezhneva, C., U.S.S.R. 66 0N 170 0W
62 Dhaba, Saudi Arabia 27 25N 35 50E
62 Dhahran, Saudi Arabia 26 20N 50 10E
65 Dhamtari, India 20 45N 81 30E
65 Dhanbad, India 23 50N 86 25E
65 Dhangarhi, Nepal 28 55N 80 40E
63 Dhank, Oman 23 33N 56 5E
65 Dhankuta, Nepal 27 0N 87 10E
64 Dhar, India 22 40N 75 5E
64 Dharmapuri, India 12 10N 78 5E
64 Dharwar, India 15 39N 75 59E
65 Dhaulagiri, Mt., Nepal 28 45N 83 25E
65 Dhenkanal, India 20 35N 85 30E
41 Dhidhimotikhon, Greece 41 18N 26 33E
41 Dhikti, Mt., Crete 35 10N 25 34E
63 Dhilban, Jordan 31 30N 35 47E
63 Dhofar, Prov., Oman 17 0N 54 10E
64 Dholpur, India 26 45N 77 58E
63 Dhour Chouer, Lebanon 33 53N 35 42E
64 Dhrol, India 22 40N 70 25E
65 Dhubri, India 26 3N 89 58E
62 Dhula, South Yemen 15 10N 48 0E
64 Dhulia, India 21 0N 74 56E
94 Diablo Heights, Panama Canal
Zone (Inset)
72 Diafarabe, Mali 14 17N 4 57W
99 Diamante, Argentina 32 0S 60 40W
98 Diamantina, Brazil 18 11S 43 45W
82 Diamantina, R., Australia 24 48S 140 0E
98 Diamantino, Brazil 14 25S 56 40W
74 Dibaya, Zaïre 6 30S 23 0E
74 Dibaya-Lubue, Zaïre 4 12S 19 54E
22 Dibden, England 50 53N 1 24W
65 Dibrugarh, India 27 38N 94 55E
90 Dickinson, U.S.A. 46 55N 102 53W
72 Diebougou, Volta 11 0N 3 15W
75 Diego Suarez, Madagascar 12 25S 49 20E
44 Diekirch, Luxembourg 49 52N 6 10E
42 Dielette, France 49 33N 1 54W
44 Diepenbeek, Belgium 50 55N 5 22E
43 Dieppe, France 49 58N 1 13E
44 Dieren, Netherlands 52 3N 6 6E
44 Diest, Belgium 50 59N 5 2E
44 Differdange, Luxembourg 49 32N 5 53E
89 Digby, Canada 44 42N 65 50W
43 Digne, France 44 6N 6 12E
48 Digranes, C., Iceland 66 5N 14 37W
65 Dihang, R., India 28 30N 95 0E
43 Dijon, France 47 20N 5 1E
61 Dikemda, U.S.S.R. 59 0N 121 35E
44 Diksmuide, Belgium 51 3N 2 52E

73 Dikwa, Nigeria 12 6N 14 0E
62 Dilam, Saudi Arabia 23 55N 47 10E
68 Dili, Portuguese Timor 8 45S 125 30E
74 Dimbelenge, Zaïre 5 28S 23 5E
72 Dimbokro, Ivory Coast 6 45N 4 30W
83 Dimboola, Australia 36 29S 142 2E
61 Dimitri Laptev Str., U.S.S.R. 73 0N 140 0E
41 Dimitovgrad, Bulgaria 42 5N 25 35E
68 Dinagat I., Philippines 10 10N 125 35E
65 Dinajpur, Bangladesh 25 40N 88 32E
44 Dinant, Belgium 50 17N 4 56E
40 Dinaric Alps, Y-slav. 44 0N 16 0E
25 Dinas Powis, Wales 51 25N 3 14W
74 Dincha, Ethiopia 6 15N 37 32E
64 Dindigul, India 10 22N 78 0E
34 Dingle, & B., Ireland 52 9N 10 16W
82 Dingo, Australia 23 40S 149 27E
72 Dinguiraye, Guinea 11 30N 10 35W
33 Dingwall, Scotland 57 36N 4 26W
72 Diourbel, Sénégal 14 40N 15 30W
68 Dipolog, Philippines 8 35N 123 25E
64 Dir, Pakistan 35 25N 71 45E
75 Dirico, Angola 17 52S 20 40E
80 Dirk Hartog I., Austral. 25 50S 113 0E
83 Dirranbandi, Australia 28 29S 148 18E
80 Disappointment, L., Australia 23 20S 123 10E
83 Discovery B., Australia 38 10S 140 40E
89 Disko B., & I., Greenland 69 0N 53 0W
23 Diss, England 52 22N 1 7E
23 Ditchling, Village & Beacon, England 50 55N 0 7W
25 Ditton Priors, England 52 29N 2 35W
64 Diu, India 20 48N 71 0E
91 Dixon, U.S.A. 41 51N 89 18W
62 Diyala, R., Iraq 34 0N 45 0E
51 Diyarbakir, Turkey 37 58N 40 25E
64 Dizak, Iran 27 20N 62 3E
62 Dizful, Iran 32 30N 48 33E
73 Djado, Niger 21 10N 12 5E
74 Djambala, Congo (Fr.) 2 25S 14 45E
72 Djanet, see Fort Charlet
74 Djang, Cameroon 5 30N 10 5E
72 Djelfa, Algeria 34 39N 3 14E
73 Djema, Central Africa 6 3N 25 0E
72 Djenne, Mali 14 0N 4 30W
72 Djerada, Morocco 34 16N 2 4W
72 Djerba I., Tunisia 33 50N 10 50E
72 Djibo, Volta 14 15N 1 35W
62 Djibouti, St., Africa 11 35N 43 0E
62 Djibouti, Djibouti 11 30N 43 5E
72 Djidjelli, Algeria 36 45N 5 50E
74 Djolu, Zaïre 0 45N 22 5E
72 Djougou, Benin 9 40N 1 45E
74 Djoum, Cameroon 2 46N 12 33E
63 Djounie (Juniyah), Leb. 33 58N 35 39E
74 Djugu, Zaïre 1 50N 30 40E
48 Djupivogur, Iceland 64 38N 14 14W
52 Dneprodzerzhinsk, U.S.S.R. 48 32N 34 30E
52 Dnepropetrovsk, U.S.S.R. 48 25N 34 55E
51 Dnepr, R., U.S.S.R. 47 0N 33 35E
51 Dnestr, R., U.S.S.R. 48 30N 25 0E
74 Doba, Chad 8 40N 16 50E
82 Dobbyn, Australia 19 40S 139 58E
47 Dobrógea, Reg., Rum. 44 30N 28 20E
23 Docking, England 52 55N 0 39E
90 Dodge City, U.S.A. 37 50N 100 4W
41 Dodecanese Is., Greece 36 40N 27 0E
74 Dodoma, Tanzania 6 0S 35 50E
44 Doetinchem, Neth. 51 58N 6 18E
18 Dogger Bank, North Sea 54 45N 2 0E
64 Dogi, Afghanistan 32 20N 62 50E
67 Dogo I., Japan 36 15N 133 20E
62 Doha, Qatar 25 15N 51 32E
64 Dohad, India 22 57N 74 20E
65 Dohazari, Bangladesh 22 10N 92 7E
41 Dojran, Yugoslavia 41 10N 22 45E
44 Dokkum, Netherlands 53 20N 6 1E
89 Dolbeau, Canada 48 25N 72 18W
43 Dôle, France 47 6N 5 30E
25 Dolgellau, Wales 52 44N 3 54W
57 Dolinsk, U.S.S.R. 47 25N 142 48E
74 Dolisie, Congo (Fr.) 4 0S 13 10E
31 Dollar, Scotland 56 9N 3 40W
40 Dolomites, Italy 46 30N 11 40E
99 Dolores, Argentina 36 15S 57 50W
88 Dolphin & Union Str., Can. 70 0N 120 0W
31 Dolphinton, Scotland 55 42N 3 28W
51 Dolya, U.S.S.R. 69 45N 132 0E
75 Dombe Grande, Angola 13 0S 13 0E
42 Domfront, France 48 35N 0 40W
95 Dominica, I., W. Indies 15 25N 61 20W
95 Dominican Rep., W.I. 19 0N 70 30W
43 Domodossola, Italy 46 6N 8 19E
43 Domrémy, France 48 40N 5 40E
27 Don, R., England 53 30N 1 15W
33 Don, R., Scotland 57 15N 2 15W
52 Don, R., U.S.S.R. 50 0N 42 0E
37 Don Benito, Spain 38 55N 5 50W
36 Donaghadee, N. Ireland 54 38N 5 32W
83 Donald, Australia 36 25S 142 57E
43 Donaueschingen, Ger. 47 58N 8 31E
45 Donauworth, Germany 48 42N 10 47E
27 Doncaster, England 53 31N 1 8W
74 Dondo, Angola 9 45S 14 32E
75 Dondo, Mozambique 19 32S 34 45E
64 Dondra Hd., Sri Lanka 6 0N 80 40E
36 Donegal, & B., Ireland 54 39N 8 6W
36 Donegal, Co., Ireland 54 52N 8 0W
47 Doneraile, Ireland 52 13N 8 37W
51 Donets, R., U.S.S.R. 48 48N 39 0E
52 Donetsk, U.S.S.R. 48 0N 37 30E
80 Dongara, Australia 29 15S 114 59E
73 Dongola, Sudan 19 8N 20 23E
74 Dongou, Congo 2 4N 17 57E
48 Donna I., Norway 66 5N 12 40E
84 Donnelly's Crossing, N.Z. 35 38S 173 33E
34 Donoughmore, Ireland 52 0N 8 50W
30 Doon, L. & R., Scotland 55 15N 4 22W
34 Doonbeg, R., Ireland 52 44N 9 31W
63 Dor, Israel 32 36N 34 55E
80 Dora, L., Australia 22 0S 122 50E
43 Dora Baltea, R., Italy 45 42N 8 0E
22 Dorchester, Dorset, Eng. 50 42N 2 26W
42 Dordogne, Dépt., France 45 0N 0 7E
43 Dordogne, R., France 44 50N 0 30E
46 Dordrecht, Netherlands 51 47N 4 40E
33 Dores, Scotland 57 22N 4 20W
72 Dori, Volta 14 0N 0 5W
23 Dorking, England 51 14N 0 20W
33 Dornoch, & F., Scotland 57 53N 4 2W
47 Dorohoi, U.S.S.R. 47 55N 26 30E
83 Dorrigo, Australia 30 22S 152 28E
22 Dorset, Co. & Hs., Eng. 50 45N 2 25W
44 Dorsten, Germany 51 40N 6 55E
44 Dortmund, Germany 51 36N 7 28E
74 Doruma, Zaïre 4 50N 27 33E
72 Dosso, Niger 13 0N 3 13E
91 Dothan, U.S.A. 31 13N 85 26W
43 Douai, France 50 22N 3 3E
74 Douala, Cameroon 4 0N 9 45E
42 Douarnenez, France 48 5N 4 20W
42 Doubs, Dépt., France 47 16N 6 35E
43 Doubs. R., France 47 0N 5 30E
72 Douentza, Mali 14 58N 2 48W
31 Douglas, Scotland 55 33N 3 50W
26 Douglas & Hd., I. of Man 54 9N 4 31W
90 Douglad, U.S.A. 31 25N 109 35W
74 Doumé, Cameroon 4 10N 13 30E
31 Doune, Scotland 56 12N 4 3W
33 Dounreay, Scotland 58 35N 3 45W
37 Douro, R., Portugal 41 8N 8 0W
37 Douro Litoral, Prov., Port. 41 10N 8 20W
27 Dove, R. & Dale, Eng. 53 5N 1 38W
83 Dover, Australia 43 26S 147 0E
23 Dover, & Str., England 51 7N 1 19E
93 Dover, Del., U.S.A. 39 19N 75 23W
93 Dover, N.H., U.S.A. 43 13N 70 55W
25 Dovey, R., Wales 52 31N 4 0W
48 Dovrefjell, mts., Norway 62 25N 9 10E
75 Dowa, Malawi 13 38S 33 58E
36 Down, Co., N. Ireland 54 22N 5 55W
23 Downham, England 52 26N 0 14E
23 Downham Market, Eng. 52 36N 0 22E
36 Downpatrick, N. Ireland 54 19N 5 41W
35 Downpatrick Hd., Ire. 54 19N 9 21W
36 Dowra, Ireland 54 11N 8 2W
65 Doyung, China 33 40N 99 30E
72 Dra, Wadi, Morocco 29 0N 8 0W
44 Drachten, Netherlands 53 7N 6 6E
41 Dragoman P., Bulgaria 43 0N 22 57E
98 Dragons' Mouths, Venezuela-Trinidad 10 40N 61 40W
43 Draguignan, France 43 38N 6 28E
100 Drake Pass, S. America 57 0S 65 0W
76 Drakensberg, mts., S. Afr. 30 0S 29 0E
41 Drama, Greece 41 9N 24 10E
49 Drammen, Norway 59 45N 10 14E
48 Dranga Jökul, mt., Ice. 66 12N 22 15W
36 Draperstown, N. Ireland 54 48N 6 50W
47 Drava. R., Yugoslavia 45 50N 18 0E
44 Drenthe, Prov., Neth. 52 53N 6 40E
46 Dresden, Germany 51 5N 13 41E
43 Dreux, France 48 42N 1 25E
27 Driffield, England 54 1N 0 27W
41 Drina, R., Yugoslavia 44 30N 19 5E
49 Drobak, Norway 59 39N 10 48E
36 Drogheda, Ireland 53 43N 6 20W
47 Drogobych, U.S.S.R. 49 28N 23 30E
35 Droichead Nua (Newbridge), Ireland 53 11N 6 48W
22 Droitwich, England 52 15N 2 10W
36 Dromara, N. Ireland 54 27N 6 1W
42 Drôme, Dépt., France 44 50N 5 10E
36 Dromore, N. Ireland 54 25N 6 8W
36 Dromore West, Ireland 54 15N 8 50W
82 Dronfield, Australia 21 12S 140 3E
27 Dronfield, England 53 18N 1 29W
36 Drum, Ireland 54 7N 7 8W
32 Drumbeg, Scotland 58 15N 5 12W
88 Drumheller, Canada 51 27N 112 58W
36 Drumlish, Ireland 53 50N 7 47W
82 Drummond Ra., Austral. 23 0S 147 15E
93 Drummondville, Can. 45 54N 72 30W
36 Drumquin, N. Ireland 54 38N 7 30W
36 Drumshanbo, Ireland 54 2N 8 2W
36 Drumsna, Ireland 53 57N 8 0W
100 Drygalski I., Antarctica 68 0S 91 0E
30 Drymen, Scotland 56 4N 4 28W
80 Drysdale R., Australia 15 0S 126 50E
92 Du Bois, U.S.A. 41 6N 78 48W
82 Duaringa, Australia 23 42S 149 42E
88 Dubawnt, L. & R., Can. 63 0N 101 30W
83 Dubbo, Australia 32 15S 148 37E
35 Dublin (Baile Atha Cliath), Ireland 53 21N 6 15W
35 Dublin, Co., Ireland 53 25N 6 20W
91 Dublin, U.S.A. 32 32N 82 57W
47 Dubno, U.S.S.R. 50 24N 25 47E
52 Dubovka, U.S.S.R. 49 3N 44 40E
72 Dubréka, Guinea 9 46N 13 31W
47 Dubrovitsa, U.S.S.R. 51 31N 26 35E
41 Dubrovnik, Yugoslavia 42 40N 18 6E
61 Dubrovskoye, U.S.S.R. 58 55N 111 0E
92 Dubuque, U.S.A. 42 30N 90 45W
82 Duchess, Australia 21 15S 139 57E
1 Ducie, I., Pacific Ocean 25 0S 125 0W
23 Duddington, England 52 36N 0 32W
65 Dudhi, India 24 15N 83 10E
61 Dudinka, U.S.S.R. 69 30N 86 0E
22 Dudley, England 52 30N 2 4W
37 Duero, R., Spain 41 31N 4 20W
27 Duffield, England 52 59N 1 30W
33 Dufftown, Scotland 57 28N 3 7W
47 Dugi Otok, I., Y.-slav. 44 0N 15 0E
44 Duisburg, Germany 51 26N 6 45E
76 Duiwelskloof, S. Africa 23 38S 30 5E
73 Duk Fadiat, Sudan 7 49N 31 31E
64 Duki, Pakistan 30 14N 68 25E
26 Dukinfield, England 53 28N 2 6W
47 Dukla P., Poland-Cz-slov. 49 25N 21 40E
72 Duku, Nigeria 10 43N 10 43E
99 Dulce, R., Argentina 28 30S 63 30W
36 Duleek, Ireland 53 40N 6 25W
82 Dululu, Australia 23 48S 150 15E
92 Duluth, U.S.A. 46 48N 92 10W
24 Dulverton, England 51 2N 3 33W
65 Dum Duma, India 27 35N 95 40E
30 Dumbarton, Scotland 55 57N 4 33W
31 Dumfries, Scot. 55 4N 3 35W
31 Dumfries and Galloway, Reg., Scotland 55 10N 4 0W
100 Dumont d'Urville, Antarctica 67 0S 140 0E
35 Dun Laoghaire, Ireland 53 15N 6 10E
47 Dunaujvaros, Hungary 47 3N 18 58E
84 Dunback, N.Z. 45 23S 170 36E
31 Dunbar, Scotland 56 0N 2 31W
31 Dunbiane, Scotland 56 11N 3 57W
35 Dunboyne, Ireland 53 26N 6 29W
33 Duncansby Hd., Scotland 58 38N 3 2W
22 Dunchurch, England 52 21N 1 18W
36 Dundalk, & B., Ireland 54 0N 6 23W
80 Dundas Str., Australia 11 0S 131 40E
31 Dundee, Scotland 56 27N 2 58W
36 Dundonald, N. Ireland 54 36N 5 50W
36 Dundrum, & B., Ireland 53 17N 6 15W
84 Dunedin, New Zealand 45 51S 170 31E
36 Dunfanaghy, Ireland 55 11N 7 59W
31 Dunfermline, Scotland 56 4N 3 27W
36 Dungannon, N. Ireland 54 31N 6 47W
35 Dungarvan & Hr., Ire. 52 5N 7 38W
23 Dungeness, England 50 54N 0 58E
36 Dungiven, N. Ireland 54 56N 6 55W
36 Dungloe, Ireland 55 0N 8 25W
83 Dungog, Australia 32 27S 151 34E
74 Dungu, Zaïre 3 48N 28 37E
31 Dunkeld, Scotland 56 34N 3 35W
43 Dunkerque, France 51 2N 2 21E
24 Dunkery Beacon, Eng. 51 11N 3 35W
72 Dunkwa, Ghana 6 0N 1 50W
35 Dunlavin, Ireland 53 3N 6 40W
35 Dunleary, see Dunlaoghaire, Ireland
36 Dunleer, Ireland 53 49N 6 22W
34 Dunloe, Gap. of, Ireland 52 0N 9 40W
30 Dunlop, Scotland 55 43N 4 32W
34 Dunmanway, Ireland 51 43N 9 6W
34 Dunmore, Ireland 53 37N 8 45W
35 Dunmore, E., Ireland 52 9N 7 0W
33 Dunnet, Scotland 58 37N 3 20W
33 Dunnet B., & Hd., Scot. 58 37N 3 28W
31 Dunning, Scotland 56 18N 3 37W
83 Dunolly, Australia 36 58S 143 44E
30 Dunoon, Scotland 55 57N 4 55W
73 Dunqul Oasis, Egypt 23 38N 31 3E
31 Duns, Scotland 55 46N 2 19W
31 Dunscore, Scotland 55 8N 3 48W
35 Dunshaughlin, Ireland 53 31N 6 31W
23 Dunstable, England 51 54N 0 31W
84 Dunstan Mts., N.Z. 44 50S 169 30E
24 Dunster, England 51 11N 3 28W
23 Dunton Green, England 51 17N 0 11E
32 Dunvegan, Scotland 57 26N 6 35W
32 Dunvegan Head, Scot. 57 32N 6 45W
63 Dura, Jordan 31 30N 35 2E
80 Durack Ra., Australia 17 0S 127 30E
43 Durance R., France 44 0N 6 0E
94 Durango, Mexico 24 12N 105 15W
37 Durango, Spain 43 15N 2 40W
90 Durango, U.S.A. 37 20N 107 55W
91 Durant, U.S.A. 33 58N 96 27W
99 Durazno, Uruguay 33 30S 56 30W
76 Durban, S. Africa 29 57S 30 59E
44 Düren, Germany 50 49N 6 29E
65 Durg, India 21 12N 81 20E
27 Durham, & Co., England 54 47N 1 36W
91 Durham, U.S.A. 36 0N 78 53W
41 Durmitor, Mt., Y.-slav. 43 20N 19 10E
33 Durness, & Kyle of, Scot. 58 34N 4 45W
41 Durres, Albania 41 20N 19 29E
83 Durrie, Australia 25 35S 140 15E
34 Durrus, Ireland 51 37N 9 32W
34 Dursey Hd., & I., Ire. 51 36N 10 16W
22 Dursley, England 51 42N 2 22W
84 D'Urville, I., N.Z. 40 55S 173 50E
60 Dushak, U.S.S.R. 37 20N 60 10E
60 Dushanbe, U.S.S.R. 38 20N 68 30E
44 Düsseldorf, Germany 51 18N 6 47E
88 Dutch Harbor, Alaska 53 40N 166 30W
66 Dutulun Shan, mts., Mongolia 48 45N 111 30E
95 Duverge, Dom. Rep. 18 15N 71 25W
50 Dvina B., U.S.S.R. 65 0N 39 30E
50 Dvina, R., U.S.S.R. 63 0N 42 45E
49 Dvina W., R., U.S.S.R. 56 35N 25 30E
64 Dwarka, India 22 20N 69 0E
76 Dwyka, S. Africa 33 10S 21 30E
33 Dyce, Scotland 57 12N 2 11W
91 Dyersburg, U.S.A. 35 5N 89 10W
89 Dyer, C., Canada 67 0N 61 0W
25 Dyfed, Co., Wales 52 0N 4 30W
31 Dysart. Scotland 56 7N 3 6W
52 Dzerzhinsk, U.S.S.R. 56 15N 43 15E
60 Dzhailma, U.S.S.R. 51 30N 61 50E
60 Dzhalal Abad, U.S.S.R. 41 0N 73 0E
61 Dzhalinda, U.S.S.R. 53 40N 124 0E
60 Dzhambul, U.S.S.R. 43 10N 71 0E
51 Dzankoi, U.S.S.R. 45 40N 34 30E
61 Dzhelinde, U.S.S.R. 70 0N 114 0E
60 Dzhetygara, U.S.S.R. 52 10N 61 0E
60 Dzhezkazgan, U.S.S.R. 47 10N 67 40E
61 Dzhugdzhur Ra., U.S.S.R. 57 30N 138 0E
66 Dzungaria, Dist., China 44 20N 88 0E
66 Dzuunmod, Mongolia 47 55N 107 0E

E

88 Eagle, Alaska 64 44N 141 29W
90 Eagle Pass, U.S.A. 28 45N 100 28W
83 Eaglehawk, Australia 36 43S 144 16E
30 Eaglesham, Scotland 55 44N 4 18W
27 Eakring, England 53 9N 0 59W
23 Ealing, Gr. London, Eng. 51 30N 0 19W
25 Eardisland, England 52 14N 2 50W
22 Earl Shilton, England 52 35N 1 20W
23 Earls Colne, England 51 56N 0 43E
31 Earlsferry, Scotland 56 11N 2 50W
31 Earlston, Scotland 55 39N 2 40W
84 Earnslaw, Mt., N.Z. 44 37S 168 28E
27 Earsdon, England 55 4N 1 30W
31 Easington Colliery, Eng. 54 49N 1 19W
31 Easington, England 54 50N 1 24W
27 Easingwold, England 54 8N 1 11W
36 Easky, Ireland 54 17N 8 55W
84 East C., New Zealand 37 39S 178 58E
91 East Pt., U.S.A. 33 38N 84 29W
23 East Anglian Hts., Eng. 52 20N 0 42E
65 East Bengal, reg., Bangla. 24 30N 90 0E
47 East Beskids, Mts., Eur. 49 8N 22 10E
67 East China Sea, Asia 29 30N 125 0E
84 East Coast, Dist., N.Z. 38 30S 177 50E
22 East Cowes, England 50 45N 1 17W
23 East Dereham, England 52 41N 0 57E
27 East Fen, England 53 5N 0 5E
23 East Grinstead, England 51 7N 0 3W
68 East Indies, reg., Asia 0 0 120 0E
27 East Kirby, England 53 5N 1 15W
31 East Linton, Scotland 56 0N 2 40W
76 East London, S. Africa 33 5S 27 58E
24 East Looe, England 50 22N 4 28W
27 East Retford, England 53 20N 0 58W
92 East St. Louis, U.S.A. 38 36N 90 3W
44 East Schelde R., Neth. 51 39N 3 50E
61 East Siberian Sea, U.S.S.R. 73 0N 160 0E
23 East Sussex, Co., England 50 55N 0 15E
83 East Toorale, Australia 30 30S 145 25E
31 East Wemyss, Scotland 56 8N 3 5W
23 Eastbourne, England 50 46N 0 16E
84 Eastbourne, N.Z. 41 50S 174 47E
23 Eastchurch, England 51 23N 0 53E
4 Easter I., Pacific Ocean 27 0S 108 30W
33 Easter Ross, dist., Scot. 57 37N 4 30W
64 Eastern Ghats, Mts., India 13 30N 79 0E
61 Eastern Sayan, Mts., U.S.SR. 54 0N 96 0E
22 Eastleigh, England 50 58N 1 21W
89 Eastmain, & R., Canada 52 20N 78 30W
22 Easton, Dorset, England 50 30N 2 28W
24 Easton, Somerset, Eng. 51 28N 2 45W
93 Easton, Pa., U.S.A. 40 42N 75 16W
27 Eastry, England 51 15N 1 19E
27 Eastwood, England 53 1N 1 16W
23 Easton, England 52 52N 0 46W
23 Eaton Socon, England 52 13N 0 18W
92 Eau Claire, U.S.A. 44 49N 91 30W
32 Eaval, Mt., Scotland 57 33N 7 12W
25 Ebbw Vale, Wales 51 47N 3 13W
45 Eberbach, Germany 49 30N 9 0E
46 Eberswalde, Germany 52 50N 13 50E
66 Ebi Nor, L., China 45 0N 82 30E
40 Eboli, Italy 40 38N 15 0E
74 Ebolowa, Cameroon 3 0N 11 11E
37 Ebro, R., Spain 41 0N 0 30E
31 Ecclefechan, Scotland 55 4N 3 16W
26 Eccles, England 53 29N 2 20W
22 Eccleshall, England 52 52N 2 14W
88 Echo Bay, Canada 66 10N 117 40W
33 Echt, Scotland 57 8N 2 21W
44 Echternach, Luxembourg 49 50N 6 15E
83 Echuca, Australia 36 3S 144 50E
37 Ecija, Spain 37 30N 5 9W
27 Eckington, England 53 21N 1 22W
98 Ecuador, S. Amer. 2 30S 77 30W
73 Ed Damer, Sudan 17 27N 34 0E
73 Ed Debba, Sudan 17 0N 31 12E
73 Ed Dueim, Sudan 13 55N 32 20E
65 Ed Dzong, Tibet 32 10N 90 20E
44 Edam, Netherlands 52 31N 5 3E
33 Eday I. & Sd., Scotland 59 12N 2 47W
74 Edd, Ethiopia 14 0N 41 30E
33 Edderton, Scotland 57 50N 4 10W
32 Eddrachillis, B., Scot. 58 19N 5 8W
44 Ede, Netherlands 52 3N 5 40E
83 Eden, Australia 37 0S 149 55E
26 Eden, R., England 54 50N 2 45W
23 Edenbridge, England 51 12N 0 4E
76 Edenburg, S. Africa 29 42S 25 58E
35 Edenderry, Ireland 53 21N 7 3W
36 Ederny, N. Ireland 54 32N 7 40W
73 Edeyin, Erg, des., Libya 27 0N 10 0E
22 Edge Hill, England 52 9N 1 35W
41 Edhessa, Greece 40 50N 22 5E
84 Edievale, New Zealand 45 20S 169 19E
31 Edinburgh, Scotland 55 57N 3 12W
41 Edirne, Turkey 41 41N 26 36E
83 Edithburgh, Australia 35 2S 137 35E
82 Edmonton, Australia 16 55S 145 45E
88 Edmonton, Canada 53 40N 113 30W
89 Edmundston, Canada 47 22N 68 22W
45 Edolo, Italy 46 11N 10 20E
41 Edremit & G., Turkey 39 35N 27 2E
88 Edson, Canada 53 35N 115 58W
74 Edward, L., see Idi Amin Dada, L.
90 Edwards Plateau, U.S.A. 30 30N 100 40W
33 Edzell, Scotland 56 49N 2 39W
44 Eekloo, Belgium 51 11N 3 34E
76 Eersterus, S. Africa 25 45S 28 15E
47 Eger, Hungary 47 57N 20 23E
80 Egerton, Mt., Australia 24 40S 118 0E
23 Egham, England 51 25N 0 35W
33 Egilsay I., Scotland 59 9N 2 56W
75 Egito, Angola 12 0S 13 50E
84 Egmont, C., N.Z. 39 12S 173 45E
84 Egmont, Mt., N.Z. 39 13S 174 7E
26 Egremont, England 54 28N 3 33W
51 Egridir, Turkey 37 55N 30 50E
73 Eguei Timmi, Chad 15 35N 16 25E
73 Egypt, N.E. Africa 26 0N 30 0E
67 Ehime, Pref., Japan 33 30N 132 30E
83 Eidsvold, Australia 25 19S 151 10E
49 Eidsvoll, Norway 60 19N 11 17E
44 Eifel, Mts., Germany 50 5N 6 35E
49 Eigersund, Norway 58 26N 6 3E
45 Eigg, Switzerland 47 29N 8 52E
32 Eigg, I. & Sd. of, Scot. 56 52N 6 15W
80 Eighty Mile Beach, Australia 19 30S 121 0E
32 Eil, L., Scotland 56 50N 5 10W
83 Eildon, L., Australia 37 6S 146 0E
82 Einasleigh, Australia 18 45S 144 15E
44 Eindhoven, Netherlands 51 27N 5 29E
45 Einsiedein, Switzerland 47 9N 8 45E
46 Eisenach, Germany 50 59N 10 21E
63 Eizariya, Jordan 31 47N 35 15E
84 Eketahuna, N.Z. 40 34S 175 40E
61 Ekimchan, U.S.S.R. 53 0N 133 0E
72 El Aaiun, Western Sahara 27 0N 13 0W
63 El Aal, Syria 32 48N 35 43E
73 El 'Alamein, Egypt 30 40N 29 0E
62 El 'Allâqi, Egypt 23 10N 32 54E
73 El Arish, Egypt 31 3N 33 40E
72 El Asnam (Orleansville), Algeria 36 2N 1 22E
62 El Bawiti, Egypt 28 27N 29 0E
72 El Bayadh (Géryville), Algeria 33 45N 1 0E
63 El Bira, Jordan 31 55N 35 13E
90 El Centro, U.S.A. 32 40N 115 38W
94 El Cuyo, Mexico 21 35N 87 50W
94 El Diaz, Mexico 21 10N 87 30W
62 El Dirr, Egypt 22 40N 32 0E
72 El Djouf, Desert, Mauritania 21 0N 8 0W
91 El Dorado, Ark., U.S.A. 33 14N 92 43W
91 El Dorado, Kan., U.S.A. 37 48N 96 56W
37 El Escorial, Spain 40 38N 4 11W
62 El Faiyum, Egypt 29 20N 30 59E
73 El Fasher, Sudan 13 37N 25 20E
94 El Fuerte, Mexico 26 36N 108 30W
95 El Gallo, Nicaragua 13 5N 84 30W
73 El Geneina, Sudan 13 27N 22 45E
73 El Geteina, Sudan 14 54N 32 30E
73 El Gezira, Prov., Sudan 15 0N 33 0E
73 El Giza, Egypt 30 0N 31 0E
72 El Golea, Algeria 30 40N 3 0E
73 El Gusbat, Libya 32 30N 14 1E
73 El Iskandariya, see Alexandria
72 El Jadida, Morocco 33 11N 8 17W
73 El Jebelein, Sudan 12 40N 32 55E
73 El Kab, Sudan 19 30N 32 46E
63 El Khalil, see Hebron
73 El Khandaq, Sudan 18 43N 30 38E
73 El Kharga, Egypt 25 30N 30 33E
73 El Mansura, Egypt 31 0N 31 20E
73 El Minya, Egypt 28 12N 30 30E
74 El Niabo, Ethiopia 4 30N 39 55E
73 El Obeid, Sudan 13 15N 30 45E
73 El Odaiya, Sudan 12 0N 27 5E
72 El Oued, Algeria 33 20N 6 40E
72 El Ouig, Mali 19 25N 0 25E
90 El Paso, U.S.A. 31 56N 106 25W
73 El Qâhira, Egypt, see Cairo
73 El Qantara, Egypt 31 0N 32 20E
73 El Qasr, Egypt 25 40N 28 42E
62 El Qattara, Egypt 30 10N 27 15E
95 El Real, Panama 8 0N 77 40W
90 El Reno, U.S.A. 35 30N 98 0W
62 El Tur, Egypt 28 14N 33 39E
74 El Wak, Kenya 3 0N 41 0E
62 El Wasta, Egypt 29 25N 31 10E
25 Elan, R., Wales 52 18N 3 34W
51 Elâzig, Turkey 38 37N 39 18E
40 Elba, I., Italy 42 50N 10 20E
41 Elbasan, Albania 41 8N 20 8E
46 Elbe, R., Germany 53 55N 8 50E
43 Elbeuf, France 49 17N 0 58E
47 Elblag, Poland 54 10N 19 22E
51 Elbrus, Mt., U.S.S.R. 43 45N 43 0E
51 Elburz, Mts., Iran 36 0N 51 30E
37 Elche, Spain 38 15N 0 45W
74 Eldoret, Kenya 0 20N 35 40E
90 Electra, U.S.A. 34 2N 98 55W
52 Elektrostal, U.S.S.R. 55 46N 38 30E
100 Elephant I., Falkland Is., Dependency 61 0S 54 0W
91 Eleuthera I., Bahamas 25 0N 76 30W
33 Elgin, Scotland 57 39N 3 20W

92 Elgin, U.S.A. 42 2N 88 15W
74 Elgon, Mt., Kenya-Uganda 1 30N 34 50E
23 Elham, England 51 9N 1 7E
31 Elie, Scotland 56 11N 2 50W
74 Elila, R., Zaïre 3 0S 27 0E
75 Elisabethville, *see* Lubumbashi
51 Elista, (Stepnoi), U.S.S.R. 46 28N 44 20E
93 Elizabeth, U.S.A. 40 35N 74 8W
57 Elizabeth C., U.S.S.R. 54 0N 143 0E
91 Elizabeth City, U.S.A. 36 17N 76 12W
49 Elk, Poland 53 50N 22 20E
92 Elkhart, U.S.A. 41 39N 85 48W
90 Elko, U.S.A. 40 58N 115 48W
27 Elland, England 53 41N 1 49W
90 Ellensburg, U.S.A. 47 2N 120 32W
26 Ellesmere Port, England 53 17N 2 55W
100 Ellesmere I., Canada 79 0N 80 0W
11 Ellice Is., *see* Tuvalu
64 Ellichpur (Achalpur), India 21 12N 77 30E
31 Ellington, England 55 14N 1 34W
33 Ellon, Scotland 57 23N 2 3W
100 Ellsworth, Antarctica 78 02 41 0W
100 Ellsworth Land, Antarctica 74 30S 85 0W
51 Elmali, Turkey 36 20N 30 0E
92 Elmira, U.S.A. 42 15N 76 54W
36 Elphin, Ireland 53 51N 8 11W
32 Elphin, Scotland 58 4N 5 3W
23 Elstree, England 51 38N 0 16W
84 Eltham, N.Z. 39 25S 174 20E
65 Eluru, India 16 50N 81 0E
37 Elvas, Portugal 38 52N 7 13W
49 Elverum, Norway 60 55N 11 34E
23 Ely, & Isle of, England 52 23N 0 16E
60 Emba, U.S.S.R. 47 0N 55 45E
60 Emba, R., U.S.S.R. 48 0N 56 0E
43 Embrun, France 44 37N 6 29E
74 Embu, Kenya 0 30S 37 30E
44 Emden, Germany 53 22N 7 12E
82 Emerald, Australia 23 30S 148 1E
88 Emerson, Canada 49 0N 97 10W
73 Emi Koussi, Mt., Chad 20 0N 19 0E
40 Emilia-Romagna, Reg., It. 44 33N 10 40E
34 Emly, Ireland 52 28N 8 20W
44 Emmeloord, Netherlands 52 43N 5 46E
44 Emmen, Netherlands 52 46N 6 50E
44 Emmerich, Germany 51 52N 6 18E
82 Emmet, Australia 24 45S 144 30E
73 Em Nahud, Sudan 12 33N 28 35E
76 Empageni, South Africa 28 43S 31 52E
91 Emporia, Kansas, U.S.A. 38 25N 96 16W
46 Ems, R., Germany 52 47N 7 18E
23 Emsworth, England 50 51N 0 56W
83 Encounter B., Australia 35 50S 139 0E
82 Endeavour Str., Austral. 11 0S 142 0E
22 Enderby, England 52 35N 1 15W
100 Enderby Ld., Antarctica 67 0S 52 0E
41 Enez, Turkey 40 40N 26 5E
23 Enfield, Gr. London, Eng. 51 39N 0 4W
45 Engadin, Dist., Switz. 46 45N 10 10E
45 Engelberg, Switzerland 46 48N 8 24E
52 Engels, U.S.S.R. 51 28N 46 6E
29 England, United Kingdom, Europe 53 0N 2 0W
65 English Bazar, India 24 58N 88 21E
13 English Channel, Europe 50 0N 2 30W
90 Enid, U.S.A. 36 25N 97 52W
44 Enkhuizen, Netherlands 52 42N 5 17E
26 Ennerdale Water, L., Eng. 54 32N 3 24W
83 Enngonia, Australia 29 24S 146 0E
34 Ennis, Ireland 52 51N 8 59W
91 Ennis, U.S.A. 32 21N 96 45W
35 Enniscorthy, Ireland 52 32N 6 43W
34 Enniskean, Ireland 51 44N 8 54W
35 Enniskerry, Ireland 53 12N 6 10W
36 Enniskillen, N. Ireland 54 19N 7 37W
34 Ennistymon, Ireland 52 57N 9 20W
44 Enschede, Netherlands 52 13N 6 53E
94 Ensenada, Mexico 31 45N 116 40W
22 Enstone, England 51 55N 1 25W
74 Entebbe, Uganda 0 3N 32 32E
99 Entre Rios, Prov., Arg. 31 0S 59 0W
80 Entrecasteaux, Pt. d', Australia 34 48S 116 0E
72 Enugu, Nigeria 6 35N 7 30E
44 Epe, Netherlands 52 22N 5 59E
43 Épernay, France 49 3N 3 55E
43 Épinal, France 48 15N 6 25E
41 Epirus, Prov., Greece 39 50N 20 20E
23 Epping, & Forest, Eng. 51 40N 0 6E
23 Epsom, England 51 19N 0 16W
75 Epukiro, & R., S.W. Africa 21 30S 19 0E
73 Equatoria, Dist., Sudan 6 0N 30 0E
71 Equatorial Guinea, Afr. 23 0N 10 0W
73 Er Rahad, Sudan 12 50N 30 47E
62 Er Roda, Egypt 27 45N 30 58E
73 Er Roseires, Sudan 11 55N 34 30E
62 Erbil, Iraq 36 12N 44 7E
61 Ercha, U.S.S.R. 69 40N 147 5E
39 Erciyas Dagi, Turkey 38 30N 36 10E
100 Erebus, Mt., Antarctica 77 0S 166 0E
51 Eregli, Turkey 41 18N 31 25E
62 Eregli, Turkey 38 30N 34 7E
46 Erfurt, Germany 50 59N 11 0E
66 Erhlien, China 43 55N 111 45E
33 Eriboll, L., Scotland 58 33N 4 38W
33 Ericht, L., Scotland 56 50N 4 20W
92 Erie, U.S.A. 42 6N 80 6W
92 Erie, L., N. America 42 0N 81 0W
32 Eriskay, & Sd. of, Scot. 57 4N 7 18W
62 Eritrea, Prov., Ethiopia 15 0N 40 0E
45 Erlangen, Germany 49 38N 11 3E
76 Ermelo, S. Africa 26 30S 29 59E
41 Ermoupolis, Greece 37 10N 24 50E
64 Ernakulam, India 9 58N 76 15E
36 Erne, L. & R., N. Ireland 54 28N 7 50W
36 Erne, Upper L., N. Ire. 54 13N 7 32W
64 Erode, India 11 24N 77 45E
36 Errigal, Mt., Ireland 55 5N 8 12W
35 Erris Hd., Ireland 54 19N 10 0W
46 Erz Gebirge (Ore Mts.), Germany 50 30N 13 0E
51 Erzincan, Turkey 39 49N 39 40E
51 Erzurum, Turkey 39 58N 41 20E
49 Esbjerg, Denmark 55 30N 8 29E
92 Escanaba, U.S.A. 45 47N 87 5W
44 Esch, Luxembourg 49 30N 6 0E
44 Eschweiler, Germany 50 49N 6 14E
94 Escobal, Panama Canal Zone (Inset)
94 Escuinapa, Mexico 22 45N 105 30W
62 Esfahan, Iran 32 40N 51 30E
63 Esh Shuna, Jordan 32 36N 35 35E
76 Eshowe, S. Africa 28 54S 31 30E
27 Esk, R. (Yorks.), Eng. 54 27N 0 52W
31 Esk, R., Scotland 55 12N 3 15W
48 Eskifjördur, Iceland 65 5N 13 55W
49 Eskilstuna, Sweden 59 20N 16 30E
51 Eskisehir, Turkey 39 20N 30 10E
37 Esla, R., Spain 42 30N 5 20W
60 Espe, U.S.S.R. 44 5N 74 0E
80 Esperance, & B., Australia 33 50S 121 57E
99 Espinhaco, Sa. do, mts., Brazil 19 0S 43 45W
99 Espirito Santo, st., Brazil 19 30S 40 30W
88 Esquimalt, Canada 48 30N 123 50W
72 Essaouira, Morocco 31 40N 9 45W
44 Essen, Belgium 51 27N 4 26E
44 Essen, Germany 51 25N 7 0W
98 Essequibo, R., Guyana 6 50N 58 30W
23 Essex, Co., England 51 45N 0 25E
45 Esslingen, Germany 48 45N 9 15E
42 Essonne, Dépt., France 48 30N 2 15E
45 Estavayer-le-Lac, Switz. 46 51N 6 52E
76 Estcourt, S. Africa 29 0S 29 55E
88 Estevan, Canada 49 12N 103 0W
27 Eston, England 54 34N 1 9W
49 Estonia, S.S.R., U.S.S.R. 58 50N 25 40E
37 Estrela, Sa. da., mts., Port. 40 20N 7 20W
37 Estremadura, Prov., Port. 39 0N 8 35W
37 Estremadura, Old Prov., Spain 39 20N 6 20W
99 Estrondo, Sa. do, hs., Brazil 8 0S 48 45W
47 Esztergom, Hungary 47 49N 18 42E
43 Étampes, France 48 26N 2 6E
43 Étaples, France 50 38N 1 40E
64 Etawah, India 26 54N 79 4E
23 Etchingham, England 51 0N 0 27E
71 Ethiopia, E. Africa 8 0N 40 0E
40 Etna, Mt., Italy 37 42N 15 0E
23 Eton, England 51 29N 0 37E
75 Etosha Pan, S.W. Africa 18 45S 16 20E
44 Ettelbrück, Luxembourg 49 51N 6 6E
45 Ettlingen, Germany 48 55N 8 22E
31 Ettrick Water, R., Scot. 55 31N 2 55W
43 Eu, France 50 0N 1 30E
41 Eubœa, *see* Evvoia, Greece
80 Eucla Basin, Austral. 31 41S 127 0E
92 Euclid, U.S.A. 41 39N 81 32W
83 Eucumbene, L., Australia 36 5S 148 40E
90 Eugene, U.S.A. 44 6N 123 8W
83 Eugowra, Australia 33 5S 148 27E
44 Eupen, Belgium 50 38N 6 3E
62 Euphrates, R., Iraq 34 0N 42 40E
42 Eure, Dépt., France 49 0N 1 20E
42 Eure-et-Loire, Dépt., Fr. 48 15N 1 20E
90 Eureka, U.S.A. 40 48N 124 0W
83 Euroa, Australia 36 49S 145 34E
75 Europa, I., Indian Oc. 23 0S 40 30E
37 Europa Pt., Gibraltar 36 2N 6 32E
44 Europoort, Netherlands 51 57N 4 10E
44 Euskirchen, Germany 50 39N 6 47E
49 Eutin, Germany 54 7N 10 38E
92 Evanston, U.S.A. 42 9N 87 43W
92 Evansville, U.S.A. 38 3N 87 27W
80 Everard, L., Australia 31 30S 135 0E
65 Everest, Mt., Himalaya, Nepal-Tibet 28 3N 87 7E
90 Everett, U.S.A. 48 0N 122 13W
91 Everglades, The, region, U.S.A. 26 0N 80 30W
22 Evesham, England 52 5N 1 57W
37 Évora, Portugal 38 37N 7 55W
43 Évreux, France 49 0N 1 5E
41 Evvoia (Eubœa), I., Greece 38 30N 23 50E
23 Ewell, England 51 20N 0 15W
94 Ewarton, Jamaica 18 10N 77 2W
83 Excelsior, Australia 33 5S 150 0E
24 Exe, R., England 50 50N 3 31W
24 Exeter, England 50 44N 3 32W
24 Exminster, England 50 40N 3 29W
24 Exmoor, England 51 10N 3 43W
24 Exmouth, England 50 37N 3 25W
80 Exmouth G., Australia 22 0S 114 20E
74 Eyasi, L., Tanzania 3 30S 35 0E
31 Eyemouth, Scotland 55 52N 2 5W
48 Eyja Fjord, Iceland 66 5N 18 27W
33 Eynhallow Sd., Scotland 59 8N 3 7W
32 Eynort, L., Scotland 57 13N 7 20W
48 Eyrarbakki, Iceland 63 5N 21 2W
80 Eyre, Australia 32 13S 126 20E
83 Eyre, L., Australia 29 20S 137 25E
80 Eyre Pen., Australia 33 30S 135 40E
34 Eyrecourt, Ireland 53 12N 8 8W
48 Eyriks Jökull, mt., Iceland 64 45N 20 20W
62 Ez Zeidab, Sudan 17 30N 33 45E

F

40 Fabriano, Italy 43 20N 12 50E
72 Fachi, Niger 19 5N 11 0E
73 Fada, Chad 17 18N 21 35E
72 Fada N'Gourma, Volta 12 5N 0 30E
61 Faddeyev I., U.S.S.R. 75 30N 144 0E
40 Faenza, Italy 44 19N 11 54E
47 Fagaras, Rumania 45 50N 24 58E
49 Fagernes, Norway 61 1N 9 5E
49 Fagersta, Sweden 60 1N 15 46E
18 Fair I., British Is. 59 30N 1 40W
88 Fairbanks, Alaska 64 59N 148 10W
22 Fairford, England 51 42N 1 48W
84 Fairlie, New Zealand 44 5S 170 48E
91 Fairmont, Minn., U.S.A. 43 40N 94 30W
91 Fairmont, W. Va., U.S.A. 39 30N 80 6W
88 Fairweather, Mt., Alaska 58 50N 137 40W
63 Faizabad, Afghanistan 37 18N 70 45E
65 Faizabad, India 26 50N 82 10E
27 Fakenham, England 52 50N 0 51E
57 Fakfak, Indonesia 2 50S 132 0E
65 Falam, Burma 22 58N 93 50E
27 Faldingworth, England 53 21N 0 22W
49 Falkenberg, Sweden 56 56N 12 30E
31 Falkirk, Scotland 55 59N 3 47W
31 Falkland, Scotland 56 15N 3 13W
99 Falkland Is., S. Atlantic 52 0S 60 0W
100 Falkland Is. Dependencies 55 0S 35 0W
49 Falköping, Sweden 58 10N 13 30E
93 Fall River, U.S.A. 41 43N 71 9W
94 Falmouth, Antigua 17 0N 61 47W
24 Falmouth, & B., Eng. 50 9N 5 4W
94 Falmouth, Jamaica 18 30N 77 42W
76 False B., S. Africa 34 15S 18 40E
49 Falster, I., Denmark 54 50N 11 55E
49 Falsterbo, Sweden 55 21N 13 3E
49 Falun, Sweden 60 38N 15 32E
62 Famagusta, Cyprus 35 10N 33 58E
99 Famatina, Mt., Arg. 28 30S 67 0W
36 Fanad Hd., Ireland 55 15N 7 37W
73 Fangak, Sudan 9 0N 30 50E
32 Fannich, L., Scotland 57 39N 5 0W
40 Fano, Italy 43 50N 13 4E
63 Fanuch, Iran 26 40N 59 35E
74 Faradje, Zaïre 4 0N 29 52E
64 Farah, Afghanistan 32 22N 62 7E
64 Farah Prov., Afghan. 32 0N 62 0E
64 Farah Rud R., Afghan. 32 30N 62 20E
72 Faranah, Guinea 10 3N 10 45W
62 Farasan Is., Red Sea 17 0N 42 0E
22 Fareham, England 50 53N 1 12W
89 Farewell, C., Greenland 60 0N 44 0W
84 Farewell, C., N.Z. 40 30S 172 40E
91 Fargo, U.S.A. 46 57N 96 47W
63 Faria, Wadi el, Jordan 32 12N 35 25E
91 Faribault, U.S.A. 44 16N 93 20W
72 Farim, Guinea-Bissau 12 27N 15 17W
22 Faringdon, England 51 39N 1 34W
91 Farmington, U.S.A. 44 40N 70 8W
23 Farnborough, Eng. 51 17N 0 46W
27 Farne Is., England 55 38N 1 37W
23 Farnham, England 51 13N 0 48W
26 Farnworth, England 53 33N 2 33W
37 Faro, Portugal 37 5N 7 54W
49 Farö, Sweden 58 0N 19 10E
13 Faroe Is., Atlantic 62 0N 7 0W
34 Farranfore, Ireland 52 10N 9 32W
82 Farrell Flat, Australia 33 50S 139 40E
41 Farsala, Greece 39 20N 22 28E
49 Farsund, Norway 58 3N 6 42E
62 Fasa, Iran 28 57N 53 35E
30 Faslane, Scotland 56 3N 4 49W
32 Fastnet Rock, Ireland 51 23N 9 37W
64 Fatehgarh, India 27 25N 79 35E
64 Fatehpur, Rajasthan, India 27 57N 74 55E
65 Fatehpur, U.P., India 26 0N 80 50E
66 Fatshan, China 23 7N 113 10E
31 Fauldhouse, Scotland 55 50N 3 44W
40 Favara, Italy 37 20N 13 40E
23 Faversham, England 51 18N 0 53E
40 Favignana, Italy 37 55N 12 20E
22 Fawley, England 50 49N 1 20W
48 Faxa Floi, Iceland 64 27N 23 0W
91 Fayetteville, N.C., U.S.A. 35 1N 78 58W
91 Fayetteville, Ark., U.S.A. 36 0N 94 5W
22 Fazeley, England 52 36N 1 42W
64 Fazilka, India 30 30N 74 2E
72 F'Dérik (Fort Gouraud), Mauritania 22 40N 12 45W
91 Fear, C., U.S.A. 33 59N 78 0W
33 Fearn, Scotland 57 47N 4 0W
84 Featherston, N Z. 41 1S 175 23E
43 Fécamp, France 49 47N 0 21E
49 Fehmarn I., Germany 54 27N 11 10E
46 Fehmarn Belt, Str., Den. 54 35N 11 20E
84 Feilding, New Zealand 40 12S 175 30E
75 Feira, Zambia 15 30S 30 15E
45 Feldkirch, Austria 47 12N 9 35E
23 Felixstowe, England 51 58N 1 23E
23 Felpham, England 50 47N 0 38W
48 Femunden L., Norway 62 30N 11 55E
66 Fenglingtu, China 34 40N 110 20E
27 Fenny Bentley, Eng. 53 4N 1 43W
22 Fenny Compton, Eng. 52 9N 1 20W
23 Fenny Stratford, Eng. 51 59N 0 42W
23 Fens, The, Eng. 52 45N 0 2E
51 Feodosiya, U.S.S.R. 45 2N 35 28E
34 Ferbane, Ireland 53 17N 7 50W
60 Fergana, U.S.S.R. 40 50N 71 55E
34 Fergus, R., Ireland 52 45N 9 0W
91 Fergus Falls, U.S.A. 46 25N 96 0W
40 Ferla, Italy 37 5N 14 55E
36 Fermanagh, Co., N. Ire. 54 22N 7 40W
34 Fermoy, Ireland 52 9N 8 15W
74 Fernando Poo., I., *see* Macias Nguema Biyoga
23 Fernhurst, England 51 3N 0 43W
90 Fernie, Canada 49 30N 115 0W
32 Fernilea, Scotland 57 18N 6 24W
64 Ferozepore, India 30 55N 75 20E
40 Ferrara, Italy 44 52N 11 40E
37 Ferrol, Spain 43 32N 8 13W
27 Ferryhill, England 54 42N 1 32W
73 Fès, Morocco 34 5N 4 55W
35 Fethard, Ireland 52 28N 7 43W
32 Fetlar I., Scotland 60 35N 0 50W
33 Fettercairn, Scotland 56 50N 2 33W
73 Fezzan, Dist., Libya 25 40N 16 0E
25 Ffestiniog, Wales 52 58N 3 56W
75 Fianarantsoa, Madagascar 21 30S 47 0E
46 Fichtel Gebirge. Mts., Germany 50 0N 12 0E
76 Ficksburg, S. Africa 28 48S 27 55E
35 Fiddown, Ireland 52 20N 7 20W
31 Fife, Reg., Scotland 56 10N 3 10W
31 Fife Ness, Scotland 56 17N 2 35W
43 Figeac, France 44 40N 2 0E
37 Figueira da Foz, Portugal 40 7N 8 54W
37 Figueras, Spain 42 17N 3 0E
72 Figuig, Morocco 32 18N 1 20W
84 Fiji, Pac. Oc. 18 0S 178 0E
23 Filby, England 52 40N 1 39E
27 Filey, & B., England 54 14N 0 18W
41 Filiatra, Greece 37 5N 21 35E
49 Filipstad, Sweden 59 42N 14 5E
45 Filisur, Switzerland 46 40N 9 40E
48 Filskivotn, Dist., Ice. 64 50N 20 45W
24 Filton, England 51 29N 2 34E
33 Findhorn, & R., Scot. 57 40N 3 36W
92 Findlay, U.S.A. 41 0N 83 32W
23 Finedon, England 52 20N 0 40W
35 Finglas, Ireland 53 22N 6 18W
75 Fingoé, Mozambique 14 55S 32 10E
42 Finistère, Dépt., France 48 13N 4 4W
37 Finisterre, C., Spain 42 51N 9 19W
49 Finland, Europe 62 20N 26 30E
50 Finland, G. of, Europe 60 0N 26 0E
88 Finlay R., Canada 55 50N 125 10W
83 Finley, Australia 35 50S 145 40E
30 Finnart, Scotland 56 7N 4 48W
36 Finn, R., Ireland 54 50N 7 55W
49 Finnmark, Norway 70 0N 25 0E
82 Finschhafen, Papua N.G. 6 33S 147 48E
33 Finstown, Scotland 59 0N 3 8W
36 Fintona, N. Ireland 54 30N 7 20W
63 Fiq, Syria 32 47N 35 41E
62 Firat (Euphrates), R., Turkey 39 0N 38 30E
64 Firozabad, India 27 5N 78 20E
73 First Cataract of Nile, Egypt 24 0N 32 50E
61 Firyuza, U.S.S.R. 38 10N 57 45E
13 Fisher Bank, Europe 61 0N 10 0W
25 Fishguard & B., Wales 51 59N 4 58W
91 Fitzgerald, U.S.A. 31 40N 83 10W
36 Fivemiletown, N. Ireland 54 23N 7 20W
90 Flagstaff, U.S.A. 35 12N 111 38W
49 Flam, Norway 60 52N 7 14E
27 Flamborough Hd., Eng. 54 9N 0 5W
44 Flandre Occidentale, Belg. 51 0N 3 0E
44 Flandre Orientale, Belg. 51 0N 3 30E
48 Flasjön, L., Sweden 64 0N 15 40E
48 Flatey I., Iceland 65 22N 22 57W
48 Flatey I., Iceland 66 12N 17 50W
48 Flateyri, Iceland 66 5N 23 30W
82 Flattery, C., Australia 15 0S 145 30E
90 Flattery, C., U.S.A. 48 30N 124 56W
95 Flatts, The, Bermuda 32 20N 64 44W
44 Flavy le Martel, France 49 43N 3 13E
23 Fleet, England 51 16N 0 50W
33 Fleet, L. & R., Scotland 57 56N 4 2W
26 Fleetwood, England 53 56N 3 2W
49 Flekkefjord, Norway 58 18N 6 39E
49 Flensburg, Germany 54 45N 9 27E
23 Fletton, England 52 34N 0 13W
45 Fleurier, Switzerland 46 55N 6 35E
44 Fleurus, Belgium 50 30N 4 33E
88 Flin Flon, Canada 54 58N 101 58W
80 Flinders B., Australia 34 25S 115 20E
83 Flinders I., Australia 40 0S 148 0E
82 Flinders R., Australia 20 35S 142 30E
83 Flinders Ras., Australia 31 0S 139 0E
92 Flint, U.S.A. 42 59N 83 45W
91 Flint R., U.S.A. 31 15N 84 15W
25 Flint, Wales 53 16N 3 10W
27 Flodden, England 55 37N 2 8W
40 Florence (Firenze), Italy 43 48N 11 18E
91 Florence, Ala., U.S.A. 34 51N 87 35W
91 Florence, S. C., U.S.A. 34 12N 79 47W
98 Florencia, Colombia 1 50N 75 50W
44 Florennes, Belgium 50 15N 4 35E
68 Flores, I., Indonesia 8 35S 121 30E
68 Flores Sea, Indonesia 6 50S 122 0E
44 Florenville, Belgium 49 40N 5 19E
99 Florianopolis, Brazil 27 35S 48 25W
91 Florida, st., U.S.A. 28 30N 81 30W
99 Florida, Uruguay 34 10S 56 25W
91 Florida Keys, Is. & B., U.S.A. 25 0N 80 30W
49 Florö, Norway 61 36N 5 0E
33 Flotta, I., Scotland 58 50N 3 8W
45 Fluela Pass, Switz. 46 48N 9 44E
44 Flushing (Vlissingen), Netherlands 51 27N 3 35E
82 Fly R., Papua N.G. 8 0S 142 0E
33 Fochabers, Scotland 57 38N 3 5W
47 Focsani, Rumania 45 39N 27 13E
40 Foggia, Italy 41 27N 15 37E
43 Foix, France 42 58N 1 30E
48 Folda Fd., Norway 67 35N 15 25E
49 Folgefonni, Norway 60 0N 6 15E
40 Foligno, Italy 42 58N 12 48E
23 Folkestone, England 51 5N 1 11E
88 Fond du Lac, Canada 59 28N 107 5W
92 Fond du Lac, Wis., U.S.A. 43 50N 88 30W
94 Fonseca, G. of, Central America 13 15N 87 40W
43 Fontainebleau, France 48 20N 2 40E
42 Fontevrault, France 47 17N 0 0
67 Foochow, China 26 10N 119 20E
45 Forbach, France 49 10N 6 52E
83 Forbes, Australia 33 24S 148 1E
30 Ford, Scotland 56 10N 5 27W
35 Ford, Ireland 52 32N 6 15W
25 Forden, England 52 34N 3 8W
22 Fordingbridge, England 50 56N 1 48W
33 Fordyce, Scotland 57 40N 2 45W
86 Forel, Mt., Greenland 67 0N 34 0W
24 Foreland Pt., England 51 14N 3 45W
42 Forest, Guernsey 49 26N 2 35W
26 Forest of Bowland, Eng. 54 0N 2 30W
22 Forest of Dean, England 51 48N 2 35W
23 Forest Row, England 51 6N 0 3E
83 Forestier Pen., Australia 43 0S 148 0E
31 Forfar, Scotland 56 40N 2 53W
40 Forli, Italy 44 14N 12 7E
33 Formartine, Dist., Scot. 57 20N 2 15W
26 Formby, & Pt., England 53 34N 3 4W
37 Formentera I., Spain 38 40N 1 33E
99 Formosa, Argentina 26 10S 58 25W
74 Formosa B., Kenya 2 50S 40 10E
67 Formosa (Taiwan) I., China 24 0N 121 0E
67 Formosa Str., China 24 0N 119 0E
43 Fornovo, Italy 44 42N 10 10E
33 Forres, Scotland 57 37N 3 36W
80 Forrest, Australia 30 50S 128 25E
82 Forsayth, Australia 18 50S 143 45E
48 Fors, Sweden 63 1N 16 38E
33 Forsinard, Scotland 58 23N 3 54W
46 Forst, Germany 51 45N 14 40E
83 Forster, Australia 32 2S 152 10E
89 Fort Albany, Ont., Can. 52 10N 81 50W
73 Fort Archambault, Chad 9 0N 18 18E
33 Fort Augustus, Scotland 57 9N 4 40W
76 Fort Beaufort, S. Africa 32 44S 26 42E
73 Fort Bretonnet, Chad 10 40N 16 50E
72 Fort Charlet (Djanet), Algeria 24 35N 9 20E
89 Fort Chimo, Canada 58 30N 67 10W
88 Fort Chipewyan, Can. 58 50N 111 0W
90 Fort Collins, U.S.A. 40 36N 105 10W
73 Fort Crampel, Cent. Africa 7 2N 19 18E
75 Fort Dauphin, Madagascar 25 0S 46 57E
94 Fort Davis, Panama Canal Zone (Inset)
95 Fort de France, Martinique 14 33N 61 2W
91 Fort Dodge, U.S.A. 42 32N 94 11W
88 Fort Frances, Canada 48 52N 93 25W
72 Fort Gouraud, *see* F'Dérik
65 Fort Hertz, *see* Putao
75 Fort Jameson, *see* Chipata
75 Fort Johnston, *see* Mangoche
72 Fort Lallemand, Algeria 31 30N 6 35E
73 Fort Lamy, *see* Ndjamena
72 Fort Laperrine (Tamanrasset), Algeria 22 45N 5 30E
91 Fort Lauderdale, U.S.A. 26 5N 80 5W
72 Fort Miribel, Algeria 29 30N 3 0E
91 Fort Myers, U.S.A. 26 39N 81 48W
88 Fort Nelson, & R., Can. 58 49N 123 0W
88 Fort Norman, Canada 65 0N 125 30W
90 Fort Peck L., U.S.A. 47 40N 107 0W
91 Fort Pierce, U.S.A. 27 35N 80 25W
74 Fort Portal, Uganda 0 48N 30 20E
88 Fort Providence, Can., 61 20N 117 30W
74 Fort Rosebery, *see* Mansa
74 Fort Rousset, Congo (Fr.) 0 35S 16 5E
88 Fort St. John, Can. 56 15N 120 50W
91 Fort Scott, U.S.A. 37 50N 94 44W
51 Fort Shevchenko, U.S.S.R. 44 37N 50 30E
88 Fort Simpson, Can. 61 45N 121 30W
88 Fort Smith, North West Territories, Canada 60 0N 112 25W
91 Fort Smith, U.S.A. 35 10N 94 30W
88 Fort Vermilion, Can. 58 30N 115 57W
75 Fort Victoria, Rhodesia 20 3S 30 50E
92 Fort Wayne, U.S.A. 41 0N 85 3W
92 Fort William, *see* Thunder Bay
32 Fort William, Scotland 56 49N 5 6W
90 Forth Worth, U.S.A. 32 50N 97 20W
88 Fort Yukon, Alaska 66 35N 145 12W
99 Fortaleza (Ceará), Brazil 3 48S 38 38W

75 Forte Roçadas, Angola 16 38S 15 22E
80 Fortescue R., Australia 22 5S 117 0E
31 Forth, Scotland 55 45N 3 42W
31 Forth, Firth of, Scotland 56 10N 2 45W
30 Forth, R., Scotland 56 8N 4 15W
33 Fortrose, Scotland 57 36N 4 8W
92 Fostoria, U.S.A. 41 8N 83 10W
31 Fothergill, England 54 43N 3 30W
23 Fotheringhay, England 52 32N 0 25W
18 Foula, I., Scotland 60 8N 2 7W
72 Foumban, Cameroon 5 50N 10 58E
43 Fourmies, France 50 0N 4 0E
41 Fournoi I., Greece 37 38N 26 50E
72 Fouta Djalon, Mt., Guinea
11 30N 12 0W
84 Foveaux Str., N.Z. 46 45S 168 15E
24 Fowey, & R., England 50 20N 4 39W
80 Fowler's B., Australia 32 0S 132 50E
26 Foxdale, I. of Man 54 12N 4 38W
89 Foxe Basin, Canada 66 30N 77 0W
89 Foxe Pen., Canada 65 0N 76 0W
36 Foxford, Ireland 53 59N 9 7W
84 Foxton, New Zealand 40 31S 175 13E
36 Foyle, L. & R., N. Ire. 55 5N 7 10W
34 Foynes, Ireland 52 37N 9 5W
23 Framlingham, England 52 12N 1 21E
41 Francavilla Fontana, It. 40 30N 17 34E
43 France, Europe 47 0N 3 0E
83 Frances, Australia 36 40S 140 55E
74 Franceville, Gabon 1 55S 13 40E
43 Franche Comté, Prov., Fr. 47 15N 6 10E
75 Francistown, Botswana 21 6S 27 32E
44 Franeker, Netherlands 53 12N 5 33E
45 Frankenthal, Germany 49 32N 8 20E
92 Frankfort, Ind., U.S.A. 40 18N 86 31W
92 Frankfort, Ken., U.S.A. 38 10N 84 50W
45 Frankfurt-on-Main, Ger. 50 5N 8 42E
46 Frankfurt-on-Oder, Ger. 52 20N 14 32E
88 Franklin B., Canada 70 0N 126 0W
90 Franklin D. Roosevelt L., U.S.A.
48 30N 119 0W
88 Franklin, Mts., Can. 66 0N 125 0W
88 Franklin Str., Canada 72 0N 96 0W
88 Franklin Terr., Canada 71 0N 100 0W
83 Frankston, Australia 38 15S 145 10E
23 Frant, England 51 5N 0 17E
100 Franz Josef Ld. U.S.S.R.
81 0N 60 0E
83 Fraser or Gt. Sandy I., Australia
25 0S 154 0E
88 Fraser R., Canada 53 30N 120 30W
33 Fraserburgh, Scotland 57 42N 2 0W
45 Frauenfeld, Switzerland 47 34N 8 54E
99 Fray Bentos, Uruguay 33 15S 58 25W
49 Fredericia, Denmark 55 36N 9 43E
89 Fredericton, Canada 45 50N 66 40W
89 Frederikshaab, Greenland
62 0N 49 30W
49 Frederikshavn, Den. 57 26N 10 19E
92 Fredonia, U.S.A. 42 25N 79 20W
49 Fredrikstad, Norway 59 16N 10 57E
95 Freeport, Bahama Is. 25 55N 78 20W
92 Freeport, U.S.A. 42 16N 89 42W
72 Freetown, Sierra Leone 8 20N 13 5W
33 Freevater Forest, Scot. 57 52N 4 43W
46 Freiburg, Germany 47 59N 7 53E
46 Freising, Germany 48 30N 11 40E
46 Freistadt, Austria 48 30N 14 30E
43 Fréjus, France 43 12N 6 45E
80 Fremantle, Australia 32 6S 115 50E
81 Fremont, U.S.A. 41 33N 96 28W
96 French Fuiana, S. Amer. 4 0N 53 0W
62 French Somal., *see* Djibouti
62 French Territory of Afars and Issas,
see Djibouti
36 Frenchpark, Ireland 53 53N 8 25W
90 Fresno, U.S.A. 36 42N 119 48W
33 Freswick, Scotland 58 35N 3 5W
31 Freuchie, Scotland 56 14N 3 8W
83 Freycinet Pen., Australia 42 0S 148 15E
75 Fria, C., S.W. Africa 18 34S 12 0E
45 Fribourg, & Cn., Switz. 46 49N 7 9E
45 Friedrichshafen, Ger. 47 38N 9 30E
84 Friendly Is., *see* Tonga Is. (Inset)
44 Friesland, Prov., Neth. 53 5N 5 50E
94 Frijoles, Panama (Inset)
23 Frimley, England 51 18N 0 43W
23 Frinton-on-Sea, England 51 50N 1 16E
99 Frio, C., Brazil 22 50S 41 50W
46 Frisian Is., Neth.-Ger. 53 30N 6 0E
40 Friuli-Venezia Giulia, Reg., Italy
46 15N 12 50E
26 Frizington, England 54 33N 3 30W
89 Frobisher & B., N.W. Terr., Canada
63 45N 68 30W
88 Frobisher, L., Canada 56 40N 108 20W
24 Frodsham, England 53 17N 2 45W
24 Frome, England 51 15N 2 19W
83 Frome, L., Australia 30 40S 139 45E
22 Frome, R., England 50 45N 2 33W
90 Front Ra., U.S.A. 40 0N 105 10W
40 Frosinone, Italy 41 40N 13 29E
48 Frostisen Mt., Norway 68 17N 17 0E
99 Froward C., Chile 55 0S 71 0W
60 Frunze, U.S.S.R. 42 55N 75 0E
45 Frutigen, Switzerland 46 34N 7 38E
94 Fuego, Vol., Guatemala
14 20N 91 15W
37 Fuenteovejuna, Spain 38 16N 5 28W
37 Fuentes de Onoro, Spain 40 37N 6 45W
37 Fundao, Portugal 40 10N 7 30W
94 Fuerte, R., Mexico 27 0N 108 30W
72 Fuerteventura, I., Canary Is.
28 25N 14 0W
48 Fuglö Sound, Norway 70 0N 20 0E
67 Fujiyama, Mt. Japan 35 30N 139 0E
66 Fukien, Prov., China 25 50N 118 0E
67 Fukui, & Pref., Japan 36 4N 136 8E
67 Fukue Shima, Japan 32 30N 128 40E
67 Fukuoka, & Pref., Japan 33 36N 130 27E
67 Fukushima, & Pref., Japan
37 30N 140 30E
46 Fulda, Germany 50 37N 9 40E
26 Fulwood, England 53 47N 2 41W
44 Fumay, France 49 59N 4 43E
72 Funchal, Madeira 32 40N 16 50E
89 Fundy, B. of, Canada 45 0N 66 0W
83 Furneaux Group, Austral. 40 0S 148 0E
26 Furness, Dist., England 54 18N 3 8W
45 Furth, Germany 49 29N 10 58E
67 Fusin, China 42 0N 121 40E
67 Fushun, China 42 1N 123 59E
84 Futuna, I., Pacific Ocean 14 3S 178 3E
67 Fuyu, China 45 15N 125 15E
30 Fyne, Loch, Scotland 56 0N 5 20W

G

74 Gabela, Angola 10 50S 14 27E
73 Gabes, Tunisia 33 53N 10 4E
74 Gabon, Africa 1 55S 12 0E
76 Gaborone, Botswana 24 38S 25 50E
41 Gabrovo, Bulgaria 42 50N 25 25E
64 Gadag, India 15 10N 75 45E
64 Gadarwara, India 22 58N 78 50E
64 Gadhada, India 21 58N 71 30E
91 Gadsden, U.S.A. 34 5N 85 59W
64 Gadwal, India 16 8N 77 56E
40 Gaeta, Italy 41 18N 13 35E
43 Gaillac, France 43 58N 1 56E
27 Gainsborough, Eng. 53 25N 0 47W
80 Gairdner, L., Australia 31 30S 136 0E
32 Gairloch, Scotland 57 43N 5 47W
33 Gairsay I., Scotland 59 4N 25 9W
75 Galangue, Angola 13 38S 16 0E
4 Galapagos Is., Pac. Oc. 0 30S 91 0W
31 Galashiels, Scotland 55 37N 2 50W
47 Galati, Rumania 45 28N 28 2E
41 Galatina, Italy 40 10N 18 10E
34 Galbally, Ireland 52 28N 8 17W
49 Galdhöpiggen, Mt., Nor. 61 40N 8 20E
94 Galeana, Mexico 30 2N 107 30W
91 Galesburg, U.S.A. 40 54N 90 20W
50 Galich, U.S.S.R. 58 22N 42 12E
37 Galicia, Old Prov., Spain 42 45N 8 0W
63 Galilee, Dist., Israel 32 52N 35 20E
63 Galilee, Sea of, *see* Kinneret, L.
62 Gallabat, Sudan 13 10N 36 30E
64 Galle, Sri Lanka 6 2N 80 13E
37 Gallego, R., Spain 42 20N 0 30W
34 Galley Hd., Ireland 51 31N 8 57W
98 Gallinas, Punta, Colombia
12 28N 71 37W
41 Gallipoli, Italy 40 1N 18 0E
41 Gallipoli, Turkey, *see* Gelibolu
48 Gällivare, Sweden 67 10N 20 32E
30 Galloway, Mull of, Scot. 54 37N 4 52W
90 Gallup, U.S.A. 35 28N 108 50W
83 Galong, Australia 34 40S 148 30E
64 Galoya, Sri Lanka 8 10N 80 55E
92 Galt, Canada 43 25N 80 20W
34 Galty Mts., Ireland 52 22N 8 13W
34 Galtymore Mt., Ireland 52 15N 8 4W
91 Galveston, U.S.A. 29 15N 95 0W
34 Galway, & Co., Ireland 53 18N 9 3W
72 Gambaga, Ghana 10 35N 0 25W
72 Gambia, & R., West Africa
13 50N 15 0W
94 Gamboa, Panama Canal Zone (Inset)
74 Gamboma, Congo (Fr.) 1 45S 16 0E
48 Gamlakarleby, *see* Kokkola, Finland
65 Gandak, R., India 26 20N 84 56E
64 Gandava, Pakistan 28 40N 67 20E
89 Gander, Newf., Canada 49 1N 54 53W
72 Gandi, Nigeria 12 55N 5 49E
65 Ganga (Ganges), R., India &
Pakistan 24 30N 88 20E
64 Ganganagar, India 29 55N 73 50E
65 Gangtok, Sikkim 27 20N 88 30E
43 Gannat, France 46 8N 3 15E
90 Gannett Pk., U.S.A. 43 10N 110 0W
75 Ganspan, S. Africa 27 55S 24 45E
72 Ganta, Liberia 7 15N 8 59W
72 Gao, Mali 16 25N 0 10W
72 Gaoua, Volta 10 20N 3 15W
72 Gaoual, Guinea 11 35N 13 25W
43 Gap, France 44 35 6 5E
34 Gap of Dunloe, Ireland 52 0N 9 40W
64 Gar Dzong, India 32 20N 79 55E
36 Gara, L., Ireland 53 54N 8 27W
42 Gard, Dépt., France 44 3N 4 20E
40 Garda, L., Italy 45 40N 10 40E
74 Gardala, Ethiopia 5 40N 36 40E
90 Garden City, U.S.A. 38 0N 100 47W
64 Gardez, Afghanistan 33 40N 69 0E
73 Gardian, Chad 15 45N 19 40E
92 Gardner, U.S.A. 42 35N 72 0W
27 Garforth, England 53 48N 1 22W
40 Gargano, Mt., Italy 41 50N 16 5E
76 Garies, S. Africa 30 31S 18 0E
40 Garigliano, R., Italy 41 18N 13 50E
30 Garliestown, Scotland 54 47N 4 22W
60 Garm, U.S.S.R. 39 25N 70 20E
45 Garmisch Partenkirchen, Germany
47 30N 11 6E
33 Garmouth, Scotland 57 40N 3 8W
43 Garonne, R., France 43 20N 1 20E
74 Garoua Malaba, Cam. 9 16N 13 25E
72 Garraway, Liberia 4 35N 8 0W
36 Garrison, Ireland 54 25N 8 5W
88 Garry, L., Canada 66 0N 100 0W
33 Garry, L., Scotland 57 5N 4 52W
74 Garsen, Kenya 2 25S 40 20E
26 Garstang, England 53 53N 2 45W
64 Gartok, Tibet, China 31 33N 80 30E
68 Garut, Java, Indonesia 7 20S 108 0E
36 Garvagh, N. Ireland 55 0N 6 41W
84 Garvie, Mts., N.Z. 45 30S 169 0E
91 Gary, U.S.A. 41 36N 87 10W
60 Gasan Kuli, U.S.S.R. 37 40N 54 20E
43 Gascony, Prov., France 43 40N 0 10E
80 Gascoyne, R., Australia 25 0S 115 0E
72 Gashaka, Nigeria 7 30N 11 30E
89 Gaspé, C., Canada 48 50N 64 5W
37 Gata, Cabo de, Spain 36 42N 2 6W
37 Gata, Sa. de, mts., Spain 40 30N 6 0W
27 Gateshead, England 54 58N 1 38W
93 Gatineau, R., Canada 47 0N 75 50W
26 Gatley, England 53 25N 2 15W
75 Gatooma, Rhodesia 18 15S 29 57E
94 Gatun, & L., Panama Canal Zone
(Inset)
64 Gaud-i-Zirreh, Afghan. 29 45N 62 0E
65 Gauhati, Assam, India 26 12N 91 50E
48 Gaula, R., Norway 63 15N 10 15E
49 Gausta, Mt., Norway 59 48N 8 40E
49 Gauja, R., U.S.S.R. 57 15N 24 50E
49 Gävle, Sweden 60 40N 17 4E
49 Gävleborg, Co., Sweden 61 0N 16 30E
83 Gawler, Australia 34 39S 138 45E
64 Gawilgarh Hills, India 21 15N 76 30E
65 Gaya, India 24 42N 85 0E
83 Gayndah, Australia 25 38S 151 40E
63 Gaza (Ghazzah), Israel 31 30N 34 28E
51 Gaziantep, Turkey 37 10N 37 30E
76 Gcuwa, S. Africa 32 20S 28 5E
47 Gdansk, Poland 54 19N 18 40E
50 Gdov, U.S.S.R. 58 40N 27 55E
47 Gdynia, Poland 54 38N 18 28E
35 Geashill, Ireland 53 14N 7 20W
73 Gebeit Mine, Sudan 21 3N 36 29E
62 Gebel Sabahi, Egypt 26 0N 34 0E
73 Gedaref, Sudan 14 0N 35 42E
63 Gedera, Israel 31 49N 34 47E
23 Gedney, England 52 47N 0 5E
74 Gedo, Ethiopia 9 0N 37 0E
49 Gedser, Denmark 54 35N 11 55E
44 Geel, Belgium 51 9N 4 59E
83 Geelong, Australia 38 8S 144 20E
44 Geeraardsbergen, Belg. 50 46N 3 53E
73 Geidam, Nigeria 12 57N 11 57E
45 Geislingen, Germany 48 37N 9 47E
74 Geita, Tanzania 2 40S 32 18E
40 Gela, Italy 37 6N 14 18E
44 Gelderland, Prov., Neth. 52 6N 6 10E
44 Geldermalsen, Neth. 51 53N 5 17E
44 Geldrop, Netherlands 51 24N 5 32E
72 Gelhak, Sudan 11 14N 32 45E
41 Gelibolu (Gallipoli), Turkey
40 30N 26 55E
44 Gelsenkirchen, Germany 51 32N 7 4E
68 Gemas, Malaya 2 35N 102 50E
44 Gembloux, Belgium 50 34N 4 41E
74 Gemena, Zaïre 3 20N 19 40E
45 Gemmi P., Switzerland 46 25N 7 39E
100 General Belgrano, Antarc. 78 0S 38 0W
99 Gen. Pico, Argentina 35 40S 63 45W
45 Geneva, & Cn., Switz. 46 12N 6 8E
45 Geneva, L. of Europe, *see* Lac Leman
44 Genk, Belgium 50 58N 5 30E
83 Genoa, Australia 37 30S 149 30E
40 Genoa, & G. (Genova), It.
44 25N 8 58E
44 Gent (Ghent), Belgium 51 5N 3 40E
76 Genyesa, S. Africa 26 30S 24 10F
80 Geographe Chan., Austral.
24 20S 113 15E
76 George, S. Africa 34 0S 22 15E
83 George, L., Australia 35 0S 149 0E
74 George, L., Uganda 0 0 30 15E
91 George, L., U.S.A. 29 20N 81 30W
93 George, L., N.Y., U.S.A. 43 40N 73 33W
83 George Town, Australia 41 5S 148 55E
68 George Town, Malaya 5 28N 100 5E
72 Georgetown, Gambia 13 30N 14 47W
94 Georgetown, Guyana 6 40N 58 15W
91 Georgia, st., U.S.A. 33 0N 83 0W
51 Georgia S.S.R., U.S.S.R. 42 0N 44 30E
89 Georgian B., Canada 45 0N 80 30W
51 Georgievsk, U.S.S.R. 44 10N 43 17E
52 Georgiu-Dezh, U.S.S.R. 51 3N 39 20E
46 Gera, Germany 50 53N 12 6E
80 Geraldton, Australia 28 48S 114 38E
63 Gerar, R., Israel 31 23N 34 35E
43 Gérardmer, France 48 0N 6 50E
46 Germany, East Europe 52 0N 13 0E
46 Germany, West Europe 51 0N 9 0E
76 Germiston, S. Africa 26 16S 28 12E
44 Gerolstein, Germany 50 12N 6 24E
37 Gerona, Spain 41 58N 2 50E
23 Gerrards Cross, England 51 35N 0 32W
42 Gers, Dépt., France 43 31N 0 10E
72 Géryville, Algeria *see* El Bayadh
92 Gettysburg, U.S.A. 39 50N 77 18W
43 Gevaudan, Dist., France 44 45N 3 30E
48 Geyser, Springs, Ice. 64 22N 20 15W
62 Gezer, Israel 31 51N 34 55E
62 Gezira, Sudan 16 20N 34 0E
72 Ghadames, Libya 30 18N 9 5E
65 Ghaghara (Gogra), R., India
26 40N 82 40E
72 Ghana, Africa 8 0N 1 30W
63 Ghar, Wadi, Jordan 31 30N 35 20E
73 Gharyan, Libya 32 10N 13 0E
72 Ghat, Libya 25 0N 10 20E
65 Ghats, Eastern, Mts., India
13 30N 79 0E
65 Ghats, Western, Mts., India
17 0N 74 0E
72 Ghazaouet (Nemours), Algeria
35 1N 1 48W
64 Ghaziabad, India 28 35N 77 45E
65 Ghazipur, India 25 39N 83 28E
63 Ghazir, Lebanon 34 1N 35 39E
44 Ghent, Belgium, *see* Gent
65 Giamda Dzong, China 30 2N 93 0E
36 Giant's Causeway, N. Ire. 55 13N 6 31W
40 Giarre, Italy 37 44N 15 10E
75 Gibeon, S.W. Africa 25 11S 17 48E
37 Gibraltar, & Str., Europe 36 10N 5 20W
27 Gibraltar Pt., England 53 7N 0 19E
80 Gibson Des., Australia 24 0S 126 0E
43 Gien, France 47 40N 2 35E
46 Giessen, Germany 50 37N 8 42E
67 Gifu, & Pref., Japan 35 30N 136 54E
26 Giggleswick, England 54 5N 2 19W
30 Gigha I., Scotland 55 42N 5 43W
37 Gijon, Spain 43 32N 5 43 W
90 Gila, R., U.S.A. 33 0N 113 0W
11 Gilbert Is., Pacific Oc. 1 0S 173 0E
82 Gilbert R., Australia 17 0S 141 30E
36 Gilford, N. Ireland 54 23N 6 21W
83 Gilgandra, Australia 31 32S 148 37E
64 Gilgit, Kashmir 35 58N 74 27E
36 Gill, L., Ireland 54 14N 8 15W
82 Gilliat, Australia 20 40S 141 28E
23 Gillingham, England 51 22N 0 33E
44 Gilly, Belgium 50 25N 4 25E
48 Gilsbakki, Iceland 64 42N 21 2W
26 Gilsland, England 55 0N 2 34W
25 Gilwern, Wales 51 49N 3 5W
74 Gimbi, Ethiopia 9 3N 35 42E
41 Giona, Mt., Greece 38 40N 22 10E
51 Giresun, Turkey 40 53 38 19E
65 Giridih, India 24 10N 86 15E
42 Gironde, Dépt., France 44 50N 0 22E
82 Giru, Australia 19 30S 147 5E
30 Girvan, & R., Scotland 55 15N 4 50W
84 Gisborne, N.Z. 38 39S 178 5E
43 Gisors, France 49 20N 1 45E
47 Giurgiu, Rumania 43 53N 25 56E
63 Giv'atayim, Israel 32 4N 34 49E
44 Givet, France 50 8N 4 49E
61 Gizhiga, U.S.S.R. 62 0N 160 27E
47 Gizycko, Poland 54 5N 21 50E
41 Gjirokaster, Albania 40 5N 20 10E
49 Gjövik, Norway 60 47N 10 43E
93 Glace Bay, Canada 46 25N 60 0W
90 Glacier National Park, U.S.A.
48 45N 114 0W
82 Gladstone, Queensland, Australia
24 0S 151 15E
83 Gladstone, S. Australia 33 5S 138 10E
49 Glama, R., Norway 61 0N 11 30E
48 Glama Jökull, Mt., Ice. 65 47N 23 0W
31 Glamis, Scotland 56 37N 3 0W
34 Glanaruddery, Mts., Ire. 52 20N 9 27W
34 Glandore, Ireland 51 33N 9 7W
34 Glanworth, Ireland 52 11N 8 21W
45 Glarner Alpen, Mts., Switzerland
46 54N 9 10E
45 Glarus, Cn., Switzerland 46 55N 9 0E
33 Glas Maol, Mt., Scotland 56 52N 3 20W
30 Glasgow, Scotland 55 52N 4 14W
92 Glasgow, U.S.A. 37 0N 85 55W
36 Glasslough, Ireland 54 20N 6 53W
24 Glastonbury, England 51 18N 2 42W
46 Glauchau, Germany 50 49 12 31E
50 Glazov, U.S.S.R. 58 9N 52 30E
32 Glen Affric, Scotland 57 16N 5 0W
30 Glen Coe, Scotland 56 40N 5 0W
93 Glen Falls, U.S.A. 43 25N 73 40W
32 Glen Garry, Scotland 57 4N 5 10W
83 Glen Innes, Australia 29 42S 151 45E
33 Glen Mor, Scotland 57 15N 4 30W
30 Glen Orchy, Scotland 56 27N 4 52W
32 Glen Shiel, Scotland 57 8N 5 20W
32 Glenamaddy, Ireland 53 40N 8 35W
35 Glenamoy, Ireland 54 14N 9 40W
35 Glenart Castle, Ireland 52 48N 6 12W
36 Glenarm, N. Ireland 54 58N 5 58W
76 Glencairn, S. Africa 34 10S 18 25E
90 Glendale, U.S.A. 34 15N 118 20W
90 Glendive, U.S.A. 47 10N 104 45W
35 Glenealy, Ireland 52 59N 6 10W
83 Glenelg, Australia 35 1S 138 30E
32 Glenelg, Scotland 57 13N 5 36W
83 Glenelg, R., Australia 37 25N 141 30E
30 Glenken, The, reg., Scot. 55 10N 4 15W
30 Glenluce, Scotland 54 53N 4 49W
83 Glenmorgan, Australia 27 15S 149 30E
83 Glenorchy, Australia 42 49S 147 18E
31 Glenrothes, Scotland 56 12N 3 11W
48 Glettinganes, Iceland 65 30N 13 30W
34 Glin, Ireland 52 34N 9 17W
34 Glinsk, Ireland 53 23N 9 49W
47 Gliwice, Poland 50 20N 18 52E
90 Globe, U.S.E. 33 36N 111 0W
46 Glockner, Gr., mt., Austria
47 0N 12 30E
46 Glogow, Poland 51 35N 16 10E
75 Glorieuses Is., Ind. Oc. 11 30N 47 20W
26 Glossop, England 53 27N 1 56W
83 Gloucester, Australia 31 58S 151 56E
22 Gloucester, & Co., Eng. 51 53N 2 14W
93 Gloversville, U.S.A. 43 4N 74 25W
46 Glückstadt, Germany 53 49N 9 29E
46 Gmund, Austria 48 45N 15 0E
46 Gmunden, Austria 47 56N 13 46E
47 Gniezno, Poland 52 30N 17 35E
22 Gnosall, England 52 48N 2 15W
68 Go Cong, Vietnam 10 25N 106 50E
64 Goa, India 15 30N 74 0E
76 Goageb, S.W. Africa 26 40S 17 15E
65 Goalpara, India 26 10N 90 40E
30 Goat Fell, mt., Scotland 55 37N 5 15W
74 Goba, Ethiopia 7 1N 39 59E
75 Goba, Mozambique 26 1S 32 10E
75 Gobabis, S.W. Africa 22 17S 19 5E
66 Gobi (Shamo) Desert, Mongolia
44 0N 108 0E
44 Goch, Germany 51 42N 6 10E
23 Godalming, England 51 11N 0 36W
65 Godavari, R., India 19 20N 76 0E
47 Godeanu, Mt., Rumania 45 25N 22 15E
64 Godhra, India 22 45N 73 56E
88 Gods Lake, Canada 54 40N 94 10W
89 Godthaab, Greenland 64 14N 51 0W
44 Goeree I., Netherlands 51 50N 3 55E
44 Goes, Netherlands 51 31N 3 55E
82 Gogango, Australia 23 40S 150 2E
44 Goggingen, Germany 48 20N 10 52E
65 Gogra, R., *see* Ghaghara, R., India
73 Gogrial, Sudan 8 30N 28 0E
99 Goiânia, Brazil 16 17S 48 16W
99 Goiás, Brazil 15 55S 50 10W
30 Goil, L., Scotland 56 8N 4 54W
64 Gojra, Pakistan 31 5N 72 35E
41 Gökçeade, I., Turkey 40 10N 26 0E
83 Gold Coast, reg., Austral. 28 0S 153 25E
49 Goldap, Poland 54 18N 22 22E
34 Golden, Ireland 52 30N 8 0W
84 Golden B., N.Z. 40 40S 172 50E
90 Golden Gate, U.S.A. 37 58N 122 30W
34 Golden Vale, Ireland 52 33N 8 20W
91 Goldsboro, U.S.A. 35 26N 77 59W
46 Goleniów, Poland 53 35N 14 50E
33 Golspie, Scotland 57 58N 3 59W
74 Goma, Zaïre 1 40S 29 42E
50 Gomel, U.S.S.R. 52 28N 31 5E
30 Gometra I., Scotland 56 30N 6 18W
94 Gomez (Palacio), Mex. 25 45N 103 28W
65 Gomoh, India 23 52N 86 10E
95 Gonaives, Haiti 19 20N 72 45W
73 Gonder, Ethiopia 12 40N 37 45E
74 Goniri, Nigeria 11 30N 12 15E
76 Good Hope, C of, S. Afr. 34 20S 18 30E
83 Goodooga, Australia 29 1S 147 28E
27 Goole, England 53 42N 0 53W
83 Goondiwindi, Australia 28 31S 150 25E
90 Goose, L., U.S.A. 42 0N 120 0W
89 Goose Bay, Canada 53 25N 60 30W
64 Gop, India 22 5N 69 50E
45 Goppingen, Germany 48 43N 9 38E
65 Gorakhpur, India 26 49N 83 30E
31 Gordon, Scotland 55 41N 2 32W
80 Gordon Downs, Australia 18 30S 129 35E
82 Gordonvale, Australia 17 5S 145 50E
73 Goré, Chad 8 0N 16 48E
73 Gore, Ethiopia 8 12N 35 32E
84 Gore, New Zealand 46 5N 168 55E
35 Goresbridge, Ireland 52 38 7 0W
37 Gorey, Jersey, Channel Is. 49 12N 2 2W
44 Gorinchem, Netherlands 51 50N 4 59E
23 Goring, England 50 50N 0 21W
40 Gorizia, Italy 45 58N 13 38E
52 Gorki (Gorkiy), U.S.S.R. 56 17N 44 0E
23 Gorleston, England 52 35N 1 44E
46 Görlitz, Germany 51 11N 15 0E
52 Gorlovka, U.S.S.R. 48 25N 37 58E
60 Gorno, Filinskoye, U.S.S.R.
60 15N 70 3E
50 Gornyatski, U.S.S.R. 67 32N 64 15E
47 Gorodok, U.S.S.R. 49 46N 23 32E
68 Gorontalo, Indonesia 0 25N 123 5E
34 Gort, Ireland 53 4N 8 49W
50 Goryn, R., U.S.S.R. 52 0N 27 0E
46 Gorzów, Poland 52 43N 15 15E
65 Gosainthan, Mt., Tibet 28 20N 85 45E
45 Göschenen, Switzerland 46 40N 8 35E
83 Gosford, Australia 33 24S 151 10E
46 Goslar, Germany 51 57N 10 28E
40 Gospic, Yugoslavia 44 35N 15 20E
22 Gosport, England 50 48N 1 9W
48 Gota Can., Sweden 58 40N 14 10E
49 Göteborg, Sweden 57 20N 11 50E
49 Göteborg & Bohus, Co., Sweden
58 15N 11 30E
46 Gotha, Germany 50 56N 10 42E
46 Gothenburg, *see* Göteborg
48 Gotland, I., Sweden 57 35N 18 30E
49 Gotska Sandon I., Swed. 58 24N 19 15E
46 Göttingen, Germany 51 33N 9 58E
47 Gottwaldov, Cz-slov. 49 15N 17 42E
73 Goubone, Chad 20 45N 17 5E
44 Gouda, Netherlands 52 1N 4 42E
89 Gouin Res., Canada 48 35N 74 40W
83 Goulburn, Australia 34 45S 149 40E
80 Goulburn Is., Australia 11 30S 133 35E
72 Goundam, Mali 16 25N 3 45W
43 Gourdon, France 44 42N 1 25E
72 Gourma-Rarous, Mali 16 55N 2 5W
43 Gournay, France 49 30N 1 45E
30 Gourock, Scotland 55 58N 4 49W
83 Gourock Ra., Australia 36 0S 149 30E
72 Gourselik, Niger 13 40N 10 40E
42 Gouville, France 49 7N 1 32W
25 Gower, Pen., Wales 51 35N 4 10W
35 Gowran, Ireland 52 38N 7 5W
99 Goya, Argentina 29 0S 59 15W
73 Goz Beida, Chad 12 20N 21 30E
62 Goz Regeb, Sudan 16 0N 35 30E
40 Gozo, I., Malta 36 2N 14 18E
76 Graaf Reinet, S. Africa 32 18S 24 37
72 Grabo, Ivory Coast 4 55N 7 25W

40 Gracac, Yugoslavia 44 20N 15 55E
95 Gracias à Dios, C., Nicaragua 15 0N 83 2W
98 Gradaús, Sa. dos, mts., Brazil 7 0S 50 0W
37 Grado, Spain 43 25N 6 10W
33 Graemsay I., Scotland 58 56N 3 17W
48 Graénalon, L., Iceland 64 10N 17 20W
83 Grafton, Australia 29 41S 153 0E
91 Grafton, U.S.A. 48 30N 97 25W
100 Graham Land, Antarc. 64 0S 65 0W
76 Grahamstown, S. Africa 33 20S 26 38E
43 Graian Alps, The Alps 45 30N 7 0E
35 Graiguenamanagh, Ire. 52 32N 6 58W
33 Grampian, Reg. Scotland 57 20N 2 50W
33 Grampians, mts., Scot. 56 42N 4 27W
99 Gran Chaco, S. America 24 0S 60 0W
40 Gran Sasso, Mt., Italy 42 30N 13 50E
94 Granada, Nicaragua 12 0N 86 0W
37 Granada, Spain 37 17N 3 37W
89 Granby, Canada 45 20N 72 43W
93 Grand L., Canada 46 0N 66 0W
90 Grand, R., S. Dakota, U.S.A. 45 45N 101 30W
72 Grand Bassam, Ivory Coast 5 10N 3 40W
94 Grand Bourg, Marie-Galante I. Fr. W. Indies 15 50N 61 20W
66 Grand Canal, China 35 0N 117 0E
90 Grand Canyon, U.S.A. 36 0N 113 40W
95 Grand Cayman I., W.I. 19 30N 81 15W
88 Grand Falls, Newf., Can. 49 0N 55 43W
88 Grand Forks, Canada 49 0N 118 30W
91 Grand Forks, U.S.A. 47 40N 97 5W
90 Grand Island, U.S.A. 41 0N 98 10W
90 Grand Junction, U.S.A. 39 2N 108 32W
72 Grand Lahou, Ivory Coast 5 6N 5 0W
88 Grand Rapids, Canada 54 25N 99 30W
92 Grand Rapids, U.S.A. 42 57N 85 38W
99 Grande, B., Argentina 51 0S 69 0W
88 Grande Prairie, Canada 55 18N 118 50W
94 Grande Terre, Guadeloupe, W.I. 16 25N 61 15W
45 Grandson, Switzerland 46 49N 6 39E
26 Grange-over-Sands, Eng. 54 12N 2 56W
31 Grangemouth, Scotland 56 1N 3 42W
27 Grangetown, England 54 40N 1 10W
90 Grangeville, U.S.A. 45 57N 116 12W
34 Graney, L. & R., Ire. 53 0N 8 40W
91 Granite City, U.S.A. 38 45N 90 0W
84 Granity, New Zealand 41 38S 171 50E
37 Granollers, Spain 41 40N 2 15E
27 Grantham, England 52 55N 0 38W
33 Grantown-on-Spey, Scot. 57 20N 3 37W
90 Grants, U.S.A. 35 10N 107 50W
90 Grants Pass, U.S.A. 42 28N 124 14W
31 Grantshouse, Scotland 55 53N 2 17W
42 Granville, France 48 52N 1 39W
98 Grao Mogol, Brazil 16 30S 42 27W
26 Grasmere, England 54 28N 3 2W
88 Gras, L. de, Canada 65 0N 118 5W
43 Grasse, France 43 43N 6 54W
45 Graubunden, Canton, Switz. 46 45N 9 30E
43 Graulhet, France 43 45N 2 0E
44 's Gravenhage, *see* The Hague, Neth.
92 Gravenhurst, Canada 44 56N 79 28W
23 Gravesend, England 51 25N 0 23E
43 Gray, France 47 25N 5 32E
26 Grayrigg, England 54 22N 2 40W
90 Grays Harbor, U.S.A. 47 0N 124 0W
23 Grays Thurrock, Eng. 51 28N 0 23E
46 Graz, Austria 47 2N 15 25E
91 Great Abaco, Bahamas 26 30N 77 20W
61 Great Anyui R., U.S.S.R. 67 0N 163 0E
83 Great Australian Basin, Australia 27 0S 145 0E
80 Great Australian Bight 33 29S 129 0E
84 Great Barrier I., N.Z. 36 8S 175 25E
82 Great Barrier Reef, Australia 19 0S 149 0E
88 Great Bear L. & R., Can. 66 0N 120 0W
90 Great Basin, U.S.A. 40 0N 116 30W
90 Great Bend, U.S.A. 38 16N 99 6W
32 Great Bernera Island, Scotland 58 15N 6 48W
34 Great Blasket I., Ireland 52 7N 10 33W
13 Great Britain, Europe 50 0 to 58 0N; 1 45E to 6 15W
76 Great Bushman Land, S. Africa 29 15S 19 30E
82 Great Divide, Australia 22 0S 145 45E
90 Great Falls, U.S.A. 47 40N 110 45W
95 Great Inagua I., Bahamas 21 0N 73 20W
64 Great Indian Desert (Thar Desert), Pakistan 28 0N 72 0E
76 Great Karroo, S. Africa 32 42S 22 20E
67 Great Khingan Mts., China 47 0N 120 0E
22 Great Malvern, England 52 7N 2 19W
75 Great Namaqualand, S.W. Africa 24 50S 17 50E
25 Great Orme's Hd., Wales 53 21N 3 52W
23 Great Ouse R., England 52 35N 0 21E
85 Great Plains, N. America 40 0N 104 0W
74 Great Ruaha, R., Tanzania 8 0S 36 40E
43 Great St. Bernard P., Italy 45 47N 7 10E
90 Great Salt L., & Desert, U.S.A. 41 0N 112 30W
80 Great Sandy Desert, Australia 20 50S 123 30E
26 Great Shunner Fell, mt., England 54 22N 2 16W
34 Great Skellig, I., Ire. 51 47N 10 32W
88 Great Slave L., & R., Can. 62 0N 113 0W
23 Great Stour R., England 51 14N 1 0E
35 Great Sugar Loaf, mt., Ire. 53 9N 6 10W
80 Great Victorian Desert, Australia 28 30S 129 0E
66 Great Wall of China 38 12N 109 0E
89 Great Whale R., Can. 55 10N 76 0W
26 Great Whernside, mt., England 54 10N 1 59W
23 Great Yarmouth, Eng. 52 40N 1 44E
95 Greater Antilles, W.I. 18 0N 76 0W
23 Greater London, Co., Eng. 51 25N 0 10W
26 Greater Manchester, Co., Eng. 53 30N 2 20W
68 Greater Sunda Is., Indon. 4 20S 112 0E
27 Greatham, England 54 39N 1 15W
37 Gredos, Sa. de, mts., Spain 40 17N 5 20W
41 Greece, Europe 39 0N 23 0E
90 Greeley, U.S.A. 40 29N 104 48W
92 Green B., U.S.A. 45 0N 87 30W
90 Green R., Utah, U.S.A. 39 30N 110 0W
91 Green Bay, U.S.A. 44 32N 88 0W
84 Green Island, N.Z. 45 50S 170 30E
100 Greenland (Dan.), N. Amer. 70 0N 40 0W
100 Greenland Sea 75 0N 5 0W
31 Greenlaw, Scotland 55 42N 2 29W
35 Greenisland, Ireland 54 42N 5 50W
30 Greenock, Scotland 55 57N 4 45W
91 Greensboro, N.C., U.S.A. 36 8N 79 54W
72 Greenville, Liberia 5 2N 9 3W
91 Greenville, Miss., U.S.A. 33 29N 91 3W
91 Greenville, S.C., U.S.A. 34 53N 82 30W
91 Greenville, Texas, U.S.A. 33 9N 96 13W
23 Greenwich, Greater London, England 51 28N 0 0
93 Greenwich, U.S.A. 41 3N 73 40W
91 Greenwood, Miss., U.S.A. 33 30N 90 9W
91 Greenwood, S.C., U.S.A. 34 14N 82 19W
83 Gregory, L., Australia 29 10S 139 20E
82 Gregory Ra., Australia 19 0S 143 15E
49 Greifswald, Germany 54 3N 13 19E
94 Grenada, I., W. Indies 12 12N 61 45W
43 Grenade, France 43 42N 1 15E
94 Grenadines, West Indies 12 30N 61 30W
83 Grenfell, Australia 33 48S 148 4E
43 Grenoble, France 45 12N 5 44E
94 Grenville, Grenada, W.I. 12 8N 61 36W
82 Grenville, C., Australia 12 0S 143 20E
31 Gretna, Scotland 55 0N 3 1W
31 Gretna Green, Scotland 55 0N 3 5W
44 Grevenmacher, Lux. 49 41N 6 25E
83 Grey Ra., Australia 28 0S 143 0E
84 Grey, R., New Zealand 42 50S 171 30E
84 Greymouth, N.Z. 42 20S 171 20E
35 Greystones, Ireland 53 8N 6 4W
84 Greytown, New Zealand 41 0S 175 30E
76 Greytown, S. Africa 29 8S 30 39E
83 Griffith, Australia 34 13S 145 46E
43 Grignan, France 44 25N 5 0E
74 Grimari, Central Africa 5 43N 20 0E
27 Grimsby, England 53 35N 0 4W
49 Grimstad, Norway 58 22N 8 35E
45 Grindelwald, Switzerland 46 38N 8 3E
76 Griqualand East, S. Afr. 30 40S 29 0E
76 Griqualand West, Dist., South Africa 28 30S 23 20E
43 Gris Nez, C., France 50 53N 1 32E
45 Grisons, Canton, Switz., *see* Graubunden
26 Grizebeck, England 54 16N 3 10W
49 Grodno, U.S.S.R. 53 40N 23 50E
46 Grodzisk, Poland 52 16N 16 36E
42 Groix, I. de, France 47 40N 3 30W
47 Grójec, Poland 51 52N 21 0E
44 Gronau, Germany 52 14N 7 0E
48 Grong, Norway 64 30N 12 20E
49 Groningen, Netherlands 53 15N 6 35E
76 Groot, R., S. Africa 33 10S 24 12E
76 Groot-Brakrivier, S. Afr. 34 0S 22 5E
81 Groote Eylandt, Austral. 14 0S 136 35E
75 Grootfontein, S.W. Africa 19 28S 18 12E
76 Grootvloer, L., S. Africa 29 50S 20 17E
46 Gross Glockner, mt., Austria 47 7N 13 0E
46 Grossenbrode, Germany 54 21N 11 4E
46 Grossenhain, Germany 51 20N 13 30E
40 Grosseto, Italy 42 46N 11 7E
88 Grouard, Canada 55 40N 116 10W
62 Grozny, U.S.S.R. 43 10N 45 34E
49 Grudziadz, Poland 53 30N 18 50E
48 Grundarf, Iceland 64 55N 23 12W
32 Gruting Voe, Scotland 60 12N 1 32W
45 Gruyères, Switzerland 46 35N 7 5E
52 Gryazi, U.S.S.R. 52 23N 39 56E
45 Gstaad, Switzerland 46 27N 7 18E
65 Gua, India 22 18N 85 20E
65 Guad-i-Zireh, Afghan. 29 50N 62 30E
94 Guadalajara, Mexico 20 40N 103 17W
37 Guadalajara, Spain 40 39N 3 5W
81 Guadalcanal, I., Pac. Oc. 9 40S 160 0E
37 Guadalhorce, R., Spain 36 40N 4 20W
38 Guadalquivir, R., Spain 36 45N 6 25W
37 Guadalupe, Sa. de, mts., Spain 39 30N 5 30W
37 Guadarrama, Sa. de, mts., Spain 41 0N 4 0W
95 Guadeloupe, I., Fr. W.I. 16 25N 61 25W
37 Guadiana, R., Spain 39 10N 4 0W
37 Guadix, Spain 37 18N 3 10W
98 Guainia R., Colombia 2 30N 69 0W
95 Guajira, Pen., Colombia 12 10N 72 10W
99 Gualeguaychu, Arg. 32 50S 58 45W
5 Guam, I., Pacific Ocean 13 25N 144 50E
94 Guamuchil, Mexico 25 30N 108 0W
94 Guanajuato, Mexico 21 10N 101 0W
95 Guane, Cuba 22 15N 83 5W
95 Guatanamo, Cuba 20 0N 75 20W
99 Guapore, R., Brazil 13 30S 62 0W
99 Guaqui, Bolivia 16 25S 68 50W
31 Guard Bridge, Scot. 56 21N 2 52W
37 Guarda, Portugal 40 30N 7 15W
71 Guardafui, C., *see* Ras Asir
94 Guatemala, Cent. Amer. 16 0N 91 0W
95 Guaviare, R., Colombia 3 50N 69 0W
98 Guayaquil, & G. Ecuador 2 7S 80 0W
94 Guaymas, Mexico 27 55N 111 0W
46 Gubin, Poland 51 56N 14 43E
49 Gudbrandsdal, val., Nor. 61 40N 9 30E
64 Gudur, India 14 7N 79 45E
43 Guebwiller, France 47 55N 7 10E
37 Guecho, Spain 43 25N 3 2W
72 Guékedou, Guinea 8 40N 10 5W
89 Guelph, Canada 43 35N 80 20W
42 Guérande, France 47 20N 2 25W
43 Guéret, France 46 10N 1 54E
37 Guernica, Spain 43 25N 2 45W
42 Guernsey I., Channel Is. 49 30N 2 37W
23 Guestling, England 50 53N 0 40E
96 Guiana, Br., S. Amer., *see* Guyana
96 Guiana, French, S. Amer. 4 0N 53 0W
75 Guibes, S.W. Africa 26 42S 16 50E
72 Guiglo, Ivory Coast 6 45N 7 30W
75 Guija, Mozambique 24 35S 33 15E
52 Gukovo, U.S.S.R. 48 5N 39 59E
23 Guildford, England 51 14N 0 33W
25 Guilsfield, Wales 52 42N 3 9W
70 Guinea, reg., W. Africa 7 0N 5 0E
72 Guinea, Africa 10 0N 11 0E
72 Guinea-Bissau, W. Africa 12 0N 15 0W
42 Guingamp, France 48 32N 3 20W
42 Guiscard, France 49 30N 3 0E
43 Guise, France 49 55N 3 40E
64 Gujarat, st., India 23 0N 71 0E
64 Gujranwala, Pakistan 32 10N 74 21E
64 Gujrat, Pakistan 32 40N 74 3E
64 Gulbarga, India 17 12N 76 59E
80 Gulf Basin, Australia 15 20S 129 0E
86 Gulf Plain, U.S.A. 30 0N 90 0W
91 Gulfport, U.S.A. 30 29N 89 6W
83 Gulgong, Australia 32 11S 149 38E
60 Gulshat, U.S.S.R. 46 45N 74 20E
74 Gulu, Uganda 2 50N 32 22E
82 Gumlu, Australia 19 53S 147 41E
72 Gummi, Nigeria 12 4N 5 9E
64 Guna, India 24 40N 77 20E
64 Gunabad, Iran 34 12N 58 40E
83 Gundagai, Australia 35 5S 148 7E
67 Gunma, Pref., Japan 36 0N 138 0E
83 Gunnedah, Australia 31 0S 150 12E
90 Gunnison, R., U.S.A. 38 30N 107 30W
64 Guntur, India 16 15N 80 18E
64 Gupis, Kashmir 36 15N 73 20E
64 Gurdaspur, India 32 4N 75 30E
64 Gurgaon, India 28 27N 76 58E
98 Gurgueia, R., Brazil 9 0S 44 0W
24 Gurnard's Head, Eng. 50 12N 5 37W
51 Gürün, Turkey 38 40N 37 20E
98 Gurupi, R., Brazil 2 30S 46 40W
51 Guryev, U.S.S.R. 47 20N 51 50E
72 Gusau, Nigeria 12 18N 6 31E
49 Gusev, U.S.S.R. 54 35N 22 20E
46 Güstrow, Germany 53 50N 12 12E
82 Guthulungra, Australia 19 52S 147 50E
94 Gutierrez, Mexico 16 45N 94 20W
96 Guyana, S. Amer. 5 0N 58 0W
43 Guyenne, Prov., France 44 40N 1 0E
83 Guyra, Australia 30 22S 151 31E
65 Gwa, Burma 17 35N 94 25E
64 Gwadar, Pakistan 25 10N 62 18E
64 Gwalior, India 26 18N 78 18E
64 Gwatar, Iran 25 8N 61 20E
25 Gwaun-Cae-Gurwen, Wales 51 46N 3 51W
36 Gweebarra, B., Ireland 54 53N 8 30W
75 Gwelo, Rhodesia 19 28S 29 40E
25 Gwent, Co., Wales 51 45N 2 55W
83 Gwydir, R., Australia 29 30S 149 0E
25 Gwynedd, Co., Wales 53 0N 4 0W
65 Gyangtse, Tibet 28 54N 89 36E
60 Gyda Pen., U.S.S.R. 71 0N 78 0E
83 Gympie, Australia 26 10S 152 40E
47 Gyöngyös, Hungary 47 50N 20 10E
47 Györ, Hungary 47 40N 17 39E
88 Gypsumville, Canada 51 53N 98 35W

H

32 Haa, The, Scotland 60 20N 1 0W
48 Haápamäkj, Finland 62 17N 24 33E
44 Haarlem, Netherlands 52 23N 4 37E
64 Hab Nadi Chauki, Pakistan 24 55N 66 50E
67 Hachinohe, Japan 40 28N 141 30E
67 Hachioji, Japan 35 30N 139 30E
23 Hackney, Greater London, England 51 32N 0 2W
31 Haddington, Scotland 55 57N 2 47W
63 Hadera, Israel 32 27N 34 55E
62 Hadhramaut, Dist., Arabia 16 30N 49 30E
23 Hadleigh, England 52 3N 0 57E
22 Hadley, England 52 42N 2 28W
23 Hadlow, England 51 12N 0 20E
26 Hadrian's Wall, England 55 0N 2 25W
67 Haeju, Korea 38 5N 125 30E
64 Hafizabad, Pakistan 32 10N 73 35E
65 Haflong, India 25 0N 93 0E
48 Hafnarfjördur, Iceland 64 5N 21 58W
73 Hagar Banga, Sudan 10 40N 22 45E
44 Hagen, Germany 51 21N 7 29E
92 Hagerstown, U.S.A. 39 40N 77 37W
49 Hagfors, Sweden 60 2N 13 34E
67 Hagi, Japan 34 36N 131 28E
34 Hags Hd., Ireland 52 57N 9 29W
42 Hague, C. de la, France 49 45N 2 0W
44 Hague, The, Netherlands 52 5N 4 18E
43 Haguenau, France 48 50N 7 50E
63 Haifa, Israel 32 50N 35 0E
62 Hail, Saudi Arabia 27 49N 42 42E
67 Hailar, China 49 17N 119 50E
89 Haileybury, Canada 47 30N 79 57W
23 Hailsham, England 50 52N 0 16E
67 Hailun, China 47 17N 127 10E
48 Hailuoto I., Finland 65 0N 24 45E
66 Hainan I. & Str., China 19 30N 109 30E
44 Hainaut, Prov., Belgium 50 32N 4 0E
66 Haiphong, Vietnam 20 57N 106 45E
95 Haiti, Hispaniola 19 0N 74 0W
47 Hajdúböszörmény, Hung. 47 42N 21 30E
47 Hajnówka, Poland 52 45N 23 32E
64 Hala, Pakistan 25 45N 68 20E
46 Halberstadt, Germany 51 53N 11 2E
49 Halden, Norway 59 5N 11 5E
64 Haldwani, India 29 15N 79 25E
51 Haleb, Syria, *see* Aleppo
22 Halesowen, England 52 27N 2 3W
89 Halifax, Canada 44 45N 64 0W
26 Halifax, England 53 44N 1 52W
82 Halifax B., Australia 18 50S 147 0E
33 Halkirk, Scotland 58 30N 3 30W
49 Halland, Co., Sweden 57 10N 12 30E
44 Halle, Belgium 50 44N 4 14E
46 Halle, Germany 51 30N 11 59E
49 Hallefors, Sweden 59 46N 14 36E
100 Hallet, Antarctica 71 30S 170 0E
100 Halley Bay, Antarctica 72 30S 25 0W
49 Hallingdal, val., Nor. 60 40N 8 50E
48 Hallnas, Sweden 64 18N 19 40E
80 Hall's Creek, Australia 18 18S 127 33E
68 Halmahera, I., Indonesia 1 0N 128 0E
49 Halmstad, Sweden 56 42N 12 47E
72 Halq el Oued, Tunisia 36 58N 10 16E
49 Hals, Denmark 57 0N 10 16E
49 Halsingborg, Sweden 56 3N 12 41E
23 Halstead, England 51 57N 0 39E
27 Haltwhistle, England 54 59N 2 28W
64 Halvad, India 23 2N 71 3E
44 Ham, France 49 44N 3 3E
62 Hama, Syria 35 10N 36 42E
67 Hamada, Japan 34 58N 132 5E
62 Hamadan, Iran 34 45N 48 48E
67 Hamamatsu, Japan 34 45N 137 50E
49 Hamar, Norway 60 50N 11 5E
48 Hamaröy, Norway 68 6N 15 35E
64 Hambantota, Sri Lanka 6 10N 81 10E
22 Hambledon, England 50 56N 1 4W
27 Hambleton Hills, Eng. 54 15N 1 15W
46 Hamburg, Germany 53 35N 9 58E
49 Häme, Co., Finland 61 30N 24 30E
49 Hameenlinna, Finland 61 0N 24 30E
46 Hameln, Germany 52 9N 9 22E
80 Hamersley Ra., Austral. 22 10S 118 0E
66 Hami, China 43 8N 93 50E
83 Hamilton, Australia 37 40S 142 0E
95 Hamilton, Bermuda 32 15N 64 46W
89 Hamilton, Canada 43 14N 80 0W
84 Hamilton, N.Z. 37 47S 175 18E
92 Hamilton, Ohio, U.S.A. 39 23N 84 30W
82 Hamilton, R., Australia 22 55S 140 25E
31 Hamilton, Scotland 55 46N 4 3W
44 Hamm, Germany 51 40N 7 49E
62 Hammam, Saudi Arabia 20 15N 46 50E
48 Hammerfest, Norway 70 45N 23 37E
23 Hammersmith, Greater London, England 51 30N 0 11W
92 Hammond, U.S.A. 41 40N 87 30W
84 Hampden, New Zealand 45 18S 170 52E
22 Hampshire, Co., England 51 8N 1 15W
22 Hampshire Downs, Eng. 51 15N 1 0W
73 Hamrat esh Sheikh, Sudan 14 45N 27 40E
40 Hamrun, Malta 35 55N 14 27E
64 Hamun-e-Helmand, L., Afghanistan 31 15N 61 15E
41 Han Pijesak, Yugoslavia 44 0N 19 0E
67 Hanamaki, Japan 39 25N 140 30E
45 Hanau, Germany 50 10N 8 50E
66 Hanchung, China 32 57N 107 7E
74 Handeni, Tanzania 5 20S 38 0E
90 Hanford, U.S.A. 36 18N 119 37W
67 Hangchow, & B., China 29 55N 120 15E
49 Hanko, Finland 59 49N 22 55E
66 Hanku, China 39 15N 117 40E
88 Hanna, Canada 51 35N 112 0W
66 Hanoi, Vietnam 20 57N 105 55E
46 Hanover, Germany 52 25N 9 45E
99 Hanover I., Chile 50 30S 75 30W
64 Hansi, India 29 5N 75 55E
66 Hantan, China 36 40N 114 30E
66 Hanyang, China 30 30N 114 20E
48 Haparanda, Finland 65 58N 24 3E
64 Hapur, India 28 45N 77 40E
62 Haql, Saudi Arabia 29 10N 35 3E
66 Har Us Nuur, L., Mongolia 48 0N 92 10E
67 Harbin, China 45 40N 126 40E
89 Harbour Grace, Canada 47 40N 53 22W
46 Harburg, Germany 53 28N 9 58E
82 Harcourt, Australia 24 17S 149 55E
49 Hardanger Fd., Norway 60 10N 6 5E
44 Harderwijk, Netherlands 52 21N 5 38E
64 Hardoi, India 27 30N 80 5E
64 Hardwar, India 30 0N 78 9E
44 Harelbeke, Belgium 50 50N 3 20E
43 Harfleur, France 49 30N 0 10E
64 Hari Rud, R., Afghan. 34 25N 64 20E
23 Haringey, Gr. London, Eng. 51 33N 0 15E
65 Haringhata, R., Bangla. 22 0N 90 0E
25 Harlech, Wales 52 50N 4 7W
44 Harlingen, Netherlands 53 11N 5 26E
90 Harlingen, U.S.A. 26 14N 97 45W
23 Harlow, England 51 47 0 8E
48 Harnösand, Sweden 62 37N 17 55E
32 Haroldswick, Scotland 60 47N 0 50W
23 Harpenden, England 51 49N 0 21W
51 Harran, Turkey 36 58N 39 3E
32 Harris, & Sd., Scotland 57 50N 7 0W
92 Harrisburg, Pa., U.S.A. 40 22N 76 48W
91 Harrisonburg, U.S.A. 38 43N 78 56W
27 Harrogate, England 54 0N 1 43W
23 Harrow, Gr. London, Eng. 51 37N 0 21W
48 Harstad, Norway 68 48N 16 25E
76 Hartbees, R., S. Africa 29 8S 20 48E
92 Hartford, Conn., U.S.A. 41 49N 72 49W
31 Harthill, Scotland 55 52N 3 45W
24 Hartland Pt., England 51 2N 4 31W
27 Hartlepool, England 54 42N 1 11W
31 Hartley, England 55 5N 1 27W
75 Hartley, Rhodesia 18 8S 30 10E
76 Harts, R., S. Africa 26 50S 25 30E
22 Harwell, England 51 32N 1 16W
23 Harwich, England 51 57N 1 18E
64 Haryana, st., India 29 0N 76 00E
46 Harz Mts., Germany 51 45N 10 40E
62 Hasa, Dist., Arabia 26 0N 49 0E
63 Hasbaiya, Lebanon 33 25N 35 41E
23 Haslemere, England 51 5N 0 41W
26 Haslingden, England 53 43N 2 19W
64 Hassan, India 13 4N 76 8E
44 Hasselt, Belgium 50 56N 5 21E
72 Hassi el Gassi, Algeria 30 40N 6 0E
72 Hassi Inifel, Algeria 29 50N 3 28E
72 Hassi Messaoud, Algeria 32 10N 6 10E
72 Hassi R'Mel, Algeria 32 20N 3 30E
23 Hastings, England 50 52N 0 35E
84 Hastings, New Zealand 39 44S 176 53E
90 Hastings, Neb., U.S.A. 40 30N 98 30W
83 Hastings Ra., Australia 31 0S 152 0E
23 Hatfield, England 51 46N 0 11W
24 Hatherleigh, England 50 49N 4 4W
64 Hathras, India 27 40N 78 35E
65 Hatia, Bangladesh 22 30N 91 5E
63 Hatsoi Ashdod, Israel 31 46N 34 42E
91 Hatteras, C., U.S.A. 35 15N 75 20W
91 Hattiesburg, U.S.A. 31 20N 89 19W
47 Hatvan, Hungary 47 40N 19 45E
49 Haugesund, Norway 59 25N 5 13E
84 Hauraki G., N.Z. 36 30S 175 5E
62 Havrun, Wadi, Iraq 33 30N 41 30E
42 Haut-Rhin, Dépt., France 48 0N 7 20E
42 Haute-Corse, Dépt., Fr. 42 15N 9 5E
42 Haute-Garonne, Dépt., Fr. 43 30N 1 10E
42 Haute-Loire, Dépt., Fr. 45 20N 3 50E
42 Haute-Marne, Dépt., Fr. 48 18N 5 7E
42 Haute-Saône, Dépt., Fr. 47 30N 6 0E
42 Haute-Savoie, Dépt., Fr. 46 4N 6 38E
42 Haute-Vienne, Dépt., Fr. 45 50N 1 12E
42 Hautes-Alpes, Dépt., Fr. 44 43N 6 40E
42 Hauts-de-Seine, Dépt., Fr. 49 0N 2 10E
42 Hautes-Pyrénées, Dépt., Fr. 43 12N 0 12E
44 Hautmont, France 50 13N 3 55E
38 Hauts Plateau, Algeria 35 0N 2 0E
95 Havana, Cuba 23 0N 82 30W
23 Havant, England 50 51N 0 59W
46 Havel, R., Germany 52 40N 12 15E
44 Havelange, Belgium 50 23N 5 15E
84 Havelock, New Zealand 41 18S 173 46E
25 Haverfordwest, Wales 51 49N 4 58W
23 Haverhill, England 52 6N 0 27E
93 Haverhill, U.S.A. 42 50N 71 2W
23 Havering, Greater London, England 51 33N 0 15E
90 Havre, U.S.A. 48 35N 109 40W
90 Hawaii, st., U.S.A. 21 0N 158 0W
90 Hawaiian, Is., Pac. Oc. 21 0N 158 0W
24 Hawarden, Wales 53 11N 2 59W
84 Hawea, L., New Zealand 44 30S 169 8E
84 Hawera, New Zealand 39 36S 174 30E
26 Hawes Water, L., England 54 31N 2 48W
31 Hawick, Scotland 55 25N 2 48W
84 Hawke B., N.Z. 39 15S 177 30E
83 Hawker, Aus,tralia 31 53S 138 25E
84 Hawke's Bay Dist., N.Z. 39 25S 176 35E
93 Hawkesbury, Ont., Can. 45 35N 74 48W
90 Hawthorne, U.S.A. 38 30N 118 50W
83 Hay, Australia 34 37S 144 45E
25 Hay, Wales 52 4N 3 5W
81 Hay, R., Australia 23 10S 137 0E
43 Hayange, France 49 20N 6 0E
26 Haydon Bridge, England 54 58N 2 14W
24 Hayle, England 50 11N 5 26W
90 Hays, U.S.A. 38 55N 99 23W
23 Hayward's Heath, Eng. 51 0N 0 5W
65 Hazaribagh, India 23 58N 85 15E
88 Hazelton, Canada 55 23N 127 45W
92 Hazleton, U.S.A. 40 59N 76 0W
22 Headington, England 51 46N 1 13W
83 Healesville, Australia 37 45S 145 33E
27 Heanor, England 53 1N 1 22W
11 Heard I., Indian Ocean 53 0S 74 0E
89 Hearst, Canada 49 40N 83 25W
23 Heathfield, England 50 58N 0 16E
27 Hebburn, England 54 59N 1 30W
26 Hebden Bridge, Eng. 53 45N 2 0W
83 Hebel, Australia 28 59S 147 59E
32 Hebrides, Inner, Scot. 56 40N 6 50W

32 Hebrides, Outer, Scot. 57 40N 7 0W
89 Hebron, Canada 58 10N 62 50W
63 Hebron, Jordan 31 32N 35 5E
48 Hede, Sweden 62 23N 13 43E
49 Hedemora, Sweden 60 18N 15 58E
84 Hedgehope, N.Z. 46 12S 168 34E
49 Hedmark, Co., Norway 61 45N 11 0E
22 Hednesford, England 52 43N 2 0W
44 Heemstede, Netherlands 52 19N 4 37E
44 Heerenveen, Netherlands 52 58N 5 55E
44 Heerlen, Netherlands 50 53N 5 58E
73 Heiban, Sudan 11 13N 30 27E
45 Heidelberg, Germany 49 26N 8 46E
76 Heidelburg, S. Africa 34 5S 20 50E
45 Heidenheim, Germany 48 41N 10 8E
76 Heilbron, S. Africa 27 8S 28 12E
45 Heilbronn, Germany 49 5N 9 19E
57 Heilungkiang, Prov., China
45 0N 130 0E
49 Heinola, Finland 61 13N 26 10E
55 Heinze Is., Burma 14 20N 97 45E
2 Hejaz, dist., Saudi Arabia 25 30N 38 30E
8 Hekla Torfa Jökull, Ice. 64 0N 19 30W
0 Helena, Mont., U.S.A. 46 40N 111 55W
0 Helensburgh, Scotland 56 1N 4 43W
4 Helensville, New Zealand 36 39S 174 28E
8 Helgeland, Dist., Norway
66 0N 13 15E
6 Heligoland I., & B., Ger. 54 11N 7 52E
1 Hellespont, see Dardanelles
6 Hellifield, England 54 1N 2 14W
7 Hellin, Spain 38 30N 1 40W
5 Helville, Madagascar 13 20S 48 12E
4 Helmand Rud R., Afghan. 30 25N 63 0E
4 Helmond, Netherlands 51 30N 5 41E
3 Helmsdale, & R., Scot. 58 7N 3 39W
7 Helmsley, England 54 14N 1 3W
9 Helsingfors, see Helsinki
9 Helsingör, Denmark 56 2N 12 35E
9 Helsinki (Helsingfors), Fin.
60 13N 24 55E
4 Helston, England 50 6N 5 17W
6 Helvellyn, mt., England 54 30N 3 0W
3 Helwân, Egypt 29 50N 31 20E
3 Hemel Hempstead, Eng. 51 45N 0 28W
9 Hemse, Sweden 57 14N 18 21E
7 Hemsworth, England 53 37N 1 21W
4 Hemyock, England 50 55N 3 14W
7 Henares, R., Spain 41 0N 2 50W
2 Hendaye, France 43 22N 1 50W
2 Henderson, Ken., U.S.A. 37 50N 87 30W
1 Henderson, N.C., U.S.A.
36 17N 78 25W
2 Henderson, Scotland 57 42N 5 47W
3 Hendon, Australia 28 2S 151 55E
Hengchun, Taiwan 22 0N 120 40E
4 Hengelo, Netherlands 52 17N 6 48E
4 Hengoed, Wales 51 39N 3 14W
6 Hengyang, China 26 30N 111 58W
4 Hénin-Lietard, France 50 25N 2 58E
3 Henley, England 51 31N 0 54W
3 Henlow, England 52 2N 0 18W
9 Henrietta Maria, C., Can. 55 0N 82 38W
5 Hentiyn Nuruu, mt., Mongolia
49 0N 108 0E
3 Henty, Australia 35 32S 147 2E
5 Henzada, Burma 17 39N 95 37E
4 Herat, Afghanistan 34 28N 62 3E
4 Herat, Prov., Afghan. 34 0N 63 0E
2 Hérault, Dépt., France 43 37N 2 57E
2 Herberton, Australia 17 28S 145 25E
4 Herbertstown, Ireland 52 32N 8 29W
Hercegnovi, Y-slav. 42 25N 18 30E
Hercegovina, Province, Yugoslavia
43 30N 17 45E
Herdhubreid, Mt., Ice. 65 10N 16 21W
Hereford, Eng. 52 4N 2 42W
Hereford & Worcester, Co., England
52 15N 2 25W
Herentals, Belgium 51 11N 4 51E
Herford, Germany 52 8N 8 40E
Herisau, Switzerland 47 24N 9 18E
Hermanus, S. Africa 34 15S 19 10E
Hermidale, Australia 31 26S 146 54E
Hermitage, N.Z. 43 45S 170 7E
Hermon, Mt., Syria-Leb. 33 25N 35 50E
Hernad, R., Hungary 48 30N 21 5E
Herne Bay, England 51 22N 1 9E
Herning, Denmark 56 8N 9 0E
Heron Bay, Can. 48 50N 86 10W
Herrera, Spain 39 12N 5 2W
Herstal, Belgium 50 38N 5 35E
Herstmonceaux, Eng. 50 53 0 21E
Hertford, & Co., Eng. 51 48N 0 4W
s'Hertogenbosch, Neth. 51 42N 5 18E
Herzliya, Israel 32 10N 34 50E
Hesse, Land, Germany 50 27N 9 10E
Hessle, England 53 44N 0 26W
Hetton-le-Hole, England 54 49N 1 26W
Hexham, England 54 58N 2 0W
Heybridge, England 51 44N 0 42E
Heysham, England 54 4N 2 54W
Heywood, Australia 38 12S 141 36E
Heywood, England 53 34N 2 19W
Hibbing, U.S.A. 47 30N 92 50W
Hidalgo del Parral, Mexico
27 0N 105 40W
Hierro I., Canary Is. 27 45N 17 58W
High Pike, mt., England 54 42N 3 4W
High River, Canada 50 30N 114 0W
High Tatra, mts., Cz-slov. 49 0N 20 0E
High Willhays, England 50 41N 4 1W
High Wycombe, England 51 38N 0 45W
Higham Ferrers, England 52 18N 0 35W
Highland, Reg., Scotland 57 30N 5 0W
22 Highley, England 52 25N 2 23W
22 Highworth, England 51 38N 1 44W
67 Hikone, Japan 35 7N 136 20E
84 Hikurangi, N.Z. 35 42S 174 17E
46 Hildesheim, Germany 52 10N 9 58E
23 Hilgay, England 52 33N 0 24E
62 Hilla, Iraq 32 39N 44 30E
44 Hillegom, Netherlands 52 18N 4 34E
23 Hillingdon, Gr. London, Eng.
51 34N 0 27W
91 Hillsboro, U.S.A. 32 0N 97 0W
36 Hillsborough, N. Ireland 54 28N 6 4E
94 Hillsborough, Carriacou, W.I.
12 14N 61 12W
83 Hillston, Australia 33 29S 145 32E
36 Hilltown, N. Ireland 54 12N 6 9W
90 Hilo, Hawaii 19 45N 155 15W
44 Hilversum, Netherlands 52 15N 5 10E
64 Himachal Pradesh, Prov., India
31 30N 77 0E
65 Himalayas, mts., Asia 29 0N 82 0E
64 Himatnagar, India 23 37N 72 57E
67 Himeji, Japan 34 56N 134 48E
67 Himi, Japan 36 55N 137 0E
82 Hinchinbrook I., Australia
18 21S 146 20E
22 Hinckley, England 52 33N 1 22W
74 Hinde Rapids, Zaïre 5 25S 27 3E
62 Hindian, R., Iran 30 20N 50 20E
26 Hindley, England 53 33N 2 35W
63 Hindu Kush, Afghanistan
36 0N 71 30E
64 Hindubagh, Pakistan 30 55N 67 42E
64 Hindupur, India 13 45N 77 25E
88 Hines Cr., Canada 56 20N 118 40W
66 Hingan, China 25 55N 110 40E
66 Hingi, China 25 10N 105 8E
64 Hingol, R., Pakistan 27 30N 66 0E
64 Hingoli, India 19 50N 77 6E
24 Hinkley Pt., England 51 13N 3 7W
48 Hinnöy, I., Norway 68 40N 16 0E
67 Hino, C., Japan 35 25N 132 45E
37 Hinojosa, Spain 38 30N 5 15W
45 Hinterrhein, R., Switz. 46 35N 9 20E
92 Hinton, U.S.A. 37 40N 80 50W
67 Hirosaki, Japan 40 35N 140 30E
67 Hiroshima, & Pref., Japan
34 30N 132 35E
43 Hirson, France 49 55N 4 3E
25 Hirwaun, Wales 51 43N 3 30W
63 Hisban, Jordan 31 48N 35 49E
95 Hispaniola, I., W.I. 17 30N 71 0W
64 Hissar, India 29 11N 75 41E
23 Hitchin, England 51 57N 0 17W
48 Hitra, I., Norway 63 30N 8 45E
49 Hjälmaren, L., Sweden 59 25N 15 50E
48 Hjeradsflói, Iceland 65 40N 14 0W
48 Hjeradsvötn, R., Iceland 65 40N 19 10W
49 Hjorring, Denmark 57 25N 10 0E
68 Ho-Chi-Minh City, Vietnam
10 40N 106 37E
66 Hoa-Binh, Vietnam 21 0N 104 25E
83 Hobart, Australia 42 49S 147 6E
90 Hobbs, U.S.A. 32 43N 103 11W
44 Hoboken, Belgium 51 11N 4 21E
49 Hobro, Denmark 56 39N 9 46E
66 Hochih, China 24 45N 107 25E
45 Hochst, Germany 50 6N 8 32E
66 Hochwan, China 30 15N 105 50E
45 Hockenheim, Germany 49 20N 8 32E
62 Hodeida, Yemen 14 50N 42 55E
88 Hodgson, Canada 51 20N 97 40W
47 Hódmezövásarhely, Hungary
46 28N 20 22E
44 Hoek van Holland, Netherlands
52 0N 4 10E
46 Hof, Germany 50 20N 11 54E
48 Hof, Iceland 64 32N 14 35W
66 Hofei, China 31 50N 117 0E
76 Hofmeyr, S. Africa 31 35S 25 45E
48 Hofs Jökull, mt., Iceland 64 45N 19 0W
48 Hofsos, Iceland 65 52N 19 19W
67 Hofu, Japan 34 0N 131 30E
62 Hofuf, Saudi Arabia 25 20N 49 40E
72 Hoggar, mts., Algeria 23 0N 6 30E
23 Hog's Back, England 51 13N 0 40W
27 Hogsthorpe, England 53 13N 0 19E
66 Hohsien, China 24 35N 111 20E
66 Hoihow (Haikow), China 20 0N 110 10E
74 Hoima, Uganda 1 25N 31 25E
67 Hokang, China 47 25N 130 35E
84 Hokitika, New Zealand 42 44S 171 2E
67 Hokkaido, I., & Pref., Japan
43 30N 143 0E
66 Hokow, China 22 55N 103 10E
23 Holbeach & Marsh, Eng. 52 48N 0 1E
83 Holbrook, Australia 35 42S 147 15E
27 Holderness, Dist., Eng. 53 48N 0 5W
90 Holdrege, U.S.A. 40 30N 99 21W
95 Holguin, Cuba 20 50N 76 20W
75 Hollams Bird I., S.W. Afr. 24 35S 14 30E
44 Holland, N., Prov., Neth. 52 29N 4 47E
44 Holland, S., Prov., Neth. 52 5N 4 30E
82 Hollandia, see Jayapura
36 Hollymount, Ireland 53 39N 9 7W
35 Hollywood, Ireland 53 6N 6 36W
90 Hollywood, U.S.A. 34 10N 118 28W
48 Holmavik, Iceland 65 42N 21 43W
27 Holmfirth, England 53 34N 1 47W
48 Holmsund, Sweden 63 42N 20 20E
63 Holon, Israel 32 2N 34 47E
89 Hólsteinsborg, Greenland 67 0N 53 20W
24 Holsworthy, England 50 48N 4 21W
23 Holt, England 52 55N 1 6E
25 Holt, Wales 53 5N 2 54W
27 Holy I., England 55 41N 1 47W
30 Holy I., Scotland 55 31N 5 4W
25 Holy I., Wales 53 18N 4 38W
25 Holyhead, & B., Wales 53 20N 4 39W
92 Holyoke, U.S.A. 42 12N 72 40W
25 Holywell, Wales 53 17N 3 15W
36 Holywood, N. Ireland 54 39N 5 50W
65 Homalin, Burma 25 0N 94 55E
72 Hombori, Mali 15 20N 1 38W
45 Homburg, Germany 49 18N 7 18E
89 Home, B., Canada 68 40N 67 0W
82 Home Hill, Australia 19 40S 147 20E
88 Homer, Alaska 59 40N 151 35W
82 Homestead, Australia 20 20S 145 40E
62 Homs, Syria 34 55N 36 43E
76 Hondeklipbaai, S. Africa 30 22S 17 18E
94 Honduras, & G. of, Central America
15 0N 86 30W
49 Hönefoss, Norway 60 10N 10 10E
43 Honfleur, France 49 24N 0 12E
66 Hong Kong, China 22 20N 114 10E
24 Honiton, England 50 48N 3 12W
67 Honjo, Japan 39 28N 140 0E
90 Honolulu, Pac. Oc. 21 20N 158 0W
67 Honshu, I., Japan 36 0N 139 0E
90 Hood, Mt., U.S.A. 45 20N 121 0W
44 Hoogeveen Netherlands 52 45N 6 30E
44 Hoogezand, Netherlands
53 11N 6 45E
82 Hook I., Australia 20 4S 149 0E
44 Hoorn. Netherlands 52 40N 5 4E
91 Hope, U.S.A. 33 43N 93 38W
100 Hope Bay, Antarctica 60 0S 57 0W
89 Hopedale, Canada 55 27N 60 22W
76 Hopefield, S. Africa 33 0S 18 22E
83 Hopetoun, Australia 35 48S 142 26E
80 Hopetoun, Australia 33 52S 120 0E
76 Hopetown, S. Africa 29 42S 24 10E
92 Hopkinsville, U.S.A. 36 55N 87 29W
90 Hoquiam, U.S.A. 47 0N 123 58W
62 Hor al Hammar, Iraq 30 50N 46 0E
49 Hordaland, Co., Norway 60 8N 6 20E
31 Horden, England 54 46N 1 18W
45 Horgen, Switzerland 47 16N 8 35E
27 Horley, England 51 11N 0 11W
46 Horn, Austria 48 40N 15 40E
48 Horn (North C.), Ice. 66 29N 22 27W
99 Horn, C., Chile 55 47S 67 0W
36 Horn Hd., Ireland 55 13N 7 57W
48 Horna, Fjord, Iceland 64 17N 15 10E
48 Hornavan, L., Seden 66 30N 18 0E
27 Horncastle, England 53 12N 0 8W
23 Horndean, England 50 55N 1 0W
92 Hornell, U.S.A. 42 20N 77 44W
83 Hornsby, Australia 33 36S 151 2E
27 Hornsea, England 53 54N 0 9W
35 Horseleap, Ireland 53 24N 7 34W
49 Horsens, Denmark 55 53N 9 45E
27 Horsforth, England 53 51N 1 38W
23 Horsham, England 51 3N 0 20W
83 Horsham, Australia 36 42S 142 13E
23 Horsham St. Faith, England
52 41N 1 15E
49 Hörten, Norway 59 25N 10 27E
26 Horton-in-Ribblesdale, England
54 10N 2 19W
88 Horton, R., Canada 69 0N 124 0W
26 Horwich, England 53 36N 2 33W
64 Hoshangabad, India 22 50N 77 58E
64 Hoshiarpur, India 31 45N 75 58E
64 Hospet, India 15 10N 76 15E
34 Hospital, Ireland 52 28N 8 28W
37 Hospitalet, Spain 41 22N 2 4E
99 Hoste, I., Argentina 55 30S 70 0W
91 Hot Springs, U.S.A. 34 25N 93 2W
48 Hoting, Sweden 64 4N 16 20E
44 Houffalize, Belgium 50 8N 5 48E
27 Houghton-le-Spring, Eng. 54 51N 1 28W
84 Houhora, New Zealand 34 49S 173 9E
93 Houlton, U.S.A. 46 15N 68 0W
91 Houma, U.S.A. 29 41N 90 43W
32 Hourn, L., Scotland 57 7N 5 35W
23 Hounslow, England 51 28N 0 23W
91 Houston, U.S.A. 29 45N 95 27W
76 Houtbaai, S. Africa 34 3S 18 27E
76 Houtkraal, S. Africa 30 30S 24 0E
66 Hovd, (Jargalant), Mongolia
48 0N 91 30E
23 Hove, England 50 49N 0 10W
83 Howard, Australia 25 18S 152 35E
27 Howden, England 53 46N 0 52W
83 Howe, C., Australia 37 30S 149 58E
33 Howe of the Mearns, Scotland
56 50N 2 30W
76 Howick, S. Africa 29 30S 30 12E
82 Howick Group, Australia 14 20S 145 30E
65 Howrah, India 22 40N 88 15E
35 Howth, & Hd., Ireland 53 23N 6 3W
33 Hoy, I. & Sd., Scotland 58 50N 3 19W
49 Höyanger, Norway 61 25N 6 5E
26 Hoylake, England 53 23N 3 12W
46 Hradec Králové, Cz-slov.
50 8N 15 52E
48 Hruta Fjord, Iceland 65 30N 21 7W
65 Hsenwi, Burma 23 15N 98 0E
65 Hsiao Khingan Shan, Mts., China
50 0N 128 0E
55 Hsi-liao, R., China 43 0N 122 0E
66 Hsuchang, China 34 0N 115 10E
67 Hualien, Taiwan 23 55N 121 30E
98 Huallaga, R., Peru 8 30S 76 10W
75 Huambo, Angola 12 35S 15 48E
98 Huancavelica, Peru 12 50S 75 0W
98 Huascaran, Mt., Peru 8 45S 77 30W
99 Huasco, Chile 28 20S 71 15W
94 Huatabampo, Mexico 26 50N 109 40W
64 Hubli, India 15 20N 75 2E
67 Huchow, China 30 46N 120 10E
27 Hucknall, England 53 3N 1 12W
27 Huddersfield, England 53 38N 1 47W
49 Hudiksvall, Sweden 61 47N 17 5E
93 Hudson, & R., U.S.A. 42 0N 74 0W
89 Hudson B., Canada 59 0N 86 0W
89 Hudson Str., Canada 62 0N 70 0W
68 Hué, Vietnam 16 33N 107 40E
37 Huelva, Spain 37 16N 6 59W
37 Huesca, Spain 42 9N 0 25W
82 Hughenden, Australia 20 58S 144 5E
66 Huhehot, China 40 50N 111 20E
98 Huila, Mt., Colombia 3 0N 76 5W
94 Huixtla, Mexico 15 15N 92 45W
65 Hukawng, Valley, Burma
26 30N 96 0E
63 Hula, L., Israel 33 4N 35 38E
89 Hull, Canada 45 30N 75 48W
27 Hull, & R., England 53 45N 0 20W
44 Hulst, Netherlands 51 17N 4 4E
67 Hulun, China, see Hailar
27 Humber, R., England 53 35N 0 20W
27 Humberside, Co., Eng. 53 50N 0 30W
88 Humboldt, Canada 52 25N 105 12W
90 Humboldt, R., U.S.A. 41 0N 117 30W
83 Hume L., Australia 36 5S 147 30E
48 Huna Floi, Iceland 65 45N 20 50W
66 Hunan, Prov., China 27 0N 111 30E
67 Hunchun, China 43 0N 130 12E
47 Hunedoara, Rumania 45 44N 22 53E
47 Hungary, Europe 47 12N 19 10E
22 Hungerford, England 51 25N 1 30W
66 Hungkiang, China 27 5N 109 20E
67 Hungnam, Korea 39 55N 127 45E
66 Hungshui, R., China 23 50N 108 0E
67 Hungtze Hu., L., China
33 20N 118 30E
27 Hunmanby, England 54 11N 0 19W
46 Hunsrück, Mts., Germany 50 0N 7 20E
27 Hunstanton, England 52 57N 0 29E
83 Hunter I., Australia 40 30S 144 46E
30 Hunterston, Scotland 55 45N 4 55W
84 Hunterville, N.Z. 39 56S 175 31E
23 Huntingdon, England 52 20N 0 12W
92 Huntington, Ind., U.S.A.
40 55N 85 28W
91 Huntington, W. Va., U.S.A.
38 21N 82 32W
84 Huntly, New Zealand 37 30S 175 8E
33 Huntly, Scotland 57 27N 2 47W
92 Huntsville, Canada 45 23N 79 13W
91 Huntsville, Alabama, U.S.A.
34 44N 86 17W
91 Huntsville, Texas, U.S.A.
30 44N 95 35W
83 Huonville, Australia 43 2S 147 0E
66 Hupei, prov., China 31 30N 113 0E
62 Hurghada, Egypt 27 15N 33 50E
30 Hurlford, Scotland 55 35N 4 29W
92 Huron, L., N. America 45 0N 82 30W
90 Huron, U.S.A. 44 25N 98 18W
23 Hurstpierpoint, England 50 56N 0 11W
48 Husavik, Iceland 66 3N 17 15W
49 Huskvarna, Sweden 57 50N 14 19E
63 Hussien Bridge, Jordan 31 43N 35 32E
90 Hutchinson, U.S.A. 38 0N 98 0W
45 Huttwil, Switzerland 47 7N 7 50E
44 Huy, Belgium 50 30N 5 16E
26 Huyton, England 53 25N 2 52W
48 Hvammr, Iceland 65 10N 21 50W
48 Hvammsfjord, Iceland 65 5N 22 30W
40 Hvar, I., Yugoslavia 43 10N 16 42E
48 Hvitá, R., Iceland 64 40N 21 30W
48 Hvitarvatn, L., Iceland 64 35N 19 50W
66 Hwai-ho, R., China 33 0N 116 0E
66 Hwainan, China 32 40N 117 30E
66 Hwaiyang, mts.. China 31 30N 115 0E
66 Hwang-ho, R., China 39 0N 107 0E
66 Hwang (Ma) R., China 34 0N 100 30E
66 Hwangshih, China 30 15N 115 0E
66 Hweitseh, China 26 50N 103 0E
66 Hyargas Nuur, Mongolia
49 0N 93 30E
26 Hyde, England 53 27N 2 5W
64 Hyderabad, India 17 25N 78 35E
64 Hyderabad, Pak. 25 20N 68 30E
43 Hyères, & Is., France 43 8N 6 6E
90 Hyndman, Pk., U.S.A. 44 0N 114 0W
67 Hyogo, Pref., Japan 35 0N 135 0E
23 Hythe, Kent, England 51 4N 1 4E
49 Hyvinkaa, Finland 60 38N 25 0E

I

34 Iar Connaught, Dist., Ire. 53 18N 9 20W
47 Iasi, Rumania 47 10N 27 37E
72 Ibadan, Nigeria 7 40N 3 50E
95 Ibagué, Colombia 4 30N 75 25W
67 Ibaraki, Pref., Japan 36 20N 140 20E
98 Ibarra, Ecuador 0 23N 78 15W
72 Ibi, Nigeria 8 7N 9 56E
98 Ibiapaba, Sa. da, mts., Brazil
4 0S 41 10W
99 Ibicuy, Argentina 33 40S 59 10W
37 Ibiza, I. & Tn., Spain 39 0N 1 30E
22 Ibstock, England 52 42N 1 23W
98 Icá, R., Brazil 3 0S 69 0W
98 Ica, Peru 14 5S 75 30W
16 Iceland, Atlantic Oc. 65 0N 17 30W
61 Icha, U.S.S.R. 55 45N 154 4E
66 Ichang, China 30 59N 111 23E
65 Ichchapuram, India 19 5N 84 40E
67 Ichinohe, Japan 40 8N 141 18E
41 Ida, Mt., Turkey 39 40N 27 15E
90 Idaho, st., U.S.A. 44 0N 115 50W
90 Idaho Falls, U.S.A. 43 30N 112 2W
45 Idar-Oberstein, Germany 49 43N 7 17E
73 Idd el Ghanam, Sudan 11 30N 24 25E
73 Idehan, Erg, Des., Libya 27 30N 12 0E
73 Idehan Marzuq, Dunes, Libya
24 50N 13 51E
72 Idelès, Algeria 23 58N 5 58E
73 Idfu, Egypt 24 57N 32 50E
41 Idhi, Mt., Crete 35 15N 24 50E
41 Idhra, I., Greece 37 20N 23 25E
74 Idi Amin Dada, L., Uganda-Zaïre
0 20S 29 35E
74 Idiofa, Zaïre 5 0S 19 45E
27 Idle, R., England 53 28N 0 58W
22 Idmiston, England 51 8N 1 43W
23 Idsworth, England 50 56N 0 56W
41 Ierapetra, Crete 35 5N 25 40E
40 Ierzu, Italy 39 42N 9 35E
75 Ifanadiana, Madagascar 21 19S 47 50E
72 Ife, Nigeria 7 30N 4 31E
72 Iferouane, Niger 19 6N 8 30E
72 Ifni, Morocco 29 15N 10 0W
61 Igarka, U.S.S.R. 67 25N 87 20E
72 Igbetti, Nigeria 8 44N 4 8E
49 Iggesund, Sweden 61 43N 17 6E
40 Iglesias, Sardinia, Italy 39 21N 8 33E
92 Ignace, Canada 49 30N 91 40W
94 Iguala, Mexico 18 30N 99 15W
99 Iguape, Brazil 24 50S 47 45W
99 Iguassu, R. & Falls, Brazil
25 30S 54 30W
99 Iguatú, Brazil 6 8S 39 15W
74 Iguéla, Gabon 2 5S 9 16E
48 Ii, & R., Finland 65 15N 25 30E
48 Iisalmi, Finland 63 35N 27 12E
72 Ijebu Ode, Nigeria 7 0N 3 58E
44 Ijmuiden, Netherlands 52 28N 4 35E
44 Ijsselmeer, Netherlands 52 45N 5 15E
41 Ikaria, I., Greece 37 35N 26 10E
67 Ikeda, Japan 34 0N 133 56E
67 Ilagan, Philippines 17 0N 121 58E
99 Ilapel, Chile 31 30S 71 0W
47 Ilawa, Poland 53 40N 19 31W
43 Ile de France, Prov., Fr. 49 0N 2 30E
43 Ile Rousse. France 42 35N 8 50E
74 Ilebo (Port Francqui), Zaïre 4 17S 20 47E
50 Ilek, R., U.S.S.R. 51 0N 55 15E
24 Ilfracombe, England 51 11N 4 7W
82 Ilfracombe, Australia 23 30S 144 28E
99 Ilhéus, Brazil 14 44S 39 18W
66 Ili, R., Sinkiang, China 43 20N 81 0E
60 Ili, R., U.S.S.R. 44 10N 77 25E
60 Ilich, U.S.S.R. 41 0N 68 20E
41 Iliodhromia I., Greece 39 10N 23 45E
72 Ilizi, Algeria 26 32N 8 33E
27 Ilkeston, England 52 59N 1 18W
26 Ilkley, England 53 55N 1 50W
42 Ille-et-Vilaine, Dépt., Fr. 48 22N 1 55W
45 Iller, R., Germany 47 48N 10 7E
98 Illmani, Mt., Bolivia 16 20S 67 40W
92 Illinois, st., & R., U.S.A. 40 15N 90 0W
50 Ilmen, L., U.S.S.R. 58 20N 31 28E
24 Ilminster, England 50 55N 2 56W
68 Iloilo, Philippines 10 40N 122 38E
72 Ilorin, Nigeria 8 30N 4 23E
50 Imandra, L., U.S.S.R. 67 40N 33 0E
67 Imabari, Japan 34 0N 133 0E
45 Immenstadt, Germany 47 33N 10 14E
27 Immingham, England 53 39N 0 13W
40 Imola, Italy 44 20N 11 40E
74 Impfondo, Congo (Fr.) 1 35N 18 10E
65 Imphal, India 24 15N 94 0E
41 Imroz, I., see Gökçeada
72 In Belbel, Algeria 27 55N 1 12E
72 In Gall, Niger 16 58N 6 57E
72 In Salah, see Ain Salah
67 Ina, Japan 35 56N 138 0E
84 Inangahua Junc., N.Z. 41 50S 171 52E
48 Inari, L., Finland 69 0N 28 0E
26 Ince, England 53 32N 2 38W
51 Ince, C., Turkey 42 2N 35 0E
31 Inchcape Rock, Scotland 56 26N 2 24W
67 Inchinomiya, Japan 35 20N 136 40E
67 Inchon, Korea 37 30N 126 38E
31 Inchture, Scotland 56 26N 3 8W
75 Incomati, R., Mozam. 25 13S 32 26E
30 Indaal, L., Scotland 55 44N 6 20W
48 Indals, R., Sweden 62 40N 16 50E
65 Indaw, Burma 24 10N 96 10E
88 Indian Head, Canada 50 32N 103 35W
5 Indian Ocean 10 0S 70 0E
91 Indian River, & Inlet, U.S.A.
28 0N 80 30W
64–65 India, Asia 22 0N 78 0E
91 Indiana, st., U.S.A. 40 0N 86 0W
91 Indianapolis, U.S.A. 39 48N 86 15W
61 Indigirka, R., U.S.S.R. 69 10N 147 20E
68 Indonesia, S.E. Asia 0 0 110 0E
64 Indore, India 22 42N 75 52E
65 Indravati, R., India 19 12N 81 30E
42 Indre, Dépt., France 47 2N 1 33E
42 Indre-et-Loire, Dépt., Fr. 47 12N 0 43E
64 Indus, R. & Delta, Pak. 24 30N 65 30E
76 Indwe, S. Africa 31 28S 27 24E
51 Inebolu, Turkey 41 58N 33 58E
74 Ingende, Zaïre 0 12S 18 57E
82 Ingham, Australia 18 22S 146 0E
26 Ingleborough, Mt. Eng. 54 10N 2 35W
83 Inglewood, Australia 28 30S 151 2E
84 Inglewood, New Zealand 39 9S 174 12E
48 Ingolfshodi, Iceland 63 50N 16 45W
46 Ingolstadt, Germany 48 47N 11 20E
93 Ingonish, Canada 46 42N 60 25W
75 Inhambane, Mozambique 24 0S 35 45E

75 Inhamingo, Mozambique 18 25S 35 0E
75 Inharrime, Mozambique 24 25S 35 1E
36 Inishfree, Bay, Ireland 55 4N 8 20W
35 Inishkea, Is., Ireland 54 7N 10 13W
34 Inishmaan, I., Ireland 53 5N 9 35W
34 Inishmore I., Ireland 53 8N 9 45W
35 Inishturk I., Ireland 53 43N 10 8W
35 Inistioge, Ireland 52 30N 7 5W
83 Injune, Australia 25 48S 148 30E
65 Inle Lake, Burma 20 30N 96 55E
46 Inn, R., Austria-Ger. 47 16N 11 0E
30 Innellan, Scotland 55 54N 4 58W
32 Inner Hebrides, Scotland 56 40N 6 50W
66 Inner Mongolia, Autonomous Reg., China 42 0N 111 0E
32 Inner Sd., Scotland 57 30N 5 55W
31 Innerleithen, Scotland 55 37N 3 6W
45 Innertkirchen, Switzerland 46 43N 8 16E
35 Inniscrone, Ireland 54 13N 9 5W
88 Innisfail, Canada 52 0N 114 0W
82 Innisfail, Australia 17 32S 146 5E
34 Innishannon, Ireland 51 46N 8 40W
45 Innsbruck, Austria 47 12N 11 20E
74 Inongo, Zaïre 1 50S 18 22E
47 Inowroclaw, Poland 52 56N 18 20E
33 Insch, Scotland 57 20N 2 39W
65 Insein, Burma 16 45N 95 30E
45 Interlaken, Switzerland 46 42N 7 53E
88 Inuvik, Canada 68 2N 135 30W
36 Inver, & B., Ireland 54 40N 8 16W
33 Inverallochy, Scotland 57 40N 1 56W
30 Inveraray, Scotland 56 14N 5 4W
33 Inverbervie, Scotland 56 50N 2 17W
84 Invercargill, N.Z. 46 28S 168 28E
83 Inverell, Australia 29 50S 151 0E
33 Invergordon, Scotland 57 42N 4 10W
31 Invergowrie, Scotland 56 29N 3 5W
31 Inverkeilor, Scotland 56 38N 2 33W
31 Inverkeithing, Scotland 56 2N 3 24W
93 Inverness, Canada 46 20N 60 15W
33 Inverness, Scotland 57 28N 4 12W
32 Invershiel, Scotland 57 13N 5 25W
33 Inverurie, Scotland 57 17N 2 22W
80 Investigator Group, Australia 33 42S 134 25E
83 Investigator Str., Austral. 35 30S 137 0E
60 Inya, U.S.S.R. 50 40N 86 55E
75 Inyanga, Rhodesia 18 12S 32 40E
41 Ioannina, Greece 39 40N 20 52E
30 Iona I., Scotland 56 20N 6 30W
41 Ionian Is. & S., Greece 38 40N 20 0E
41 Ios I., Greece 36 42N 25 20E
91 Iowa, st., U.S.A. 42 15N 93 30W
91 Iowa City, U.S.A. 41 45N 91 40W
66 Ipin, China 29 15N 104 0E
68 Ipoh, Malaya 4 32N 101 0E
74 Ippy, Central Africa 6 5N 21 7E
23 Ipswich, England 52 4N 1 10E
83 Ipswich, Australia 27 38S 152 45E
98 Iquique, Chile 20 20S 70 5W
98 Iquitos, Peru 3 48S 73 12W
41 Iraklion, (Candia), Crete 35 20N 25 10E
62 Iran (Persia), Asia 33 50N 54 0E
94 Irapuato, Mexico 20 50N 101 28W
62 Iraq, S.W. Asia 33 30N 45 0E
95 Irazu, Vol., Costa Rica 10 0N 83 43W
63 Irbid, Jordan 32 34N 35 50E
95 Ireland I., Bermudas 32 21N 64 52W
29 Ireland, Europe 53 0N 8 0W
29 Ireland, N., British Isles 54 40N 6 50W
61 Iret, U.S.S.R. 60 5N 154 5E
74 Iringa, Tanzania 7 50S 35 30E
94 Iriona, Honduras 16 0N 84 58W
18 Irish Sea, British Isles 53 50N 5 0W
61 Irkineyeva, U.S.S.R. 58 30N 97 0E
61 Irkutsk, U.S.S.R. 52 20N 104 0E
26 Irlam, England 53 26N 2 27W
83 Iron Baron, Australia 33 0S 137 0E
47 Iron Gate, Rum.-Y-slav. 44 43N 22 25E
83 Iron Knob, Australia 32 41S 137 0E
91 Iron Mt., U.S.A. 45 54N 88 0W
22 Ironbridge, England 52 38N 2 27W
65 Irrawaddy, R. & Delta, Burma 16 0N 95 0E
26 Irthing, R., England 55 0N 2 37W
23 Irthlingborough, England 52 20N 0 37W
60 Irtysh, R., U.S.S.R. 59 0N 69 30E
37 Irun, Spain 43 20N 1 50W
30 Irvine, Scotland 55 37N 4 39W
36 Irvinestown, N. Ireland 54 28N 7 40W
83 Irymple, Australia 34 4S 142 1E
48 Isa Fjord, Iceland 66 10N 23 0W
48 Isafjördur, Iceland 66 10N 23 15W
74 Isangi, Zaïre 0 50N 24 10E
46 Isar, R., Germany 48 40N 12 30E
40 Ischia I., Italy 40 46N 13 54E
43 Iseo, Italy 45 39N 10 2E
43 Isère, Dépt., France 45 25N 5 40E
60 Ishim, & R., U.S.S.R. 56 15N 69 30E
67 Ishinomaki, Japan 38 26N 141 18E
64 Ishkuman, Kashmir 36 40N 73 45E
91 Ishpeming, U.S.A. 46 30N 87 40W
74 Isiolo, Kenya 0 19N 37 39E
76 Isipingo Beach, S. Africa 30 0S 30 55E
74 Isiro (Paulis), Zaïre 2 53N 27 58E
61 Isitskoye, U.S.S.R. 60 55N 125 0E
51 Iskenderun, & G., Turkey 36 48N 36 17E
39 Iskur R., Bulgaria 43 0N 24 0E
64 Islamabad, Pakistan 33 40N 73 20E
36 Island Magee, Pen., N. Ire. 54 50N 5 45W
30 Islay, I. & Sd., Scotland 55 45N 6 15W
27 Isle of Axholme, England 53 33N 0 50W
26 Isle of Man, Br. Isles 54 10N 4 35W
95 Isle of Pines, Cuba 21 45N 82 50W
22 Isle of Purbeck, England 50 38N 2 0W
30 Isle of Whithorn, Scot. 54 42N 4 23W
22 Isle of Wight, Co., Eng. 50 40N 1 20W
92 Isle Royale, U.S.A. 48 0N 88 40W
73 Isma'iliya, Egypt 31 0N 32 0E
73 Isna, Egypt 25 12N 32 30E
51 Isnik Gölü, L., Turkey 40 30N 30 0E
74 Isoka, Zambia 10 10S 32 42E
62 Isparta, Turkey 37 30N 31 5E
63 Israel, S.W. Asia 32 0N 35 0E
43 Issoudun, France 47 0N 2 0E
60 Issyk Kul, L., U.S.S.R. 42 50N 77 30E
51 Istanbul, Turkey 41 1N 28 56E
40 Istra, Dist., Y-slav. 45 18N 13 50E
99 Itabira, Brazil 19 30S 43 10W
99 Itacoatiara, Brazil 3 0S 58 20W
40 Italy, Europe 42 0N 13 0E
22 Itchen, R., England 51 0N 1 20W
92 Ithaca, U.S.A. 42 28N 76 28W
41 Ithaki, Greece 38 25N 20 43E
67 Iturup I., U.S.S.R. 45 0N 148 0E
99 Ivai, R., Brazil 23 30S 53 20W
48 Ivalo, & R., Finland 68 38 27 35E
83 Ivanhoe, Australia 32 55S 144 20E
52 Ivanovo, U.S.S.R. 57 5N 41 0E
89 Ivigtut, Greenland 62 0N 47 30W
37 Iviza, & I., see Ibiza
72 Ivory Coast, Africa 7 0N 5 0W
43 Ivrea, Italy 45 30N 7 50E
43 Ivry, France 48 55N 1 30E
67 Iwakuni, Japan 34 10N 132 10E
67 Iwanuma, Japan 38 7N 140 58E
67 Iwate, Pref., Japan 39 30N 140 20E
76 Ixopo, S. Africa 30 10S 30 5E
44 Izegem, Belgium 50 55N 3 13E
50 Izhevsk, U.S.S.R. 56 50N 53 0E
47 Izmail, U.S.S.R. 45 21N 28 40E
41 Izmir, & G., Turkey 38 21N 27 8E
51 Izmit, Turkey 40 45N 29 50E
63 Izr'a, Syria 32 52N 36 15E
67 Izumo, Japan 35 25N 133 0E

J

62 Jabal At Tuwaiq, mts., Saudi Arabia 22 30N 46 0E
62 Jabal Shammar, Mts., Saudi Arabia 27 30N 42 30E
64 Jabalpur, India 23 10N 80 0E
41 Jablanica, Mt., Albania 41 20N 20 30E
46 Jablonec, Cz-slov. 50 43N 15 10E
62 Jabrin, Saudi Arabia 23 10N 48 32E
37 Jaca, Spain 42 35N 0 32W
99 Jachal, Argentina 30 5S 69 10W
83 Jackson, Australia 26 40S 149 35E
84 Jackson B., N.Z. 43 58S 168 40E
92 Jackson, Mich., U.S.A. 42 15N 84 29W
91 Jackson, Miss., U.S.A. 32 20N 90 13W
91 Jackson, Tenn., U.S.A. 35 36N 88 45W
84 Jacksons, New Zealand 42 46S 171 33E
91 Jacksonville Fla., U.S.A. 30 28N 81 40W
91 Jacksonville, Ill., U.S.A. 39 44N 90 16W
95 Jacmel, Haiti 18 15N 72 35W
64 Jacobabad, Pakistan 28 20N 68 27E
63 Jacob's Well, Jordan 32 12N 35 17E
99 Jacui, R., Brazil 30 0S 52 0W
73 Jado, Libya 32 0N 12 0E
74 Jadotville, see Likasi
37 Jaén, Spain 37 48N 3 43W
63 Jaffa, see Tel Aviv-Jaffa
64 Jaffna, Sri Lanka 9 45N 80 0E
65 Jagdalpur, India 19 1N 82 7E
76 Jagersfontein, S. Africa 29 40S 25 28E
73 Jaghbub, Libya 29 42N 24 38E
64 Jagraon, India 30 40N 75 40E
62 Jahrum, Iran 28 27N 53 30E
68 Jailolo Passage, Indonesia 0 30N 129 20E
64 Jaipur, India 27 0N 75 50E
72 Jajere, Nigeria 11 58N 10 25E
68 Jakarta, Indonesia 6 9S 106 49E
94 Jalapa Enriquez, Mexico 19 32N 96 55W
64 Jalgaon, India 20 57N 76 30E
64 Jalna, India 19 45N 75 50E
37 Jalon, R., Spain 41 26N 1 35W
65 Jalpaiguri, India 26 15N 88 0E
95 Jamaica, I., West Indies 18 15N 77 30W
65 Jamalpur, India 25 20N 86 30E
68 Jambi, Indonesia 1 40S 103 35E
89 James, B., Canada 53 30N 81 0W
90 James, R., S. Dak., U.S.A. 43 40N 97 40W
80 James Ra., Australia 24 10S 132 40E
83 Jamestown, Australia 33 11S 138 30E
90 Jamestown, North Dakota, U.S.A. 46 58N 98 38W
92 Jamestown, N.Y., U.S.A. 42 8N 79 17W
64 Jamkhandi, India 16 30N 75 5E
64 Jammu, India 32 50N 74 58E
64 Jammu and Kashmir, Asia 34 0N 77 0E
64 Jamnagar, India 22 30N 70 5E
65 Jamshedpur, India 22 50N 86 10E
48 Jämtland, Co., Sweden 62 45N 14 30E
100 Jan Mayen I., Arctic Oc. 71 0N 8 0W
64 Jand, Pakistan 33 30N 71 57E
83 Jandowae, Australia 26 40S 151 2E
92 Janesville, U.S.A. 42 48N 88 59W
63 Janin, Jordan 32 28N 35 18E
99 Januaria, Brazil 15 30S 44 30W
64 Jaora, India 23 42N 75 5E
67 Japan, E. Asia 36 0N 138 0E
67 Japan Sea, E. Asia 40 0N 134 30E
37 Jarama, R., Spain 40 50N 3 30W
63 Jarash, Jordan 32 17N 35 54E
62 Jarir, Wadi, Si. Arabia 24 10N 42 0E
47 Jaroslaw, Poland 50 0N 22 40E
27 Jarrow, England 54 59N 1 30W
65 Jarwa, India 27 52N 82 36E
63 Jask, Iran 25 52N 57 50E
47 Jaslo, Poland 49 45N 21 30E
47 Jaszbereny, Hungary 47 37N 19 58E
37 Jativa, Spain 39 1N 0 32W
98 Jauja, Peru 11 45S 75 25W
65 Jaunpur, India 25 42N 82 55E
68 Java I., Indonesia 7 0S 110 0E
68 Java Sea, Indonesia 5 0S 111 30E
68 Jayapura, Indonesia 2 28S 140 38E
65 Jaynagar, India 26 43N 86 9E
62 Jeb Aneiza, Mt., Iraq 32 10N 39 20E
73 Jebel Abyad, Plat. of, Sudan 17 30N 28 40E
63 Jebel 'Ajlun, mts., Jordan 32 20N 35 50E
63 Jebel el Leja, Syria 33 17N 36 5E
62 Jebel Ibrahim, mt., Si. Arabia 20 26N 41 15E
63 Jebel Sanmini, mt., Lebanon 33 56N 35 55E
31 Jedburgh, Scotland 55 29N 2 32W
47 Jedrzejów, Poland 50 35N 20 15E
91 Jefferson City, U.S.A. 38 40N 92 18W
91 Jeffersonville, U.S.A. 38 22N 85 49W
72 Jega, Nigeria 12 15N 4 23E
46 Jelenia Góra, Poland 50 50N 15 45E
49 Jelgava, U.S.S.R. 56 39N 23 45E
44 Jemeppe, Belgium 50 37N 5 29E
46 Jena, Germany 51 0N 11 30E
61 Jennette I., U.S.S.R. 77 25N 157 20E
91 Jennings, U.S.A. 30 15N 92 45W
83 Jeparit, Australia, 36 10S 142 5E
37 Jerez, Spain 36 42N 6 10W
82 Jericho, Australia 23 38S 146 6E
63 Jericho, Jordan 31 51N 35 28E
83 Jerilderie, Australia 35 20S 145 40E
93 Jersey City, U.S.A. 40 50N 74 10W
42 Jersey I., Channel Is. 49 17N 2 10W
63 Jerusalem, Israel 31 47N 35 13E
68 Jesselton, see Kota Kinabalu
65 Jessore, Bangladesh 23 12N 89 10E
44 Jette, Belgium 50 52N 4 18E
65 Jeypore, India 18 45N 82 32E
63 Jezziné, Lebanon 33 33N 35 34E
64 Jhal Jhao, Pakistan 26 20N 65 30E
64 Jhalawar, India 24 35N 76 10E
64 Jhang Maghiana, Pak. 31 8N 72 15E
64 Jhansi, India 25 40N 78 49E
65 Jharsuguda, India 21 50N 84 5E
64 Jhelum, & R., Pak. 32 58N 73 45E
65 Jiachan, Tibet, China 31 40N 81 5E
62 Jidda, Saudi Arabia 21 30N 39 0E
46 Jihlava, & R., Cz-slov. 49 21N 15 38E
94 Jimenez, Mexico 27 10N 104 55W
73 Jima, Ethiopia 7 50N 37 0E
83 Jindabyne, Australia 36 30S 148 35E
74 Jinja, Uganda 0 30N 33 15E
47 Jiu, R., Rumania 44 50N 23 50E
99 Joao Pessöa, Brazil 7 12S 35 0W
42 Jobourg, France 49 49N 1 54W
64 Jodhpur, India 26 10N 73 0E
50 Joensuu, Finland 62 40N 29 49E
43 Joeuf, France 49 12N 6 0E
76 Johannesburg, S. Africa 26 15S 28 4E
33 John o'Groats, Scotland 58 38N 3 5W
91 Johnston City, U.S.A. 36 29N 82 20W
74 Johnston Falls, see Mambilima
30 Johnstone, Scotland 55 50N 4 30W
35 Johnstown, Ireland 52 46N 7 34W
92 Johnstown, U.S.A. 40 20N 78 52W
68 Johor Baharu, Malaya 1 35N 103 40E
43 Joigny, France 48 0N 3 25E
48 Jokkmokk, Sweden 66 32N 19 56E
92 Joilet, U.S.A. 41 36N 88 0W
89 Joliette, Canada 46 1N 73 40W
68 Jolo I., Philippines 6 3N 121 3E
91 Jonesboro, U.S.A. 35 50N 90 45W
49 Jönköping, Sweden 57 48N 14 12E
89 Jonquière, Canada 48 27N 71 10W
91 Joplin, U.S.A. 36 58N 94 30W
63 Jordan, R., Jordan-Israel 32 15N 35 32E
62 Jordan, S.W. Asia 32 0N 37 0E
65 Jorhat, India 26 42N 94 15E
48 Jörn, Sweden 65 8N 20 0E
72 Jos, Nigeria 9 53N 8 51E
80 Joseph Bonaparte G., Australia 13 45S 129 0E
49 Jötunheimen, Mts., Nor. 61 35N 8 20E
63 Jouaïya, Lebanon 33 14N 35 20E
63 Joub Jennine, Lebanon 33 38N 35 48E
88 Juan de Fuca Str., North America 48 30N 124 30W
75 Juan de Nova I., Madagascar 17 10S 43 45E
99 Juan Fernandez, I., Pacific Ocean 33 15S 79 0W
99 Juazeiro, Brazil 9 30S 40 30W
73 Juba, Sudan 5 0N 31 35E
70 Juba, R., East Africa 1 45N 42 42E
72 Juby, C., Morocco 27 50N 13 45W
37 Júcar, R., Spain 40 5N 2 10W
94 Juchitan, Mexico 16 30N 95 15W
63 Judaea, Wilderness of, Jordan 31 25N 35 18E
63 Judaean Hills, Jordan 31 45N 35 15E
66 Juikin, China 26 5N 115 25E
99 Juiz de Fora, Brazil 21 35S 43 40W
99 Jujuy, Argentina 24 5S 65 30W
82 Julia Creek, Australia 20 40S 141 55E
46 Julian Alps, Y-slav. 46 15N 13 40E
89 Julianehaab Greenland 60 40N 45 40W
44 Jülich, Germany 50 56N 6 20E
64 Jullundur, India 31 20N 75 40E
62 Jumaima, Saudi Arabia 29 40N 43 37E
44 Jumet, Belgium 50 28N 4 27E
64 Jumna, R., see Yamuna
64 Junagadh, India 21 34N 70 30E
91 Junction City, U.S.A. 39 5N 96 58W
82 Jundah, Australia 24 56S 143 5E
88 Juneau, Alaska 58 13N 134 0W
83 Junee, Australia 34 53S 147 36E
45 Jungfrau, mt., Switz. 46 30N 7 50E
99 Junin, Argentina 34 25S 61 0W
42 Jura, Dépt., France 46 46N 5 40E
30 Jura, I. & Sd., Scotland 55 57N 5 55W
43 Jura Mts., France-Switz. 46 40N 6 5E
80 Jurien Bay, Australia 30 20S 115 0E
98 Juruá, R., Brazil 6 0S 68 0W
43 Jussey, France 47 50N 5 55E
73 J'Uweinat, mt., Egypt 22 40N 25 0E
49 Jylland (Jutland), Den. 56 10N 9 0E
48 Jyvaskyla, Finland 62 12N 25 47E

K

64 K2 Mt., Kashmir 36 0N 77 0E
68 Kabaena, I., Indonesia 5 15S 122 0E
72 Kabala, Sierra Leone 9 38N 11 37W
74 Kabale, Uganda 1 1S 30 0E
74 Kabalo, Zaïre 6 0S 27 0E
74 Kabambare, Zaïre 4 40S 27 44E
51 Kabardino-Balkar, A.S.S.R., U.S.S.R. 43 30N 43 30E
74 Kabarega Falls, Uganda 2 24N 31 55E
74 Kabinda, Zaïre 6 3S 24 20E
75 Kabompo, R., Zambia 13 30S 24 30E
74 Kabongo, Zaïre 7 18S 25 40E
82 Kabra, Australia 23 25S 150 25E
64 Kabul, & R., Afghanistan 34 30N 69 13E
75 Kabwe, Zambia 13 39S 28 38E
60 Kachiry, U.S.S.R. 53 20N 75 55E
72 Kaddi, Nigeria 13 40N 5 40E
83 Kadina, Australia 33 58S 137 48E
52 Kadiyevka, U.S.S.R. 48 17N 38 17E
73 Kadugli, Sudan 11 0N 29 45E
72 Kaele, Cameroon 10 15N 14 15E
67 Kaesong, Korea 38 0N 126 40E
74 Kafakumba, Zaïre 9 40S 23 40E
51 Kafan, U.S.S.R. 39 10N 46 15E
72 Kafanchan, Nigeria 9 49N 8 20E
63 Kafr Kanna, Israel 32 45N 35 20E
75 Kafue, & R., Zambia 15 45S 28 25E
74 Kafulwe, Zambia 9 0S 29 10E
60 Kagan, U.S.S.R. 39 50N 64 30E
47 Kagul, U.S.S.R. 45 50N 28 15E
67 Kagoshima, & Pref., Japan 31 48N 130 40E
74 Kahama, Tanzania 3 50S 32 25E
83 Kahmoomulga, Austral. 25 58S 145 51E
72 Kaiama, Nigeria 9 36N 4 1E
84 Kaiapoi, New Zealand 43 24S 172 40E
98 Kaieteur Falls Fs., Guyana 5 5N 59 0W
66 Kaifeng, China 34 45N 114 40E
84 Kaikohe, New Zealand 35 25S 173 49E
84 Kaikoura, & Ra., N.Z. 42 23S 173 43E
65 Kailas Ra., Tibet 31 0N 82 0E
84 Kaimanawa Mts., N.Z. 39 0S 176 15E
84 Kaipara Hr., N.Z. 36 22S 174 10E
72 Kairouan, Tunisia 35 48N 10 8E
47 Kaiserslautern, Germany 49 29N 7 46E
84 Kaitaia, New Zealand 35 7S 173 17E
84 Kaitangata, N.Z. 46 18S 170 0E
48 Kajaani, Finland 64 15N 27 45E
82 Kajabbi, Australia 20 0S 140 0E
73 Kajo Kaji, Sudan 3 58N 31 40E
73 Kaka, Sudan 10 38N 32 10E
84 Kakanui, Mts., N.Z. 45 15S 170 35E
51 Kakhovka Res., U.S.S.R. 46 30N 33 50E
64 Kalabagh, Pakistan 33 0N 71 30E
41 Kalábaka, Greece 39 40N 21 35E
75 Kalabo, Zambia 14 58S 22 33E
52 Kalach, U.S.S.R. 50 38N 41 10E
65 Kaladan, R., Burma 21 15N 93 0E
75 Kalahari, des., Africa 23 0S 22 0E
61 Kalakan, U.S.S.R. 55 20N 116 55E
41 Kalamata, Greece 37 2N 22 7E
92 Kalamazoo, U.S.A. 42 15N 85 35W
92 Kalamazoo, R., U.S.A. 42 35N 86 0W
64 Kalat, Pakistan 29 5N 66 32E
63 Kalbuh, Wadi, Oman 22 0N 57 50E
74 Kalemie (Albertville), Zaïre 5 55S 29 9E
65 Kalewa, Burma 23 5N 94 20E
48 Kalfafellsstadur, Iceland 64 11N 15 45W
66 Kalgan, China 40 50N 114 50E
80 Kalgoorlie, Australia 30 40S 121 28E
41 Kaliakra, C., Bulgaria 43 23N 28 26E
74 Kalima, Zaïre 2 38S 26 37E
68 Kalimantan, prov., Indonesia 0 30S 115 0E
52 Kalinin, U.S.S.R. 56 47N 35 55E
61 Kalinina, U.S.S.R. 60 0N 108 10E
49 Kaliningrad, U.S.S.R. 54 42N 20 30E
90 Kalispell, U.S.A. 48 18N 114 27W
47 Kalisz, Poland 51 48N 18 5E
74 Kaliua, Tanzania 5 0S 31 59E
48 Kalix, R., Sweden 67 30N 21 15E
53 Kallia, Jordan 31 46N 35 29E
48 Kallsjön, L., Sweden 63 35N 13 10E
49 Kalmar, & Co., Sweden 56 42N 16 20E
51 Kalmyk, A.S.S.R., U.S.S.R. 46 30N 45 30E
60 Kalmykovo, U.S.S.R. 49 0N 51 50E
47 Kalocsa, Hungary 46 31N 18 58E
75 Kalomo, Zambia 16 54S 26 30E
46 Kalovy Vary, Cz-slov. 50 15N 12 55E
52 Kaluga, U.S.S.R. 54 35N 36 20E
65 Kalutara, Sri Lanka 6 35N 80 0E
52 Kalyazin, U.S.S.R. 57 18N 37 45E
50 Kama, R., U.S.S.R. 60 0N 56 0E
67 Kamaishi, Japan 39 20N 142 0E
62 Kamaran I., Red Sea 15 28N 42 30E
61 Kamchatka, Pen., U.S.S.R. 56 0N 160 0E
60 Kamen, U.S.S.R. 53 50N 81 30E
51 Kamenets-Podolski, U.S.S.R. 48 45N 26 10E
47 Kamenka Bugskaya, Pol. 50 8N 24 16E
60 Kamensk-Uralskiy, U.S.S.R. 56 30N 62 50E
52 Kamensk Shakhtinskiy, U.S.S.R. 48 23N 40 20E
61 Kamenskoye, U.S.S.R. 62 40N 165 0E
30 Kames, Scotland 55 54N 5 15W
74 Kamina, Zaïre 8 40S 25 3E
88 Kamloops, Canada 50 40N 120 20W
44 Kamp Lintfort, Ger. 51 30N 6 38E
74 Kampala, Uganda 0 20N 32 30E
44 Kampen, Netherlands 52 34N 5 54E
68 Kampot, Cambodia 10 30N 104 0E
88 Kamsack, Canada 51 40N 102 0W
52 Kamyshin, U.S.S.R. 50 10N 45 30E
67 Kanagawa, Pref., Japan 35 25N 139 20E
74 Kananga (Luluabourg), Zaïre 5 55S 22 18E
50 Kanash, U.S.S.R. 55 48N 47 32E
67 Kanazawa, Japan 36 40N 136 48E
65 Kanchenjunga, Mt., Nepal 27 45N 88 15E
66 Kanchow, China 25 50N 114 45E
74 Kanda Kanda, Zaïre 6 55S 23 33E
64 Kandahar, Afghanistan 31 42N 65 40E
64 Kandahar, Prov., Afghan 31 0N 65 0E
50 Kandalaksha, U.S.S.R. 67 3N 32 30E
64 Kandalu, Afghanistan 29 55N 63 20E
84 Kandavu I., Fiji Is. 19 0S 178 15E
45 Kandersteg, Switzerland 46 28N 7 40E
72 Kandi, Benin 11 15N 3 0E
64 Kandla, India 23 0N 70 7E
83 Kandos, Australia 32 55S 150 0E
64 Kandy, Sri Lanka 7 20N 80 35E
83 Kangaroo I., Australia 35 45S 137 15E
74 Kango, Gabon 0 11N 10 5E
61 Kangotovo, U.S.S.R. 63 30N 87 40E
89 Kaniapiskau, R., Can. 56 20N 68 40W
92 Kankakee, U.S.A. 41 7N 87 50W
72 Kankan, Guinea 10 27N 9 15W
65 Kanker, India 20 10N 81 40E
66 Kan-kiang, R., China 27 0N 115 0E
64 Kannod, India 22 45N 76 40E
72 Kano, Nigeria 11 58N 8 20E
80 Kanowna, Australia 30 30S 121 37E
64 Kanpur, India 26 30N 80 23E
90 Kansas, st., & R., U.S.A. 38 30N 98 30W
91 Kansas City, U.S.A. 39 4N 94 37W
66 Kansen, China 37 45N 92 55E
61 Kansk, U.S.S.R. 56 20N 95 30E
66 Kansu, Prov., China 39 0N 105 0E
66 Kantse, China 31 30N 100 25E
34 Kanturk, Ireland 52 11N 8 52W
75 Kanye, Botswana 24 58S 25 25E
75 Kaoko Otavi, S.W. Afr. 18 12S 13 45E
72 Kaolack, Sénégal 14 10N 15 47W
74 Kapanga, Zaïre 8 15S 22 32E
60 Kapchagai, U.S.S.R. 44 10N 77 25E
46 Kapela, Mts., Y-slav. 44 40N 15 40E
84 Kapiti, I., New Zealand 40 45S 174 55E
47 Kaposvár, Hungary 46 20N 17 40E
68 Kapuas, R., Indon. 0 5S 110 30E
83 Kapunda, Australia 34 20S 138 57E
84 Kapuni, New Zealand 39 30S 174 5E
92 Kapuskasing, Canada 49 25N 82 25W
60 Kara, U.S.S.R. 69 15N 65 26E
60 Kara Bogaz Gol., L., U.S.S.R. 41 30N 53 30E
60 Kara-Kalpak, A.S.S.R., U.S.S.R. 42 0N 60 0E
60 Kara Kum, Des., U.S.S.R. 39 40N 60 0E
60 Kara Sea, U.S.S.R. 75 0N 62 0E
64 Karachi, Pakistan 25 0N 67 0E
60 Karaganda, U.S.S.R. 49 50N 73 10E
64 Karaikal, India 10 55N 79 50E
64 Karaikkudi, India 10 2N 78 45E
60 Karakas, U.S.S.R. 48 26N 83 27E
64 Karakoram Ra. & P., India 35 0N 78 0E
51 Karaköse (Agri), Turkey 39 45N 43 0E
84 Karamea Bight, N.Z. 41 40S 172 0E
76 Karasburg, S.W. Africa 28 0S 18 44E
60 Karasino, U.S.S.R. 66 50N 86 50E
60 Karauzyak, U.S.S.R. 43 35N 59 25E
62 Karbala, Iraq 32 47N 44 2E
47 Karcag, Hungary 47 20N 21 0E
41 Kardhitsa, Greece 39 20N 21 55E
49 Kardla, U.S.S.R. 58 58N 22 46E
73 Kareima, Sudan 18 35N 31 50E
50 Karelian A.S.S.R., U.S.S.R. 64 0N 34 0E
74 Karema, Tanzania 6 45S 30 30E
60 Kargat, U.S.S.R. 55 20N 80 30E
75 Kariba Gorge & Lake, Africa 16 30S 29 15E
75 Karibib, S.W. Africa 22 0S 15 50E
68 Karimata Str., Indonesia 2 0S 109 0E
64 Karimnagar, India 18 28N 79 5E
60 Karkaralinsk, U.S.S.R. 49 27N 75 37E
82 Karkar I., Papua N.G. 4 40S 146 0E
62 Karkheh R., Iran 33 0N 47 30E
51 Karkinitsk, Gulf of, U.S.S.R. 46 0N 33 0E

63 Karkur, Israel 32 28N 35 0E
46 Karl Marx Stadt (Chemnitz), Germany 50 49N 12 50E
40 Karlovac, Yugoslavia 45 26N 15 34E
49 Karlsborg, Sweden 58 30N 14 29E
49 Karlskroga, Sweden 59 21N 14 26E
49 Karlskrona, Sweden 56 13N 15 37E
49 Karlshamn, Sweden 56 17N 14 50E
45 Karlsruhe, Germany 49 3N 8 26E
49 Karlstad, Sweden 59 21N 13 20E
54 Karnai, India 29 35N 76 58E
65 Karnaphuli Reservoir, Bangladesh 22 40N 92 20E
64 Karnataka, st., India 14 0N 76 0E
41 Karnobat, Bulgaria 42 40N 27 0E
83 Karoonda, Australia 35 0S 140 5E
74 Karonga, Malawi 9 57S 33 55E
66 Karora, Sudan 17 44N 38 15E
41 Karpathos I., Greece 35 47N 27 10E
50 Karpinsk, U.S.S.R. 59 45N 59 45E
64 Karram R., India 32 45N 71 0E
76 Karreeberge, S. Africa 30 50S 22 0E
51 Kars, Turkey 40 50N 43 0E
50 Karsakpay, U.S.S.R. 47 55N 66 50E
40 Karst, Plat., Yugoslavia 45 35N 14 0E
50 Karshi, U.S.S.R. 39 5N 65 50E
50 Karsun, U.S.S.R. 54 10N 47 15E
50 Kartaly, U.S.S.R. 53 15N 60 50E
74 Karungu, Tanzania 0 45S 34 10E
54 Karur, India 10 55N 78 5E
54 Karwar, India 14 55N 74 13E
74 Kasai, R., Zaïre 4 0S 19 30E
74 Kasama, Zambia 10 10S 31 12E
74 Kasanga, Tanzania 8 23S 31 12E
74 Kasangulu, Zaïre 4 15S 15 15E
75 Kasempa, Zambia 13 15S 25 43E
52 Kashan, Iran 34 0N 51 30E
50 Kashgar, China 39 30N 76 10E
57 Kashing, China 30 50N 120 45E
54 Kashmir & Jammu, st., Asia 34 45N 76 0E
52 Kasimov, U.S.S.R. 54 58N 41 28E
48 Kaskinen (Kaskö), Finland 62 22N 21 13E
38 Kaslo, Canada 49 58N 117 0W
74 Kasongo, Zaïre 4 18S 26 40E
74 Kasongo-Lunda, Zaïre 6 32S 16 59E
46 Kassal, Germany 51 22N 9 30E
73 Kassala, Sudan 15 35N 36 27E
51 Kastamonu, Turkey 41 35N 34 2E
41 Kastoria, Greece 40 31N 21 18E
74 Kasulu, Tanzania 4 29S 30 7E
83 Katamatite, Australia 36 5S 145 40E
74 Katanga, reg., see Shaba
54 Katangi, India 21 56N 79 50E
80 Katanning, Australia 33 40S 117 32E
36 Katesbridge, Ireland 54 18N 6 8W
65 Katha, Burma 24 16N 96 13E
80 Katherine, Australia 14 30S 132 15E
54 Kathgotlam, India, see Haldwani
54 Katihar, India 25 40N 87 40E
65 Katmandu, Nepal 27 58N 85 23E
75 Katombora, Zambia 18 0S 25 30E
83 Katoomba (Blue Mountains), Australia 33 42S 150 18E
47 Katowice, Poland 50 18N 19 2E
30 Katrine, L., Scotland 56 15N 4 30W
49 Katrineholm, Sweden 59 3N 16 12E
72 Katsina, Nigeria 13 0N 7 35E
57 Katsuura, Japan 35 10N 140 20E
49 Kattegat, Europe 56 50N 11 15E
44 Katwijk-aan-Zee, Neth. 52 12N 4 25E
51 Katylyktakh, U.S.S.R. 68 55N 134 10E
90 Kauai, I., Hawaiian Is. 22 0N 159 40W
48 Kauliranta, Finland 66 28N 23 46E
49 Kaunas, U.S.S.R. 54 54N 23 54E
72 Kaura Namoda, Nigeria 12 40N 6 30E
48 Kautokeino, Norway 69 0N 23 8E
41 Kavála, Greece 41 0N 24 4E
82 Kavieng, Papua N.G. 3 0S 151 0E
57 Kawagoe, Japan 36 0N 139 30E
55 Kawardha, India 21 58N 81 15E
57 Kawasaki, Japan 35 40N 139 35E
84 Kawerau, New Zealand 38 5S 176 50E
84 Kawhia Hr., New Zealand 38 5S 174 40E
65 Kawthoolei, state, Burma 18 0N 97 0E
65 Kayah, State, Burma 19 0N 97 30E
72 Kayes, Mali 14 15N 11 27W
51 Kayseri, Turkey 38 52N 35 30E
1 Kazache, U.S.S.R. 70 50N 137 0E
0 Kazakhstan, S.S.R., U.S.S.R. 49 0N 70 0E
50 Kazan, U.S.S.R. 55 48N 49 0E
1 Kazanluk, Bulgaria 42 39N 25 27E
9 Kazanskaya, U.S.S.R. 49 33N 41 25E
7 Kazatin, U.S.S.R. 49 45N 28 35E
2 Kazerun, Iran 29 30N 51 40E
1 Kazbek Mt., U.S.S.R. 42 48N 44 29E
0 Kazym R., U.S.S.R. 63 30N 69 2E
2 Ke-Macina Mali 14 5N 5 20W
1 Kea, I., Greece 37 36N 24 22E
6 Keady, N. Ireland 54 15N 6 41W
0 Keal, Loch na, Scotland 56 29N 6 5W
8 Kebnekaise, Mt., Sweden 68 0N 18 30E
8 Kediri, Indonesia 7 44S 112 5E
2 Kedougou, Sénégal 12 35N 12 10W
6 Keele, England 53 2N 2 17W
7 Keelung (Chilung), China 25 10N 121 45E
2 Keene, U.S.A. 42 58N 72 16W
5 Keetmanshoop, S.W. Africa 26 30S 18 5E
8 Keewatin, Terr., Canada 63 20N 88 30W
41 Kefallinia (Cephalonia), I., Greece 38 15N 20 33E
63 Kefar Sava, Israel 32 10N 34 55E
72 Keffi, Nigeria 8 58N 7 47E
48 Keflavik, Iceland 64 2N 22 35W
45 Kehl, Germany 48 34N 7 50E
26 Keighley, England 53 52N 1 54W
76 Keimoes, S. Africa 28 40S 20 55E
33 Keith, Scotland 57 33N 2 57W
67 Kelang, Malaya 3 0N 101 35E
51 Kelkit R., Turkey 40 9N 38 0E
33 Kellas, Scotland 57 33N 3 24W
74 Kellé, Congo (Fr.) 0 7S 14 20E
72 Kellé, Niger 14 18N 10 10E
80 Kellerberrin, Australia 31 34N 117 42E
90 Kellogg, U.S.A. 47 37N 116 13W
35 Kells, Ireland 52 33N 7 18W
36 Kells, see Ceannus Mor
36 Kells, N. Ireland 54 49N 6 14W
88 Kelowna, Canada 49 56N 119 26W
23 Kelsale, England 52 15N 1 30E
25 Kelsall, England 53 14N 2 44W
84 Kelso, New Zealand 45 53S 169 16E
31 Kelso, Scotland 55 37N 2 27W
68 Keluang, Malaya 1 50N 103 30E
23 Kelvedon, England 51 50N 0 43E
50 Kem, & R., U.S.S.R. 65 0N 34 40E
60 Kemerovo, U.S.S.R. 55 35N 86 7E
48 Kemi & R., Finland 65 48N 24 43E
48 Kemijärvi, Finland 66 42N 27 30E
33 Kemnay, Scotland 57 14N 2 28W
83 Kempsey, Australia 31 5N 152 53E
23 Kempston, England 52 7S 0 30W
45 Kempten, Germany 47 45N 10 20E
31 Ken, L., & R., Scotland 55 0N 4 0W
26 Kendal, England 54 20N 2 45W
83 Kendall, Australia 31 33S 152 36E
68 Kendari, Indonesia 4 0S 122 35E
72 Kenema, Sierra Leone 7 55N 11 13W
65 Keng Tawng, Burma 20 50N 98 25E
74 Kenge, Zaïre 5 0S 16 55E
65 Keng Tung, Burma 21 5N 99 30E
76 Kenhardt, S. Africa 29 28S 21 6E
22 Kenilworth, England 52 21N 1 34W
72 Kenitra, Morocco 34 15N 6 40W
34 Kenmare, & R., Ireland 51 53N 9 35W
93 Kennebec, R., U.S.A. 45 0N 69 50W
95 Kennedy, C., (C. Canaveral), U.S.A. 28 28N 80 31W
90 Kennewick, U.S.A. 46 12N 119 8W
88 Keno Hill, Canada 64 0N 135 40W
91 Kenogami, R., Canada 50 0N 85 0W
89 Kenora, Canada 49 48N 94 20W
92 Kenosha, U.S.A. 42 40N 87 49W
24 Kent, Co., England 51 10N 0 45E
24 Kentisbeare, England 50 51N 3 18W
91 Kentucky, R., U.S.A. 37 30N 83 30W
91 Kentucky, st., U.S.A. 37 20N 85 0W
89 Kentville, Canada 45 6N 64 29W
71 Kenya, Africa 0 30S 38 30E
74 Kenya, Mt., Kenya 0 12S 37 30E
91 Keokuk, U.S.A. 40 27N 91 28W
64 Kerala, st., India 10 0N 77 0E
83 Kerang, Australia 35 47S 143 59E
51 Kerch, & Str., U.S.S.R. 45 12N 36 35E
63 Kerem Maharal, Israel 32 39N 35 0E
5 Kerguelen I., Indian Oc. 49 30S 69 40E
74 Kericho, Kenya 0 24S 35 14E
67 Kerinci, mt., Indonesia 1 35S 100 40E
73 Kerkenna, I., Tunisia 34 48N 11 12E
60 Kerki, U.S.S.R. 37 50N 65 25E
41 Kérkira I. (Corfu), Gr. 39 30N 19 50E
84 Kermadec Is., Pacific Oc. 31 0S 178 0W
62 Kerman, Iran 30 15N 57 0E
62 Kermanshah, Iran 34 18N 47 5E
41 Kerme G., Turkey 36 55N 27 45E
30 Kerrera, I., Scotland 56 24N 5 32W
88 Kerrobert, Canada 52 0N 109 10W
34 Kerry, Co., Ireland 52 5N 9 30W
34 Kerry Hd., Ireland 52 20N 9 55E
25 Kerry, Wales 52 30N 3 15W
36 Kesh, N. Ireland 54 31N 7 43W
48 Keski Suomen, Co., Finland 63 0N 25 15E
26 Keswick, England 54 36N 3 7W
60 Ket, R., U.S.S.R. 58 50N 85 0E
72 Keta, Ghana 5 49N 1 0E
68 Ketapang, Indonesia 1 55S 110 0E
47 Ketrzyn, Poland 54 5N 21 21E
23 Kettering, England 52 20N 0 42W
26 Kettlewell, England 54 8N 2 2W
92 Kewanee, U.S.A. 41 17N 89 56W
91 Keweenaw, B., U.S.A. 47 0N 88 0W
92 Keweenaw Pen., U.S.A. 47 0N 88 0W
36 Key, L., Ireland 54 0N 8 15W
95 Key West, U.S.A. 24 40N 82 45W
23 Keynsham, England 51 25N 2 30W
61 Kezhma, U.S.S.R. 59 15N 100 57E
63 Kfar Ata, Israel 32 48N 35 7E
61 Khabarovsk, U.S.S.R. 48 20N 135 5E
62 Khaibar, Saudi Arabia 26 2N 39 28E
65 Khairagarh, India 21 15N 81 0E
64 Khairpur, & Prov., Pakistan 27 32N 68 45E
41 Khalkis, Greece 38 25N 23 40E
60 Khalmer-Sede, U.S.S.R. 67 25N 78 50E
61 Khalmer Yu, U.S.S.R. 68 0N 65 10E
65 Khamba Dzong, Tibet, China 28 25N 88 30E
62 Khamis Mushait, Si. Arabia 18 15N 42 45E
64 Khanapur, India 15 25N 74 30E
62 Khanaqin, Iraq 34 30N 45 25E
64 Khandwa, India 21 59N 76 25E
64 Khanewal, Pakistan 30 25N 71 55E
66 Khangai, Mts., Mongolia 47 0N 99 0E
41 Khania, Crete 35 20N 24 0E
64 Khanpur, Pakistan 28 35N 70 30E
63 Khanu, Iran 28 0N 57 45E
66 Khara Usu Nur, see Har Us Nuur
65 Kharagpur, India 22 20N 87 20E
64 Kharda, India 18 40N 75 40E
64 Khargon, India 21 45N 75 35E
52 Kharkov, U.S.S.R. 49 50N 36 15E
73 Khartoum, Sudan 15 40N 32 52E
64 Khash, Afghanistan 31 28N 62 40E
64 Khash Desert, Afghan. 31 45N 62 30E
73 Khashm el Girba, Sudan 14 52N 35 30E
41 Khaskovo, Bulgaria 41 56N 25 30E
61 Khatanga, U.S.S.R. 72 0N 102 40E
61 Khatyn, U.S.S.R. 62 10N 174 55E
64 Khed Brahma, India 24 7N 73 5E
72 Khemis Miliana (Affreville), Algeria 36 14N 2 20E
72 Khenchela, Algeria 35 25N 7 12E
72 Khenifra, Morocco 32 58N 5 46W
51 Kherson, U.S.S.R. 46 47N 32 43E
61 Kheta R., U.S.S.R. 71 0N 97 0E
66 Khetinsiring, Tibet, China 33 0N 91 40E
61 Khilok, U.S.S.R. 51 30N 110 50E
67 Khingan Mts., China 47 0N 119 30E
41 Khios, Greece 38 20N 26 0E
66 Khirgiz Nur, see Hyargas Nuur
62 Khirsan R., Iran 31 15N 51 10E
61 Khiuma I., U.S.S.R. 59 0N 22 30E
60 Khiva, U.S.S.R. 41 27N 60 10E
62 Khoi, Iran 38 39N 45 0E
64 Khojak P., Afghanistan 30 57N 66 40E
61 Khonu, U.S.S.R. 66 36N 143 10E
62 Khor Dhahiya, South Yemen 18 50N 51 35E
41 Khora Sfakion, Crete 35 15N 24 10E
60 Khorog, U.S.S.R. 37 50N 71 50E
57 Khotan, China 37 8N 79 57E
47 Khotin, U.S.S.R. 48 31N 26 27E
72 Khouribga, Morocco 32 58N 6 50W
65 Khulna, Bangladesh 22 45N 89 34E
62 Khurramabad, Iran 36 37N 51 12E
64 Khush, Afghanistan 32 55N 62 10E
64 Khushab, Pakistan 32 25N 72 20E
63 Khushniye, Syria 33 0N 35 49E
47 Khust, U.S.S.R. 48 10N 23 18E
64 Khyber P., Pak. Afghan. 34 0N 71 15E
66 Kialing, R., China 33 0N 103 30E
83 Kiama, Australia 34 38S 150 58E
74 Kiambi, Zaïre 7 18S 27 59E
67 Kiamusze, China 46 20N 130 40E
66 Kian, China 27 0N 114 50E
66 Kiangling, China 30 25N 112 20E
66 Kiang-si, Prov., China 27 45N 115 30E
67 Kiangsu, Prov., China 33 0N 120 0E
67 Kiaohsien, China 36 5N 120 40E
74 Kibombo, Zaïre 3 54S 25 54E
23 Kibworth Beauchamp, England 52 33N 0 59W
88 Kicking Horse P., Can. 51 30N 116 10W
22 Kidderminster, England 52 23N 2 15W
22 Kidlington, England 51 49N 1 18W
26 Kidsgrove, England 53 6N 2 15W
25 Kidwelly, Wales 51 45N 4 17W
49 Kiel, B. & Can., Ger. 54 18N 10 5E
47 Kielce, Poland 50 52N 20 38E
27 Kielder, England 55 14N 2 35W
51 Kiev, U.S.S.R. 50 24N 30 28E
72 Kiffa, Mauritania 16 48N 11 15W
74 Kigali, Rwanda 1 58S 30 0E
74 Kigoma, Tanzania 4 49S 29 45E
66 Kikiang, China 29 0N 106 10E
41 Kikinda, Yugoslavia 45 47N 20 31E
41 Kikladhes (Cyclades) Arch., Greece 37 30N 25 15E
82 Kikori, Papua N.G. 7 45S 144 10E
74 Kikwit, Zaïre 4 50S 18 45E
90 Kilauea, Mt., Hawaii, I. 19 40N 155 30W
35 Kilbeggan, Ireland 53 21N 7 30W
30 Kilbirnie, Scotland 55 45N 4 42W
30 Kilbrennan Sd., Scot. 55 40N 5 23W
34 Kilbrittain, Ireland 51 40N 8 42W
35 Kilcock, Ireland 53 24N 6 40W
34 Kilcoe, Ireland 51 33N 9 26W
34 Kilconnell, Ireland 53 20N 8 25W
83 Kilcoy, Australia 27 0S 152 28E
30 Kilcreggan, Scotland 56 0N 4 50W
35 Kilcullen, Ireland 53 8N 6 45W
35 Kildare, & Co., Ireland 53 9N 6 54W
32 Kildonan & Strath, Scot. 58 10N 3 50W
34 Kildorrery, Ireland 52 14N 8 26W
34 Kilfenora, Ireland 53 0N 9 13W
30 Kilfinan, Scotland 55 57N 5 19W
34 Kilfinnane, Ireland 52 21N 8 30W
34 Kilgarvan, Ireland 51 45N 9 28W
74 Kilimanjaro, Mt., Tanzania 3 0S 37 0E
74 Kilindini, Kenya 4 10S 39 30E
47 Kiliya, U.S.S.R. 45 28N 29 16E
35 Kilkea, Ireland 52 57N 6 55W
34 Kilkee, Ireland 52 40N 9 37W
36 Kilkelly, Ireland 53 53N 8 50W
35 Kilkenny, & Co., Ireland 52 39N 7 13W
24 Kilkhampton, England 50 53N 4 30W
34 Kilkieran B., Ireland 53 17N 9 50W
34 Kilkishen, Ireland 52 49N 8 45W
35 Kill, Kildare, Ireland 53 15N 6 36W
34 Killadysert, Ireland 52 42N 9 7W
35 Killala, & B., Ireland 54 11N 9 13W
34 Killaloe, Ireland 52 49N 8 28W
36 Killard Pt., N. Ireland 54 19N 5 32W
83 Killarney, Australia 28 27S 152 1E
34 Killarney, Ireland 52 4N 9 30W
35 Killary Hr., Ireland 53 35N 9 57W
34 Killeagh, Ireland 51 56N 8 0W
35 Killeigh, Ireland 53 13N 7 26W
35 Killenaula, Ireland 52 35N 7 40W
36 Killeshandra, Ireland 54 0N 7 30W
33 Killiecrankie P., Scot. 56 43N 3 44W
34 Killimor, Ireland 53 9N 8 17W
30 Killin, Scotland 56 27N 4 20W
41 Killini, Mt., Greece 37 57N 22 31E
27 Killinghall, England 54 1N 1 33W
34 Killorglin, Ireland 52 6N 9 48W
36 Killough, N. Ireland 54 16N 5 40W
35 Killucan, Ireland 53 30N 7 10W
35 Killurin, Ireland 52 20N 6 34W
36 Killybegs, Ireland 54 36N 8 30W
36 Killyleagh, N. Ireland 54 24N 5 40W
30 Kilmacolm, Scotland 55 54N 4 34W
35 Kilmacthomas, Ireland 52 12N 7 28W
35 Kilmaganny, Ireland 52 26N 7 20W
34 Kilmallock, Ireland 52 27N 8 11W
30 Kilmarnock, Scotland 55 37N 4 29W
30 Kilmaurs, Scotland 55 37N 4 33W
34 Kilmeedy, Ireland 52 25N 8 55W
30 Kilmelford, Scotland 56 16N 5 30W
34 Kilmihill, Ireland 52 44N 9 18W
83 Kilmore, Australia 37 20S 144 55E
35 Kilmore, Ireland 52 12N 6 35W
33 Kilmuir, Scotland 57 44N 4 7W
34 Kilmurry, Ireland 52 47N 9 30W
34 Kilnaleck, Ireland 53 52N 7 20W
30 Kilninver, Scotland 56 20N 5 30W
74 Kilosa, Tanzania 6 40S 37 2E
36 Kilrea, N. Ireland 54 48N 6 34W
31 Kilrenny, Scotland 56 15N 2 40W
34 Kilronan, Ireland 53 8N 9 40W
35 Kilsheelan, Ireland 52 23N 7 37W
31 Kilsyth, Scotland 55 58N 4 3W
35 Kiltealy, Ireland 52 34N 6 45W
35 Kiltamagh, Ireland 53 51N 9 0W
74 Kilwa, Zaïre 9 15S 28 15E
74 Kilwa Kisiwani, Tanzania 8 58S 39 12E
74 Kilwa Kivinje, Tanzania 8 45S 39 15E
30 Kilwinning, Scotland 55 40N 4 42W
34 Kilworth, Ireland 52 10N 8 15W
34 Kilworth, Mts., Ireland 52 14N 8 15W
80 Kimba, Australia 33 10S 136 22E
76 Kimberley, S. Africa 28 42S 24 59E
68 Kinabalu, Mt., Malaysia 5 55N 116 45E
33 Kinbrace, Scotland 58 16N 3 56W
92 Kincardine, Canada 44 8N 81 38W
33 Kincardine, Scotland 57 51N 4 21W
72 Kindia Guinea 10 0N 12 52W
74 Kindu-Port Empain, Zaïre 3 0S 25 25E
52 Kineshma, U.S.S.R. 57 30N 42 0E
22 Kineton, England 52 10N 1 30W
83 King I., Australia 39 55S 144 0E
80 King Sd., Australia 16 30S 123 15E
89 King Frederick VI Coast, Greenland 63 0N 43 0W
89 King George Is., Canada 57 30N 80 0W
98 King George V Falls, Fs. Guyana 3 0N 58 0W
80 King Leopold Ra., Australia 17 0S 125 30E
88 King William I., Canada 69 0N 97 0W
76 King William's Town, S. Africa 32 50S 27 17E
30 Kingairloch, Dist., Scot. 56 37N 5 30W
83 Kingaroy, Australia 26 35S 151 38E
31 Kinghorn, Scotland 56 4N 3 10W
49 Kingisepp, U.S.S.R. 58 15N 22 15E
90 Kingman, U.S.A. 35 15N 114 10W
23 King's Lynn, England 52 45N 0 24E
35 Kings, R., Ireland 52 33N 7 20W
22 Kingsbury, England 52 33N 1 41W
83 Kingscote, Australia 35 40S 137 45E
89 Kingston, Canada 44 23N 76 37W
23 Kingston, England 51 23N 0 17W
95 Kingston, Jamaica 18 0N 76 47W
84 Kingston, New Zealand 45 15S 168 47E
93 Kingston, U.S.A. 41 55N 74 0W
27 Kingston-upon-Hull, see Hull
83 Kingston South East, Australia 36 50S 139 52E
95 Kingstown, St. Vincent, W.I. 13 10N 61 15W
90 Kingsville, U.S.A. 27 30N 97 55W
24 Kingswood, England 51 26N 2 21W
67 Kingtehchen, China 28 45N 118 50E
22 Kington, England 52 12N 3 2W
33 Kingussie, Scotland 57 5N 4 4W
35 Kinitty, Ireland 53 6N 7 44W
66 Kingyang, China 36 10N 107 35E
67 Kinhwa, China 28 55N 119 30E
74 Kinkala, Congo (Fr.) 4 18S 14 48E
84 Kinleith, New Zealand 38 25S 176 0E
32 Kinloch, Scotland 57 0N 6 18W
33 Kinloch, Sutherland, Scotland 58 17N 4 50W
30 Kinloch Rannoch, Scot. 56 41N 4 12W
33 Kinloss, Scotland 57 38N 3 37W
36 Kinlough, Ireland 54 27N 8 16W
35 Kinnegad, Ireland 53 28N 7 8W
63 Kinneret, Israel 32 43N 35 33E
63 Kinneret, L., (Sea of Galilee), Israel 32 50N 35 25E
31 Kinross, Scot. 56 12N 3 25W
34 Kinsale, & Hr., Ireland 51 43N 8 31W
34 Kinsale, Old Head of, Ireland 51 37N 8 32W
66 Kinsha, R., see Yangtze R.
74 Kinshasa (Leopoldville), Zaïre 4 40S 15 30E
91 Kinston, U.S.A. 35 15N 77 34W
32 Kintaravay, Scotland 58 4N 6 42W
33 Kintore, Scotland 57 14N 2 20W
30 Kintyre, Mull of, Scot. 55 17N 5 48W
30 Kintyre, Pen. & Dist., Scotland 55 35N 5 35W
34 Kinvara, Ireland 53 5N 8 48W
74 Kioga, L., see Kyoga, L., Uganda
41 Kiparissia & G., Greece 37 15N 21 32E
35 Kippure, Mt., Ireland 53 10N 6 15W
75 Kipushi, Zaïre 11 55S 27 20E
45 Kirchheim, Germany 48 38N 9 29E
36 Kircubbin, N. Ireland 54 30N 5 33W
61 Kirensk, U.S.S.R. 57 55N 108 30E
55 Kirgiz Steppe, U.S.S.R. 50 0N 70 0E
60 Kirgizia, S.S.R., U.S.S.R. 42 0N 75 0E
50 Kirillov, U.S.S.R. 59 58N 38 10E
67 Kirin, China 43 50N 127 2E
67 Kirin, Prov., China 44 20N 128 0E
41 Kirkagaç, Turkey 39 0N 27 45E
27 Kirkburton, England 53 36N 1 42W
26 Kirkby, England 53 29N 2 55W
27 Kirkby-in-Ashfield, Eng. 53 6N 1 15W
26 Kirkby Lonsdale, England 54 12N 2 38W
27 Kirkby Moorside, Eng. 54 17N 0 55W
26 Kirby Stephen, Eng. 54 27N 2 23W
31 Kirkcaldy, Scotland 56 6N 3 9W
30 Kirkcolm, Scotland 54 59N 5 4W
31 Kirkconnel, Scotland 55 23N 4 0W
30 Kirkcowan, Scotland 54 53N 4 38W
31 Kirkcudbright, Scotland 54 49N 4 3W
48 Kirkenes, Norway 69 40N 30 1E
26 Kirkham, Lancs., Eng. 53 48N 2 54W
31 Kirkintilloch, Scotland 55 56N 4 9W
48 Kirkjubaejar, Iceland 63 50N 18 1W
89 Kirkland Lake, Canada 48 15N 80 0W
41 Kirklareli, Turkey 41 45N 27 15E
31 Kirkliston, Scotland 55 55N 3 27W
31 Kirkmichael, Scotland 56 43N 3 31W
91 Kirksville, U.S.A. 40 10N 92 40W
51 Kirkuk, Iraq 35 30N 44 21E
33 Kirkwall, Scotland 58 58N 2 57W
76 Kirkwood, S. Africa 33 20S 25 25E
50 Kirov, U.S.S.R. 58 38N 49 30E
51 Kirovabad, U.S.S.R. 40 48N 46 35E
50 Kirovgrad, U.S.S.R. 57 30N 60 0E
51 Kirovograd, U.S.S.R. 48 35N 32 20E
60 Kirovsk, U.S.S.R. 38 0N 60 25E
31 Kirriemuir, Scotland 56 40N 3 0W
52 Kirsanov, U.S.S.R. 52 40N 42 35E
51 Kirsehir, Turkey 39 20N 34 0E
23 Kirtling, England 52 11N 0 29E
27 Kirton, England 52 56N 0 3W
48 Kiruna, Sweden 67 50N 20 8E
74 Kirundu, Zaïre 0 50S 25 40E
74 Kisangani (Stanleyville), Zaïre 0 40N 25 18E
62 Kiseiba, Egypt 22 30N 30 0E
60 Kiselevsk, U.S.S.R. 54 10N 86 35E
47 Kishinev, U.S.S.R. 47 2N 28 52E
64 Kishtwar, India 33 25N 75 57E
74 Kisii, Kenya 0 42S 34 44E
74 Kisiju, Tanzania 7 15S 39 28E
47 Kiskörös, Hungary 46 40N 19 20E
47 Kiskunhalas, Hungary 46 28N 19 21E
72 Kissidougou, Guinea 9 0N 10 0W
74 Kisumu, Kenya 0 2S 34 57E
63 Kiswe, Syria 33 23N 36 14E
72 Kita, Mali 13 5N 9 25W
60 Kitab, U.S.S.R. 39 25N 66 55E
67 Kitakami, R., Japan 39 30N 141 8E
67 Kitakyushu, Japan 33 52N 130 45E
74 Kitale, Kenya 1 0N 35 5E
89 Kitchener, Canada 43 30N 80 41W
74 Kitega, Burundi 3 28S 29 59E
48 Kitenen, R., Finland 67 45N 26 40E
41 Kithira, Greece 36 10N 22 57E
41 Kithira, I., Greece 36 15N 23 0E
41 Kithnos, I., Greece 37 27N 24 28E
88 Kitimat, Canada 54 5N 128 30W
74 Kitui, Kenya 1 10S 38 0E
75 Kitwe, Zambia 12 55S 28 10E
45 Kitzingen, Germany 49 40N 10 7E
66 Kiuchuan, China 39 50N 98 15E
66 Kiukiang, China 29 45N 116 0E
48 Kivalo, mts., Finland 66 10N 26 3E
74 Kivu, L., Zaïre 2 0S 29 5E
50 Kizel, U.S.S.R. 59 0N 57 40E
51 Kizil, R., Turkey 40 30N 34 15E
60 Kizil Kiva, U.S.S.R. 40 20N 72 25E
63 Kizyl Arvat, U.S.S.R. 38 55N 56 30E
51 Kizlyar, U.S.S.R. 43 52N 46 45E
13 Kjolen, Mts., Europe 66 0N 15 0E
46 Kladno, Czechoslovakia 50 13N 14 2E
46 Klagenfurt, Austria 46 39N 14 19E
49 Klaipeda, U.S.S.R. 55 42N 21 6E
90 Klamath Falls, U.S.A. 42 15N 121 46W
90 Klamath R., U.S.A. 42 30N 123 10W
49 Klar, R., Sweden 60 45N 13 0E
46 Klatovy, Cz-slov. 49 20N 13 20E
76 Klawer, S. Africa 31 45S 18 40E
76 Klerksdorp, Transvaal 26 45S 27 11E
44 Kleve, Germany 51 48N 6 9E
52 Klin, U.S.S.R. 56 30N 36 45E
76 Klipplaat, S. Africa 33 0S 24 15E
46 Klodzko, Poland 50 28N 16 35E
88 Klondike, Canada 64 5N 139 0W
45 Klosters, Switzerland 46 54N 9 50E
72 Klouto, Togo 7 0N 0 59E
61 Klyuchevsk, U.S.S.R. 55 45N 160 27E
27 Knaresborough, England 54 1N 1 27W

90 Las Vegas, N. Mexico, U.S.A. 35 35N 105 20W
65 Lashio, Burma 22 58N 97 58E
31 Lasswade, Scotland 55 53N 3 8W
74 Lastoursville, Gabon 0 48S 12 59E
40 Lastovo I., Yugoslavia 42 47N 16 53E
99 Latacunga, Ecuador 0 45S 78 30W
62 Latakia, Syria 35 27N 35 58E
33 Latheron, Scotland 58 17N 3 22W
40 Latium, Prov., Italy 42 0N 12 20E
83 Latrobe, Tasmania 41 5S 146 40E
64 Latur, India 18 35N 76 42E
49 Latvia, S.S.R., U.S.S.R. 56 50N 24 0E
84 Lau or Eastern Group, Fiji 17 0S 178 0W
31 Lauder, & Dale, Scotland 55 43N 2 44W
46 Lauenberg, Germany 53 22N 10 34E
25 Laugharne, Wales 51 47N 4 28W
83 Launceston, Australia 41 24S 147 5E
24 Launceston, England 50 39N 4 22W
65 Launglon Bok Is. (S. Moscos Is.), Burma 13 50N 97 50E
82 Laura, Australia 15 45S 144 30E
91 Laurel, U.S.A. 31 45N 89 0W
33 Laurencekirk, Scotland 56 50N 2 28W
45 Lausanne, Switzerland 46 31N 6 39E
46 Lausitz (Lusatian), mts., Cz-slov. 50 40N 15 0E
68 Laut I., Indonesia 3 30S 116 15E
45 Lauterbrunnen, Switz. 46 36N 7 54E
42 Laval, France 48 4N 0 46W
43 Lavaur, France 43 40N 1 50E
23 Lavendon, England 52 11N 0 39W
) Laverton, Australia 28 36S 122 27E
41 Lavrion, Greece 37 41N 24 2E
65 Lawng Pit, Mts., Burma 26 15N 98 15E
72 Lawra, Ghana 10 39N 2 51W
91 Lawrence, Kan., U.S.A. 38 59N 95 16W
93 Lawrence, Mass., U.S.A. 42 46N 71 2W
34 Lawrence, N.Z. 46 0S 169 45E
90 Lawton, U.S.A. 34 35N 98 30W
26 Laxey, I. of Man, Eng. 54 15N 4 23W
36 Laytown, Ireland 53 40N 6 15W
43 Le Blanc, France 46 40N 1 3E
43 Le Cateau, France 50 8N 3 30E
44 Le Chesne, France 49 31N 4 45E
43 Le Creusot, France 46 52N 4 25E
94 Le François, Martinique, Fr. W.I. 14 35N 60 55W
42 Le Havre, France 49 32N 0 5E
72 Le Kef, Tunisia 36 12N 8 47E
45 Le Locle, Switzerland 47 3N 6 44E
74 Le Marinel, Zaïre 10 25S 25 25E
99 Le Maire Str., Arg. 55 0S 65 0W
42 Le Mans, France 48 0N 0 15E
94 Le Moule, Guadeloupe I. 16 17N 61 22W
43 Le Puy, France 45 3N 3 53E
44 Le Quesnoy, France 50 15N 3 37E
43 Le Touquet, France 50 20N 1 45E
42 Le Verdon, France 45 33N 1 5W
43 Le Vigan, France 44 0N 3 32E
3 Lea, R., England 51 38N 0 1W
7 Leadenham, England 53 13N 0 33W
7 Leadgate, England 54 52N 1 48W
1 Leadhills, Scotland 55 27N 3 48W
0 Leadville, U.S.A. 39 20N 106 18W
5 Lealui, Zambia 15 10S 23 20E
2 Leamington, England 52 17N 1 32W
4 Leane, L., Ireland 52 0N 9 30W
0 Learmonth, Australia 22 30S 114 10E
3 Leatherhead, England 51 18N 0 20W
4 Leavenworth, U.S.A. 39 16N 94 59W
4 Lebanon, Mo., U.S.A. 37 43N 93 44W
1 Lebanon, Tenn., U.S.A. 36 13N 86 15W
3 Lebanon Mts., Lebanon 33 45N 35 45E
2 Lebanon, S.W. Asia 33 30N 35 40E
7 Lebrija, Spain 36 50N 6 2W
9 Lebu, Chile 37 47S 73 45W
1 Lecce, Italy 40 11N 18 12E
5 Lecco, Italy 45 51N 9 24E
5 Lech, R., Germany 47 45N 10 45E
3 Lectoure, France 43 55N 0 32E
7 Leczyca, Poland 52 2N 19 30E
4 Ledeberg, Belgium 51 3N 3 40E
7 Ledesma, Spain 41 0N 6 0W
3 Leduc, Canada 53 20N 113 30W
2 Lee, England 50 47N 1 11W
4 Lee, R., Ireland 51 54N 8 50W
7 Leeds, Yorkshire, Eng. 53 49N 1 33W
5 Leek, England 53 6N 2 2W
4 Leer, Germany 53 15N 7 22E
3 Leeton, N.S.W. 34 23S 146 28E
4 Leeuwarden, Neth. 53 13N 5 48E
) Leeuwin, C., Australia 34 21S 115 2E
5 Leeward Is., West Indies 17 0N 64 0W
3 Legaspi, Philippines 13 10N 123 46E
) Leghorn (Livorno), Italy 43 34N 10 20E
5 Legnica, Poland 51 12N 16 10E
4 Leh, India 34 10N 77 50E
4 Lehinch, Ireland 52 56N 9 20W
3 Leicester, & Co., Eng. 52 37N 1 6W
2 Leichhardt Ra., Austral. 20 46S 147 40E
4 Leiden, Netherlands 52 10N 4 30E
4 Leie, R., Belgium 51 0N 3 30E
5 Leigh, Lancs., England 53 30N 2 31W
2 Leigh, Worcs., England 52 10N 2 21W
3 Leigh Creek, Australia 30 25S 138 20E
3 Leighton Buzzard, Eng. 51 55N 0 38W
5 Leine, R., Germany 52 35N 9 40E
4 Leinster, Prov., Ireland 52 55N 6 55W
5 Leipzig, Germany 51 20N 12 21E
7 Leiria, Portugal 39 46N 8 50W
23 Leiston, England 52 13N 1 35E
31 Leith, Scotland 55 59N 3 10W
23 Leith Hill, England 51 10N 0 23W
31 Leitholm, Scotland 55 42N 2 16W
29 Leitrim, & Co., Ireland 54 0N 8 3W
44 Lek, R., Netherlands 51 56N 4 50E
44 Lelystad, Netherlands 52 32N 5 28E
45 Leman (Geneva), L., Switz. 46 28N 6 30E
44 Lemmer, Netherlands 52 49N 5 42E
49 Lemvig, Denmark 56 33N 8 20E
61 Lena R., U.S.S.R. 64 30N 127 0E
35 Lenadoon Pt., Ireland 54 19N 9 3W
30 Lendalfoot, Scotland 55 12N 4 55W
60 Leninabad, U.S.S.R. 40 10N 69 50E
51 Leninakan, U.S.S.R. 41 0N 43 40E
50 Leningrad, U.S.S.R. 60 0N 30 25E
52 Leninsk, U.S.S.R. 48 40N 45 15E
60 Leninsk Kuznetskiy, U.S.S.R. 55 15N 86 15E
60 Leninogorsk, U.S.S.R. 50 30N 83 45E
45 Lenk, Switzerland 46 28N 7 27E
51 Lenkoran, Azerbaijan 38 46N 48 50E
30 Lennox Hills, Scotland 56 2N 4 15W
30 Lennoxtown, Scotland 55 58N 4 14W
44 Lens, France 50 27N 2 49E
40 Lentini, Italy 37 20N 15 0E
72 Léo, Volta 11 3N 2 2W
46 Leoben, Austria 47 22N 15 4E
22 Leominster, England 52 14N 2 44W
94 León, Mexico 21 5N 101 50W
94 Leon, Nicaragua 12 25N 86 47W
37 Leon, & Prov., Spain 42 35N 5 35W
83 Leongatha, Victoria 39 0S 146 0E
80 Leonora, Australia 28 49S 121 19E
74 Léopoldville, *see* Kinshasa
50 Lepel, U.S.S.R. 54 45N 28 30E
61 Lepikha, U.S.S.R. 64 45N 126 55E
94 Lerdo, Mexico 25 35N 103 35W
72 Lere, Nigeria 10 22N 8 31E
37 Lerida, Spain 41 38N 0 38E
32 Lerwick, Scotland 60 9N 1 10W
43 Les Andelys, France 49 18N 1 30E
95 Les Cayes, Haiti 18 0N 74 0W
42 Les Landes, Dist., France 44 20N 1 5W
42 Les Pieux, France 49 30N 1 50W
42 Les Sables d'Olonne, Fr. 46 34N 1 50W
23 Lesbury, England 55 25N 1 37W
41 Leskovac, Yugoslavia 42 55N 21 59E
31 Leslie, Scotland 56 12N 3 12W
31 Lesmahagow, Scotland 55 38N 3 55W
76 Lesotho, Africa 29 30S 28 0E
61 Lesozavodsk, U.S.S.R. 45 25N 133 30E
95 Lesser Antilles, W. Indies 14 0N 61 30W
88 Lesser Slave L., Canada 55 30N 115 30W
68 Lesser Sunda Is., *see* Nusa Tenggara
44 Lessines, Belgium 50 43N 3 50E
41 Lésvos I., Greece 39 10N 26 34E
46 Leszno, Poland 51 53N 16 37E
76 Letaba, S. Africa 23 45S 31 40E
23 Letchworth, England 51 58N 0 13W
88 Lethbridge, Canada 49 45N 112 48W
68 Lèti Is., East Indies 8 0S 128 0E
98 Leticia, Colombia 4 0S 70 0W
65 Letpadan, Burma 17 45N 96 0E
36 Letterkenny, Ireland 54 57N 7 43W
31 Leuchars. Scotland 56 23N 2 53W
45 Leuk, Switzerland 46 20N 7 38E
45 Leukerbad, Switzerland 46 22N 7 38E
44 Leuven, Belgium 50 53N 4 42E
44 Leuze, Belgium 50 37N 3 36E
52 Lev Tolstoy, U.S.S.R. 53 13N 39 27E
48 Levanger, Norway 63 47N 11 35E
43 Levanto, Italy 44 10N 9 35E
30 Leven, L., Argyll, Scot. 56 40N 5 5W
31 Leven, L., Kinross, Scot. 56 10N 3 25W
80 Levêque, C., Australia 16 15S 122 55E
44 Leverkusen, Germany 51 2N 6 59E
84 Levin, New Zealand 40 35S 175 15E
89 Levis, Canada 46 45N 71 15W
41 Lévka Ori, Mt., Crete 35 20N 24 0E
41 Levkás I., Greece 38 40N 20 35E
84 Levuka, Fiji Is. 17 34S 179 0E
23 Lewes, England 50 52N 0 1E
32 Lewis, Butt of, Scotland 58 30N 6 16W
32 Lewis I., Scotland 58 10N 6 40W
90 Lewis Ra., U.S.A. 48 15N 114 0W
23 Lewisham, Greater London, England 51 26N 0 5E
90 Lewiston, Idaho, U.S.A. 46 27N 117 2W
90 Lewistown, Mont., U.S.A. 47 11N 109 30W
92 Lexington, U.S.A. 38 2N 84 37W
26 Leyland, England 53 41N 2 42W
68 Leyte I., Philippines 10 30N 125 0E
43 Lezignan, France 43 10N 2 50E
52 Lgov, U.S.S.R. 51 41N 35 17E
64 Lhasa, Tibet 29 42N 91 10E
67 Liaoning, prov., China 42 0N 125 0E
67 Liaotung, G. of, China 40 30N 121 30E
67 Liaotung, Pen., China 40 0N 122 40E
67 Liaoyüan, China 43 52N 123 28E
88 Liard, R., Canada 61 15N 122 30W
74 Libenge, Zaïre 3 40N 18 55E
46 Liberec, Cz-slov. 50 47N 15 7E
72 Liberia, W. Africa 6 0N 9 30W
74 Libreville, Gabon 0 25N 9 25E
73 Libya, N. Africa 27 0N 16 0E
73 Libyan Des., N. Africa 27 0N 27 0E
62 Libyan Plateau, Egypt 31 0N 26 0E
40 Licata, Italy 37 8N 13 58E
22 Lichfield, England 52 41N 1 49W
75 Lichinga, Mozambique 13 8S 35 30E
76 Lichtenburg, S. Africa 26 10S 26 18E
49 Lida, U.S.S.R. 53 53N 25 15E
49 Lidköping, Sweden 58 31N 13 14E
46 Liechtenstein, Europe 47 2N 10 0E
44 Liège, & Prov., Belgium 50 38N 5 30E
46 Lienz, Austria 46 50N 12 10E
49 Liepája, U.S.S.R. 56 30N 21 0E
44 Lier, Belgium 51 9N 4 34E
45 Liestal, Switzerland 47 29N 7 44E
35 Liffey, R., Ireland 53 20N 6 31W
36 Lifford, Ireland 54 49N 7 29W
40 Liguria, prov., Italy 44 20N 8 30E
40 Ligurian Sea, Medit. S. 43 20N 8 40E
65 Lihwa, China 30 5N 100 20E
74 Likasi (Jadotville), Zaïre 10 52S 26 47E
74 Likati, Zaïre 3 20N 24 0E
66 Likiang, China 26 50N 100 5E
43 Lille, France 50 38N 3 0E
49 Lille Bælt, Denmark 55 8N 10 0E
49 Lillehammer, Norway 61 10N 10 29E
49 Lillesand, Norway 58 12N 8 23E
22 Lilleshall, England 52 45N 2 22W
49 Lilleström, Norway 59 56N 11 7E
88 Lillooet, Canada 50 44N 122 0W
75 Lilongwe, Malawi 14 0S 33 40E
49 Lim Fjord, Denmark 56 38N 8 23E
98 Lima, Peru 12 10S 77 5W
92 Lima, U.S.A. 40 40N 84 5W
62 Limassol, Cyprus 34 20N 33 0E
36 Limavady, N. Ireland 55 3N 6 56W
44 Limbourg, Prov., Belg. 51 0N 5 30E
44 Limburg, Germany 50 25N 8 5E
44 Limburg, Prov., Neth. 51 15N 6 0E
29 Limerick, & Co., Ireland 52 40N 8 37W
34 Limerick Junction, Ire. 52 30N 8 12W
41 Limnos, I., Greece 39 50N 25 10E
43 Limoges, France 45 51N 1 15E
95 Limón, Costa Rica 10 0N 83 2W
43 Limousin, Prov., France 45 35N 1 30E
43 Limoux, France 43 0N 2 15E
75 Limpopo, R., Mozam. 25 10S 33 30E
23 Limpsfield, England 51 15N 0 1E
74 Limuru, Kenya 1 6S 36 38E
99 Linares, Chile 36 0S 71 35W
94 Linares, Mexico 24 50N 99 20W
37 Linares, Spain 38 10N 3 42W
28 Lincoln, & Co., England 53 16N 0 33W
84 Lincoln, New Zealand 43 37S 172 30E
91 Lincoln, Neb., U.S.A. 40 55N 96 46W
27 Lincolnshire Wolds, Eng. 53 30N 0 20W
45 Lindau, Germany 47 33N 9 40E
49 Lindesnes, C., Norway 57 58N 7 3E
92 Lindsay, Canada 44 28N 78 53W
68 Lingayen Gulf, Phil. 16 30N 120 20E
63 Lingeh, Iran 26 35N 54 47E
44 Lingen, Germany 52 36N 7 19E
23 Lingfield, England 51 11N 0 1W
68 Lingga, Arch., E. Indies 0 0 104 37E
72 Linguéré, Senegal 15 25N 15 5W
67 Lini, China 35 10N 118 30E
49 Linköping, Sweden 58 24N 15 35E
31 Linlithgow, Scotland 55 58N 3 38W
25 Linney Head, Wales 51 37N 5 4W
30 Linnhe, L., Scotland 56 35N 5 30W
66 Linsia, China 35 40N 102 30E
23 Linslade, England 51 55N 0 40W
45 Linth, R., Switzerland 47 0N 9 0E
23 Liston, Cambs., England 52 6N 0 19E
66 Lintsing, China 36 55N 116 0E
43 Lions, G. of France 43 0N 4 0E
40 Lipari Is., Italy 38 40N 15 7E
52 Lipetsk, U.S.S.R. 52 45N 39 45E
47 Lipno, Poland 52 50N 19 15E
44 Lippe, R., Germany 51 40N 7 20E
74 Lira, Uganda 2 15N 32 55E
37 Liria, Spain 39 35N 0 35W
74 Lisala, Zaïre 2 15N 21 37E
36 Lisbellaw, N. Ireland 54 20N 7 32W
37 Lisbon, Portugal 38 43N 9 10W
36 Lisburn, N. Ireland 54 31N 6 3W
34 Liscannor, & B., Ireland 52 55N 9 27W
34 Liscarroll, Ireland 52 15N 8 44W
34 Lisdoonvarna, Ireland 53 2N 9 18W
24 Liskeard, England 50 28N 4 26W
83 Lismore, Australia 28 47S 153 20E
34 Lismore, Ireland 52 8N 7 58W
36 Lisnaskea, N. Ireland 54 15N 7 28W
23 Liss, England 51 3N 0 53W
44 Lisse, Netherlands 52 17N 4 33E
92 Listowel, Canada 43 45N 80 57W
34 Listowel, Ireland 52 28N 9 28W
66 Litang, China 23 25N 108 10E
26 Litherland, England 53 29N 3 0W
83 Lithgow, Australia 33 30S 150 14E
41 Lithinon, C., Crete 35 0N 24 45E
49 Lithuania, S.S.R., U.S.S.R. 55 35N 24 0E
46 Litomerice, Cz-slov. 50 33N 14 10E
91 Little Abaco I., Bahamas 26 51N 77 45W
100 Little America, Antarc. 79 0S 164 0W
76 Little Bushman Ld., S. Africa 29 0S 18 30E
46 Little Carpathians, mts., Czechoslovakia 48 30N 17 20E
92 Little Current, Canada 45 58N 81 59W
76 Little Karroo, S. Africa 33 44S 22 0E
67 Little Khinyan, mts., China 48 0N 128 0E
32 Little Minch, Scotland 57 37N 6 50W
90 Little Missouri R., U.S.A. 46 0N 104 0W
64 Little Rann, India 23 25N 71 25E
91 Little Rock, U.S.A. 34 50N 92 25W
43 Little St. Bernard, Mt., Fr. 45 40N 6 47E
26 Littleborough, England 53 38N 2 8W
23 Littlehampton, England 50 48N 0 32W
23 Littleport, England 52 27N 0 18E
66 Liuchow, China 24 21N 109 5E
75 Liuwa Plain, Zambia 14 30S 22 35E
83 Liverpool, Australia 33 59S 150 52E
89 Liverpool, Canada 44 0N 65 0W
26 Liverpool, England 53 25N 3 0W
83 Liverpool Ra. & Pl., Australia 31 40S 150 30E
31 Livingston, Scotland 55 52N 3 33W
90 Livingston, U.S.A. 45 43N 110 41W
75 Livingstone, Zambia 17 48S 25 58E
74 Livingstonia, Malawi 10 33S 34 5E
40 Livorno, *see* Leghorn
99 Livramento, Brazil 30 50S 55 30W
74 Liwale, Tanzania 9 45S 38 0E
34 Lixnaw, Ireland 52 24N 9 38W
24 Lizard Pt., England 49 58N 5 11W
40 Ljubljana, Yugoslavia 46 4N 14 50E
48 Ljungan, R., Sweden 62 30N 14 30E
49 Ljungby, Sweden 56 55N 13 56E
49 Ljusdal, Sweden 61 50N 16 5E
49 Ljusna, Sweden 61 16N 17 12E
49 Ljusnan, R., Sweden 62 0N 15 20E
25 Llanaelhaiarn, Wales 52 59N 4 24W
25 Llanafan-fawr, Wales 52 12N 3 29W
25 Llanarth, Wales 52 12N 4 19W
25 Llanarthney, Wales 51 51N 4 9W
25 Llanberis, Wales 53 6N 4 4W
25 Llanddewi-Brefi, Wales 52 11N 3 57W
25 Llandeilo, Wales 51 53N 3 59W
25 Llandogo, Wales 51 43N 2 42ES
25 Llandovery, Wales 51 59N 3 48W
25 Llandrillo, Wales 52 56N 3 27W
25 Llandrindod Wells, Wales 52 15N 3 23W
25 Llandudno, Wales 53 20N 3 51W
25 Llandygwydd, Wales 52 3N 4 33W
25 Llandyrnog, Wales 53 10N 3 19W
25 Llandyssul, Wales 52 3N 4 20W
25 Llanelli, Wales 51 41N 4 8W
37 Llanes, Spain 43 30N 4 50W
25 Llanfaelog, Wales 53 13N 4 29W
25 Llanfair Caereinion, Wales 52 39N 3 20W
25 Llanfairfechan, Wales 53 15N 3 58W
25 Llangefni, Wales 53 15N 4 20W
25 Llangelynin, Wales 52 39N 4 7W
25 Llangennech, Wales 51 41N 4 10W
25 Llangollen, Wales 52 58N 3 11W
25 Llanharan, Wales 51 32N 3 28W
25 Llanidloes, Wales 52 26N 3 32W
25 Llanllyfni, Wales 53 2N 4 18W
25 Llannor, Wales 52 55N 4 25W
90 Llano Estacado (Staked Plains) U.S.A. 33 30N 103 0W
25 Llanon, Wales 52 17N 4 9W
96 Llanos, Reg., Columbia & Ven. 5 0N 67 0W
99 Llanquihue, L., Chile 41 2S 72 55W
25 Llanrhidian, Wales 51 36N 4 11W
25 Llanrwst, Wales 53 9N 3 48W
25 Llanstephan, Wales 51 46N 4 24W
25 Llantrisant, Wales 51 32N 3 25W
25 Llantwit-Major, Wales 51 24N 3 29W
25 Llanwenog, Wales 52 6N 4 11W
25 Llanystymdwy, Wales 52 56N 4 17W
25 Llethr, Mt., Wales 52 47N 3 58W
25 Lleyn Penin, Wales 52 55N 4 35W
88 Lloydminster, Canada 53 20N 110 3W
99 Llullaillaco, Mt., Chile 24 40S 68 30W
31 Loanhead, Scotland 55 53N 3 10W
76 Lobatse, Botswana 25 15S 25 30E
75 Lobito, Angola 12 0S 13 0E
98 Lobos Is., Peru 6 15S 81 0W
45 Locarno, Switzerland 46 11N 8 48E
32 Lochaber, Dist., Scotland 57 0N 5 0W
30 Lochaline, Scotland 56 32N 5 47W
30 Lochans, Scotland 54 52N 5 1W
32 Lochcarron, Scotland 57 25N 5 30W
30 Lochdonhead, Scotland 56 27N 5 40W
44 Lochem, Netherlands 52 10N 6 26W
43 Loches, France 47 10N 1 0E
31 Lochgelly, Scotland 56 7N 3 18W
30 Lochgilphead, Scotland 56 3N 5 25W
30 Lochgoilhead, Scotland 56 10N 4 54W
32 Lochinver, Scotland 58 9N 5 15W
31 Lochmaben, Scotland 55 8N 3 27W
33 Lochnagar, Mt., Scotland 56 56N 3 15W
30 Lochranza, Scotland 55 42N 5 18W
30 Lochwinnoch, Scotland 55 47N 4 39W
33 Lochy, L., & R., Scot. 56 57N 4 55W
92 Loch Haven, U.S.A. 41 7N 77 33W
31 Lockerbie, Scotland 55 6N 3 22W
83 Lockhart, Australia 35 10S 146 48E
91 Lockport, U.S.A. 43 10N 78 45W
63 Lod (Lydda), Israel 31 57N 34 54E
43 Lodi, Italy 45 20N 9 32E
74 Lodja, Zaïre 3 38S 23 35E
74 Lodwar, Kenya 2 58N 35 25E
47 Lódz, Poland 51 48N 19 22E
76 Loeriesfontein, S. Africa 30 56S 19 28E
48 Lofoten Is., Norway 68 30N 15 0E
27 Loftus, England 54 33N 0 52W
90 Logan, U.S.A. 41 42N 111 47W
86 Logan, Mt., Yukon, Canada 60 48N 138 40W
92 Logansport, U.S.A. 40 48N 86 20W
74 Loge, R., Angola 7 35S 14 15E
37 Logrono, Spain 42 25N 2 21W
65 Lohardaga, India 23 30N 84 36E
62 Loheia, Yemen 15 45N 42 40E
66 Loho, China 33 30N 114 0E
45 Lohr, Germany 49 59N 9 33E
65 Loikaw, Burma 19 43N 97 20E
49 Loimaa, Finland 60 51N 22 53E
42 Loir-et-Cher, Dépt., Fr. 47 33N 1 50E
42 Loire, Dépt., France 45 40N 4 5E
43 Loire, R., France 47 40N 2 30E
42 Loire-Atlant., Dépt., Fr. 47 32N 1 48W
42 Loiret, Dépt. France 48 5N 2 20E
98 Loja, Ecuador 4 0S 79 16W
37 Loja, Spain 37 10N 4 15W
44 Lokeren, Belgium 51 6N 3 59E
74 Lokitaung, Kenya 4 18N 35 45E
48 Lokka Res., Finland 68 00N 27 30E
48 Lökken, Norway 63 8N 9 45E
72 Lokoja, Nigeria 7 48N 6 43E
74 Lokolama, Zaïre 2 10S 19 50E
49 Lolland, Denmark 54 50N 11 30E
65 Lolungchung, China 30 45N 96 10E
41 Lom, Bulgaria 43 52N 23 20E
40 Lombardy, Prov., Italy 45 22N 9 50E
68 Lomblen I., Indonesia 8 30S 123 32E
68 Lombok, I., Indonesia 8 35S 116 30E
72 Lome, Togo 6 8N 1 10E
74 Lomela & R., Zaïre 2 5S 23 52E
74 Lomié, Cameroon 3 13N 13 38E
30 Lomond, L., Scotland 56 4N 4 34W
89 London, Canada 43 0N 81 21W
23 London, Greater, Eng. 51 30N 0 5W
36 Londonderry, & Co., N. Ireland 55 0N 7 18W
99 Londrina, Brazil 23 30S 50 45W
91 Long Bay, U.S.A. 33 30N 78 30W
90 Long Beach, Calif., U.S.A. 33 50N 118 6W
22 Long Eaton, England 52 53N 1 15W
93 Long I., U.S.A. 40 50N 73 0W
30 Long, L., Scotland 56 5N 4 52W
25 Long Mt., Wales 52 38N 3 3W
23 Long Melford, England 52 5N 0 44E
22 Long Mynd, mt., Eng. 52 30N 2 56W
23 Long Sutton, England 52 47N 0 9E
68 Long Xuyen, Vietnam 10 15N 105 25E
32 Longa I., Scotland 57 45N 5 50W
65 Longdam, China 28 15N 98 15E
83 Longford, Australia 41 47S 147 4E
36 Longford, & Co., Ireland 53 44N 7 46W
31 Longforgan, Scotland 56 28N 3 8W
89 Longlac, Canada 49 45N 86 25W
65 Longling, China 24 35N 98 35E
90 Longmont, U.S.A. 40 14N 105 10W
82 Longreach, Australia 23 29S 144 13E
26 Longridge, England 53 50N 2 37W
33 Longside, Scotland 57 30N 1 57W
26 Longton (Lancs.), Eng. 53 43N 2 48W
26 Longton (Staffs.), England 53 0N 2 8W
26 Longtown, Cumb., Eng. 55 0N 2 58W
44 Longuyon, France 49 27N 5 35E
91 Longview, U.S.A. 32 28N 94 29W
43 Longwy, France 49 31N 5 46E
43 Lons le Saunier, France 46 42N 5 31E
48 Lönsdal, Norway 66 45N 15 30E
34 Loop Hd., Ireland 52 34N 9 56W
66 Lop Nor, L., China 40 0N 90 0E
74 Lopez, C., Gabon 0 47S 8 40E
65 Lora, R., Afghanistan 32 0N 67 15E
92 Lorain, U.S.A. 41 29N 82 10W
64 Loralai, Pakistan 30 25N 68 30E
37 Lorca, Spain 37 40N 1 41W
81 Lord Howe I., Pac. Oc. 31 0S 159 0E
82 Lorengau, Papua N.G. 2 0S 147 0E
40 Loreto, Italy 43 26N 13 40E
42 Lorient, France 47 45N 3 22W
30 Lorn, Firth of, Scot. 56 20N 5 40W
83 Lorne, Australia 38 35S 144 0E
45 Lorrach, Germany 47 37N 7 38E
45 Lorraine, reg., France 48 58N 6 0E
99 Los Andes, Chile 32 42S 70 25W
99 Los Angeles, Chile 37 42S 72 20W
90 Los Angeles, U.S.A. 33 50N 118 22W
94 Los Mochis, Mexico 25 50N 109 0W
61 Loshkalakh, U.S.S.R. 62 40N 147 5E
40 Losinj, I., Yugoslavia 44 55N 14 45E
33 Lossiemouth, Scotland 57 44N 3 16W
42 Lot, Dépt., France 44 52N 1 48E
43 Lot, R., France 44 30N 1 45E
99 Lota, Chile 37 15S 73 20W
73 Lotagipi Swamp, Sudan & Kenya 4 28N 35 0E
42 Lot-et-Garonne, Dépt., Fr. 44 33N 0 22E
31 Lothian, Reg., Scotland 55 50N 3 0W
74 Loto, Zaïre 2 18S 23 0E
45 Lotschberg Tunnel, Switz. 46 25N 7 40E
48 Lotta, R., U.S.S.R. 68 30N 29 0E
42 Loudeac, France 48 5N 2 45W
72 Louga, Senegal 15 38N 16 7W
22 Loughborough, England 52 45N 1 12W
36 Loughbrickland, N. Ire. 54 19N 6 19W
25 Loughor, Wales 51 39N 4 5W
34 Loughrea, Ireland 53 14N 8 35W
36 Loughros More B., Ireland 54 47N 8 34W
37 Louie, Portugal 37 8N 8 0W
76 Louis Trichardt, S. Africa 25 5S 29 50E
82 Louisiade Arch., Papua N.G. 10 0S 153 0E
91 Louisiana, st., U.S.A. 31 0N 92 0W
92 Louisville, U.S.A. 38 16N 85 48W
42 Lourdes, France 43 15N 0 3W
75 Lourenco Marques, *see* Maputo
27 Louth, England 53 24N 0 2W
36 Louth, & Co., Ireland 53 56N 6 31W
44 Louvain, *see* Leuven
43 Louviers, France 49 15N 1 10E
43 Lovere, Italy 45 50N 10 5E

49 Loviisa, Finland 60 25N 26 20E
93 Lowell, U.S.A. 42 44N 71 15W
46 Lower Austria, prov., Austria 48 0N 16 0E
94 Lower California, Mex. 28 0N 113 30W
84 Lower Hutt, N.Z. 41 10S 174 55E
46 Lower Saxony, Länd, Ger. 52 45N 9 0E
61 Lr. Tunguska, R., U.S.S.R. 64 0N 98 0E
23 Lowestoft, England 52 29N 1 47E
47 Lowicz, Poland 52 3N 19 59E
31 Lowther Hills, Scotland 55 20N 3 40W
83 Loxton, Australia 34 28S 140 31E
78 Loyalty Is., Pac. Oc. 20 20S 168 0E
66 Loyang, China 34 55N 112 15E
42 Lozère, Dépt., France 44 28N 3 30E
74 Luacano, Angola 11 15S 21 40E
74 Luanda, Angola 8 58S 13 9E
66 Luang Prabang, Laos 19 52N 101 50E
75 Luangwa, R., Zambia 12 0S 32 28E
75 Luanshya, Zambia 13 8S 28 25E
74 Luashi, Zaïre 11 3S 23 38E
74 Luau, Angola 10 39S 22 14E
75 Lubango, Angola 15 0S 13 30E
90 Lubbock, U.S.A. 33 37N 101 50W
46 Lübeck, & B., Germany 53 52N 10 41E
47 Lublin, Poland 51 18N 22 32E
75 Lubumbashi (Elisabethville), Zaïre 11 30S 27 31E
35 Lucan, Ireland 53 21N 6 27W
88 Lucania, Mt., Alaska 61 10N 140 20W
40 Lucca, Italy 43 52N 10 35E
30 Luce B., Scotland 54 45N 4 45W
94 Lucea, Jamaica 18 25N 78 10W
68 Lucena, Philippines 14 0N 121 35E
37 Lucena, Spain 37 28N 4 28W
47 Luzenéc, Cz-slov. 48 18N 19 42E
66 Luchow, China 29 5N 105 0E
75 Lucira, Angola 14 0S 12 35E
46 Luckenwalde, Germany 52 15N 13 10E
65 Lucknow, India 26 57N 80 59E
42 Luçon, France 46 30N 1 10W
75 Lüderitz, S.W. Africa 26 40S 15 19E
64 Ludhiana, India 30 53N 76 2E
91 Ludington, U.S.A. 43 55N 86 29W
22 Ludlow, England 52 22N 2 42W
49 Ludvika, Sweden 60 15N 15 5E
45 Ludwigsburg, Germany 48 53N 9 11E
45 Ludwigshafen, Germany 49 30N 8 27E
74 Luebo, Zaïre 5 10S 21 24E
75 Luena, Angola 11 45S 19 58E
74 Lufira, R., Zaïre 9 20S 27 0E
91 Lufkin, U.S.A. 31 17N 94 46W
45 Lugano, Switzerland 46 1N 8 48E
45 Lugano, L. di., Switz. 46 2N 8 57E
52 Lugansk, *see* Voroshilovgrad
75 Lugenda, R., Mozam. 12 30S 36 20E
35 Lugnaquillia, Mt., Ire. 52 57N 6 25W
37 Lugo, Spain 43 2N 7 34W
47 Lugoj, Rumania 45 38N 21 57E
60 Lugovoi, U.S.S.R. 43 10N 72 50E
22 Lugwardine, England 52 4N 2 38W
33 Luichart, L., Scotland 57 38N 4 44W
66 Luichow Pen., China 20 40N 110 0E
30 Luing, I., Scotland 56 15N 5 40W
45 Luino, Italy 45 59N 8 43E
74 Luisa, Zaïre 7 40S 22 30E
75 Lukanga Swamp, Zambia 14 30S 27 50E
74 Lukenie, R., Zaïre 3 0S 18 30E
74 Lukolela, Zaïre 1 30S 17 8E
47 Lukow, Poland 51 58N 22 22E
48 Lule, R., Sweden 66 20N 21 0E
48 Lulea, Sweden 65 33N 22 8E
66 Luliang Mts., China 37 30N 111 0E
74 Lulonga, R., Zaïre 1 0N 18 40E
74 Lulua, R., Zaïre 6 20S 22 40E
74 Luluabourg, *see* Kananga
75 Lumai, Angola 13 20S 21 25E
75 Lumbala, Angola 14 12S 21 20E
33 Lumphanan, Scotland 57 8N 2 41W
84 Lumsden, N.Z. 45 41S 168 29E
49 Lund, Sweden 55 44N 13 6E
75 Lundazi, Zambia 12 30S 33 20E
24 Lundy, I., Bristol Chan. 51 11N 4 40W
26 Lune, R., England 54 10N 2 40W
46 Lüneburg, Germany 53 13N 10 22E
43 Lunel, France 43 40N 4 5E
93 Lunenburg, Canada 44 25N 64 32W
43 Luneville, France 48 39N 6 30E
48 Lungholt, Iceland 63 30N 18 5W
67 Lungkow, China 37 38N 120 25E
65 Lungleh, India 22 55N 92 45E
74 Luofu, Zaïre 0 1N 29 15E
40 Luqa, Malta 35 50N 14 27E
43 Lure, France 47 40N 6 30E
36 Lurgan (Craigavon), N. Ireland 54 28N 6 20W
75 Lusaka, Zambia 15 3S 28 30E
74 Lusambo, Zaïre 4 55S 23 20E
74 Lushoto, Tanzania 4 50S 38 10E
35 Lusk, Ireland 53 32N 6 10W
30 Luss, Scotland 56 6N 4 38W
67 Lü-ta (Dairen-Port Arthur), China 39 0N 121 33E
23 Luton, England 51 52N 0 25W
47 Lutsk, U.S.S.R. 50 50N 25 15E
22 Lutterworth, England 52 27N 1 14W
74 Luwingu, Zambia 10 15S 30 2E
44 Luxembourg, Prov., Belg. 49 58N 5 30E
44 Luxembourg, Lux. 49 37N 6 8E
44 Luxembourg, Europe 49 45N 6 20E
73 Luxor, Egypt 25 40N 32 38E
42 Luz, France 42 50N 0 2W
45 Luzern, & Cn., Switz. 47 3N 8 18E
46 Luzické Hory (Lusatian Mts.), Cz-slov., *see* Lausitz mts.
68 Luzon, I., Philippines 16 30N 121 0E
47 Lvov, U.S.S.R. 49 51N 24 0E
61 Lyakhov Is., U.S.S.R. 73 30N 143 0E
33 Lybster, Scotland 58 18N 3 16W
51 Lycian Taurus, Mts., Tur. 37 0N 30 30E
23 Lydd, England 50 56N 0 54E
63 Lydda, *see* Lod
76 Lydenburg, S. Africa 25 0S 30 27E
24 Lydford, England 50 38N 4 7W
48 Lyeksele, Sweden 64 32N 18 40E
84 Lyell, & Ra., N.Z. 41 46S 172 4E
24 Lyme Bay, England 50 38N 2 55W
24 Lyme Regis, England 50 43N 2 57W
22 Lymington, England 50 47N 1 34W
26 Lymm, England 53 23N 2 30W
47 Lyna, R., Poland 54 17N 21 0E
92 Lynchburg, U.S.A. 37 28N 79 12W
22 Lyndhurst, England 50 51N 1 36W
83 Lynd Ra., Australia 25 35S 149 20E
22 Lyneham, England 51 30N 1 57W
24 Lynmouth, England 51 14N 3 50W
92 Lynn, U.S.A. 42 30N 71 0W
43 Lyonnais, Prov., France 45 50N 4 20E
42 Lyons, France 45 47N 4 50E
26 Lytham, England 53 45N 2 58W
84 Lyttelton, New Zealand 43 38S 172 46E
52 Lyubertsy, U.S.S.R. 55 41N 37 54E

M

66 Ma, R., *see* Hwang
62 Ma'an, Jordan 30 15N 35 37E
49 Maarianhamina, Finland 60 12N 20 0E
44 Maas, R., Netherlands 51 48N 5 30E
44 Maaseik, Belgium 51 7N 5 47E
44 Maastricht, Netherlands 50 52N 5 42E
73 Maatin-es-Sarra, Libya 21 45N 22 0E
74 Mabirou, Congo (Fr.) 1 10S 15 48E
27 Mablethorpe, England 53 21N 0 14E
91 McAlester, U.S.A. 34 58N 95 50W
66 Macao, & Port. Terr., China 22 15N 113 35E
98 Macapá, Brazil 0 5N 52 0W
26 Macclesfield, England 53 16N 2 8W
86 McClure Str., Can. 74 20N 120 0W
91 McComb, U.S.A. 31 30N 90 27W
83 Macdonald, L., Australia 23 30S 128 40E
80 Macdonnell Ranges, Australia 23 30S 133 0E
88 Macdougall L., Canada 66 20N 98 30W
33 Macduff, Scotland 57 41N 2 29W
41 Macedonia, Prov., Greece 40 45N 23 0E
41 Macedonia, Yugoslavia 41 30N 21 30E
98 Maceio, Brazil 9 30S 35 40W
72 Macenta, Guinea 8 35N 9 20W
40 Macerata, Italy 43 18N 13 33E
34 Macgillacuddy's Reeks, Mts., Ireland 52 0N 9 48W
98 Machala, Ecuador 3 10S 79 59W
30 Machars, The, dist., Scot. 54 45N 4 30W
61 Machevna, U.S.S.R. 61 5N 172 0E
93 Machias, U.S.A. 44 45N 67 30W
65 Machilipatnam, India 16 12N 81 12E
72 Macius Nguema Biyoga, I., W. Africa 3 25N 8 45E
83 Macintyre, R., Australia 28 32S 150 25E
82 Mackay, Australia 21 6S 149 14E
80 Mackay, L., Australia 23 0S 131 0E
92 McKeesport, U.S.A. 40 22N 79 41W
88 Mackenzie, Terr., Can. 64 30N 115 0W
88 Mackenzie Mts., Canada 64 0N 130 0W
82 Mackenzie R., Australia 23 30S 148 45E
88 Mackenzie R., Canada 62 0N 122 0W
83 Macksville, Australia 30 40S 152 56E
83 Maclean, Australia 29 29S 153 15E
83 Macleay R., Australia 30 56S 153 0E
88 McLennan, Canada 55 50N 117 0W
100 McMurdo, & Sd., Antarctica 78 0S 166 0E
88 McMurray, Canada 56 35N 111 30W
90 McPherson, U.S.A. 38 25N 97 45W
83 McPherson Ra., Australia 28 20S 153 0E
43 Mâcon, France 46 21N 4 45E
91 Macon, U.S.A. 32 40N 83 28W
75 Macondo, Angola 12 40S 23 48E
83 Macquarie, Hr., Austral. 42 2S 145 10E
100 Macquarie, I., S. Ocean 54 0S 159 0E
83 Macumba R., Australia 27 0S 136 0E
61 Madaba, Jordan 31 42N 35 48E
73 Madagali, Nigeria 10 56N 13 33E
74 Madagascar I., Africa 19 0S 46 0E
73 Madama, Niger 21 35N 13 50E
82 Madang, Papua N.G. 5 15S 145 46E
72 Madaoua, Niger 14 5N 6 27E
65 Madaripur, Bangladesh 23 10N 90 10E
40 Maddalena I., Italy 41 20N 9 22E
94 Madden L., Panama 9 15N 79 35W
32 Maddy, L., Scotland 57 36N 7 6W
72 Madeira, I., Atlant. Oc. 32 40N 17 20W
98 Madeira, R., Brazil 6 0S 61 0W
94 Madera, Mexico 29 15N 107 55W
64 Madhya Pradesh, st., Ind. 23 0N 78 0E
62 Madinat al Shaab, S. Yemen 13 0N 44 45E
74 Madingou, Congo (Fr.) 4 10S 13 33E
92 Madison, Wis., U.S.A. 43 15N 89 30W
68 Madiun, Indonesia 7 27S 111 30E
64 Madras, India 13 2N 80 22E
94 Madre, Sa., mts., Mex. 25 0N 106 0W
68 Madre, Sa., mts., Phil. 17 30N 122 0E
99 Madre de Dios, I., Chile 50 30S 75 30W
37 Madrid, Spain 40 27N 3 42W
68 Madura, I., Indonesia 7 0S 114 0E
64 Madurai, India 9 50N 78 5E
65 Mae Hong Son, Thailand 19 25N 98 5E
25 Maesteg, Wales 51 36N 3 40W
76 Maevatanana, Madag. 16 57S 46 50E
75 Mafeking, S. Africa 25 48S 25 30E
83 Maffra, Australia 38 4S 147 0E
63 Mafraq, Jordan 32 21N 36 12E
61 Magadan, U.S.S.R. 59 40N 150 50E
74 Magadi, Kenya 1 40S 36 20E
98 Magangue, Colombia 9 15N 74 50W
72 Magburaka, Sierra Leone 8 41N 11 45W
98 Magdalena, R., Colombia 9 0N 74 40W
46 Magdeburg, Germany 52 8N 11 35E
68 Magelang, Indonesia 7 45S 110 20E
99 Magellan's Str., Chile 52 20S 69 0W
45 Maggia, R., Switzerland 46 17N 8 40E
45 Maggiore, L., Italy 46 0N 8 40E
36 Maghera, N. Ireland 54 51N 6 40W
36 Magherafelt, N. Ireland 54 45N 6 38W
50 Magnitogorsk, U.S.S.R. 53 20N 59 0E
93 Magog, Canada 45 20N 72 0W
36 Maguires' Bridge, N. Ire. 54 18N 7 28W
64 Mahabaleshwar, India 17 58N 73 50E
68 Mahakam, R., Indonesia 0 25N 116 30E
75 Mahalapye, Botswana 23 0S 26 48E
73 Mahalla el Kubra, Egypt 31 10N 31 0E
65 Mahanadi, R., India 20 30N 84 30E
64 Mahbubnagar, India 16 45N 77 55E
73 Mahdia, Tunisia 35 30N 11 2E
84 Maheno, New Zealand 45 8S 170 50E
84 Mahia Pen., N.Z. 39 12S 177 53E
74 Mai-Ndombe, L., Zaïre 2 0S 18 30E
62 Maidan-i-Naftan, Iran 32 0N 49 27E
23 Maidenhead, England 51 31N 0 42W
23 Maidstone, England 51 15N 0 32E
72 Maiduguri, Nigeria 12 0N 13 5E
65 Maijdi, Bangladesh 22 45N 91 25E
65 Maikala, Ra., India 21 50N 81 0E
64 Maimana, Afghanistan 35 55N 64 35E
45 Main, R., Germany 49 50N 9 30E
42 Maine, Prov., France 48 10N 0 0
91 Maine, st., U.S.A. 45 0N 68 30W
42 Maine-et-Loire, Dépt., France 47 17N 0 23W
33 Mainland, I., Orkneys, Scotland 59 0N 3 0W
32 Mainland, I., Shetlands, Scotland 60 15N 1 20W
43 Maintenon, France 48 35N 1 38E
75 Maintirano, Madag. 18 3S 44 5E
45 Mainz, Germany 50 0N 8 15E
99 Maipo Vol., Chile 34 0S 70 0W
83 Maitland, Australia 32 49S 151 38E
67 Maizuru, Japan 35 25N 135 25E
68 Majene, Indonesia 3 29S 119 4E
62 Majma'a, Saudi Arabia 25 52N 45 28E
37 Majorca, I., *see* Mallorca
75 Majunga, Madag. 15 40S 46 25E
72 Maka-Koulibentane, Sénégal 13 40N 14 13W
75 Makarikari Salt Pan, Botswana 20 45S 26 20E
68 Makasar, *see* Ujung Pandang 5 10S 119 20E
68 Makasar, Str. of, Indonesia 3 0S 117 0E
51 Makat, U.S.S.R. 47 40N 53 25E
72 Makeni, Sierra Leone 8 56N 12 5W
52 Makeyevka, U.S.S.R. 48 0N 38 0E
51 Makhachkala, U.S.S.R. 42 58N 47 40E
66 Makhai, China 38 30N 93 40E
47 Makó, Hungary 46 16N 20 27E
74 Makokou, Gabon 0 35N 12 55E
61 Makorovo, U.S.S.R. 57 30N 107 40E
64 Makrai, India 22 2N 77 0E
63 Makran, dist., Iran 26 0N 60 30E
64 Makran Coast Ra., Pakistan 25 30N 64 0E
60 Maksimoyarskoye, U.S.S.R. 58 50N 87 5E
64 Malabar Coast, India 12 0N 75 25E
68 Malacca, Str. of, Malaya 4 0N 100 0E
37 Maladetta, Mt., Spain 42 40N 0 30E
37 Malaga, Spain 36 46N 4 47W
75 Malagasy Rep., Africa 19 0S 46 0E
35 Malahide, Ireland 53 27N 6 10W
73 Malakal, Sudan 9 37N 31 45E
64 Malakand, Pakistan 34 30N 72 0E
68 Malaku (Moluccas), Is., Indonesia 2 0S 127 30E
61 Malamyzh, U.S.S.R. 50 0N 136 50E
68 Malang, Indonesia 8 0S 112 34E
74 Malanje, Angola 9 30S 16 17E
49 Mälaren L., Sweden 59 30N 16 50E
51 Malatya, Turkey 38 37N 38 35E
74 Malawi, E. Africa 12 30S 33 40E
75 Malawi, L., *see* Nyasa L.
55 Malay Pen., S.E. Asia 4 30N 102 0E
68 Malaya, st., S.E. Asia 4 0N 103 0E
68 Malaysia, S.E. Asia 4 0N 110 0E
51 Malazgirt, Turkey 39 13N 42 30E
82 Malbon, Australia 21 5S 140 17E
47 Malbork, Poland 54 3N 19 10E
80 Malcolm, Australia 28 58S 121 30E
44 Maldegem, Belgium 51 12N 3 27E
55 Maldive Is., Indian Ocean 5 0N 73 0E
23 Maldon, England 51 43N 0 41E
64 Malegaon, India 20 35N 74 25E
48 Malgomaj, L., Sweden 64 45N 16 5E
73 Malha, Sudan 15 8N 25 10E
26 Malham Tarn, England 54 6N 2 11W
37 Malhao, Sa. do, mts., Port. 37 25N 8 0W
90 Malheur, L., U.S.A. 43 20N 118 50W
72 Mali, West Africa 18 0N 1 0W
65 Mali, R., Burma 26 30N 97 50E
36 Malin Hd. & Pen., Ire. 55 23N 7 22W
66 Malipo, China 23 25N 104 45E
32 Mallaig, Scotland 57 0N 5 48W
73 Mallawi, Egypt 27 44N 30 44E
37 Mallorca I., Balaeric Is., Spain 39 30N 3 0E
34 Mallow, Ireland 52 9N 8 38W
25 Malltraeth B., Wales 53 7N 4 25W
48 Malmberget, Sweden 67 13N 20 32E
44 Malmédy, Belgium 50 26N 6 2E
22 Malmesbury, England 51 36N 2 6W
49 Malmö, Sweden 55 38N 12 57E
49 Malmöhus, Co., Sweden 55 45N 13 15E
40 Malta, I., Medit. Sea 35 54N 14 28E
27 Maltby, England 53 25N 1 12W
27 Malton, England 54 10N 0 45W
64 Malvan, India 16 0N 73 30E
61 Maly I., U.S.S.R. 74 20N 140 30E
74 Mambilima Falls, Zambia 10 45S 28 45E
43 Mamers, France 48 20N 0 20E
72 Mamfe, Cameroon 5 59N 9 40E
98 Mamore, R., Bolivia 16 30S 63 20W
72 Mamou, Guinea 10 15N 12 0W
72 Man, Ivory Coast 7 30N 7 40W
26 Man, I. of, British Isles 54 10N 4 35W
65 Man-Na, Burma 23 25N 97 20E
37 Manacor, Mallorca, Spain 39 37N 3 46E
68 Manado, Indonesia 1 35N 124 50E
94 Managua, Nicaragua 12 0N 86 20W
75 Manakara, Madagascar 22 5S 48 5E
62 Manakha, Yemen 15 2N 43 50E
82 Manam I., Papua N.G. 4 10S 145 0E
75 Mananjary, Madagascar 21 10S 48 28E
75 Manantenina, Madagas. 24 6S 47 20E
84 Manapouri, New Zealand 45 30S 167 33E
65 Manasarowar L., China 30 40N 81 20E
66 Manass, China 44 20N 86 20E
98 Manaus, Brazil 3 0S 60 10W
42 Manche, Dépt., France 48 57N 1 20W
26 Manchester, England 53 28N 2 15W
93 Manchester, U.S.A. 43 0N 71 22W
66 Manchouli, China 49 40N 117 0E
67 Manchuria, reg., China 44 30N 126 0E
55 Manchurian Plain, China 45 0N 125 0E
74 Manda, Tanzania 10 37S 34 52E
75 Mandabé, Madagascar 21 0S 44 55E
49 Mandal, Norway 58 0N 7 22E
65 Mandalay, Burma 22 0N 96 12E
41 Mandalya, G., Turkey 37 15N 27 15E
68 Mandar G., Indonesia 3 30S 119 30E
64 Mandi, India 31 40N 76 55E
65 Mandla, India 22 45N 80 26E
64 Mandya, India 12 30N 76 50E
62 Manfalut, Egypt 27 20N 31 0E
40 Manfredonia, G. of, Italy 41 39N 15 54E
47 Mangalia, Rumania 43 50N 28 37E
64 Mangalore, India 12 58N 75 0E
84 Mangaweka, N.Z. 39 47S 175 43E
34 Mangerton, Mt. Ireland 51 57N 9 29W
68 Manggar, Indonesia 3 0S 108 15E
65 Mangin Ra., Burma 24 15N 95 45E
75 Mangoche (Fort Johnston), Malawi 14 25S 35 16E
68 Mangole, I., Indonesia 1 45S 126 0E
60 Mangyshlak, Pen., U.S.S.R. 43 40N 52 30E
91 Manhattan, U.S.A. 39 20N 96 40W
65 Mani, Tibet, China 34 45N 87 10E
89 Manicouagan R., Can. 50 25N 68 32W
68 Manila, Philippines 14 30N 121 12E
68 Manila Bay, Phil. 14 20N 120 30E
83 Manilla, Australia 30 45S 150 36E
65 Manipur, st., India 24 44N 94 0E
41 Manisa, Turkey 38 38N 27 24E
92 Manistee, U.S.A. 44 19N 86 15W
88 Manitoba, L. & Prov., Canada 51 0N 98 55W
91 Manitowoc, U.S.A. 44 10N 87 42W
98 Manizales, Columbia 5 30N 75 56W
91 Mankato, U.S.A. 44 10N 94 0W
72 Mankono, Ivory Coast 8 10N 6 10W
75 Mankoya, Zambia 14 58S 24 57E
83 Manly, Australia 33 48S 151 20E
83 Manna Hill, Australia 32 29S 140 0E
64 Mannar, & G., Sri Lanka 9 0N 79 49E
45 Mannheim, Germany 49 32N 8 32E
23 Manningtree, England 51 56N 1 3E
83 Mannum, Australia 34 57S 139 12E
75 Manombo, Madagascar 22 55S 43 30E
74 Manono, Zaïre 7 19S 27 23E
36 Manorhamilton, Ireland 54 19N 8 10W
43 Manosque, France 43 50N 5 45E
37 Manresa, Spain 41 46N 1 51E
74 Mansa, Zambia 11 7S 28 54E
89 Mansel I., Canada 62 10N 80 0W
83 Mansfield, Australia 37 4S 146 5E
27 Mansfield, England 53 9N 1 12W
92 Mansfield, U.S.A. 40 45N 82 38W
27 Mansfield Woodhouse, England 53 12N 1 11W
98 Manta, Ecuador 1 0S 80 40W
43 Mantes, France 49 0N 1 45E
64 Manthani, India 18 40N 79 35E
98 Mantiqueira, Sa. da, mts., Brazil 22 0S 44 30W
48 Mänttä, Finland 61 59N 24 32E
40 Mantua, Italy 45 8N 10 47E
84 Manukau, N.Z. 37 0S 174 40E
82 Manus I., Papua N.G. 2 0S 147 0E
74 Manyara, L., Tanzania 3 40S 35 50E
51 Manych-Gudila L., U.S.S.R. 46 17N 42 55E
74 Manyoni, Tanzania 5 55S 35 0E
64 Manzai, Pakistan 32 25N 70 12E
37 Manzanares, Spain 39 0N 3 22W
95 Manzanillo, Cuba 20 25N 77 10W
94 Manzanillo, Mexico 19 12N 104 12W
76 Manzini, Swaziland 26 30S 31 20E
73 Mao, Chad 14 45N 15 50E
75 Maputo, Mozambique 25 59S 32 42E
62 Maqna, Saudi Arabia 28 30N 35 0E
74 Maquela do Zombo, Ang. 6 2S 15 22E
99 Maquinchao, Argentina 41 0S 68 30W
33 Mar, Dist., Scotland 57 8N 2 55W
99 Mar, Sa. do, mts., Brazil 23 0S 45 0W
99 Mar Chiquita, L., Arg. 30 30S 62 40W
99 Mar del Plata, Argentina 38 0S 57 39W
98 Maraca, I., Brazil 2 10N 50 20W
98 Maracaby Fall, Fs., Brazil 0 10S 66 50W
98 Maracaibo & L., of, Venezuela 10 37N 71 40W
98 Maracay, Venezuela 10 15N 67 35W
51 Maragheh, Iran 37 25N 46 10E
98 Marajo, I., Brazil 1 0S 49 30W
74 Maralal, Kenya 1 0N 36 38E
80 Maralinga, Australia 30 15S 131 30E
75 Marandellas, Rhodesia 18 5S 31 35E
98 Maranhao, st., Brazil 5 0S 44 30W
83 Maranoa, R., Australia 27 40S 148 0E
98 Maranón, R. Peru 4 40S 75 30W
51 Maras, Turkey 37 50N 36 58E
82 Marathon, Australia 20 51S 143 32E
41 Marathon, Greece 38 10N 23 55E
37 Marbella, Spain 36 33N 4 53W
80 Marble Bar, Australia 21 5S 119 43E
43 Marburg, Germany 50 45N 8 50E
23 March, England 52 32N 0 6E
44 Marche, Belgium 50 14N 5 21E
43 Marche, Prov., France 46 10N 1 40E
37 Marchena, Spain 37 23N 5 27W
40 Marches, Prov., Italy 43 20N 13 20E
44 Marchin, Belgium 50 26N 5 12E
64 Mardan, Pakistan 34 20N 72 0E
51 Mardin, Turkey 37 20N 41 0E
82 Mareeba, Australia 17 0S 145 27E
42 Marennes, France 45 50N 1 5W
27 Marfleet, England 53 45N 0 15W
25 Margam, Wales 51 34N 3 44W
94 Margarita, Panama Canal Zone (Inset)
98 Margarita, I., Venezuela 11 0N 64 0W
23 Margate, England 51 23N 1 25E
76 Margate, S. Africa 30 50S 30 15E
50 Mari, A.S.S.R., U.S.S.R. 56 30N 48 0E
83 Maria I., Australia 42 39S 147 57E
84 Maria van Diemen, C., N.Z. 34 29S 172 36E
5 Mariana Is., Pac. Oc. 18 0N 146 0E
90 Marias, R., U.S.A. 48 30N 111 30W
40 Maribor, Yugoslavia 46 15N 15 40E
89 Maricourt, Canada 61 30N 72 0W
94 Marie Galante I., W.I. 16 0N 61 15W
44 Mariembourg, Belgium 50 6N 4 31E
92 Marietta, U.S.A. 39 28N 81 28W
60 Mariinsk, U.S.S.R. 56 10N 87 20E
98 Marilia, Brazil 22 0S 50 0W
37 Marin, Spain 42 22N 8 46W
92 Marinette, U.S.A. 45 3N 87 38W
92 Marion, Ind., U.S.A. 40 35N 85 37W
92 Marion, Ohio, U.S.A. 40 33N 83 13W
43 Maritime Alps, France 44 10N 6 52E
41 Maritsa, R., Bulgaria 42 10N 24 20E
44 Marken, Netherlands 52 27N 5 6E
22 Market Bosworth, Eng. 52 37N 1 24W
22 Market Drayton, Eng. 52 55N 2 30W
23 Market Harborough, Eng. 52 29N 0 55W
27 Market Rasen, England 53 23N 0 21W
27 Market Weighton, Eng. 53 52N 0 40W
100 Markham, Mt., Antarc. 82 0S 160 0E
31 Markinch, Scotland 56 12N 3 8W
50 Marks, U.S.S.R. 51 43N 46 45E
44 Marl, Germany 51 40N 7 6E
82 Marlborough, Australia 22 46S 149 52E
22 Marlborough, England 51 25N 1 43W
84 Marlborough, dist., N.Z. 41 46S 173 30
44 Marle, France 49 43N 3 47E
23 Marlow, England 51 35N 0 46W
64 Marmagao, India 15 25N 73 45E
43 Marmande, France 44 30N 0 10E
41 Marmara, Sea of, Turkey 40 40N 28 0
40 Marmolada, Mt., Italy 46 20N 11 55E
42 Marne, Dépt., France 49 12N 4 5E
43 Marne, R., France 48 30N 5 0E
75 Maroantsetra, Madagascar 15 28S 49 4
98 Maroni, R., S. America 5 50N 54 0W
83 Maroochydore, Australia 26 35S 153 1
83 Maroona, Australia 37 30S 142 57E
73 Maroua, Cameroon 10 50N 14 5E
75 Marovoay, Madagascar 16 10S 46 35E
76 Marquard, S. Africa 28 35S 27 30E
92 Marquette, U.S.A. 46 30N 87 27W
72 Marrakech, Morocco 31 32N 8 0W
83 Marree, Australia 29 35S 137 55E
75 Marromeu, Mozambique 18 8S 35 45E
75 Marrupa, Mozambique 13 5S 37 40E
73 Marsa Brega, Libya 30 30N 19 45E
74 Marsa Fatma, Ethiopia 14 50N 40 15
73 Marsa Susa, Libya 32 45N 21 48E
74 Marsabit, Kenya 2 10N 38 0E
42 Marseilles, France 43 21N 5 22E
91 Marsh I., U.S.A. 29 40N 91 50W
72 Marshall, Liberia 6 8N 10 22W
91 Marshall, Mo., U.S.A. 39 11N 93 16W
4 Marshall Is., Pac. Oc. 9 30N 167 0E
91 Marshalltown, U.S.A. 42 5N 93 0W
92 Marshfield, U.S.A. 44 47N 90 10W
27 Marske by the Sea, Eng. 54 36N 1 1W
49 Marstrand, Sweden 57 53N 11 35E
65 Martaban, & G., Burma 16 42N 97 4
73 Marte, Nigeria 12 23N 13 46E
44 Martelange, Belgium 49 50N 5 44E

3 Martha's Vineyard, I., U.S.A. 41 27N 70 43W
5 Martigny, Switzerland 46 7N 7 5E
3 Martigues, France 43 20N 5 2E
5 Martinique, I., Fr. W.I. 14 40N 61 0W
4 Marton, N.Z. 40 5S 175 14E
7 Martos, Spain 37 44N 3 58W
3 Marvejois, France 44 35N 3 15E
4 Marwar, India 25 40N 73 30E
0 Mary, U.S.S.R. 37 40N 61 43E
2 Mary Kathleen, Austral. 20 40S 139 55E
3 Maryborough, Queens., Australia 25 32S 152 30E
3 Maryborough, Victoria, Australia 37 0S 143 48E
1 Maryland, st., U.S.A. 39 30N 77 0W
6 Maryport, England 54 43N 3 31W
3 Marywell, Scotland 56 35N 2 31W
3 Marzuq, Libya 25 50N 13 50E
3 Masada, Israel 31 20N 35 19E
4 Masaka, Uganda 0 20S 31 48E
4 Masasi, Tanzania 11 0S 39 0E
8 Masbate, I., Phil. 12 15N 123 30E
2 Mascara, Algeria 35 28N 0 2E
6 Maseru, Lesotho 29 35S 27 20E
3 Mashhad, Iran 36 15N 59 30E
7 Mashike, Japan 43 48N 141 20E
4 Mashkel, R., Iran 27 7N 63 0E
4 Mashki Chah, Pakistan 29 0N 62 25
4 Masi Manimba, Zaïre 4 40S 18 5E
1 Masillon, U.S.A. 40 52N 81 28W
4 Masindi, Uganda 1 40N 31 40E
3 Masira, G., Oman 20 0N 58 0E
4 Mask, L., Ireland 53 36N 9 20W
1 Mason City, U.S.A. 43 11N 93 17W
0 Massa, Italy 44 1N 10 12E
3 Massachusetts, st., U.S.A. 42 20N 72 0
3 Massenya, Chad 11 45N 16 25E
3 Massif Central, mts., Fr. 44 50N 3 0E
5 Massinga, Mozambique 23 15S 35 22E
4 Masterton, N.Z. 40 51S 175 41E
4 Mastuj, Pakistan 36 20N 72 35E
4 Mastung, Pakistan 29 50N 66 42E
7 Masuda, Japan 34 48N 131 58E
7 Masurian Lakes, Poland 53 45N 21 40E
3 Mata da Corda, Sa. da, mts., Brazil 17 30S 45 30W
4 Matadi, Zaïre 5 55S 13 13E
4 Matagalpa, Nicaragua 13 5N 85 36W
2 Matagami, L., Canada 49 50N 77 35W
4 Matale, Sri Lanka 7 37N 80 40E
2 Matam, Sénégal 15 34N 13 17W
4 Matamoros, Mex. 25 50N 97 27W
9 Matane, Canada 48 48N 67 37W
5 Matanzas, Cuba 23 0N 80 40W
4 Matara, Sri Lanka 5 58N 80 30E
3 Mataram, Indonesia 8 35S 116 18E
7 Mataro, Spain 41 37N 2 30E
4 Matehuala, Mexico 23 50N 100 39W
0 Matera, Italy 40 40N 16 38E
4 Mathura, India 27 39N 77 48E
7 Matlock, England 53 9N 1 32W
3 Mato Grosso, plateau & st., Brazil 15 0S 56 0W
0 Matopo, S. Africa 20 0S 30 0E
7 Matozinhos, Portugal 41 15N 8 42W
3 Matrah, Oman 23 31N 58 27E
5 Matsang, R., Tibet, China 29 30N 89 0E
7 Matsue, Japan 35 28N 133 5E
7 Matsumoto, Japan 36 8N 138 0E
7 Matsuyama, Japan 33 56N 132 56E
4 Mattagami, R., Canada 49 40N 81 40W
4 Mattancheri, India 9 50N 76 15E
5 Matterhorn, mt., Switz. 45 58N 7 30E
2 Mattoon, U.S.A. 39 28N 88 27W
4 Matun, Afghanistan 33 15N 69 55E
5 Maturin, Venezuela 9 42N 63 18W
0 Matylka, U.S.S.R. 63 55N 82 0E
Maubeuge, France 50 18N 3 58E
5 Mauganj, India 24 50N 81 55E
5 Maughold Hd., I. of Man 54 18N 4 20W
Maui I., Hawaiian Is. 21 0N 156 30W
2 Mauleon, France 43 15N 1 0W
4 Maumtuck Mts., Ireland 53 33N 9 35W
5 Maun, Botswana 20 0S 23 30E
5 Maunmagan Is., Burma 14 10N 97 45E
3 Maures, Mts., France 43 20N 6 30E
Mauritania, Africa 20 0N 10 0W
Mauritius. I., Indian Oc. 20 20S 57 10E
2 Maushij, Yemen 13 44N 43 17E
0 Mawson, Antarctica 67 0S 62 0E
Maxesibeni, S. Africa 30 50S 29 20E
May, C., U.S.A. 38 58N 75 0W
May, I. of, Scotland 56 13N 2 41W
May Pen., Jamaica 17 55N 77 12W
Maya R., U.S.S.R. 58 20N 135 0E
Mayaguana I., Bahamas 22 12N 73 0W
Mayaguez, Puerto Rico 18 10N 67 0W
Maybole, Scotland 55 21N 4 41W
Mayenne, Dépt., France 48 17N 0 40W
Maykop, U.S.S.R. 44 38N 40 11E
Maynooth, Ireland 53 23N 6 35W
Mayo, Co., Ireland 53 46N 9 0W
Maysville, Ky., U.S.A. 38 40N 83 45W
Mayum La, pass, Tibet, China 30 20N 82 20E
Mazabuka, Zambia 15 50S 27 45E
Mazamet, France 43 30N 2 20E
Mazar-i-Sharif, Afghan. 36 50N 67 0E
Mazarron, Spain 37 39N 1 17W
Mazaruni, R., Guyana 6 0N 60 0W
Mazatlan, Mexico 23 20N 106 20W
Mbabane, Swaziland 26 30S 31 30E
Mbaiki, Central Africa 4 0N 18 0E
74 Mbala, Zambia 8 49S 31 20E
74 Mbale, Uganda 1 10N 34 0E
74 Mbalmayo, Cameroon 3 33N 11 33E
74 Mbandaka (Coquilhatville), Zaïre 0 3S 18 20E
74 Mbanza Ngungu, Zaïre 5 12S 14 53E
74 Mbuji-Mayi, Zaïre 6 10S 23 29E
40 Mdina, Malta 35 54N 14 22E
90 Mead, L., U.S.A. 36 10N 114 20W
92 Meadville, U.S.A. 41 39N 80 7W
33 Mealfuarvonie, Mt., Scot. 57 16N 4 46W
29 Meath, Co., Ireland 53 37N 6 35W
43 Meaux, France 48 59N 2 52E
62 Mecca, Saudi Arabia 21 20N 40 13E
44 Mechelen, Belgium 51 2N 4 29E
72 Mecheria, Algeria 33 35N 0 15W
68 Medan, Indonesia 3 45N 98 45E
72 Medéa, Algeria 36 12N 2 50E
98 Medellin, Colombia 6 10N 75 40W
72 Médenine, Tunisia 33 15N 10 35E
72 Mederdra, Mauritania 17 0N 15 35W
90 Medford, U.S.A. 42 25N 123 0W
47 Medias, Rumania 46 5N 24 21E
90 Medicine Front Ra., U.S.A. 41 0N 105 40W
88 Medicine Hat, Canada 50 0N 110 30W
62 Medina, Saudi Arabia 24 20N 39 55E
37 Medina, Spain 41 18N 4 52W
37 Medina Sidonia, Spain 36 30N 5 58W
5 Mediterranean Sea 36 0N 15 0E
42 Médoc, Dist., France 45 15N 1 0W
52 Medveditsa, R., U.S.S.R. 50 20N 44 0E
61 Medvezhi Is., U.S.S.R. 71 0N 161 0E
23 Medway, R., England 51 13N 0 25E
80 Meekatharra, Australia 26 30S 118 27E
64 Meerut, India 29 0N 77 45E
74 Mega, Ethiopia 3 57N 38 30E
93 Megantic, Canada 45 30N 70 42W
40 Megara, Greece 38 0N 23 20E
65 Meghalaya, st., India 25 30N 91 0E
63 Megiddo, Israel 32 37N 35 9E
39 Megiste (Kastellórizon), Greece 36 8N 29 35E
41 Mehadia, Rumania 44 55N 22 22E
62 Meheisa, Sudan 19 37N 33 0E
64 Mehsana, India 23 39N 72 26E
43 Mehun, France 47 15N 2 12E
65 Meiktila, Burma 20 56N 95 58E
43 Meiningen, Germany 50 35N 10 25E
45 Meiringen, Switzerland 46 45N 8 10E
46 Meissen, Germany 51 11N 13 23E
74 Meiyganga, Cameroon 6 20N 14 10E
99 Mejillones, Chile 23 15S 70 32W
74 Mekambo, Gabon 1 5N 13 50E
73 Mekele, Ethiopia 13 30N 39 20E
64 Mekhtah, Pakistan 30 30N 69 15E
72 Meknes, Morocco 34 0N 5 25W
55 Mekong, R., S.E. Asia 16 30N 104 50E
64 Melagiri Hills, India 12 25N 77 30E
68 Melaka, Malaya 2 20N 102 12E
83 Melbourne, Australia 37 45S 144 50E
50 Melekess, U.S.S.R. 54 20N 49 30E
73 Melfi, Chad 11 0N 17 59E
88 Melfort, Canada 53 0N 104 56W
72 Melilla, Morocco 35 17N 2 55W
52 Melitopol, U.S.S.R. 46 53N 35 20E
46 Melk, Austria 48 15N 15 20E
22 Melksham, England 51 22N 2 9W
48 Mellansel, Sweden 63 26N 18 12E
49 Mellerud, Sweden 58 40N 12 28E
76 Melmoth, S. Africa 28 35S 31 20E
99 Melo, Uruguay 32 15S 54 0W
83 Melrose, Australia 32 40S 146 58E
31 Melrose, Scotland 55 36N 2 45W
48 Melstadur, Iceland 65 20N 20 55W
23 Melton, England 52 6N 1 21E
23 Melton Mowbray, Eng. 52 45N 0 52W
43 Melun, France 48 35N 2 40E
62 Melut, Sudan 10 30N 32 20E
32 Melvaig, Scotland 57 48N 5 49W
33 Melvich, Scotland 58 34N 3 55W
81 Melville B., Australia 12 5S 136 45E
82 Melville C., Australia 14 20S 144 50E
80 Melville, I., Australia 11 30S 131 0E
89 Melville, L., Canada 53 40N 59 0W
89 Melville Pen., Canada 67 40N 84 0W
36 Melvin, L., Ireland 54 27N 8 10W
45 Memmingen, Germany 47 59N 10 12E
91 Memphis, U.S.A. 35 10N 89 49W
25 Menai Bridge & Str., Wales 53 14N 4 10W
72 Ménaka, Mali 16 0N 2 10E
68 Menam, R., Thailand 15 0N 100 30E
92 Menasha, U.S.A. 44 18N 88 28W
43 Mende, France 44 33N 3 30E
24 Mendip Hills, England 51 17N 2 40W
90 Mendocino, C., U.S.A. 40 25N 124 25W
65 Mendong Gomba, Tibet, China 31 0N 85 15E
99 Mendoza, Argentina 32 45S 68 39W
41 Menemen, Turkey 38 18N 27 10E
40 Menfi, Italy 37 35N 12 55E
68 Menggala, Indonesia 4 25S 105 26E
67 Mengtsz, China 23 22N 103 45E
44 Menin, Belgium 50 48N 3 8E
83 Menindee, Australia 32 22S 142 22E
83 Meningie, Australia 35 38S 139 27E
65 Menkong, China 28 40N 98 15E
92 Menominee, U.S.A. 45 15N 87 37W
92 Menominee, R., U.S.A. 45 50N 88 12W
75 Menongue, Angola 14 45S 17 59E
37 Menorca I., Balearic Is., Spain 40 0N 4 0E
68 Mentawai Is., Indonesia 2 30S 99 30E
43 Menton, France 43 50N 7 30E
73 Menzel Temime, Tunisia 36 50N 11 0E
80 Menzies, Australia 29 42S 121 2E
63 Me'ona, Israel 33 0N 35 15E
44 Meppel, Netherlands 52 42N 6 12E
41 Merabéllou B., Greece 35 15N 25 50E
40 Merano, Italy 46 39N 11 12E
83 Merbein, Australia 34 10S 142 0E
64 Mercara, India 12 40N 75 40E
90 Merced, U.S.A. 37 16N 120 26W
99 Mercedes, Argentina 29 15S 58 10W
99 Mercedes, Arg. 33 5S 65 21W
99 Mercedes, Uruguay 33 58S 58 5W
84 Mercer, New Zealand 37 15S 175 5E
89 Mercy C., Canada 65 0N 62 30W
22 Mere, England 51 6N 2 16W
73 Méréke, Central Africa 7 35N 23 0E
68 Mergui, Burma 12 30N 98 40E
94 Mérida, Mexico 20 55N 89 40W
37 Merida, Spain 38 56N 6 25W
98 Mérida, Venezuela 8 30N 71 2W
22 Meriden, England 52 26N 1 38W
92 Meriden, U.S.A. 41 28N 72 54W
44 Merksem, Belgium 51 17N 4 25E
73 Merowe, Sudan 18 57N 32 15E
80 Merredin, Australia 31 29S 118 23E
92 Merrill, U.S.A. 45 16N 89 40W
83 Merriwa, Australia 32 10S 150 28E
83 Merriwagga, Australia 33 47S 145 43E
83 Merrygoen, Australia 31 55S 149 10E
44 Mersch, Luxembourg 49 44N 6 7E
31 Merse, The, Scotland 55 40N 2 25W
46 Merseburg, Germany 51 22N 12 0E
26 Mersey, R., England 53 20N 2 55W
26 Merseyside, Co., Eng. 53 25N 2 55W
51 Mersin, Turkey 36 52N 34 29E
68 Mersing, Malaya 2 30N 103 50E
25 Merthyr Tydfil, Wales 51 45N 3 22W
37 Mertola, Portugal 37 39N 7 39W
23 Merton, Greater London, England 51 23N 0 9W
74 Meru, Kenya 0 2N 37 35E
44 Merzig, Germany 49 27N 6 39E
90 Mesa, U.S.A. 33 25N 111 50W
74 Mesewa, Ethiopia 15 35N 39 25E
73 Meshra el Req, Sudan 8 25N 29 18E
45 Mesocco, Switzerland 46 24N 9 14E
41 Mesolongion, Greece 38 25N 21 25E
62 Mesopotamia, Dist., S.W. Asia 32 30N 45 0E
40 Messina, & Str., Italy 38 13N 15 33E
75 Messina, S. Africa 22 18S 29 50E
41 Messini, Greece 37 0N 22 0E
41 Mesta, R., Greece 41 10N 25 0E
98 Meta, R., Colombia 5 50N 70 0W
31 Methil, Scotland 56 11N 3 1W
84 Methven, N.Z. 43 37S 171 40E
31 Methven, Scotland 56 24N 3 36W
75 Metil, Mozambique 16 24S 39 0E
64 Mettur Dam, India 11 45N 77 45E
63 Metulla, Israel 33 17N 35 34E
43 Metz, France 49 10N 6 10E
42 Meurthe-et-Moselle, Dépt., France 48 53N 5 53E
42 Meuse, Dépt., France 49 3N 5 53E
44 Meuse, R., Fr., Belgium 50 29N 5 5E
24 Mevagissey, & B., Eng. 50 15N 4 40W
27 Mexborough, England 53 30N 1 17W
98 Mexiana I., Brazil 0 0 49 30W
94 Mexicali, Mexico 32 40N 115 30W
86 Mexican Plat., Mexico 23 0N 104 0W
94 Mexico, Cent. Amer. 23 0N 102 0W
94 Mexico City, Mexico 19 25N 99 5W
94 Mexico, G. of, Mexico 25 0N 89 0W
43 Mèze, France 43 30N 3 30E
50 Mezen, R., U.S.S.R. 64 34N 46 30E
47 Mezökovesd, Hungary 47 44N 20 35E
47 Mezötúr, Hungary 47 0N 20 45E
64 Mhow, India 22 25N 75 51E
91 Miami, Fla., U.S.A. 25 55N 80 23W
75 Miandrivazo, Madag. 19 40S 45 40E
51 Mianeh, Iran 37 27N 47 39E
64 Mianwali, Pakistan 32 33N 71 43E
75 Miarinarivo, Madag. 18 50S 46 58E
60 Miass, U.S.S.R. 55 00N 60 00E
92 Michigan City, U.S.A. 41 40N 86 58W
92 Michigan, L., N. America 44 0N 87 0W
92 Michigan, st., U.S.A. 45 0N 85 30W
89 Michikamau, L., Canada 54 0N 64 0W
94 Michipicoten, I., Canada 47 45N 86 0W
52 Michurinsk, U.S.S.R. 53 0N 40 30E
26 Mickle Fell, mt., Eng. 54 36N 2 10W
27 Mickleover, England 52 55N 1 32W
31 Mid Calder, Scotland 55 53N 3 23W
44 Middelburg, Netherlands 51 31N 3 37E
91 Middlesboro, U.S.A. 36 42N 83 40W
27 Middlesbrough, England 54 34N 1 16W
94 Middlesex, Belize 16 50N 88 40W
23 Middleton, England 52 43N 0 29E
22 Middleton Cheney, Eng. 52 5N 1 10W
27 Middleton-on-the-Wolds, England 53 50N 0 35W
93 Middletown, N.Y., U.S.A. 41 29N 74 28W
92 Middletown, Ohio, U.S.A. 39 30N 84 7W
26 Middlewich, England 53 12N 2 28W
25 Mid-Glamorgan, Co., Wales 51 40N 3 50W
92 Midland, Mich., U.S.A. 43 35N 84 15W
90 Midland, Texas, U.S.A. 32 0N 102 8W
80 Midland Junc., Austral. 31 40S 116 0E
34 Midleton, Ireland 51 54N 8 7W
65 Midnapore, India 22 18N 87 30E
4 Midsomer Norton, Eng. 51 17N 2 29W
11 Midway I., Pac. Oc. 28 0N 178 0W
67 Mie, Pref., Japan 34 20N 136 30E
47 Miedzyrzec, Poland 52 0N 22 45E
37 Mieres, Spain 43 16N 5 48W
63 Migdal, Israel 32 50N 35 30E
41 Mikinai, Greece 37 45N 22 45E
74 Mikindani, Tanzania 10 0S 40 0E
49 Mikkeli, Finland 61 43N 27 25E
48 Mikkeli, Co., Finland 62 0N 28 0E
41 Mikonos I., Greece 37 30N 25 24E
67 Mikura Shima, I., Japan 33 50N 139 30E
40 Milan, Italy 45 28N 9 12E
83 Milang, Australia 35 39S 139 0E
62 Milas, Turkey 37 20N 27 50E
40 Milazzo, Italy 38 14N 15 14E
23 Mildenhall, England 52 21N 0 29E
83 Mildura, Australia 34 13S 142 5E
83 Miles, Australia 26 35S 150 18E
90 Miles City, U.S.A. 46 30N 105 47W
25 Milford Haven, Wales 51 41N 5 9W
22 Milford-on-Sea, Eng. 50 44N 1 34W
84 Milford Sd., N.Z. 44 35S 167 50E
90 Milk R., N. America 49 0N 107 0W
43 Millau, France 44 8N 3 10E
91 Milledgeville, U.S.A. 33 0N 83 20W
83 Millicent, Australia 37 50S 140 25E
91 Millinocket, U.S.A. 45 44N 68 31W
83 Millmerran, Australia 27 52S 151 8E
26 Millom, England 54 12N 3 16W
30 Millport, Scotland 55 45N 4 55W
34 Millstreet, Ireland 52 3N 9 4W
34 Milltown, Ireland 52 10N 9 42W
76 Milnerton, S. Africa (Inset) 33 5S 18 29E
30 Milngavie, Scotland 55 57N 4 19W
41 Milos, I., Greece 36 40N 24 27E
83 Milparinka, Australia 29 46S 141 57E
84 Milton, New Zealand 46 8S 169 59E
23 Milton Keynes, England 52 3N 0 45W
34 Miltown Malbay, Ire. 52 53N 9 22W
24 Milverton, England 51 2N 3 15W
92 Milwaukee, U.S.A. 43 5N 88 5W
67 Mimitsu, Japan 32 55N 131 30E
66 Min Kiang, R., China 26 40N 117 30E
62 Mina al Ahmadi, Kuwait 29 0N 47 0E
63 Minab, Iran 27 7N 57 7E
99 Minas (Lavelleja), Uruguay 34 20S 54 48W
93 Minas Basin, Canada 45 14N 64 20W
37 Minas de Rio Tinto, Spain 37 45N 6 36W
98 Minas Gerais, st., Brazil 19 15S 45 0W
67 Minato, Japan 36 24N 140 38E
32 Minch, The, Scotland 58 10N 5 50W
22 Minchinhampton, Eng. 51 42N 2 10W
68 Mindanao, I., Philippines 8 0N 125 0E
46 Minden, Germany 52 18N 8 57E
91 Minden, U.S.A. 32 44N 93 19W
68 Mindoro, I., Philippines 12 40N 121 0E
35 Mine Hd., Ireland 52 0N 7 33W
24 Minehead, England 51 14N 3 30W
90 Mineral Wells, U.S.A. 32 50N 98 10W
51 Mingechaur Res., U.S.S.R. 40 45N 46 30E
65 Mingin, Burma 22 55N 94 30E
32 Minginish, Dist., Scot. 57 17N 6 15W
32 Mingulay I., Scotland 56 49N 7 35W
37 Minho, & Prov., Port. 41 25N 8 20W
37 Minho, R., Spain 43 10N 7 30W
67 Minhow, *see* Foochow
91 Minneapolis, U.S.A. 45 0N 93 30W
91 Minnesota, st., U.S.A. 46 0N 94 30W
37 Minorca I., *see* Menorca
83 Minore, Australia 32 15S 148 25E
90 Minot, U.S.A. 48 15N 101 10W
50 Minsk, U.S.S.R. 54 0N 27 30E
47 Minsk Mazowiecki, Pol. 52 10N 21 30E
61 Minusinsk, U.S.S.R. 53 50N 92 15E
65 Minutang, India 28 20N 96 30E
62 Minwakh, South Yemen 15 59N 49 28E
66 Minya Konka, mt., China 30 0N 101 15E
89 Miquelon I., St. Pierre & Miquelon, North America 47 0N 56 30W
73 Mir, Niger 14 6N 11 58E
94 Miraflores, Panama Canal Zone (Inset)
64 Miraj, India 16 57N 74 46E
64 Miram Shah, Pakistan 33 0N 70 0E
37 Miranda, Portugal 41 33N 6 20W
37 Miranda, Spain 42 40N 2 53W
43 Mirande, France 43 30N 0 20E
43 Mirecourt, France 48 20N 6 5E
62 Mirfa, U.A.E. 24 0N 53 24E
68 Miri, Sarawak, Malaysia 4 30N 114 5E
82 Miriam Vale, Australia 24 20S 151 39E
99 Mirim, L., S. America 33 0S 53 0W
100 Mirny, Antarctica 66 30S 96 0E
64 Mirpur Khas, Pakistan 25 33N 68 0E
65 Mirzapur, India 25 8N 82 39E
93 Miscou, I., Canada 48 0N 64 32W
67 Mishan, China 45 30N 131 30E
63 Mishmar Aiyalon, Israel 31 57N 34 58E
47 Miskolc, Hungary 48 8N 20 46E
73 Misratah, Libya 32 20N 15 7E
92 Missinaibi, R., Canada 49 30N 83 15W
91 Mississippi R., U.S.A. 35 0N 90 0W
91 Mississippi, st., U.S.A. 33 0N 89 30W
91 Mississippi Delta, U.S.A. 29 15N 90 30W
90 Missoula, U.S.A. 46 57N 113 58W
90 Missouri, R., U.S.A. 42 0N 98 30W
91 Missouri, st., U.S.A. 38 0N 92 30W
89 Mistassini, L., Canada 51 0N 73 35W
24 Misterton, England 50 51N 2 35W
98 Misti, Vol., Peru 16 30S 71 0W
40 Mistretta, Italy 38 0N 14 20E
67 Misumi, Japan 32 34N 130 32E
73 Misurata, Libya, *see* Misratah
25 Mitchel Troy, Wales 51 46N 2 45W
83 Mitchell, Australia 26 30S 147 58E
90 Mitchell, U.S.A. 43 45N 98 2W
82 Mitchell, R., Australia 16 0S 142 30E
34 Mitchelstown, Ireland 52 17N 8 15W
41 Mitilini, Greece 39 8N 26 36E
67 Mito, Japan 36 28N 140 26E
98 Mitú, Colombia 1 0N 70 0W
75 Mitsinjo, Madagascar 15 35S 45 45E
83 Mittagong, Australia 34 25S 150 25E
74 Mitumba Mts., Zaïre 7 0S 27 0E
74 Mitwaba, Zaïre 8 37S 27 28E
74 Mitzick, Gabon 0 45N 11 40E
67 Miyagi, Pref., Japan 38 15N 141 0E
67 Miyake Jima, Japan 34 0N 139 30E
67 Miyako, Japan 39 40N 141 45E
67 Milyakonojo, Japan 31 30N 131 0E
67 Miyasu, Japan 35 40N 135 8E
67 Miyazaki, & Pref., Japan 31 58N 131 30E
72 Mizdah, Libya 31 40N 13 2E
34 Mizen Hd., Ireland 51 27N 9 49W
65 Mizoram, st., India 23 20N 93 0E
49 Mjölby, Sweden 58 19N 15 4E
49 Mjosa L., & R., Norway 60 40N 11 0E
46 Mlada Boleslav, Cz-slov. 50 28N 15 0E
70 Mlanje, mt., Mozambique 16 0S 35 55E
47 Mlawa, Poland 53 6N 20 20E
74 Moanda, Gabon 1 5S 13 0E
35 Moate, Ireland 53 24N 7 42W
91 Moberley, U.S.A. 39 28N 92 27W
91 Mobile, U.S.A. 30 47N 88 10W
74 Mobutu Sese Seko, L., E. Africa 1 45N 31 0E
76 Mochudi, Botswana 24 25S 26 5E
98 Mocoa, Colombia 1 15N 76 45W
43 Modane, France 45 20N 6 25E
76 Modder, R., S. Africa 28 48S 26 15E
40 Modena, Italy 44 38N 10 54E
90 Modesto, U.S.A. 37 36N 120 58W
40 Modica, Italy 36 54N 14 50E
83 Moe, Australia 38 12S 146 19E
44 Moers, Germany 51 27N 6 39E
31 Moffat, Scotland 55 18N 3 25W
71 Mogadishu, Somali Republic 2 1N 45 25E
72 Mogador, *see* Essaouira
67 Mogami, R., Japan 38 50N 140 0E
65 Mogaung, Burma 25 26N 96 55E
50 Mogilev, U.S.S.R. 54 17N 30 30E
51 Mogilev-Podolski, U.S.S.R. 48 25N 27 50E
75 Mogincual, Mozambique 15 30S 40 22E
61 Mogocha, U.S.S.R. 53 40N 119 50E
65 Mogok, Burma 23 0N 96 30E
47 Mohacs, Hungary 45 59N 18 40E
75 Mohembo, Botswana 18 15S 21 43E
34 Moher Cliffs, Ireland 52 58N 9 26W
32 Moidart, L. & Dist., Scot. 56 50N 5 52W
60 Mointy, U.S.S.R. 47 40N 73 45E
36 Moira, N. Ireland 54 29N 6 14W
49 Moisäkula, U.S.S.R. 58 2N 25 12E
89 Moisie, Canada 50 17N 66 0W
43 Moissac, France 44 8N 1 0E
61 Moiyero R., U.S.S.R. 67 30N 104 0E
90 Mojave Desert, U.S.A. 35 0N 116 20W
67 Moji, Japan 33 56N 131 0E
65 Mokokchung, India 26 15N 94 25E
67 Mokpo, Korea 34 50N 126 30E
44 Mol, Belgium 51 11N 5 7E
25 Mold, Wales 53 10N 3 9W
51 Moldavia S.S.R., U.S.S.R. 47 40N 28 0E
48 Molde, Norway 62 45N 7 8E
23 Mole, R., England 51 18N 0 20W
75 Molepolole, Botswana 24 28S 25 28E
40 Molfetta, Italy 41 12N 16 40E
92 Moline, U.S.A. 41 30N 90 25W
74 Moliro, Zaïre 8 5S 30 30E
40 Molise, Reg., Italy 41 30N 14 30E
49 Molndal, Sweden 57 35N 12 0E
90 Molokai, I., Hawaiian Is. (Inset)
83 Molong, Australia 33 0S 149 0E
68 Molucca Sea, Indonesia 4 0S 126 0E
68 Moluccas, Indonesia, *see* Maluku
71 Mombasa, Kenya 4 0S 39 40E
41 Momchilgrad, Bulgaria 41 33N 25 23E
98 Mompos, Colombia 9 15N 74 25W
49 Mön, I., Denmark 54 57N 12 23E
65 Mon, R., Burma 20 30N 94 30E
32 Monach Is., Scotland 57 31N 7 40W
43 Monaco, Europe 43 46N 7 23E
33 Monadhliath Mts., Scot. 57 8N 4 20W
36 Monaghan, & Co., Ire. 54 14N 6 58W
32 Monar, L. & Forest, Scot. 57 26N 5 4W
35 Monasterevan, Ireland 53 10N 7 7W
73 Monastir, Tunisia 35 40N 10 50E
35 Monavullagh, Mts., Ire. 52 10N 7 40W
37 Moncayo, Mt., Spain 41 47N 1 50W
44 Mönchen-Gladbach, Ger. 51 13N 6 26E
37 Monchique, Portugal 37 16N 8 40W
37 Monchique, Sa. de, mts., Portugal 37 20S 8 40W
94 Monclova, Mexico 27 0N 101 20W
93 Moncton, Canada 46 10N 65 0W
37 Mondego, R., Portugal 40 30N 7 50W
40 Mondovi, Italy 44 25N 7 50E
34 Moneygall, Ireland 52 53N 7 58W
37 Monforte, Spain 42 30N 7 33W
65 Mong Pawk, Burma 22 0N 99 20E
65 Mong Ton, Burma 20 20N 98 55E
65 Mong Wa, Burma 21 25N 100 25E
65 Mong Kung, Burma 21 50N 97 35E
73 Mongalla, Sudan 5 10N 31 50E
80 Monger, L., Australia 29 10S 117 0E
65 Monghyr, India 25 20N 86 22E
73 Mongo, Chad 12 14N 18 43E

66 Mongolia, Asia 45 20N 105 30E
73 Mongororo, Chad 12 1N 22 28E
75 Mongu, Zambia 15 16S 23 3E
31 Monifieth, Scotland 56 29N 2 49W
34 Monivea, Ireland 53 28N 8 42W
74 Monkoto, Zaïre 1 30S 20 45E
22 Monmouth, Wales 51 48N 2 43W
22 Monmouth, Co., *see* Gwent
40 Monopoli, Italy 40 57N 17 18E
91 Monroe, La., U.S.A. 32 30N 92 1W
92 Monroe, Mich., U.S.A. 41 54N 83 27W
72 Monrovia, Liberia 6 15N 10 43W
44 Mons, Belgium 50 26N 3 58E
75 Mont Aux Sources, S. Africa 28 54S 28 50E
43 Mont Blanc, Fr. & Italy 45 52N 6 50E
43 Mont Cenis, mt., France 45 20N 7 5E
42 Mont de Marsan, France 43 58N 0 34W
43 Mont Dore, mt., France 45 32N 2 30E
43 Mont du Cantal, mt., Fr. 45 10N 2 20E
93 Mont Joli, Canada 48 35N 68 10N
93 Mont Laurier, Canada 46 35N 75 30W
43 Mont Mézenc, mt., Fr. 44 45N 4 35E
43 Mont St. Michel, France 48 40N 1 32W
37 Montalban, Spain 40 50N 0 48W
90 Montana, St., U.S.A. 47 0N 109 0W
43 Montargis, France 48 0N 2 40E
43 Montauban, France 44 1N 1 20E
43 Montbeliard, France 47 32N 6 48E
43 Montbrison, France 45 35N 4 0E
43 Montceau, France 46 40N 4 25E
44 Montcornet, France 49 42N 4 0E
43 Montdidier, France 49 40N 2 30E
40 Monte Argentario, mt., Italy 42 25N 11 10E
80 Monte Bello Is., Austral. 20 30S 115 30E
43 Monte Carlo, Monaco 43 46N 7 23E
99 Monte Caseros, Arg. 30 10S 57 50W
40 Monte Cimone, mt., Italy 44 10N 10 40
43 Monte Cinto, mt., France 42 20N 9 10E
40 Monte Rosa, Italy & Switz. 46 0N 8 0E
40 Monte S. Angelo, Italy 41 40N 16 0E
95 Montego Bay, Jamaica 18 30N 77 50W
43 Montélimar, France 44 34N 4 48E
94 Montemorelos, Mexico 25 8N 99 30W
40 Montenegro, Fed. Unit, Yugoslavia 42 52N 19 20E
43 Montereau, France 48 20N 3 0E
90 Monterey, U.S.A. 36 39N 121 45W
94 Monterrey, Mexico 25 42N 100 22W
98 Montes Claros, Brazil 16 20S 43 0W
37 Montes de Toledo, Spain 39 30N 4 30W
74 Monteverde, Angola 8 45S 16 45E
99 Montevideo, Uruguay 34 50S 56 15W
42 Montfort, France 48 10N 2 0W
91 Montgomery, U.S.A. 32 17N 86 20W
25 Montgomery, Wales 52 33N 3 9W
64 Montgomery, Pakistan, *see* Sahiwal
45 Monthey, Switzerland 46 15N 6 56E
45 Montigny les Metz, Fr. 49 6N 6 9E
37 Montijo, Portugal 38 40N 8 56W
37 Montilla, Spain 37 36N 4 40W
43 Montluçon, France 46 21N 2 37E
43 Montmédy, France 49 35N 5 25E
43 Montmorillon, France 46 23N 0 50E
82 Monto, Australia 24 58S 151 0E
37 Montoro, Spain 38 0N 4 30W
93 Montpelier, Ver., U.S.A. 44 15N 72 30W
43 Montpellier, France 43 40N 3 50E
93 Montreal, Canada 45 42N 73 50W
42 Montreiul, France 50 30N 1 48E
45 Montreux, Switzerland 46 27N 6 54E
31 Montrose, Scotland 56 43N 2 28W
90 Montrose, U.S.A. 38 30N 107 53W
95 Montserrat, I., W.I. 16 30N 62 0W
74 Monveda, Zaïre 3 0N 21 35E
65 Monywa, Burma 22 5N 95 8E
75 Monze, Zambia 16 23S 27 28E
64 Monze C., Pakistan 24 47N 66 37E
37 Monzon, Spain 41 53N 0 12E
35 Mooncoin, Ireland 52 18N 7 16W
35 Moone, Ireland 52 58N 6 49W
83 Moonie, R., Australia 28 0S 149 20E
83 Moonta, Australia 34 6S 137 32E
80 Moore, L., Australia 30 0S 117 30E
31 Moorfoot Hills, Scotland 55 45N 3 5W
91 Moorhead, U.S.A. 47 0N 96 42W
83 Mooroopna, Australia 36 30S 145 25E
93 Moosehead L., U.S.A. 45 45N 69 48W
88 Moosejaw, Canada 50 24N 105 25W
72 Mopti, Mali 14 34N 4 0W
64 Moradabad, India 28 50N 78 54E
75 Morafenobe, Madag. 17 50S 44 53E
75 Moramanga, Madag. 18 58S 48 15E
94 Morant Point, Jamaica 17 55N 76 10W
32 Morar, & L., Scotland 56 57N 5 40W
64 Moratuwa, Sri Lanka 6 45N 80 0E
41 Morava, R., Yugoslavia 44 10N 21 20E
46 Moravia, Dist., Cz-slov. 49 27N 16 55E
46 Moravian Hts., Cz-slov. 49 20N 15 20E
42 Morbihan, Dépt., France 47 55N 2 45W
42 Morcenx, France 44 0N 1 0W
88 Morden, Canada 49 12N 98 10W
52 Mordovian, A.S.S.R., U.S.S.R. 54 20N 44 30E
33 More L., Scotland 58 18N 4 50W
48 Möre and Romsdal, Co., Norway 62 30N 8 0E
26 Morecambe, & B., Eng. 54 5N 2 52W
83 Moree, Australia 29 25S 149 46E
45 Morel, Switzerland 46 23N 8 2E
94 Morelia, Mexico 19 48N 101 0W
82 Morella, Australia 23 0S 143 47E
37 Morena, Sa. de, mts., Spain 38 20N 4 40W
83 Moreton I., Austral. 27 0S 153 15E
43 Morez, France 46 32N 6 0E
83 Morgan, Australia 34 3S 139 40E
91 Morgantown, U.S.A. 39 43N 79 59W
45 Morges, Switzerland 46 31N 6 30E
67 Morioka, Japan 39 48N 141 8E
83 Morkalla, Australia 34 18S 141 4E
42 Morlaix, France 48 38N 3 51W
27 Morley, England 53 46N 1 36W
83 Mornington, Australia 38 15S 145 5E
36 Mornington, Ireland 53 42N 6 17W
82 Mornington I., Austral. 16 30S 139 20E
68 Moro G., Philippines 7 0N 123 0E
82 Morobe, Papua N.G. 7 57S 147 50E
72 Morocco, N. Africa 32 0N 5 0W
74 Morogoro, Tanzania 7 0S 37 50E
75 Morombé, Madagascar 21 38S 43 27E
95 Moron, Cuba 21 0N 78 45W
37 Moron, Spain 37 5N 5 30W
74 Morondava, Madag. 20 25S 44 30E
74 Moroto, Uganda 2 50N 34 0E
27 Morpeth, England 55 10N 1 42W
51 Morphou, Cyprus 35 17N 32 56E
84 Morrinsville, N.Z. 37 38S 175 30E
91 Morristown, U.S.A. 36 25N 83 18W
52 Morshansk, U.S.S.R. 53 28N 41 48E
42 Mortagne, France 47 0N 1 0W
22 Mortimer's Cross, Eng. 52 15N 2 47W
83 Mortlake, Australia 38 4S 142 50E
83 Moruya, Australia 35 55S 150 2E
33 Morven, Mt., Scotland 58 12N 3 40W
83 Morwell, Australia 38 12S 146 8E
24 Morwenstow, England 50 53N 4 32W
90 Moscow, U.S.A. 46 47N 117 2W
52 Moscow, U.S.S.R. 55 50N 37 40E
42 Moselle Dépt., France 49 5N 6 45E
46 Moselle, R., W. Europe 50 10N 7 10E
90 Moses Lake, U.S.A. 41 5N 119 0W
84 Mosgiel, New Zealand 45 53S 177 21E
74 Moshi, Tanzania 3 10S 37 30E
48 Mosjöen, Norway 66 0N 13 15E
48 Moskenstraumen, Norway 67 45N 13 0E
52 Moskva, R., U.S.S.R. 55 45N 36 0E
95 Mosquito Coast, Nicaragua 13 0N 84 0W
49 Moss, Norway 59 26N 10 40E
83 Moss Vale, Australia 34 38S 150 29E
84 Mossburn, New Zealand 45 40S 168 15E
76 Mosselbaai, S. Africa 34 10S 22 9E
74 Mossendjo, Congo (Fr.) 2 55S 12 55E
83 Mossgiel, Australia 33 5S 144 33E
99 Mossoró, Brazil 5 0S 37 15W
75 Mossuril, Mozambique 14 57S 40 42E
46 Most, Czechoslovakia 50 31N 13 38E
41 Mostar, Yugoslavia 43 21N 17 46E
36 Mostrim, Ireland 53 42N 7 38W
47 Mosty, U.S.S.R. 53 30N 24 30E
25 Mostyn, England 53 18N 3 14W
62 Mosul, Iraq 36 5N 43 15E
73 Mota, Ethiopia 11 5N 37 50E
49 Motala, & Can., Sweden 58 30N 15 20E
31 Motherwell, Scotland 55 47N 4 0W
65 Motihari, India 26 45N 85 0E
37 Motril, Spain 36 45N 3 34W
41 Moudhros, Greece 39 53N 25 18E
45 Moudon, Switzerland 46 41N 6 49E
74 Mouila, Gabon 1 50S 11 0E
73 Mouka, Central Africa 7 18N 21 50E
43 Moulins, France 46 36N 3 21E
65 Moulmein, Burma 16 30N 97 52E
73 Moundou, Central Africa 8 40N 16 10E
90 Mount Adams, Mt., U.S.A. 46 12N 121 35W
83 Mount Barker, S. Australia 35 8S 138 52E
80 Mount Barker, W. Australia 34 40S 117 50E
34 Mount Bellow Bridge, Ire. 53 29N 8 27W
75 Mount Darwin, Rhodesia 16 30S 31 35E
82 Mount Douglas, Australia 21 35S 146 50E
83 Mount Gambier, Austral. 37 45S 140 45E
80 Mount Goldsworthy, Australia 20 25S 119 39E
90 Mount Hood, Mt., U.S.A. 45 15N 121 40W
83 Mount Hope, Australia 32 48S 146 0E
82 Mount Isa, Australia 20 40S 139 30E
90 Mount Lassen, Mt., U.S.A. 40 32N 121 15W
64 Mount Lavinia, Sri Lanka 6 50N 79 50E
83 Mount Lofty Ras, Austral. 35 0S 139 30E
84 Mount Maunganui, N.Z. 37 35S 176 30E
82 Mount Morgan, Austral. 23 35S 150 28E
90 Mount Rainier, Mt., U.S.A. 46 48N 121 43W
90 Mount Shasta, Mt., U.S.A. 41 30N 122 1W
82 Mount Surprise, Austral. 18 10S 144 17E
90 Mount Taylor, Mt., U.S.A. 35 20N 107 35W
80 Mount Tom Price, Austral. 22 40S 118 9E
92 Mount Vernon, U.S.A. 38 22N 88 44W
80 Mount Whaleback, Australia 24 38S 113 33E
90 Mount Whitney, Mt., U.S.A. 36 25N 118 13W
24 Mount's B., England 50 4N 5 25W
25 Mountain Ash, Wales 51 42N 3 23W
36 Mountcharles, Ireland 54 38N 8 14W
35 Mountmellick, Ireland 53 8N 7 17W
35 Mountrath, Ireland 53 0N 7 29W
72 Mourdhia, Mali 14 35N 7 25W
36 Mourne Mts., N. Ireland 54 8N 6 2W
36 Mourne, R., N. Ireland 54 45N 7 24W
44 Mouscron, Belgium 50 45N 3 15E
73 Moussoro, Chad 13 48N 16 48E
43 Moutiers, France 45 30N 6 30E
36 Moville, Ireland 55 11N 7 2W
36 Moy, N. Ireland 54 27N 6 41W
72 Moyamba, Sierra Leone 8 15N 12 30W
34 Moylough, Ireland 53 29N 8 35W
98 Moyobamba, Peru 6 5S 77 5W
75 Mozambique, Africa 15 3S 40 43E
75 Mozambique, Port. prov., Africa 19 0S 35 0E
70 Mozambique Channel, Indian Ocean 18 0S 42 0E
74 Mpanda, Tanzania 6 22S 30 40E
75 Mpangwe, Zambia 14 8S 32 10E
75 Mpika, Zambia 11 54S 31 32E
74 Mpwapwa, Tanzania 6 30S 36 30E
73 Msaken, Tunisia 35 49N 10 33E
75 Msoro, Zambia 13 35S 32 0E
74 Mtwara, Tanzania 10 16S 40 10E
74 Muanda, Zaïre 6 0S 12 20E
68 Muang Khong Kaen, Thailand 16 59N 102 40E
68 Muang Nakhon Sawan, Thailand 15 40N 100 5E
68 Muang Phetchabun, Thailand 16 30N 101 10E
66 Muang Phitsanulak, Thailand 16 45N 100 3E
68 Muang Ubon, Thailand 15 20N 104 55E
68 Muar, Malaya 2 0N 102 40E
68 Muaraenim, Indonesia 3 35S 103 50E
68 Muaratewe, Indonesia 0 55S 114 50E
62 Mubarraz, Saudi Arabia 25 29N 49 40E
74 Mubende, Uganda 0 40N 31 21E
74 Mubi, Nigeria 10 16N 13 17E
22 Much Wenlock, Eng. 52 35N 2 33W
32 Muck I., Scotland 56 49N 6 13W
83 Mudgee, Australia 32 33S 149 32E
36 Muff, Ireland 55 4N 7 16W
75 Mufulira, Zambia 12 40S 28 2E
51 Mugla, Turkey 37 15N 28 30E
73 Muglad, Sudan 11 10N 27 35E
65 Mugu, Nepal 29 50N 82 30E
73 Muhammad Qol, Sudan 20 58N 37 0E
46 Mühlhausen, Germany 51 14N 10 26E
35 Muine Bheag, Ireland 52 41N 6 48W
31 Muirdrum, Scotland 56 31N 2 40W
31 Muirhead, Scotland 55 45N 4 5W
76 Muizenberg, S. Africa 34 7S 18 27E
63 Mujib, Wadiel, Jordan 31 28N 35 45E
47 Mukachevo, U.S.S.R. 48 27N 22 45E
62 Mukalla, South Yemen 14 38N 49 0E
67 Mukden, *see* Shenyang
65 Muktinath, Nepal 28 37N 83 55E
64 Muktsar, India 30 40N 74 30E
46 Mulde, R., Germany 51 30N 12 38E
94 Muleje, Mexico 26 50N 112 15W
93 Mulgrave, Canada 45 40N 61 30W
37 Mulhacen, Mt., Spain 36 45N 2 47W
44 Mulheim, Germany 51 0N 7 4E
43 Mulhouse, France 47 46N 7 19E
65 Muli, China 28 20N 100 40E
30 Mull I., Scotland 56 28N 6 0W
30 Mull of Galloway, Scot. 54 37N 4 52W
36 Mull of Kintyre, Scot. 55 17N 5 48W
30 Mull of Oa, Scotland 55 35N 6 20W
36 Mullagh, Ireland 53 49N 6 56W
35 Mullaghareirk Mts., Ire. 52 18N 9 10W
64 Mullaitivu, Sri Lanka 9 15N 80 50E
32 Mullardoch, L., Scotland 57 20N 5 0W
35 Mullet Pen., Ireland 54 10N 10 4W
80 Mullewa, Australia 28 33S 115 28E
35 Mullinahone, Ireland 52 32N 7 30W
35 Mullinavat, Ireland 52 22N 7 10W
35 Mullingar, Ireland 53 31N 7 19W
83 Mullumbimby, Austral. 28 30S 153 10E
64 Multan, Pakistan 30 3N 71 30E
25 Mumbles, The, Wales 51 35N 3 50W
25 Mumbles Hd., Wales 51 34N 3 59W
75 Mumbwa, Zambia 15 0S 27 2E
68 Muna I., Indonesia 5 0S 122 35E
64 Munabao, India 25 45N 70 15E
92 Muncie, U.S.A. 40 15N 85 22W
46 Münden, Germany 51 25N 9 40E
83 Mungallala, R., Austral. 26 25S 147 34E
82 Mungana, Australia 17 8S 144 27E
74 Mungbere, Zaïre 2 35N 28 35E
83 Mungindi, Australia 28 55S 149 0E
75 Munhango, Angola 12 15S 18 35E
46 Munich, Germany 48 9N 11 30E
92 Munising, U.S.A. 46 25N 87 0W
45 Munsingen, Switzerland 46 54N 7 37E
44 Münster, Germany 51 58N 7 39E
34 Munster, Prov., Ireland 52 25N 8 30W
44 Munstereifel Germany 50 33N 6 47E
48 Muonio, Finland 68 20N 23 0E
75 Mupa, Angola 16 5S 15 50E
62 Muqainama, Si. Arabia 22 9N 48 51E
46 Mur, R., Cent., Europe 46 30N 16 30E
50 Murashi, U.S.S.R. 59 30N 49 0E
43 Murat, France 45 10N 2 55E
84 Murchison, New Zealand 41 45S 172 23E
74 Murchison Falls, *see* Kabarega
80 Murchison. R., Austral. 27 35S 115 0E
80 Murchison Ra., Austral. 20 0S 135 0E
37 Murcia, Spain 38 0N 1 8W
37 Murcia, Prov., Spain 38 35N 1 50W
47 Mures, R., Rumania 46 0N 22 10E
43 Muret, France 43 26N 1 16E
64 Murghab, R., Afghan. 35 4N 64 5E
83 Murgon, Australia 26 5S 151 55E
46 Muritz, L., Germany 53 30N 12 25E
50 Murmansk, U.S.S.R. 69 0N 33 50E
52 Murom, U.S.S.R. 55 31N 42 4E
67 Muroran, Japan 42 20N 141 5E
83 Murray Bridge, Australia 35 2S 139 8E
93 Murray Hr., Canada 46 0N 62 32W
83 Murray, R., Australia 34 30S 141 40E
64 Murree, Pakistan 33 50N 73 25E
45 Murren, Switzerland 46 33N 7 58E
34 Murrough, Ireland 53 8N 9 17W
83 Murrumbidgee R., Australia 34 37S 144 30E
83 Murrumburrah, Austral. 34 35S 147 30E
83 Murrurundi, Australia 31 42S 150 51E
83 Murtoa, Australia 36 42S 142 28E
31 Murton, England 54 51N 1 22W
84 Murupara, New Zealand 38 25S 176 45E
65 Murwara, India 23 46N 80 28E
83 Murwillumbah, Austral. 28 21S 153 2E
73 Murzuq, Libya 25 53N 13 38E
46 Mürzzuschalg, Austria 47 5N 15 35E
51 Mus, Turkey 38 50N 41 28E
64 Musa Qala, Afghan. 32 23N 64 48E
41 Musala, Mt., Bulgaria 42 15N 23 35E
63 Musallim, Wadi, Oman 22 0N 56 30E
63 Muscat, Oman 23 40N 58 38E
63 Muscat & Oman, *see* Oman
78 Musgrave Ras., Austral. 26 10E 131 30E
91 Muskegon, U.S.A. 43 13N 86 10W
91 Muskegon, R., U.S.A. 43 25N 85 40W
91 Muskogee, U.S.A. 35 46N 95 32W
73 Musmar, Sudan 18 6N 35 40E
74 Musoma, Tanzania 1 31S 33 58E
62 Mussa Ali, Ethiopia 12 25N 42 15E
31 Musselburgh, Scotland 55 54N 3 3W
90 Musselshell, R., U.S.A. 46 35N 108 30W
64 Mussooree, India 30 23N 78 10E
94 Mustique, I., W.I. 12 50N 61 10W
83 Muswellbrook, Australia 32 18S 151 0E
62 Mut, Egypt 25 27N 29 0E
67 Mutankiang, Manchuria 44 34N 129 45E
75 Mutana, Angola 16 40S 15 1E
61 Mutarai, U.S.S.R. 61 20N 100 55E
74 Mutshatsha, Zaïre 10 35S 24 20E
67 Mutsu B., Japan 41 8N 141 0E
82 Muttaburra, Australia 22 30S 144 30E
34 Mutton I., Ireland 52 50N 9 33W
62 Muwaih, Saudi Arabia 22 35N 41 32E
74 Muxima, Angola 9 25S 13 52E
55 Muyun Kum, U.S.S.R. 47 0N 65 0E
64 Muzaffarabad, Kashmir 34 30N 73 25E
64 Muzaffarnagar, India 29 27N 77 40E
65 Muzaffarpur, India 26 15N 85 29E
60 Muzhi, U.S.S.R. 65 25N 64 40E
66 Muztagh, Mt., China 36 30N 87 22E
74 Mwanza, Tanzania 2 30S 33 1E
74 Mwaya, Tanzania 9 30S 33 58E
74 Mweka, Zaïre 4 12S 21 56E
74 Mwenga, Zaïre 3 7S 28 27E
74 Mweru, L., Zaïre 9 0S 28 50E
74 Mweru Marsh, Zambia 8 40S 29 40E
75 Mwinilunga, Zambia 11 43N 24 27E
68 My Tho, Vietnam 10 0N 106 48E
74 Myadhi, Gabon 1 16N 13 10E
65 Myaungmya, Burma 16 27N 94 58E
41 Mycenae, Greece 37 45N 22 45E
66 Myingyan, Burma 21 35N 94 40E
66 Myitkyina, Burma 25 50N 97 15E
65 Mymensingh, Pakistan, *see* Nasirabad
25 Mynydd du, Wales 51 45N 3 45W
25 Mynydd Epynt, Mt., Wales 52 3N 3 30W
25 Mynydd Prescelly, Mt., Wales 51 56N 4 45W
48 Myrdals Jökull, mts., Ice. 63 40N 19 0W
64 Mysore, India 12 18N 76 37E
52 Mytishchi, U.S.S.R. 55 54N 37 47E
48 Myvatn, L., Iceland 65 35N 16 55W

N

46 Naab, R., Germany 49 40N 12 10E
49 Naantali, Finland 60 32N 21 55E
44 Naaldwijk, Netherlands 52 0N 4 15E
63 Na'ar, Jordan 31 53N 35 50E
35 Naas, Ireland 53 14N 6 39W
76 Nababeep, S. Africa 29 35S 17 35E
65 Nabadwip, India 23 25N 88 20E
62 Naband, Iran 27 12N 52 38E
73 Nabeul, Tunisia 36 30N 10 40E
63 Nabulus, Jordan 32 13N 35 15E
75 Nacala, Mozambique 14 40S 40 40E
94 Nacaome, Honduras 13 40N 87 35W
74 Nachingwea, Tanzania 10 32S 38 48E
49 Nacka, Sweden 59 17N 18 14E
94 Nacozari, Mexico 30 30N 109 50W
64 Nadiad, India 22 41N 72 56E
47 Nadvornaya, U.S.S.R. 48 37N 24 30E
60 Nadym, & R., U.S.S.R. 65 30N 73 0E
72 Nafada, Nigeria 11 0N 11 20E
68 Naga, Philippines 13 37N 123 5E
65 Nagaland, st. India 26 0N 94 30E
74 Nagalle, Ethiopia 5 20N 39 30E
67 Nagano, & Pref., Japan 36 38N 138 6E
67 Nagaoka, Japan 37 30N 138 55E
65 Nagapattinam, India 10 40N 79 50E
64 Nagar Parkar, Pak. 24 30N 70 35E
67 Nagasaki, & Pref., Jap. 32 40N 129 48E
67 Nagashima, Japan 34 10N 136 15E
65 Nagchu Dzong, Tibet, China 31 25N 91 57E
64 Nagercoil, India 8 12N 77 33E
34 Nagles mts., Ireland 52 3N 8 30W
67 Nagoya, Japan 35 17N 137 0E
64 Nagpur, India 21 5N 79 5E
47 Nagykorös, Hungary 46 55N 19 48E
67 Naha, Japan 26 10N 127 45E
63 Naharayim, Jordan 32 38N 35 34E
63 Nahariya, Israel 33 0N 35 6E
63 Nahr Bisri, R., Lebanon 33 34N 35 25E
63 Nahr ed Dâmour, R., Leb. 33 44N 35 35E
63 Nahr El-Litani, R., Leb. 33 20N 35 20E
99 Nahuel Huapi L., Arg. 41 0S 71 40W
89 Nain, Canada 56 38N 62 0W
64 Nainpur, India 22 30N 80 10E
29 Nairn, Scotland 57 36N 3 51W
33 Nairn R., Scotland 57 25N 4 10W
74 Nairobi, Kenya 1 15S 36 49E
74 Naivasha, Kenya 0 50S 36 30E
67 Najin, Korea 42 10N 130 10E
67 Nakadori Shima, Japan 33 0N 129 5E
67 Nakamura, Japan 33 0N 133 0E
67 Nakatsu, Japan 33 40N 131 15E
51 Nakhichevan, & A.S.S.R., U.S.S.R. 39 20N 45 30E
67 Nakhodka, U.S.S.R. 42 50N 132 50E
68 Nakhon Ratchasima, Thailand 15 0N 105 40E
68 Nakhon Si Thammarat, Thailand 8 30N 100 6E
92 Nakina, Canada 50 8N 86 35W
62 Nakhl, Egypt 29 55N 33 43E
75 Nakop, S.W. Africa 28 1S 20 1E
49 Nakskov, Denmark 54 45N 11 12E
74 Nakuru, Kenya 0 10S 36 0E
51 Nalchik, U.S.S.R. 43 24N 43 32E
64 Nalgonda, India 17 4N 79 8E
64 Nallamalai Hs., India 16 0N 79 0E
73 Nalut, Libya 31 55N 11 2E
66 Nam Dinh, Vietnam 20 20N 106 15E
65 Nam Tso L., Tibet 30 45N 90 30E
60 Namangan, U.S.S.R. 41 30N 71 45E
76 Namaqualand, Dist., S. Africa 29 45S 18 0E
83 Nambour, Australia 26 31S 152 50E
83 Nambucca Heads, Australia 30 40S 152 48E
66 Namcha Barwa, Mt., China 29 50N 95 10E
70 Namib Des., Namibia 24 0S 15 0E
75 Namibia (South West Africa), Africa 22 0S 17 30E
83 Namoi, R., Australia 30 20S 150 30E
90 Nampa, U.S.A. 43 32N 116 35W
48 Namsen, R., Norway 64 40N 12 45E
48 Namsos, Norway 64 25N 11 30E
65 Namtu, Burma 23 0N 97 25E
44 Namur, & Prov., Belgium 50 28N 4 52E
75 Namutoni, S.W. Africa 18 50S 17 0E
75 Namwala, Zambia 15 50S 26 12E
66 Nan Ling, mts., China 25 30N 112 30E
55 Nan Shan, mts., China 38 30N 98 0E
88 Nanaimo, Canada 49 7N 123 58W
83 Nanango, Australia 26 40S 152 1E
67 Nanao, Japan 37 0N 137 0E
66 Nanchang, China 28 22N 115 49E
66 Nanchung, China 31 0N 105 20E
43 Nancy, France 48 44N 6 10E
64 Nanda Devi, mt., India 30 45N 80 0E
65 Nander, India 19 10N 77 16E
84 Nandi, Viti Levu, Fiji 17 40S 177 20E
64 Nandurbar, India 21 20N 74 15E
64 Nanga Parbat, mt., India 35 10N 75 0E
64 Nangrahar Prov., Afghan. 35 0N 71 0E
67 Nanking, China 32 5N 118 55E
80 Nannine, Australia 26 50S 118 16E
66 Nanning, China 22 50N 107 58E
67 Nanping, China 26 45N 118 15E
42 Nantes, France 47 17N 1 34W
92 Nanticoke, U.S.A. 41 10N 76 0W
43 Nantua, France 46 10N 5 35E
93 Nantucket I., U.S.A. 41 5N 70 5W
57 Nantung, China 31 50N 120 55E
26 Nantwich, England 53 5N 2 31W
66 Nanyang, China 33 1N 112 37E
74 Nanyuki, Kenya 0 1N 37 3E
37 Náo, C., Spain 38 25N 0 15E
67 Naoetsu, Japan 37 6N 138 9E
90 Napa, U.S.A. 38 24N 122 17W
84 Napier, New Zealand 39 37S 176 52E
40 Naples, (Napoli), Italy 40 53N 14 18E
67 Nara, & Pref., Japan 34 30N 135 40E
83 Naracoorte, Australia 36 55S 140 50E
63 Naradhan, Australia 33 30S 146 27E
65 Narasapur, India 16 50N 81 48E
65 Narayanganj, Bangla. 23 35N 90 30E
64 Narayanpet, India 16 50N 77 12E
25 Narberth, Wales 51 48N 4 45W
43 Narbonne, France 43 12N 3 1E
22 Narborough, England 52 34N 1 12W
41 Nardo, Italy 40 10N 18 0E
49 Narew, R., Poland 53 12N 21 50E
64 Narmada R., India 22 0N 75 15E
55 Narodnaya Mt., U.S.S.R. 65 10N 60 5E
83 Narooma, Austral. 36 14S 150 4E
83 Narrabri, Australia 30 26S 149 47W
83 Narrandera, Australia 34 46S 146 0E
80 Narrogin, Australia 32 50S 117 12E
83 Narromine, Australia 32 1S 148 8E
64 Narsinghpur, India 23 0N 79 6E
50 Narva, Estonia, U.S.S.R. 59 25N 28 5
48 Narvik, Norway 68 27N 17 30E
50 Naryan-Mar, U.S.S.R. 68 0N 53 0E
60 Narymskoye, U.S.S.R. 49 15N 84 15E

50 Naryn, U.S.S.R. 41 30N 76 10E
48 Nasa, mt., Norway 66 32N 16 0E
23 Naseby, England 52 23N 1 0W
91 Nashua, U.S.A. 42 46N 71 30W
91 Nashville, U.S.A. 36 0N 86 50W
54 Nasik, India 20 0N 74 0E
55 Nasirabad, Bangladesh 24 50N 90 25E
54 Nasirabad, India 26 14N 74 44E
73 Nassar City, Egypt, *see* Kôm Ombo
91 Nassau, Bahamas 25 2N 77 25W
73 Nasir, Sudan 8 30N 33 2E
73 Nasser, L., Egypt 24 0N 32 40E
49 Nässjö, Sweden 57 38N 14 45E
99 Natal, Brazil 5 48S 35 20W
76 Natal Prov., S. Africa 28 40S 30 30E
89 Natashquan, & R., Can. 50 14N 61 46W
91 Natchez, U.S.A. 31 35N 91 20W
91 Natchitoches, U.S.A. 31 40N 93 3W
83 Natimuk, Australia 36 52S 142 0E
74 Natron, L., Tanzania 2 0S 36 0E
30 Naturaliste, C., Australia 33 35S 115 1E
46 Naumburg, Germany 51 10N 11 45E
55 Nauntanwa, India 27 20N 83 25E
54 Naushahra, Pakistan 34 0N 72 0E
56 Naushki, U.S.S.R. 50 30N 106 0E
37 Navalcarnero, Spain 40 15N 4 0W
36 Navan, *see* An Uaimh
89 Navarino I., Chile 55 0S 67 30W
7 Navarra, Prov., Spain 43 0N 1 45W
33 Naver, L. & R., Scot. 58 18N 4 20W
94 Navojoa, Mexico 27 10N 109 25W
50 Navolok, U.S.S.R. 62 50N 40 0E
1 Nápaktos, Greece 38 23N 21 26E
1 Návplion, Greece 37 30N 22 50E
54 Navsari, India 20 58N 72 45E
63 Nawa, Syria 32 54N 36 3E
54 Nawabshah, Pakistan 26 20N 68 25E
55 Nawakot, Nepal 28 2N 83 55E
51 Nayakhon, U.S.S.R. 62 5N 159 0E
41 Naxos, I., Greece 37 5N 25 29E
89 Nazare, Brazil 12 52S 39 15W
63 Nazareth, Israel 32 42N 35 17E
94 Nazas, R., Mexico 25 30N 104 0W
23 Naze, The, England 51 52N 1 19E
55 Nazir Hat, Bangladesh 22 40N 91 50E
74 Ndalatando, Angola 9 12S 14 48E
73 Ndélé, Central Africa 8 30N 20 37E
73 Ndjamena, Chad 12 3N 15 3E
74 N'Djolé, Gabon 0 10S 10 45E
75 Ndola, Zambia 12 54S 28 35E
36 Neagh, L., N. Ireland 54 35N 6 25W
25 Neath, & R., Wales 51 40N 3 47W
3 Nebine, Cr., Australia 28 30S 146 50E
50 Nebit Dag., U.S.S.R. 39 50N 54 30E
0 Nebraska, st., U.S.A. 42 15N 100 30W
91 Nebraska City, U.S.A. 40 44N 95 55W
45 Neckar, R., Germany 48 37N 9 15E
89 Necochea, Argentina 38 30S 58 50W
2 Needles, The, England 50 40N 1 35W
4 Neemuch, India 24 25N 74 50E
8 Neepawa, Canada 50 19N 99 30W
92 Negaunee, U.S.A. 46 30N 87 32W
3 Negev, Israel 30 50N 34 50E
61 Negoiu, mt., Rumania 45 20N 25 0E
4 Negombo, Sri Lanka 7 10N 79 54E
41 Negotin, Yugoslavia 44 15N 22 34E
5 Negrais, C., Burma 16 0N 94 18E
9 Negro R., Argentina 40 0S 64 0W
8 Negro R., Brazil 1 0S 63 0W
8 Negros, I., Philippines 10 0N 123 0E
63 Neh, Iran 31 30N 59 58E
56 Neikiang, China 29 45N 104 25E
0 Neilston, Scotland 55 47N 4 26W
6 Neisse, R., Pol.-Ger. 51 27N 14 59E
8 Neiva, Colombia 3 0N 75 25W
2 Nejd, reg., Si. Arabia 25 15N 45 0E
4 Nekemte, Ethiopia 9 4N 36 30E
9 Nekso, Denmark 55 4N 15 8E
61 Nelka, U.S.S.R. 57 50N 136 0E
4 Nellore, India 14 30N 80 1E
1 Nelma, U.S.S.R. 47 30N 139 0E
8 Nelson, Canada 49 25N 117 17W
6 Nelson, England 53 50N 2 14W
4 Nelson, New Zealand 41 18S 173 20E
3 Nelson, C., Australia 38 18S 141 40E
4 Nelson, Dist., N.Z. 41 20S 173 23E
8 Nelson, R., Canada 56 22N 95 0W
6 Nelspruit, S. Africa 25 29S 30 59E
2 Néma, Mauritania 16 30N 7 0W
9 Neman, R., U.S.S.R. 55 5N 23 0E
2 Nemours, Algeria, *see* Ghazaouet
3 Nemours, France 48 16N 2 40E
1 Nemui, U.S.S.R. 55 35N 136 0E
7 Nemuro, Japan 43 20N 145 30E
3 Nene, R., England 52 38N 0 50W
4 Nenagh, Ireland 52 53N 8 12W
5 Nepal, Asia 28 0N 83 40E
5 Nepalganj, Nepal 28 0N 81 30E
0 Nephi, U.S.A. 39 43N 111 50W
5 Nephin, mt., Ireland 54 0N 9 22W
5 Nephin Beg Ra., Ireland 54 0N 9 35W
1 Neretva, R., Y-slav. 43 10N 17 53E
1 Nerchinsk, U.S.S.R. 52 1N 116 25E
1 Nerchinski Zavod, U.S.S.R. 51 10N 119 35E
7 Nerva, Spain 37 43N 6 30W
8 Nes, Iceland 65 50N 17 18W
4 Nesle, France 49 45N 2 53E
3 Ness, L. & R., Scotland 57 15N 4 28W
5 Neston, England 53 17N 3 4W
9 Nesttun, Norway 60 17N 5 31E
3 Netanya, Israel 32 20N 34 51E
2 Netherdale, Australia 21 10S 148 33E
4 Netherlands, Europe 52 20N 6 0E
7 Nettleham, England 53 15N 0 28W
46 Neu Brandenburg, Ger. 53 35N 13 15E
45 Neuchâtel, & Cn., Switz. 47 0N 6 56E
45 Neuchâtel, Lac de, Switz. 46 55N 6 50E
44 Neufchâteau, Belgium 49 50N 5 26E
43 Neufchâtel, France 49 42N 1 30E
44 Neufchâtel sur Aisne, Fr. 49 27N 4 0E
46 Neumünster, Germany 54 5N 10 0E
45 Neunkirchen, Germany 49 20N 7 0E
99 Neuquen & R., Arg. 39 5S 68 50W
46 Neuruppin, Germany 52 52N 12 48E
44 Neuss, Germany 51 13N 6 39E
46 Neusiedler, L., of, Austria 47 58N 16 47E
45 Neustadt, Germany 47 53N 8 14E
46 Neustrelitz, Germany 53 19N 13 0E
44 Neuwied, Germany 50 27N 7 30E
50 Neva, R., U.S.S.R. 59 55N 31 0E
91 Nevada, U.S.A. 37 51N 94 28W
90 Nevada, st., U.S.A. 39 30N 118 0W
37 Nevada, Sa. de, mts., Spain 37 10N 3 20W
95 Nevada de Chita, Colombia 6 30N 72 0W
61 Nevelski mt., U.S.S.R. 50 0N 143 25E
43 Nevers, France 47 3N 3 12E
83 Nevertire, Australia 31 38S 147 50E
94 Nevis I., W. Indies 17 0N 62 30W
32 Nevis, L., Scotland 57 0N 5 45W
31 New Abbey, Scotland 54 58N 3 37W
91 New Albany, U.S.A. 38 20N 85 50W
98 New Amsterdam, Guyana 6 12N 57 30W
91 New Bedford, U.S.A. 41 30N 71 0W
35 New Birmingham, Ire. 52 36N 7 38W
90 New Braunfels, U.S.A. 29 40N 98 13W
26 New Brighton, England 53 27N 3 4W
84 New Brighton, N.Z. 43 29S 172 43E
93 New Britain, U.S.A. 41 35N 72 50W
82 New Britain. I., Papua N.G. 6 0S 150 0E
89 New Brunswick, Prov., Canada 46 30N 66 30W
81 New Caledonia, I., Pacific Ocean 21 15S 165 0E
37 New Castile, prov., Spain 40 5N 3 20W
92 New Castle, U.S.A. 41 2N 80 20W
30 New Cumnock, Scot. 55 24N 4 3W
83 New England Ra., Austral. 30 0S 152 0E
22 New Forest, England 50 52N 1 48W
31 New Galloway, Scotland 55 4N 4 9W
93 New Glasgow, Canada 45 35N 62 57W
78 New Guinea, I., E. Indies 5 0S 140 0E
91 New Hampshire, st., U.S.A. 43 20N 71 30W
82 New Hanover, I., Pacific Ocean 2 18S 150 0E
93 New Haven, U.S.A. 41 15N 72 58W
81 New Hebrides, Is., Pacific Ocean 16 0S 166 30E
91 New Iberia, U.S.A. 30 0N 91 46W
82 New Ireland, I., Papua N.G. 3 0S 152 0E
93 New Jersey, st., U.S.A. 39 50N 74 30W
93 New London, U.S.A. 41 20N 72 5W
30 New Luce, Scotland 54 56N 4 51W
90 New Mexico, st., U.S.A. 34 40N 106 0W
26 New Mills, England 53 22N 2 0W
30 Newmilns, Scotland 55 36N 4 19W
83 New Norfolk, Australia 42 45S 146 59E
91 New Orleans, U.S.A. 30 0N 90 0W
84 New Plymouth, N.Z. 39 2S 174 5E
91 New Providence, Bahamas 25 0N 77 25W
25 New Quay, Wales 52 12N 4 22W
25 New Radnor, Wales 52 14N 3 9W
23 New Romney, England 50 59N 0 56E
35 New Ross, Ireland 52 25N 6 57W
27 New Rossington, England 53 30N 1 4W
61 New Siberian Is., U.S.S.R. 75 30N 140 0E
83 New South Wales, st., Australia 32 20S 147 0E
25 New Tredegar, Wales 51 43N 3 15W
91 New Ulm, U.S.A. 44 19N 94 35W
88 New Westminster, Can. 49 12N 122 50W
93 New York, & st., U.S.A. 40 45N 74 0W
84 New Zealand 40 0S 173 0E
74 Newala, Tanzania 11 0S 39 0E
27 Newark, England 53 5N 0 49W
93 Newark, Del., U.S.A. 39 45N 75 45W
93 Newark, N.J., U.S.A. 40 45N 74 0W
92 Newark, Ohio, U.S.A. 40 8N 82 30W
91 New Bern, U.S.A. 35 7N 77 4W
27 Newbiggin-by-the-Sea, England 55 12N 1 30W
31 Newbigging, Scotland 55 42N 3 33W
36 Newbliss, Ireland 54 9N 7 8W
35 Newbridge, *see* Droichead Nua
25 Newbridge-on-Wye, Wales 52 13N 3 26W
31 Newburgh, Scotland 56 21N 3 14W
93 Newburgh, U.S.A. 41 33N 74 0W
27 Newburn, England 54 58N 1 44W
22 Newbury, England 51 24N 1 19W
83 Newcastle, Australia 32 59S 151 49E
35 Newcastle, Ireland 53 5N 6 4W
36 Newcastle, N. Ireland 54 13N 5 54W
25 Newcastle Emlyn, Wales 52 4N 4 28W
80 Newcastle Waters, Australia 17 1S 133 42E
27 Newcastle-on-Tyne, Eng. 54 58N 1 36W
26 Newcastle-under-Lyme, England 53 1N 2 16W
80 Newdegate, Australia 33 0S 119 30E
22 Newent, England 51 56N 2 24W
89 Newfoundland, prov., Canada 49 0N 56 0W
23 Newham, Greater London, England 51 31N 0 3E
23 Newhaven, England 50 47N 0 3E
23 Newington, England 51 6N 1 8E
91 Newman, U.S.A. 33 32N 84 35W
23 Newmarket, England 52 15N 0 24E
34 Newmarket, Ireland 52 10N 9 0W
94 Newmarket, Jamaica 18 8N 77 53W
34 Newmarket-on-Fergus, Ireland 52 46N 8 54W
22 Newnham, England 51 48N 2 27W
22 Newport, Salop, Eng. 52 46N 2 23W
25 Newport, Monmouth, Wales 51 35N 3 0W
35 Newport, & B., Mayo, Ireland 53 53N 9 33W
34 Newport, Tipperary, Ire. 52 43N 8 24W
31 Newport, Scotland 56 27N 2 56W
91 Newport, Ark., U.S.A. 35 44N 91 17W
91 Newport, Ken., U.S.A. 39 3N 84 28W
93 Newport, R.I., U.S.A. 41 30N 71 17W
93 Newport, Vt. U.S.A. 44 47N 72 12W
91 Newport News, U.S.A. 37 6N 76 25W
23 Newport Pagnell, Eng. 52 5N 0 43W
24 Newquay, England 50 25N 5 6W
36 Newry, N. Ireland 54 10N 6 18W
91 Newton, Iowa, U.S.A. 41 43N 93 4W
91 Newton, Kansas, U.S.A. 38 6N 97 17W
24 Newton Abbot, England 50 32N 3 37W
27 Newton Aycliffe, England 54 36N 1 33W
30 Newton Stewart, Scot. 54 57N 4 28W
26 Newton-le-Willows, Eng. 53 27N 2 37W
33 Newtonhill, Scotland 57 1N 2 9W
31 Newtown, Scotland 55 34N 2 38W
25 Newtown, Wales 52 30N 3 22W
36 Newtown Forbes, Ireland 53 46N 7 50W
36 Newtown Hamilton, N. Ireland 54 12N 6 34W
36 Newtown Monasterboice, Ireland 53 46N 6 26W
36 Newtownabbey, Ireland 54 40N 5 55W
36 Newtownards, N. Ireland 54 36N 5 42W
36 Newtownbutler, N. Ireland 54 11N 7 21W
36 Newtowncunningham, Ireland 54 59N 7 31W
35 Newtownmountkennedy, Ireland 53 6N 6 6W
36 Newtownstewart, N. Ireland 54 43N 7 23W
50 Nezhin, Ukraine, U.S.S.R. 51 3N 32 5E
75 Ngami, Ll (Former), Botswana 20 35S 22 35E
73 Ngaoundere, Cameroon 7 23N 13 20E
84 Ngapara, New Zealand 44 57S 170 46E
66 Ngoring, Nor, L., China 35 0N 97 15E
74 Ngudu, Tanzania 3 25S 32 2E
73 Nguigmi, Niger 14 20N 13 20E
68 Nha Trang, Vietnam 12 15N 109 15E
83 Nhill, Australia 36 18S 141 40E
81 Nhulunbuy, Australia 12 18S 137 0E
92 Niagara Falls, N. America 43 12N 79 0W
72 Niamey, Niger 13 31N 2 20E
68 Nias, Is., East Indies 1 0N 97 20E
94 Nicaragua, & L., Central America 12 30N 85 0W
41 Nicastro, Italy 39 0N 16 18E
43 Nice, France 43 45N 7 17E
35 Nicobar Is., India 8 0N 93 20E
62 Nicosia, Cyprus 35 7N 33 2E
27 Nidd, R., England 54 2N 1 40W
46 Nienburg, Germany 52 38N 9 10E
76 Nieu Bethesda, S. Africa 31 55S 24 30E
44 Nieuwpoort, Belgium 51 9N 2 46E
42 Nièvre, Dépt., France 47 17N 3 40E
51 Nigde, Turkey 38 0N 34 40E
72 Niger, W. Africa 15 0N 9 0E
72 Niger, R., W. Africa 16 0N 0 20E
72 Niger Delta, Nigeria 4 0N 5 0E
72 Nigeria, W. Africa 9 30N 8 0E
33 Nigg, B., Scotland 57 42N 4 0W
84 Nightcaps, New Zealand 45 58S 168 3E
67 Niigata, & Pref., Japan 38 0N 139 5E
90 Niihau, Hawaii 21 45N 160 10W
44 Nijkerk, Netherlands 52 14N 5 29E
44 Nijmegen, Netherlands 51 50N 5 52E
67 Nikko, Japan 36 50N 139 30E
51 Nikolayev, U.S.S.R. 46 58N 32 7E
61 Nikolayevski, Siberia 53 30N 140 10E
51 Nikopol, U.S.S.R. 47 20N 34 20E
41 Niksic, Yugoslavia 42 47N 18 57E
73 Nile, R., N.E. Africa 27 20N 31 0E
73 Nile, prov., Sudan 20 0N 33 0E
43 Nîmes, France 43 51N 4 21E
83 Nimmitabel, Australia 36 42S 149 0E
83 Nindigully, Australia 28 27S 149 0E
67 Ningan, China 44 30N 129 45E
67 Ningpo, China 30 0N 121 40E
66 Ningsia, *see* Yinchwan
66 Ningsia Hui, Autonomous Region, China 37 0N 106 0E
65 Ningtsin, China 29 50N 98 25E
66 Ningtu, China 26 50N 115 30E
44 Ninove, Belgium 50 51N 4 2E
72 Nioro, Mali 15 30N 9 30W
42 Niort, France 46 22N 0 43W
88 Nipawin, Canada 53 20N 104 0W
89 Nipigon, & B., Canada 49 10N 88 20W
89 Nipigon, L., Canada 49 40N 88 30W
62 Niriz, Iran 29 15N 54 5E
65 Nirmali, India 26 25N 86 30E
41 Nis, Yugoslavia 43 17N 21 53E
99 Niterói, Brazil 22 52S 42 55W
31 Nith, R., Scotland 55 27N 3 58W
31 Nithsdale, Scotland 55 13N 3 45W
47 Nitra, Czechoslovakia 48 20N 18 4E
84 Niuafo'ou, I., Pacific Ocean (Inset)
44 Nivelles, Belgium 50 36N 4 20E
43 Nivernais, Prov., France 47 20N 3 25E
64 Nizamabad, India 18 45N 78 7E
61 Nizhne Kolymsk, U.S.S.R. 68 35N 160 55E
61 Nizhneudinsk, U.S.S.R. 55 0N 99 25E
50 Nizhniy Tagil, U.S.S.R. 57 45N 60 0E
72 Nkambe, Camer. 6 35N 10 40E
74 Nkhata Bay, Malawi 11 35S 34 20E
75 Nkhota Kota, Malawi 13 0S 34 20E
65 Nmai, mts., Burma 25 45N 98 0E
65 Noakhali, *see* Maijdi
36 Nobber, Ireland 53 49N 6 45W
67 Nobeoka, Japan 32 35N 131 40E
94 Nogales, Mexico 31 30N 111 0W
90 Nogales, U.S.A. 31 25N 111 0W
43 Nogent le Rotou, Fr. 48 20N 0 50E
52 Noginsk, U.S.S.R. 55 50N 38 28E
61 Noginsk, U.S.S.R. 64 30N 90 50E
42 Noirmoutier, I. de, Fr. 47 0N 2 17W
61 Nokhtuisk, U.S.S.R. 60 10N 117 15E
88 Nokomis, Canada 51 10N 105 10W
64 Nok Kundi, Pakistan 28 55N 62 55E
83 Noondoo, Australia 28 35S 148 25E
44 Noord Beveland I., Neth. 51 35N 3 45E
44 Noord Brabant, prov. Netherlands 51 40N 5 0E
44 Noord Holland, prov., Netherlands 52 30N 4 45E
76 Noordhoek, S. Africa 34 7S 18 25E
44 Noordoost Polder, Neth. 52 45N 5 45E
92 Noranda, Canada 48 20N 79 0W
42 Nord, Dépt., France 50 27N 3 20E
88 Nordegg, Canada 52 0N 116 47W
23 Nordelph, England 52 34N 0 18E
46 Norderney I., Germany 53 43N 7 12E
46 Nordhausen, Germany 51 30N 10 43E
44 Nordhorn, Germany 52 29N 7 3E
13 Nordkinn, C., Europe 71 3N 28 0E
48 Nordland, Co., Norway 66 30N 14 30E
61 Nordvik, U.S.S.R. 73 45N 110 57E
28 Norfolk, Co., England 52 42N 1 0E
91 Norfolk, Neb., U.S.A. 42 6N 97 28W
91 Norfolk, Va., U.S.A. 36 55N 76 12W
23 Norfolk Broads, Eng. 52 45N 1 30E
78 Norfolk I., Pacific Ocean 29 0S 167 55E
27 Norham, England 55 42N 2 10W
82 Norman R., Australia 19 20S 142 25E
82 Normanby, I., Papua N.G. 10 0S 151 0E
82 Normanby, R., Australia 15 0S 145 0E
42 Normandy, Prov., France 49 0N 0 0
82 Normanton, Australia 17 52S 140 58E
27 Normanton, England 53 42N 1 25W
48 Norrbotten, Co., Sweden 66 40N 20 0E
49 Nörresundby, Denmark 57 5N 9 52E
49 Norrköping, Sweden 58 39N 16 6E
80 Norseman, Australia 32 8S 121 45E
61 Norsk, U.S.S.R. 52 30N 130 5E
98 Norte, Sa. do, mts., Brazil 12 0S 59 0W
32 North Ballachulish, Scot. 56 42N 5 9W
88 North Battleford, Can. 52 48N 108 6W
89 North Bay, Canada 46 20N 79 30W
90 North Bend, U.S.A. 43 28N 124 15W
31 North Berwick, Scotland 56 3N 2 43W
68 North Bunguran Is., Indonesia 4 40N 108 0E
93 North C., Canada 47 0N 60 28W
84 North C., New Zealand 34 22S 173 1E
49 North C., Norway 71 0N 26 0E
91 North Carolina, st., U.S.A. 35 30N 79 0W
30 North Channel, U.K. 55 0N 5 30W
92 North Chan., L. Huron 46 5N 83 0W
90 North Dakota, st., U.S.A. 47 30N 100 0W
22 North Dorset Downs, England 50 40N 2 30W
22 North Downs, England 51 18N 0 20E
13 North Dvina R., U.S.S.R. 62 30N 43 0E
65 North East Frontier Agency, *see* Arunachal Pradesh
33 North Esk R., Scotland 56 54N 2 45W
13 North European Plain 57 0N 26 0E
23 North Foreland, England 51 23N 1 28E
49 North Frisian Is., Ger. 55 0N 8 20E
84 North I., New Zealand 38 0S 176 0E
67 North Korea, st., Asia 40 0N 127 0E
65 North Moscos Is., *see* Heinze Is.
51 North Ossetian, A.S.S.R., U.S.S.R. 43 0N 44 10E
68 North Pageh, I., Indon. 3 0S 100 10E
24 North Petherton, Eng. 51 6N 3 0W
90 North Platte R., U.S.A. 42 30N 105 0W
31 North Queensferry, Scot. 56 1N 3 22W
46 North Rhine-Westphalia, Land, Germany 51 0N 7 0E
32 North Roe, dist., Scot. 60 35N 1 20W
33 North Ronaldsay, I., & Firth, Scotland 59 25N 2 25W
88 North Saskatchewan R. Canada 54 0N 112 30W
13 North Sea, Europe 56 0N 3 0E
27 North Somercotes, Eng. 53 26N 0 9E
34 North Sd., Ireland 53 10N 9 48W
33 North Sd., Scotland 59 17N 2 45W
84 North Taranaki Bight, New Zealand 38 50S 174 0E
92 North Tonawanda, U.S.A. 43 0N 78 50W
32 North Tolsta, Scotland 58 21N 6 14W
48 North Tröndelag, Co., Norway 64 15N 12 0E
32 North Uist, I., Scotland 57 37N 7 20W
95 North Village, Bermuda 32 19N 64 47W
23 North Walsham, England 52 49N 1 24E
80 North-West C., Austral. 21 42S 114 10E
32 North-West Highlands, Scotland 57 30N 5 2W
89 North-West River, Can. 53 45N 60 10W
27 North Yorkshire, Co., Eng. 54 20N 1 0W
73 Northern Darfur, prov., Sudan 15 0N 25 0E
73 Northern Kassala, prov., Sudan 15 0N 30 0E
84 Northland, Dist., N.Z. 35 30S 174 0E
88 Northwest Terr.. Canada 65 0N 97 0W
27 North York Moors, Eng. 54 25N 0 50W
27 Northallerton, England 54 21N 1 27W
80 Northam, Australia 31 40S 116 40E
24 Northam, England 51 2N 4 13W
80 Northampton, Australia 28 24S 114 37E
28 Northampton, & Co., England 52 14N 0 54W
65 Northern Circars, India 17 30N 82 30E
36 Northern Ireland, U.K. 54 40N 6 50W
80 Northern Terr., Australia 19 30S 134 0E
23 Northfleet, England 51 27N 0 20E
22 Northleach, England 51 50N 1 51W
83 Northumberland, C., Australia 38 0S 140 30E
28 Northumberland, Co., England 55 13N 2 0W
82 Northumberland Is., Australia 21 45S 150 20E
93 Northumberland Str., Canada 46 20N 64 15W
26 Northwich, England 53 16N 2 32W
27 Norton, England 54 8N 0 47W
92 Norwalk, U.S.A. 41 8N 82 46W
48 Norway, Europe 65 30N 12 0E
16 Norwegian Sea 70 0N 0 2E
23 Norwich, England 52 38N 1 19E
67 Noshiro, & R., Japan 40 12N 140 0E
60 Nosok, U.S.S.R. 69 20N 82 20E
75 Nossi Bé, I., Madag. 13 25S 48 15E
75 Nossi Mitsio, Madag. 12 55S 48 20E
76 Nossob, R., Botswana 25 0S 20 20E
47 Notec, R., Europe 53 5N 17 10E
40 Noto, Sicily, Italy 36 59N 15 10E
28 Nottingham, & Co., Eng. 52 58N 1 8W
72 Nouadhibou (Port Etienne), Mauritania 21 0N 17 0W
76 Noupoort, South Africa 31 10S 24 57E
44 Nouzonville, France 49 49N 4 45E
74 Nova Chaves, Angola 10 20S 21 26E
68 Nova Sagres, Port. Timor 8 20S 127 30E
93 Nova Scotia, Prov., Can. 45 0N 64 0W
60 Novaya Lyalya, U.S.S.R. 59 0N 60 50E
60 Novaya Zemlya, Is., U.S.S.R. 75 0N 55 0E
47 Nové Zámky, Cz-slov. 48 2N 18 8E
50 Novgorod, U.S.S.R. 58 30N 31 10E
41 Novi Pazar, Yugoslavia 43 8N 20 30E
41 Novi Sad, Yugoslavia 45 17N 19 44E
60 Novo Kuznetsk, U.S.S.R. 53 30N 87 10E
74 Novo Redondo, Angola 11 3S 13 46E
52 Novocherkassk, U.S.S.R. 47 22N 40 8E
47 Novograd Volynsk, U.S.S.R. 50 6N 27 33E
60 Novokazalinsk, U.S.S.R. 45 50N 62 5E
50 Novokuybyshevsk, U.S.S.R. 53 10N 49 52E
60 Novokuznetsk. U.S.S.R. 54 0N 87 10E
100 Novolazarevskaya, Antarctica 70 45S 2 0E
52 Novomoskovsk, U.S.S.R. 54 5N 38 15E
51 Novorossiysk, U.S.S.R. 44 40N 37 50E
52 Novoshakhtinsk, U.S.S.R. 47 45N 39 55E
60 Novosibirsk, U.S.S.R. 55 10N 83 5E
50 Novouzensk, U.S.S.R. 50 30N 48 10E
40 Novska, Yugoslavia 45 22N 16 59E
60 Novy Port, U.S.S.R. 67 40N 73 20E
65 Nowgong, India 26 22N 92 40E
83 Nowra, Australia 34 51S 150 38E
47 Nowy Sacz, Poland 49 39N 20 42E
46 Nowy Tomysl, Poland 52 20N 16 5E
43 Noyon, France 49 35N 3 0E
75 Nsanje, Malawi 16 55S 35 15E
73 Nubian Des., Sudan 21 0N 33 0E
98 Nudo Coropuna, mt., Peru 16 0S 72 30W
88 Nueltin, L., Canada 59 40N 99 30W
90 Nueces, R., U.S.A. 28 40N 99 0W
94 Nueva Rosita, Mexico 28 0N 101 20W
94 Nuevo Laredo, Mexico 27 25N 99 35W
84 Nuhaka, New Zealand 39 0S 177 47E
62 Nukha, U.S.S.R. 41 28N 47 5E
73 Nukheila, Oasis, Sudan 19 7N 26 15E
84 Nuku'alofa, Tonga Is. 21 9S 175 14W
60 Nukus, U.S.S.R. 42 30N 60 0E
80 Nullarbor Plain, Austral. 30 40S 129 30E
73 Numan, Nigeria 9 29N 12 3E
67 Numata, Japan 36 45N 139 4E
67 Numazu, Japan 35 10N 138 50E
83 Numurkah, Australia 36 3S 145 30E
22 Nuneaton, England 52 31N 1 28W
74 Nunivak Is., Alaska 60 0N 166 0W
44 Nunspeet, Netherlands 52 22N 5 46E
40 Nuoro, Sardinia, Italy 40 20N 9 20E
83 Nuriootpa, Australia 34 27S 139 0E

45 Nürnberg (Nuremberg), Germany 49 28N 11 7E
68 Nusa Tenggara, Prov., Indonesia 7 40S 118 0E
62 Nusaybin, Turkey 37 3N 41 10E
64 Nushki, Pakistan 29 35N 65 57E
76 Nuweveldberge, mts., S. Africa 32 10S 21 45E
80 Nuyts, Pt., Australia 35 1S 116 40E
80 Nyabing, Australia 33 30S 118 10E
74 Nyahanga, Tanzania 2 10S 33 32E
83 Nyah, Australia 35 8S 143 26E
73 Nyala, Sudan 12 2N 24 58E
65 Nyalam Dz., Tibet, China 28 10N 85 50E
73 Nyamlell, Sudan 9 0N 27 3E
74 Nyahururu, Kenya 0 2N 36 27E
75 Nyasa, L., E. Africa 12 0S 34 30E
74 Nyasaland, E. Africa, *see* Malawi
49 Nybro, Sweden 56 43N 15 55E
60 Nyda, U.S.S.R. 66 40N 73 28E
66 Nyenchen Tanghla, Ra., Asia 30 30N 90 0E
74 Nyeri, Kenya 0 34S 37 0E
47 Nyiregyhaza, Hungary 47 47N 21 43E
49 Nyköbing, Denmark 54 51N 11 50E
49 Nylöping, Sweden 58 46N 17 0E
75 Nylstroom, S. Africa 24 40S 28 0E
83 Nymagee, Australia 32 7S 146 20E
49 Nynashamn, Sweden 58 55N 17 57E
83 Nyngan, Australia 31 39S 147 13E
45 Nyon, Switzerland 46 24N 6 15E
39 Nyons, France 44 20N 5 5E
47 Nysa, Poland 50 40N 17 22E
67 Nyudo, C., Japan 40 0N 139 30E
74 Nzega, Tanzania 4 12S 33 11E
72 Nzérekoré, Guinéa 7 46N 8 58W

O

31 Oa, Mull of, Scotland 55 35N 6 20W
22 Oadby, England 52 37N 1 7W
90 Oahu, Hawaii 21 30N 158 0W
83 Oakbank, Australia 32 58S 140 50E
22 Oakengates, England 52 42N 2 29W
83 Oakey, Australia 27 28S 151 33E
23 Oakham, England 52 40N 0 47W
90 Oakland, U.S.A. 37 55N 122 5W
84 Oamaru, New Zealand 45 1S 171 0E
100 Oasis, Antartica 77 0S 101 0E
100 Oates Coast, Antarctica 70 0S 165 0E
94 Oaxaca, Mexico 17 15N 96 38W
60 Ob, G. of, U.S.S.R. 70 0N 73 0E
60 Ob, R., U.S.S.R. 62 40N 66 0E
92 Oba, Canada 48 50N 84 10W
84 Oban, New Zealand 46 55S 168 10E
30 Oban, Scotland 56 25N 5 27W
44 Oberhausen, Germany 51 28N 6 50E
83 Oberon, Australia 33 40S 149 50E
68 Obi Is., Indonesia 1 40S 128 0E
98 Obidos, Brazil 1 48S 55 37W
62 Obock, Djibouti 12 0N 43 15E
34 O'Briensbridge, Ireland 52 46N 8 30W
72 Obuasi, Ghana 6 17N 1 40W
98 Ocaña, Colombia 8 0N 73 35W
37 Ocaña, Spain 39 55N 3 30W
30 Ochil Hills, Scotland 56 15N 3 40W
61 October Revolution I., U.S.S.R. 79 30N 97 0E
62 Oda, Gebel, Sudan 20 15N 36 50E
48 Odadahraun, Iceland 65 10N 17 0W
49 Odda, Norway 60 3N 6 35E
48 Oddeyri, Iceland 65 40N 18 5W
76 Odendaalsrus, S. Africa 27 53S 26 45E
49 Odense, Denmark 55 22N 10 23E
49 Oder, R., Poland 53 3N 14 20E
90 Odessa, U.S.A. 31 50N 102 25W
51 Odessa, U.S.S.R. 46 37N 30 16E
72 Odienné, Ivory Coast 9 30N 7 15W
23 Odiham, England 51 16N 0 57W
47 Odorhei, Rumania 46 20N 25 20E
41 Odzak, Yugoslavia 45 3N 18 18E
75 Odzi, Rhodesia 19 0S 32 20E
40 Ofanto, R., Italy 41 10N 16 50E
45 Ofenpass, Switzerland 46 40N 10 20E
35 Offaly, Co., Ireland 53 10N 7 30W
45 Offenbach, Germany 50 7N 8 51E
45 Offenburg, Germany 48 28N 7 57E
45 Oftringen, Switzerland 47 20N 7 56E
67 Ogaki, Japan 35 25N 136 30E
72 Ogbomosho, Nigeria 8 5N 4 10E
90 Ogden, U.S.A. 41 22N 111 50W
91 Ogdensburg, U.S.A. 44 42N 75 20W
67 Oginohama, Japan 38 27N 141 30E
40 Oglio, R., Italy 46 0N 10 20E
82 Ogmore, Australia 22 37S 149 35E
25 Ogmore Vale, Wales 51 35N 3 32W
84 Ohakune, New Zealand 39 26S 175 25E
44 Ohey, Belgium 50 26N 5 8E
91 Ohio, R., U.S.A. 39 45N 81 30W
91 Ohio, st., U.S.A. 40 40N 82 30W
46 Ohre R., Cz-slov. 50 10N 12 30E
41 Ohrid, Yugoslavia 41 10N 20 50E
76 Ohrigstad, S. Africa 24 35S 30 32E
35 Oilgate, Ireland 52 25N 6 30W
61 Oimyakon, U.S.S.R. 63 20N 143 5E
60 Oirot-Tura, U.S.S.R. 52 0N 86 3E
42 Oise, Dépt., France 49 35N 2 12E
43 Oise R., France 49 20N 3 0E
44 Oisterwijk, Netherlands 51 35N 5 12E
67 Oita, & Pref., Japan 33 10N 131 30E
99 Ojos del Salado, mt., Arg. 27 0S 68 0W
75 Okahandja, S.W. Africa 22 0S 16 52E
84 Okarito, New Zealand 43 15S 170 10E
75 Okavango Swamp, Botswana 19 30S 23 0E
67 Okayama, & Pref., Japan 34 40N 133 6E
67 Okazaki, Japan 34 55N 137 10E
91 Okeechobee, L., U.S.A. 27 0N 80 50W
24 Okehampton, England 50 45N 4 0W
72 Okene, Nigeria 7 32N 6 11E
64 Okha, India 22 25N 69 0E
61 Okha, U.S.S.R. 53 40N 142 50E
61 Okhotsk, U.S.S.R. 59 25N 143 10E
61 Okhotsk, Sea of, U.S.S.R. 57 0N 149 0E
67 Oki Is., Japan 36 17N 133 10E
75 Okiep, S. Africa 29 41S 17 59E
67 Okinawa, I., Japan 26 30N 128 0E
90 Oklahoma City, U.S.A. 35 40N 97 20W
90 Oklahoma, st., U.S.A. 35 40N 97 0W
72 Okrika, Nigeria 4 47N 7 4E
51 Oktabrsk, U.S.S.R. 49 20N 57 15E
84 Okuru, New Zealand 43 55S 168 58E
48 Olafsvik, Iceland 64 52N 23 45W
49 Oland I., Sweden 56 50N 16 40E
83 Olary, Australia 32 8S 140 7E
99 Olavarria, Argentina 37 0S 60 20W
40 Olbia, Sardinia, Italy 40 55N 9 30E
37 Old Castile, Prov. Spain 42 0N 4 0W
36 Old Castle, Ireland 53 46N 7 10W
33 Old Deer, Scotland 57 30N 2 3W
35 Old Head of Kinsale, Ire., *see* Kinsale
30 Old Kilpatrick, Scotland 55 56N 4 34W
62 Old Sennar, Sudan 13 52N 33 32E
22 Oldbury, England 52 30N 1 59W
44 Oldenburg, Germany 53 10N 8 15E
26 Oldham, England 53 34N 2 7W
44 Oldenzaal, Netherlands 52 19N 6 55E
92 Olean, U.S.A. 42 7N 78 27W
61 Olekma, R., U.S.S.R. 57 30N 121 30E
33 Oldmeldrum, Scotland 57 20N 2 19W
61 Olekminsk, U.S.S.R. 60 40N 120 30E
61 Olenek, R., U.S.S.R. 72 30N 122 30E
42 Oleron, I.d', France 46 0N 1 20W
47 Olésnica, Poland 51 13N 17 22E
61 Olga, U.S.S.R. 43 50N 135 20E
76 Olifants R., S. Africa 24 0S 31 25E
76 Olifantshoek, S. Africa 27 50S 22 55E
63 Olives, Mt. of Israel 31 47N 35 14E
27 Ollerton, England 53 12N 1 1W
23 Olney, England 52 0N 0 42W
46 Olomouc, Cz-slov. 49 35N 17 8E
42 Oloron, France 43 10N 0 40W
61 Olovyannaya, U.S.S.R. 50 55N 115 30E
49 Olsztyn, Poland 53 45N 20 30E
45 Olten, Switzerland 47 22N 7 54E
90 Olympia, U.S.A. 47 2N 122 50W
41 Olympia, Ruins of, Gr. 37 40N 21 39E
41 Olympus, Mt., Greece 40 2N 22 25E
86 Olympus, Mt., U.S.A. 48 7N 124 0W
36 Omagh, N. Ireland 54 35N 7 18W
91 Omaha, U.S.A. 41 28N 96 12W
63 Oman, Arabia 22 0N 52 0E
63 Oman, G. of, S.W. Asia 24 30N 59 0E
68 Ombai Str., East Indies 8 15S 124 45E
22 Ombersley. England 52 17N 2 12W
74 Omboue, Gabon 1 35S 9 15E
40 Ombrone, R., Italy 42 40N 11 3E
73 Omdurman, Sudan 15 50N 32 45E
67 Ominato, Japan 41 25N 141 8E
44 Ommen, Netherlands 52 32N 6 26E
61 Omolon, R., U.S.S.R 64 30N 161 0E
67 Omoto, Japan 39 57N 142 0E
66 Ompor, U S.S.R. 49 50N 117 0E
60 Omsk, U.S.S.R. 55 0N 73 30E
47 Omul, Mt., Rumania 45 20N 25 20E
75 Omuramba Omatako, R., South-West Africa 20 0S 17 50E
67 Omuta, Japan 33 0N 130 26E
75 Ondangua, S.W. Africa 18 0S 16 0E
66 Ondörhaan, Mongolia 47 30N 110 15E
48 Ondverdarnes, Iceland 64 52N 24 0W
50 Onega, & G. of, & R., U.S.S.R. 60 40N 37 30E
84 Onehunga, New Zealand 36 58S 174 50E
61 Onekotan, I., U.S.S.R. 49 30N 154 30E
61 Onguren, U.S.S.R. 54 0N 108 0E
72 Onitsha, Nigeria 6 8N 6 55E
67 Onomichi, Japan 34 30N 133 5E
80 Onslow, Australia 21 44S 115 1E
91 Onslow Bay, U.S.A. 34 30N 77 0W
67 Ontake, Mt., Japan 35 57N 137 30E
90 Ontario, U.S.A. 43 50N 117 0W
92 Ontario, L., N. America 43 40N 78 0W
89 Ontario, Prov., Canada 50 0N 86 0W
92 Ontonagon, U.S.A. 46 58N 89 12W
80 Oodnadatta, Australia 27 30S 135 30E
80 Ooldea, Australia 30 30S 131 55E
44 Oosterhout, Netherlands 51 38N 4 51E
64 Ootacamund, India 11 30N 76 40E
76 Ootse, Botswana 25 0S 25 40E
74 Opala, Zaïre 1 13S 24 45E
64 Opanake, Sri Lanka 6 30N 80 35E
47 Opava, Czechoslovakia 49 57N 17 50E
80 Ophthalmia Ra., Austral. 23 14S 119 30E
37 Oporto, Portugal 41 10N 8 38W
49 Oppland, Dist., Norway 61 10N 10 0E
84 Opua, New Zealand 35 13S 174 0E
84 Opunake, New Zealand 39 27S 173 52E
62 Oqair, Saudi Arabia 25 45N 50 10E
63 Or Yehuda, Israel 32 1N 34 53E
48 Oraefa Jokull, mt., Ice. 64 10N 16 20W
47 Oradea, Rumania 47 3N 21 57E
64 Orai, India 26 3N 79 30E
72 Oran, Algeria 35 45N 0 38W
99 Oran, Argentina 23 5S 64 15W
83 Orange, Australia 33 13S 149 0E
43 Orange, France 44 10N 4 50E
91 Orange, U.S.A. 30 5N 93 47W
76 Orange, R., S.W. Africa 28 40S 16 30E
76 Orange Free State, Prov., South Africa 28 20S 27 0E
91 Orangeburg, U.S.A. 33 30N 80 51W
75 Orangemouth, S.W. Afr. 23 38S 16 24E
92 Orangeville, Canada 43 58N 80 2W
46 Oranienburg, Germany 52 43N 13 14E
76 Oranjefontein, S. Africa 23 30S 27 30E
34 Oranmore, Ireland 53 16N 8 57W
45 Orbe, Switzerland 46 44N 6 30E
40 Orbetello, Italy 42 25N 11 5E
83 Orbost, Australia 37 40S 148 28E
44 Orchies, France 50 28N 3 14E
66 Ordos, Desert, China 39 30N 108 0E
51 Ordzhonikidze, U.S.S.R. 43 20N 44 30E
46 Ore Mts., Germany, *see* Erz Gebirge
48 Orebro, & Co., Sweden 59 20N 15 18E
90 Oregon, St., U.S.A. 43 45N 120 30W
52 Orekhovo-Zuyevo, U.S.S.R. 55 0N 39 2E
52 Orel, U.S.S.R. 53 3N 36 8E
50 Orenburg, U.S.S.R. 51 42N 55 7E
37 Orense, Spain 42 19N 7 53W
23 Orford, England 52 6N 1 33E
44 Origny Ste. Benoite, Fr. 49 50N 3 30E
37 Orihuela, Spain 38 8N 0 58W
92 Orillia, Canada 44 42N 79 30W
98 Orinoco, Delta of, Ven. 9 0N 61 0W
98 Orinoco R., Venezuela 8 0N 64 50W
65 Orissa, Prov., India 21 0N 85 0E
40 Oristano, Italy 39 57N 8 39E
48 Orkanger, Norway 63 16N 9 57E
48 Orkla, R., Norway 63 0N 9 40E
76 Orkney, S. Africa 27 0S 26 35E
33 Orkneys Is., & Co., Scotland 59 5N 3 0W
100 Orkneys, South, Islands, Southern Ocean 61 0S 46 0W
91 Orlando, U.S.A. 28 30N 81 0W
43 Orléanais, Prov., France 47 50N 2 0E
43 Orléans, France 47 57N 1 53E
72 Orléansville, *see* El Asnam
64 Ormara, Pakistan 25 13N 64 37E
68 Ormoc, Philippines 11 5N 124 30E
84 Ormond, N.Z. 38 30S 177 55E
26 Ormskirk, England 53 34N 2 53W
45 Ornans, France 47 7N 6 8E
42 Orne, Dépt., France 48 40N 0 15W
48 Örnsköldsvik, Sweden 63 18N 18 44E
40 Orosei, Italy 40 20N 9 40E
83 Orroroo, Australia 32 45S 137 30E
45 Orsieres, Switzerland 46 2N 7 10E
50 Orsk, U.S.S.R. 51 8N 58 30E
47 Orsova, Rumania 44 42N 22 22E
45 Orta, L., Italy 45 48N 8 28E
37 Ortigueira, Spain 43 40N 7 50W
40 Ortles, Mt., Italy 46 19N 10 38E
26 Orton, England 54 28N 2 35W
40 Ortona, Italy 42 20N 14 22E
98 Oruro, Bolivia 17 50S 67 25W
40 Orvieto, Italy 42 45N 12 5E
23 Orwell, R., England 52 10N 1 0E
41 Oryakhovo, Bulgaria 43 43N 23 55E
91 Osage, R., U.S.A. 38 0N 94 0W
67 Osaka, & Pref., Japan 34 40N 135 39E
92 Oshawa, Canada 44 0N 78 59W
75 Oshikango, S.W. Africa 17 9S 16 10E
72 Oshogbo, Nigeria 7 55N 4 50E
74 Oshwe, Zaïre 3 10S 19 35E
41 Osijek, Yugoslavia 45 32N 18 42E
61 Osinino, U.S.S.R. 71 0N 148 57E
91 Oskaloosa, U.S.A. 41 17N 92 44W
49 Oskarshamn, Sweden 57 18N 16 23E
49 Oslo, Norway 59 54N 10 50E
49 Oslo Fjord, Norway 59 0N 10 30E
64 Osmanabad, India 18 6N 76 4E
51 Osmaniye, Turkey 37 7N 36 15E
44 Osnabrück, Germany 52 19N 8 2E
45 Osogna, Switzerland 46 18N 8 58E
99 Osorno, Chile 40 30S 73 0W
44 Oss, Netherlands 51 47N 5 32E
83 Ossa, Mt., Australia 41 47S 146 0E
27 Ossett, England 53 40N 1 35W
44 Ostend, Belgium 51 14N 2 56E
49 Öster Dal, R., Seden 61 30N 13 50E
49 Östergötland, Sweden 58 20N 15 30E
48 Östersund, Sweden 63 14N 14 40E
49 Östfold, Co., Norway 59 30N 11 0E
40 Ostia, Italy 41 40N 12 20E
47 Ostrava, Cz.slov. 49 55N 18 19E
47 Ostróda, Poland 53 40N 20 1E
47 Ostróg, U.S.S.R. 50 20N 26 30E
47 Ostroleka, Poland 53 1N 21 34E
47 Ostrów, Poland 51 40N 17 50E
47 Ostrów Mazowiecka, Pol. 52 48N 21 55E
47 Ostrowiec, Poland 51 0N 21 25E
67 Osumi Chan. (Van Diemen Str.), Japan 30 55N 131 0E
26 Oswaldtwistle, England 53 44N 2 27W
91 Oswego, U.S.A. 43 25N 76 33W
22 Oswestry, England 52 15N 3 5W
67 Ota, Japan 36 42N 140 30E
84 Otago, Dist., N.Z. 45 20S 169 50E
84 Otaki, New Zealand 40 38S 175 10E
67 Otaru, Japan 43 10N 141 0E
75 Otavi, S.W. Africa 19 35S 17 25E
75 Otjiwarongo, S.W. Afr. 20 22S 16 37E
27 Otley, England 53 56N 1 31W
84 Otorohanga, N.Z. 38 10S 175 12E
41 Otranto, & Str., Italy 40 11N 18 28E
67 Otsu, Japan 35 0N 136 0E
93 Ottawa, & R., Canada 45 20N 75 41W
91 Ottawa, U.S.A. 38 40N 95 20W
89 Ottawa Is., Canada 59 30N 81 0W
22 Otter, R., England 50 48N 3 15W
24 Ottery St. Mary, Eng. 50 45N 3 16W
91 Ottumwa, U.S.A. 41 5N 92 20W
72 Oturkpo, Nigeria 7 10N 8 15E
47 Otwock, Poland 52 10N 21 20E
91 Ouachita, Mts., U.S.A. 34 58N 94 20E
91 Ouachita, R., U.S.A. 32 30N 92 5W
73 Ouadda, Central Africa 8 15N 22 20E
72 Ouagadougou, Volta 12 25N 1 30W
72 Ouallene, Algeria 24 30N 1 20E
74 Ouanda Djalé, Central Africa 8 55N 22 53E
74 Ouango, Central Africa 4 19N 22 30E
72 Ouargla, Algeria 31 50N 5 20E
72 Ouarzazate, Morocco 31 0N 6 40W
74 Oubangi, R., Congo (Fr.) 1 0N 17 30E
44 Oudenaarde, Belgium 50 51N 3 37E
44 Oudensbock, Neth. 51 35N 4 30E
75 Oudtshoorn, S. Africa 33 32S 22 8E
74 Ouesso, Congo (Fr.) 1 40N 16 10E
72 Ouezzane, Morocco 34 51N 5 42W
44 Ougrée, Belgium 50 37N 5 30E
72 Ouidah, Benin 6 25N 2 0E
72 Oujeft, Mauritania 20 0N 13 0W
72 Ouled Djellal, Algeria 34 20N 6 30E
23 Oulton Broad, England 52 28N 1 44E
48 Oulu, Co., Finland 64 53N 25 23E
48 Oulu, L. & R., Finland 64 20N 27 15E
48 Ounas, R., Finland 67 45N 24 55E
23 Oundle, England 52 29N 0 27W
44 Our, R., Germany 50 3N 6 8E
99 Ouro Preto, Brazil 20 17S 43 48W
44 Ourthe, R., Belgium 50 13N 5 33W
33 Ousdale, Scotland 58 10N 3 34W
23 Ouse, Great, R., Cambs., England 52 21N 0 6E
23 Ouse, R., Sussex, Eng. 50 50N 0 5E
27 Ouse, R., Yorks., Eng. 54 0N 1 10W
32 Out Skerries, Scotland 60 25N 0 44W
32 Outer Hebrides, Scot. 57 40N 7 0W
83 Ouyen, Australia 35 0S 142 30E
99 Ovalle, Chile 30 35S 71 17W
75 Ovamboland, reg., S.W. Africa 17 40S 16 0E
37 Ovar, Portugal 40 50N 8 40W
33 Overbister, Scotland 59 16N 2 33W
44 Overijssel, Prov., Neth. 52 24N 6 33E
48 Overtornea, Sweden 66 25N 23 32E
37 Oviedo, Spain 43 25N 5 53W
84 Owaka, New Zealand 46 30S 169 48E
91 Owatonna, U.S.A. 44 8N 93 34W
92 Owen Sound, Canada 44 40N 81 0W
82 Owen Stanley Ra., Papua 9 0S 148 0E
91 Owensboro, U.S.A. 37 47N 87 7W
92 Owosso, U.S.A. 43 2N 84 12W
36 Ox Mts., *see* Slieve Gamph
49 Oxelösund, Sweden 58 43N 17 15E
22 Oxford, & Co., England 51 45N 1 15W
84 Oxford, New Zealand 43 20S 172 10E
83 Oxleys Pk., Australia 31 50S 150 20E
33 Oykel R., Scotland 57 58N 4 40W
72 Oyo, Nigeria 7 58N 3 59E
43 Oyonnax, France 46 15N 5 40E
83 Oyster B., Australia 42 10S 148 0E
68 Ozamiz, Philippines 8 10N 123 40E
91 Ozark Plateau, U.S.A. 37 0N 92 30W
91 Ozarks, L. of the, U.S.A. 38 0N 93 0W

P

65 Paan, China 29 55N 99 5E
76 Paarl, Cape Prov. 33 45S 18 59E
48 Paatsi, R., U S.S.R. 68 55N 29 0E
64 Pab Hills, Pakistan 26 20N 66 45E
32 Pabbay I., & Sd., Scot. 57 47N 7 14W
65 Pabna, Bangladesh 24 0N 89 10E
95 Pacaraima, Sa, mts., Venezuela 4 0N 63 0W
98 Pacasmayo, Peru 7 28S 79 30W
64 Pachpadra, India 25 57N 72 0E
94 Pachuca, Mexico 20 13N 98 45W
4 Pacific Ocean 45 0S to 60 0N, 120 0E to 75 0W
68 Padang, Indonesia 1 5S 100 25E
46 Paderborn, Germany 51 47N 8 52E
26 Padiham, England 53 48N 2 20W
88 Padlei, Canada 62 10N 97 5W
24 Padstow, & B., England 50 32N 4 57W
46 Padua (Padova), Italy 45 23N 11 51E
91 Paducah, U.S.A. 37 1N 88 29W
84 Paeroa, New Zealand 37 18S 175 39E
46 Pag I., Yugoslavia 44 20N 15 0E
68 Pagadian, Philippines 7 55N 123 30E
71 Pagalu, I. Atlant. 1 35S 5 35E
90 Page, U.S.A. 37 0N 111 25W
84 Pago Pago, Samoa 14 5S 171 48W
68 Pahandut, Indonesia, *see* Palangkaraya
84 Pahiatua, New Zealand 40 27S 175 48E
62 Pahlevi, Iran 37 37N 49 8E
67 Paicheng, China 45 40N 122 30E
24 Paignton, England 50 26N 3 33W
49 Päijänne, L., Finland 61 40N 25 30E
42 Paimboeuf, France 47 20N 2 0W
42 Paimpol, France 48 42N 3 2W
30 Paisley, Scotland 55 51N 4 25W
22 Painswick, England 51 47N 2 11W
90 Painted Desert, U.S.A. 36 0N 111 10W
65 Paiyu, China 31 10N 98 45E
68 Pakanbaru, Indonesia 0 30N 101 35E
66 Pakhoi, China 21 30N 109 12E
64 Pakistan, Asia 30 0N 70 0E
64 Pakistan, West *see* Pakistan
65 Pakistan, East *see* Bangladesh
65 Pakokku, Burma 21 15N 95 6E
68 Pakse, Laos 15 5N 105 47E
64 Paktya, prov., Afghan. 33 0N 69 0E
64 Palam, India 19 0N 77 0E
37 Palamos, Spain 41 52N 3 13E
68 Palangkaraya (Pahandut), Indonesia 2 25S 114 0E
64 Palanpur, India 24 15N 72 30E
75 Palapye, Botswana 22 30S 27 28E
91 Palatka, U.S.A. 29 37N 81 42W
5 Palau Is., Pacific Ocean 7 20N 135 0E
68 Palawan, I., Philippines 9 30N 119 0E
49 Paldiski, U.S.S.R. 59 23N 24 9E
68 Paleleh, Indonesia 1 0N 122 0E
68 Palembang, Indonesia 3 0S 104 47E
37 Palencia, Spain 42 1N 4 35W
40 Palermo, Italy 38 8N 13 18E
63 Palestine, *see* Israel and Jordan
91 Palestine, U.S.A. 31 46N 95 40W
64 Palghat, India 11 1N 76 59E
23 Palgrave, England 52 22N 1 6E
64 Pali, India 25 45N 73 10E
64 Palitana, India 21 48N 71 49E
46 Palk Bay, Sri Lanka 9 20N 80 0E
46 Palk Str., India 10 0N 80 0E
45 Pallanza, Italy 45 58N 8 35E
34 Pallaskenry, Ireland 52 38N 8 52W
82 Palm Is., Australia 18 45S 146 35E
37 Palma, Balearic Is., Spain 39 37N 2 40
72 Palma, I., Canary Is. 28 50N 17 50W
40 Palmas, G. of, Italy 38 50N 8 25E
84 Palmerston, N.Z. 45 30S 170 45E
84 Palmerston North, N.Z. 40 18S 175 36E
40 Palmi, Italy 38 20N 15 55E
98 Palmira, Colombia 3 40N 76 20W
62 Palmyra, Syria 34 20N 37 55E
64 Palni Hs., India 10 30N 77 30E
94 Palo Seco, Trinidad 10 5N 61 32W
51 Palu, Turkey 38 37N 40 0E
43 Pamiers, France 43 5N 1 40E
55 Pamir, mts., Cent. Asia 37 0N 73 0E
90 Pampa, U.S.A. 35 32N 101 0W
98 Pampas, The, Argentina 36 20S 62 0W
37 Pampiona, Spain 42 48N 1 37W
95 Panama, & G., Panama 9 3N 79 30W
95 Panama Canal Zone, Pan. 9 3N 79 45
95 Panama, Cent. Amer. 9 0N 80 0W
91 Panama City, U.S.A. 30 13N 85 14W
41 Pancevo, Yugoslavia 44 55N 20 42E
64 Pandharpur, India 17 36N 75 24E
22 Pangbourne, England 51 29N 1 6W
68 Pangkal Pinang, Indon. 2 0S 106 8E
64 Pangon Tso, L., Tibet 33 50N 78 50E
65 Pangyang, Burma 22 10N 98 45E
64 Panjim, Goa, India 15 30N 73 45E
64 Panna, India 24 45N 80 15E
64 Pannani, India 10 40N 75 55E
40 Pantelleria, I., Italy 36 50N 12 0E
94 Panuco, R., Mexico 21 30N 98 30W
72 Panyam, Nigeria 9 27N 9 8E
66 Packi, China 34 30N 106 50E
66 Paoshan, China 25 16N 99 35E
66 Pao-ting, China 39 0N 115 47E
66 Paotow, China 40 45N 110 1E
73 Paoua, Central Africa 7 25N 16 30E
47 Pápa, Hungary 47 20N 17 30E
32 Papa Stour I., Scotland 60 19N 1 40W
32 Papa Stronsay, Scotland 59 9N 2 34W
33 Papa Westray I., Scot. 59 21N 2 54W
94 Papantla, Mexico 20 27N 97 15W
30 Paps of Jura, Scotland 55 55N 6 0W
82 Papua New Guinea 7 0S 145 0E
82 Papua, G. of, New Guinea 8 30S 145
98 Para, st., Brazil 4 0S 52 30W
98 Pará, *see* Belém
68 Paracel Is., S. China Sea 16 30N 111 3
91 Paragould, U.S.A. 36 4N 90 29W
98 Paraguaná, Pen. de, Ven. 12 0N 70 0W
99 Paraguari, Paraguay 25 30S 57 15W
99 Paraguay R., S. Amer. 23 0S 58 0W
97 Paraguay, S. Amer. 21 0S 60 0W
98 Paraiba, st., Brazil 7 12S 38 0W
49 Parainen, Finland 60 21N 22 17E
72 Parakou, Benin 9 30N 2 35E
98 Paramaribo, Surinam 5 45N 55 15W
61 Paramushir I., U.S.S.R. 50 10N 156 0
99 Paraná, Argentina 32 0S 60 30W
99 Paraná R., Argentina 29 0S 59 30W
99 Parana, St., Brazil 24 0S 52 0W
99 Paranagua, Brazil 25 45S 48 30W
98 Paranaiba, R., Brazil 18 40S 48 30W
99 Paranapanema, R., Brazil 22 30S 52 0
99 Paranpiacaba, Sa., mts., Brazil 24 30S 49 0W
83 Paratoo, Australia 32 45S 139 15E
43 Paray le Monial, France 46 25N 4 5E
64 Parbhani, India 19 30N 77 0E
46 Parchim, Germany 53 30N 11 50E
46 Pardubice, Cz-slov. 50 0N 15 45E
98 Parecis, Sa. dos, mts., Brazil 13 50S 59 0W
61 Paren, U.S.S.R. 62 30N 163 0E
92 Parent, Canada 47 50N 74 40W
95 Paria, G. of, S. America 10 15N 62 0
95 Parintins, Brazil 2 30S 56 20W
43 Paris, France 48 52N 2 18E
91 Paris, U.S.A. 33 42N 95 34W
91 Park, Ra., U.S.A. 40 0N 106 30W
76 Park Rynie. S. Africa 30 20S 30 25E
92 Parkersburg, U.S.A. 39 18N 81 35W
83 Parkes, Australia 33 0S 148 6E
40 Parma, Italy 44 48N 10 19E
98 Parnaiba, Brazil 3 10S 41 40W
98 Parnaiba, R., Brazil 6 45S 44 0W
41 Parnassos, Mt., Greece 38 30N 22 40
49 Pärnu, U.S.S.R. 58 24N 24 37E
83 Paroo R., Australia 30 0S 144 40E
64 Paropamisus Ra., Afghan. 34 40N 63
41 Paros, I., Greece 37 3N 25 10E

24 Parracombe, England 51 20N 3 50W
83 Parramatta, Australia 33 48S 151 0E
100 Parry Is. Arctic Ocean 78 30N 112 0W
91 Parsons, U.S.A., 37 18N 95 18W
42 Parthenay, France 46 40N 0 18W
35 Partry, Mts., Ireland 53 40N 9 24W
98 Paru, R., Brazil 1 0N 54 40W
65 Parvatipuram, India 18 56N 83 30E
64 Parwan, Prov., Afghan, 35 0N 69 0E
90 Pasadena, Calif., U.S.A. 34 0N 118 0W
91 Pasadena, Texas, U.S.A. 29 42N 95 23W
42 Pas-de-Calais, Dépt., Fr. 50 27N 2 15E
91 Pascagoula, U.S.A. 30 30N 88 30W
90 Pasco, U.S.A., 46 16N 119 3W
68 Pasir Mas, Malaya 6 0N 102 20E
64 Pasni, Pakistan 25 15N 63 25E
30 Pass of Brander, Scot. 56 24N 5 8W
47 Pass of the Tarters, U.S.S.R. 48 20N 24 50E
35 Passage E., Ireland 52 13N 6 59W
34 Passage W., Ireland 51 55N 8 26W
46 Passau, Germany 48 33N 13 21E
40 Passero, C., Sicily, Italy 36 41N 15 10E
99 Passo Fundo, Brazil 28 10S 52 25W
98 Pastaza, R., Ecuador 3 30S 76 40W
98 Pasto, Colombia 1 12N 77 25W
48 Pasvik R., U.S.S.R. 69 15N 29 30E
99 Patagonia, S. Argentina 45 0S 69 0W
64 Patan, India 23 56N 72 5E
23 Patcham, England 50 52N 0 9W
83 Patchewollock, Austral. 36 27S 142 0E
84 Patea, New Zealand 39 45S 174 28E
72 Pategi, Nigeria 8 50N 5 45E
40 Paterno, Italy 37 35N 14 50E
93 Paterson, U.S.A. 40 59N 74 10W
90 Pathfinder Res., U.S.A. 42 10N 105 50W
64 Patiala, India 30 22N 76 28E
65 Patkai Bum, mts., India 26 39N 95 0E
41 Patmos, I., Greece 37 18N 26 35E
65 Patna, Bihar, India 25 40N 85 10E
41 Pátrai, Greece 38 15N 21 47E
27 Patrington, England 53 42N 0 1W
40 Patti, Italy 38 10N 14 55E
65 Patuakhali, Bangladesh 22 20N 90 15E
42 Pau, France 43 21N 0 23W
65 Pauk, Burma 21 25N 94 30E
74 Paulis, see Isiro
96 Paulistana, Brazil 8 0S 41 15W
98 Paulo Afonso Rapids, Brazil 9 20S 37 40W
76 Paulpietersburg, S. Africa 27 25S 30 50E
40 Pavia, Italy 45 11N 9 11E
60 Pavlodar, U.S.S.R. 52 25N 77 10E
52 Pavlograd, U.S.S.R. 48 40N 36 0E
52 Pavlovo, U.S.S.R. 56 0N 43 10E
52 Pavlovsk, U.S.S.R. 50 32N 40 7E
52 Pavlovskiy-Posad, U.S.S.R. 55 47N 38 40E
93 Pawtucket, U.S.A. 41 55N 71 25W
68 Payakumbah, Indonesia 0 20S 100 40E
45 Payerne, Switzerland 46 50N 6 56E
90 Payette, U.S.A. 44 6N 116 55W
89 Payne, L., Canada 59 30N 74 30W
)9 Paysandú, Uruguay 32 19S 58 0W
90 Payson, U.S.A. 40 4N 111 45W
41 Pazardzhik, Bulgaria 42 12N 24 19E
88 Peace, R., Canada 58 47N 114 0W
88 Peace River, Canada 56 0N 117 18W
83 Peak Hill, N.S.W., Australia 32 36S 148 9E
80 Peak Hill, W.A., Australia 25 42S 118 47E
27 Peak, The, England 53 25N 1 52W
90 Pearl City, Hawaii 21 15N 157 55W
41 Pec, Yugoslavia 42 41N 20 14E
50 Pechenga, U.S.S.R. 69 30N 31 25E
50 Pechora, G. of, U.S.S.R. 68 40N 54 0E
90 Pecos, & R., U.S.A. 31 25N 103 35W
47 Pécs, Hungary 46 4N 18 13E
31 Peebles, Scotland 55 39N 3 11W
93 Peekskill, U.S.A. 41 15N 73 57W
26 Peel, Isle of Man 54 13N 4 43W
26 Peel Fell, mt., England 55 19N 2 34W
83 Peel R., Australia 30 58S 150 30E
49 Peene, R., Germany 53 52N 13 40E
84 Pegasus B., New Zealand 43 13S 173 0E
55 Pegu, Burma 17 33N 96 25E
55 Pegu Yoma, mts., Burma 19 0N 96 0E
57 Pehan, China 49 10N 126 20E
56 Pei Kiang, China 24 10N 113 10E
58 Pekalongan, Indonesia 6 50S 109 45E
92 Pekin, U.S.A. 40 30N 89 43W
56 Peking, China 39 49N 116 30E
47 Peleaga, mt., Rumania 45 17N 22 58E
88 Pelly, R., Canada 62 20N 133 0W
41 Peloponnese, Pen., Greece 37 50N 22 0E
99 Pelotas, Brazil 31 45S 52 20W
42 Pelvoux, Mt., France 44 52N 6 10E
58 Pematang Siantar, Indon. 3 0N 99 15E
75 Pemba, Mozambique 13 0S 40 42E
70 Pemba I., Tanzania 0 5S 39 40E
80 Pemberton, Australia 34 28S 115 59E
22 Pembridge, England 52 13N 2 54W
92 Pembroke, Canada 45 40N 77 10W
28 Pembroke, Wales 51 41N 4 55W
28 Pembrey, Wales 51 42N 4 16W
37 Penalara, Mt., Spain 40 55N 3 50W
28 Penarth, Wales 51 27N 3 12W
99 Penas, G. de, Chile 47 30S 75 0W
24 Pencoed, Wales 51 31N 3 30W
0 Pend Oreille L., U.S.A. 47 20N 116 30W
2 Pendembu, Sierra Leone 8 6N 10 45W
6 Pendle Hill, Hs., Eng. 53 52N 2 20W
0 Pendleton, U.S.A. 45 42N 118 47W
63 Pendzhikent, U.S.S.R. 39 20N 67 30E
66 Pengpu, China 32 50N 117 50E
83 Penguin, Australia 41 4S 146 7E
37 Peniche, Portugal 39 20N 9 22W
31 Penicuik, Scotland 55 50N 3 11W
27 Penistone, England 53 32N 1 38W
67 Penki, China 41 15N 122 40E
25 Penmaenmawr, Wales 53 16N 3 56W
42 Penmarch, Pte. de ,Fr. 47 50N 4 30W
92 Penn Yan, U.S.A. 42 40N 77 0W
64 Penner R., India 14 40N 80 10E
26 Pennines, mts., England 54 20N 2 10W
92 Pennsylvania, st., U.S.A. 41 10N 77 30W
83 Penola, Australia 37 12S 140 51E
80 Penong, Australia 32 0S 133 0E
83 Penrith, Australia 33 48S 150 40E
26 Penrith, England 54 40N 2 47W
24 Penryn, England 50 10N 5 7W
91 Pensacola, U.S.A. 30 30N 87 15W
100 Pensacola Mts., Antarctica 84 0S 45 0W
83 Penshurst, Australia 37 55S 142 25E
88 Penticton, Canada 49 30N 119 30W
82 Pentland, Australia 20 37S 145 27E
33 Pentland Firth, Scot. 58 41N 3 0W
31 Pentland Hills, Scotland 55 47N 3 35W
22 Penybont, Wales 52 16N 3 15W
26 Pen-y-ghent, mt., Eng. 54 8N 2 10W
25 Pen-y-groes, Wales 51 48N 4 3W
52 Penza, U.S.S.R. 53 8N 45 0E
24 Penzance, England 50 8N 5 33W
61 Penzhina G., U.S.S.R. 61 0N 163 0E
61 Penzhino, U.S.S.R. 63 50N 168 3E
92 Peoria, U.S.A. 40 40N 89 35W
37 Perdido, mt., Spain 42 45N 0 15W
51 Perekop, U.S.S.R. 46 0N 33 0E
51 Pereyaslav Khmelnitski, U.S.S.R. 50 5N 31 28E
99 Pergamino, Argentina 33 45S 60 40W
43 Perigueux, France 45 16N 0 42E
98 Perija, Sa. de mts., Colombia 9 30N 73 3W
62 Perim I., Red Sea 12 40N 43 17E
50 Perm, U.S.S.R. 58 0N 55 15E
98 Pernambuco (Recife), Brazil 8 20S 35 0W
98 Pernambuco, st., Brazil 8 0S 39 0W
41 Pernik, Bulgaria 42 37N 23 4E
43 Peronne, France 49 55N 2 55E
52 Perovo, U.S.S.R. 55 40N 37 45E
43 Perpignan, France 42 43N 2 55E
24 Perranporth, England 50 20N 5 9W
24 Perranzabuloe, England 50 18N 5 7W
90 Perryton, U.S.A. 36 25N 100 55W
22 Pershore, England 52 7N 2 4W
62 Persia, see Iran
62 Persian G., S.W. Asia 27 0N 51 0E
80 Perth, Australia 32 0S 115 50E
92 Perth, Canada 44 52N 76 28W
31 Perth, Scotland 56 24N 3 27W
93 Perth Amboy, U.S.A. 40 30N 74 25W
96 Peru, S. America 88 0S 75 0W
40 Perugia, Italy 43 8N 12 25E
50 Pervomaisk, U.S.S.R. 47 58N 31 0E
40 Pesaro, Italy 43 57N 12 55E
40 Pescara, Italy 42 30N 14 18E
64 Peshawar, Pakistan 34 3N 71 30E
63 Petah Tiqva, Israel 32 5N 34 52E
44 Petange, Luxembourg 49 33N 5 55E
100 Peter 1st, I., S. Ocean 69 0S 91 0W
92 Peterborough, Canada 44 21N 78 27W
83 Peterborough, Australia 32 58S 138 49E
23 Peterborough, England 52 35N 0 14W
22 Peterchurch, England 52 3N 2 58W
33 Peterculter, Scotland 57 7N 2 20W
33 Peterhead, Scotland 57 32N 1 47W
27 Peterlee, England 54 45N 1 18W
92 Petersburg, U.S.A. 37 13N 77 25W
23 Petersfield, England 51 0N 0 56W
89 Petitsikapau, L., Canada 54 40N 66 30W
64 Petlad, India 22 30N 72 40E
94 Peto, Mexico 20 3N 89 0W
84 Petone, New Zealand 41 5S 174 50E
92 Petoskey, U.S.A. 45 20N 84 58W
41 Petrich, Bulgaria 41 25N 23 12E
92 Petrolia, Canada 42 54N 82 5W
61 Petropavlovsk-Kamchatsky, U.S.S.R. 53 10N 158 30E
99 Petropolis, Brazil 22 30S 43 10W
41 Petrograd, see Zrenjanin
47 Petroseni, Rumania 45 30N 23 28E
41 Petrovaradin, Yugoslavia 45 15N 19 58E
52 Petrovsk, U.S.S.R. 52 23N 45 18E
61 Petrovsk, U.S.S.R. 51 20N 108 50E
50 Petrozavodsk, U.S.S.R. 61 50N 34 25E
76 Petrusburg, S. Africa 29 0S 25 20E
36 Pettigo, Ireland 54 38N 7 50W
23 Petworth, England 50 59N 0 37W
61 Pevek, U.S.S.R. 69 35N 170 50E
22 Pewsey, Vale of, Eng. 51 20N 1 48W
43 Pézenas, France 43 28N 3 50E
45 Pfafers-Dorf, Switzerland 46 58N 9 28E
45 Pfaffikon, Switzerland 47 21N 8 48E
45 Pforzheim, Germany 48 50N 8 25E
64 Phagwara, India 31 10N 75 40E
64 Phalodi, India 27 5N 72 25E
68 Phan Rang, Vietnam 11 38N 109 4E
68 Phan Thiet, Vietnam 11 0N 108 9E
68 Phanom Dang Raek, mts., Thailand 14 30N 104 0E
66 Phari, Tibet, China 27 53N 89 10E
93 Philadelphia, U.S.A. 39 55N 75 18W
72 Philippeville, see Skikda
44 Philippeville, Belgium 50 12N 4 33E
82 Philippi, L., Australia 24 20S 138 55E
68 Philippines, Asia 13 0N 123 0E
76 Philippolis, S. Africa 30 15S 25 16E
35 Philipstown, see Daingean
76 Philipstown, S. Africa 30 28S 24 28E
83 Phillip I., Australia 38 22S 145 18E
68 Phnom Penh, Cambodia 11 40N 105 0E
90 Phœnix, U.S.A. 33 45N 111 50W
4 Phœnix Is., Pacific Ocean 4 0S 171 0W
68 Phu Quoc, I., Vietnam 10 20N 104 0E
40 Piacenza, Italy 45 0N 9 40E
83 Pialba, Australia 25 18S 152 50E
47 Piatra Neamt, Rum. 46 59N 26 20E
99 Piaui, R., Brazil 7 55S 42 30W
99 Piaui, st., Brazil 6 30S 42 30W
98 Piaui, Sa. do, mts., Brazil 10 0S 43 0W
40 Piazza, Italy 37 20N 14 20E
37 Pic de Aneto, mt., Spain 42 35N 0 45E
43 Picardy, Prov., France 49 50N 3 0E
91 Picayune, U.S.A. 30 43N 89 43W
99 Pichilemu, Chile 34 20S 72 5W
27 Pickering, England 54 15N 0 45W
27 Pickering, Vale of, Eng. 54 12N 0 45W
37 Pico Guina, mt., Spain 42 50N 6 45W
37 Picos de Europa, mts. Sp. 43 15N 5 0W
83 Picton, Australia 34 5S 150 38E
92 Picton, Canada 43 59N 77 0W
84 Picton, New Zealand 41 20S 174 1E
93 Pictou, Canada 45 45N 63 5W
23 Pidley, England 52 23N 0 4W
64 Pidurutalagala, mt., Sri Lanka 7 0N 80 50E
91 Piedmont Plat., U.S.A. 34 0N 82 0W
40 Piedmont, Prov., Italy 45 0N 7 40E
94 Piedras Negras, Mex. 28 50N 100 35W
90 Pierre, U.S.A. 44 30N 100 15W
45 Pierrefontaine, France 47 14N 6 32E
76 Piet Retief, S. Africa 27 2S 30 52E
75 Pietermaritzburg, S. Africa 29 38S 30 28E
75 Pietersburg, S. Africa 23 45S 29 30E
47 Pietrosul, mt., Rumania 47 36N 24 56E
47 Pietrosul, mt., Rumania 47 7N 25 13E
90 Pike's Pk., mt., U.S.A. 38 50N 105 0W
76 Piketberg, South Africa 32 54N 18 42E
49 Pila, Poland 53 10N 16 48E
99 Pilar, C., Chile 52 40S 75 0W
80 Pilbara, Australia 21 13S 118 21E
99 Pilcomayo, R., S. Amer. 22 30S 62 20W
64 Pilibhit, India 28 20N 79 58E
47 Pilica, R., Poland 51 25N 20 45E
41 Pilion, mt. Greece 39 23N 23 0E
41 Pilos, Greece 36 55N 21 45E
68 Pinang, I., Malaya 5 20N 100 12E
95 Pinar del Rio, Cuba 22 30N 84 30W
47 Pinczów, Poland 50 30N 20 35E
72 Pindiga, Nigeria 9 58N 10 53E
41 Pindus Mts., Greece 39 30N 21 30E
91 Pine Bluff, U.S.A. 34 5N 91 58W
80 Pine Creek, Australia 13 40S 131 37E
82 Pine Hill, Australia 23 42S 147 0E
50 Pinega, R., U.S.S.R. 63 48N 45 0E
40 Pinerolo, Italy 44 53N 7 23E
75 Pinetown, South Africa 29 48S 30 54E
68 Ping, R., Thailand 16 30N 99 40E
66 Pingliang, China 35 30N 106 50E
37 Pinhel, Portugal 41 46N 6 57W
24 Pinhoe, England 50 44N 3 28W
41 Pinios R., Greece 39 37N 22 23E
67 Pinkiang, China see Harbin
83 Pinnaroo, Australia 35 5S 141 0E
99 Pino Hachado P., Chile 38 45S 71 0W
100 Pionerskaya, Antarctica 69 30S 97 0E
47 Piotrków, Poland 51 25N 19 40E
93 Pipmuacan, L., Can. 49 40N 70 20W
92 Piqua, U.S.A. 40 10N 84 15W
41 Piraievs, Greece 37 57N 23 30E
98 Pirapora, Brazil 17 25S 44 50W
41 Pirgos, Greece 37 38N 21 32E
41 Pirin Pl., Bulgaria 41 40N 23 20E
45 Pirmasens, Germany 49 12N 7 36E
41 Pirot, Yugoslavia 43 10N 22 39E
42 Pirou, France 49 12N 1 31W
40 Pisa, Italy 43 42N 10 25E
40 Pisciotta, Italy 40 7N 15 12E
98 Pisco, Peru 13 55S 76 10W
46 Pisek, Czechoslovakia 49 20N 14 8E
37 Pisuerga, R., Spain 42 45N 4 20W
90 Pit, R., U.S.A. 41 30N 120 45W
72 Pita, Guinea 11 0N 12 15W
4 Pitcairn I., Pacific Ocean 24 55S 131 0W
48 Pitea & R., Sweden 65 24N 21 30E
47 Pitesti, Rumania 44 52N 24 55E
65 Pithapuram, India 17 0N 82 20E
31 Pittenweem, Scotland 56 12N 2 44W
91 Pittsburg, Kan., U.S.A. 37 8N 94 40W
92 Pittsburgh, Pa., U.S.A. 40 30N 79 52W
93 Pittsfield, U.S.A. 42 28N 73 20W
83 Pittsworth, Australia 27 41S 151 37E
98 Piura, Peru 5 20S 80 35W
45 Piz Bernina, Pk., Switz. 46 22N 9 55E
40 Pizzo, Italy 38 42N 16 10E
89 Placentia, & B., Newf. 47 14N 54 2W
30 Pladda I., Scotland 55 25N 5 7W
90 Plainview, U.S.A. 34 15N 101 44W
91 Plant City, U.S.A. 28 3N 82 15W
37 Plasencia, Spain 40 3N 6 3W
43 Plateau de Langres, Fr. 47 45N 5 30E
90 Plateau du Coteau du Missouri, U.S.A. 47 0N 100 0W
90 Platte R., U.S.A. 41 0N 99 0W
46 Plauen, Germany 50 30N 12 7E
99 Plaza Huincal, Argentina 39 0S 69 0W
68 Pleiku, Vietnam 14 0N 108 15E
84 Plenty, Bay of, N.Z. 37 45S 177 0E
50 Plesetsk, U.S.S.R. 62 40N 40 10E
93 Plessisville, Canada 46 15N 71 48W
41 Pleven, Bulgaria 43 22N 24 41E
47 Plock, Poland 52 37N 19 40E
32 Plockton, Scotland 57 20N 5 39W
41 Ploësti, Rumania 44 58N 26 0E
41 Plovdiv, Bulgaria 42 7N 24 48E
75 Plumtree, Rhodesia 20 27S 27 55E
24 Plymouth, England 50 22N 4 10W
95 Plymouth, Montserrat. W.I. 16 38N 62 5W
24 Plympton, England 50 23N 4 2W
24 Plymstock, England 50 22N 4 4W
25 Plynlimon, mt., Wales 52 29N 3 47W
46 Plzeň, Czechoslovakia 49 48N 13 20E
40 Po, R., Italy 45 2N 9 20E
60 Pobedy Pk., Mt., U.S.S.R. 42 10N 79 57E
90 Pocatello, U.S.A. 43 10N 111 0W
27 Pocklington, England 53 56N 0 46W
61 Podkamennaya Tunguska, U.S.S.R. 61 40N 90 5E
52 Podolsk, U.S.S.R. 55 20N 37 40E
72 Podor, Sénégal 16 30N 14 50W
76 Pofadder, South Africa 29 10S 19 22E
76 Point, C., S. Africa 34 22S 18 30E
94 Point Fortin, Trinidad 11 0N 61 50W
26 Point of Ayre, I. of Man 54 25N 4 22W
74 Pointe Noire, Congo (Fr.) 4 48S 12 0E
94 Point Saline, Grenada, W.I. 12 12N 61 40W
43 Poitiers, France 46 38N 0 20E
43 Poitou, Prov., France 46 40N 0 10W
44 Poix Terron, France 49 40N 4 38E
64 Pokaran, India 27 0N 71 50E
83 Pokataroo, Australia 29 34S 148 50E
40 Pola, Yugoslavia, see Pula
47 Poland, Europe 52 20N 20 0E
24 Polden Hills, England 51 5N 2 50W
74 Poli, Cameroon 8 34N 12 54E
43 Poligny, France 46 50N 5 40E
68 Polillo I., Philippines 14 50N 121 50E
41 Poliyiros, Greece 40 15N 23 10E
64 Pollachi, India 10 40N 77 0E
61 Polnovat, U.S.S.R. 63 50N 66 10E
50 Polotsk, U.S.S.R. 55 30N 28 42E
24 Polruan, England 50 17N 4 36W
52 Poltava, U.S.S.R. 49 37N 34 30E
50 Polyarny, U.S.S.R. 69 0N 33 10E
37 Pombal, Portugal 39 55N 8 40W
91 Ponca City, U.S.A. 36 43N 97 13W
95 Ponce, Puerto Rico 18 7N 66 48W
65 Pondicherry, India 12 0N 79 50E
76 Pondoland, dist., S. Africa 31 10S 29 40E
37 Ponferrada, Spain 42 34N 6 35W
76 Pongola, R., S. Africa 27 28S 32 7E
65 Ponnyadaung, mts., Burma 22 0N 94 0E
50 Ponoi, & R., U.S.S.R. 67 0N 41 15E
42 Pons, France 45 35N 0 35W
43 Pont-à-Mousson, France 48 58N 6 0E
42 Pont-l'Abbé, France 47 50N 4 16W
43 Pont St. Esprit, France 44 18N 4 40E
99 Ponta Grossa, Brazil 25 0S 50 10W
25 Pontardawe, Wales 51 43N 3 51W
43 Pontarlier, France 46 52N 6 20E
91 Pontchartrain, L., U.S.A. 30 10N 90 10W
41 Pontedera, Italy 43 40N 10 40E
27 Pontefract, England 53 41N 1 20W
37 Pontevedra, Spain 42 29S 8 37W
74 Ponthierville (Ubundu), Zaïre 0 22S 25 30E
92 Pontiac, U.S.A. 42 40N 83 20W
68 Pontianak, Indonesia 0 12S 109 29E
40 Pontine Is., Italy 40 58N 13 0E
51 Pontine Mts., Turkey 40 40N 39 0E
42 Pontivy, France 48 5N 3 0W
43 Pontoise, France 49 5N 2 5E
43 Pontremoli, Italy 44 22N 9 50E
45 Pontresina, Switzerland 46 30N 9 53E
25 Pontypool, Wales 51 43N 3 1W
25 Pontypridd, Wales 51 36N 3 19W
22 Poole, England 50 43N 1 59W
32 Poolewe, Scotland 57 46N 5 36W
64 Poona, see Pune
83 Poopelloe, L., Australia 31 30S 144 0E
98 Poopó, L., Bolivia 19 0S 67 0W
98 Popayan, Colombia 2 10N 76 45W
44 Poperinge, Belgium 50 51N 2 44E
61 Popigai, U.S.S.R. 72 55N 106 5E
91 Poplar Bluff, U.S.A. 36 45N 90 27W
83 Poplita, L., Australia 33 0S 141 50E
94 Popocatepetl, Mt., Mex. 18 45N 99 40W
74 Popokabaka, Zaïre 5 40S 16 33E
64 Porbandar, India 21 37N 69 46E
88 Porcupine R., Alaska 67 0N 143 0W
49 Pori, Finland 61 30N 21 35E
48 Porjus, Sweden 67 0N 19 50E
49 Porkkala, Finland 60 15N 24 30E
24 Porlock Hill, England 51 12N 3 40W
42 Pornic, France 47 10N 2 10W
61 Poronaisk, U.S.S.R. 49 25N 142 57E
45 Porrentruy, Switzerland 47 25N 7 4E
40 Porreta P., Italy 44 0N 11 10E
48 Porsangen Fjord, Norway 70 45N 26 0E
83 Port Adelaide, Australia 34 50S 138 42E
88 Port Alberni, Canada 49 20N 124 50W
75 Port Alfred, S. Africa 33 36S 26 58E
82 Port Alma, Australia 23 38S 150 53E
95 Port Antonio, Jamaica 18 12N 76 28W
83 Port Arthur, Australia 43 10S 147 40E
92 Port Arthur, see Thunder Bay
91 Port Arthur, U.S.A. 29 56N 94 5W
30 Port Askaig, Scotland 55 51N 6 6W
95 Port-au-Prince, Haiti 18 40N 72 20W
83 Port Augusta, Australia 32 22S 137 49E
89 Port aux Basques, Can. 47 43N 59 20W
30 Port Bannatyne, Scotland 55 52N 5 5W
75 Port-Berge, Madagascar 15 38S 47 40E
37 Port Bou, Spain 42 25N 3 5E
65 Port Canning, Bangladesh 22 25N 88 40E
89 Port Cartier, Canada 50 10N 66 50W
84 Port Chalmers, N.Z. 45 45S 170 40E
30 Port Charlotte, Scotland 55 44N 6 24W
43 Port de Bouc, France 43 23N 5 0E
95 Port de Paix, Haiti 19 50N 72 50W
68 Port Dickson, Malaya 2 43N 101 45E
82 Port Douglas, Australia 16 30S 145 30E
94 Port Elizabeth, Bequia I. 13 0N 61 15W
76 Port Elizabeth, S. Africa 33 58S 25 42E
30 Port Ellen, Scotland 55 37N 6 12W
26 Port Erin, Isle of Man 54 6N 4 47W
72 Port Étienne, see Nouadhibou
83 Port Fairy, Australia 38 18S 142 15E
74 Port Francqui, see Ilebo
74 Port Gentil, Gabon 0 47S 8 40E
30 Port Glasgow, Scotland 55 56N 4 41W
72 Port Harcourt, Nigeria 4 45N 7 20E
89 Port Hawkesbury, Can. 45 35N 64 40W
80 Port Hedland, Australia 20 16S 118 36E
93 Port Hood, Canada 46 2N 61 30W
92 Port Huron, U.S.A. 42 59N 82 30W
83 Port Jackson, Australia 33 55S 151 12E
68 Port Kelang, Malaya 3 0N 101 20E
83 Port Kembla, Australia 34 29S 150 56E
35 Port Laoise, Ireland 53 3N 7 15W
91 Port Lavoca, U.S.A. 28 35N 96 50W
80 Port Lincoln, Austral. 34 40S 135 47E
30 Port Logan, Scotland 54 42N 4 57W
42 Port Louis, France 47 40N 3 0W
82 Port Macdonnell, Austral. 38 0S 140 39E
83 Port Macquarie, Australia 31 29S 153 0E
82 Port Moresby, Papua N.G. 9 15S 147 12E
88 Port Nelson, Canada 57 2N 93 0W
75 Port Nolloth, S. Africa 29 12S 16 55E
94 Port of Spain, Trinidad 10 40N 61 23W
31 Portpatrick, Scotland 54 50N 5 8W
83 Port Phillip, B., Australia 38 17S 144 40E
83 Port Pirie, Australia 33 10S 138 0E
88 Port Radium, see Echo Bay
73 Port Safaga, Egypt 26 48N 34 0E
73 Port Said, Egypt 31 28N 32 6E
43 Port St. Louis, France 43 20N 4 50E
75 Port Shepstone, S. Africa 30 45S 30 30E
88 Port Simpson, Canada 54 20N 130 28W
92 Port Stanley, Canada 42 40N 81 12W
73 Port Sudan, Sudan 19 40N 37 20E
25 Port Talbot, Wales 51 36N 3 48W
43 Port Vendres, France 42 30N 3 5E
68 Port Weld, Malaya 4 45N 100 40E
36 Portaferry, N. Ireland 54 23N 5 31W
92 Portage, U.S.A. 43 36N 89 28W
88 Portage la Prairie, Can. 50 0N 98 25W
37 Portalegre, Portugal 39 18N 7 27W
35 Portarlington, Ireland 53 10N 7 11W
42 Portbail, France 49 20N 1 42W
36 Portglenone, N. Ireland 54 52N 6 29W
25 Porthcawl, Wales 51 29N 3 42W
25 Porthmadog, Wales 52 54N 4 7W
24 Portishead, England 51 29N 2 47W
33 Portknockie, Scotland 57 42N 2 48W
83 Portland, N.S.W., Australia 33 25S 150 0E
83 Portland, Vic., Austral. 38 13S 141 35E
93 Portland, Me., U.S.A. 43 42N 70 18W
90 Portland, Ore., U.S.A. 45 35N 122 37W
83 Portland B., Australia 38 29S 142 0E
24 Portland, Bill of, Eng. 50 30N 2 27W
24 Portland, I. of, England 50 33N 2 27W
94 Portland Pt., Jamaica 17 40N 77 0W
89 Portland Promontory, Canada 58 40N 79 30W
25 Portmadoc, see Porthmadog
34 Portmagee, Ireland 51 53N 10 24W
35 Portmarnock, Ireland 53 26N 6 8W
99 Porto Alegre, Brazil 30 7S 50 55W
75 Porto Alexandre, Angola 16 0S 11 40E
40 Porto Empedocle, Italy 37 20N 13 25E
72 Porto Novo, Benin 6 27N 2 40E
72 Porto Santo I., Madeira 33 0N 16 40W
40 Porto Torres, Italy 40 51N 8 22E
98 Porto Velho, Brazil 8 50S 63 56W
40 Portoferraio, Italy 42 48N 10 20E
40 Portoscuso, Italy 39 10N 8 25E
98 Portoviejo, Ecuador 0 55S 80 30W
32 Portree, Scotland 57 25N 6 11W
34 Portroe, Ireland 52 53N 8 22W
36 Portsalon, Ireland 55 13N 7 37W
33 Portskerra, Scotland 58 35N 3 55W
23 Portslade, England 50 51N 0 13W
22 Portsmouth, England 50 47N 1 7W
93 Portsmouth, N.H., U.S.A. 43 15N 71 0W
92 Portsmouth, Ohio, U.S.A. 38 46N 83 5W
91 Portsmouth, Va., U.S.A. 36 48N 76 25W
33 Portsoy, Scotland 57 41N 2 40W
48 Porttipahta Res., Finland 68 10N 26 30E
37 Portugal, Europe 39 40N 8 0W
75 Portuguese E. Africa, see Mozambique
72 Portuguese Guinea, see Guinea-Bissau
34 Portumna, Ireland 53 7N 8 12W
49 Porvoo, Finland 60 30N 25 40E
99 Posados, Argentina 27 30S 56 0W
72 Poste Maurice Cortier (Bidon 5), Algeria 22 20N 1 15E

76 Postmasburg, S. Africa 28 25S 23 1E
61 Potapovskoye, U.S.S.R. 68 40N 86 55E
40 Potenza, Italy 40 41N 15 50E
84 Poteriteri L., N.Z. 46 0S 166 0E
75 Potgietersrus, South Africa 24 10S 29 3E
51 Poti, U.S.S.R. 42 20N 41 30E
72 Potiskum, Nigeria 11 39N 11 2E
92 Potomac, R., U.S.A. 39 10N 77 20W
98 Potosi, Bolivia 19 45S 65 45W
66 Potow, China 38 20N 117 0E
46 Potsdam, Germany 52 19N 13 15E
23 Potters Bar, England 51 42N 0 11W
64 Pottuvil, Sri Lanka 6 55N 81 50E
35 Poulaphouca Falls. & Res., Ireland 53 7N 6 35W
26 Poulton-le-Fylde, Eng. 53 51N 2 59W
50 Povenets, U.S.S.R. 62 48N 35 0E
84 Poverty B., N.Z. 38 42S 178 0E
37 Povóa de Varzim, Port. 41 28N 8 45W
90 Powder R., U.S.A. 45 20N 105 40W
90 Powell, L., U.S.A. 37 20N 110 35W
80 Powell Creek, Australia 18 0S 133 50
25 Powys, Co., Wales 52 20N 3 30W
66 Poyang, L., China 29 0N 116 25E
67 Poyarkova, U.S.S.R. 49 35N 128 45E
41 Pozarevac, Yugoslavia 44 39N 21 10E
46 Poznan, Poland 52 23N 16 57E
37 Pozoblanco, Spain 38 35N 5 1W
43 Prades, France 42 40N 2 28E
46 Prague, Czechoslovakia 50 8N 14 25E
46 Praha, see Prague
41 Prahova, R., Rumania 45 0N 25 40E
85 Prairies, N. America 43 0N 97 0W
40 Prato, Italy 43 53N 11 7E
90 Pratt, U.S.A. 37 42N 98 46W
37 Pravia, Spain 43 30N 6 10W
99 Pre-Cordilleras, mts., Arg. 29 0S 68 0W
80 Premier Downs, Austral. 30 30S 126 30E
49 Prenzlau, Germany 53 18N 13 52E
65 Preparis I., & Chans., India 15 0N 93 40E
47 Prerov, Czechoslovakia 49 27N 17 4E
26 Prescot, England 53 26N 2 49W
93 Prescott, Canada 44 46N 75 32W
90 Prescott, U.S.A. 34 24N 112 30W
90 Presidio, U.S.A. 29 35N 104 20W
47 Presov, Czechoslovakia 49 1N 21 33E
93 Presque Isle, U.S.A. 46 35N 68 3W
25 Prestatyn, Wales 53 20N 3 24W
25 Presteigne, Wales 52 16N 3 1W
26 Preston, England 53 47N 2 43W
31 Preston, Scotland 55 48N 2 18W
90 Preston, U.S.A. 42 6N 111 50W
31 Prestonpans, Scotland 55 57N 2 59W
26 Prestwich, England 53 32N 2 17W
30 Prestwick, Scotland 55 30N 4 36W
76 Pretoria, S. Africa 25 36S 28 12E
41 Preveza, Greece 38 58N 20 46E
46 Pribram, Czechoslovakia 49 42N 14 0E
90 Price, U.S.A. 39 33N 110 46W
76 Prieska, S. Africa 29 40S 22 38E
41 Prilep, Yugoslavia 41 19N 21 34E
88 Prince Albert, Canada 53 15N 105 47W
88 Prince Albert Pen., Can. 71 0N 115 0W
89 Prince Charles I., Can. 67 0N 76 0W
93 Prince Edward I., Prov., Canada 46 30N 63 30W
71 Prince Edward Is., Ind. Oc. 45 30S 38 0E
88 Prince George, Canada 54 0N 123 0W
88 Prince of Wales I., Alaska 55 30N 132 30W
88 Prince of Wales I., Can. 73 0N 99 0W
88 Prince Rupert, Canada 54 20N 130 25W
23 Princes Risborough, England 51 43N 0 51W
94 Princes Town, Trinidad 10 15N 61 28W
82 Princess Charlotte B., Australia 14 0S 144 0E
92 Princeton, U.S.A. 37 14N 87 54W
24 Princetown, England 50 33N 4 0W
71 Principé I., West Africa 1 45N 7 20E
50 Pripyat R., U.S.S.R. 52 10N 27 10E
50 Pripyat Marshes, Poland 51 53N 27 5E
41 Pristina, Yugoslavia 42 39N 21 9E
43 Privas, France 44 46N 4 40E
41 Prizren, Yugoslavia 42 12N 20 46E
94 Progreso, Mexico 21 31N 89 37W
60 Prokopyevsk, U.S.S.R. 53 58N 86 30E
65 Prome, Burma 18 52N 95 25E
43 Propriano, Corsica, Fr. 41 44N 8 55E
82 Proserpine, Australia 20 27S 148 40E
46 Prostejov, Cz-slov. 49 5N 17 0E
83 Proston, Australia 26 2S 151 32E
43 Provence, Prov., France 43 55N 6 10E
93 Providence, U.S.A. 41 42N 71 23W
91 Providence Channels, Bahama 26 0N 78 0W
88 Provideniya, U.S.S.R. 64 25N 173 15W
43 Provins, France 48 37N 3 15E
90 Provo, U.S.A. 40 18N 111 36W
26 Prudhoe, England 54 57N 1 51W
88 Prudhoe Bay, Alaska 70 20N 149 40W
47 Pruszków, Poland 52 9N 20 49E
47 Prut, R., Rum.-U.S.S.R. 46 20N 28 32E
47 Przemysl, Poland 49 44N 22 49E
47 Przeworsk, Poland 50 5N 22 45E
60 Przhevalsk, U.S.S.R. 42 30N 78 30E
50 Pskov, U.S.S.R. 57 30N 28 30E
27 Pudsey, England 53 47N 1 41W
94 Puebla, Mexico 19 11N 98 15W
90 Pueblo, U.S.A. 38 18N 104 48W
37 Pueblonuevo, Spain 38 16N 5 16W
37 Puente Genil, Spain 37 24N 4 17W
66 Puerh, China 23 0N 100 53E
94 Puerto Barrios, Guat. 15 50N 88 35W
95 Puerto Berrio Colombia 6 30N 74 30W
95 Puerto Cabello, Ven. 10 22N 67 58W
95 Puerto Cabezas, Nicar. 14 5N 83 20W
95 Puerto Colombia, Col. 11 0N 75 0W
94 Puerto Corte's, Honduras 15 50N 88 0W
72 Puerto de Cabras, Canary Is. 28 40N 13 30W
99 Puerto Deseado, Arg. 47 0S 68 0W
98 Puerto Esperanca, Brazil 19 25S 57 25W
99 Puerto Madryn, Arg. 43 0S 65 0W
98 Puerto Maldonado, Peru 12 25S 69 0W
99 Puerto Montt, Chile 41°22S 72 40W
94 Puerto Morelos, Mexico 21 0N 86 0W
95 Puerto Rico, I., W.I. 18 15N 66 30W
4 Puerto Rico Trough, Atlantic Ocean 20 0N 65 0W
98 Puerto Suarez, Bolivia 19 0S 57 45W
98 Puerto Wilches, Col. 7 25N 73 45W
50 Pugachev, U.S.S.R. 52 0N 48 50E
90 Puget Sd., U.S.A. 48 0N 122 30W
93 Puge-Théniers, France 44 0N 7 0E
37 Puigcerda, Spain 42 23N 1 53E
84 Pukekohe, New Zealand 37 12S 174 55E
40 Pula, Yugoslavia 44 53N 13 53E
98 Pulacayo, Bolivia 20 25S 66 40W
92 Pulaski, Va., U.S.A. 37 0N 80 54W
47 Pulawy, Poland 51 28N 22 0E
23 Pulham Market, England 52 25N 1 13E
64 Pulicat, L. of, India 13 45N 80 12E
90 Pullman, U.S.A. 46 45N 117 0W
47 Pultusk, Poland 52 45N 21 9E
98 Puna I., Ecuador 3 0S 80 20W
99 Puna d'Atacama, Plat., Argentina 25 0S 67 0W
66 Punakha, Bhutan 28 0N 89 15E
64 Punch, India 33 40N 74 12E
64 Pune, India 18 25N 73 57E
64 Punjab, Prov., India 31 45N 74 30E
98 Puno, Peru 15 50S 70 12W
99 Punta Arenas, Chile 53 6S 71 5W
94 Puntarenas, Costa Rica 9 58N 84 40W
60 Pur R., U.S.S.R. 65 30N 78 0E
22 Purbeck I., England 50 38N 2 0W
65 Puri, India 19 50N 85 57E
22 Purley, England 51 29N 1 4W
44 Purmerend, Netherlands 52 30N 4 56E
65 Purnea, India 26 0N 87 38E
65 Purulia, India 23 20N 86 15E
98 Purus, R., Brazil 7 40S 66 0W
67 Pusan, Korea 35 12N 129 0E
61 Pushchino, U.S.S.R. 54 25N 158 10E
50 Pushkino, U.S.S.R. 51 16N 47 9E
65 Putao (Fort Hertz), Burma 27 24N 97 28E
84 Putaruru, N.Z. 38 3S 175 46E
40 Putignano, Italy 40 52N 17 10E
64 Puttalam, Sri Lanka 8 1N 79 55E
44 Putten, Netherlands 52 17N 5 37E
98 Putumayo, R., Col. 2 15S 72 0W
42 Puy-de-Dôme, Dépt., Fr. 45 40N 2 52E
90 Puyallup, U.S.A. 47 15N 122 22W
25 Pwllheli, Wales 52 54N 4 26W
67 Pyongyang, N. Korea 39 0N 126 0E
90 Pyramid L., U.S.A. 38 47N 120 0W
37 Pyrenees, mts., Europe 42 30N 1 0E
42 Pyrénées Orientales, dépt., France 42 30N 2 30E

Q

63 Qabatiya, Jordan 32 25N 35 16E
62 Qadhima, Saudi Arabia 22 15N 39 15E
62 Qal' at el Mudauwara, Saudi Arabia 29 28N 36 3E
64 Qal'eh Shaharak, Afghan. 34 10N 64 20E
63 Qalqilyah, Jordan 32 10N 34 58E
76 Qamata, S. Africa 32 1S 27 30E
62 Qamr B., South Yemen 16 0N 52 30E
73 Qara, Egypt 29 38N 26 30E
63 Qasr Dabà, Jordan 31 36N 36 2E
73 Qasr Farafra, Egypt 27 2N 28 0E
62 Qasr Umm Ramad, Saudi Arabia 23 10N 49 0E
63 Qatana, Syria 33 27N 36 5E
62 Qatar Sheikhdom, Arabia 25 30N 51 0E
62 Qatif, Saudi Arabia 26 30N 50 0E
63 Qatrana Sta., Jordan 31 12N 36 2E
62 Qattara Depression, Egypt 30 0N 28 0E
51 Qazvin, Iran 36 15N 50 0E
73 Qena, Egypt 26 10N 32 37E
64 Qila Safed, Pakistan 29 3N 61 27E
64 Qila Saifullah, Pakistan 30 45N 68 20E
63 Qiryat Gat, Israel 31 36N 34 46E
62 Qishm, & I., Iran 26 45N 56 0E
62 Qishn, South Yemen 15 30N 51 30E
62 Qizan, Saudi Arabia 16 58N 42 35E
51 Qizil Uzun, R., Iran 37 0N 48 40E
83 Quambatook, Australia 35 55S 143 45E
83 Quambone, Australia 30 56S 148 0E
68 Quan Long, Vietnam 7 10N 105 15E
83 Quandialla, Australia 34 2S 147 50E
68 Quang Ngai, Vietnam 15 2N 109 20E
68 Quang Tri, Vietnam 16 45N 107 7E
88 Quatsino, Canada 50 30N 127 40W
75 Que Que, Rhodesia 18 54S 29 45E
83 Queanbeyan, Australia 35 23S 149 17E
89 Quebec, & Prov., Can. 46 50N 71 30W
88 Queen Charlotte Is., Can. 53 0N 132 0W
88 Queen Charlotte Sd., Can. 51 0N 128 0W
88 Queen Maud G., Can. 68 25N 101 30W
100 Queen Maud Land, Antarc. 74 0S 15 0E
26 Queensbury, England 53 46N 1 50W
83 Queenscliff, Australia 38 12S 144 35E
82 Queensland, st., Australia 24 0S 145 0E
83 Queenstown, Australia 41 1S 145 38E
76 Queenstown, S. Africa 31 55S 27 1E
74 Quela, Angola 9 10 16 56E
75 Quelimane, Mozambique 17 55S 36 58E
67 Quelpart, see Cheju Do. I.
94 Queretaro, Mexico 20 47N 100 12W
88 Quesnel, Canada 52 25N 122 30W
64 Quetta, Pakistan 30 7N 66 55E
68 Quezon City, Philippines 14 50N 120 35E
68 Qui Nhon, Vietnam 13 37N 109 10E
74 Quibaxi, Angola 8 24S 14 27E
98 Quibdo, Colombia 6 0N 76 50W
42 Quiberon, France 47 31N 3 7W
75 Quilengues, Angola 14 12S 14 12E
64 Quilon, India 9 0N 76 40E
83 Quilpie, Australia 26 33S 144 17E
34 Quilty, Ireland 52 50N 9 27W
42 Quimper, France 48 0N 4 7W
42 Quimperlé, France 47 52N 3 37W
34 Quin, Ireland 52 50N 8 52W
91 Quincy, Ill., U.S.A. 39 55N 91 23W
93 Quincy, Mass., U.S.A. 42 15N 71 0W
37 Quintanar, Spain 39 35N 3 5W
83 Quirindi, Australia 31 27S 150 38E
98 Quito, Ecuador 0 20S 78 45W
62 Qum, Iran 34 30N 50 50E
62 Qumisheh, see Shahriza, Iran
32 Quoich, L., Scotland 57 4N 5 20W
83 Quondong, Australia 33 0S 140 15E
83 Quorn, Australia 32 30S 137 55E
92 Quorn, Canada 49 30N 91 0W
66 Qurug Tagh, mts., China 41 30N 90 0E
73 Quseir, Egypt 26 8N 34 20E

R

49 Raahe, Finland 64 40N 24 30E
63 Ra'anana, Israel 32 10N 34 53E
32 Raasay I. & Sd., Scot. 57 25N 6 3W
40 Rabat, Malta 35 53N 14 22E
72 Rabat, Morocco 34 0N 6 42W
82 Rabaul, Papua N.G. 4 15S 152 12E
62 Rabigh Qasr, Si. Arabia 22 54N 39 1E
89 Race, C., Canada 46 40N 53 15W
63 Rachaya, Syria 33 30N 35 50E
72 Rachid, Mauritania 18 45N 11 45W
91 Racine, U.S.A. 42 41N 87 49W
47 Radauti, Rumania 47 53N 25 48E
26 Radcliffe, Lancs., Eng. 53 35N 2 19W
27 Radcliffe, Notts., Eng. 52 57N 1 3W
47 Radekhov, U.S.S.R. 50 25N 24 40E
91 Radford, U.S.A. 37 8N 80 33W
83 Radium Hill, Australia 32 30S 140 35E
22 Radley, England 51 42N 1 14W
25 Radnor Forest, Wales 52 19N 3 20W
47 Radom, Poland 51 24N 21 24E
41 Radomir, Bulgaria 42 37N 23 4E
47 Radomsko, Poland 51 5N 19 28E
24 Radstock, England 51 17N 2 25W
24 Radyr, Wales 51 32N 3 16W
88 Rae, Canada 62 45N 115 50W
65 Rae Bareli, India 26 20N 81 5E
89 Rae Isthmus, Canada 66 40N 87 30W
84 Raetihi, New Zealand 39 27S 175 20E
99 Rafaela, Argentina 31 10S 61 25W
73 Raga, Sudan 8 30N 25 45E
64 Ragama, Sri Lanka 7 0N 79 50E
82 Raglan, Australia 23 48S 150 45E
84 Raglan, New Zealand 37 55S 174 55E
40 Ragusa, Sicily 37 0N 14 48E
73 Rahad el Berdi, Sudan 11 20N 23 40E
64 Raichur, India 16 15N 77 24E
63 Raifoun, Syria 33 58N 35 33E
65 Raigarh, India 21 56N 83 25E
83 Railton, Australia 41 25S 146 25E
90 Rainier, Mt., U.S.A. 46 42N 121 40W
88 Rainy L., Canada 48 40N 93 0W
64 Raipipla, India 21 45N 73 30E
65 Raipur, India 21 16N 81 42E
65 Raj Nandgaon, India 21 0N 81 0E
68 Raja Ampat Arch., Indon. 1 0S 129 30E
65 Rajahmundry, I., India 16 0N 81 46E
64 Rajapalaiyim, India 9 20N 77 30E
64 Rajasthan, Prov., India 27 15N 73 0E
64 Rajgarh, India 24 3N 76 35E
64 Rajkot, India 22 15N 70 54E
65 Rajshahi, Bangladesh 24 30N 88 35E
84 Rakaia, & R., N.Z. 43 45S 172 1E
64 Rakaposhi, Kashmir 36 10N 74 0E
49 Rakvere, U.S.S.R. 59 20N 26 30E
91 Raleigh, U.S.A. 35 46N 78 43W
91 Raleigh Bay, U.S.A. 34 50N 76 0W
63 Ram Allah, Jordan 31 55N 35 11E
62 Ramadi, Iraq 33 26N 43 15E
64 Ramanathapuram (Ramnad), India 9 10N 78 57E
63 Ramat David, Israel 32 41N 35 11E
63 Ramat Gan, Israel 32 5N 34 48E
63 Ramat Hakovesh, Israel 32 12N 34 56E
63 Ramat Hashofet, Israel 32 39N 34 59E
43 Rambouillet, France 48 40N 1 50E
65 Ramechhap, Nepal 27 20N 86 5E
65 Ramgarh, Bihar, India 23 23N 85 30E
64 Ramgarh, Rajasthan, India 27 25N 70 20E
63 Ramishk, Iran 26 59N 58 47E
63 Ramla, Israel 31 55N 34 52E
64 Ramnad, see Ramanathapuram
47 Râmnicu Sărat, Rum. 45 26N 27 3E
47 Râmnicu Valcea, Rum. 45 6N 24 20E
76 Ramotswa, Botswana 24 50S 25 50E
64 Rampur, India 28 50N 79 10E
65 Rampur Hat, India 24 15N 87 45E
65 Ramree, I., Burma 19 10N 93 50E
26 Ramsbottom, England 53 38N 2 20W
23 Ramsey, England 51 55N 1 12E
26 Ramsey, & B., I. of Man 54 19N 4 24W
25 Ramsey I., Wales 51 51N 5 20W
23 Ramsgate, England 51 20N 1 26E
64 Ramtek, India 21 20N 79 15E
65 Ranaghat, India 23 5N 88 35E
99 Rancagua, Chile 34 18S 70 45W
65 Ranchi, India 23 29N 85 18E
90 Randall Res., U.S.A. 43 25N 99 30W
36 Randalstown, N. Ireland 54 45N 6 20W
49 Randers, Denmark 56 30N 10 0E
48 Ranea, & R., Sweden 65 52N 22 20E
84 Rangaunu B., N.Z. 34 51S 173 15E
65 Rangia, India 26 30N 91 20E
84 Rangiora, New Zealand 43 26S 172 37E
65 Rangoon, & R., Burma 16 55N 96 25E
65 Rangpur, Bangladesh 25 42N 89 22E
64 Ranibennur, India 14 40N 75 35E
65 Raniganj, India 23 35N 87 4E
64 Raniwara, India 24 50N 72 10E
83 Rankins Springs, Austral. 33 45S 146 12E
41 Rankovicévo (Kraljevo), Yugoslavia 43 43N 20 40E
64 Rann of Kutch, India 24 0N 70 0E
82 Rannes, Australia 24 6S 150 11E
30 Rannoch, L. & Dist., Scotland 56 41N 4 15W
30 Rannoch Moor, Scotland 56 37N 4 43W
75 Ranohiro, Madagascar 22 30S 45 25E
43 Rapallo, Italy 44 20N 9 18E
36 Raphoe, Ireland 54 52N 7 32W
90 Rapid City, U.S.A. 44 0N 103 20W
33 Rapness, Scotland 59 15N 2 51W
45 Rapperswil, Switzerland 47 15N 8 49E
51 Raqqa, Syria 36 2N 39 0E
73 Ras Abu Shagara, Egypt 21 0N 37 30E
62 Ras al Hadd. C., Oman 22 30N 59 48E
63 Ras al Madraka. C., Oman 19 0N 57 47E
71 Ras Asir, C., Somali Rep. 11 50N 51 12E
73 Ras Banas, C., Egypt 24 0N 35 45E
74 Ras Dashen, mt., Ethiopia 13 8N 37 45E
73 Ras el Milh, C., Egypt 31 55N 25 10E
73 Ras Hadarba, C., Sudan 22 0N 36 50E
72 Ras Lanuf, Libya 30 30N 18 30E
62 Ras Rakan, C., Tr. States 26 7N 51 20E
99 Rasa, Pt., Argentina 40 30S 62 0W
73 Rashad, Sudan 11 55N 31 0E
62 Rasht, Iran 37 18N 49 40E
74 Rat Is., Alaska 50 15N 177 30E
64 Ratangarh, India 28 4N 74 56E
34 Ráth Luirc (Charleville), Ireland 52 21N 8 40W
35 Rathangan, Ireland 53 13N 7 0W
35 Rathcoole, Ireland 53 17N 6 29W
34 Rathcormac, Ireland 52 5N 8 19W
35 Rathdowney, Ireland 52 52N 7 36W
35 Rathdrum, Ireland 52 55N 6 13W
46 Rathenow, Germany 52 36N 12 22E
34 Rathkeale, Ireland 52 31N 8 57W
36 Rathlin I., N. Ireland 55 17N 6 12W
34 Rathmore, Kerry, Ireland 52 5N 9 12W
36 Rathmullen, Ireland 55 7N 7 32W
35 Rathnew, Ireland 53 0N 6 5W
35 Rathvilly, Ireland 52 54N 6 42W
45 Ratische Alpen, Switz. 46 50N 10 10E
64 Ratlam, India 23 21N 75 2E
64 Ratnagiri, India 17 1N 73 22E
35 Ratoath, Ireland 53 30N 6 27W
90 Raton, U.S.A. 36 57N 104 30W
31 Rattray, Scotland 56 36N 3 20W
33 Rattray Hd., Scotland 57 40N 1 53W
48 Raufarhofn, Iceland 66 30N 15 53W
84 Raukumara Ra., N.Z. 38 0S 178 0E
49 Rauma, Finland 61 10N 21 20E
49 Raumo, see Rauma.
23 Raunds, England 52 22N 0 32W
62 Ravar, Iran 31 10N 56 50E
40 Ravenna, Italy 44 26N 12 14E
45 Ravensburg, Germany 47 48N 9 35E
82 Ravenshoe, Australia 17 45S 145 30E
80 Ravensthorpe, Australia 33 31S 120 7E
64 Ravi, R., Pakistan 31 0N 73 20E
64 Rawalpindi, Pakistan 33 40N 73 2E
80 Rawlinna, Australia 31 0S 125 25E
80 Rawlinson Ra., Australia 25 0S 129 0E
27 Rawmarsh, England 53 27N 1 20W
26 Rawtenstall, England 53 42N 2 18W
89 Ray, C., Canada 47 42N 59 25W
65 Rayagada, India 19 5N 83 15E
63 Rayâk, Lebanon 33 52N 36 0E
23 Rayleigh, England 51 36N 0 38E
88 Raymond, Canada 49 28N 112 42W
42 Raz, Pte. du, France 48 2N 4 47W
41 Razgrad, Bulgaria 43 33N 26 33E
42 Ré, I. de, France 46 16N 1 25W
23 Reading, England 51 27N 0 57W
90 Reading, U.S.A. 40 25N 75 46W
33 Reay, Scotland 58 33N 3 48W
73 Rebiana, Libya 24 12N 22 10E
98 Recife (Pernambuco), Brazil 8 5S 35 0W
90 Red Bluff, U.S.A. 40 15N 122 25W
88 Red Deer, Canada 52 14N 113 55W
88 Red Lake, Canada 51 10N 93 45W
91 Red Lake, U.S.A. 48 0N 95 0W
91 Red R., U.S.A. 31 30N 92 30W
66 Red R., Vietnam & China 22 10N 104 0E
70 Red Sea, Arabia-Africa 20 0N 39 0E
73 Red Sea, prov., Sudan 20 0N 35 0E
94 Red Tank, Panama Canal Zone (Inset).
47 Red Tower Pass, Rumania 45 38N 24 20E
25 Red Wharf B., Wales 53 18N 4 10W
23 Redbridge, Gr. London, Eng. 51 35N 0 7E
27 Redcar, England 54 38N 1 4W
83 Redcliffe, Australia 27 12S 153 0E
83 Redcliffs, Australia 34 12S 142 4E
90 Redding, U.S.A. 40 35N 122 25W
22 Redditch, England 52 18N 1 58W
27 Rede R., England 55 18N 2 20W
23 Redhill, England 51 14N 0 10W
90 Redlands, U.S.A. 34 2N 117 12W
27 Redmile, England 52 54N 0 48W
42 Redon, France 47 40N 2 5W
37 Redondela, Spain 42 15N 8 35W
37 Redondo, Portugal 38 40N 7 35W
24 Redruth, England 50 14N 5 14W
91 Redwing, U.S.A. 44 35N 92 40W
34 Ree, L., Ireland 53 30N 7 57W
84 Reefton, New Zealand 42 1S 171 50E
46 Regensburg, Germany 49 0N 12 5E
40 Reggio, Calabria, Italy 38 7N 15 41E
40 Reggio, Emilia Romagna, Italy 44 41N 10 39E
88 Regina, Canada 50 30N 104 37W
75 Rehoboth, S.W. Africa 23 18S 17 1E
63 Rehovot, Israel 31 55N 34 48E
46 Reichenbach, Germany 50 37N 12 18E
23 Reigate, England 51 13N 0 11W
43 Reims, France 49 18N 4 0E
88 Reindeer L., Canada 57 30N 102 28W
84 Rejnga C., New Zealand 34 28S 172 36E
37 Reinosa, Spain 43 3N 4 11W
76 Reitz, S. Africa 27 50S 28 35E
61 Rekiniki, U.S.S.R. 60 50N 163 20E
68 Rembang, Indonesia 6 38S 111 15E
43 Remiremont, France 48 0N 6 35E
44 Remscheid, Germany 51 11N 7 12E
49 Rendsburg, Germany 54 19N 9 41E
29 Renfrew, Scot. 55 53N 4 23W
68 Rengat, Indonesia 0 30S 102 40E
47 Reni, U.S.S.R. 45 30N 28 19E
32 Renish Pt., Scotland 57 44N 6 59W
62 Renk, Sudan 11 50N 32 50E
44 Renkum, Netherlands 51 58N 5 43E
83 Renmark, Australia 34 9S 140 48E
42 Rennes, France 48 10N 1 41W
90 Reno, U.S.A. 39 35N 119 45W
40 Reno, R., Italy 44 38N 11 30E
22 Repton, England 52 50N 1 32W
90 Republican R., U.S.A. 40 10N 99 0W
37 Requena, Spain 39 34N 1 14W
99 Resistencia, Argentina 27 30S 59 0W
47 Resita, Rumania 45 18N 21 53E
84 Resolution I., N.Z. 45 35S 166 40E
25 Resolven, Wales 51 43N 3 42W
43 Rethel, France 49 30N 4 20E
41 Rethimnon, Crete, Greece 34 45N 24 30E
76 Retreat, S. Africa 34 5S 18 20E
71 Réunion I., Indian Ocean 21 15S 56 0E
37 Réus, Spain 41 9N 1 5E
45 Reutlingen, Germany 48 30N 9 15E
43 Revel, France 43 26N 2 0E
88 Revelstoke, Canada 50 59N 118 5W
86 Revilla Gigedo Is., Pacific Ocean 18 50N 111 0W
44 Revin, France 49 57N 4 39E
65 Rewa, India 24 35N 81 25E
64 Rewari, India 28 18N 76 43E
48 Reykafjord, Iceland 66 0N 21 20W
48 Reykjahlid, Iceland 65 40N 16 55W
48 Reykjanæs, Iceland 63 50N 22 40W
48 Reykjavik, Iceland 64 10N 21 53W
80 Reynolds Ra., Australia 22 30S 133 0E
94 Reynosa, Mexico 26 0N 98 0W
51 Reza'iyeh, Iran 37 40N 45 0E
45 Rhätikon, mts., The Alps 46 50N 10 0E
25 Rhayader, Wales 52 18N 3 31W
44 Rheine, West Germany 52 17N 7 25E
44 Rheydt, Germany 51 12N 6 27E
44–45 Rhine (Rhein), R., Ger. 50 45N 7 10E
46 Rhineland Palatinate, Land, Germany 50 55N 6 50E
91 Rhinelander, U.S.A. 45 48N 89 27W
30 Rhins, The, Scotland 54 50N 5 3W
25 Rhiw, Wales 52 49N 4 37W
91 Rhode I., st., U.S.A. 41 20N 71 20W
41 Rhodes, see Ródhos.
75 Rhodesia, Africa 19 0S 30 0E
41 Rhodope Mts., Bulgaria 41 40N 24 10E
25 Rhondda, Wales 51 40N 3 29W
42 Rhône, Dept. & R., Fr. 45 58N 4 35E
25 Rhos-on-Sea, Wales 53 18N 3 46W
25 Rhosllanerchrugog, Wales 53 3N 3 4W
32 Rhu Coigach, Scotland 58 6N 5 27W
25 Rhuddlan, Wales 53 17N 3 28W
32 Rhum I., Scotland 57 0N 6 20W
25 Rhyl, Wales 53 20N 3 28W
25 Rhymney, Wales 51 45N 3 17W
33 Rhynie, Scotland 57 20N 2 50W
64 Riasi, Kashmir 33 10N 74 45E
37 Ribadéo, Spain 43 35N 7 0W
64 Ribat, Pakistan 29 50N 60 55E
37 Ribatejo, Prov., Portugal 39 10N 8 30W
26 Ribble, R., England 53 56N 2 20W
49 Ribe, Denmark 55 20N 8 43E
99 Ribeirao Preto, Brazil 21 15S 47 40W
44 Ribemont, France 49 48N 2 55E
43 Riberac, France 45 15N 0 15E
98 Riberalta, Bolivia 11 0S 66 0W
84 Riccarton, New Zealand 43 31S 172 28E
93 Richibucto, Canada 46 39N 65 5W
90 Richland, U.S.A. 46 25N 119 30W
82 Richmond, Australia 20 45S 142 13E
23 Richmond, Greater London, England 51 27N 0 17W
27 Richmond, Yorks., Eng. 54 24N 1 45W
84 Richmond, New Zealand 41 20S 173 14E
91 Richmond, Ind., U.S.A. 39 47N 85 0W

91 Richmond, Ky., U.S.A. 37 45N 84 18W
91 Richmond, Va., U.S.A. 37 30N 77 28W
83 Richmond Ra., Australia 29 0S 152 45E
23 Rickmansworth, England 51 40N 0 27W
46 Ried, Austria 48 15N 13 30E
46 Riesen Geb., mts., Poland 50 50N 16 0E
76 Rietfontein, S. Africa 26 45S 20 0E
40 Rieti, Italy 42 25N 12 50E
48 Rifstangi, Iceland 66 32N 16 0W
73 Rig Rig, Chad 14 15N 14 26E
49 Riga, & G., U.S.S.R. 56 58N 24 12E
49 Riihimaki, Finland 60 44N 24 45E
40 Rijeka, Yugoslavia 45 1N 14 22E
44 Rijn, R., Netherlands 52 5N 4 30E
44 Rijssen, Netherlands 52 18N 6 31E
44 Rijswijk, Netherlands 52 3N 4 20E
65 Rima, China 28 25N 97 5E
40 Rimini, Italy 44 2N 12 38E
89 Rimouski, Canada 48 25N 68 30W
34 Rineanna (Shannon Airport), Ireland 52 42N 8 57W
31 Ringford, Scotland 54 55N 4 3W
48 Ringköbing, Denmark 56 15N 8 15E
49 Ringvassöy I., Norway 69 53N 19 25E
35 Ringville, Ireland 52 3N 7 37W
22 Ringwood, England 50 50N 1 48W
41 Rinia I., Greece 37 15N 25 20E
99 Rio Claro, Brazil 22 20S 47 35W
94 Rio Claro, Trinidad 10 12N 61 15W
99 Rio Cuarto, Argentina 33 0S 64 0W
99 Rio de Janeiro, & st., Brazil 22 5S 43 12W
99 Rio de la Plata, S. Amer. 35 0S 57 0W
99 Rio Gallegos, Arg. 51 40S 69 10W
90 Rio Grande, New Mexico, U.S.A. 34 20N 106 48W
94 Rio Grande, R., Mexico 29 0N 107 0W
94 Rio Grande de Santiago, Mexico 22 0N 103 35W
94 Rio Grande del Norte, Mexico 25 55N 97 12W
99 Rio Grande do Norte, st., Brazil 5 30S 36 0W
99 Rio Grande do Sul, & st., Brazil 32 0S 52 0W
98 Riobamba, Ecuador 1 40S 78 48W
98 Riohacha, Colombia 11 33N 72 45W
43 Riom, France 45 52N 3 5E
58 Riouw Arch., Indonesia 0 50N 104 50E
27 Ripley, England 53 3N 1 24W
27 Ripon, England 54 9N 1 32W
62 Riq'ai, Saudi Arabia 29 0N 46 33E
25 Risca, Wales 51 36N 3 6W
63 Rishon le Zion, Israel 31 58N 34 47E
26 Rishton, England 53 46N 2 26W
49 Risör, Norway 58 43N 9 10E
40 Riva, Italy 45 54N 10 52E
43 Rivarolo, Italy 45 20N 7 45E
72 River Cess, Liberia 5 30N 9 25W
99 Rivera, Uruguay 31 0S 55 40W
75 Riversdale, S. Africa 34 10S 21 35E
90 Riverside, U.S.A. 33 55N 117 25W
83 Riverton, Australia 34 0S 138 50E
88 Riverton, Canada 51 5N 97 0W
84 Riverton, New Zealand 46 20S 168 5E
93 Riviere au Renard, Can. 49 5N 64 25W
40 Riviera di Levante, Italy 44 23N 9 15E
40 Riviera di Ponente, Italy 43 58N 8 0E
93 Rivière du Loup, Can. 47 50N 69 27W
94 Rivière Pilote, Martinique, W.I. 14 30N 60 50W
62 Riyadh, Saudi Arabia 24 40N 46 50E
62 Rize, Turkey 40 59N 40 30E
40 Rizzuto, C., Italy 38 54N 17 5E
49 Rjukan Fos., Norway 59 54N 8 40E
22 Road Weedon, England 52 14N 1 6W
43 Roanne, France 46 4N 4 2E
91 Roanoke, & R., U.S.A. 37 18N 80 1W
34 Roaringwater B., Ireland 51 30N 9 30W
94 Robert, Martinique, W.I. 14 40N 60 57W
75 Robert Williams, Angola 12 40S 15 45E
80 Robertson Ra., Australia 23 20S 121 0E
72 Robertsport, Liberia 6 45N 11 26W
35 Robertstown, Ireland 53 16N 6 50W
93 Roberval, Canada 48 24N 72 20W
27 Robin Hood's B., Eng. 54 25N 0 31W
80 Robinson Ranges, Austral. 25 40S 119 0E
88 Robson, Mt., Canada 53 15N 118 0W
37 Roca, Cabo de, Portugal 38 46N 9 30W
43 Rocamadour, France 44 46N 1 40E
26 Rochdale, England 53 38N 2 11W
43 Rochechouart, France 45 50N 0 45E
44 Rochefort, Belgium 50 12N 5 15E
42 Rochefort, France 45 57N 0 57W
23 Rochester, England 51 22N 0 29E
91 Rochester, Minn., U.S.A 44 2N 92 29W
93 Rochester, N.H., U.S.A. 43 18N 71 0W
91 Rochester, N.Y., U.S.A. 43 12N 77 40W
23 Rochford, England 51 36N 0 42E
35 Rochfortbridge, Ireland 53 25N 7 19W
91 Rock Island, U.S.A. 41 30N 90 32W
90 Rock Springs, U.S.A. 41 38N 109 13W
13 Rockall I., Atlantic Oc. 57 37N 13 42W
18 Rockall Deep, Atlantic Ocean 56 45N 11 0W
26 Rockcliffe, England 54 58N 3 0W
36 Rockcorry, Ireland 54 7N 7 0W
91 Rockford, U.S.A. 42 19N 89 8W
82 Rockhampton, Australia 23 28S 150 31E
23 Rockingham, & For., Eng. 52 30N 0 40W
91 Rockland, U.S.A. 44 10N 69 10W
91 Rocky Mount, U.S.A. 35 57N 75 52W
90 Rocky Mts., N. America 40 0N 110 0W
44 Roden, Netherlands 53 7N 6 20E
43 Rodez, France 44 22N 2 39E
41 Ródhos I., Greece 36 21N 28 77E
23 Roding R., England 51 43N 0 16E
80 Roebourne, Australia 20 43S 117 10E
80 Roebuck B., Australia 18 10S 122 0E
44 Roermonde, Netherlands 51 12N 6 0E
89 Roes Welcome, Sd., Can. 65 0N 87 0W
44 Roeselare, Belgium 50 57N 3 7E
49 Rogaland, Co., Norway 59 0N 6 30E
43 Rogliano, Corsica, France 42 55N 9 25E
64 Rohri, Pakistan 27 47N 68 50E
64 Rohtak, India 28 57N 76 30E
44 Roisel, France 49 58N 3 6E
94 Rojo, C., Mexico 21 30N 97 20W
91 Rolla, U.S.A. 37 59N 91 46W
82 Rollingstone, Australia 19 0S 146 15E
83 Roma, Australia 26 32S 148 49E
49 Roma, Sweden 57 35N 18 27E
89 Romaine, R., Canada 51 40N 63 40W
47 Roman, Rumania 46 50N 26 29E
61 Roman, U.S.S.R. 60 25N 112 10E
43 Romans, France 45 2N 5 1E
45 Romanshorn, Switz. 47 35N 9 22E
40 Rome, Italy 41 53N 12 33E
91 Rome, Ga., U.S.A. 34 15N 85 8W
91 Rome, N.Y., U.S.A. 43 15N 75 30W
43 Romilly, France 48 30N 3 46E
23 Romney Marsh, England 51 0N 0 54E
45 Romont, Switzerland 46 42N 6 54E
43 Romorantin, France 47 20N 1 45E
48 Romsdal, val., Norway 62 30N 7 50E
22 Romsey, England 50 59N 1 29W
32 Rona, I., Scotland 57 33N 6 0W
32 Ronay, I., Scotland 57 30N 7 10W
37 Roncesvalles & P., Spain 43 1N 1 20W
37 Ronda, Spain 36 48N 5 9W
49 Rondane, Plat., Norway 61 66N 95 7E
49 Rönne, Denmark 55 5N 14 41E
44 Ronse, Belgium 50 44N 3 36E
64 Roorkee, India 29 45N 78 20E
100 Roosevelt I., Antarctica 80 0S 161 0E
36 Roosky, Ireland 53 50N 7 47W
80 Roper R., Australia 14 58S 134 0E
43 Roquefort, France 43 58N 3 0E
98 Roraima, mt., Venezuela 5 45N 62 0W
98 Roraima, state, Brazil 2 30N 62 0W
48 Röros, Norway 62 35N 11 22E
45 Rorschach, Switzerland 47 29N 9 29E
99 Rosario, Argentina 33 3S 60 40W
94 Rosario, Mexico 23 0N 105 40W
99 Rosario de la Frontera, Argentina 25 45S 65 0W
37 Rosas, Spain 42 18N 3 10E
42 Roscoff, France 48 40N 4 0W
36 Roscommon, & Co., Ire. 53 38N 8 8W
34 Roscrea, Ireland 52 58N 7 48W
95 Roseau, Dominica, W.I. 15 15N 61 15W
83 Rosebery, Australia 41 52S 145 38E
90 Roseburg, U.S.A. 43 13N 123 20W
82 Rosedale, Australia 24 38S 151 53E
33 Rosehearty, Scotland 57 42N 2 8W
62 Roseires, Sudan 11 50N 34 30E
33 Rosemarkie, Scotland 57 35N 4 8W
46 Rosenheim, Germany 47 55N 12 5E
88 Rosetown, Canada 51 30N 108 10W
73 Rosetta, Egypt 31 20N 30 21E
83 Rosewood, Australia 27 38S 152 20E
49 Röskilde, Denmark 55 39N 12 3E
52 Roslavl, U.S.S.R. 53 57N 32 40E
22 Ross on Wye, England 51 54N 2 34W
84 Ross, New Zealand 42 55S 170 52E
100 Ross Dependency, Antarctica 70 0S 170 0E
100 Ross Ice Shelf, Antarc. 82 0S 175 0W
100 Ross Sea, Antarctica 75 0S 178 0E
36 Rossan Pt., Ireland 54 42N 8 49W
34 Rosscarbery & B., Ireland 51 34N 9 1W
36 Rosses Bay, Ireland 55 2N 8 30W
36 Rosses Point, Ireland 54 17N 8 34W
88 Rossland, Canada 49 5N 117 35W
35 Rosslare & Hr., Ireland 52 15N 6 20W
72 Rosso, Mauritania 16 40N 15 45W
52 Rossosh, U.S.S.R. 50 17N 39 30E
88 Rosthern, Canada 52 58N 106 10W
46 Rostock, Germany 54 3N 12 7E
52 Rostov, U.S.S.R. 47 12N 39 40E
48 Rosvatn L., Norway 65 40N 14 0E
90 Roswell, U.S.A. 33 28N 104 36W
31 Rosyth, Scotland 56 2N 3 25W
27 Rothbury & For., Eng. 55 19N 1 52W
23 Rother, R., Kent, England 51 1N 0 37E
27 Rotherham, England 53 26N 1 20W
33 Rothes, Scotland 57 33N 3 13W
30 Rothesay, Scotland 55 50N 5 3W
46 Rothhaar, G., mt., Ger. 51 6N 8 10E
23 Rothwell, Northants, England 52 25N 0 48W
27 Rothwell, Yorks., Eng. 53 46N 1 29W
84 Rotoroa, L., N.Z. 41 50S 172 39E
84 Rotorua, & L., N.Z. 38 13S 176 20E
44 Rotterdam, Netherlands 51 55N 4 30E
23 Rottingdean, England 50 48N 0 3W
45 Rottweil, Germany 48 12N 8 20E
84 Rotuma I., Pacific Oc. 12 0S 177 0E
43 Roubaix, France 50 43N 3 4E
43 Rouen, France 49 28N 1 7E
34 Rough Pt., Ireland 52 19N 10 0W
34 Roundstone, Ireland 53 24N 9 55W
35 Roundwood, Ireland 53 4N 6 14W
33 Rousay, I., Scotland 59 9N 3 4W
43 Roussillon, Dist., France 42 40N 2 40E
89 Rouyn, Canada 48 6N 79 0W
48 Rovaniemi, Finland 66 35N 25 40E
40 Rovereto, Italy 45 53N 11 2E
40 Rovigo, Italy 45 2N 11 41E
40 Rovinj, Yugoslavia 45 18N 13 40E
47 Rovno, U.S.S.R. 50 30N 26 22E
31 Rowanburn, Scotland 55 5N 2 54W
68 Roxas, Philippines 11 40N 122 45E
84 Roxburgh, New Zealand 45 30S 169 27E
29 Roxburgh, Scot. 55 34N 2 30W
23 Royston, Herts., England 52 3N 0 1W
26 Royton, Lancs., England 53 34N 2 7W
44 Rozoy-sur-Serre, France 49 40N 4 8E
52 Rtishchevo, U.S.S.R. 52 27N 43 50E
25 Ruabon, Wales 52 59N 3 3W
84 Ruahine Ra., N.Z. 39 45S 176 0E
22 Rubery, England 52 24N 1 59W
30 Rubha a' Mhail, C., Scot. 55 57N 6 7W
40 Rubicone, R., Italy 44 9N 12 29E
63 Rud-i-Khoran R., Iran 29 0N 56 30E
50 Rudnichny, U.S.S.R. 59 40N 52 20E
64 Rudok, Tibet, China 33 30N 79 40E
74 Rudolf, L., see Turkana, L.
43 Rudolstadt, Germany 50 45N 11 55E
42 Ruffec, France 46 0N 0 18E
74 Rufiji, R., Tanzania 8 0S 38 0E
72 Rufisque, Sénégal 14 42N 17 8W
22 Rugby, England 52 21N 1 17W
22 Rugeley, England 52 45N 1 54W
46 Rügen I., Germany 54 32N 13 30E
46 Rühr, R., Germany 51 25N 8 0E
74 Ruki R., Zaïre 0 10S 18 30E
74 Rukwa, L., Tanzania 8 5S 33 0E
32 Rum I., see Rhum
80 Rum Jungle, Australia 13 20S 131 12E
47 Rumania, Europe 45 40N 25 20E
73 Rumbek, Sudan 6 50N 29 30E
84 Runanga, New Zealand 42 25S 171 15E
26 Runcorn, England 53 21N 2 44W
74 Rungwa & R., Tanzania 6 40S 33 50E
65 Rupa, India 27 15N 92 25E
89 Rupert, R., Canada 51 30N 78 40W
75 Rusape, Rhodesia 18 32S 32 5E
41 Rusé (Ruschuk), Bulgaria 43 53N 25 57E
35 Rush, Ireland 53 31N 6 7W
23 Rushden, England 52 17N 0 37W
60 Russian S.F.S.R., Europe and Asia 58 0N 80 0E
60 Russkaya Polyana, U.S.S.R. 54 5N 74 0E
76 Rustenburg, S. Africa 25 34S 27 10E
62 Rutba, Iraq 33 4N 40 15E
47 Ruthenia, reg., U.S.S.R. 48 30N 23 40E
30 Rutherglen, Scotland 55 48N 4 13W
25 Ruthin, Wales 53 8N 3 18W
33 Ruthven, Scotland 57 4N 4 2W
91 Rutland, U.S.A. 43 47N 72 55W
74 Rutshuru, Zaïre 1 0S 29 28E
44 Ruurlo, Netherlands 52 5N 6 27E
74 Ruwenzori, Mt., Uganda 0 40N 29 50E
52 Ruzayevka, U.S.S.R. 54 10N 44 55E
47 Ruzomberok, Cz. 49 12N 19 15E
74 Rwanda, Africa 2 0S 30 0E
30 Ryan, L., Scotland 55 0N 5 4W
52 Ryazan, U.S.S.R. 54 35N 39 45E
52 Ryazhsk, U.S.S.R. 53 43N 40 0E
62 Rybache, U.S.S.R. 46 40N 81 20E
50 Rybachi Pen., U.S.S.R. 69 40N 32 0E
50 Rybinsk (Shcherbakov), U.S.S.R. 58 0N 38 51E
50 Rybinsk Res., U.S.S.R. 58 30N 37 50E
22 Ryde, England 50 44N 1 11W
23 Rye, & B., England 50 58N 0 44E
27 Ryhope, England 54 53N 1 21W
83 Rylstone, Australia 32 40S 149 58E
47 Rypin, Poland 53 0N 19 30E
67 Ryukyu Is., Japan 26 30N 128 0E
52 Rzhev, U.S.S.R. 56 20N 34 25E

S

45 Saanen, Switzerland 46 29N 7 17E
46 Saar, Land, Germany 49 38N 6 33E
45 Saar (Sarre), R., Fr. & Germany 49 20N 6 45E
45 Saarbrücken, Germany 49 19N 7 0E
44 Saarburg, Germany 49 38N 6 33E
44 Saarlouis, Germany 49 18N 6 44E
45 Saas Fee, Switzerland 46 8N 7 56E
68 Sabah, state, Malaysia 6 0N 117 0E
63 Sabastiya, Jordan 32 16N 35 11E
62 Sabha, Wadi, Si. Arabia 23 50N 50 0E
94 Sabinas, Mexico 27 40N 101 10W
94 Sabinas Hidalgo, Mex. 26 25N 100 15W
40 Sabine Mts., Italy 42 20N 12 50E
91 Sabine R., U.S.A. 31 45N 93 45W
93 Sable, C., Canada 43 28N 65 50W
91 Sable, C., U.S.A. 25 15N 81 5W
89 Sable, I., Canada 43 57N 60 00W
63 Sabzawar, Iran 36 25N 57 55E
63 Sabzawar, Afghanistan 33 12N 62 0E
45 Säckingen, Germany 47 35N 7 55E
90 Sacramento, & R., U.S.A. 38 37N 121 25W
90 Sacramento Mts., U.S.A. 32 20N 105 0W
27 Sacriston, England 54 49N 1 38W
37 Sadaba, Spain 42 20N 1 15W
30 Saddell, Scotland 55 31N 5 30W
35 Saddle Hd., Ireland 54 0N 10 10W
67 Sado, I., Japan 38 0N 138 15E
65 Sadon, Burma 25 25N 97 50E
49 Säffle, Sweden 59 9N 12 55E
23 Saffron Walden, England 52 1N 0 15E
72 Safi, Morocco 32 15N 9 15W
67 Saga, & Pref., Japan 33 18N 130 6E
65 Sagaing, Burma 21 58N 95 56E
67 Sagami B., Japan 35 0N 139 30E
64 Sagar, India 23 50N 78 50E
25 Sageston, Wales 51 41N 4 48W
91 Saginaw, & B., U.S.A. 43 29N 84 0W
37 Sagres, Portugal 37 1N 8 57W
95 Sagua la Grande, Cuba, 22 58N 80 2W
93 Saguenay, R., Canada 48 18N 70 0W
37 Sagunto, Spain 39 42N 0 18W
37 Sahagúna, Spain 42 20N 5 0W
63 Sahah, Jordan 31 51N 36 0E
72 Sahara Atlas, mts., Algeria 34 0N 3 0E
72 Sahara, Des., N. Africa 20 0N 12 0E
64 Saharanpur, India 29 57N 77 38E
64 Sahiwal, Pakistan 30 48N 73 5E
63 Saidabad, Iran 29 27N 55 48E
64 Saidapet, India 13 0N 80 15E
74 Sa'id Bundas, Sudan 8 24N 24 48E
64 Saidu, Pakistan 34 50N 72 15E
68 Saigon, see Ho-Chi-Minh City
62 Saihut, South Yemen 15 25N 51 20E
66 Saikhoa Ghat, India 28 5N 95 0E
50 Saimaa, L., Finland 61 20N 28 0E
31 St. Abb's, Scotland 55 54N 2 7W
31 St. Abb's Hd., Scotland 55 55N 2 8W
43 St. Affrique, France 43 58N 2 55E
24 St. Agnes, & Hd., Eng. 50 19N 5 15W
23 St. Albans, England 51 46N 0 20W
91 St. Albans, U.S.A. 44 50N 73 0W
22 St. Albans Hd., England 50 35N 2 4W
44 St. Amand, France 50 26N 3 27E
43 St. Amand-Montrond, France 46 40N 2 30E
44 St. Amandsberg, Belgium 51 5N 3 42E
43 St. André, France 44 0N 6 30E
75 St. André, C., Madagascar 16 0S 44 25E
31 St. Andrews, Scotland 56 20N 2 48W
42 St. Anne, Channel Is. 49 44N 2 10W
26 St. Annes, England 53 46N 3 4W
95 St. Ann's, & B., Jamaica 18 10N 77 15W
83 St. Arnaud, Australia 36 33S 143 15E
25 St. Asaph, Wales 53 17N 3 26W
89 St. Augustin, Canada 51 30N 58 30W
91 St. Augustine, U.S.A. 29 58N 81 21W
24 St. Austell, England 50 20N 4 48W
45 St. Avold, France 49 8N 6 41E
94 St. Barthélemy I., W.I. 17 56N 62 45W
26 St. Bees & Hd., England 54 31N 3 39W
88 St. Boniface, Canada 49 50N 97 0W
31 St. Boswells, Scotland 55 34N 2 39W
42 St. Brelade's, Jersey, Channel Is. 49 12N 2 13W
25 St. Bride's B., Wales 51 48N 5 11W
42 St. Brieuc, France 48 34N 2 45W
43 St. Calais, France 47 55N 0 40E
94 St. Catherine, Mt., Grenada, W.I. 12 13N 61 40W
22 St. Catherine's Point, England 50 35N 1 19W
43 St. Céré, France 44 50N 1 50E
92 St. Clair L., Canada-U.S.A. 42 38N 82 30W
43 St. Claude, France 46 22N 5 50E
91 St. Cloud, U.S.A. 45 28N 94 10W
24 St. Columb Major, Eng. 50 26N 4 56W
95 St. Croix, I., W. Indies 17 45N 64 45W
33 St. Cyrus, Scotland 56 47N 2 25W
25 St. Davids, & Hd., Wales 51 53N 5 16W
95 St. David's I., Bermudas 32 23N 64 38W
43 St. Dié, France 48 20N 7 0E
43 St. Dizier, France 48 40N 5 8E
88 St. Elias, Mt., Canada 60 40N 140 0W
43 St. Étienne, France 45 27N 4 22E
94 St. Eustatius I., W.I. 17 30N 63 30W
93 St. Félicien, Canada 48 38N 72 30W
43 St. Florent, France 42 40N 9 15E
43 St. Flour, France 45 0N 3 10E
45 St. Gallen, & Canton, Switzerland 47 26N 9 21E
43 St. Gaudens, France 43 5N 0 45E
95 St. George, Bermudas 32 25N 64 43W
90 St. George, U.S.A. 37 10N 113 35W
95 St. George's, Grenada, W.I. 12 5N 61 40W
44 St. Georges, Belgium 50 36N 5 22E
43 St. Germain, Yvelines, France 48 52N 2 5E
24 St. Germans, England 50 24N 4 19W
42 St. Gilles, France 46 41N 2 0W
43 St. Girons, France 43 0N 1 8E
25 St. Govan's Hd., Wales 51 35N 4 56W
75 St. Helena B., S. Africa 32 40S 18 0E
5 St. Helena I., S. Atlan. Oc. 10 20S 7 50W
26 St. Helens, Eng. 53 28N 2 43W
90 St. Helens, U.S.A. 45 50N 122 52W
42 St. Helier, Jersey 49 15N 2 8W
43 St. Hippolyte, France 47 20N 6 50E
44 St. Hubert, Belgium 50 2N 5 22E
89 St. Hyacinthe, Canada 45 40N 73 0W
45 St. Ingbert, Germany 49 16N 7 6E
24 St. Ives, & B., Corn., Eng. 50 14N 5 30W
23 St. Ives, Hunts., England 52 19N 0 4W
43 St. Jean, France 45 20N 6 20E
93 St. Jean, L., Canada 48 39N 72 10W
42 St. Jean de Luz, France 43 25N 1 40W
93 St. Jerôme, Canada 45 57N 74 0W
93 St. John, N.B., Canada 45 18N 65 55W
93 St. John, R., U.S.A. 46 42N 69 35W
95 St. John's, Antigua, W.I. 17 0N 61 50W
89 St. John's Newf'd., Can. 47 37N 52 40W
36 St. Johnston, Ireland 54 56N 7 29W
91 St. Joseph, U.S.A. 39 49N 94 50W
89 St. Joseph, L., Canada 51 10N 90 50W
92 St. Joseph R., U.S.A. 42 8N 85 30W
43 St. Junien, France 45 50N 0 55E
24 St. Just, England 50 7N 5 41W
18 St. Kilda, I., Atlantic Oc. 57 50N 8 40W
84 St. Kilda, N.Z. 45 53S 170 31E
94 St. Kitts I., West Indies 17 20N 62 49W
93 St. Lawrence, G. of, Can. 48 0N 62 0W
93 St. Lawrence, R., Canada 49 0N 68 30W
23 St. Leonards, England 50 51N 0 33E
42 St. Lô, France 49 12N 1 5W
72 St. Louis, Senegal 16 0N 16 27W
91 St. Louis, U.S.A. 38 40N 90 20W
94 St. Lucia, I. & Chan., Wind. Is., W. Indies 14 0N 61 0W
76 St. Lucia, L., S. Africa 27 45S 32 30E
94 St. Maarten I., Neth. W.I. 18 5N 63 0W
32 St. Magnus B., Scotland 60 23N 1 35W
42 St. Malo, France 48 42N 2 2W
95 St. Marc, Haiti, W.I. 19 0N 72 50W
42 St. Martin, Jersey, Channel Is. 49 15N 2 5W
43 St. Martin, France 44 2N 7 15E
95 St. Martin I., W.I. 18 15N 63 0W
83 St. Mary Pk., Australia 31 30S 138 40E
83 St. Mary's, Australia 41 30S 148 15E
24 St. Mary's I., England 49 55N 6 18W
42 St. Mathieu, Pte. de, Fr. 48 20N 4 50W
43 St. Maur, France 48 44N 2 30E
45 St. Maurice, Switzerland 46 14N 7 1E
25 St. Mellons, England 51 31N 3 8W
24 St. Michael's Mt., Eng. 50 7N 5 29W
31 St. Monance, Scotland 56 12N 2 45W
45 St. Moritz, Switzerland 46 30N 9 51E
42 St. Nazaire, France 47 20N 2 13W
23 St. Neots, England 52 13N 0 16W
44 St. Niklaas, Belgium 51 10N 4 8E
43 St. Omer, France 50 42N 2 12E
43 St. Paul, France 42 50N 2 30E
91 St. Paul, U.S.A. 44 58N 93 6W
40 St. Paul's Bay, Malta 36 57N 14 24E
42 St. Peter Port, Channel Is. 49 30N 2 35W
91 St. Petersburg, U.S.A. 27 49N 82 44W
89 St. Pierre and Miquelon, Fr. Overseas Terr., N. Amer. 46 49N 56 15W
46 St. Polten, Austria 48 10N 15 38E
43 St. Quentin, France 49 54N 3 13E
43 St. Raphael, France 43 22N 6 50E
43 St. Rémy, France 43 43N 4 50E
42 St. Servan, France 48 40N 2 0W
42 St. Sever, France 43 47N 0 40W
93 St. Stephen, Canada 45 12N 67 18W
92 St. Thomas, Canada 42 45N 81 20W
95 St. Thomas, I., W. Indies 18 20N 65 0W
44 St. Trond, Belgium 50 49N 5 11E
43 St. Tropez, France 43 18N 6 35E
43 St. Valéry-en-Caux, Fr. 49 52N 0 45E
43 St. Valéry sur Somme, Fr. 50 10N 1 40E
43 St. Vallier, France 45 12N 4 50E
37 St. Vincent, C., Portugal 37 0N 9 0W
83 St. Vincent, G. Australia 35 0S 138 0E
94 St. Vincent I., W. Indies 13 17N 61 15W
44 St. Vith, Belgium 50 17N 6 5E
43 St. Yrieix, France 45 32N 1 15E
94 Sainte Anne, Guadeloupe, Fr. W.I. 16 13N 61 23W
94 Sainte Anne, Martinique, Fr. W.I. 14 25N 60 52W
75 Ste. Marie, I., Madag. 16 55S 50 0E
94 Sainte Marie, Martinique, Fr. W.I. 14 46N 61 0W
44 Sainte Ménéhould, France 49 10N 4 52E
94 Sainte Rose, Guadeloupe, W.I. 16 18N 61 40W
42 Saintes, France 45 47N 0 40W
36 Saintfield, N. Ireland 54 28N 5 50W
42 Saintonge, Dist., France 45 30N 0 40W
65 Sairang, India 23 50N 92 40E
67 Saitama, Pref., Japan 36 20N 139 45E
62 Saiun, South Yemen 15 52N 48 55E
98 Sajama, Mt., Bolivia 17 30S 68 30W
67 Sakai, Japan 34 30N 135 30E
67 Sakashima Gunto, Is., Jap. 25 0N 124 0E
67 Sakata, Japan 38 58N 139 56E
61 Sakhalin, U.S.S.R. 52 0N 143 0E
76 Sakrivier, S. Africa 31 10S 20 28E
49 Sala, Sweden 59 56N 16 30E
99 Salado, R., Argentina 29 0S 63 0W
72 Salaga, Ghana 8 35N 0 45W
37 Salamanca, Spain 40 59N 5 40W
82 Salamaua, Papua N.G. 7 10S 147 0E
41 Salamis, Greece 37 58N 23 30E
98 Salaverry, Peru 8 12S 79 0W
68 Salayar, I., Indonesia 6 12S 120 25E
43 Salbris, France 47 22N 2 8E
37 Saldaña, Spain 42 30N 4 48W
83 Sale, Australia 38 7S 147 0E
26 Sale, England 53 26N 2 19W
72 Salé, Morocco 33 29N 6 47W
60 Salekhard, U.S.S.R. 66 30N 66 50E
64 Salem, India 11 35N 78 0E
93 Salem, Mass., U.S.A. 42 30N 71 0W
90 Salem, Ore., U.S.A. 44 48N 123 0W
40 Salerno, Italy 40 42N 14 50E
26 Salford, England 53 29N 2 18W
90 Salida, U.S.A. 38 25N 106 0W
75 Salima, Malawi 13 50S 34 30E
90 Salina, U.S.A. 38 57N 97 58W
94 Salina Cruz, Mexico 16 23N 95 25W
90 Salinas & R., U.S.A. 36 40N 121 42W
99 Salinas Grandes, Arg. 29 15S 63 30W
43 Salins, France 46 59N 5 50E
83 Salisbury, Australia 34 45S 138 35E
22 Salisbury, England 51 5N 1 47W
75 Salisbury, Rhodesia 17 50S 31 2E
91 Salisbury, Md., U.S.A. 38 25N 75 33W
91 Salisbury, N.C., U.S.A. 35 42N 80 30W

22 Salisbury Plain, England 51 14N 1 57W
62 Sallom, Sudan 19 22N 37 6E
90 Salmon, & R., U.S.A. 45 10N 113 50W
90 Salmon River Mts., U.S.A. 44 45N 120 0W
49 Salo, Finland 60 22N 23 3E
43 Salo, Italy 45 40N 10 30E
43 Salon, France 43 40N 5 5E
22 Salop, Co., England 52 48N 2 50W
64 Salsette, I., India 18 30N 72 10E
51 Salsk, U.S.S.R. 46 10N 41 30E
43 Salsomaggiore, Italy 44 50N 10 0E
48 Salt Fd., Norway 67 10N 14 10E
90 Salt Fork R., Texas, U.S.A. 33 15N 101 0W
90 Salt Lake City, U.S.A. 40 45N 111 50W
99 Salta, Argentina 24 47S 65 20W
24 Saltash, England 50 25N 4 12W
27 Saltburn, England 54 35N 0 58W
30 Saltcoats, Scotland 55 38N 4 47W
35 Saltee Is., Ireland 52 7N 6 35W
27 Saltergate, England 54 20N 0 40W
94 Saltillo, Mexico 25 28N 101 0W
99 Salto, Uruguay 31 25S 58 0W
98 Salto Augusto, Falls, Fs., Brazil 8 30S 58 0W
90 Salton Sea, U.S.A. 33 20N 115 45W
72 Saltpond, Ghana 5 15N 1 3W
23 Saltwood, England 51 4N 1 5E
73 Salum, G. of, Egypt 31 30N 25 10E
65 Salur, India 18 36N 83 12E
40 Saluzzo, Italy 44 40N 7 30E
99 Salvador (Bahia), Brazil 12 50S 38 25W
94 Salvadore, C. Amer. 13 45N 88 50W
65 Salween, R., China-Burma 19 30N 97 40E
46 Salzburg, & prov., Austria 47 46N 13 1E
46 Salzgitter, Germany 52 7N 10 19E
60 Sama, U.S.S.R. 60 25N 60 27E
61 Samagaltai, U.S.S.R. 51 40N 95 0E
63 Samar, Jordan 32 40N 35 47E
68 Samar, I., Philippines 11 30N 125 0E
82 Samarai, Papua N.G. 10 30S 151 0E
63 Samaria, Dist., Jordan 32 21N 35 15E
63 Samaria, Mts. of, Jordan 32 15N 35 15E
68 Samarinda, Indonesia 0 48S 117 18E
60 Samarkand, U.S.S.R. 39 45N 66 55E
62 Samarra, Iraq 34 30N 43 55E
62 Samawa, Iraq 31 15N 45 15E
65 Sambalpur, India 21 32N 83 59E
68 Sambas, Indonesia 1 35N 109 20E
75 Sambava, Madagascar 14 10S 50 3E
64 Sambhal, India 28 40N 78 35E
64 Sambhar, India 26 55N 74 45E
40 Sambiase, Italy 38 57N 16 16E
47 Sambor, U.S.S.R. 49 30N 23 15E
44 Sambre, R., Fr.-Belg. 50 20N 4 15E
74 Same, Tanzania 4 1S 37 45E
51 Samnan, Iran 35 31N 53 20E
41 Samos, I., Greece 37 41N 26 50E
41 Samothraki, I., Greece 40 28N 25 38E
68 Sampit, Indonesia 2 23S 113 0E
66 Samshui, China 23 15N 112 55E
51 Samsun, Turkey 41 20N 36 12E
68 Samut Songkhram, Thailand 13 20N 100 0E
72 San Mali 13 15N 4 45W
95 San Andres, I., Colombia 12 30N 81 35W
90 San Andres, Mts., U.S.A. 33 0N 106 40W
94 San Andres Tuxtla, Mex. 18 25N 95 15W
90 San Angelo, U.S.A. 31 25N 100 28W
99 San Antonio Oeste, Arg. 40 40S 65 5W
99 San Antonio, Chile 33 30S 71 40W
90 San Antonio, U.S.A. 29 27N 98 32W
95 San Antonio, C., Cuba 21 58N 85 0W
91 San Antonio, R., U.S.A. 28 45N 97 30W
91 San Benito, U.S.A. 26 5N 97 45W
90 San Bernardino, U.S.A. 34 11N 117 25W
68 San Bernardino Str., Philippines 12 30N 124 17E
91 San Blas, C., U.S.A. 29 40N 85 20W
68 San Carlos, Philippines 11 0N 124 20E
99 San Carlos de Bariloche, Argentina 41 20N 71 0W
90 San Clemente I., U.S.A. 32 50N 118 30W
99 San Cristobal, Argentina 30 25S 61 10W
94 San Cristobal, Mexico 17 14N 92 32W
95 San Cristobal, Venezuela 7 30N 72 15W
78 San Cristobal, I., Solomon Is. 11 0S 162 0E
90 San Diego, U.S.A. 32 45N 117 12W
99 San Felipe, Chile 32 40S 70 45W
95 San Felipe, Venezuela 10 10N 68 50W
37 San Feliu, Spain 41 45N 3 0E
94 San Fernando, Mexico 24 50N 98 2W
37 San Fernando, Spain 36 36N 6 14W
95 San Fernando, Trinidad 10 10N 61 28W
98 San Fernando, Venezuela 7 50N 67 30W
90 San Francisco, U.S.A. 37 40N 122 25W
95 San Francisco de Macoris, Dominican Republic 19 15N 70 5W
99 San Ignacio, Bolivia 16 10S 61 0W
90 San Joaquin, R., U.S.A. 37 0N 120 0W
94 San Jorge B., Mexico 31 0N 113 30W
99 San Jorge, G. de, Arg. 46 0S 66 30W
98 San José, Bolivia 18 0S 60 30W
95 San José, Costa Rica 9 50N 84 2W
68 San Jose, Philippines 10 45N 122 0E
90 San Jose, Cal., U.S.A. 37 20N 122 50W
99 San José, Uruguay 34 7S 57 0W
99 San Juan, Argentina 31 38S 68 38W
95 San Juan, Puerto Rico 18 27N 66 10W
90 San Juan Mts., U.S.A. 37 30N 107 0W
99 San Julian, Argentina 49 20S 67 35W
99 San Lorenzo, Mt., Arg. 47 30S 72 0W
94 San Lucas, C., Mexico 23 0N 110 0W
99 San Luis, Argentina 33 24S 66 15W
90 San Luis Obispo, U.S.A. 35 18N 120 38W
94 San Luis Potosi, Mex. 22 10N 100 37W
40 San Marino, Italy 43 58N 12 30E
90 San Mateo, U.S.A. 37 30N 122 15W
99 San Matias, G. de, Arg. 41 30S 64 0W
94 San Miguel, Salvador 13 25N 88 10W
99 San Nicolas, Argentina 33 20S 60 10W
94 San Pedro, Mexico 26 0N 102 58W
99 San Pedro, Paraguay 24 0S 57 10W
95 San Pedro de Macoris, Dominican Republic 18 30N 69 20W
94 San Pedro Sula, Honduras 15 35N 88 0W
99 San Rafael, Argentina 34 30S 68 20W
40 San Remo, Italy 43 50N 7 50E
94 San Salvador, Salvador 13 59N 89 18W
95 San Salvador I., Bahama 24 0N 74 30W
37 San Sebastian, Spain 43 20N 1 58W
40 San Severo, Italy 41 40N 15 20E
94 San Vicente, Salvador 13 45N 88 50W
37 San Vicente de la Barquera, Spain 43 28N 4 30W
62 San'a, Yemen 15 25N 44 15E
63 Sanamein, Syria 33 5N 36 10E
68 Sanana, I., Indonesia 2 20S 126 0E
95 Sanchez, Dominican Republic 19 10N 69 35W
43 Sancoins, France 46 50N 2 58E
95 Sancti Spiritus, Cuba 22 0N 78 0W
68 Sandakan, Malaysia 6 0N 118 12E
68 Sandalwood I., Indonesia 10 0S 120 0E
33 Sanday, I. & Sd., Orkneys, Scotland 59 12N 2 30W
26 Sandbach, England 53 8N 2 23W
83 Sandgate, Australia 27 26S 152 57E
23 Sandgate, England 51 4N 1 7E
23 Sandhurst, England 51 21N 0 48W
49 Sandnes, Norway 58 50N 5 45E
74 Sandoa, Zaïre 9 48S 22 4E
47 Sandomierz, Poland 50 40N 21 42E
65 Sandoway, Burma 18 14N 94 30E
90 Sandpoint, U.S.A. 48 27N 116 35W
32 Sandray, Hebrides, Scot. 56 53N 7 30W
23 Sandringham, England 52 49N 0 30E
80 Sandstone, Australia 27 55S 119 25E
91 Sandusky, U.S.A. 41 25N 82 45W
49 Sandviken, Sweden 60 38N 16 58E
23 Sandwich, England 51 16N 1 22E
23 Sandy, England 52 8N 0 18W
82 Sandy, C., Australia 24 45S 152 30E
64 Sandy Desert, Pakistan 28 0N 65 0E
91 Sanford, U.S.A. 28 48N 81 27W
88 Sanford, Mt., Alaska 62 5N 143 30W
64 Sangamner, India 19 35N 74 10E
61 Sangatolon, U.S.S.R. 61 50N 149 30E
68 Sangihe Is., Indonesia 3 57N 125 14E
64 Sangli, India 16 55N 74 25E
74 Sangmelina, Cameroon 2 57N 12 1E
37 Sangonera, R., Spain 37 40N 2 0W
90 Sangre de Cristo Ra., U.S.A. 37 30N 105 20W
94 Sangre Grande, Trinidad 10 36N 61 8W
74 Sangwa, Zaïre 5 30S 26 5E
74 Sankuru, R., Zaïre 4 0S 21 0E
37 Sanlúcar la Mayor, Spain 36 46N 6 21W
37 Sanlúcar de Barrameda, Spain 36 40N 6 28W
47 Sanok, Poland 49 35N 22 14E
31 Sanquhar, Scotland 55 22N 3 55W
72 Sansanné-Mango, Togo 10 28N 0 25E
94 Santa Ana, Salvador 14 0N 89 35W
90 Santa Ana, U.S.A. 33 40N 117 48W
90 Santa Barbara, U.S.A. 34 30N 119 40W
90 Santa Barbara Is., U.S.A. 33 15N 118 30W
90 Santa Blanca Pk., U.S.A. 33 20N 105 45W
90 Santa Catalina I., U.S.A. 33 10N 119 0W
99 Santa Catarina I., Brazil 27 45S 48 20W
95 Santa Clara, Cuba 22 30N 79 40W
90 Santa Clara, U.S.A. 37 22N 122 3W
98 Santa Cruz, Bolivia 17 50S 63 26W
72 Santa Cruz, Canary Is. 28 25N 16 19W
90 Santa Cruz, U.S.A. 36 57N 122 0W
90 Santa Cruz I., U.S.A. 34 5N 119 50W
81 Santa Cruz Is., Pac. Oc. 10 20S 168 0E
94 Santa Eugenia, Pt., Mex. 27 50N 115 5W
99 Santa Fé, Argentina 31 40S 60 45W
90 Santa Fe, U.S.A. 35 40N 105 50W
99 Santa Inés I., Chile 54 0S 73 0W
74 Santa Isabel, Equatorial Guinea 3 45N 8 50E
99 Santa Maria, Brazil 29 30S 53 40W
90 Santa Maria, U.S.A. 34 50N 120 28W
41 Santa Maria di Leuca, C., Italy 39 50N 18 23E
95 Santa Marta, Colombia 11 13N 74 12W
95 Santa Marta, Sa. Nevada de, mts., Colombia 11 0N 73 0W
90 Santa Monica, U.S.A. 34 5N 118 31W
99 Santa Rosa, Argentina 36 35S 64 0W
94 Santa Rosa, Honduras 14 50N 88 45W
90 Santa Rosa, U.S.A. 38 25N 122 45W
94 Santa Rosalia, Mexico 27 10N 112 32W
66 Santai, China 31 20N 104 30E
37 Santander, Spain 43 28N 3 52W
98 Santarém, Brazil 3 12S 54 30W
37 Santarém, Portugal 39 17N 8 43W
91 Santee, R., U.S.A. 33 30N 80 15W
99 Santiago, Chile 33 35S 70 40W
95 Santiago, Dominican Republic 19 25N 70 40W
37 Santiago, Spain 42 54N 8 31W
95 Santiago de Cuba, Cuba 20 5N 75 48W
99 Santiago del Estero, Arg. 27 45S 64 27W
74 Santo Antonio do Zaire, Angola 5 50S 12 10E
98 Santo Antonio Falls, Brazil 9 0S 64 0W
95 Santo Domingo, Dominican Republic 18 32N 69 50W
37 Santona, Spain 43 28N 3 29W
99 Santos, Brazil 24 0S 46 10W
67 Santuaho, China 26 50N 119 50E
74 Sanza Pombo, Angola 7 16S 15 5E
99 São Borja, Brazil 28 30S 56 0W
98 São Francisco R., Brazil 8 45S 40 0W
98 São Luiz (Maranhao), Brazil 2 45S 44 10W
98 São Manuel R., Brazil 11 0S 55 35W
99 São Paulo, & st., Brazil 23 35S 46 30W
98 São Roque, C., Brazil 5 0S 35 0W
74 São Salvador do Congo, Angola 6 30S 14 25E
99 São Sebastião I., Brazil 24 0S 45 30W
99 São Tomé, C., de, Brazil 22 0S 41 10W
43 Saône, R., France 46 10N 3 50E
42 Saône-et-Loire, Dept., Fr. 46 42N 4 25E
72 Sapele, Nigeria 5 50N 5 40E
67 Sapporo, Japan 43 1N 141 15E
73 Saqota, Ethiopia 12 30N 38 45E
41 Sar Planina, Mts., Y-slav. 42 0N 20 45E
41 Sarajevo, Yugoslavia 43 56N 18 46E
63 Sarakhs, U.S.S.R. 36 35N 61 2E
65 Sarangarh, India 21 30N 82 57E
52 Saransk, U.S.S.R. 54 13N 45 5E
52 Sarapul, U.S.S.R. 56 35N 53 47E
91 Sarasota, U.S.A. 27 15N 82 29W
91 Saratoga Springs, U.S.A. 43 6N 73 50W
52 Saratov, U.S.S.R. 51 35N 45 59E
68 Saravane, Laos 15 35N 106 25E
68 Sarawak, St., Malaysia 2 40N 113 15E
65 Sarda, R., India 28 55N 80 30E
72 Sardalas, Libya 25 48N 10 40E
40 Sardinia, I., Italy 40 20N 9 5E
63 Sardarshahr, India 28 30N 74 30E
48 Sarektjakko, Mt., Nor. 67 30N 17 30E
50 Sarema, I., U.S.S.R. 58 20N 22 45E
45 Sargans, Switzerland 47 4N 9 30E
64 Sargodha, Pakistan 32 10N 72 35E
60 Sargumei, U.S.S.R. 45 20N 74 53E
82 Sarina, Australia 21 22S 149 13E
43 Sarlat, France 44 52N 1 10E
99 Sarmiento, Argentina 45 30S 69 0W
45 Sarnen, Switzerland 46 54N 8 14E
92 Sarnia, Canada 43 0N 82 30W
47 Sarny, U.S.S.R. 51 18N 26 40E
41 Saros, G. of, Turkey 41 37N 26 35E
49 Sarpsborg, Norway 59 16N 11 12E
45 Sarrebourg, France 48 44N 7 2E
42 Sartène, Corsica, France 41 38N 8 55E
42 Sarthe, Dépt., France 48 5N 0 3E
60 Sartynya, U.S.S.R. 63 25N 63 7E
62 Sarur, Oman 23 20N 58 7E
42 Sarzeau, France 47 30N 2 50W
65 Sasaram, India 24 56N 84 0E
72 Sasebo, Japan 33 6N 129 50E
64 Saser, Mt., Kashmir 35 0N 77 45E
88 Saskatchewan, Prov., Can. 54 0N 106 0W
88 Saskatchewan R., Can. 53 20N 104 30W
88 Saskatoon, Canada 52 10N 106 38W
61 Saskylakh, U.S.S.R. 72 0N 114 40E
61 Sasnovka, U.S.S.R. 54 20N 109 50E
52 Sasovo, U.S.S.R. 54 25N 41 55E
72 Sassandra, & R., Ivory Coast 5 0N 6 0W
40 Sassari, Italy 40 45N 8 35E
46 Sassnitz, Germany 54 33N 13 35E
47 Sasyk, L., U.S.S.R. 45 32N 29 12E
72 Satadougou, Mali 12 40N 11 25W
64 Satara, India 17 50N 74 0E
64 Satmala Hills, Andhra Pradesh, India 19 30N 78 30E
64 Satmala Hills, Maharashtra, India 20 20N 74 30E
65 Satna, India 24 40N 80 50E
47 Sátoraljaújhely, Hungary 48 25N 21 40E
64 Satpura Hills, India 22 0N 77 0E
47 Satu Mare, Hungary 47 50N 23 0E
48 Saudharkrókur, Iceland 65 45N 19 37W
62 Saudi Arabia, S.W. Asia 25 0N 45 0E
44 Sauer, R., Luxembourg 49 51N 6 17E
43 Saulieu, France 47 20N 4 15E
92 Sault Ste. Marie, Canada 46 35N 84 22W
91 Sault Ste. Marie, U.S.A. 46 30N 84 24W
42 Saumur, France 47 18N 0 10W
48 Saurbœr, Iceland 64 21N 21 35W
74 Saurimo, Angola 9 45S 20 30E
40 Sava, R., Yugoslavia 46 14N 14 20E
84 Savaii I., Samoa (Inset)
72 Savalou, Benin 8 0N 2 9E
95 Savanna la Mar., Jamaica 18 14N 78 6W
91 Savannah, & R., U.S.A. 32 0N 81 5W
68 Savannakhet, Laos 16 35N 105 0E
75 Save, R., Mozambique 21 16S 34 0E
51 Saveh, Iran 35 0N 50 10E
72 Savelugu, Ghana 9 38N 0 4W
43 Saverne, France 48 40N 7 15E
43 Savigliano, Italy 44 40N 7 40E
42 Savoie, Dépt., France 45 33N 6 20E
40 Savona, Italy 44 21N 8 32E
68 Sawah Lunto, Indon. 0 30S 100 48E
64 Sawai Madhopur, India 26 5N 76 22E
67 Sawara, Japan 35 58N 140 36E
90 Sawatch Ra., U.S.A. 38 30N 106 30W
23 Sawbridgeworth, Eng. 51 49N 0 10E
36 Sawel, Mt., N. Ireland 54 47N 7 2W
73 Sawknah, Libya 29 10N 16 0E
75 Sawmills, Rhodesia 19 30S 28 2E
68 Sawu I., Indonesia 10 30S 122 0E
23 Saxmundham, England 52 13N 1 29E
72 Say, Niger 12 57N 2 25E
61 Sayan Mts., U.S.S.R. 54 0N 98 0E
63 Sayda (Sidon), Lebanon 33 33N 35 21E
63 Saynshand, Mongolia 45 0N 110 8E
92 Sayre, Pa., U.S.A. 41 57N 76 35W
41 Sazan, Albania 40 30N 19 20E
46 Sazava, R., Cz-slov. 49 42N 15 10E
64 Sazin, Kashmir 35 35N 73 25E
26 Scafell Pikes, England 54 28N 3 13W
27 Scalby & Ness, C., Eng. 54 18N 0 24W
32 Scalloway, Scotland 60 7N 1 22W
32 Scalpay I., Inner Hebrides 57 18N 6 0W
32 Scalpay I., Outer Hebrides, Scotland 57 51N 6 40W
48 & 49 Scandinavia Europe 65 0N 15 0E
33 Scapa Flow, Scotland 58 53N 3 2W
30 Scarba I., Scotland 56 10N 5 42W
27 Scarborough, England 54 13N 0 25W
34 Scariff, Ireland 52 55N 8 30W
32 Scarp, I., Scotland 58 1N 7 8W
34 Scattery I., Ireland 52 38N 9 30W
45 Schaffhausen & Canton, Switzerland 47 43N 8 38E
89 Schefferville, Canada 54 50N 66 55W
44 Schelde, R., Belgium 51 10N 4 15E
93 Schenectady, U.S.A. 42 47N 73 55W
44 Scheveningen, Neth. 52 7N 4 20E
44 Schiedam, Netherlands 51 55N 4 24E
31 Schiehallion, Scotland 56 39N 4 9W
44 Schiermonnikoog, Neth. 53 30N 6 15E
40 Schio, Italy 45 40N 11 20E
44 Schleiden, Germany 50 32N 6 26E
46 Schleswig, Germany 54 50N 9 30E
46 Schleswig Holstein, Länd, Germany 54 30N 9 36E
61 Schmidt I., U.S.S.R. 81 0N 91 0E
45 Schorndorf, Germany 48 47N 9 32E
44 Schoten, Belgium 51 15N 4 30E
44 Schouwen I., Neth. 51 41N 3 53E
45 Schramberg, Germany 48 13N 8 23E
92 Schreiber, Canada 48 50N 87 20W
45 Schwabischer Alb (Swabian Jura), mts., Germany 48 30N 9 30E
45 Schwäbisch Gmünd, Germany 48 48N 9 47E
68 Schwaner Ra., Indonesia 0 35S 112 30E
67 Schwangcheng, China 45 30N 126 20E
45 Schwarzwald (Black Forest), Germany 48 15N 8 10E
45 Schweinfurt, Germany 50 3N 10 12E
76 Schweizer Reneke, S. Africa 27 10S 25 20E
45 Schwenningen, Germany 48 4N 8 30E
45 Schwyz, & Cn., Switz. 47 2N 8 39E
40 Sciacca, Italy 37 30N 13 0E
40 Scilla, Italy 38 18N 15 44E
24 Scilly, Isles of, England 49 55N 6 20W
83 Scone, Australia 31 58S 150 57E
31 Scone, Scotland 56 25N 3 24W
29 Scotland, U.K. 56 0N 4 0W
100 Scott, Antarctica 78 15S 167 0E
90 Scottsbluff, U.S.A. 41 55N 103 37W
83 Scottsdale, Australia 41 9S 147 30E
36 Scrabby, Ireland 53 53N 7 32W
91 Scranton, U.S.A. 41 25N 75 30W
31 Scremerston, England 55 44N 1 59W
30 Scridain L., Scotland 56 22N 6 10W
27 Scunthorpe, England 53 33N 0 35W
23 Seaford, England 50 46N 0 7E
32 Seaforth L., Scotland 57 53N 6 38W
27 Seaham, England 54 50N 1 20W
26 Seaton, Cumb., England 54 41N 3 32W
24 Seaton, Devon, England 50 42N 3 3W
90 Seattle, U.S.A. 47 45N 122 20W
94 Sebastien Vizcaino B., Mexico 28 30N 115 0W
51 Sebin Karahisar, Turkey 40 20N 38 21E
44 Seclin, France 50 33N 3 2E
73 Second Cataract of Nile, Sudan 21 45N 31 12E
84 Secretary I., N.Z. 45 13S 166 58E
64 Secunderabad, India 17 40N 78 35E
91 Sedalia, U.S.A. 38 40N 93 20W
83 Sedan, Australia 34 33S 139 20E
43 Sedan, France 49 40N 5 0E
26 Sedbergh, England 54 18N 2 35W
84 Seddon, N.Z. 41 42S 174 5E
84 Seddonville, N.Z. 41 30S 172 0E
27 Sedgefield, England 54 40N 1 27W
72 Sedihou, Sénégal 12 50N 15 30W
63 Sedom, Israel 31 4N 35 24E
60 Sedov Pk., U.S.S.R. 73 30N 54 10E
75 Seeheim, S.W. Africa 26 48S 17 50E
50 Seg L., U.S.S.R. 63 20N 33 20E
72 Ségou, Mali 13 28N 6 16W
37 Segovia, Spain 40 58N 4 7W
37 Segre, R., Spain 42 10N 1 25E
72 Séguéla, Ivory Coast 8 5N 6 30W
37 Segura, R., Spain 38 8N 0 38W
64 Sehore, India 22 39N 77 4E
30 Seil I., Scotland 56 18N 5 37W
48 Seiland, Norway 70 30N 23 15E
61 Seimchan, U.S.S.R. 62 50N 152 30E
48 Seinäjoki, Finland 62 47N 22 58E
42 Seine, R., France 48 57N 2 25E
42 Seine-et-Marne, Dépt., Fr. 48 53N 3 0E
42 Seine-Maritime, Dépt., Fr. 49 40N 1 5E
42 Seine-St Denis, Dépt., Fr. 49 0N 2 30E
76 Sekoma, Botswana 24 35S 23 55E
72 Sekondi-Takoradi, Ghana 4 56N 1 43W
27 Selby, England 53 48N 1 5W
40 Sele, R., Italy 40 31N 15 0E
66 Selenge Mörön, R., China 49 0N 102 0E
43 Sélestat, France 48 18N 7 30E
72 Sélibaby, Mauritania 15 20N 12 15W
73 Selima Oasis, Sudan 21 20N 29 35E
88 Selkirk, Canada 50 8N 96 40W
31 Selkirk, Scotland 55 34N 2 51W
88 Selkirk Ra., Canada 51 0N 117 0W
91 Selma, U.S.A. 32 30N 86 59W
23 Selsey, England 50 44N 0 47W
23 Selsey Bill, England 50 43N 0 48W
75 Selukwe, Rhodesia 19 37S 30 0E
82 Selwyn, Australia 21 37S 140 32E
41 Seman, R., Albania 40 50N 19 50E
68 Semarang, Indonesia 6 55S 110 40E
91 Seminole, U.S.A. 35 10N 96 45W
60 Semipalatinsk, U.S.S.R. 50 30N 80 20E
60 Semiyarsk, U.S.S.R. 50 58N 78 40E
46 Semmering P., Austria 47 39N 15 50E
62 Semna, Sudan 20 28N 31 7E
44 Semois, R., Belgium 49 48N 5 12E
45 Sempach, Switzerland 47 9N 8 12E
43 Semur, France 47 30N 4 20E
75 Senanga, Zambia 15 59S 23 15E
67 Sendai, Japan 38 15N 141 0E
92 Seneca, L., U.S.A. 42 30N 77 0W
72 Sénégal, Africa 14 45N 15 0W
72 Senegal, R., Mali 13 55N 11 0W
70 Senegambia, Dist., West Africa 15 0N 14 0W
76 Senekal, O.F.S. 28 20S 27 40E
65 Senge Khambab (Indus), R., Tibet 32 30N 81 0E
40 Senigallia, Italy 43 43N 13 12E
48 Senja I., Norway 69 25N 17 30E
43 Senlis, France 49 10N 2 35E
98 Sena Madureira, Brazil 9 0S 68 45W
73 Sennar, Sudan 13 42N 33 57E
89 Senneterre, Canada 48 25N 77 15W
43 Sens, France 48 12N 3 18E
41 Senta, Yugoslavia 45 59N 20 1E
37 Séo de Urgel, Spain 42 18N 1 28E
67 Seoul, Korea 37 49N 127 15E
82 Sepik, R., Papua N.G. 4 0S 143 0E
89 Sept Iles, Canada 50 10N 63 30W
90 Sequoia National Park, U.S.A. 36 20N 118 30W
44 Seraing, Belgium 50 36N 5 33E
65 Serampore, India 22 44N 88 30E
68 Serang, Indonesia 5 55S 106 15E
41 Serbia Fed. Unit, Yugoslavia 43 20N 21 20E
52 Serdobsk, U.S.S.R. 52 33N 44 8E
68 Seremban, Malaya 2 35N 102 10E
75 Serenje, Zambia 13 2S 30 50E
41 Sereth, R., see Siret, R.
99 Sergipe, st., Brazil 10 40S 37 30W
68 Seria, Malaysia 4 30N 114 25E
41 Serifos, I., Greece 37 11N 24 30E
60 Serny Zavod, U.S.S.R. 40 5N 59 10E
60 Serov, U.S.S.R. 59 45N 60 20E
75 Serowe, Botswana 22 19S 27 1E
98 Serpents Mouth, Ven. 10 0N 61 30W
52 Serpukhov, U.S.S.R. 54 52N 37 40E
41 Serrai, Greece 41 0N 23 30E
43 Serres, France 44 22N 5 42E
75 Serule, Botswana 21 52S 27 32E
75 Sesfontein, S.W. Africa 19 7S 13 39E
37 Sestao, Spain 43 23N 3 5W
43 Sète, France 43 21N 3 40E
72 Sétif, Algeria 36 10N 5 23E
72 Settat, Morocco 33 0N 7 35W
74 Setté Cama, Gabon 2 32S 9 57E
26 Settle, England 54 4N 2 18W
37 Setubal, & B. of, Port. 38 33N 8 53W
88 Seul, L., Canada 50 25N 92 30W
62 Sevan L., U.S.S.R. 40 15N 45 20E
51 Sevastopol, U.S.S.R. 44 37N 33 30E
34 Seven Heads, C., Ireland 51 32N 8 40W
23 Sevenoaks, England 51 16N 0 12E
43 Sévérac, France 44 20N 3 5E
24 Severn Beach, England 51 34N 2 39W
22 Severn R., England 51 40N 2 35W
22 Severn Stoke, England 52 5N 2 13W
61 Severnaya Zemlya, U.S.S.R. 79 30N 97 0E
61 Severo-Yeniseisky, U.S.S.R. 60 25N 93 25E
50 Severodvinsk, U.S.S.R. 64 45N 40 0E
50 Severouralsk, U.S.S.R. 60 10N 59 30E
90 Sevier, R. & L., U.S.A. 39 0N 113 20W
37 Seville, Spain 37 27N 5 58W
88 Seward, Alaska 60 0N 149 30W
5 Seychelle Is., Indian Oc. 4 30S 55 30E
48 Seydisfjordur, Iceland 65 15N 13 52W
83 Seymour, Australia 36 58S 145 10E
43 Sézanne, France 48 40N 3 45E
47 Sfântu Gheorghe, Rum. 45 50N 25 50E
73 Sfax, Tunisia 34 49N 10 42E
44 's Gravenhage, Netherland, see The Hague
32 Sgurr Mor, Mt., Scotland 57 42N 5 0W
32 Sgurr na Ciche, Scotland 57 0N 5 29W
32 Sgurr na Lapaich Mt., Scotland 57 21N 5 14W
74 Shaba, reg., Zaïre 9 50S 26 0E
65 Shaba Gomba, China 32 10N 89 0E
75 Shabani, Rhodesia 20 15S 30 14E
62 Shabicha, Iraq 30 52N 43 45E
100 Shackleton, Antarctica 79 0S 39 0W

60 Shadrinsk, U.S.S.R. 56 15N 64 0E
22 Shaftesbury, England 51 1N 2 12W
64 Shahgarh, India 27 15N 69 50E
73 Shahhat (Cyrene), Libya 32 40N 21 30E
63 Shahr-i-Zabul, Afghanistan 31 0N 61 20E
63 Shahrig, Pakistan 30 12N 67 35E
62 Shahriza, Iran 32 0N 51 57E
64 Shajapur, India 23 20N 76 15E
52 Shakhty, U.S.S.R. 47 40N 40 10E
72 Shaki, Nigeria 8 41N 3 21E
74 Shala, L., Ethiopia 7 30N 38 30E
73 Shallal, El, Egypt 24 0N 33 0E
66 Shamo, Desert, see Gobi Desert
74 Shamo, L., Ethiopia 5 50N 37 40E
75 Shamva, Rhodesia 17 15S 31 40E
65 Shan State, Burma 21 5N 100 0E
34 Shanagolden, Ireland 52 35N 9 6W
72 Shanga, Nigeria 11 1N 4 40E
75 Shangani, R., Rhodesia 18 37S 28 0E
67 Shanghai, China 31 15N 121 35E
66 Shangiao, China 28 20N 116 15E
66 Shangkiu, China 34 35N 116 0E
22 Shanklin, I. of W., Eng. 50 38N 1 12W
84 Shannon, N.Z. 40 35S 175 40E
34 Shannon, R. Ireland 52 36N 9 40W
34 Shannonbridge, Ireland 53 18N 8 1W
66 Shan-si, Prov., China 37 30N 112 0E
61 Shantar I., U.S.S.R. 55 0N 137 30E
66 Shan-tung, Prov., China 36 30N 119 30E
67 Shaohing, China 30 2N 120 30E
67 Shaowu, China 27 25N 117 0E
66 Shaoyang, China 27 15N 111 15E
26 Shap, England 54 31N 2 43W
33 Shapinsay, I. & Sd., Scot. 59 3N 2 51W
64 Sharja, U.A.E. 25 17N 55 18E
63 Sharkh, Oman 21 20N 59 5E
92 Sharon, U.S.A. 41 18N 80 30W
63 Sharon, Plain of. Israel 32 20N 34 55E
63 Sharqiya, Jordan 32 11N 35 15E
66 Sha-si, China 30 25N 112 12E
88 Shaunavon, Canada 49 30N 108 40W
93 Shawinigan, Can. 46 45N 73 0W
91 Shawnee, U.S.A. 35 16N 96 59W
64 Shazia, Tibet, China 33 10N 82 40E
47 Shchara, R., U.S.S.R. 53 20N 25 10E
91 Sheboygan, U.S.A. 43 47N 87 43W
93 Shediac, Canada 46 18N 64 28W
35 Sheefry Hills, Ireland 53 40N 9 40W
36 Sheelin, L., Ireland 53 49N 7 17W
36 Sheep Haven, Ireland 55 12N 7 53W
34 Sheeps Hd., Ireland 51 31N 9 50W
23 Sheerness, England 51 26N 0 45E
63 Shefar'am, Israel 32 48N 35 10E
27 Sheffield, England 52 23N 1 28W
66 Shehung, China 30 45N 105 0E
34 Shehy Mts., Ra., Ireland 51 47N 9 15W
63 Sheikh Miskin, Syria 32 50N 36 10E
65 Shekar Dzong, China 28 45N 87 0E
66 Sheklung, China 23 4N 113 50E
93 Shelburne, Canada 43 49N 65 19W
61 Shelekhov G., U.S.S.R. 59 50N 157 0E
83 Shellharbour, Australia 34 35S 150 57E
91 Shenandoah, U.S.A. 40 48N 95 22W
92 Shenandoah, R., U.S.A. 38 30N 78 40W
72 Shendi, Sudan 16 57N 33 46E
23 Shenfield, England 51 39N 0 21E
66 Shensi, Prov., China 35 0N 109 0E
65 Shentsa, Tibet, China 30 52N 88 30E
67 Shenyang, China 41 50N 124 0E
64 Sheopur Kalan, India 25 40N 76 40E
47 Shepetovka, U.S.S.R. 50 10N 27 0E
83 Shepparton, Australia 36 25S 145 28E
23 Sheppey I., England 51 23N 0 50E
22 Shepshed, England 52 47N 1 18W
24 Shepton Mallet, England 51 11N 2 31W
22 Sherborne, England 50 57N 2 32W
22 Sherborne St. John, Eng. 51 17N 1 7W
72 Sherbro, I., Sierra Leone 7 25N 12 40W
93 Sherbrooke, Canada 45 21N 71 57W
27 Sherburn, England 53 47N 1 15W
36 Shercock, Ireland 54 0N 6 54W
23 Shere, England 51 13N 0 28W
22 Sherfield English, Eng. 51 1N 1 35W
90 Sheridan, U.S.A. 44 48N 106 56W
23 Sheringham, England 52 57N 1 14E
34 Sherkin I., Ireland 51 28N 9 25W
91 Sherman, U.S.A. 33 40N 96 40W
88 Sherridon, Canada 55 10N 101 20W
44 s'Hertogenbosch, Neth. 51 42N 5 18E
27 Sherwood Forest, Eng. 53 12N 1 10W
61 Shestakovo, U.S.S.R. 68 25N 147 5E
32 Shetland Is., & Reg., Scotland 60 20N 1 20W
60 Shevchenko, U.S.S.R. 43 25N 51 30E
91 Sheyenne R., U.S.A. 47 30N 98 15W
32 Shiant Is., & Sd., Scot. 57 54N 6 20W
63 Shibam, South Yemen 16 0N 48 45E
93 Shickshock Mts., Can. 48 55N 66 30W
32 Shiel, L., Scotland 56 50N 5 30W
22 Shifnal, England 52 39N 2 22W
67 Shiga, Pref., Japan 35 15N 135 50E
73 Shigaib, Sudan 15 5N 23 35E
65 Shigatse, Tibet, China 29 27N 88 55E
66 Shihkiachwang, China 38 0N 114 30E
66 Shihlu, China 19 10N 109 0E
64 Shikarpur, Pakistan 28 3N 68 40E
67 Shikoku I., Japan 33 30N 133 30E
27 Shildon, England 54 37N 1 39W
61 Shilka, U.S.S.R. 51 48N 116 0E
35 Shillelagh, Ireland 52 45N 6 30W
65 Shillong, India 25 30N 91 55E
63 Shilo, Jordan 32 4N 35 16E
67 Shimada, Japan 34 45N 138 10E
67 Shimane. Pref., Japan 35 0N 132 0E
67 Shimabara, Japan 32 40N 130 25E
67 Shimizu, Japan 35 6N 138 10E
64 Shimoga, India 13 57N 75 32E
67 Shimonoseki, Japan 33 58N 131 0E
33 Shin, L. & R., Scotland 58 5N 4 30W
64 Shindand, Afghan. 33 15N 62 10E
67 Shinjo, Japan 38 55N 140 26E
74 Shinkolobwe, Zaïre 11 10S 26 40E
34 Shinrone, Ireland 53 0N 7 58W
74 Shinyanga, Tanzania 3 38S 33 20E
67 Shio, C., Japan 33 30N 135 45E
67 Shiogama, Japan 38 16N 141 5E
41 Shipka, Bulgaria 42 40N 25 25E
64 Shipki La, India 31 45N 78 40E
26 Shipley, England 53 50N 1 47W
93 Shippigan, Canada 47 44N 64 48W
22 Shipston-on-Stour, Eng. 52 4N 1 39W
63 Shiqma, R., Israel 31 35N 34 35E
62 Shir Kuh, mt., Iran 31 32N 54 10E
62 Shiraz, Iran 29 38N 52 38E
75 Shire, R., Malawi 16 30S 35 15E
27 Shirebrook, England 53 13N 1 11W
66 Shiukwan, China 25 0N 113 5E
64 Shivpuri, India 25 30N 77 36E
67 Shizuoka, & Pref., Japan 34 59N 138 30E
41 Shkodër, Albania 42 3N 19 38E
41 Shkumbin, R., Albania 41 0N 19 24E
23 Shoeburyness, England 51 31N 0 48E
64 Sholapur, India 17 40N 76 0E
23 Shoreham-by-Sea, Eng. 50 50N 0 17W
75 Shoshong, Botswana 22 59S 26 41E
91 Shreveport, U.S.A. 32 30N 93 50W
22 Shrewsbury, England 52 43N 2 44W
22 Shropshire, Co., see Salop
62 Shuqra, South Yemen 13 25N 45 37E
62 Shushtar, Iran 32 0N 48 47E
52 Shuya, U.S.S.R. 56 53N 41 28E
65 Shwebo, Burma 22 36N 95 50E
50 Shyaulyali (Siauliai), U.S.S.R. 56 0N 23 20E
64 Shyok, & R., Kashmir 34 15N 78 5E
64 Siahan Ra., Pakistan 27 30N 64 30E
66 Siakwan, China 25 45N 100 10E
64 Sialkot, Pakistan 32 36N 74 37E
57 Siam, see Thailand
68 Siam, G. of, S.E. Asia 11 0N 101 0E
66 Sian, China 34 15N 109 0E
66 Siang, R., China 26 45N 112 30E
65 Siang, R., see Dihang, R.
66 Siangfan, China 32 15N 112 2E
66 Siang-tan, China 27 48N 112 45E
68 Siargao I., Philippines 9 50N 126 0E
50 Siauliai (Shyaulyali), U.S.S.R. 56 0N 23 20E
40 Sibenik, Yugoslavia 43 46N 15 54E
60 Siberia, N. Asia 62 0N 110 0E
68 Siberut, I., Indonesia 1 30S 98 45E
74 Sibiti, Congo (Fr.) 3 38S 13 9E
41 Sibiu, Rumania 45 43N 24 11E
23 Sible Hedingham, Eng. 51 58N 0 37E
68 Sibolga, Indonesia 1 50N 98 45E
65 Sibsagar, India 27 0N 94 42E
68 Sibu, Sarawak, Malaysia 2 25N 111 50E
68 Sibuko Bay, Malaysia 4 10N 118 0E
68 Sibuyan, I. Philippines 12 30N 122 30E
68 Sibuyan Sea, Philippines 12 30N 122 30E
66 Sichang, China 28 15N 101 45E
40 Sicily, I., Italy 37 40N 14 0E
73 Sidi Barrâni, Egypt 31 35N 26 0E
72 Sidi-Bel Abbes, Algeria 35 12N 0 42W
32 Sidlaw Hills, Scotland 56 30N 3 15W
24 Sidmouth, England 50 41N 3 14W
90 Sidney, U.S.A. 41 18N 103 0W
73 Sidra, G. of, Libya 31 30N 19 0E
44 Sieg, R., Germany 50 48N 7 15E
44 Siegburg, Germany 50 48N 7 12E
44 Siegen, Germany 50 51N 8 5E
40 Siena, Italy 43 20N 11 20E
66 Sienyang, China 34 20N 108 48E
72 Sierra Leone, W. Africa 8 20N 12 0W
90 Sierra Nevada, Mts., U.S.A. 39 0N 119 0W
41 Sifnos, I., Greece 36 50N 24 40E
47 Sighet, Rumania 47 54N 23 57E
47 Sighisoara, Rumania 46 13N 24 50E
27 Sighty Crag, mt., Eng. 55 8N 2 34W
48 Siglufjordur, Iceland 66 10N 18 58W
43 Sigmaringen, Germany 48 2N 9 13E
44 Signy l'Abbaye, France 49 40N 4 25E
49 Sigtuna, Sweden 59 40N 17 38E
37 Siguenza, Spain 41 0N 2 30W
72 Siguiri, Guinea 11 34N 9 5W
68 Sihanoukville, see Kompong Som
72 Sikasso, Mali 11 25N 5 45W
61 Sikhote Alin Ra., U.S.S.R. 47 0N 137 0E
66 Si-kiang, R., China 23 30N 110 30E
41 Sikinos, I., Greece 36 40N 25 5E
65 Sikkim, N.E. India 27 30N 88 30E
37 Sil, R., Spain 42 21N 7 0W
65 Silchar, India 24 50N 93 2E
65 Silgarhi Doti, Nepal 29 15N 81 0E
65 Silghat, India 26 40N 93 0E
62 Silifke, Turkey 36 20N 34 0E
65 Siliguri, India 26 45N 88 25E
41 Silistra, Bulgaria 44 5N 27 20E
49 Siljan, L., & mt., Sweden 60 52N 14 50E
49 Silkeborg, Denmark 56 10N 9 32E
26 Silsden, England 53 55N 1 55W
94 Silver City, Panama Canal Zone (Inset)
90 Silver City, U.S.A. 32 50N 108 20W
34 Silvermines, Ireland 52 48N 8 15W
45 Silvrettahorn, mt., Switz. 46 55N 10 10E
50 Simbirsk, see Ulyanovsk
92 Simcoe, Canada 42 52N 80 20W
61 Simenga, U.S.S.R. 62 47N 107 50E
68 Simeulue I., Indonesia 2 45N 96 0E
51 Simferopol, U.S.S.R. 44 55N 34 5E
65 Simikot, Nepal 30 0N 81 45E
64 Simla, India 31 5N 77 17E
48 Simo L. & R., Finland 66 10N 27 0E
27 Simonside, mt., England 55 15N 2 0W
76 Simonstown, C. Prov. 34 15S 18 28E
45 Simplon P. & Tunnel, Switzerland 46 17N 8 7E
81 Simpson Des., Australia 25 0S 137 0E
61 Simushir, I., U.S.S.R. 47 20N 152 30E
73 Sinai, Pen., Egypt 28 40N 33 40E
94 Sinaloa, Mexico 25 50N 107 55W
72 Sinawan, Libya 31 0N 10 30E
33 Sinclairs B., Scotland 58 30N 3 7W
64 Sind Sagar Doab, Plat., Pakistan 32 0N 71 30E
37 Sines, Portugal 37 58N 8 53W
62 Singa, Sudan 13 15N 33 59E
68 Singapore, I., Asia 1 0N 104 30E
68 Singaraja, Indonesia 8 0S 115 15E
45 Singen, Germany 47 45N 8 48E
74 Singida, Tanzania 4 50S 34 50E
41 Singitkós, G., Greece 40 5N 24 0E
83 Singleton, Australia 32 33S 151 10E
68 Singora, Thailand, see Songkhla
66 Singtai, China 37 25N 114 45E
66 Sinhailien, China 34 30N 119 10E
66 Sinhsien, China 38 40N 112 15E
66 Sining, China 36 40N 100 45E
73 Sinkat, Sudan 19 0N 37 0E
66 Sinkiang-Uigur, A.R., China 40 30N 87 0E
40 Sinni, R., Italy 40 5N 16 20E
75 Sinoia, Rhodesia 17 20S 30 2E
51 Sinop, Turkey 42 0N 35 7E
66 Sinsiang, China 35 15N 113 55E
68 Sintang, Indonesia 0 10N 111 35E
37 Sintra, Portugal 38 45N 9 30W
66 Sinuiju, China 40 0N 124 40E
66 Sinyang, China 32 7N 114 10E
45 Sion, Switzerland 46 15N 7 23E
36 Sion Mills, Ireland 54 47N 7 29W
91 Sioux City, U.S.A. 42 40N 96 17W
91 Sioux Falls, U.S.A. 43 35N 96 48W
91 Sious Lookout, Canada 50 10N 92 30W
94 Siparia, Trinidad 10 50N 61 30W
68 Sipora, I., Indonesia 2 5S 99 40E
81 Sir Edward Pellew Group, Australia 15 30S 137 10E
40 Siracusa, Italy 37 7N 15 18E
65 Sirajganj, Bangladesh 23 56N 89 57E
74 Sire, Ethiopia 9 10N 37 5E
47 Siret, R., Rumania 45 40N 27 20E
62 Sirhan, Wadi, Jordan 30 45N 38 30E
64 Sirohi, India 24 46N 72 50E
64 Sironj, India 24 8N 77 50E
41 Siros I., Greece 37 30N 24 55E
64 Sirsa, India 29 4N 75 1E
40 Sisak, Yugoslavia 45 30N 16 20E
68 Sisaket, Thailand 15 10N 104 25E
44 Sissonne, France 49 36N 3 52E
64 Sistan, reg., Afghan. 31 0N 61 30E
43 Sisteron, France 44 10N 5 58E
65 Sitapur, India 27 15N 81 0E
88 Sitka, Alaska 57 6N 135 12W
65 Sittang R., Burma 18 0N 97 0E
44 Sittard, Netherlands 50 59N 5 48E
23 Sittingbourne, England 51 20N 0 43E
51 Sivas, Turkey 39 50N 37 2E
51 Sivrihisar, Turkey 39 35N 31 30E
73 Siwa, Egypt 29 18N 25 38E
65 Siwalik Ra., Nepal 27 0N 84 0E
65 Siwan, India 26 15N 84 20E
34 Sixmilebridge, Ireland 52 45N 8 46W
36 Sixmilecross, N. Ireland 54 34N 7 7W
73 Sixth Cataract, Sudan 16 20N 33 2E
23 Sizewell, England 52 13N 1 25E
49 Sjælland, Denmark 55 30N 11 30E
48 Sjönsta, Norway 67 10N 15 50E
48 Skaga Fjord, Iceland 66 0N 19 30W
49 Skagastölstindane, Mt., Norway 61 25N 8 0E
48 Skagaströnd, Iceland 65 50N 20 12W
49 Skagen, Denmark 57 45N 10 35E
49 Skagen (The Skaw), Den. 57 48N 10 40E
49 Skagerrak, Scandinavia 57 30N 9 0E
88 Skagway, Alaska 59 22N 135 8W
49 Skara, Sweden 58 26N 13 23E
49 Skaraborg, Co., Sweden 58 45N 14 0E
64 Skardu, India 35 15N 75 40E
33 Skateraw, Scotland 57 1N 2 9W
49 Skaw, The, see Skagen
88 Skeena, R., Canada 55 0N 128 30W
27 Skegness, England 53 10N 0 20E
48 Skellefte, R., Sweden 65 30N 19 15E
48 Skellefteå, Sweden 64 48N 20 53E
48 Skelleftestrand, Sweden 64 43N 21 14E
27 Skellingthorpe, England 53 15N 0 35W
26 Skelmersdale, England 53 34N 2 49W
27 Skelton, England 54 33N 0 59W
35 Skerries, Ireland 53 36N 6 4W
25 Skerries, The, Wales 53 26N 4 37W
34 Skibbereen, Ireland 51 34N 9 14W
26 Skiddaw, mt., England 54 38N 3 5W
49 Skien, Norway 59 14N 9 32E
47 Skierniewice, Poland 52 0N 20 20E
72 Skikda (Philippeville), Algeria 36 55N 6 58E
26 Skipton, England 53 58N 2 2W
41 Skiros, I., Greece 38 45N 24 38E
49 Skive, Denmark 56 33N 9 2E
49 Skjalfandafljót, R., Ice. 65 30N 17 30W
48 Skjalfandi, Fd., Iceland 66 0N 17 30W
49 Skoghall, Sweden 59 23N 13 7E
25 Skomer I., Wales 51 44N 5 18W
41 Skopje, Yugoslavia 42 1N 21 26E
49 Skövde, Sweden 58 15N 13 59E
61 Skovorodino, U.S.S.R. 54 0N 125 0E
49 Skudeneshavn, Norway 59 10N 5 10E
46 Skwierzyna, Poland 52 35N 15 30E
32 Skye, I., Scotland 57 25N 6 20W
36 Slane, Ireland 53 43N 6 32W
35 Slaney, R., Ireland 52 52N 6 45W
47 Slatina, Rumania 44 23N 24 23E
60 Slavgorod, U.S.S.R. 53 20N 79 0E
46 Slavkov (Austerlitz), Czechoslovakia 49 10N 16 52E
51 Slavyansk, U.S.S.R. 48 50N 37 35E
34 Slea Hd., Ireland 52 7N 10 30W
27 Sleaford, England 53 0N 0 23W
32 Sleat, Sd., Scot. 57 6N 5 55W
32 Sleat, Pt. of, Scotland 57 1N 6 0W
44 Sliedrecht, Netherlands 51 51N 4 45E
40 Sliema, Malta 35 56N 14 18E
36 Slieve Anierin, mt., Ire. 54 5N 7 57W
34 Slieve Aughty, mts., Ire. 53 5N 8 32W
34 Slieve Bernagh, mt., Ire. 52 50N 8 30W
35 Slieve Bloom, mts., Ire. 53 4N 7 40W
36 Slieve Donard, mt., N. Ire. 54 8N 5 53W
34 Slieve Felim, mt., Ireland 52 40N 8 5W
36 Slieve Gamph (Ox. Mts.), Ireland 54 6N 9 0W
36 Slieve Gullion, mt., N. Ire. 54 6N 6 27W
36 Slieve League, mt., Ire. 54 40N 8 35W
34 Slieve Mish, mt., Ireland 52 13N 9 55W
34 Slieve Miskish, mt., Ire. 51 40N 9 55W
35 Slieve More, mt., Ireland 54 1N 10 4W
35 Slieve Snaght, mt., Ire. 55 0N 8 18W
36 Slieve Tooey, mt., Ire. 54 46N 8 39W
35 Slievenamon, mt., Ire. 52 25N 7 37W
36 Sligo & Co., Ireland 54 16N 8 28W
36 Sligo B., Ireland 54 18N 8 40W
32 Slioch, Mt., Scotland 57 40N 5 12W
48 Slite, Sweden 57 41N 18 43E
41 Sliven, Bulgaria 42 41N 26 20E
47 Slonim, U.S.S.R. 53 2N 25 19E
23 Slough, England 51 30N 0 35W
47 Slovakia, Dist., Cz-slov. 48 50N 20 0E
47 Slovakian Ore Mts., Czechoslovakia 48 30N 19 30E
46 Slovenia, Fed. Unit, Yugoslavia 46 0N 15 0E
47 Sluch, R., U.S.S.R. 50 48N 27 10E
34 Slyne Hd., Ireland 53 25N 10 11W
34 Smerwick Hr., Ireland 52 13N 10 34W
22 Smethwick, England 52 29N 1 58W
36 Smithborough, Ireland 54 13N 7 8W
76 Smithfield, S. Africa 30 13S 25 37E
92 Smith's Falls, Canada 44 55N 76 0W
83 Smithton, Australia 41 58S 145 2E
83 Smithton & Gladstone, Australia 31 0S 153 0E
90 Smoky Hill R., U.S.A. 38 55N 100 30W
48 Smöla, I., Norway 63 23N 8 3E
50 Smolensk, U.S.S.R. 54 40N 31 50E
41 Smolikas, mt., Greece 40 15N 21 0E
41 Smolyan, Bulgaria 41 36N 24 38E
41 Smyrna, see Izmir
26 Snaefell, mt., Isle of Man 54 14N 4 26W
48 Snaefell Mt., Iceland 64 47N 15 30W
48 Snaefells Jökull, mt., Ice. 64 47N 23 45W
27 Snainton, England 54 14N 0 33W
90 Snake R., U.S.A. 43 30N 116 50W
44 Sneek, Netherlands 53 2N 5 41E
76 Sneeuwberge Mts., C. Prov., S. Africa 31 55S 24 30E
46 Snezka, mt., Poland 50 40N 15 55E
32 Snizort, L., Scotland 57 34N 6 30W
48 Snöhetta, mt., Norway 62 10N 9 40E
25 Snowdon, mt., Wales 53 4N 4 10W
88 Snowdrift, Canada 62 10N 110 0W
83 Snowy Mts., Australia 36 30S 148 20E
83 Snowy R., Australia 37 0S 148 23E
47 Snyatyn, U.S.S.R. 48 30N 25 40E
75 Soalala, Madagascar 16 3S 45 30E
32 Soay I. & Sd., Scotland 57 9N 6 13W
99 Sobral, Brazil 3 46S 40 30W
57 So-ch'e, China 38 15N 77 0E
4 Society Is., Pacific Ocean 17 30S 151 0W
90 Socorro, U.S.A. 34 3N 106 50W
63 Socotra I., E. Africa 12 37N 54 0E
49 Söderhamn, Sweden 61 20N 17 0E
49 Söderköping, Sweden 58 28N 16 20E
49 Södermanland, Co., Swed. 59 2N 17 20E
49 Södertalje, Sweden 59 12N 17 35E
44 Soest, Netherlands 52 10N 5 19E
41 Sofia, Bulgaria 42 40N 23 30E
61 Sofiiski, U.S.S.R. 52 10N 133 55E
49 Sogndalsfjöra, Norway 61 15N 7 4E
49 Sogne and Fjordane, Co., Norway 61 30N 6 30E
49 Sogne Fd., Norway 61 8N 6 0E
73 Sohag, Egypt 26 30N 31 43E
23 Soham, England 52 20N 0 20E
37 Soignies, Belgium 50 35N 4 5E
43 Soissons, France 49 25N 3 19E
47 Sokal, U.S.S.R. 50 30N 24 16E
72 Sokodé, Togo 8 55N 1 12E
47 Sokólka, Poland 53 28N 23 30E
72 Sokolo, Mali 14 50N 6 18W
72 Sokoto, Nigeria 13 3N 5 15E
50 So Iletsk, U.S.S.R. 51 20N 54 50E
68 Solano, Philippines 16 40N 121 15E
22 Solent, The, England 50 45N 1 30W
79 Solfonn, Mt., Norway 60 2N 6 57E
22 Solihull, England 52 26N 1 47W
98 Solimoes, R., Brazil 2 30S 66 30W
44 Solingen, Germany 51 11N 7 5E
48 Solleftea, Sweden 63 8N 17 5E
81 Solomon Is., Pacific Oc. 7 0S 158 0E
82 Solomon Sea, Papua N.G. 8 0S 153 0E
45 Solothurn, Switzerland 47 14N 7 33E
45 Solothurn, Canton, Switz. 47 19N 7 42E
49 Sölvesborg, Sweden 56 5N 14 35E
26 Solway Firth, Irish Sea 54 50N 3 40W
75 Solwezi, Zambia 12 18S 26 20E
70 Somali Pen., E. Africa 7 0N 44 0E
71 Somali Rep., E. Africa 4 0N 45 0E
94 Sombrerete, Mexico 23 35N 103 35W
23 Somerby, England 52 42N 0 49W
91 Somerset, U.S.A. 37 5N 84 45W
24 Somerset, Co., England 51 5N 3 0W
76 Somerset E., S. Africa 32 42S 25 45E
95 Somerset, & I., Bermuda 32 18N 64 52W
88 Somerset, I., Canada 73 0N 95 0W
76 Somerset W., S. Africa 34 3S 18 50E
23 Somersham, England 52 24N 0 1W
24 Somerton, England 51 4N 2 43W
47 Somes, R., Rumania 47 42N 23 10E
42 Somme, Dépt., France 49 55N 1 53E
43 Somme, R., France 50 15N 1 30E
43 Sommières, France 43 50N 4 0E
41 Somovit, Bulgaria 43 40N 24 45E
23 Sompting, England 50 51N 0 20W
49 Sonderborg, Denmark 54 58N 9 49E
89 Sondre Stromfjord, Greenland 67 10N 50 10W
45 Sondrio, Italy 46 10N 9 52E
64 Sonepat, India 29 0N 77 0E
65 Sonepur, India 20 55N 83 45E
74 Songea, Tanzania 11 0S 35 45E
68 Songkhla (Singora), Thailand 7 25N 100 40E
73 Songo, Sudan 10 0N 24 15E
94 Sonora R., Mexico 29 5N 111 0W
94 Sonsonate, Salvador 13 45N 89 50W
45 Sonthofen, Germany 47 31N 10 17E
67 Soochow, China 31 20N 120 40E
47 Sopot, Poland 54 14N 18 17E
48 Sör Trondelag, Co., Nor. 63 0N 9 30E
89 Sorel, Canada 45 57N 73 10W
63 Soreq, R., Israel 31 50N 34 50E
40 Sorgono, Italy 40 0N 9 0E
37 Soria, Spain 41 48N 2 28W
32 Sorisdale, Scotland 56 40N 6 28W
99 Sorocaba, Brazil 23 30S 47 20W
47 Soroki, U.S.S.R. 48 8N 28 12E
74 Soroti, Uganda 2 0N 33 45E
48 Söröy Sound, Norway 70 25N 23 0E
48 Soroya, I., Norway 70 40N 22 30E
47 Sosnowiec, Poland 50 20N 19 30E
41 Soudhas B., Greece 35 31N 24 10E
94 Soufrière, St. Lucia, W.I. 13 45N 61 4W
49 Sound, The, Denmark 56 7N 12 30E
88 Souris, Canada 49 35N 100 30W
90 Souris R., U.S.A. & Canada 48 30N 101 30W
73 Sousse, Tunisia 35 51N 10 38E
42 Soustons, France 43 44N 1 10W
76 South Africa, Africa 30 0S 24 0E
84 South Auckland, Bay of Plenty, Dist., N.Z. 38 0S 176 0E
80 South Australia, st. 29 40S 135 0E
26 South Barrule, mt., Isle of Man 54 8N 4 40W
91 South Bend, U.S.A. 41 44N 86 17W
23 South Benfleet, England 51 33N 0 34E
91 South Carolina, st., U.S.A. 34 0N 81 0W
68 South China Sea 10 0N 112 0E
90 South Dakota, st., U.S.A. 45 20N 100 0W
24 South Dorset Downs, England 50 45N 2 38W
23 South Downs, Ra., Eng. 50 55N 0 30W
27 South Elkington, England 53 22N 0 5W
23 South Foreland, England 51 8N 1 23E
94 South Gamboa, Panama Canal Zone (Inset).
100 South Georgia, I., Falkland Is. Dep. 54 30S 36 0W
25 South Glamorgan, Co., Wales 51 30N 3 20W
23 South Hayling, England 50 47N 0 56W
74 South Horr, Kenya 2 20N 36 48E
100 South Ice, Antarctica 81 30S 28 0W
84 South Invercargill, N.Z. 46 28S 168 22E
84 South I., New Zealand 44 30S 170 0E
27 South Kirby, England 53 35N 1 25W
24 South Molton, England 51 1N 3 51W
65 South Moscos Is., see Launglon Bok Is.
88 South Nahanni & R., Canada 61 5N 123 30W
68 South Naturna Is., Indon. 2 50N 108 25E
100 South Orkneys, Is., Falkland Is. Dep. 60 30S 45 0W
68 South Pagai I., Indonesia 3 0S 100 20E
90 South Platte R., U.S.A. 40 25N 104 0W
33 South Ronaldsay, Scot. 58 47N 2 58W
100 South Sandwich Is., Falkland Is. Dep. 59 0S 27 0W
88 South Saskatchewan R., Canada 51 0N 109 0W
100 South Shetlands, Is., Falkland Is. Dep. 60 30S 60 0W
27 South Shields, England 55 0N 1 27W
32 South Uist I., Scotland 57 15N 7 22W
75 South West Africa, see Namibia
84 South West C., N.Z. 47 32S 167 30E
62 South Yemen, Asia 15 0N 47 00E
27 South Yorkshire, Co., England 53 30N 1 25W
22 Southampton, England 50 55N 1 24W
89 Southampton I., Canada 64 30N 84 0W
22 Southampton Water, Eng. 50 52N 1 21W
23 Southborough, England 51 8N 0 17E

84 Southbridge, N.Z. 43 45S 172 17E
23 Southend-on-Sea, Eng. 51 33N 0 43E
30 Southend, Scotland 55 18N 5 38W
84 Southern Alps, N.Z. 43 30S 170 30E
80 Southern Cross, Australia 31 9S 119 21E
88 Southern Indian L., Can. 57 15N 99 0W
73 Southern Darfur, prov., Sudan 10 0N 25 0E
73 Southern Kardofan, prov., Sudan 12 0N 30 0E
4 Southern Ocean 60 0S 128 0E
75 Southern Rhodesia, *see* Rhodesia.
31 Southern Uplands, Scot. 55 30N 4 0W
84 Southland, Dist., N.Z. 44 50S 167 30E
26 Southport, England 53 39N 2 59W
83 Southport, Australia 28 0S 153 30E
23 Southwark, Greater London, England 51 29N 0 5W
27 Southwell, England 53 5N 0 57W
23 Southwick, England 50 50N 0 14W
23 Southwold, England 52 19N 1 42E
49 Sovetsk, U.S.S.R. 55 6N 21 50E
61 Sovetskaya Gavan (Soviet Harbour), U.S.S.R. 48 55N 140 5E
27 Sowerby, England 54 13N 1 19W
44 Spa, Belgium 50 30N 5 53E
37 Spain, Europe 39 50N 3 40W
83 Spalding, Australia 33 27S 138 30E
23 Spalding, England 52 47N 0 9W
46 Spandau, Germany 52 35N 13 7E
90 Spanish Fork, U.S.A. 40 6N 111 40W
72 Spanish Sahara, *see* Western Sahara
95 Spanish Town, Jamaica, W.I. 18 0N 76 59W
90 Sparks, U.S.A. 39 30N 119 37W
91 Spartanburg, U.S.A. 34 58N 81 57W
41 Sparti, Greece 37 7N 22 18E
40 Spartivento, C., Italy 38 56N 8 57E
40 Spartivento, C., Italy 37 58N 16 7E
67 Spassk-Dalni, U.S.S.R. 44 45N 132 55E
41 Spatha, C., Greece 35 40N 23 50E
33 Spean Bridge, Scotland 56 53N 4 55W
94 Speightstown, Barbados, W.I. 13 15N 59 8W
83 Spencer, C., Australia 35 20S 136 50E
83 Spencer G., Australia 34 0S 137 0E
27 Spennymoor, England 54 43N 1 35W
84 Spenser Mts., N.Z. 42 0S 172 30E
36 Sperrin Mts., N. Ireland 54 50N 7 5W
46 Spessart Mts., Germany 50 10N 9 25E
33 Spey, R., Scotland 57 40N 3 5W
45 Speyer, Germany 49 22N 8 28E
35 Spiddal, Ireland 53 14N 9 19W
40 Spinazzola, Italy 41 0N 16 5E
23 Spithead, England 50 43N 0 56W
100 Spitsbergen (Svalbard), Arctic Ocean 80 0N 20 0E
40 Split, Yugoslavia 43 32N 16 30E
45 Splugen Pass, Switzerland 46 30N 9 20E
90 Spokane, U.S.A. 47 48N 118 25W
40 Spoleto, Italy 42 46N 12 47E
41 Sporades Is., N., Greece 39 20N 24 0E
68 Spratly I., S. China Sea 8 45N 111 30E
46 Spree, R., Germany 51 30N 14 30E
46 Spremberg, Germany 51 33N 14 21E
75 Springbok, S. Africa 29 48S 17 57E
91 Springfield, Ill., U.S.A. 39 23N 89 42W
93 Springfield, Mass., U.S.A. 42 0N 73 0W
91 Springfield, Ohio, U.S.A. 39 42N 84 15W
90 Springfield, Ore., U.S.A. 44 0N 123 0W
93 Springhill, Canada 45 45N 64 0W
76 Springs, Trans., S. Afr. 26 14S 28 21E
82 Springsure, Australia 24 2S 148 0E
90 Springville, Utah, U.S.A. 40 13N 111 35W
27 Sproatley, England 53 46N 0 9W
75 Spungabera, Mozam. 20 28S 32 47E
27 Spurn Hd., England 53 37N 0 8E
88 Squamish, Canada 49 45N 123 10W
40 Squillace, Italy 38 50N 16 26E
61 Sredinny Ra., U.S.S.R. 57 0N 159 0E
61 Sredne Kolymsk, U.S.S.R. 67 20N 153 25E
61 Sredne Tambovskoye, U.S.S.R. 50 50N 137 50E
61 Sredne Vilyuisk, U.S.S.R. 63 50N 123 10E
41 Sremska Mitrovica, Yugoslavia 44 59N 19 35E
68 Srepok, R., Khmer Rep. & Vietnam 13 30N 107 0E
61 Sretensk, U.S.S.R. 52 10N 117 50E
64 Sri Lanka, Asia 8 0N 80 45E
64 Srinagar, Kashmir 34 5N 74 55E
40 Srnetica, Yugoslavia 44 25N 16 35E
49 Stade, Germany 53 38N 9 31E
30 Staffa, I., Scotland 56 26N 6 22W
22 Stafford & Co., England 52 40N 2 4W
27 Staindrop, England 54 35N 1 49W
23 Staines, England 51 25N 0 30W
27 Stainforth, England 53 37N 0 59W
26 Stainmore Forest, Eng. 54 29N 2 5W
52 Stalingrad, *see* Volgograd
52 Stalino, U.S.S.R., *see* Donetsk
26 Stalybridge, England 53 29N 2 3W
82 Stamford, Australia 21 15S 143 46E
93 Stamford, U.S.A. 41 5N 73 30W
27 Stamford Bridge, Eng. 54 0N 0 54W
75 Standerton, S. Africa 27 0S 29 30E
26 Standish, England 53 35N 2 39W
76 Stanger, S. Africa 29 22S 31 15E
26 Stanhope, England 54 45N 2 0W
41 Stanke Dimitrov, Bulgaria 42 27N 23 9E
83 Stanley, Australia 40 45S 145 20E
27 Stanley, England 54 53N 1 42W
74 Stanleyville, *see* Kisangani
26 Stanlow, England 53 16N 2 45W
27 Stannington, England 55 7N 1 41W
61 Stanovoy Ra., U.S.S.R. 55 0N 130 0E
83 Stanthorpe, Australia 28 40S 152 0E
88 Stanton, Canada 69 40N 128 40W
27 Stapleford, England 52 56N 1 16W
41 Stara-Zagora, Bulgaria 42 22N 25 41E
46 Stargard, Poland 53 19N 15 1E
52 Staritsa, U.S.S.R. 56 33N 34 59E
47 Starogard, Poland 53 59N 18 30E
47 Staroskonstantinov, U.S.S.R. 49 45N 27 8E
24 Start Bay, England 50 14N 3 35W
24 Start Pt., England 50 14N 3 38W
61 Stary Kheidzhan, U.S.S.R. 60 0N 144 50E
99 Staten I., (I. de los Estados), Argentina 54 50S 64 30W
91 Staunton, U.S.A. 38 11N 79 0W
49 Stavanger, Norway 58 58N 5 32E
27 Staveley, England 53 16N 1 20W
44 Stavelot, Belgium 50 25N 5 56E
44 Staveren, Netherlands 52 53N 5 25E
49 Stavern, Norway 59 0N 10 3E
50 Stavropol, U.S.S.R. 45 5N 42 0E
83 Stawell, Australia 37 0S 142 48E
74 Stefanie, L., *see* Chew Bahir
45 Steffisburg, Switzerland 46 48N 7 40E
48 Steinkjer, Norway 63 59N 11 40E
76 Stella, South Africa 26 35S 24 45E
93 Stellarton, Canada 45 32N 62 45W
75 Stellenbosch, S. Africa 34 0S 18 55E
40 Stelvio Pass, Italy 46 32N 10 20E
43 Stenay, France 49 30N 5 15E
46 Stendal, Germany 52 38N 11 50E
31 Stenhousemuir, Scotland 56 2N 3 46W
51 Stepnoi, U.S.S.R., *see* Elista
51 Stepnoi Divnoe, U.S.S.R. 46 0N 43 20E
60 Stepnyak, U.S.S.R. 53 5N 70 55E
76 Sterkstroom, S. Africa 31 32S 26 32E
90 Sterling, U.S.A. 40 38N 103 15W
50 Sterlitamak, U.S.S.R. 53 34N 55 47E
46 Stettin, *see* Szczecin
88 Stettler, Canada 52 20N 112 45W
91 Steubenville, U.S.A. 40 24N 80 37W
23 Stevenage, England 51 54N 0 11W
91 Stevens Point, U.S.A. 44 40N 89 35W
30 Stevenston, Scotland 55 38N 4 45W
84 Stewart I., N.Z. 47 0S 168 0E
88 Stewart River, Canada 63 0N 139 30W
30 Stewarton, Scotland 55 40N 4 30W
38 Stewartstown, N. Ireland 54 35N 6 40W
46 Steyr, Austria 48 1N 14 21E
76 Steytlerville, S. Africa 33 20S 24 16E
88 Stikine, R., Canada 57 40N 132 0W
91 Stillwater, Minn., U.S.A. 45 2N 92 54W
91 Stillwater, Okla., U.S.A. 36 5N 97 7W
41 Stip, Yugoslavia 41 41N 22 10E
31 Stirling, Scotland 56 7N 3 55W
80 Stirling Ra., Australia 34 27S 118 0E
31 Stobo, Scotland 55 38N 3 18W
46 Stockerau, Austria 48 25N 16 15E
49 Stockholm, & Co., Sweden 59 21N 18 3E
26 Stockport, England 53 25N 2 10W
27 Stocksbridge, England 53 30N 1 36W
27 Stockton on Tees, Eng. 54 34N 1 20W
90 Stockton, U.S.A. 37 58N 121 18W
32 Stoer, Pt. of, Scotland 58 15N 5 22W
23 Stoke Mandeville, Eng. 51 46N 0 47W
26 Stoke-on-Trent, Eng. 53 2N 2 12W
27 Stokesley, England 54 27N 1 12W
48 Stokkseyri, Iceland 63 47N 20 52W
41 Stolac, Yugoslavia 43 5N 18 0E
44 Stolberg, Germany 50 47N 6 12E
61 Stolbovoi, I., U.S.S.R. 74 10N 135 30E
61 Stolbovoye, U.S.S.R. 64 50N 153 50E
26 Stone, England 52 54N 2 9W
31 Stonehaven, Scotland 56 57N 2 12W
22 Stonehouse, England 51 45N 2 18W
31 Stonehouse, Scotland 55 42N 4 0W
88 Stonewall, Canada 50 10N 97 20W
61 Stony Tunguska, R., U.S.S.R. 62 0N 97 0E
48 Storuman L., Sweden 65 10N 16 30E
48 Stora Lulevatten, Sweden 67 10N 19 30E
48 Stora Sjöffallet, Sweden 67 30N 18 30E
48 Storavan, L., Sweden 66 0N 18 30E
49 Store Bælt, Denmark 55 30N 11 0E
48 Storen, Norway 63 0N 10 20E
48 Storisandur, Dist., Ice. 65 10N 20 0W
83 Storm B., Australia 42 10S 147 22E
32 Stornoway, Scotland 58 12N 6 21W
48 Storolfshvoll, Iceland 63 48N 20 15W
47 Storozhinets, U.S.S.R. 48 14N 24 45E
48 Storsjön L., Sweden 63 15N 14 22E
23 Stort, R., England 51 56N 0 11E
48 Storuman, L., Sweden 65 15N 17 0E
22 Stour, R. (Dorset), Eng. 50 52N 2 10W
23 Stour, R. (Essex), Eng. 51 57N 1 0E
23 Stour R. (Suffolk), Eng. 52 5N 0 40E
22 Stourbridge, England 52 25N 2 9W
22 Stourport, England 52 21N 2 17W
22 Stow-on-the-Wold, Eng. 51 55N 1 42W
23 Stowmarket, England 52 11N 0 59E
36 Strabane, N. Ireland 54 49N 7 25W
33 Strachan, Scotland 57 1N 2 31W
30 Strachur, Scotland 56 9N 5 3W
36 Stradbally, Laois, Ire. 53 2N 7 10W
35 Stradbally, Waterford, Ire. 52 7N 7 28W
83 Strahan, Australia 42 5S 145 15E
49 Stralsund, Germany 54 18N 12 58E
76 Strand, South Africa 34 5S 18 45E
36 Strangford, & L., N. Ire. 54 21N 5 43W
36 Stranorlar, Ireland 54 48N 7 47W
30 Stranraer, Scotland 54 54N 5 1W
43 Strasbourg, France 48 35N 7 46E
92 Stratford, Canada 43 20N 81 12W
84 Stratford, New Zealand 39 22S 174 20E
22 Stratford-on-Avon, Eng. 52 11N 1 43W
33 Strath Dearn, Scotland 57 26N 4 10W
31 Strath Earn, Scotland 56 20N 3 50W
33 Strath Halladale, Scot. 58 30N 3 51W
33 Strath Spey, Scotland 57 18N 3 32W
31 Strath Tay, Scotland 56 40N 3 40W
83 Strathalbyn, Australia 35 18S 138 59E
31 Strathaven, Scotland 55 40N 4 3W
33 Strathbogie, Dist., Scot. 57 25N 2 45W
30 Strathclyde, Reg., Scotland 56 0N 5 0W
33 Strathdon, Scotland 57 12N 3 4W
31 Strathmiglo, Scotland 56 16N 3 15W
33 Strathmore, Dist., Scot. 56 40N 3 10W
33 Strathmore R., Scotland 58 25N 4 40W
33 Strathpeffer, Scotland 57 37N 4 30W
24 Stratton, England 50 49N 4 31W
22 Stratton St. Margaret, England 51 35N 1 45W
48 Straumnes, Iceland 66 27N 23 7W
80 Streaky B., Australia 32 37S 134 10E
24 Street, England 51 7N 2 43W
61 Strelka, U.S.S.R. 58 5N 93 5E
43 Stresa, Italy 45 55N 8 30E
27 Stretford, England 53 27N 2 19W
33 Strichen, Scotland 57 35N 2 5W
36 Strokestown, Ireland 53 47N 8 9W
40 Stromboli, I. Italy 38 50N 15 17E
32 Stromeferry, Scotland 57 20N 5 37W
33 Stromness, Scotland 58 59N 3 20W
48 Ströms Vattudal L., Swed. 64 0N 15 30E
49 Strömstad, Sweden 58 59N 11 10E
48 Strömsund, Sweden 63 52N 15 39E
33 Stronsay F. & I., Scot. 59 3N 2 35W
23 Strood, England 51 23N 0 30E
22 Stroud, England 51 45N 2 11W
49 Struer, Denmark 56 30N 8 35E
41 Struma, R., Bulgaria 41 50N 23 14E
25 Strumble Hd., Wales 52 2N 5 4W
41 Strumica, Yugoslavia 41 30N 22 41E
47 Stry, U.S.S.R. 49 18N 23 50E
80 Stuart Ra., Australia 29 30S 135 30E
68 Stung-Treng, Khmer Rep. 13 42N 105 55E
80 Sturt, R., Australia 19 30S 127 40E
76 Stutterheim, S. Africa 32 33S 27 28E
45 Stuttgart, Germany 48 49N 9 15E
91 Stuttgart, U.S.A. 34 32N 91 32W
48 Stykkisholmur, Iceland 65 5N 22 45W
47 Styr, R., U.S.S.R. 51 5N 25 40E
46 Styria, Prov., Austria 47 18N 15 0E
62 Suakin, Sudan 19 30N 37 25E
65 Süanhwa, China 40 40N 115 5E
65 Subarnarekha R., India 22 30N 86 45E
41 Subotica, Yugoslavia 46 2N 19 33E
47 Suceava, Rumania 47 32N 26 20E
67 Suchan, U.S.S.R. 43 5N 133 0E
66 Süchow, Kiangsu, China 34 17N 117 15E
34 Suck, R., Ireland 53 25N 8 12W
98 Sucre, Bolivia 19 0S 65 20W
73 Sudan, Africa 15 30N 31 0E
70 Sudan Reg, Africa 11 0N 8 0E
92 Sudbury, Canada 46 35N 81 10W
22 Sudbury, Suffolk, Eng. 52 3N 0 45E
73 Sudd, Reg., Sudan 8 0N 30 0E
46 Sudeten Highlands, Ger. 50 0N 17 20E
37 Sueca, Spain 39 13N 0 20W
73 Suez, Egypt 30 0N 32 30E
73 Suez Canal, Egypt 30 30N 32 15E
73 Suez, G. of, Egypt 29 0N 33 0E
23 Suffolk, Co., England 52 15N 1 0E
35 Sugar Loaf, Gt., mt., Ire. 53 7N 6 10W
83 Sugarloaf Pt., Australia 32 30S 152 30E
35 Suir, R., Ireland 52 18N 7 20W
52 Sukhinichi, U.S.S.R. 54 15N 35 17E
50 Sukhona, R., U.S.S.R. 59 30N 42 0E
62 Sukhumi, U.S.S.R. 43 10N 41 5E
89 Sukkertoppen, Greenland 65 40N 53 0W
64 Sukkur, Pakistan 27 45N 68 56E
62 Sulaiyil, Saudi Arabia 20 30N 45 25E
64 Sulaiman Range, Asia 31 0N 70 10E
62 Sulaimaniya, Iran 35 32N 45 25E
68 Sulawesi, I., Indonesia 2 0S 120 0E
47 Sulina Mouth, Danube, Rumania 45 0N 29 40E
48 Sulitjelma, mt., Norway 67 2N 16 30E
98 Sullana, Peru 5 0S 80 30W
65 Sultanpur, India 26 8N 82 5E
68 Sulu Arch., Philippines 6 0N 121 0E
68 Sulu Sea, Philippines 8 0N 120 0E
73 Suluq (Soluk), Libya 31 44N 20 14E
45 Sulzbach, Germany 49 17N 7 2E
68 Sumatra, I., Indonesia 0 30N 101 0E
68 Sumba I., *see* Sandalwood I.
68 Sumbawa I., Indonesia 8 30S 118 0E
74 Sumbawanga, Tanzania 8 0S 31 38E
32 Sumburgh Hd., Scotland 59 53N 1 16W
41 Sumen, Bulgaria 43 17N 26 55E
35 Summerhill, Ireland 53 30N 6 44W
93 Summerside, Canada 46 25N 63 50W
46 Sumperk, Czechoslovakia 49 59N 17 0E
91 Sumter, U.S.A. 33 55N 80 17W
52 Sumy, U.S.S.R. 50 58N 34 45E
32 Sunart, Dist., Scotland 56 42N 5 30W
30 Sunart, L., Scotland 56 40N 5 50W
83 Sunbury, Australia 37 48S 144 50E
93 Sunbury, U.S.A. 40 50N 76 50W
57 Sunda Sea, Indonesia 6 30S 118 0E
68 Sunda Str., Indonesia 6 0S 105 43E
65 Sundarbans, E. Pak. 22 10N 89 30E
65 Sundargarh, India 22 10N 84 7E
27 Sunderland, England 54 55N 1 23W
23 Sundridge, England 51 15N 0 11E
48 Sundsvall, Sweden 62 21N 17 18E
23 Sunninghill, England 51 24N 0 39W
67 Suo B., Japan 33 56N 131 35E
65 Supaul, India 26 10N 86 35E
91 Superior, Wis., U.S.A. 46 40N 92 1W
92 Superior, L., N. America 47 30N 88 0W
50 Sura, R., U.S.S.R. 55 0N 46 30E
68 Surabaya, Indonesia 7 12S 112 48E
68 Surakarta, Indonesia 7 45S 110 50E
64 Suratgarh, India 29 15N 74 0W
83 Surat, Australia 27 13S 149 1E
64 Surat, India 21 12N 73 5E
68 Surat Thani, Malaya 9 5N 99 25E
44 Sure R., Luxembourg 49 50N 6 0E
60 Surgut, U.S.S.R. 61 27N 73 7E
65 Suri, India 23 55N 87 30E
64 Suriapet, India 17 5N 79 30E
96 Surinam (Netherlands Guiana), S. America 4 0N 56 0W
23 Surrey, Co., England 51 5N 0 20W
45 Sursee, Switzerland 47 12N 8 6E
73 Surt, Libya 31 10N 16 50E
92 Susquehanna, R., U.S.A. 42 0N 76 0W
93 Sussex, Canada 45 42N 65 33W
23 Sussex E., Co., England 50 55N 0 16E
23 Sussex W., Co., England 50 54N 0 32W
76 Sutherland, S. Africa 32 21S 20 44E
64 Sutlej, R., India 30 7N 73 30E
23 Sutton, England 51 21N 0 11W
23 Sutton Bridge, England 52 46N 0 12E
22 Sutton Coldfield, England 52 32N 1 47W
27 Sutton-in-Ashfield, Eng. 53 8N 1 15W
67 Suttsu, Japan 42 47N 140 5E
76 Suurberge, C. Prov. 33 8S 25 30E
84 Suva, Fiji Is. 18 5S 178 20E
47 Suwalki, Poland 54 6N 22 53E
63 Suweilih, Jordan 32 2N 35 50E
52 Suzdal, U.S.S.R. 56 27N 40 20E
100 Svalbard (Spitsbergen), Arctic Ocean 78 0N 15 0E
48 Svartisen, mt., Norway 66 55N 13 30E
49 Svealand, Dist., Sweden 59 55N 15 0E
49 Sveg, Sweden 62 2N 14 27E
49 Svendborg, Denmark 55 7N 10 38E
60 Sverdlovsk, U.S.S.R. 56 52N 60 32E
100 Sverdrup I., Arctic Oc. 80 0N 100 0W
50 Svir, R., U.S.S.R. 61 0N 34 0E
41 Svishtov, Bulgaria 43 36N 25 23E
61 Svobodny, U.S.S.R. 51 30N 128 5E
48 Svolvær, Norway 68 20N 14 30E
46 Swabian Jura, mts., Germany, *see* Schwabishe Alb.
22 Swadlincote, England 52 47N 1 34W
23 Swaffham, England 52 38N 0 40E
75 Swakopmund, S.W. Afr. 22 33S 14 35E
27 Swale, R., England 54 13N 1 28W
83 Swan Hill, Australia 35 15S 143 31E
22 Swanage, England 50 36N 1 57W
36 Swanlinbar, Ireland 54 11N 7 42W
83 Swansea, Australia 33 3S 151 35E
25 Swansea, & B., Wales 51 38N 3 57W
76 Swartberge, S. Africa 33 15S 22 0E
66 Swatow, China 23 30N 116 50E
75 Swaziland, S.E. Afr. 26 30S 31 30E
16 Sweden, Europe 63 0N 16 0E
88 Swift Current, Canada 50 20N 107 49W
36 Swilly, L. & R., Ireland 55 14N 7 33W
22 Swindon, England 51 33N 1 47W
36 Swinford, Ireland 53 55N 8 58W
46 Swinoujscie, Poland 53 54N 14 16E
26 Swinton, Lancs., Eng. 53 31N 2 21W
27 Swinton, Yorks., Eng. 53 28N 1 20W
45 Switzerland, Europe 46 50N 8 10E
35 Swords, Ireland 53 28N 6 14W
83 Sydney, Australia 33 55S 151 12E
89 Sydpröven, Greenland 60 30N 45 20W
50 Syktyvkar, U.S.S.R. 61 45N 50 40E
48 Sylarna Mt., Sweden 63 2N 12 20E
65 Sylhet, Bangladesh 24 50N 91 52E
48 Sylt, I., Denmark 55 0N 8 19E
60 Sym, U.S.S.R. 60 20N 87 55E
31 Symington, Scotland 55 35N 3 36W
22 Symonds Yat, England 51 50N 2 38W
60 Syr Darya, R., U.S.S.R. 44 40N 65 0E
40 Syracuse, *see* Siracusa
91 Syracuse, U.S.A. 43 0N 76 10W
62 Syria, S.W. Asia 35 0N 38 0E
62 Syrian Des., Si. Arabia 32 0N 40 0E
50 Syzran, U.S.S.R. 53 12N 48 30E
46 Szczecin, Poland 53 25N 14 31E
46 Szczecnek, Poland 53 43N 16 41E
66 Szechwan, Prov., China 30 0N 104 0E
47 Szeged, Hungary 46 17N 20 9E
47 Székesfehérvár, Hungary 47 17N 18 24E
47 Szentes, Hungary 46 39N 20 19E
67 Szeping, China 43 15N 124 15E
47 Szolnok, Hungary 47 15N 20 10E
46 Szombathely, Hungary 47 17N 16 27E

T

66 Ta Liang Shan, mts., China 28 0N 102 20E
76 Table, Mt., S. Africa 34 1S 18 27E
46 Tabor, Czechoslovakia 49 23N 14 29E
74 Tabora, Tanzania 5 0S 33 0E
72 Tabou, Ivory Coast 4 30N 7 20W
62 Tabriz, Iran 38 3N 46 24E
67 Tachima, Japan 37 9N 139 48E
68 Tacloban, Philippines 10 15N 124 55E
98 Tacna, Peru 18 5S 70 20W
90 Tacoma, U.S.A. 47 15N 122 12W
99 Tacuarembo, Uruguay 31 30S 56 0W
98 Tacutu, R., S. America 3 0N 59 40W
27 Tadcaster, England 53 54N 1 18W
72 Tademait, Plat. du, Alg. 28 28N 2 0E
60 Tadzhikistan, Rep., U.S.S.R. 39 0N 72 6E
67 Taegu, Korea 35 48N 129 30E
63 Tafa, Syria 32 44N 36 4E
37 Tafalla, Spain 42 30N 1 42W
52 Taganrog, U.S.S.R. 47 16N 38 55E
52 Taganrog Gulf, U.S.S.R. 46 50N 37 57E
35 Taghmon, Ireland 52 21N 6 43W
88 Tagish, Canada 60 20N 134 0W
37 Tagus (Tajo) R., Spain 40 40N 2 12W
68 Tahan, Mt., Malaya 4 15N 102 50E
66 Tahcheng, China 46 45N 83 10E
4 Tahiti, Pacific Ocean 17 50S 149 40W
90 Tahoe, L., U.S.A. 39 0N 120 0W
62 Tahiri, Iran 27 35N 52 20E
73 Tahta, Egypt 26 44N 31 32E
67 Tai Shan, mts., China 36 0N 118 30E
67 Taichung, Taiwan 24 10N 120 35E
62 Taif, Saudi Arabia 21 0N 41 2E
84 Taihape, New Zealand 39 42S 175 49E
60 Tailakovy, U.S.S.R. 59 20N 74 5E
83 Tailem Bend, Australia 35 12S 139 29E
62 Taima, Saudi Arabia 27 23N 39 20E
61 Taimyr Pen., U.S.S.R. 75 0N 100 0E
33 Tain, Scotland 57 48N 4 3W
67 Tainan, Taiwan 23 0N 120 22E
41 Tainaron (Matapan), C., Greece 36 20N 22 30E
67 Taipei, Taiwan 25 0N 121 38E
68 Taiping, Malaya 4 55N 100 45E
67 Taira, Japan 37 4N 140 58E
61 Taishet, U.S.S.R. 56 0N 98 5E
99 Taitao Pen., Chile 46 0S 75 0W
66 Taitung, China 30 45N 117 40E
67 Taitung, Taiwan 22 55N 121 5E
67 Taiwan (Formosa), China 24N 121 0E
66 Tai-yüan, China 38 2N 112 20E
62 Ta'izz, Yemen 13 43N 44 7E
37 Tajo, R., Spain 40 40N 2 12W
73 Tajura, Libya 32 51N 13 27E
55 Ta-Khingan Shan, China 50 0N 120 0E
55 Ta-Liang Shan, China 28 20N 103 0E
67 Takamatsu, Japan 34 15N 134 0E
67 Takana, Japan 34 0N 135 6E
67 Takaoka, Japan 36 40N 137 4E
84 Takapuna, New Zealand 36 47S 174 47E
67 Takasaki, Japan 36 10N 139 0E
67 Takata, Japan 37 12N 138 12E
74 Takaungu, Kenya 3 35S 39 45E
67 Takefu, Japan 35 57N 136 5E
67 Taketoyo, Japan 34 56N 137 0E
66 Takla-Makan, China 39 45N 85 0E
61 Tala, U.S.S.R. 72 50N 113 57E
98 Talara, Peru 4 20S 81 10W
60 Talas, U.S.S.R. 42 45N 72 0E
68 Talaud, Is., Indonesia 4 10N 126 50E
37 Talavera, Spain 39 59N 4 46W
68 Talayan, Philippines 6 55N 124 25E
99 Talca, Chile 35 18S 71 45W
99 Talcahuano, Chile 36 35S 73 12W
65 Talcher, India 20 55N 85 3E
60 Taldy Kurgan, U.S.S.R. 45 5N 78 50E
64 Talguppa, India 14 10N 74 45E
66 Tali, China 25 57N 100 7E
74 Tali Post, Sudan 5 55N 30 44E
68 Taliabu, Indonesia 1 45S 125 0E
32 Talladale, Scotland 57 41N 5 20W
91 Tallahassee, U.S.A. 30 30N 84 10W
83 Tallangatta, Australia 36 8S 147 5E
49 Tallinn, U.S.S.R. 59 29N 24 58E
34 Tallow, Ireland 52 6N 7 59W
62 Talodi, Sudan 10 42N 30 22E
99 Taltal, Chile 25 40S 70 35W
83 Talwood, Australia 28 25S 149 25E
25 Tal-y-Lyn, Wales 52 40N 3 53W
72 Tamale, Ghana 9 30N 0 50W
24 Tamar, R., England 50 45N 4 22W
75 Tamatave, Madagascar 17 50S 49 40E
72 Tambacounda, Sénégal 13 10N 13 40W
82 Tambo, Australia 24 54S 146 14E
52 Tambov, U.S.S.R. 52 43N 41 30E
37 Tamega, R., Portugal 41 15N 8 0W
72 Tamgak Mts., Niger 19 10N 8 35E
65 Tamil Nadu, st., India 11 0N 78 0E
45 Tamins, Switzerland 46 50N 9 22E
91 Tampa, & B., U.S.A. 28 10N 82 20W
49 Tampere, Finland 61 34N 23 38E
94 Tampico, Mexico 22 20N 98 12W
72 Tamsagout, Mali 24 5N 6 35W
83 Tamworth, Australia 31 8S 151 0E
22 Tamworth, England 52 38N 1 42W
48 Tana Fjord, Norway 70 45N 28 20E
73 Tana L., Ethiopia 12 0N 37 20E
74 Tana R., Kenya 1 0S 40 0E
80 Tanami Desert, Australia 20 0S 136 0E
75 Tananarive, Madagascar 19 0S 47 20E
40 Tanaro, R., Italy 44 47N 8 10E
83 Tanbar, Australia 25 30S 141 58E
74 Tandah, Ethiopia 10 0N 40 45E
99 Tandil, Argentina 37 8S 59 10W
64 Tando Adam, Pak. 25 40N 68 34E
67 Tanega Shima, I., Japan 30 40N 131 0E
72 Tanezrouft, Dist., Algeria 22 30N 2 0E
71 Tanganyika, *see* Tanzania
74 Tanganyika, L., Cent. Afr. 6 30S 29 40E
66 Tanghla Ra., Mts., China 33 0N 92 0E
72 Tangier, N. Africa 35 46N 5 47W
66 Tangshan, China 39 45N 118 0E
64 Tanjore, *see* Thanjavur
68 Tanjungpandan, Indon. 2 45S 107 40E
68 Tanjungselor, Indon. 2 50N 116 40E
73 Tanta, Egypt 30 50N 30 84E

83 Tanunda, Australia 34 30S 139 0E
22 Tanworth, England 52 20N 1 50W
71 Tanzania, Africa 6 0S 34 30E
67 Taonan, China 45 29N 122 57E
72 Taourirt, Morocco 34 20N 3 2W
66 Tapa, Mts., China 31 50N 109 0E
98 Tapajos, R., Brazil 6 30S 57 30W
51 Tarabulus, Lebanon, *see* Tripoli
73 Tarabulus, Libya, *see* Tripoli
68 Tarakan, Indonesia 3 15N 117 30E
84 Taranaki, Dist., N.Z. 39 0S 174 50E
32 Taransay, I. & Sd., Scot. 57 54N 7 1W
40 Taranto, & G., Italy 40 30N 17 14E
43 Tarare, France 45 52N 4 30E
84 Tararua Ra., N.Z. 40 47S 175 30E
43 Tarascon, France 43 50N 4 40E
72 Tarat, Algeria 26 4N 9 7E
84 Tarawera, N.Z. 39 2S 176 35E
34 Tarbert, Ireland 52 35N 9 22W
30 Tarbert & L.W., Argyll, Scotland 55 58N 5 25W
32 Tarbert, & L., W & E, Harris, Scotland 57 55N 6 50W
42 Tarbes, France 43 13N 0 1E
30 Tarbet, Scotland 56 13N 4 44W
80 Tarcoola, Australia 30 48S 134 52E
83 Taree, Australia 31 48S 152 17E
72 Tarfaya, Morocco 27 55N 12 55W
37 Tarifa, Spain 36 2N 5 37W
62 Tarim, South Yemen 16 15N 49 22E
66 Tarim Basin, China 40 30N 85 0E
66 Tarim R., China 41 0N 85 0E
51 Tarkhankut C., U.S.S.R. 45 25N 32 30E
72 Tarkwa, Ghana 5 23N 2 0W
68 Tarlac, Philippines 15 25N 120 35E
26 Tarleton, England 53 41N 2 51W
42 Tarn, Dépt., France 43 50N 2 10E
42 Tarn-et-Garonne, Dépt., France 44 10N 1 10E
47 Tarnow, Poland 50 1N 21 2E
47 Tarnowskie Góry, Poland 50 30N 19 0E
72 Taroudant, Morocco 30 30N 9 0W
37 Tarragona, Spain 41 7N 1 13E
37 Tarrasa, Spain 41 30N 2 0E
51 Tarsus, Turkey 37 0N 34 50E
47 Tartars, P. of the, U.S.S.R. 48 20N 24 30E
61 Tartary Str., U.S.S.R. 53 10N 141 30E
50 Tartu, U.S.S.R. 58 22N 26 40E
73 Tasawah, Libya 26 0N 13 30E
89 Taschereau, Canada 48 45N 78 45W
60 Tashauz, U.S.S.R. 42 7N 59 30E
60 Tashkent, U.S.S.R. 41 7N 69 15E
60 Tashkumyr, U.S.S.R. 41 40N 72 20E
70 Tasili Plateau, N. Africa 25 30N 8 0E
48 Tasjön, L., Sweden 64 15N 16 0E
84 Tasman B., N.Z. 41 0S 173 30E
84 Tasman Mts., N.Z. 41 0S 172 30E
83 Tasman Pen., Australia 43 0S 147 40E
84 Tasman Sea, Australasia 38 0S 163 0E
83 Tasmania, I., Australia 42 0S 146 30E
47 Tatabanya, Hungary 47 35N 18 30E
50 Tatar, A.S.S.R., U.S.S.R. 55 30N 51 30E
60 Tatarsk, U.S.S.R. 55 30N 76 3E
67 Tateyama, Japan 35 0N 139 58E
66 Ta-tung, China 40 0N 113 20E
51 Tatvan, Turkey 38 33N 42 12E
46 Tauern Mts., Austria 47 15N 12 40E
84 Taumarunui, N.Z. 38 55S 175 15E
76 Taung, South Africa 27 32S 24 45E
65 Taunggyi, Burma 20 55N 97 3E
65 Taungun & P., Burma 18 50N 94 20E
24 Taunton, England 51 1N 3 5W
46 Taunus Mts., Germany 50 18N 8 20E
84 Taupo & L., N.Z. 38 47S 175 50E
49 Taurage, U.S.S.R. 55 15N 22 18E
84 Tauranga, New Zealand 37 40S 176 12E
40 Taurianova, Italy 38 22N 16 1E
51 Taurus Mts., Turkey 37 30N 34 30E
60 Tavda, U.S.S.R. 58 7N 65 8E
37 Tavira, Portugal 37 5N 7 40W
24 Tavistock, England 50 34N 4 10W
64 Tavoy, Burma 13 49N 98 22E
24 Taw, R., England 50 57N 3 55W
73 Taweisha, Sudan 12 25N 26 55E
68 Tawitawi, I., Phil. 5 15N 120 0E
36 Tawnyinah, Ireland 53 55N 8 45W
31 Tay, Firth of, Scotland 56 27N 2 45W
31 Tayport, Scotland 56 26N 2 53W
31 Tayside, Reg., Scotland 56 30N 3 30W
68 Taytay, Philippines 10 40N 119 25E
60 Taz R., U.S.S.R. 65 40N 82 40E
51 Tbilisi, U.S.S.R. 41 45N 44 48E
74 Tchibanga, Gabon 2 45S 11 12E
84 Te Anau, L., N.Z. 45 12S 167 48E
84 Te Awamutu, N.Z. 38 1S 175 20E
84 Te Kuiti, New Zealand 38 20S 175 11E
72 Tébessa, Algeria 35 38N 8 5E
68 Tebingtinggi, Indonesia 3 30S 103 0E
47 Tecuci, Rumania 45 20N 27 25E
26 Tees, R., England 54 39N 1 9W
27 Teesside, England 54 34N 1 16W
68 Tegal, Indonesia 7 0S 108 35E
25 Tegid, L., Wales 52 55N 3 37W
72 Tegina, Nigeria 10 5N 6 11E
94 Tegucigalpa, Honduras 14 20N 87 12W
90 Tehachapi P., U.S.A. 35 5N 119 30W
66 Tehchow, China 37 35N 116 15E
62 Tehran, Iran 35 37N 51 22E
66 Tehtsin, China 28 45N 98 10E
94 Tehuantepec, & G., Mex. 16 40N 95 35W
25 Teifi, R., Wales 52 2N 4 20W
24 Teign, R., England 50 40N 3 40W
24 Teignmouth, England 50 33N 3 31W
37 Tejo (Tagus), R., Port. 39 15N 8 30W
84 Tekapo, L., N.Z. 43 55S 170 30E
41 Tekirdag, Turkey 41 0N 27 25E
63 Tel Aviv-Jaffa, Israel 32 4N 34 45E
94 Tela, Honduras 15 45N 87 25W
68 Telanaipura, Indonesia *see* Jambi
51 Telavi, U.S.S.R. 42 0N 43 30E
49 Telemark, Co., Norway 59 32N 8 20E
22 Telford, England 52 42N 2 29W
64 Tellicherry, India 11 45N 75 43E
68 Telok Anson, Malaya 3 50N 101 0E
50 Telpos Iz, Mt., U.S.S.R. 64 12N 59 30E
49 Telsiai, U.S.S.R. 56 2N 22 30E
68 Teluk Betung, Indon. 5 30S 105 20E
84 Temuka, N.Z. 44 14S 171 17E
72 Tema, Ghana 5 41N 0 0
94 Temax, Mexico 21 15N 88 50W
76 Tembuland, dist., S. Afr. 31 40S 28 0E
22 Teme, R., England 52 23N 3 7W
60 Temir, U.S.S.R. 49 3N 57 3E
60 Temir Tau, U.S.S.R. 53 15N 87 40E
92 Temiskaming, Canada 46 50N 79 0W
83 Temora, Australia 34 29S 147 33E
91 Temple, U.S.A. 31 3N 97 27W
82 Temple B., Australia 12 15S 143 3E
34 Templemore, Ireland 52 47N 7 49W
36 Tempo, N. Ireland 54 23N 7 27W
99 Temuco, Chile 39 0S 72 0W
65 Tenali, India 16 15N 80 30E
22 Tenbury, England 52 18N 2 36W
43 Tenda, France 44 6N 7 39E
72 Tenerife, I., Canary Is. 28 30N 18 0W
37 Tenes, Algeria 36 36N 0 32W
66 T'eng Ch'ung, China 25 5N 98 25E
66 Tengkow, China 40 0N 106 20E
64 Tenkasi, India 8 45N 77 10E
80 Tennant Creek, Austral. 19 30S 134 15E
43 Tenneins, France 44 22N 0 20E
91 Tennessee, R., U.S.A. 34 45N 87 30W
91 Tennessee, st., U.S.A. 35 40N 86 30W
67 Tenryu, R., Japan 35 30N 137 56E
23 Tenterden, England 51 5N 0 41E
83 Tenterfield, Australia 29 0S 152 0E
98 Teofilo Otoni, Brazil 17 50S 41 30W
94 Tepic, Mexico 21 20N 104 50W
46 Teplice, Czechoslovakia 50 39N 13 50E
72 Téra, Niger 14 0N 0 57E
40 Teramo, Italy 42 39N 13 46E
83 Terang, Australia 38 7S 142 59E
98 Teresina, Brazil 5 2S 42 45W
83 Terewah or Narran, L., Australia 29 52S 147 35E
44 Tergnier, France 49 49N 3 17E
63 Termez, U.S.S.R. 37 25N 67 12E
40 Termini, Italy 37 57N 13 45E
40 Termoli, Italy 42 0N 15 3E
68 Ternate, I., Indonesia 0 45N 127 20E
40 Terni, Italy 42 35N 12 40E
47 Ternopol, U.S.S.R. 49 30N 25 40E
91 Terre Haute, U.S.A. 39 29N 87 20W
34 Terryglass, Ireland 8 14N 53 3W
44 Terschelling, I., Neth. 53 23N 5 20E
37 Teruel, Spain 40 22N 1 6W
41 Tesanj, Yugoslavia 44 40N 18 0E
88 Teslin, Canada 60 20N 132 45W
72 Tessalit, Mali 20 5N 0 57E
72 Tessaoua, Niger 13 55N 8 18E
22 Test, R., England 51 3N 1 32W
22 Tetbury, England 51 38N 2 9W
75 Tete, Mozambique 16 10S 33 37E
41 Teteven, Bulgaria 42 58N 24 15E
90 Teton, Mts., U.S.A. 43 45N 110 45W
41 Tetovo, Yugoslavia 42 1N 21 2E
22 Tettenhall, England 52 35N 2 7W
72 Tetuan, Morocco 35 32N 5 22W
99 Teuco R., Argentina 24 0S 62 0W
31 Teviot, R., Scotland 55 20N 2 57W
83 Tewantin, Australia 26 27S 153 3E
22 Tewkesbury, England 51 59N 2 8W
91 Texarkana, U.S.A. 33 28N 94 11W
83 Texas, Australia 28 43S 151 3E
90 Texas, st., U.S.A. 31 15N 98 30W
44 Texel, I., Netherlands 53 5N 4 48E
65 Tezpur, India 26 50N 92 40E
76 Thaba Nchu, S. Africa 29 10S 26 57E
76 Thabana Ntlenyana, mt., Lesotho 29 12S 29 22E
63 Thaih, U.A.E. 23 57N 54 0E
57 Thailand (Siam), Asia 15 0N 101 0E
64 Thal, Pakistan 33 30N 70 30E
65 Thala Pass, Burma 28 15N 98 10E
68 Thale Luang, Thailand 7 30N 100 15E
83 Thallon, Australia 28 36S 149 0E
23 Thame, England 51 45N 0 59W
23 Thame R., England 51 52N 0 47W
84 Thames, N.Z. 37 3S 175 32E
22 Thames, R., England 51 29N 0 40E
64 Thana, India 19 30N 72 58E
23 Thanet, I., England 51 21N 1 20E
64 Thanjavur, India 10 45N 79 17E
43 Thann, France 47 46N 7 5E
64 Thar Des., India 27 30N 72 20E
64 Tharad, India 24 30N 71 30E
65 Tharrawaddy, Burma 17 42N 95 57E
41 Thasos, I., Greece 40 40N 24 40E
22 Thatcham, England 51 24N 1 16W
45 Thawil, Switzerland 47 18N 8 32E
66 Thazi, Burma 21 0N 96 5E
90 The Dalles, U.S.A. 45 35N 121 15W
44 The Hague ('s Gravenhage), Netherlands 52 5N 4 18E
80 The Johnston Lakes, Australia 32 30S 120 40E
88 The Pas, Canada 53 40N 101 20W
24 The Quantocks, England 51 8N 3 10W
49 The Skaw, *see* Skagen
36 The Skerries Is., N. Ire. 55 14N 6 40W
49 The Sound, Denmark 56 7N 12 30E
24 The Sound, England 50 17N 4 10W
83 The Warburton, R., Austral. 27 50S 138 0E
83 Theodore, Australia 25 0S 150 1E
41 Thermopylae, P., Greece 38 48N 22 45E
41 Thessaloniki, Greece 40 38N 23 0E
41 Thessaly, Dist., Greece 39 30N 22 20E
23 Thetford, England 52 24N 0 45E
93 Thetford Mines, Canada 46 15N 71 5W
76 Theunissen, S. Africa 28 30S 26 40E
43 Thiers, France 45 50N 3 32E
65 Thimphu, Bhutan 27 31N 89 45E
48 Thingvallavatn, Iceland 64 10N 21 5W
43 Thionville, France 49 20N 6 10E
41 Thira, I., Greece 36 24N 25 26E
27 Thirsk, England 54 14N 1 22W
48 Thjorsá R., Iceland 64 20N 19 15W
88 Thompson, R., Canada 51 0N 119 0W
82 Thomson, R., Australia 23 50S 144 0E
74 Thomson's Falls, *see* Nyahururu
45 Thonon, France 46 20N 6 30E
52 Thorez, U.S.S.R. 48 0N 38 38E
65 Thori, India 27 23N 84 30E
48 Thórisvatn L., Iceland 64 10N 18 7W
48 Thorlákshöfn, Iceland 63 50N 21 20W
27 Thornaby-on-Tees, Eng. 54 33N 1 18W
23 Thorndon, England 52 16N 1 8E
27 Thorne, England 53 37N 0 58W
27 Thornham, England 52 59N 0 35E
31 Thornthwaite, England 54 36N 3 13W
26 Thornton-Cleveleys, Eng. 53 50N 3 4W
23 Thorpe, England 52 38N 1 20E
48 Thorshöfn, Iceland 66 12N 15 15W
42 Thouars, France 47 0N 0 18W
41 Thrace, Prov., Greece 41 27N 26 30E
23 Thrapston, England 52 24N 0 32W
84 Three Kings I., N.Z. 34 0S 172 0E
26 Threshfield, England 54 5N 2 2W
80 Throssell Ra., Australia 22 0S 122 0E
44 Thuin, Belgium 50 20N 4 17E
100 Thule, Greenland 76 22N 69 0W
45 Thun, Switzerland 46 46N 7 39E
92 Thunder Bay, Canada 48 20N 89 23W
45 Thunersee, Switzerland 46 42N 7 40E
45 Thur, R., Switzerland 47 37N 8 40E
45 Thurgau, Canton, Switz. 47 38N 9 4E
46 Thuringian Forest, Ger. 50 35N 11 0E
23 Thurlby, England 52 45N 0 21W
34 Thurles, Ireland 52 40N 7 53W
23 Thurrock, England 51 28N 0 20E
81 Thursday, I., Australia 10 35S 142 10E
45 Thusis, Switzerland 46 43N 9 26E
74 Thysville, *see* Mbanza Ngungu
73 Tibati, Cameroon 6 30N 12 52E
40 Tiber, R., Italy 43 33N 12 10E
63 Tiberias, Israel 32 47N 35 32E
73 Tibesti, Dist., Sahara 20 30N 17 0E
65 Tibert, A.R., China 32 30N 88 0E
63 Tibnin, Lebanon 33 11N 35 24E
94 Tiburon, I., Mexico 29 0N 112 30W
72 Tichit, Mauritania 19 20N 8 55W
45 Ticino, Canton, Switz. 46 20N 8 45E
40 Ticino, R., Italy 45 20N 8 53E
72 Tidjikja, Mauritania 18 25N 11 55W
44 Tiel, Netherlands 51 54N 5 26E
44 Tielt, Belgium 51 0N 3 20E
44 Tienen, Belgium 50 49N 4 57E
55 Tien Shan, mts., Asia 43 40N 86 0E
66 Tienshui, China 34 45N 105 15E
66 Tientsin, China 39 0N 117 5E
66 Tientu, China 18 30N 109 30E
100 Tierra del Fuego Terr., South America 54 0S 68 0W
37 Tietar, R., Spain 40 0N 5 45W
93 Tignish, Canada 46 55N 64 15W
62 Tigris, R., Iraq 32 30N 46 0E
65 Tigu, Tibet 28 45N 91 40E
65 Tigyaing, Burma 23 45N 96 10E
94 Tijuana, Mexico 32 30N 117 30W
51 Tikhoretsk, U.S.S.R. 45 55N 40 10E
61 Tiksi, U.S.S.R. 71 50N 129 0E
44 Tilburg, Netherlands 51 34N 5 6E
23 Tilbury, England 51 27N 0 23E
61 Tilichiki, U.S.S.R. 60 50N 166 0E
31 Till, R., England 55 35N 2 0W
72 Tillabéri Niger 14 15N 1 40E
31 Tillicoultry, Scotland 56 9N 3 44W
41 Tilos I., Greece 36 22N 27 21E
83 Tilpa, Australia 30 58S 144 30E
33 Tilt, R., Scotland 56 50N 3 48W
50 Timan Ridge, U.S.S.R. 64 30N 51 30E
84 Timaru, New Zealand 44 20S 171 21E
83 Timboon, Australia 38 32S 143 0E
72 Timbuktu, *see* Tombouctou
62 Timerein, Sudan 15 57N 36 30E
72 Timimoun, Algeria 29 10N 0 10E
47 Timisoara, Rumania 45 43N 21 8E
89 Timmins, Canada 48 30N 81 30W
41 Timok, R., Yugoslavia 43 30N 22 18E
34 Timoleague, Ireland 51 39N 8 46W
68 Timor, I., Indonesia 9 30S 125 0E
80 Timor Sea, Indian Ocean 14 0S 120 0E
35 Tinahely, Ireland 52 48N 6 28W
72 Tindouf, Algeria 27 30N 8 15W
65 Tindzhe Dzong, China 28 25N 88 10E
67 Ting-hai, China 30 10N 122 12E
72 Tinjoub, Algeria 29 20N 5 40W
49 Tinnoset, Norway 59 42N 9 3E
99 Tinogasta, Argentina 28 0S 67 30W
41 Tinos I., Greece 37 38N 25 10E
24 Tintagel, England 50 40N 4 45W
25 Tintern, Wales 51 42N 2 41W
83 Tintinara, Australia 35 58S 140 1E
65 Tipongpani, India 27 15N 95 50E
34 Tipperary, & Co., Ire. 52 29N 8 8W
22 Tipton, England 52 32N 2 3W
41 Tirane, Albania 41 20N 19 50E
45 Tirano, Italy 46 15N 10 15E
47 Tiraspol, U.S.S.R. 46 50N 29 30E
63 Tirat Karmel, Israel 32 46N 34 58E
51 Tirebolu, Turkey 40 59N 38 50E
30 Tiree I., Scotland 56 30N 6 55W
47 Tîrgoviste, Rumania 44 58N 25 30E
47 Tirgu-Jiu, Rumania 45 0N 23 20E
47 Tirgu Mures, Rumania 46 31N 24 38E
64 Tirodi, India 21 35N 79 35E
40 Tirso, R., Italy 40 0N 8 45E
64 Tiruchchirappalli, India 10 52N 78 40E
64 Tirunelveli, India 8 45N 77 45E
64 Tiruvannamalai, India 12 15N 79 10E
88 Tisdale, Canada 52 50N 104 10W
49 Tisted, Denmark 56 58N 8 40E
47 Tisza, R., Hungary 47 50N 21 0E
98 Titicaca, L., Bolivia-Peru 16 0S 69 30W
41 Titograd, Yugoslavia 42 30N 19 19E
41 Titov Veles, Yugoslavia 41 40N 21 49E
41 Titovo Uzice, Y-slav. 43 55N 19 50E
74 Titule, Zaïre 3 5N 25 25E
92 Titusville, U.S.A. 41 38N 79 40W
24 Tiverton, England 50 55N 3 31W
40 Tivoli, Italy 41 58N 12 25E
48 Tjeggelvas, L., Sweden 66 30N 18 0E
94 Tlacotalpan, Mexico 18 50N 95 40W
94 Tlaxcala, Mexico 19 23N 98 10W
94 Tlaxiaco, Mexico 17 15N 97 40W
72 Tlemcen, Algeria 34 55N 1 20W
68 Toba, L., Indonesia 2 30N 98 57E
64 Toba Kakar, Hills, Pak. 31 20N 68 40E
94 Tobago, I., W. Indies 11 17N 60 40W
36 Tobercurry, Ireland 54 3N 8 44W
30 Tobermory, Scotland 56 38N 6 4W
60 Tobol R., U.S.S.R. 54 0N 63 30E
60 Tobolsk, U.S.S.R. 58 10N 68 30E
82 Tobriand or Kiriwina Is., Papua N.G. 8 35S 151 0E
73 Tobruk, Libya, *see* Tubruq
98 Tocantins, R., Brazil 3 30S 49 30W
45 Toce, R., Italy 46 13N 8 19E
67 Tochigi, Pref., Japan 36 40N 139 45E
99 Tocopilla, Chile 22 12S 70 20W
83 Tocumwal, Australia 35 54S 145 56E
26 Todmorden, England 53 42N 2 5W
72 Togba, Mauretania 7 40N 10 20W
50 Togliatti, U.S.S.R. 53 37N 49 18E
72 Togo, W. Africa 7 45N 1 0E
74 Toinya, Sudan 6 17N 29 46E
47 Tokaj, Hungary 48 7N 21 22E
84 Tokanui, New Zealand 46 51S 169 0E
84 Tokarahi, New Zealand 44 56S 170 39E
51 Tokat, Turkey 40 27N 36 32E
4 Tokelau Is., Pac. Oc. 9 0S 172 0W
60 Tokmak, U.S.S.R. 42 55N 75 45E
67 Tokushima, & Pref., Jap. 34 0N 134 30E
67 Tokuyama, Japan 34 0N 131 50E
67 Tokyo, & Pref. Japan 35 48N 139 45E
37 Toledo, Spain 39 55N 4 0W
92 Toledo, U.S.A. 41 47N 83 30W
72 Tolga, Algeria 34 49N 5 26E
98 Tolima, Mt., Colombia 4 0N 75 0W
37 Tolosa, Spain 43 9N 2 5W
68 Tolo, G. of, Indonesia 2 0S 121 30E
94 Toluca, Mexico 19 25N 99 37W
66 Tolun, China 42 30N 116 30E
37 Tomar, Portugal 39 35N 8 28W
47 Tomaszów, Mazowiecki, Poland 51 30N 20 0E
98 Tombador, Sa. do, mts., Brazil 12 0S 57 10W
72 Tombouctou, Mali 16 50N 3 0W
32 Tomdoun, Scotland 57 3N 5 3W
37 Tomelloso, Spain 39 13N 2 1W
68 Tomini G., Indonesia 0 0 120 30E
33 Tomintoul, Scotland 57 16N 3 24W
61 Tommot, U.S.S.R. 59 0N 126 30E
41 Tomorrit, Mt., Albania 40 40N 20 30E
60 Tomsk, U.S.S.R. 56 30N 85 5E
94 Tonala, Mexico 16 10N 94 0W
45 Tonale P., Italy 46 18N 10 36E
23 Tonbridge, England 51 11N 0 16E
24 Tone, R., England 51 0N 3 22W
22 Tong, England 52 40N 2 17W
84 Tonga (Friendly) Is., Pacific Ocean 19 50S 175 0W
76 Tongaat, South Africa 29 35S 31 5E
84 Tongatapu I., Pac. Oc. 21 0S 175 20W
44 Tongeren, Belgium 50 37N 5 28E
68 Tongian Is., Indonesia 0 20S 122 30E
83 Tongio, Australia 37 10S 147 35E
99 Tongoy, Chile 30 10S 71 45W
90 Tongue, R., U.S.A. 45 20N 106 3W
64 Tonk, India 26 10N 76 0E
66 Tonkin, G. of, China 20 0N 109 0E
68 Tonlé Sap, Cambodia 12 30N 105 30E
43 Tonnerre, France 47 52N 3 58E
49 Tönning, Germany 54 19N 8 58E
90 Tonopah, U.S.A. 38 4N 117 13W
49 Tonsberg, Norway 59 15N 10 25E
25 Tonyrefail, Wales 51 35N 3 26W
90 Tooele, U.S.A. 40 32N 113 22W
34 Toomevara, Ireland 52 50N 8 3W
83 Toora, Australia 38 40S 146 20E
83 Toowoomba, Australia 27 30S 152 0E
64 Top, Afghanistan 34 15N 68 35E
50 Top, L., U.S.S.R. 65 30N 32 0E
91 Topeka, U.S.A. 39 0N 95 40W
60 Topki, U.S.S.R. 55 40N 85 40E
94 Topolobampo, Mexico 25 45N 108 48W
24 Tor B., England 50 25N 3 33W
24 Torbay, England 50 28N 3 32W
37 Tordesillas, Spain 41 30N 5 0W
61 Torei, U.S.S.R. 50 45N 104 45E
46 Torgau, Germany 51 35N 12 58E
44 Torhout, Belgium 51 4N 3 7E
40 Torino, *see* Turin
73 Torit, Sudan 4 29N 32 32E
37 Tormes, R., Spain 41 10N 6 0W
48 Torne, R., Sweden 67 30N 22 0E
48 Torneträsk, L., Sweden 68 20N 19 25E
48 Tornio, & R., Finland 65 57N 24 12E
99 Toro, Cor del, Chile 29 10S 69 0W
41 Toronaios, G., Greece 40 0N 23 35E
83 Toronto, Australia 32 58S 151 30E
92 Toronto, Canada 43 42N 79 30W
74 Tororo, Uganda 0 43N 34 13E
24 Torquay, England 50 28N 3 32W
37 Tôrre de Moncorvo, Port. 41 12N 7 10W
37 Torrelavega, Spain 43 20N 4 5W
83 Torrens, L., Australia 31 0S 137 40E
82 Torrens Creek, Austral. 20 48S 145 3E
94 Torreon, Mexico 25 30N 103 12W
94 Torres, Mexico 28 40N 110 55W
82 Torres Strait, Australia 10 0S 142 30E
37 Torres Vedras, Portugal 39 3N 9 19W
37 Torrevieja, Spain 37 59N 0 40W
32 Torridon, & L., Scot. 57 33N 5 30W
93 Torrington, U.S.A. 41 50N 73 5W
42 Torteval, Guernsey, Channel Is. 49 26N 2 38W
43 Tortona, Italy 44 55N 8 55E
83 Torrowangee, Australia 31 25S 141 30E
37 Tortosa, Spain 40 48N 0 47E
98 Tortuga I., Venezuela 11 0N 65 30W
47 Torun, Poland 53 2N 18 37E
52 Torzhok, U.S.S.R. 57 10N 34 55E
67 Tosa B., Japan 33 15N 133 30E
24 Totnes, England 50 25N 3 54W
83 Tottenham, Australia 32 10S 147 20E
67 Tottori, & Pref., Japan 35 30N 134 10E
72 Toubkal, Djebel, Morocco 31 15N 7 20W
72 Touggourt, Algeria 33 5N 6 0E
43 Toul, France 48 42N 5 53E
43 Toulon, France 43 9N 5 55E
43 Toulouse, France 43 37N 1 18E
43 Touraine, Dist., France 47 20N 0 40E
43 Tourcoing, France 50 46N 3 3E
44 Tournai, Belgium 50 37N 3 23E
43 Tournus, France 46 35N 4 50E
43 Tours, France 47 24N 0 41E
76 Touws, South Africa 33 32S 20 32E
76 Touwsrivier, S. Africa 33 20S 20 2E
23 Towcester, England 52 8N 1 0W
82 Townshend I., Australia 22 15S 150 38E
82 Townsville, Australia 19 15S 146 47E
25 Towy, R., Wales, *see* Tywi
25 Towyn, *see* Tywyn
67 Toyama, B. & Pref., Jap. 36 40N 137 10E
67 Toyohashi, Japan 34 40N 137 28E
51 Trabzon, Turkey 40 58N 39 50E
93 Tracadie, Canada 47 30N 65 0W
37 Trafalgar, C., Spain 36 13N 6 7W
88 Trail, Canada 49 6N 117 58W
41 Trajan's Gate, Bulgaria 42 21N 23 46E
47 Trajan's Wall, Rumania 44 18N 28 20E
34 Tralee, & B., Ireland 52 16N 9 43W
35 Tramore & B., Ireland 52 9N 7 10W
49 Tranås, Sweden 58 5N 14 58E
68 Trang, Malaya 7 30N 99 40E
83 Trangie, Australia 31 58S 148 2E
40 Trani, Italy 41 17N 16 27E
76 Transkei, S. Africa 32 0S 28 0E
75 Transvaal, Prov., S. Afr. 25 20S 28 30E
47 Transylvania, reg., Rum. 46 18N 24 30E
47 Transylvanian Alps, Rum. 45 35N 24 30E
40 Trapani, Italy 38 1N 12 55E
83 Traralgon, Australia 38 17S 146 35E
37 Tras os Montes E Alto-Douro, Prov., Portugal 41 25N 7 20W
40 Trasimeno, L., Italy 43 8N 12 5E
68 Trat, Cambodia 12 20N 102 30E
83 Traveller's L., Australia 33 14S 142 0E
84 Travers, Mt., N.Z. 42 1S 172 45E
92 Traverse City, U.S.A. 44 50N 85 40W
41 Travnik, Yugoslavia 44 12N 17 38E
40 Trebbia, R., Italy 44 50N 9 30E
46 Trebic, Czechoslovakia 49 15N 15 50E
41 Trebinje, Yugoslavia 42 43N 18 17E
46 Trebon, Czechoslovakia 49 0N 14 50E
25 Tredegar, Wales 51 46N 3 16W
25 Treharris, Wales 51 38N 3 17W
99 Treinta y Tres, Uruguay 33 30S 54 0W
44 Trélon, France 50 5N 4 6E
49 Trelleborg, Sweden 55 21N 13 2E
25 Tremadog, & B., Wales 52 55N 4 8W
37 Tremp, Spain 42 10N 0 50E
27 Trent, R., England 53 33N 0 44W
40 Trentino-Alto-Adige, Reg., Italy 46 5N 11 0E
40 Trento, Italy 46 3N 11 5E
92 Trenton, Canada 44 6N 77 37W
93 Trenton, U.S.A. 40 17N 74 39W
89 Trepassey, Canada 46 34N 53 25W
99 Tres Arroyos, Argentina 38 30S 60 30W
99 Tres Puntas, C., Arg. 47 30S 65 0W
43 Treviglio, Italy 45 35N 9 40E
40 Treviso, Italy 45 41N 12 18E
24 Trevose Hd., England 50 33N 5 3W
43 Trévoux, France 46 0N 4 50E
64 Trichur, India 10 30N 76 15E
83 Trida, Australia 32 58S 144 59E
45 Trier, Germany 49 45N 6 40E
40 Trieste, Italy 45 39N 13 50E
41 Trikkala, Greece 39 35N 21 42E

35 Trim, Ireland 53 35N 6 47w
64 Trincomalee, Sri Lanka 8 40N 81 12E
98 Trinidad, Bolivia 14 30s 65 12w
95 Trinidad, Cuba 21 55N 80 7w
90 Trinidad, U.S.A. 37 5N 104 30w
94 Trinidad, I., W. Indies 10 5N 61 0w
94 Trinidad & Tobago, *see* Inset
99 Trinidad I., Argentina 39 0s 62 0w
94 Trinité, Martinque, Fr., W.I. 14 42N 60 58w
94 Trinity R., U.S.A. 31 30N 95 3w
73 Trinkitat, Sudan 17 30N 37 50E
51 Tripoli, Lebanon 34 40N 36 0E
73 Tripoli, Libya 32 58N 13 12E
41 Tripolis, Greece 37 29N 22 37E
73 Tripolitania, Libya 30 0N 14 0E
65 Tripura, Prov., India 24 0N 91 40E
5 Tristan da Cuñha, Atlantic Ocean 38 0s 12 20w
64 Trivandrum, India 8 40N 76 50E
47 Trnava, Czechoslovakia 48 20N 17 30E
82 Trobriand or Kiriwina Is., Papua 8 40s 152 0E
40 Troglav, Mt., Yugoslavia 43 53N 16 20E
93 Trois Rivières, Canada 46 25N 72 45w
60 Troitsk, U.S.S.R. 54 20N 61 28E
67 Troitskoye, U.S.S.R. 49 43N 136 50E
48 Trolladyngja Mt., Ice. 64 49N 17 29w
49 Trollhätten, Sweden 58 11N 12 15E
76 Trompsburg, S. Africa 30 0s 25 40E
48 Troms, Co., Norway 69 15N 20 0E
48 Tromsö, Norway 69 34N 18 49E
99 Tronador, Mt., Chile 41 30s 71 30w
48 Trondelag, N., Co., Nor. 65 0N 12 0E
48 Trondheim, & Fd., Nor. 63 25N 10 23E
51 Troodos, Mt., Cyprus 35 0N 32 45E
30 Troon, Scotland 55 33N 4 38w
31 Trossachs, Scotland 56 13N 4 23w
32 Trotternish, dist., Scot. 57 35N 6 15w
88 Trout L., Canada 60 40N 121 40w
43 Trouville, France 49 20N 0 10E
22 Trowbridge, England 51 20N 2 12w
91 Troy, Ala., U.S.A. 31 45N 85 58w
93 Troy, N.Y., U.S.A. 42 48N 73 37w
41 Troy, Ancient City, Turkey 39 47N 26 18E
43 Troyes, France 48 19N 4 2E
66 Trucial States, *see* United Arab Emirates
98 Trujillo, Peru 8 7s 78 50w
37 Trujillo, Spain 39 29N 5 53w
95 Trujillo, Venezuela 9 25N 70 20w
83 Trundle, Australia 32 47s 147 40E
93 Truro, Canada 45 21N 63 30w
24 Truro, England 50 15N 5 4w
36 Truskmore, Mt., Ireland 54 22N 8 23w
46 Trutnov, Czechoslovakia 50 37N 15 54E
66 Tsaidam, dist., China 37 30N 95 30E
66 Tsamkong, China 21 15N 110 10E
65 Tsanga, China 30 40N 100 25E
65 Tsangpo, R., China 30 0N 83 0E
75 Tsau, Botswana 20 5s 22 50E
63 Tsefat, Israel 32 57N 35 29E
60 Tselinograd, U.S.S.R. 51 45N 71 5E
76 Tses, S.W. Africa 25 50s 18 10E
75 Tshane, Botswana 24 5s 21 54E
74 Tshikapa, Zaïre 6 17s 21 0E
66 Tsiaotso, China 35 11N 13 10E
75 Tsihombe, Madagascar 25 9s 45 34E
52 Tsimlyansk Res., U.S.S.R. 48 0N 42 30E
66 Tsi-nan, China 36 45N 117 0E
66 Tsinghai, prov., China 36 0N 96 0E
67 Tsingkiang, China 33 45N 119 0E
66 Tsin Ling Shan, mts., China 34 20N 108 0E
66 Tsingshih, China 29 30N 112 0E
66 Tsingsi, China 23 25N 105 20E
67 Tsingtao, China 36 7N 120 25E
66 Tsining, China 35 30N 116 35E
67 Tsitsihar, China 47 20N 124 0E
51 Tskhinvali, U.S.S.R. 42 15N 43 30E
52 Tsna, R., U.S.S.R. 53 20N 41 40E
63 Tstl, Syria 32 50N 35 58E
67 Tsu, Japan 34 38N 136 28E
67 Tsu Shima I., Japan 34 20N 129 15E
67 Tsugaru Str., Japan 41 30N 141 0E
75 Tsumeb, S.W. Africa 19 11s 17 47E
66 Tsunyi, China 27 38N 107 0E
67 Tsuruga, Japan 35 42N 136 4E
67 Tsuruoka, Japan 38 40N 139 52E
67 Tsuyama, Japan 35 7N 134 0E
34 Tuam, Ireland 53 31N 8 50w
4 Tuamoto Arch., Pac. Oc. 17 0s 144 0w
51 Tuapse, U.S.S.R. 44 0N 39 0E
84 Tuatapere, New Zealand 46 5s 167 41E
99 Tubarao, Brazil 28 25s 49 0w
63 Tubas, Jordan 32 20N 35 22E
45 Tübingen, Germany 48 30N 9 0E
73 Tubruq, Libya 32 0N 23 45E
94 Tucacas, Venezuela 10 48N 68 18w
90 Tucson, U.S.A. 32 12N 110 48w
99 Tucumán, Argentina 26 48s 65 30w
90 Tucumcari, U.S.A. 35 12N 103 45w
37 Tudela, Spain 42 4N 1 39w
25 Tudweiliog, Wales 52 54N 4 35w
83 Tuen, Australia 28 33s 145 57E
61 Tugur, U.S.S.R. 53 40N 136 55E
73 Tukrah, Libya 32 30N 20 20E
74 Tukuyu, Tanzania 9 0s 33 40E
64 Tukzar, Afghanistan 35 35N 66 25E
63 Tul Karm, Jordan 32 19N 35 2E
94 Tula, Mexico 22 55N 99 45w
52 Tula, U.S.S.R. 54 18N 37 35E
66 Tulan, China 37 20N 98 20E
90 Tulare, & L., U.S.A. 36 0N 119 40w
98 Tulcan, Ecuador 0 50N 77 50w
47 Tulcea, Rumania 45 10N 28 47E
75 Tulear, Madagascar 23 20N 43 45E
34 Tulla, Ireland 52 52N 8 46w
35 Tullamore, Ireland 53 17N 7 29w
43 Tulle, France 45 17N 1 41E
43 Tullins, France 45 18N 5 30E
35 Tullow, Ireland 52 47N 6 42w
73 Tulmaythah, Libya 32 40N 20 55E
91 Tulsa, U.S.A. 36 5N 96 0w
61 Tulun, U.S.S.R. 54 45N 100 20E
98 Tumaco, Colombia 1 40N 78 45w
83 Tumbarumba, Australia 35 54s 148 0E
64 Tumkur, India 13 15N 77 6E
31 Tummel, L. & R., Scot. 56 42N 3 57w
64 Tump, Pakistan 26 3N 62 18E
72 Tumu, Ghana 11 0N 2 0w
83 Tumut, Australia 35 17s 148 9E
23 Tunbridge Wells, Eng. 51 8N 0 17E
83 Tuncurry, Australia 32 0s 152 18E
74 Tunduru, Tanzania 11 10s 37 30E
66 Tung Ting, L., China 29 0N 112 30E
65 Tunga Pass, China 29 5N 94 10E
64 Tungabhadra, R., India 15 30N 76 50E
74 Tungaru, Sudan 10 10N 30 50E
66 Tunghing, China 21 45N 107 15E
67 Tunghwa, China 41 40N 126 20E
66 Tungjen, China 27 50N 108 30E
66 Tungkwan, China 34 37N 110 0E
67 Tungliao, China 43 30N 122 20E
48 Tungnafells J., mts., Ice. 64 30N 18 20w
65 Tungpu, China 31 40N 98 25E
66 Tungtze, China 28 25N 106 0E
66 Tunhwang, China 40 25N 94 15E
73 Tunis, Tunisia 36 48N 10 13E
73 Tunisia, North Africa 34 0N 9 0E
67 Tunki, China 29 45N 118 15E
48 Tunnsjöen, L., Sweden 64 40N 14 0E
23 Tunstall, England 52 7N 1 28E
91 Tupelo, U.S.A. 34 23N 88 59w
65 Tura, India 25 20N 90 25E
61 Tura, U.S.S.R. 64 20N 99 40E
62 Turaba, Saudi Arabia 28 22N 43 14E
55 Turanain Pl., U.S.S.R. 44 0N 63 0E
47 Turek, Poland 52 0N 18 30E
66 Turfan, China 43 40N 88 55E
66 Turfan Depression, China 42 45N 90 0E
41 Turgovishte, Bulgaria 43 17N 26 38E
51 Turgutlu, Turkey 38 30N 27 40E
67 Turi Rog., U.S.S.R. 45 5N 131 45E
37 Turia, R., Spain 39 45N 1 12w
40 Turin (Torino), Italy 45 2N 7 43E
47 Turka, U.S.S.R. 49 10N 23 0E
74 Turkana, L., Kenya 3 30N 36 0E
60 Turkestan, U.S.S.R. 43 12N 68 10E
51 Turkey, Asia & Eur. 39 0N 33 0E
60 Turkmenistan, S.S.R., U.S.S.R. 39 0N 60 0E
95 Turks Is., W. Indies 21 15N 71 10w
49 Turku, Finland 60 30N 22 19E
49 Turku Pori, Co., Finland 61 15N 22 10E
44 Turnhout, Belgium 51 21N 4 47E
47 Turnu Magurele, Rum. 43 45N 24 50E
47 Turnu Severin, Rum. 44 38N 22 58E
33 Turriff, Scotland 57 33N 2 27w
91 Tuscaloosa, U.S.A. 33 14N 87 31w
40 Tuscany, reg., Italy 43 35N 11 20E
52 Tushino, U.S.S.R. 55 50N 37 26E
22 Tutbury, England 52 52N 1 42w
41 Tutrakan, Bulgaria 44 0N 26 34E
45 Tuttlingen, Germany 48 0N 8 50E
61 Tuva, A.S.S.R., U.S.S.R. 51 30N 95 0E
11 Tuvaln, Is., Pac. Oc. 7 40s 178 0E
94 Tuxpan, Mexico 20 50N 97 23w
94 Tuxtla, Mexico 16 50N 93 15w
51 Tuz, L., Turkey 38 45N 33 15E
41 Tuzla, Yugoslavia 44 35N 18 20E
31 Tweed, R., Scotland 55 38N 2 20w
27 Tweedmouth, England 55 46N 2 1w
90 Twin Falls, U.S.A. 42 30N 114 35w
83 Twofold B., Australia 37 0s 150 0E
26 Tyldesley, England 53 32N 2 29w
91 Tyler, U.S.A. 32 18N 95 17w
30 Tyndrum, Scotland 56 26N 4 42w
26 Tyne, R., England 54 58N 2 0w
31 Tyne, R., Scotland 55 58N 2 40w
27 Tyne & Wear, Co., Eng. 55 0N 1 35w
27 Tynemouth, England 55 1N 1 28w
63 Tyre, Lebanon 33 17N 35 12E
83 Tyrell, L., Australia 35 23s 142 50E
49 Tyri Fd., Norway 60 8N 10 3E
46 Tyrol, Prov., Austria 46 58N 11 40E
36 Tyrone, Co., N. Ireland 54 40N 7 15w
40 Tyrrhenian Sea, Medit. S. 40 30N 12 0E
48 Tys Fjord, Norway 68 5N 16 30E
25 Tywi, R., Wales 51 50N 3 50w
25 Tywyn, Wales 52 34N 4 5w
76 Tzaneen, South Africa 23 45s 30 5E
66 Tzekung, China 29 30N 104 20E
66 Tzepo, China 36 20N 118 30E
65 Tzuchien, China 27 45N 98 35E

U

63 Uassem, Syria 32 59N 36 2E
74 Ubangi, R., Congo, *see* Oubangi, R.
67 Ube, Japan 33 55N 131 20E
37 Ubeda Baeza, Spain 38 0N 3 25w
98 Uberaba, Brazil 19 50s 47 50w
98 Uberlandia, Brazil 19 0s 48 22w
98 Ucayali, R., Peru 8 30s 74 20w
60 Uchinya, U.S.S.R. 60 5N 65 15E
61 Uchur R., U.S.S.R. 58 0N 131 0E
23 Uckfield, England 50 58N 0 6E
64 Udaipur, India 24 48N 73 42E
56 Udaipur Garhi, Nepal 27 0N 86 30E
49 Uddevalla, Sweden 58 23N 11 57E
31 Uddingston, Scotland 55 50N 4 3w
48 Uddjaur, L., Sweden 65 55N 17 50E
72 Udi, Nigeria 6 20N 7 30E
40 Udine, Italy 46 2N 13 18E
64 Udipi, India 13 15N 74 40E
50 Udmurt A.S.S.R., U.S.S.R. 57 0N 52 30E
66 Udon Thani, Thailand 17 45N 102 0E
67 Ueda, Japan 36 27N 138 7E
61 Uelen, U.S.S.R. 66 0N 170 10w
46 Uelzen, Germany 53 0N 10 30E
50 Ufa, U.S.S.R. 54 50N 55 53E
50 Ufa, R., U.S.S.R. 56 0N 57 0E
74 Uganda, E. Africa 2 0N 32 30E
61 Uglegorsk, U.S.S.R. 49 10N 142 5E
61 Ugolyak, U.S.S.R. 64 40N 120 10E
32 Uig, Scotland 58 13N 7 1w
90 Uintah Mts., U.S.A. 40 45N 110 0w
32 Uist, *see* North Uist, South Uist
76 Uitenhage, S. Africa 33 47s 25 28E
44 Uithuizen, Netherlands 53 24N 6 41E
38 Ujda, Morocco 34 45N 2 0w
74 Ujiji, Tanzania 4 59s 29 43E
67 Ujiyamada, Japan 34 25N 136 50E
64 Ujjain, India 23 10N 75 45E
47 Ujpest, Hungary 47 36N 19 9E
74 Ukerewe I., Tanzania 2 0s 32 0E
65 Ukhrul, India 25 10N 94 20E
50 Ukhta, U.S.S.R. 63 55N 54 0E
90 Ukian, U.S.A. 39 12N 123 10w
50 Ukmerge, U.S.S.R. 55 15N 24 40E
51 Ukraine S.S.R., U.S.S.R. 49 20N 32 0E
66 Ulan-Bator, Mongolia 48 0N 106 59E
61 Ulan Ude, U.S.S.R. 51 50N 107 20E
67 Ulanhot, China 46 10N 121 45E
41 Ulcinj, Yugoslavia 42 0N 19 10E
76 Ulco, South Africa 28 20s 24 15E
48 Uleaborg, *see* Oulu
83 Ulladulla, Australia 35 22s 150 28E
32 Ullapool, Scotland 57 54N 5 9w
26 Ullswater, L., England 54 35N 2 50w
45 Ulm, Germany 48 27N 9 58E
83 Ulmarra, Australia 29 36s 152 55E
49 Ulricehamn, Sweden 57 50N 13 24E
35 Ulster, U.K. 54 32N 7 0w
36 Ulster Canal, N. Ireland 54 15N 7 0w
60 Ulutau, U.S.S.R. 48 50N 67 5E
30 Ulva, I., Scotland 56 30N 6 12w
26 Ulverston, England 54 13N 3 6w
83 Ulverstone, Australia 41 5s 146 8E
50 Ulyanovsk, U.S.S.R. 54 12N 48 25E
66 Ulyasutay, Mongolia 47 50N 96 40w
51 Uman, U.S.S.R. 48 30N 30 5E
65 Umaria, India 23 35N 80 50E
64 Umarkot, Pakistan 25 12N 69 58E
82 Umboi I., Papua N.G. 5 30s 148 0E
45 Umbrail Pass, Switzerland 46 35N 10 20E
40 Umbria, reg., Italy 43 0N 12 40E
48 Ume, R., Sweden 64 15N 19 30E
48 Umea, Sweden 63 49N 20 20E
76 Umkomaas, S. Africa R. 30 12s 30 48E
73 Umm Dam, Sudan 13 50N 31 0E
62 Umm Lajj, Saudi Arabia 25 0N 37 23E
63 Umm Qays, Jordan 32 40N 35 40E
73 Umm Ruwaba, Sudan 12 50N 31 10E
75 Umtali, Rhodesia 18 59s 32 41E
76 Umtata, S. Africa 31 40s 28 42E
76 Umzinto, S. Africa 30 15s 30 40E
40 Unac, R., Yugoslavia 44 50N 16 15E
88 Unalaska, Alaska 54 0N 164 30w
98 Uncia, Bolivia 18 30s 66 25w
83 Ungarie, Australia 33 30s 147 10E
89 Ungava B., Canada 59 30N 68 0w
89 Ungava Peninsula, Canada 60 0N 75 0w
88 Unimak I. & Pass, Alaska 54 30N 164 30w
91 Union, U.S.A. 34 43N 81 32w
92 Union City, U.S.A. 36 30N 89 2w
60-61 Union of Soviet Socialist Republics 60 0N 90 0E
76 Uniondale, S. Africa 33 35s 23 19E
92 Uniontown, U.S.A. 39 56N 79 45w
63 United Arab Emirates, Asia 23 0N 54 0E
16 United Kingdom, Europe 55 0N 2 0w
90 United States of America, N. America 39 0N 96 0w
64 Unnao, India 26 45N 80 50E
36 Unshin R., Ireland 54 8N 8 26w
32 Unst, I., Scotland 60 45N 0 50w
45 Unterwalden, Cn., Switz. 46 55N 8 15E
74 Upemba, L., Zaïre 8 40s 26 22E
76 Upington, S. Africa 28 18s 21 12E
84 Upolu I., Samoa (Inset)
46 Upper Austria, Austria 48 15N 15 10E
25 Upper Chapel, Wales 52 3N 3 26w
63 Upper Galilee, Dist., Israel 33 2N 35 20E
84 Upper Hutt, N.Z. 41 8s 175 5E
90 Upper Klamath L., U.S.A. 42 30N 122 0w
36 Upper L., Erne, N. Ire. 54 13N 7 32w
73 Upper Nile, dist., Sudan 10 0N 33 0E
61 Upper Taimyr R., U.S.S.R. 73 40N 96 0E
72 Upper Volta, Africa 12 0N 1 0w
49 Uppsala, & Co., Sweden 59 52N 17 35E
26 Upton, England 53 14N 2 52w
22 Upton-on-Severn, Eng. 52 4N 2 12w
98 Uraba, G. of, Colombia 8 30N 77 0w
50 Ural Mts., U.S.S.R. 59 0N 60 0E
51 Ural, R., U.S.S.R. 49 10N 52 0E
83 Uralla, Australia 30 40s 151 30E
50 Uralsk, U.S.S.R. 51 12N 51 20E
88 Uranium City, Canada 59 40N 108 30w
83 Uranquinty, Australia 35 10s 146 40E
67 Urawa, Japan 36 0N 139 30E
40 Urbino, Italy 43 46N 12 41E
51 Urda, U.S.S.R. 48 43N 48 27E
94 Ures, Mexico 29 20N 110 30w
51 Urfa, Turkey 37 15N 39 5E
46 Urfahr, Austria 48 15N 14 20E
66 Urga, *see* Ulan Bator
60 Urgench, U.S.S.R. 41 40N 60 30E
45 Uri, Canton, Switzerland 46 50N 8 40E
44 Urk, Netherlands 52 40N 5 37E
35 Urlingford, Ireland 52 44N 7 33w
62 Urmia, L., Iran 37 40N 45 30E
26 Urmston, England 53 28N 2 22w
98 Urubamba, R., Peru 13 0s 72 30w
99 Uruguaiana, Brazil 29 45s 57 0w
96 Uruguay, S. Amer. 33 0s 55 0w
99 Uruguay, R., S. America 28 30s 56 0w
66 Urumchi, China 44 0N 88 0E
67 Urup, I., U.S.S.R. 46 0N 150 0E
42 Urville, France 49 40N 1 45w
50 Usa, R., U.S.S.R. 66 29N 61 0E
62 Usak, Turkey 38 43N 29 28E
75 Usakos, S.W. Africa 21 58s 15 30E
74 Useko, Tanzania 5 9s 32 22E
42 Ushant I., France 48 30N 5 0w
99 Ushuaia, Argentina 54 45s 68 15w
25 Usk, & R., Wales 51 42N 2 53w
51 Usküdar, Turkey 41 0N 29 5E
52 Usman, U.S.S.R. 52 5N 39 40E
61 Usole Sibirskoye, U.S.S.R. 52 40N 103 40E
99 Uspallata P., Argentina 32 45s 70 0w
60 Uspenski, U.S.S.R. 48 50N 72 55E
43 Ussel, France 45 30N 2 15E
67 Ussuri R., Asia 46 30N 133 30E
61 Ussuriysk, U.S.S.R. 43 40N 131 50E
61 Ust Bolsheretsk, U.S.S.R. 52 40N 156 30E
60 Ust Ishim, U.S.S.R. 57 45N 71 10E
61 Ust Kamchatsk, U.S.S.R. 56 10N 162 0E
60 Ust Kamenogorsk, U.S.S.R. 50 0N 82 20E
61 Ust Kut, U.S.S.R. 56 50N 105 10E
61 Ust Maya, U.S.S.R. 60 30N 134 20E
60 Ust Port, U.S.S.R. 70 0N 84 10E
61 Ust Tungir, U.S.S.R. 55 25N 120 15E
60 Ust Urt, Plat., U.S.S.R. 43 10N 55 0E
50 Ust Usa, U.S.S.R. 66 0N 56 30E
61 Ust-chaun, U.S.S.R. 68 30N 170 50E
46 Usti nad Labem, Cz-slov. 50 40N 14 7E
40 Ustica I., Italy 38 42N 13 14E
61 Ustye, U.S.S.R. 57 40N 94 50E
94 Usumacinta, R., Central America 17 0N 91 0w
90 Utah, st., U.S.A. 39 40N 111 30w
90 Utah, L., U.S.A. 40 20N 111 45w
74 Utete, Tanzania 8 0s 38 50E
91 Utica, U.S.A. 43 0N 75 12w
67 Uto, Japan 32 35N 130 48E
44 Utrecht, & Prov., Neth. 52 6N 5 8E
37 Utrera, Spain 37 14N 5 50w
67 Utsonomiya, Japan 36 30N 139 56E
65 Uttar Pradesh, st., India 27 20N 80 30E
66 Uttaradit, Thailand 17 42N 100 1E
26 Uttoxeter, England 52 53N 1 52w
49 Uudenmaa, Co., Finland 60 30N 25 0E
48 Uusikaarlepyy, Finland 63 35N 22 30E
49 Uusikaupunki, Finland 60 50N 21 25E
90 Uvalde, U.S.A. 29 14N 99 45w
50 Uvaly Uplands, U.S.S.R. 60 0N 51 15E
60 Uvat, U.S.S.R. 59 5N 68 50E
74 Uvinza, Tanzania 5 0s 30 27E
74 Uvira, Zaïre 3 19s 29 2E
61 Uvs Nuur, Mongolia 50 15N 92 30E
67 Uwajima, Japan 33 10N 132 30E
98 Uyuni, Salar de, Bolivia 20 0s 68 0w
60 Uzbekistan, S.S.R., U.S.S.R. 38 0N 68 0E
43 Uzerche, France 45 22N 1 30E
43 Uzès, France 44 0N 4 20E
47 Uzhgorod, U.S.S.R. 48 36N 22 18E
46 Uznam, I., Ger.-Poland 54 0N 14 0E

V

76 Vaal, R., S. Africa 26 45s 25 30E
48 Vaasa, & Co., Finland 63 9N 21 30E
47 Vác, Hungary 47 50N 19 10E
64 Vadodara, India 22 22N 73 17E
48 Vadsö, Norway 70 3N 29 50E
45 Vaduz, Liechtenstein 47 9N 9 32E
47 Vah, R., Czechoslovakia 49 10N 18 30E
43 Val-de-Marne, Dépt., Fr. 49 0N 2 30E
42 Val d'Oise, Dépt., France 49 10N 2 10E
89 Val d'Or, Canada 48 7N 77 47w
45 Valais, Canton, Switz. 46 10N 7 30E
50 Valdai Hill, U.S.S.R. 58 0N 33 0E
37 Valdepenas, Spain 38 44N 3 26w
99 Valdés Pen., Argentina 42 30s 64 0w
88 Valdez, Alaska 61 14N 146 10w
99 Valdivia, Chile 40 3s 73 35w
91 Valdosta, U.S.A. 30 51N 83 21w
42 Vale, Channel Is. 49 30N 2 30w
43 Valence, France 44 58N 4 59E
37 Valencia, Prov., & G., Spain 39 28N 0 23w
94 Valencia, Venezuela 10 37N 68 0w
43 Valenciennes, France 50 20N 3 32E
94 Valera, Venezuela 9 20N 70 30w
49 Valga, U.S.S.R. 57 41N 26 0E
43 Valinco, G. of, France 41 45N 8 30E
47 Valjevo, Yugoslavia 44 18N 19 55E
94 Valladolid, Mexico 20 30N 88 10w
37 Valladolid, Spain 41 40N 4 45w
37 Vallecas, Spain 40 23N 3 41w
90 Vallejo, U.S.A. 38 12N 122 12w
99 Vallenar, Chile 28 35s 70 45w
40 Valletta, Malta 35 55N 14 29E
90 Valley City, U.S.A. 47 0N 98 0w
93 Valleyfield, Canada 45 10N 74 15w
45 Vallorbe, Switzerland 46 43N 6 20E
37 Valls, Spain 41 15N 1 10E
49 Valmiera, U.S.S.R. 57 30N 25 27E
41 Valona, *see* Vlone
99 Valparaiso, Chile 33 5s 71 50w
76 Vals, R., South Africa 27 30s 26 45E
43 Valtellina, R., Italy 46 9N 9 50E
95 Valverde, Dom. Rep. 19 30N 71 10w
37 Valverde, Spain 37 30N 6 45w
51 Van, & L., Turkey 38 30N 43 30E
80 Van Diemen G., Austral. 12 0s 132 0E
88 Vancouver, Canada 49 14N 122 50w
92 Vancouver, U.S.A. 45 47N 122 46w
88 Vancouver I., Canada 49 30N 126 0w
76 Vanderbijlpark, S. Africa 26 40s 27 50E
49 Vänern, L., Sweden 58 47N 13 50E
49 Vänersborg, Sweden 58 26N 12 27E
74 Vänga, Kenya 4 33s 39 5E
48 Vännäs, Sweden 63 57N 19 30E
42 Vannes, France 47 42N 2 43w
48 Vannöy I., Norway 70 6N 19 50E
76 Vanrhynsdorp, S. Africa 31 32s 18 46E
49 Vansbro, Sweden 60 36N 14 12E
80 Vansittart B., Australia 13 50s 126 30E
84 Vanua Levu, Pac. Oc. 16 45s 179 20E
42 Var, Dépt., France 43 25N 6 5E
45 Varallo Sesia, Italy 45 50N 8 16E
65 Varanasi (Banaras), India 25 19N 82 57E
40 Varazdin, Yugoslavia 46 19N 16 21E
49 Varberg, Sweden 57 12N 12 19E
41 Vardar, R., Yugoslavia 41 30N 22 20E
47 Varena, U.S.S.R. 54 7N 24 30E
43 Varennes, Allier, France 46 20N 3 28E
43 Varennes, Meuse, France 49 15N 5 0E
40 Varese, Italy 45 49N 8 50E
49 Värmland, Co., Sweden 59 45N 13 0E
41 Varna, Bulgaria 43 10N 28 0E
49 Värnamo, Sweden 57 10N 14 3E
35 Vartry Res., Ireland 53 3N 6 12w
64 Vasht, Iran 28 15N 61 15E
49 Västeras, Sweden 59 37N 16 38E
49 Väster-dal, R., Sweden 60 30N 14 0E
48 Vasterbotten, Sweden 65 0N 17 0E
48 Västernorrland, Co., Sweden 63 0N 17 30E
49 Vastervik, Sweden 57 48N 16 32E
49 Västmanland, Co., Swed. 59 45N 16 20E
40 Vasto, Italy 42 8N 14 50E
32 Vaternish Pt., Scotland 57 36N 6 40w
32 Vatersay, I., Scotland 56 56N 7 32w
48 Vatna Jökull, mts., Ice. 64 30N 16 30w
75 Vatomandry, Madagascar 19 17s 48 55E
47 Vatra-Dornei, Rumania 47 20N 25 30E
49 Vättern, L., Sweden 58 25N 14 30E
42 Vaucluse, Dépt., France 44 7N 5 3E
45 Vaud, Canton, Switzerland 46 33N 6 30E
98 Vaupes, R., S. America 1 15N 71 0w
49 Växjö, Sweden 56 56N 14 48E
98 Veadeiros, Chapada dos, plat., Brazil 15 0s 48 0w
47 Vedea, R., Rumania 44 0N 25 20E
44 Veendam, Netherlands 53 6N 6 52E
48 Vega Fjord, Norway 65 30N 12 0E
48 Vega I., Norway 65 42N 11 50E
44 Veghel, Netherlands 51 37N 5 33E
88 Vegreville, Canada 53 35N 112 10w
37 Vejer, Spain 36 14N 5 59w
49 Vejle, Denmark 55 47N 9 30E
40 Velebit Planina, mts., Yugoslavia 44 40N 15 30E
37 Velez-Malaga, Spain 36 48N 4 5w
37 Velez Rúbio, Spain 37 45N 2 5w
50 Velikaya R., U.S.S.R. 57 0N 28 50E
50 Velikiy Ustyug, U.S.S.R. 60 47N 46 20E
50 Velikiye Luki, U.S.S.R. 56 25N 30 35E
40 Velletri, Italy 41 43N 12 50E
64 Vellore, India 13 0N 79 5E
44 Velzen, Netherlands 52 27N 4 40E
42 Vendée, Dépt., France 46 30N 1 35E
43 Vendôme, France 47 44N 1 0E
40 Veneto, reg., Italy 46 0N 12 0E
40 Venezia, *see* Venice
96 Venezuela, S. America 8 40N 67 0w
98 Venezuela, G. of, Ven. 11 30N 71 0w
64 Vengurla, India 15 45N 73 35E
40 Venice, & G., Italy 45 27N 12 20E
65 Venkatapuram, India 18 20N 80 30E
44 Venlo, Netherlands 51 22N 6 10E
43 Ventimiglia, Italy 43 51N 7 50E
22 Ventnor, I. of Wight, Eng. 50 36N 1 13w
49 Ventspils, U.S.S.R. 57 29N 21 33E
37 Vera, Spain 37 8N 1 53w
94 Veracruz, Mexico 19 13N 96 18w
64 Veraval, India 21 2N 70 17E
40 Vercelli, Italy 45 19N 8 28E
46 Verden, Germany 52 58N 9 18E
46 Verdon, R., France 43 47N 6 10E
43 Verdun, France 49 12N 5 20E
75 Vereeniging, S. Africa 26 42s 27 52E
42 Vergara, Spain 43 8N 2 23w
61 Verkh, Vilyuisk, U.S.S.R. 63 25N 120 5E
61 Verkhne Kolymsk, U.S.S.R. 65 48N 150 30E
61 Verkhoyansk, U.S.S.R. 68 0N 133 30E
61 Verkhoyansk, Ra., U.S.S.R. 65 0N 132 0E
88 Vermilion, Canada 53 20N 110 40w
91 Vermont, st., U.S.A. 44 0N 72 40w
88 Vernon, Canada 50 15N 119 20w
90 Vernon, U.S.A. 34 12N 99 18w

41 Véroia, Greece 40 35N 22 15E
40 Verona, Italy 45 26N 11 0E
43 Versailles, France 48 48N 2 7E
72 Vert, C., Sénégal 14 45N 17 30W
44 Verviers, Belgium 50 35N 5 52E
24 Veryan & B., England 50 13N 4 56W
52 Veselyy Res., U.S.S.R. 47 0N 41 0E
43 Vesoul, France 47 41N 6 8E
48 Vest, Fjorden, Norway 68 0N 15 0E
49 Vest-Agder, Co., Norway 58 30N 7 0E
48 Vesteralen, Norway 69 15N 15 45E
49 Vestfold, Co., Norway 59 15N 10 10E
48 Vestmannæyjär, Iceland 63 27N 20 15W
48 Vestvagöy I., Norway 68 15N 13 50E
40 Vesuvius, Mt., Italy 40 50N 14 28E
47 Veszprem, Hungary 47 8N 17 55E
49 Vetlanda, Sweden 57 30N 15 8E
50 Vetluga R., U.S.S.R. 57 0N 45 25E
45 Vevey, Switzerland 46 28N 6 52E
37 Viana, Portugal 38 20N 8 0W
37 Viana do Castello, Port. 41 40N 8 50W
49 Viborg, Denmark 56 28N 9 12E
40 Vicenza, Italy 45 35N 11 37E
37 Vich, Spain 41 56N 2 15E
98 Vichada, R., Colombia 4 30N 70 0W
52 Vichuga, U.S.S.R. 57 20N 41 50E
43 Vichy, France 46 10N 3 28E
91 Vicksburg, U.S.A. 32 12N 90 47W
83 Victor Hr., Australia 35 50S 138 40E
83 Victoria, st., Australia 37 0S 145 0E
72 Victoria, Cameroon 4 0N 9 12E
90 Victoria, Canada 48 28N 123 20W
72 Victoria, Guinea 10 57N 14 50W
40 Victoria, Malta 36 1N 14 18E
68 Victoria, Sabah, Malaysia 5 15N 115 40E
91 Victoria, U.S.A. 28 46N 97 0W
75 Victoria Falls, Rhodesia 17 59S 25 57E
88 Victoria I., Canada 70 30N 109 0W
74 Victoria, L., Africa 1 0S 33 0E
100 Victoria Ld., Antarctica 80 0S 160 0E
66 Victoria, Mt., Burma 21 15N 94 5E
68 Victoria Point, Burma 10 0N 98 30E
80 Victoria, R., Australia 15 40S 131 0E
80 Victoria River Downs, Australia 16 22S 131 8E
76 Victoria W., S. Africa 31 37S 23 5E
93 Victoriaville, Canada 46 0N 72 5W
41 Vidin, Yugoslavia 43 59N 22 52E
99 Viedma, L., Argentina 49 30S 72 30W
43 Viella, Spain 42 43N 0 47E
46 Vienna (Wien), Austria 48 12N 16 20E
43 Vienne, France 45 32N 4 57E
43 Vienne R., France 47 10N 0 20E
42 Vienne, Dépt., France 46 23N 0 20E
66 Vientiane, Laos 18 6N 102 30E
95 Vieques, I., Puerto Rico 18 10N 65 30W
45 Vierwaldstattersee (L. of Lucerne), Switzerland 47 2N 8 10E
44 Viersen, Germany 51 16N 6 24E
57 Vietnam, Asia 15 0N 108 0E
94 Vieux Fort, St. Lucia, W.I. 13 45N 60 58W
68 Vigan, Philippines 17 32N 120 20E
37 Vigo, Spain 42 12N 8 42W
65 Vijayawada, India 16 30N 80 39E
41 Vijose, R., Albania 40 40N 20 21E
48 Vikna I., Norway 65 0N 11 0E
50 Vikulovo, U.S.S.R. 56 50N 70 40E
75 Vila Arriaga, Angola 14 35S 13 30E
75 Vila Coutinho, Mozam. 14 34S 34 21E
37 Vila Franca, Portugal 39 0N 8 58W
75 Vila General Machado, Angola 11 58S 17 22E
76 Vila Luiza, Mozambique 25 40S 32 35E
75 Vila Nova de Seles, Angola 11 35S 14 22E
75 Vila Pereira d'Eça, Angola 16 48S 15 50E
37 Vila Real, Portugal 41 17N 7 42W
76 Vila de Sena, Mozàm. 17 23S 34 40E
74 Vila Verissimo Sarmento, Angola 8 15S 20 50E
42 Vilaine, R., France 47 50N 1 50W
48 Vilhelmina, Sweden 64 38N 16 50E
61 Viliga, U.S.S.R. 61 20N 156 20E
49 Viljandi, U.S.S.R. 58 23N 25 38E
94 Villa Ahumada, Mex. 30 35N 106 30W
99 Villa Encarnación, Para. 27 20S 56 0W
99 Villa Maria, Argentina 32 20S 63 15W
46 Villach, Austria 46 37N 13 45E
37 Villagarcia, Spain 42 34N 8 46W
94 Villahermosa, Mexico 18 0N 92 55W
37 Villalba, Spain 43 19N 7 43W
37 Villanueva de la Serena, Spain 39 0N 5 49W
37 Villarreal, Spain 39 50N 0 1W
99 Villarrica, Paraguay 25 45S 56 30W
37 Villarrobledo, Spain 39 20N 2 30W
45 Villars, Switzerland 46 18N 7 6E
37 Villaviciosa, Spain 43 30N 5 30W
42 Ville de Paris, Dépt., France 49 0N 2 15E
43 Villefranche, Alpes-Maritimes, France 43 43N 7 20E
43 Villefranche, Aveyron, Fr. 44 20N 2 0E
43 Villefranche, Rhône, Fr. 46 0N 4 40E
37 Villena, Spain 38 42N 0 52W
43 Villeneuve, France 44 22N 0 40E
44 Villerupt, France 49 28N 5 55E
43 Villeurbanne, France 45 42N 4 55E
50 Vilnius, U.S.S.R. 54 42N 25 15E
44 Vilvoorde, Belgium 50 56N 4 28E
61 Vilyui R., U.S.S.R. 63 58N 125 0E
61 Vilyuisk, U.S.S.R. 63 20N 121 20E
99 Vina del Mar, Chile 33 0S 71 30W
37 Vinaroz, Spain 40 25N 0 30E
91 Vincennes, U.S.A. 38 49N 87 30W
Vinh, Vietnam 18 55N 105 49E
68 Vinh Loi, Vietnam 9 29N 105 50E
41 Vinkovci, Yugoslavia 45 20N 18 45E
47 Vinnitsa, U.S.S.R. 49 10N 28 30E
64 Viramgam, India 23 12N 72 3E
42 Virandeville, France 49 35N 1 44W
88 Virden, Canada 49 50N 100 55W
99 Vírgenes, C., Argentina 52 15S 68 10W
95 Virgin Is., W. Indies 18 20N 65 0W
36 Virginia, Ireland 53 50N 7 5E
76 Virginia, S. Africa 27 53S 26 45E
91 Virginia, st., U.S.A. 37 15N 79 0W
44 Virton, Belgium 49 35N 5 33E
64 Virudhungar, India 9 30N 77 55E
40 Vis I., Yugoslavia 43 0N 16 10E
90 Visalia, U.S.A. 36 23N 119 16W
68 Visayan Sea, Philippines 11 30N 123 30E
49 Visby, Sweden 57 41N 18 20E
88 Viscount Melville Sd., Canada 75 0N 110 0W
44 Visé, Belgium 50 44N 5 42E
41 Visegrad, Yugoslavia 43 47N 19 15E
37 Viseu, Portugal 40 40N 7 53W
65 Vishakhapatnam, India 17 44N 83 16E
76 Vishoek, South Africa (Inset) 34 8S 18 40E
40 Viso, Mt., Italy 44 45N 7 10E
45 Visp, Switzerland 46 19N 7 54E
47 Vistula, R., *see* Wisla
50 Vitebsk, U.S.S.R. 55 15N 30 20E
40 Viterbo, Italy 42 26N 12 10E
84 Viti Levu, I., Pac. Oc. 18 0S 178 0E
61 Vitim, & R., U.S.S.R. 59 45N 112 25E
98 Vitoria, Brazil 20 15S 40 15W
37 Vitoria, Spain 42 52N 2 35W
42 Vitré, France 48 10N 1 18W
43 Vitry le Francois, France 48 42N 4 30E
40 Vittoria, Italy 37 0N 14 30E
40 Vittorio Veneto, Italy 45 58N 12 19E
37 Vivero, Spain 43 40N 7 34W
43 Viviers, France 44 26N 4 40E
65 Vizianagaram, India 18 8N 83 24E
44 Vlaardingen, Neth. 51 55N 4 21E
52 Vladimir, U.S.S.R. 56 2N 40 35E
47 Vladimir Volynski, U.S.S.R. 50 50N 24 18E
61 Vladivostok, U.S.S.R. 42 58N 131 50E
44 Vlieland, I., Netherlands 53 15N 4 57E
44 Vlissingen, *see* Flushing
41 Vlöre (Vlöne), Albania 40 30N 19 31E
46 Vltava, R., Cz-slov. 49 20N 14 10E
57 Vogelkop Pen., Indon. 1 25S 133 0E
46 Vogels Berg, mt., Ger. 50 37N 9 30E
43 Voghera, Italy 45 0N 9 0E
75 Vohémar, Madagascar 13 25S 50 0E
75 Vohipeno, Madagascar 22 21S 47 51E
74 Voi, Kenya 3 20S 38 35E
43 Voiron, France 45 21N 5 38E
48 Vojmsjön, L., Sweden 65 0N 16 30E
48 Volda, Norway 62 12N 6 5E
44 Volendam, Netherlands 52 30N 5 4E
50 Volga, R., U.S.S.R. 57 30N 42 0E
52 Volgograd (Stalingrad), U.S.S.R. 48 42N 44 28E
50 Volkhov, R., U.S.S.R. 59 30N 32 0E
45 Volklingen, Germany 49 15N 6 51E
47 Volkovysk, U.S.S.R. 53 10N 24 30E
76 Volksrust, S. Africa 27 20S 29 58E
61 Volochanka, U.S.S.R. 70 55N 94 10E
61 Volochayevka, U.S.S.R. 48 27N 134 40E
50 Vologda, U.S.S.R. 59 10N 39 57E
41 Vólos, & G., Greece 39 26N 22 57E
50 Volsk, U.S.S.R. 52 5N 47 30E
72 Volta, R., W. Africa 5 40N 0 23E
40 Volterra, Italy 43 23N 10 54E
40 Voltri, Italy 44 26N 8 45E
40 Volturno, R., Italy 41 3N 14 0E
52 Volzhskiy, U.S.S.R. 48 53N 44 55E
44 Voorburg, Netherlands 52 4N 4 18E
48 Vopnafjördur, Iceland 65 45N 14 50W
46 Vorarlberg, Prov., Austria 47 15N 10 0E
50 Vorkuta, U.S.S.R. 67 30N 64 10E
52 Voronezh, U.S.S.R. 51 37N 39 10E
52 Voroshilovgrad, U.S.S.R. 48 35N 39 29E
52 Voroshilovsk, U.S.S.R., *see* Kommunarsk
42 Vosges, Dépt., France 48 5N 6 25E
43 Vosges, Mts., France 48 20N 7 0E
49 Voss, Norway 60 38N 6 28E
100 Vostok, Antarctica 78 30S 107 0E
100 Vostok I., Antarctica 72 0S 97 0E
50 Votkinsk, U.S.S.R. 57 5N 53 50E
37 Vouga, R., Portugal 40 45N 8 0W
43 Vouziers, France 49 20N 4 44E
43 Voves, France 48 18N 1 35E
51 Voznesensk, U.S.S.R. 47 30N 32 0E
61 Voznesenskaya, U.S.S.R. 55 15N 95 50E
50 Voznesenye, U.S.S.R. 61 6N 35 20E
41 Vranje, Yugoslavia 42 33N 21 55E
41 Vratsa, Bulgaria 43 13N 23 30E
41 Vrbas, R., Yugoslavia 45 0N 17 22E
76 Vrede, S. Africa 27 30S 29 15E
76 Vredendal, South Africa 31 35S 18 25E
75 Vredenburg, S. Africa 32 55S 18 0E
45 Vrin, Switzerland 46 40N 9 6E
41 Vrsac, Yugoslavia 45 10N 21 15E
76 Vryburg, S. Africa 26 48S 24 44E
76 Vryheid, S. Africa 27 50S 30 40E
44 Vught, Netherlands 51 39N 5 17E
40 Vulcano, I., Italy 38 29N 15 0E
50 Vyatka, R., U.S.S.R. 57 30N 49 30E
50 Vyatskiye Polyany, U.S.S.R. 56 15N 51 30E
52 Vyazma, U.S.S.R. 55 15N 34 20E
50 Vyborg, U.S.S.R. 60 45N 28 40E
50 Vychegda, R., U.S.S.R. 61 30N 48 0E
25 Vyrnwy, L. & R., Wales 52 46N 3 30W
52 Vyshniy Volochek, U.S.S.R. 57 30N 34 30E
50 Vytegra, U.S.S.R. 61 15N 36 40E

W

72 Wa, Ghana 10 5N 2 27W
44 Waal, R., Netherlands 51 33N 5 40E
44 Waalwijk, Netherlands 51 42N 5 2E
92 Wabash, & R., U.S.A. 40 54N 85 48W
88 Wabiskaw, R., Canada 57 40N 115 30W
47 Wabrzezno, Poland 53 15N 19 0E
90 Waco, U.S.A. 31 50N 97 0W
73 Wad Banda, Sudan 13 3N 27 58E
73 Wad Medani, Sudan 14 23N 33 58E
44 Wadden Zee, Neth. 53 15N 5 0E
23 Waddesdon, England 51 51N 0 51W
88 Waddington, Mt., Can. 51 20N 125 25W
24 Wadebridge, England 50 31N 4 49W
45 Wadenswil, Switzerland 47 13N 8 40E
23 Wadhurst, England 51 4N 0 21E
63 Wadi es Sir, Jordan 31 57N 35 50E
73 Wadi Halfa, Sudan 21 52N 31 22E
25 Waenfawr, Wales 53 7N 4 10W
44 Wageningen, Neth. 51 58N 5 40E
89 Wager Bay, Canada 65 45N 91 0W
89 Wager, B., Canada 65 45N 90 0W
83 Wagga Wagga, Australia 35 10S 147 23E
80 Wagin, Australia 33 19S 117 20E
72 Wagin, Nigeria 12 42N 7 10E
68 Wahai, Indonesia 2 50S 129 35E
84 Waiau, New Zealand 42 54S 173 0E
84 Waihi, New Zealand 37 19S 175 58E
84 Waikaremoana L., N.Z. 38 45S 177 5E
84 Waikato, R., N.Z. 37 18S 174 43E
83 Waikerie, Australia 34 1S 140 0E
84 Waikokopu, N.Z. 39 0S 177 58E
84 Waikouaiti, N.Z. 45 38S 170 41E
84 Waimarino, New Zealand 39 7S 175 26E
84 Waimate, New Zealand 44 45S 171 7E
64 Wainganga, R., India 21 30N 80 0E
88 Wainwright, Canada 52 57N 111 0W
84 Waiouru, New Zealand 39 28S 175 36E
84 Waipara, New Zealand 43 3S 172 46E
84 Waipawa, New Zealand 39 54S 176 36E
84 Waipiro, New Zealand 38 2S 178 25E
84 Waipukurau, N.Z. 40 0S 176 31E
84 Wairoa, N.Z. 39 0S 177 31E
84 Waitaki, R., N.Z. 44 52S 171 14E
84 Waitara, New Zealand 38 57S 174 12E
84 Waiuku, New Zealand 37 6S 174 38E
66 Waiyeng, China 23 10N 114 30E
67 Wajima, Japan 37 28N 137 0E
74 Wajir, Kenya 1 57N 40 10E
67 Wakamatsu, Honshu, Japan 37 30N 139 58E
67 Wakamatsu, Kyushu, Japan 33 58N 130 50E
67 Wakasa B., Japan 35 50N 135 30E
84 Wakatipu, L., N.Z. 45 0S 168 30E
67 Wakayama, & Pref., Jap. 34 10N 135 12E
11 Wake I., Pacific Ocean 19 0N 167 0E
27 Wakefield, England 53 41N 1 30W
84 Wakefield, N.Z. 41 25S 173 7E
67 Wakkanai, Japan 45 20N 141 49E
76 Wakkerstroom, S. Africa 27 30S 30 12E
83 Wakool, & R., Australia 35 30S 144 20E
23 Walberswick, England 52 18N 1 39E
46 Walbrzych, Poland 50 45N 16 18E
83 Walcha, Australia 31 0S 151 38E
44 Walcheren, I., Neth. 51 39N 3 35E
49 Walcz, Poland 53 17N 16 27E
45 Wald, Switzerland 47 19N 8 54E
25 Wales, Gt. Britain 52 0N 3 30W
83 Walgett, Australia 30 15S 147 32E
83 Walhalla, Australia 37 48S 146 30E
90 Walker, L., U.S.A. 38 45N 118 42W
82 Walkerston, Australia 21 11S 149 8E
90 Walla Walla, U.S.A. 46 6N 118 25W
90 Wallace, U.S.A. 47 35N 115 58W
92 Wallaceburg, Canada 42 33N 82 26W
47 Wallachia, reg., Rum. 44 42N 25 20E
83 Wallaroo, Australia 33 56S 138 0E
26 Wallasey, England 53 26N 3 5W
83 Wallerawang, Australia 33 25S 150 0E
22 Wallingford, England 51 36N 1 8W
32 Walls, Scotland 60 13N 1 34W
27 Wallsend, England 54 59N 1 32W
83 Wallsend, Australia 33 0S 151 10E
83 Wallumbilla, Australia 26 30S 149 5E
23 Walmer, England 51 11N 1 24E
76 Walmer, South Africa 34 0S 25 25E
22 Walsall, England 52 35N 1 59W
90 Walsenburg, U.S.A. 37 42N 104 47W
23 Walsoken, England 52 40N 0 11E
27 Waltham, England 53 32N 0 6W
23 Waltham Abbey, England 51 39N 0 0
23 Waltham Forest, Greater London, England 51 37N 0 2E
26 Walton-le-Dale, England 53 45N 2 41W
23 Walton-on-the-Naze, Eng. 51 50N 1 18E
75 Walvis Bay, S.W. Africa 22 40S 14 30E
65 Wampo, Tibet, China 31 25N 86 35E
64 Wana, Pakistan 32 25N 69 30E
83 Wanbi, Australia 34 48S 140 30E
83 Wandoan, Australia 25 58S 149 59E
23 Wandsworth, Greater London, England 51 27N 0 12W
84 Wanganui, New Zealand 39 53S 175 7E
83 Wangaratta, Australia 36 25S 146 23E
66 Wanhsien, China 31 3N 108 30E
75 Wankie, Rhodesia 18 23S 26 25E
95 Wanks, R., Cent. America 15 0N 83 5W
22 Wantage, England 51 35N 1 22W
64 Warangal, India 17 57N 79 36E
83 Waratah, Australia 41 32S 145 48E
83 Warburton, Australia 37 58S 145 57E
84 Ward, New Zealand 41 58S 174 2E
33 Ward Hill, Scotland 58 54N 3 23W
76 Warden, S. Africa 27 50S 29 1E
64 Wardha, India 20 53N 78 36E
22 Wardington, England 52 8N 1 17W
26 Wardle, England 53 39N 2 38W
23 Ware, England 51 49N 0 2W
22 Wareham, England 50 40N 2 8W
83 Warialda, Australia 29 32S 150 30E
27 Warkworth, England 55 22N 1 38W
84 Warkworth, N.Z. 36 28S 174 35E
22 Warley, England 52 29N 2 3W
76 Warmbad, South Africa 24 50S 28 10E
75 Warmbad, S.W. Africa 28 23S 18 40E
22 Warminster, England 51 12N 2 12W
49 Warnemünde, Germany 54 10N 12 0E
83 Warragul, Australia 38 7S 146 0E
83 Warrego, R., Australia 29 20S 145 50E
83 Warren, Australia 31 33S 147 58E
92 Warren, Ohio, U.S.A. 41 8N 80 57W
91 Warren, Pa., U.S.A. 41 54N 79 12W
83 Warrenville, Australia 25 40S 147 20E
72 Warri, Nigeria 5 35N 5 57E
80 Warrina, Australia 28 7S 136 0E
26 Warrington, England 53 24N 2 36W
83 Warrnambool, Australia 38 18S 142 29E
47 Warsaw (Warszawa), Pol. 52 16N 21 0E
27 Warsop, England 53 13N 1 9W
47 Warszawa, *see* Warsaw
47 Warta (Warthe), R., Poland 51 20N 19 0E
83 Warwick, Australia 28 15S 152 10E
22 Warwick, & Co., Eng. 52 18N 1 35W
90 Wasatch Ra., U.S.A. 39 30N 111 30W
27 Washington, England 54 54N 1 31W
92 Washington, D.C., U.S.A. 38 58N 77 0W
91 Washington, N.C., U.S.A. 35 32N 76 54W
90 Washington, st., U.S.A. 47 45N 121 0W
64 Washir, Afghanistan 32 15N 63 50E
44 Wassenaar, Netherlands 52 8N 4 24E
43 Wassy, France 48 30N 5 0E
26 Wast Water, L., Eng. 54 26N 3 19W
92 Waswanipi, L., & R., Canada 49 30N 76 25W
24 Watchet, England 51 1N 3 18W
75 Waterberg, S.W. Africa 20 23S 17 9E
76 Waterberge, mts., South Africa 24 30S 28 0E
93 Waterbury, U.S.A. 41 32N 73 0W
35 Waterford, & Co., Ire. 52 15N 7 7W
34 Watergrasshill, Ireland 52 1N 8 21W
44 Waterloo, Belgium 50 43N 4 24E
26 Waterloo, England 53 29N 2 59W
72 Waterloo, Sierra Leone 8 26N 13 8W
91 Waterloo, U.S.A. 42 30N 92 16W
32 Waternish, Scotland 57 32N 6 35W
93 Watertown, N.Y., U.S.A. 43 57N 75 50W
90 Watertown, S.D., U.S.A. 44 58N 97 4W
76 Waterval-Boven, S. Africa 25 40S 30 20E
34 Waterville, Ireland 51 49N 10 11W
93 Waterville, U.S.A. 44 30N 69 0W
93 Watervliet, U.S.A. 42 40N 73 40W
23 Watford, England 51 39N 0 23W
95 Watling's I., Bahamas 24 0N 74 35W
23 Watlington, Norfolk, England 52 40N 0 24E
23 Watlington, Oxford, England 51 39N 1 1W
88 Watrous, Canada 51 40N 105 30W
74 Watsa, Zaïre 3 0N 29 30E
33 Watten, Scotland 58 29N 3 18W
45 Wattwil, Switzerland 47 20N 9 6E
73 Wau, & R., Sudan 7 50N 28 2E
83 Wauchope, Australia 31 27S 152 44E
91 Waukegan, U.S.A. 42 23N 87 51W
92 Wausau, U.S.A. 45 0N 89 30W
80 Wave Hill, Australia 17 32S 130 58E
23 Waveney, R., England 52 21N 1 13E
84 Waverley, N.Z. 39 46S 174 35E
44 Wavre, Belgium 50 43N 4 37E
91 Waxahachie, U.S.A. 32 23N 96 52W
44 Waxweiler, Germany 50 6N 6 22E
91 Waycross, U.S.A. 31 10N 82 25W
64 Wazi Khwa, Afghanistan 32 5N 68 15E
64 Wazirabad, Pakistan 32 30N 74 5E
23 Weald, The, England 51 9N 0 20E
26 Wear, R., England 54 48N 1 33W
26 Weaver, R., England 53 0N 2 31W
90 Weatherford, U.S.A. 32 45N 97 47W
91 Webster City, U.S.A. 42 30N 93 48W
68 Weda, Indonesia 1 15N 127 50E
100 Weddell Sea, Antarctica 68 0S 40 0W
83 Wedderburn, Australia 36 28S 143 37E
22 Wednesbury, England 52 33N 2 2W
22 Wednesfield, England 52 36N 2 3W
83 Wee Waa, Australia 30 3S 149 30E
44 Weert, Netherlands 51 16N 5 44E
67 Weifang, China 36 45N 119 0E
67 Weihai, China 37 30N 122 0E
46 Weimar, Germany 50 59N 11 15E
45 Weinheim, Germany 49 37N 8 45E
66 Weining, China 27 0N 103 50E
90 Weiser, U.S.A. 44 15N 117 3W
65 Weisi, China 27 10N 99 15E
62 Wejh, Saudi Arabia 26 15N 36 30E
47 Wejherowo, Poland 54 36N 18 15E
76 Welkom, South Africa 28 0S 26 45E
92 Welland, & Can., Canada 43 0N 79 6W
23 Welland, R., England 52 40N 0 30W
82 Wellesley Is., Australia 16 45S 139 30E
44 Wellin, Belgium 50 5N 5 6E
23 Wellingborough, Eng. 52 19N 0 42W
83 Wellington, Australia 32 30S 148 58E
22 Wellington, Salop., Eng. 52 42N 2 30W
24 Wellington, Som., Eng. 50 58N 3 14W
76 Wellington, South Africa 33 35S 19 0E
91 Wellington, U.S.A. 37 14N 97 26W
84 Wellington, & Dist., N.Z. 41 15S 176 46E
99 Wellington I., Chile 49 30S 75 0W
35 Wellington Bridge, Ire. 52 15N 6 45W
24 Wells, England 51 13N 2 38W
80 Wells, L., Australia 27 0S 123 35E
46 Wels, Austria 48 10N 14 0E
25 Welshpool, Wales 52 39N 3 9W
23 Welwyn, England 51 48N 0 13W
22 Wem, England 52 52N 2 44E
90 Wenatchee, U.S.A. 47 25N 120 25W
67 Wenchow, China 27 59N 120 32E
23 Wendover, England 51 47N 0 45W
45 Wengen, Switzerland 46 28N 7 56E
82 Wenlock, R., Australia 12 15S 142 0E
22 Wenlock Edge, England 52 30N 2 46W
27 Wensleydale, England 54 18N 2 10W
23 Wensum, R., England 52 47N 0 55E
83 Wentworth, Australia 34 10S 141 50E
22 Weobley, England 52 9N 2 53W
76 Wepener, South Africa 29 46S 27 1E
46 Werra, R., Germany 51 10N 10 0E
83 Werribee, Australia 38 0S 144 40E
83 Werris Creek, Austral. 31 8S 150 36E
44 Wesel, Germany 51 41N 6 39E
46 Weser, R., Germany 52 30N 9 0E
65 West Bengal, St., India 23 0N 87 0E
47 West Beskids, Mts., Czechoslovakia 49 30N 19 20E
27 West Bridgford, England 52 56N 1 8W
22 West Bromwich, England 52 31N 1 59W
32 West Burra I., Scotland 60 7N 1 5W
31 West Calder, Scotland 55 52N 3 34W
13 West Dvina R., Europe 55 40N 28 0E
44 West Flanders, Belgium 50 58N 3 0E
91 West Frankfort, U.S.A. 37 49N 88 46W
46 West Germany, Europe 51 0N 9 0E
25 West Glamorgan, Co., Wales 51 45N 3 55W
23 West Grinstead, Eng. 50 58N 0 18W
30 West Kilbride, Scotland 55 42N 4 51W
26 West Kirby, England 53 23N 3 11W
31 West Linton, Scotland 55 45N 3 24W
24 West Looe, England 50 20N 4 27W
22 West Midlands, Co., England 52 30N 1 55W
75 West Nicholson, Rhodesia 21 1S 29 20E
64 West Pakistan, Asia 27 0N 67 0W
91 West Palm Beach, U.S.A. 26 40N 80 12W
93 West Pt., C., Canada 49 50N 64 40W
27 West Rasen, England 53 23N 0 23W
44 West Schelde, R., Neth. 51 23N 3 50E
60 West Siberian Plain, U.S.S.R. 62 0N 76 0E
23 West Sussex, Co., Eng. 50 53N 0 30W
92 West Virginia, st., U.S.A. 39 0N 81 0W
83 West Wyalong, Australia 33 56S 147 10E
27 West Yorkshire, Co., Eng. 53 45N 1 30W
23 Westbourne, England 50 22N 0 56W
83 Westbury, Australia 41 32S 147 0E
22 Westbury, Salop., Eng. 52 41N 2 57W
22 Westbury, Wilts., England 51 15N 2 11W
46 Wester Wald, mts., Ger. 50 40N 8 0E
23 Westerham, England 51 16N 0 5W
80 Western Australia, st., Australia 25 0S 121 30E
64 Western Ghats, mts., India 15 0N 74 0E
32 Western Isles, Reg., Scot. 57 45N 7 0W
72 Western Sahara, Africa 25 0N 13 0W
84 Western Samoa, Pacific Ocean (Inset)
61 Western Sayan, U.S.S.R. 52 30N 94 0E
44 Westfriesche Eil anden, Netherlands 53 30N 5 15E
26 Westhoughton, England 53 34N 2 30W
84 Westland Dist., N.Z. 43 0S 170 0E
35 Westmeath, Co., Ireland 53 30N 7 30W
26 Westmorland, *see* Cumbria
22 Weston, England 52 51N 2 2W
24 Weston-super-Mare, Eng. 51 21N 2 58W
35 Westport, & B., Ireland 53 48N 9 32W
84 Westport, New Zealand 41 50S 171 52E
33 Westray, I. & Firth, Scot. 59 17N 2 58W
31 Westruther, Scotland 55 45N 2 34W
68 Wetar I., Indonesia 7 50S 126 20E
88 Wetaskiwin, Canada 52 58N 113 20W
27 Wetherby, England 53 57N 1 24W
44 Wetteren, Belgium 51 0N 3 53E
46 Wetzlar, Germany 50 34N 8 27E
82 Wewak, Papua N.G. 3 40S 143 30E
35 Wexford, & Co., Ireland 52 19N 6 28W
35 Wexford Hr., Ireland 52 20N 6 23W
23 Wey, R., England 51 18N 0 30W
27 Weybourne, England 52 58N 1 8E
23 Weybridge, England 51 22N 0 28W
88 Weyburn, Canada 49 40N 104 56W
89 Weymont, Canada 47 50N 73 50W
22 Weymouth, England 50 36N 2 28W
84 Whakatane, New Zealand 37 59S 177 0E
89 Whale R., Canada 55 25N 76 0W
100 Whales, B. of, Antarc. 78 30S 165 0W
26 Whaley Bridge, England 53 20N 1 59W
32 Whalsay I., Scotland 60 21N 0 58W
84 Whangamomona, N.Z. 39 8S 174 44E
84 Whangarei, N.Z. 35 41S 174 20E
26 Wharfedale, England 54 8N 2 0W
90 Wheeler Pk., U.S.A. 39 20N 114 30W
92 Wheeling, U.S.A. 40 0N 80 38W
26 Whernside, mt., England 54 15N 2 24W
26 Whiston, England 53 25N 2 45W

31 Whitburn, Scot., U.K. 55 52N 3 41W
27 Whitby, England 54 29N 0 38W
24 Whitchurch, Devon, Eng. 50 31N 4 7W
22 Whitchurch, Hants., Eng. 51 15N 1 21W
26 Whitchurch, Salop., Eng. 52 58N 2 41W
25 Whitchurch, Wales 51 32N 3 15W
82 Whitecliffs, N.Z. 43 26S 171 55E
47 White Crisul, R., Rum. 46 18N 22 20E
41 White Drin, R., Y.-slav. 42 30N 20 34E
31 White Esk, R., Scotland 55 15N 3 10W
22 White Horse Vale, Eng. 51 39N 1 35W
84 White I., New Zealand 37 29S 177 14E
47 White Mts., Cz-slov. 49 0N 17 40E
90 White Mts., U.S.A. 37 15N 118 15W
73 White Nile, *see* Bahr el Abiad
73 White Nile, prov., Sudan 13 0N 32 0E
50 White Russia (Byelorussia), S.S.R., U.S.S.R. 53 50N 30 0E
50 White Sea, U.S.S.R. 65 30N 37 30E
31 Whiteadder, R., Scotland 55 50N 2 25W
91 Whitefish B., U.S.A. 47 0N 85 0W
34 Whitegate, Ireland 51 49N 8 14W
26 Whitehaven, England 54 33N 3 36W
88 Whitehorse, Canada 60 40N 135 5W
31 Whitekirk, Scotland 56 2N 2 36W
83 Whitemark, Australia 40 4S 148 0E
83 Whitfield, Australia 36 50S 146 23E
30 Whithorn, Scotland 54 44N 4 24W
84 Whitianga, N.Z. 36 50S 175 40E
25 Whitland, Wales 51 49N 4 37W
27 Whitley B., England 55 3N 1 26W
90 Whitney, Mt., U.S.A. 36 45N 118 30W
23 Whitstable, England 51 21N 1 2E
82 Whitsunday I., Australia 20 15S 149 4E
88 Whittier, Alaska 60 5N 140 50W
27 Whittington, Derby, Eng. 53 17N 1 24W
22 Whittington, Salop., Eng. 52 53N 2 59W
23 Whittlesey, England 52 33N 0 7W
27 Whitwell, England 53 16N 1 11W
26 Whitworth, England 53 39N 2 11W
88 Wholdaia L., Canada 60 40N 104 20W
83 Whyalla, Australia 33 0S 137 28E
83 Whyjonta, Australia 29 40S 142 25E
91 Wichita, U.S.A. 37 48N 97 12W
90 Wichita Falls, U.S.A. 33 58N 98 36W
33 Wick, Scotland 58 27N 3 8W
23 Wickford, England 51 37N 0 31E
35 Wicklow, & Co., Ireland 52 58N 6 2W
35 Wicklow Mts., Ireland 53 5N 6 25W
31 Widdrington, England 55 15N 1 35W
24 Widemouth, England 50 45N 4 34W
26 Widnes, England 53 21N 2 46W
47 Wieliczka, Poland 49 59N 20 5E
47 Wielun, Poland 51 12N 18 45E
46 Wien, *see* Vienna
46 Wiener Neustadt, Austria 47 48N 16 13E
45 Wiesbaden, Germany 50 5N 8 14E
26 Wigan, England 53 33N 2 38W
22 Wight, Isle of, Co., Eng 50 40N 1 20W
22 Wigmore, England 52 19N 2 52W
22 Wigston, England 52 35N 1 6W
26 Wigton, England 54 50N 3 9W
30 Wigtown, Scot. 54 52N 4 27W
30 Wigtown B., Scotland 54 48N 4 17W
45 Wil, Switzerland 47 28N 9 3E
83 Wilcannia, Australia 31 36S 143 20E
47 Wilhelmshaven, Germany 43 34N 8 8E
100 Wilkes, Antarctica 66 0S 111 0E
93 Wilkes Barre, U.S.A. 41 18N 75 48W
100 Wilkes Basin, Antarctica 77 0S 138 0E
88 Wilkie, Canada 52 20N 108 40W
44 Willebroek, Belgium 51 5N 4 20E
95 Willemstadt, Neth., Antilles 12 0N 69 0W
22 Willenhall, England 52 36N 2 3W
28 Willesborough, England 51 8N 0 55E
88 Williams L., Canada 52 20N 122 10W
92 Williamson, U.S.A. 37 38N 82 10W
92 Williamsport, U.S.A. 41 19N 77 7W
83 Williamstown, Australia 37 45S 144 49E
23 Willingdon, England 50 47N 0 16E
27 Willington, England 54 43N 1 41W
45 Willisau, Switzerland 47 7N 8 0E
76 Williston, South Africa 31 20S 20 59E
90 Williston, U.S.A. 48 2N 104 3W
24 Williton, England 51 10N 3 18W
76 Willowmore, S. Africa 33 10S 23 37E
83 Willunga, Australia 35 27S 138 32E
83 Wilmington, Australia 32 30S 138 0E
24 Wilmington, England 50 46N 3 8W
93 Wilmington, Del., U.S.A. 39 47N 75 35W
91 Wilmington, N.C., U.S.A. 34 12N 77 50W
26 Wilmslow, England 53 19N 2 14W
22 Wilnecote, England 52 37N 1 39W
91 Wilson, U.S.A. 35 44N 77 55W
83 Wilson's Promontory, Australia 39 1S 146 29E
22 Wilton, England 51 5N 1 51W
22 Wiltshire, Co., England 51 18N 1 55W
44 Wiltz, Luxembourg 49 58N 5 57E
80 Wiluna, Australia 26 30S 120 4E
22 Wimborne Minster, Eng. 50 48N 1 58W
76 Winburg, S. Africa 28 25S 27 22E
24 Wincanton, England 51 3N 2 25W
23 Winchelsea, England 50 56N 0 42E
22 Winchester, England 51 4N 1 19W
92 Winchester, U.S.A. 39 18N 78 10W
90 Wind River Ra., U.S.A. 43 45N 109 40W
83 Windera, Australia 25 59S 151 37E
26 Windermere & L., Eng. 54 20N 2 57W
75 Windhoek, S.W. Africa 22 37S 17 8E
83 Windsor, Australia 33 40S 150 45E
93 Windsor, Nova Scotia, Canada 45 0N 64 8W
93 Windsor, Ontario, Can. 42 17N 83 0W
23 Windsor, England 51 28N 0 36W
76 Windsorton, S. Africa 28 20S 24 50E
95 Windward Is., W. Indies 13 30N 61 0W
95 Windward Passage, W. Indies 20 0N 73 30W
31 Windygates, Scotland 56 12N 3 1W
91 Winfield, U.S.A. 37 20N 97 15W
83 Wingen, Australia 31 55S 150 55E
83 Wingham, Australia 31 42S 152 3E
23 Wingham, England 51 16N 1 12E
89 Winisk, R., Canada 54 40N 87 0W
72 Winneba, Ghana 5 25N 0 36W
90 Winnemucca, U.S.A. 40 59N 117 45W
88 Winnipeg, Canada 49 55N 97 15W
88 Winnipeg, L., Canada 52 0N 98 0W
88 Winnipegosis, L., Can. 52 30N 99 50W
92 Winona, U.S.A. 44 0N 91 44W
26 Winsford, England 53 12N 2 31W
44 Winschoten, Netherlands 53 10N 7 3E
23 Winslow, England 51 56N 0 53W
90 Winslow, U.S.A. 35 5N 100 45W
91 Winston Salem, U.S.A. 35 8N 80 24W
44 Winterswyk, Neth. 51 58N 6 44E
45 Winterthur, Switzerland 47 30N 8 42E
82 Winton, Australia 22 23S 143 2E
84 Winton, New Zealand 46 10S 168 21E
27 Wirksworth, England 53 6N 1 35W
26 Wirral Pen., England 53 20N 3 5W
23 Wisbech, England 52 39N 0 9E
91 Wisconsin Rapids, U.S.A. 44 26N 89 43W
92 Wisconsin, st., U.S.A. 45 0N 90 0W
47 Wisla (Vistula) R., Pol. 53 0N 18 55E
49 Wismar, Germany 53 54N 11 23E
43 Wissembourg, France 49 0N 7 58E
75 Witbank, South Africa 25 52S 29 8E
23 Witham, England 51 48N 0 38E
27 Witham R., England 53 7N 0 13W
27 Withern, England 53 20N 0 8E
27 Withernsea, England 53 45N 0 1E
23 Witley, England 51 9N 0 39W
22 Witney, England 51 48N 1 29W
46 Wittenberge, Germany 53 0N 11 41E
46 Wittenburg, Germany 51 52N 12 45E
80 Wittenoom, Australia 22 15S 118 20E
44 Wittlich, Germany 49 59N 6 52E
47 Wlocklawek, Poland 52 36N 19 5E
47 Wlodawa, Poland 51 30N 23 30E
23 Woburn, England 51 59N 0 36W
23 Woburn Sands, England 52 1N 0 38W
83 Wodonga, Australia 36 3S 146 57E
23 Woking, England 51 18N 0 34W
23 Wokingham, England 51 24N 0 50W
45 Wolhusen, Switzerland 47 4N 8 5E
46 Wolin, I., Poland 53 40N 14 37E
88 Wollaston, L., Canada 58 20N 103 20W
88 Wollaston Pen., Canada 69 30N 113 0W
83 Wollongong, Australia 34 25S 151 0E
76 Wolmaransstad, S. Africa 27 20S 26 0E
83 Wolseley, Australia 36 20S 141 0E
26 Wolsingham, England 54 44N 1 52W
44 Wolvega, Netherlands 52 53N 6 0E
22 Wolverhampton 52 36N 2 8W
23 Wolverton, England 52 3N 0 47W
27 Wombwell, England 53 32N 1 24W
83 Wondai, Australia 26 12S 151 48E
67 Wonsan, Korea 39 20N 127 25E
83 Wonthaggi, Australia 38 28S 145 38E
23 Woodbridge, England 52 7N 1 20E
83 Woodend, Australia 37 20N 144 33E
34 Woodford, Ireland 53 3N 8 24W
82 Woodlark I., Pac. Oc. 9 0S 152 45E
23 Woodley, England 51 26N 0 54W
80 Woodroffe, Mt., Austral. 26 16S 131 30E
80 Woods, L., Australia 18 0S 133 0E
88 Woods, L., of the, Canada-U.S.A. 49 30N 94 30W
83 Woodside, Australia 38 45S 147 0E
93 Woodstock, N.B., Can. 46 12N 67 45W
92 Woodstock, Ont., Can. 43 7N 80 46W
84 Woodville, New Zealand 40 19S 175 59E
24 Wookey Hole, England 51 14N 2 40W
22 Wool, England 50 41N 2 14W
24 Woolacombe, England 51 11N 4 12W
83 Woolgoolga, Australia 30 7S 153 12E
83 Woombye, Australia 26 40S 152 58E
81 Woomera, Australia 31 5S 136 50E
93 Woonsocket, U.S.A. 42 1N 71 30W
83 Wooroorooka, Australia 27 59S 145 58E
67 Woosung, China 31 20N 121 25E
22 Wootton Bassett, Eng. 51 32N 1 55W
76 Worcester, South Africa 33 40S 19 28E
22 Worcester, Eng. 52 11N 2 13W
91 Worcester, U.S.A. 42 18N 71 45W
22 Worfield, England 52 34N 2 22W
26 Workington, England 54 38N 3 34W
27 Worksop, England 53 19N 1 8W
44 Workum, Netherlands 52 59N 5 27E
44 Wormerveer, Netherlands 52 30N 4 45E
45 Worms, Germany 49 40N 8 20E
23 Wortham, England 52 22N 1 3E
23 Worthing, England 50 48N 0 22W
74 Wota, Ethiopia 7 4N 35 51E
22 Wotton-under-Edge, Eng. 51 38N 2 21W
73 Wour, Chad. 21 20N 15 48E
61 Wrangel I., U.S.S.R. 71 30N 180 0E
88 Wrangell, Alaska 56 30N 132 52W
88 Wrangell Mts., Alaska 61 40N 143 30W
32 Wrath, C., Scotland 58 38N 5 0W
22 Wrekin, Mt., England 52 40N 2 33W
25 Wrexham, Wales 53 4N 3 0W
68 Wright, Philippines 11 45N 125 0E
88 Wrigley, Canada 63 0N 123 30W
24 Writhlington, England 51 18N 2 16W
46 Wroclaw (Breslau), Poland 51 6N 17 0E
23 Wrotham, England 51 18N 0 20E
22 Wroughton, England 51 32N 1 48W
66 Wu Kiang, R., China 27 30N 107 30E
55 Wu Yis Shan, mts., China 28 0N 118 0E
66 Wuchang, China 30 45N 114 25E
66 Wu-chow, China 23 35N 110 49E
66 Wuhan, China 30 45N 114 15E
66 Wu-hu, China 31 12N 118 20E
64 Wun, India 20 0N 79 0E
65 Wuntho, Burma 24 0N 95 30E
44 Wuppertal, Germany 51 15N 7 15E
45 Würzburg, Germany 49 45N 9 59E
67 Wusih, China 31 30N 120 5E
66 Wuwei, China 38 0N 102 25E
83 Wyandra, Australia 27 15S 145 58E
83 Wycheproof, Australia 36 0S 143 17E
25 Wye, R., Wales 52 15N 3 27W
23 Wymondham, England 52 45N 0 42W
23 Wymondham, England 52 33N 1 8E
76 Wynberg, South Africa 34 0S 18 27E
84 Wyndham, New Zealand 46 20S 168 51E
80 Wyndham, Australia 15 18S 127 58E
25 Wynnstay, Wales 52 36N 3 33W
83 Wynnum, Australia 28 0S 152 58E
83 Wynyard, Australia 41 0S 145 45E
90 Wyoming, St., U.S.A. 43 30N 107 30W
83 Wyong, Australia 33 5S 151 25E
26 Wyre, R., England 53 54N 2 48W
22 Wyre Forest, England 52 23N 2 25W

X

75 Xai-Xai, Mozambique 25 2S 33 34E
41 Xánthi, Greece 41 5N 24 55E
75 Xinavane, Mozambique 25 2S 32 47E
98 Xingu, R., Brazil 6 0S 53 0W

Y

66 Yaan, China 30 10N 101 50E
83 Yaapeet, Australia 35 48S 142 0E
63 Ya'bad, Israel 32 27N 35 10E
74 Yaballo, Ethiopia 4 57N 38 8E
63 Yabis, Wadi, Jordan 32 25N 35 40E
61 Yablonovy Ra., U.S.S.R. 52 0N 114 0E
64 Yadgir, India 16 50N 77 0E
65 Yakiang, China 30 2N 101 10E
90 Yakima, U.S.A. 46 40N 120 35W
72 Yako, Volta 12 58N 2 11W
73 Yakoma, Zaïre 4 0N 22 17E
67 Yakoshih, China 49 30N 120 45E
61 Yakutsk, U.S.S.R. 62 0N 129 0E
61 Yakut, A.S.S.R., U.S.S.R. 66 0N 130 0E
88 Yakutat, Alaska 59 38N 139 40W
82 Yalleroi, Australia 24 3S 145 42E
83 Yallourn, Australia 38 10S 146 18E
51 Yalta, U.S.S.R. 44 28N 34 10E
67 Yalu R., Korea 40 40N 126 20E
66 Yalung, R., China 27 30N 101 45E
67 Yamagata, & Pref., Jap. 38 10N 140 6E
67 Yamaguchi, & Pref., Jap. 34 8N 131 30E
60 Yamal Pen., U.S.S.R. 70 0N 70 0E
67 Yamanashi, Pref., Japan 35 30N 138 30E
50 Yaman Tau, Mt., U.S.S.R. 54 0N 59 0E
83 Yamba, N.S.W., Austral. 29 25S 152 15E
73 Yambio, Sudan 4 38N 28 24E
41 Yambol, Bulgaria 42 30N 26 33E
66 Yamdrok Tso L., China 29 0N 90 30E
65 Yamethin, Burma 20 29N 96 18E
83 Yamma Yamma, L., Australia 26 20S 141 25E
64 Yamuna, R. (Jumna), India 27 10N 79 0E
61 Yana R., U.S.S.R. 69 0N 135 0E
83 Yanac, Australia 36 4S 141 12E
65 Yandoon, Burma 17 0N 95 40E
66 Yangchuan, China 38 5N 113 0E
66 Yangtze (Kinsha) R., China 32 30N 98 0E
66 Yang-tze-kiang, R., China 31 45N 121 15E
91 Yankton, U.S.A. 42 58N 97 26W
83 Yanna, Australia 26 55S 146 5E
73 Yao, Chad 12 58N 17 32E
72 Yaoundé, Cameroon 4 0N 11 20E
94 Yaqui, R., Mexico 27 30N 110 0W
82 Yaraka, Australia 24 53S 144 3E
23 Yare, R., England 52 35N 1 28E
62 Yarim, Yemen 14 14N 43 23E
57 Yarkand, China 38 15N 77 0E
64 Yarkhun, R., Pak. 36 30N 72 30E
31 Yarm, England 54 31N 1 20W
93 Yarmouth, Canada 43 50N 66 20W
52 Yaroslavl, U.S.S.R. 57 40N 40 0E
83 Yarram, Australia 38 29S 146 40E
83 Yarraman, Australia 26 50S 151 59E
31 Yarrow, Scotland 55 32N 3 0W
61 Yartsevo, U.S.S.R. 60 20N 90 0E
83 Yass, Australia 34 50S 148 58E
88 Yathkyed L., Canada 62 45N 98 0W
63 Yatta, Jordan 31 28N 35 5E
67 Yawata, Japan 33 54N 130 56E
23 Yaxley, England 52 31N 0 14W
64 Yazdan, Iran 33 30N 60 45E
91 Yazoo City, U.S.A. 32 51N 90 26W
91 Yazoo, R., U.S.A. 32 48N 90 45W
65 Ye-Byu, Burma 14 10N 98 15E
47 Yedintsy, U.S.S.R. 48 5N 27 20E
52 Yegoryevsk, U.S.S.R. 55 23N 39 2E
67 Yehsien, China 37 10N 119 55E
51 Yeysk, U.S.S.R. 46 38N 38 10E
72 Yeji, Ghana 8 11N 0 41W
52 Yelets, U.S.S.R. 52 42N 38 33E
72 Yelimane, Mali 15 4N 10 30W
32 Yell I. & Sd., Scotland 60 35N 1 5W
67 Yellow Sea, China 35 30N 123 0E
88 Yellowhead P., Canada 52 40N 117 45W
88 Yellowknife, & R., Can. 62 14N 114 2W
90 Yellowstone National Park, U.S.A. 44 15N 110 0W
90 Yellowstone R., U.S.A. 46 20N 107 0W
62 Yemen, Arabia 16 0N 44 30E
52 Yenakiyevo, U.S.S.R. 48 20N 38 10E
66 Yenan, China 37 5N 108 55E
62 Yenbo, Saudi Arabia 24 0N 38 20E
60 Yenisey, G. & R., U.S.S.R. 72 20N 80 0E
61 Yeniseysk, U.S.S.R. 58 25N 91 30E
67 Yenki, China 43 10N 129 25E
66 Yenki, China 42 30N 86 0E
67 Yentai, China, *see* Chefoo
24 Yeo, R., England 51 0N 2 48W
64 Yeola, India 20 0N 74 25E
64 Yeotmal, India 20 26N 78 4E
24 Yeovil, England 50 57N 2 38W
82 Yeppoon, Australia 23 0S 150 45E
60 Yerbent, U.S.S.R. 39 30N 58 50E
51 Yerevan, U.S.S.R. 40 10N 44 20E
61 Yermakovo, U.S.S.R. 52 35N 126 20E
61 Yerofei Paulovich, U.S.S.R. 54 0N 122 0E
98 Yerupaja, Mt., Peru 10 20S 77 0W
24 Yes Tor, England 50 43N 3 57W
61 Yessei, U.S.S.R. 68 25N 102 10E
42 Yeu, I. d', France 46 43N 2 20W
51 Yevpatoriya, U.S.S.R. 45 15N 33 20E
52 Yevstratovskiy, U.S.S.R. 50 7N 39 44E
62 Yezd, Iran 31 55N 54 22E
41 Yiannitsa, Greece 40 45N 22 22E
66 Yinchwan (Ningsia), China 38 45N 106 5E
66 Yingtan, China 28 20N 116 25E
65 Yinmabin, Burma 22 10N 94 55E
74 Yirol, Sudan 6 30N 30 30E
41 Yithion, Greece 36 40N 22 40E
66 Yiyang, China 28 45N 112 30E
48 Ylitornio, Finland 66 25N 23 45E
48 Ylivieska, Finland 64 2N 24 30E
72 Yobe, R., Nigeria 13 0N 12 0E
68 Yogyakarta, Indonesia 7 50S 110 24E
74 Yokadouma, Cameroon 3 35N 14 50E
73 Yoko, Cameroon 5 35N 12 28E
67 Yokohama, Japan 35 25N 139 35E
67 Yokosuka, Japan 35 18N 139 36E
67 Yokote, Japan 39 20N 140 30E
73 Yola, Nigeria 9 10N 12 37E
67 Yonago, Japan 35 30N 133 20E
67 Yonezawa, Japan 37 57N 140 4E
91 Yonkers, U.S.A. 41 0N 73 57W
42 Yonne, Dépt., France 47 50N 3 45E
43 Yonne, R., France 48 0N 3 20E
80 York, Australia 31 50S 116 48E
27 York, England 53 58N 1 5W
82 York, C., Australia 10 50S 142 30E
89 York Factory, Canada 56 4N 92 35W
80 York Sd., Australia 14 57S 125 5E
27 York Wolds, England 54 0N 0 40W
83 Yorke Pen., Australia 34 45S 137 38E
28 Yorkshire, Co., England 54 4N 1 15W
88 Yorkton, Canada 51 17N 102 35W
90 Yosemite National Park, U.S.A. 37 30N 119 30W
50 Yoshkar Ola, U.S.S.R. 56 40N 47 50E
34 Youghal & Bay, Ireland 51 57N 7 51W
83 Young, Australia 34 18S 148 18E
91 Youngstown, U.S.A. 41 2N 80 43W
51 Yozgat, Turkey 39 53N 34 48E
44 Ypres, Belgium 50 50N 2 52E
48 Ystad, Sweden 55 25N 13 48E
25 Ystwyth, R., Wales 52 20N 3 48W
33 Ythan, R., Scotland 57 26N 2 15W
94 Yucatan, Dist., Mexico 19 30N 89 30W
94 Yucatan Str., Mexico 22 0N 86 20W
60 Yudino, U.S.S.R. 55 10N 67 55E
46-47 Yugoslavia, Europe 44 30N 18 0E
66 Yukiang, R., China 22 50N 109 0E
86 Yukon R., Alaska 65 0N 154 0W
88 Yukon, Terr. Canada 61 45N 133 30W
66 Yungan, China 26 0N 117 0E
67 Yunkia, China, *see* Wenchow
66 Yulin, China 18 25N 109 20E
90 Yuma, U.S.A. 32 40N 114 35W
66 Yunnan, Prov., China 25 30N 102 0E
67 Yushan, China 28 46N 119 3E
67 Yushan, Mt., Taiwan 23 30N 121 5E
66 Yushu, China 33 10N 96 10E
66 Yutze, China 37 45N 112 25E
67 Yuzhno Sakhalinsk, U.S.S.R. 46 50N 143 30E
42 Yvelines, Dépt., France 49 0N 1 50E
45 Yverdon, Switzerland 46 47N 6 39E
43 Yvetot, France 49 38N 0 45E

Z

44 Zaandam, Netherlands 52 27N 4 48E
63 Zabdani, Syria 33 44N 36 7E
62 Zabid, Yemen 14 8N 43 15E
94 Zacapa, Guatemala 15 0N 89 35W
94 Zacatecas, Mexico 22 52N 102 15W
94 Zacoalco, Mexico 20 5N 103 33W
40 Zadar, Yugoslavia 44 9N 15 15E
37 Zafra, Spain 38 28N 6 28W
62 Zagazig, Egypt 30 33N 31 12E
52 Zagorsk, U.S.S.R. 56 23N 28 10E
40 Zagreb, Yugoslavia 45 47N 15 58E
51 Zagros Mts., Iran 33 45N 47 0E
64 Zahidan, Iran 29 35N 60 50E
63 Zahlah, Lebanon 33 50N 35 55E
74 Zaïre, Rep. of, Africa 3 0S 23 0E
74 Zaïre, R., Africa 2 0N 22 0E
60 Zaisan, L., U.S.S.R. 48 10N 83 35E
41 Zákinthos, & I., Greece 37 48N 20 57E
47 Zaleshchiki, U.S.S.R. 48 48N 25 45E
75 Zambezi, Zambia 13 38S 23 7E
75 Zambezi, R., Africa 18 50S 36 20E
74-75 Zambia, Africa 15 0S 28 0E
68 Zamboanga, Philippines 6 55N 122 0E
52 Zametchino, U.S.S.R. 53 30N 42 38E
94 Zamora, Mexico 20 0N 102 10W
37 Zamora, Spain 41 30N 5 49W
47 Zamosc, Poland 50 43N 23 18E
44 Zandvoort, Netherlands 52 21N 4 33E
74 Zanzibar I., E. Africa 6 0S 39 17E
72 Zaouiet el-Kahla, Algeria 27 10N 6 40E
99 Zapala, Argentina 39 0S 70 0W
52 Zaporozhye, U.S.S.R. 47 45N 35 10E
37 Zaragoza, Spain 41 38N 0 50W
99 Zárate, Argentina 34 0S 59 0W
72 Zaria, Nigeria 11 0N 7 25E
46 Zary, Poland 51 37N 15 10E
73 Zarzis, Libya 33 30N 11 0E
61 Zashiversk, U.S.S.R. 67 25N 142 40E
64 Zaskar Mts., Kashmir & India 33 0N 77 20E
76 Zastron, South Africa 30 10S 27 3E
61 Zavitinsk, U.S.S.R. 50 10N 129 20E
47 Zawiercie, Poland 50 20N 19 30E
47 Zdunska Wola, Poland 51 38N 19 0E
44 Zeebrugge, Belgium 51 19N 3 12E
44 Zeeland, Prov., Neth. 51 30N 3 50E
76 Zeerust, South Africa 25 33S 26 1E
62 Zeila, Somali Rep. 11 0N 43 30E
44 Zeist, Netherlands 52 5N 5 15E
47 Zelenogradsk, U.S.S.R. 54 53N 20 29E
44 Zelzate, Belgium 51 12N 3 49E
73 Zemio, Central Africa 5 3N 25 11E
41 Zemun, Yugoslavia 44 51N 20 25E
51 Zenjan, Iran 36 39N 48 30E
46 Zerbst, Germany 51 59N 12 8E
45 Zermatt, Switzerland 46 1N 7 44E
45 Zerriez, Switzerland 46 43N 10 6E
29 Zetland Co., *see* Shetland
61 Zeya, & R., U.S.S.R. 54 10N 127 20E
51 Zeytin, Turkey 37 53N 36 53E
37 Zezere, R., Portugal 40 10N 7 40W
47 Zhabinka, U.S.S.R. 52 17N 24 3E
52 Zhdanov, U.S.S.R. 47 2N 37 36E
50 Zhitomir, U.S.S.R. 50 20N 28 42E
50 Zhlobin, U.S.S.R. 53 0N 30 0E
47 Zhmerinka, U.S.S.R. 49 1N 28 2E
61 Zhupanovo, U.S.S.R. 53 50N 159 35E
46 Zielona Gora, Poland 51 57N 15 31E
44 Zierikzee, Netherlands 51 40N 3 55E
73 Ziguei, Chad 14 45N 15 48E
72 Ziguinchor, Sénégal 12 25N 16 20W
63 Zikhron Yaagov, Israel 32 35N 34 57E
62 Zilfi, Saudi Arabia 26 30N 45 22E
47 Zilina, Czechoslovakia 49 15N 18 50E
73 Zillah, Libya 28 29N 17 50E
66 Zilling Tso, L., China 31 45N 89 0E
61 Zima, U.S.S.R. 54 0N 102 5E
72 Zinder, Niger 13 45N 9 3E
62 Zira, Iran 28 12N 51 29E
41 Zlatograd, Bulgaria 41 20N 25 0E
50 Zlatoust, U.S.S.R. 55 5N 59 25E
73 Zillah, Libya 28 29N 17 50E
46 Znojmo, Czechoslovakia 48 50N 16 2E
45 Zofingen, Switzerland 47 18N 7 57E
75 Zomba, Malawi 15 23S 35 19E
73 Zongo, Zaïre 4 10N 18 50E
51 Zonguldak, Turkey 41 30N 32 0E
73 Zouar, Chad 20 28N 16 32E
72 Zouérabe, Mauritania 22 35N 12 30W
41 Zrenjanin, Yugoslavia 45 23N 20 26E
45 Zug, & Cn., Switzerland 47 11N 8 31E
45 Zugersee, L., Switzerland 47 10N 8 30E
44 Zuid Holland, Neth. 51 50N 4 30E
75 Zumbo, Mozambique 15 30S 30 24E
72 Zungeru, Nigeria 9 57N 6 45E
45 Zürich, & Canton, Switz. 47 22N 8 32E
45 Zürichsee, (L. of Zürich), Switzerland 47 15N 8 38E
40 Zurrieq, Malta 35 52N 14 26E
44 Zutphen, Netherlands 52 18N 6 12E
73 Zuwarah, Libya 32 50N 12 5E
60 Zverinogolovskoye, U.S.S.R. 54 30N 62 30E
60 Zverovo, U.S.S.R. 71 40N 83 20E
47 Zvolen, Czechoslovakia 48 33N 19 10E
46 Zwettl, Austria 48 40N 15 10E
46 Zwickau, Germany 50 42N 12 25E
46 Zweibrücken, Germany 49 14N 7 22E
45 Zweisimmen, Switzerland 46 32N 7 24E
44 Zwolle, Netherlands 52 22N 6 7E
47 Zyrardow, Poland 52 0N 20 30E
60 Zyryanovsk, U.S.S.R. 49 20N 85 12E

PRINTED IN GREAT BRITAIN BY GEORGE PHILIP PRINTERS LIMITED, LONDON

A satellite view of an area on the Nepal-Chinese border. On the higher mountains, snow has melted first from the warmer southward-facing slopes. (Photo NASA)